PROSE AND POETRY OF ENGLAND

Prose and Poetry of

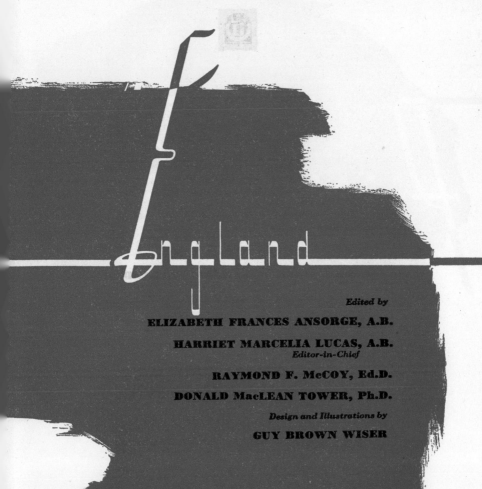

England

Edited by

ELIZABETH FRANCES ANSORGE, A.B.

HARRIET MARCELIA LUCAS, A.B.
Editor-in-Chief

RAYMOND F. McCOY, Ed.D.

DONALD MacLEAN TOWER, Ph.D.

Design and Illustrations by

GUY BROWN WISER

Syracuse, New York

THE L. W. SINGER COMPANY

The Prose and Poetry Series

PROSE AND POETRY OF ENGLAND

PROSE AND POETRY OF AMERICA

PROSE AND POETRY FOR APPRECIATION

PROSE AND POETRY FOR ENJOYMENT

PROSE AND POETRY ADVENTURES

PROSE AND POETRY JOURNEYS

PROSE AND POETRY OF TODAY

PROSE AND POETRY OF THE WORLD

8–43

CONTENTS

THE TWENTIETH CENTURY (1900–1943)

MODERN ENGLISH LITERATURE REFLECTS THE DIVERSITY AND STRENGTH OF A GREAT COMMONWEALTH

"There'll always be an England."

It is balanced with common sense and humor.

III   ENGLISHMEN ARE TRUE TO TRADITIONS OF COURAGE AND RIGHT

Twentieth-century Englishmen have faced the test of two wars.

They are realizing the need for international understanding and fellowship.

THE FOUNDATION PERIODS (449–1492)

THE FOUNDATIONS OF ENGLISH CULTURE WERE LAID IN THE TEN CENTURIES BEFORE COLUMBUS DISCOVERED AMERICA

"To sing a song that old was sung."

THE AGE OF ELIZABETH (1492–1620)

THE YEARS BETWEEN THE DISCOVERY OF AMERICA BY COLUMBUS AND THE LANDING OF THE PILGRIMS WITNESSED ENGLAND'S COMING OF AGE

"The spacious times of great Elizabeth."

THE SEVENTEENTH AND EIGHTEENTH CENTURIES
(1620–1780)

WHILE AMERICAN COLONIES WERE BEING SETTLED, ENGLAND WAS PASSING THROUGH A SERIES OF RELIGIOUS, POLITICAL, AND SOCIAL STRUGGLES

"So many men, so many minds."

I DIFFERENCES BETWEEN PURITAN AND CAVALIER
BROUGHT CIVIL WAR

THE AGE OF ROMANTICISM (1780–1840)

STIMULATED BY THE AMERICAN AND FRENCH REVOLUTIONS, ENGLISH WRITERS RENOUNCED CLASSICISM AND DISCOVERED A NEW FREEDOM OF THOUGHT

"Would you have your songs endure?
Build on the human heart!"

THE VICTORIAN ERA (1840–1900)

ENGLISH ARTS FLOURISHED IN THE PEACEFUL HALF-CENTURY THAT BROUGHT EXPANSION AND PROSPERITY TO BOTH SIDES OF THE ATLANTIC

"Proper words in proper places."

APPENDIX

THE TWENTIETH CENTURY
1900-1943

"THERE'LL ALWAYS BE AN ENGLAND"

H

Love of country is inborn with the British.

ENGLAND IS MY VILLAGE

JOHN LLEWELLYN RHYS

WHEN the Old Man came into the ante-room the young officers began to rise in their chairs but he waved them back with an impatient gesture. It was warm and comfortable in there and the tenor of idle chatter continued: one could hear the crackle of a newspaper page and the sound of bidding from the four who were playing a Chinese game in the corner, their minds apparently intent on the little walls of white blocks on the table before them.

Beneath the Wing Commander's arm were a number of files. On the outside of the files was a map. Robert recognized its shape and his heart kicked inside him. And now every pilot in the Squadron was watching the senior officer, watching him without movement of head, watching him while seeming to read, watching him while crying "Three Characters." [1] The Old Man nodded, first at one, then another, and finally at Robert. Silently they rose to their feet, leaving their circle of friends, their reading, their Chinese game, and filed into the neighboring room. When they had gone the lazy murmur of conversation continued, watchers filled the places at the game, another officer picked up the copy of *The Field* that Robert had been reading.

The Wing Commander stood by the grand piano waiting for them to gather about him. It had been a guest-room before the war but now the fripperies had been removed and the tall windows were stark with gas-proof screens. He looked suddenly older, Robert thought. Now his hair shone with grey, new lines emphasized the hardness of his features. But his voice was unchanged, harsh, imperious.

[1] "THREE CHARACTERS"—A term used in playing the Chinese game, *mah jong.*

1

"Gentlemen! The show's tomorrow." He paused and looked slowly at the circle of pilots. "The target you know. Here's the latest from Intelligence and a few other little details I want you to know."

Robert heard his instructions and memorized them with an ease born of practice, but the words seemed meaningless, rattling like hail on the roof of his mind.

"Any questions?"

But they were all old hands and no naïve youngsters among them wanted to make themselves heard.

"Well . . . good luck! I know you'll put up a good show," his voice was suddenly shy, "I wish they'd let me come with you."

They went back to the ante-room, went on talking, reading, playing the Chinese game. Robert sat down by a friend. They had been together for years but were in different squadrons.

"If anything," Robert's voice was quiet as he flipped the pages of a magazine, "if anything were . . . to slip up . . . tomorrow, would you attend to the odd detail?"

"Of course, old boy." The other puffed his pipe alight, swung the match till it was extinguished.

"Tomorrow?"

"Yes."

"Tough show?"

"Tough enough."

It was almost day as Robert walked over to Flights with the Squadron Leader, and cold with the half light lying dead on the roofs of the camouflaged hangars and the windsock flapping drearily on its pole. The erks [2] were beginning to start up the motors, which clattered protestingly to life, back-firing and juddering on their bearers.

"Looks like a good day, sir?"

The Leader of the raid looked up, then kicked his heel into the turf. "Yes: hope this frost holds off. I hope to hunt next week." It was a lot too clear, Robert thought. He hoped there was more cloud over there.

"You got some leave, sir?"

"Yes, I'm lucky. Six days."

"I'll say you're lucky." Not too much cloud, he thought, cov-

[2] ERKS—Mechanics.

ering the target and only too likely to be full of ice this time of year.

"Have you been out with the local pack?"[3] the older man went on.

"No, I can't get anyone to mount me."[4] He wondered if they'd have any of the new twin fighters waiting for them. They hadn't been seen yet, and were supposed to be very fast and to carry cannons.

"That *is* the trouble," said the Squadron Leader. When Robert got to his machine only the starboard engine had been started. Impatiently he watched the efforts of the crew. If only they'd get that engine running, he thought, if only they'd get it running. If only they'd get it running. He went up to the fitter.

"You haven't over-doped?"

"No, sir. She'll go now."

Still she refused to start. He climbed up the ladder into the cockpit.

"Got your throttle setting right?"

"Yes, sir," said the Corporal, "she'll start in a minute."

The Second Pilot was inside, busy at the navigator's table.

"All set?" Robert asked.

"Bombs, petrol[5] and everything hunky-dory, sir," the Sergeant answered.

If only they'd start that engine, he thought, if only they'd get it going and we could take off.

At last the motor roared to life and he climbed into his seat, ran up the engines, pulled up the ladder and waved away the chocks.

As he waited on the aerodrome, his airscrews throwing long flickering shadows, he kicked the heavy rudder violently from side to side. Where were the others? Where were the others? They would be late off the ground and there'd be a row. Then he glanced at his watch and found to his surprise that it was five minutes to zero hour. Behind him the wireless operator was hidden by his tall set and the gunners were amidships waiting to take up their positions once the machine was airborne. The Second Pilot leaned over the navigating table, setting his maps and charts and instruments.

---

[3] LOCAL PACK—A return to the hunting subject—"Have you been out with the hunt club here?"   [4] ANYONE TO MOUNT ME—Robert has no horse.
[5] PETROL—British term for *gasoline*.

And now the other machines were taxi-ing towards him, huge heavily laden monoplanes, grim against the dawn, moving fast over the close-cut turf, beating down clean thick lines through the white frost. He glanced down at the controls, felt the various cocks, checked the cylinder-head temperatures, the hydraulic and brake pressures. Then, when all was ready, he pushed open the throttles, the noise increasing till it filled the long narrow compartment, beating mercilessly upon his ears, drowning the scream of the hydraulic gear.

She was heavy with full petrol and a belly full of bombs, but as he felt her becoming airborne he brought the wheel gently back and he bumped up into the air.

They flew in tight formation and far below patches of fog lay pressed into the valleys. The sun threw skinny shadows, exaggerating the place of the leafless trees in the landscape, and blue smoke rose in stiff columns from farm chimneys, a bitter blue against the slight haze. Looking down at this scene of unreal cleanness Robert found it hard to believe it was War. This is an exercise, he thought, Redland against Blueland, and we shall meet the "enemy" fighter pilots in Mess tonight and have a terrific party.

As they approached the coast he noticed a familiar seaside town to the north. It was lifeless now, the blatant lettering on every house and shop and boarding screaming to empty streets, to deserted beaches and amusement parks.

The sea was calm, edged with white froth. The calm was a good thing, he thought, for the rubber dinghy [6] they carried in the wing was not designed to weather a gale.

Always before, the coast had been the meeting-place of land and sea, a convenient opportunity for obtaining a navigational "fix" or position. But now, as he glanced at the little boats askew on the beaches like burnt matches on a bar floor, he thought, "This is the edge of England." Then he looked ahead at the hard cold grey of the North Sea and edged a little closer to the Squadron Leader's aircraft.

From time to time Robert switched on his microphone and spoke to each gunner in his turret. They were alert and cheerful and behind him the Second Pilot worked at his check navigation,

[6] RUBBER DINGHY—Life raft.

4

taking sights, drifts, bearings, his face expressionless, his movements slow and sure so that he might have been in a classroom.

Sometimes they saw fishing-boats whose crews waved frantically, and tiny minesweepers busy at their deadly task and
once a convoy with destroyers like sheepdogs on its flanks. The
weather was fine, with high lumps of cumulus,[7] and they began
to climb.

In a little while the Second Pilot came forward and held up
eight fingers. Robert nodded. Eight minutes. He felt cold
inside his guts, his teeth were chattering, he wished they were
in the thick of it, and grinned at his companion. The target came
into view, a smudge on the horizon. The Leader began to give
his orders over the radio and they started a big circle so as to
attack from out of the sun. As they came up the sky filled with
anti-aircraft fire. The Second Pilot had switched on his microphone and Robert could hear him jeering at the enemy gunners,
for the shooting was poor, though some of the bursts were un-
comfortably close.

They came over the target and released their bombs. Robert
watched the sky unceasingly for enemy fighters, turning a little
and holding up his thumb against the sun, squinting round the
edge of the glove, wondering if any aircraft were lurking in its
glare waiting for the anti-aircraft to cease before diving to the
attack.

The Second Pilot was busy with the camera recording the
hits far below, whistling as he worked. A burst of Archie[8] off
the port wing-tip made the machine rock violently. The Second
Pilot kept absolutely motionless for a few seconds. Robert
looked out along the wing where little strips of fabric were
fluttering back from the leading edge but the machine still flew
perfectly and he moved the wheel gingerly, grinning as the
ailerons responded. The Second Pilot turned slowly back to his
task.

Soon they were out of range of the ground guns and Robert
saw one of the other machines break formation and rock its
wings. He spoke to the gunners.

"Keep your eyes skinned. There's a fighter about somewhere."
Then he saw it, a lone enemy machine, a single-seat fighter with

---

[7] CUMULUS—Rounded cloud masses.
[8] ARCHIE—Anti-aircraft fire.

square wing-tips. It came up quite slowly, lazily, flying on to the tail of one of the bombers. It was so simple a maneuver that it might have been a pupil on his circuit at a flying training school. As it turned off, short jabs of black smoke jerked themselves from the back cockpit of the bomber. The fighter turned slowly onto its side. First smoke, then flames, poured from its

engine, splashing down the fuselage. In the bright sunshine, against the blue sea, the flames were orange, and the machine fell slowly, twisting, turning, diving.

"Here they come!" said the Second Pilot, and Robert saw that the sky seemed to be filled with fighters. They broke up and began to attack. Robert watched two circling him from the front. As they turned the flank his rear gunner switched on his microphone and Robert could hear him swearing. He used one obscene word after another. They were meaningless, uttered without expression, repeated over and over again like the rhyme of a child. Tracers from the enemy streamed overhead, curved in graceful trajectory and dropped out of sight. Then the gunner was silent. Robert heard the rattle of his guns and his voice, jubilant.

"Got him, sir."

"Good. Keep your eyes skinned."

The middle gunner reported a machine. "But he's yellow, sir. Keeps out of range."

"Be patient," Robert said.

Now a twin-engined aircraft came up on the beam, accompanied by one of the smaller fighters, which attacked from the rear. A burst of fire shattered the roof over the Second Pilot's head. The front gunner coolly brought his guns to bear. The twin was an ugly brute, the first Robert had seen with extended stabilizers on the tail. He was frightened now, his mouth dry, his hands wet inside the silk lining of his gloves.

The gunners reported unceasingly. They were flying at full throttle and Robert looked despairingly ahead for cloud, but the nearest cumulus was miles away. Attack after attack came up, filled the air with tracer, turned lazily away. The middle gunner brought down another fighter before he was hit in the leg. Robert sent the Second Pilot back in his place.

One burst of machine-gun-fire shattered half the instrument panel, sent a shower of broken glass over his knees. Darkness filled his eyes, but in his mind he could still see the face of the enemy gunner, red and foolishly grim as he fired from the rear cockpit of the fighter. The wheel went limp in his hands, the strain of months of war, the nag of responsibility, lifted from his consciousness. This is good, he thought, this is good. To relax, to relax, to relax.

Then his vision cleared and he pulled the aircraft level. To his surprise the fighters had vanished and at his side was the Squadron Leader's machine, which he thought he had seen go down. The enemy must have run out of ammunition. He began to sing, thumping his hands on the wheel.

They were separated from the others and flew in tight formation, the Squadron Leader turning his head from time to time and grinning and doing a thumbs up. They lost height till they were just above the sea, their patterned shadows sliding effortlessly over mile after mile of water desolation. On crossing the coast the senior officer altered course for base. They flew at a few hundred feet over the sleepy countryside, their shadows now vaulting hedge and haystack, silently, climbing ridge and col,[9] dropping easily into shallow valleys.

The sun was still high in the sky and the country had never been more lovely. Not pretty, Robert thought, in the frills of summer, but beautiful in the starkness of winter. As he looked, first to the north at the black rich earth of the fens, marshalled by dykes, then south to the flatness of Suffolk, woolly with leaf-stripped trees, each feature of the country fitted into its place in his mind, each town he knew, hazy and grey with the mist of a winter's afternoon, each stretch of river, pregnant now with flood, each change of character from county to county. How familiar, he thought. How well I know it all. Truly, England is my village.

Soon the little lake shaped like an elephant's trunk appeared and they dived low over the hangars, then broke away, dropped their wheels and came in to land. There were no other machines about and the camp seemed strangely deserted.

A little later they walked into the Mess. It was warm and comfortable in there and the words and phrases of the many conversations jumbled themselves into a haze of sound. At the table by the fire there was an empty chair at the Chinese game. When Robert saw the other players he stopped in his stride. There was Nails, who got his on the first show, and Dick, who went down in flames, and Thistle his second pilot, and Badger, who was lost in the North Sea in December.

"Come on!" Badger said. "We're waiting for you."

"But I thought . . ." Robert said. "I thought . . ."

Badger was smiling.

[9] COL—A pass between adjacent peaks in a mountain chain.

DID YOU READ WITH UNDERSTANDING?

Read the story through once, before answering the questions. If necessary, reread it as you consider each point.

1. How much does the reader learn about the setting of the story? Would you guess that it took place near the beginning of the war? Why or why not? How much is it necessary for the reader to know about the *place?* How does he learn it?

2. What indicates that the Wing Commander has come in on business of importance? What place do you think was indicated on the map that

Robert recognized? Does it matter that the reader never learns what the objective was? Discuss.

3. What details in the two introductory sections of the story point toward a tragic conclusion?

4. What indicates Robert's nervousness before the flight takes off? Notice the flight noises that accompany the take-off. What are some of the sounds that are mentioned? Do you think that Robert had been in active combat before? How can you tell? What indicates that Robert was a skillful pilot and managed his craft well? Discuss.

5. Summarize the results of the fight in the air so far as Robert observed them. What planes fell? Who accounted for them?

6. What indicates that Robert has been hit? What details—or omission of details—indicate that Robert's return journey is not a routine flight? Discuss. What is the only plane to accompany him? What are Robert's feelings as England takes shape below them? Is there anything unusual about the landing? Discuss.

7. What is the significance of the players seated about the game table? What message do they convey to Robert? to the reader? Do you think Robert's plane crashed, or did the Second Pilot bring it in? How can you tell? What feeling is left with the reader by the words, "Badger was smiling"? Were you surprised at the ending? Or were you prepared for it? Does the story gain in meaning at the second reading?

8. Why do you think the author chose for his title, "England Is My Village"? What features of the story are emphasized by this title?

9. What traits of character do you notice in these English fliers? Do you think they behaved much as Americans would under similar circumstances? Was Robert cowardly or brave? How do you judge?

WHEN GREEN BUDS HANG

A. E. HOUSMAN

WHEN green buds hang in the elm like dust
    And sprinkle the lime like rain,
Forth I wander, forth I must,
    And drink of life again.

5   Forth I must by hedgerow bowers
    To look at the leaves uncurled,
And stand in the field where cuckoo flowers
    Are lying about the world.

7. CUCKOO FLOWERS—Wood sorrel or "ragged robin."

9

FOR INTERPRETATION

1. Why is "like dust" an appropriate description of elm buds? Have you ever seen a budded lime tree? If so, describe it. If not, how do you think it looks, with its buds described as sprinkling the tree "like rain"?

2. How does early spring make the poet feel? What does he want to do? Express it in his words.

LOVELIEST OF TREES

A. E. HOUSMAN

L   LOVELIEST of trees, the cherry now
        Is hung with bloom along the bough,
        And stands about the woodland ride,
        Wearing white for Eastertide.

B1 5 Now, of my threescore years and ten,
        Twenty will not come again,
        And take from seventy springs a score,
        It only leaves me fifty more.

L   And since to look at things in bloom
    10 Fifty springs are little room,
U   About the woodlands I will go
        To see the cherry hung with snow.

FOR INTERPRETATION

Throughout this book you will find poems marked in the margin with letter symbols such as those used above. These symbols form a guide to *choral reading*. They are fully explained in the *Appendix*.

1. How old is the poet on the day he enjoys the cherry blossoms? Explain the reference to his "three score years and ten." Check with the dates of his biography. Did he live to be seventy?

2. Do fifty springs seem a short time to you to look forward to? Why did it seem so to the poet?

3. What points of similarity do you notice between this poem and the preceding one? Discuss.

REAL PROPERTY

HAROLD MONRO

Tell me about that harvest-field.
Oh! Fifty acres of living bread.
The color has painted itself in my heart.
The form is patterned in my head.

5   So now I take it everywhere;
See it whenever I look round;
Hear it growing through every sound,
Know exactly the sound it makes—
Remembering, as one must all day,
10   Under the pavement the live earth aches.

Trees are at the farther end,
Limes all full of the mumbling bee;
So there must be a harvest-field
Whenever one thinks of a linden tree.

15   A hedge is about it, very tall,
Hazy and cool, and breathing sweet.
Round paradise is such a wall
And all the day, in such a way,
In paradise the wild birds call.

20   You only need to close your eyes
And go within your secret mind,
And you'll be into paradise:
I've learnt quite easily to find
Some linden trees and drowsy bees,
25   A tall sweet hedge with the corn behind.

I will not have the harvest mown;
I'll keep the corn and leave the bread.
I've bought that field; it's now my own:
I've fifty acres in my head.

25. CORN—Except in American usage, the word *corn* means any small grain, such as wheat.

11

30   I take it as a dream to bed.
I carry it about all day. . . .

Sometimes when I have found a friend
I give a blade of corn away.

FOR INTERPRETATION

1. Technically, or legally, speaking, what is "real property"? What are the first lines to tell us that in this instance the real property exists only in the poet's imagination?
2. What lines in the second stanza suggest how the poet got possession of his property? Describe the field and its surroundings.
3. What do lines 26 and 27 mean? How did the poet "buy" the field? How can he give a blade away? Who speaks line 1?
4. Explain in your own words the meaning of the poem. What do you learn from it about the author? Why do you think he chose the title?

WEATHERS

THOMAS HARDY

L		This is the weather the cuckoo likes,
L_1		And so do I;
G_1		When showers betumble the chestnut spikes,
G_2		And nestlings fly:
G_3	5	And the little brown nightingale bills his best,
M		And they sit outside at "The Travelers' Rest,"
G		And maids come forth spring-muslin drest,
U		And citizens dream of the south and west,
L_1		And so do I.
B	10	This is the weather the shepherd shuns,
B_1		And so do I;
B		When beeches drip in browns and duns,
		And thresh, and ply;
B_1		And hill-hid tides throb, throe on throe,
B_2	15	And meadow rivulets overflow,
B_3		And drops on gate-bars hang in a row,
B_4		And rooks in families homeward go,
B_1		And so do I.

12

FOR INTERPRETATION

1. What season does the first stanza suggest? with what details? If this were an American poem, what birds would be mentioned instead of the cuckoo and nightingale? Would any other words be different? If so, which ones?

2. What season does the second stanza suggest? with what words? What word would an American poet use instead of *shepherd?* What other words in this stanza would be changed if the poem were Americanized?

3. In line 13 *thresh* and *ply* are verbs. (Look up *ply* if you don't know a meaning that would fit here.) What picture is suggested by lines 12 and 13?

4. Do Americans feel the same way the poet did about these two kinds of weather? Discuss.

THE SOUTH COUNTRY

HILAIRE BELLOC

When I am living in the Midlands
    That are sodden and unkind,
I light my lamp in the evening:
    My work is left behind;
5 And the great hills of the South Country
    Come back into my mind.

The great hills of the South Country
    They stand along the sea;
And it's there walking in the high woods
10   That I could wish to be,
And the men that were boys when I was a boy
    Walking along with me.

The men that live in North England
    I saw them for a day:
15 Their hearts are set upon the waste fells,
    Their skies are fast and gray;
From their castle-walls a man may see
    The mountains far away.

13

The men that live in West England
20 They see the Severn strong,
A-rolling on rough water brown
  Light aspen leaves along.
They have the secret of the rocks,
  And the oldest kind of song.

25 But the men that live in the South Country
  Are the kindest and most wise,
They get their laughter from the loud surf,
  And the faith in their happy eyes
Comes surely from our Sister the Spring
30 When over the sea she flies;
The violets suddenly bloom at her feet,
  She blesses us with surprise.

I never get between the pines
  But I smell the Sussex air
35 Nor I never come on a belt of sand
  But my home is there.
And along the sky the line of the Downs
  So noble and so bare.

A lost thing could I never find,
40 Nor a broken thing mend:
And I fear I shall be all alone
  When I get towards the end.
Who will there be to comfort me
  Or who will be my friend?

45 I will gather and carefully make my friends
  Of the men of the Sussex Weald;
They watch the stars from silent folds,
  They stiffly plow the field.
By them and the God of the South Country
50 My poor soul shall be healed.

If I ever become a rich man,
  Or if ever I grow to be old,

24. OLDEST KIND OF SONG—This district borders on Wales, and is the setting
for many of the legends of King Arthur.

14

I will build a house with deep thatch
To shelter me from the cold,
55   And there shall the Sussex songs be sung
And the story of Sussex told.

I will hold my house in the high wood
Within a walk of the sea,
And the men that were boys when I was a boy
60   Shall sit and drink with me.

FOR INTERPRETATION

1. What part of England is called "the Midlands"? What kind of district does it seem to be? What keeps the poet from concentrating on his work?

2. What is the South Country like? How much do you learn about it in the second stanza?

3. What is the North Country like? What kind of men live there?

4. What is West England like? What occupation is suggested by the line, "They have the secret of the rocks"? The "oldest kind of song" (l. 24) probably refers to what language and what legends?

5. What are the men of the South Country like? Do you think the poet's preference for them is due to real superiority in the men, or to the fact that the South Country is his home country? Discuss.

6. Name the important features of South Country landscape that are mentioned in various parts of the poem. What besides the familiar landscape does the poet hope to enjoy in his old age?

7. Has the writer succeeded in making the South Country landscape seem the most pleasant part of England? Discuss.

PRELUDE

JOHN MILLINGTON SYNGE

STILL south I went and west and south again,
Through Wicklow from the morning till the night,
And far from cities, and the sights of men,
Lived with the sunshine and the moon's delight.

2. WICKLOW—A sparsely settled country district of Ireland, south of Dublin.

5   I knew the stars, the flowers, and the birds,
     The gray and wintry sides of many glens,
     And did but half remember human words,
     In converse with the mountains, moors, and fens.

FOR INTERPRETATION

1. From the poem "Prelude" what kind of country would one expect to find in Wicklow? What do the lines tell you about the way the poet learned to know the district? What tells you that he was alone much of the time?

2. Did the poet enjoy his experience? How can you tell?

THE LITTLE WAVES OF BREFFNY

EVA GORE-BOOTH

M   THE grand road from the mountain goes shining to the sea,
B   And there is traffic in it, and many a horse and cart;
LG   But the little roads of Cloonagh are dearer far to me,
LG1   And the little roads of Cloonagh go rambling through my heart.

16

DB   5 A great storm from the ocean goes shouting o'er the hill,

MG   And there is glory in it, and terror on the wind;

DB   But the haunted air of twilight is very strange and still,

LGI   And the little winds of twilight are dearer to my mind.

B   The great waves of the Atlantic sweep storming on their way,

L   10 Shining green and silver with the hidden herring shoal;

G   But the little waves of Breffny have drenched my heart in spray,

LGI   And the little waves of Breffny go stumbling through my soul.

FOR INTERPRETATION

1. What makes the reader feel—without having to be told—that "The Little Waves of Breffny" is a poem about Ireland?

2. Where do you think "the little roads of Cloonagh" go? How do they differ from the "grand road to the sea"?

3. What kind of wind does the poet like best? Does she like other winds too? How can you tell?

4. Even if you cannot find it on a map, can you tell what "Breffny" is? Is it a sea? a lake? a river? a bay?

5. In how many ways has the poet told us that she prefers little things to great ones? What kind of person do you think she would be? Discuss.

THE LAKE ISLE OF INNISFREE

WILLIAM BUTLER YEATS

Mr. Yeats has told us how he came to write this poem: "I had still the ambition, formed . . . in my teens, of living in imitation of Thoreau on Innisfree, a little island in Lough Gill, and when walking through Fleet Street, very homesick, I heard a little tinkle of water and saw a fountain in a shop window which balanced a little ball upon its jet, and began to remember lake water. From the sudden remembrance came my poem 'Innisfree.'"

17

I WILL arise and go now, and go to Innisfree,
And a small cabin build there, of clay and wattles made;
Nine bean rows will I have there, a hive for the honey bee,
And live alone in the bee-loud glade.

5 And I shall have some peace there, for peace comes dropping
     slow,
   Dropping from the veils of the morning to where the cricket
     sings;
   There midnight's all a-glimmer, and noon a purple glow,
   And evening full of the linnet's wings.

   I will arise and go now, for always night and day
10 I hear lake water lapping with low sounds by the shore;
   While I stand on the roadway, or on the pavements gray,
   I hear it in the deep heart's core.

FOR INTERPRETATION

1. Most high school students are familiar with Henry Thoreau's experiment in living "the simple life" on the shores of Walden pond and with the book that tells about his life there. What details in Yeats's description of his dream-home on Innisfree sound somewhat like Thoreau's American home in the woods? Which details in Yeats's picture are definitely Irish?

2. Where was Yeats living when he wrote the poem? Which stanza in the poem mentions the kind of sound that reminded him of his boyhood dream? What feeling does the poem leave with the reader? Which expressions contribute most powerfully to that feeling? Quote them.

3. Have you had a similar experience to that of the poet—does a certain sound or a certain scent flash over you a scene or experience from your childhood? Which is usually more effective in stirring up memories —scent, or sound, or sight? Do you think it true that most poems grow out of *memories*, or out of *dreams?* Discuss.

TO A LONDON THREE-YEAR-OLD

JAMES HILTON

You were not born in time to know
How evening came to London then;

The peacetime dusk, the skies aglow,
The City streets alive with men
5   Smoking cigars and selling stock,
Hurrying to catch the six o'clock.

Beneath the stars, in this dark hour,
You cannot guess, nor will you soon,
How Big Ben, like a golden moon,
10   Shone on the people from his tower—
Shone on the crowds of Englishmen
Who roamed the streets of London then.

You have not seen a rainy night
Beneath the lamps, when every drop
15   Flashed as it fell, and when the light
Streamed from some small late-closing shop
On mud-brown pavements and the walls
Of warehouses around St. Paul's.

Yet 'twas this place, whose somber tones
20   Are all that you can now surmise,
That built its courage in your bones
And sealed its brightness in your eyes.

FOR INTERPRETATION

1. This poem was written in 1943. What time is meant by the word
then in the second line of the poem? Why does the poet in his descrip-

19

tion of London as it was *then* choose dusk, evening, and night for his scenes? Are the contrasts less apparent by daylight? Discuss.

2. What is Big Ben? Why has this London three-year-old never seen Big Ben shining from his tower?

3. What are the most important differences between a rainy night in London *then* and *now?*

4. What kind of London does today's child see?

5. In what sense can the thought of the last four lines be true? How does the somberness of war-time London symbolize *courage* and *brightness?* Discuss.

THE SOLDIER

RUPERT BROOKE

B1 IF I should die, think only this of me;
   That there's some corner of a foreign field
   That is for ever England. There shall be
   In that rich earth a richer dust concealed;
  5 A dust whom England bore, shaped, made aware,
   Gave, once, her flowers to love, her ways to roam,
B   A body of England's, breathing English air,
   Washed by the rivers, blest by suns of home.

   And think, this heart, all evil shed away,
  10 A pulse in the eternal mind, no less
   Gives somewhere back the thoughts by England given;
LG Her sights and sounds; dreams happy as her day
   And laughter, learnt of friends; and gentleness,
U   In hearts at peace, under an English heaven.

FOR INTERPRETATION

1. Explain the meaning of the first three lines. What is the "richer dust" of line 4? How much of the soldier remains in some foreign field?· What part returns to England? How?

2. What meaning does Brooke seem to give to immortality (lines 9–14)?

3. What are the things about England he has appreciated most? Might one of our soldiers overseas think these same thoughts, substituting America and American for England and English? Discuss.

EXTENDED ACTIVITIES

LOVE OF COUNTRY IS INBORN WITH THE BRITISH

HOW LITERATURE REFLECTS THE TIMES

MODERN ENGLISH LITERATURE REFLECTS THE DIVERSITY AND STRENGTH
OF A GREAT COMMONWEALTH

The first two score years of the twentieth century have been a bewildering period for the world and especially difficult for the nations of
great empire. To understand something of the problems of modern
England and to appreciate the scope of modern English literature, it is
well for us to have clearly in mind the significance of certain terms by
which men refer to the island empire. In primer-like style then, let us
define our terms:

England, strictly speaking, refers to the southern part of the island of
Great Britain, not including the southwestern portion known as
Wales.

Great Britain is the name for the whole island which comprises England,
Scotland, and Wales. *Ireland* is a separate island, now divided into
two political units—Northern Ireland, which is united with the government of Great Britain, and the Irish Free State, which is independent.

The United Kingdom is the term used to indicate Great Britain and
Ireland.

The British Empire has been defined as an "association of political
communities united under common allegiance to the British Crown,
comprising Great Britain and Northern Ireland; the self-governing
Dominions; India; the Colonies; the Protectorates, Dependencies,
and Mandates." The total area of the Empire is over thirteen million square miles, or an expanse of territories one hundred times the
size of the United Kingdom.

The self-governing *Dominions* include Canada, Australia, South Africa,
New Zealand, and the Irish Free State. India is not entirely self-
governing, though it has been offered Dominion status.

The smaller units are too many and complex for special mention, but
they include besides the larger colonies such isolated spots as Malta
and Gibraltar.

Great Britain likes to refer to this vast empire as a "Commonwealth
of Nations." And indeed the Dominions and Colonies have virtually the
rank of independent nations. They are united by a common loyalty, and
in times of crisis give themselves freely for common defense. In all parts

21

of the Empire, English is the official language; and the term *English literature* may be understood to include the literary productions written anywhere in the Empire. The terms *British* and *Britisher* are often used loosely to designate any white citizen of the British Empire, just as *English* and *Englishman* are sometimes used with a broad, rather than an exact, reference.

A realization of the complexity of the British commonwealth prepares one for the diversity of its literature—especially its modern literature, which draws from the whole far-flung British scene. Rudyard Kipling was one of the first writers to realize the tremendous range of subjects for writers offered by life in the outposts. He wrote ballads and stories of privates in Delhi and Kohinoor, of officers in Lahore, of native women, of servants and water boys. He wrote about the plight of small lads sent "home," across thousands of miles of water, for schooling—separated from their parents through all the years of boyhood. Other writers, of course, followed the lead; and all the phases of foreign living became familiar to the folks back home. No portion of the Empire has missed its chance to serve as the setting for story, history, biography, verse, or play. Besides the works of roving Englishmen, there has been added a considerable body of verse and prose by Dominion-born British—by Australians, for example, or New Zealanders—so that recent literature is truly representative of the scope of the Empire.

Within our century, the unity and strength of this commonwealth of nations has been proved in two great wars. In 1914, one after another, the Dominions and Colonies declared their intentions of fighting along with Great Britain. Troops were rushed to England and France from every section of the globe. In 1939 there was the same eager rush to the colors, the Irish Free State alone trying to preserve neutrality. Fighting and suffering in a common cause has brought about the closest kind of sympathy between the peoples of the Empire. And whole-hearted working together gave England strength to survive what the world feared would be total destruction.

Both war periods and the uneasy interlude between have left the sharpest impress on creative literature. The second World War gives promise of producing even more enduring work than the first one. The English have stretched their horizons. New literature looks at life from a vantage point that brings the whole world—not just Britain's chunk of it—into range. A survey of its field will disclose not only what the Britisher is like and what he does but also what he sees in others and what are his aspirations for a new world.

MEN OF THE BRITISH ISLES KNOW A COMMON LOVE
OF THE HOMELAND

Notwithstanding broadening international interests, the first and deepest devotion of any son of the United Kingdom is given to his homeland. Love of country—the home country—is inborn with the British. At heart the people are attached to the soil. It is one of the tragedies of modern life that folks who know land and love to work it have been crowded into cities. Ireland and Great Britain are tiny in proportion to the millions of souls they maintain. And more than two-thirds of the smaller island is bog and water. In consequence a change-over from agricultural living long ago sent rural-minded folks into factories and centers of commerce. The United Kingdom is one of the most highly concentrated industrial and trade centers of the world. But the folks in London and Manchester and Dublin and Belfast have not outgrown their love of the land. In their dreams they hear the call of the little springs of Devon or of the great hills of the South Country. In the heart of the islander there is hidden a picture of Sligo in the west of Ireland, of Wicklow in the east, of Loch Katrine in Scotland, or of a once-green valley in Wales.

British lyric poetry is lightened by such bits of country landscape—of cherry trees in bloom, of roads that wind through woodlands where the "shy-eyed delicate deer troop down to the pools to drink." The soldier tramping some foreign field or flying the lanes of air dreams of a frost-nipped woods at home or of rain on hedge-row buds. To possess those fields in peace or to leave them to his children he counts it worth his chance to die.

FOR ACQUAINTANCE WITH AUTHORS

HILAIRE BELLOC (1870–   )—"THE SOUTH COUNTRY"

Hilaire Belloc was born in Paris, the son of a French barrister and his English wife. He was educated in England, however, and there is little French left with him except his name and his Gallic wit. At Oxford his career was distinguished. He began to write immediately after graduation and has been successful at whatever he tried his hand: verse, children's stories, history, essay, and even light novels. He was a devoted friend of G. K. Chesterton; and George Bernard Shaw in fun christened the combination "Chester-belloc." The two argued and wrote much together.

RUPERT BROOKE (1887–1915)—"THE SOLDIER"

What would you think if the captain of your football team had won prizes for poetry, honors in scholarship, and fostered revivals of Eliza-bethan plays? And, if in addition, he was tall, handsome, vivacious, and charming? You'd remember him, wouldn't you, especially if later he went into military service and died as a soldier at the age of twenty-eight?

And so it is with Britishers of the first-war generation. Rupert Brooke is well remembered, not only for his poetry but for the brilliant promise of his life. He was one of those singularly favored by the gods. His father was housemaster at Rugby, and Rupert was educated there. Far from being hampered by his father's position, he was a leader in all

23

pranks. Everyone knew him for his boisterous sense of mischief as well as for his
verse and football playing.

At Cambridge, Brooke dabbled in radical campus politics, college theatricals,
and journalism. His brilliant writing
even then won him the friendship of
other poets, de la Mare, Gosse, and Drinkwater. His unusual academic standing
earned him a fellowship at Cambridge
and with the publication of his *Poems* in
1911 he seemed assured of success. He
wrote and lectured until 1914, but with
the outbreak of war he immediately enlisted and received a commission in the
Royal Naval Division. On his way to the
Dardanelles after a winter's training he
died on board ship of an infection follow-
ing sunstroke. "The Soldier" was written only a few months before his
death. The shock of his death touched all who knew him. His work,
although excellent, still showed more promise than achievement. We can
only speculate as to the verse and man England might have had if Brooke
had lived.

EVA GORE-BOOTH (1870–1926)—"THE LITTLE WAVES OF BREFFNY"

A poet devoted to her homeland was Eva Gore-Booth, daughter of
a baronet, who from her early twenties gave herself and her writing
talents entirely to Ireland. The great W. B. Yeats wrote in praise of her
first book of poems and greeted each succeeding volume with the warmest
criticism. Miss Gore-Booth busied herself also with the promotion of
woman suffrage and trade unions. In 1914 she was a leader in the Women's
Peace Crusade. Two years later her sensitive nature was deeply hurt
when her sister Constance, who had taken an active part in the Irish Rebellion of Easter week, was condemned to death. The sentence was afterwards commuted to life imprisonment, but the poet's active life from
then on was greatly curtailed. Toward the end of her life she went to
Italy where she turned increasingly toward religious subjects in her
poetry. Her health had always been frail, but she composed verse nearly
to her last day.

THOMAS HARDY (1840–1928)—"WEATHERS"

Stone, music, and Greek literature fashioned the life of Thomas Hardy.
The son of a prosperous stone mason, he was early destined for his
father's trade. The home environment was pleasant; the child, delicate
and precocious, learned to read before he could talk plainly. A few years
in grammar school, some French lessons from a tutor, and his own

reading made up his formal education. At sixteen he was apprenticed to a local ecclesiastical architect, sympathetic enough to let him read more Greek stories than architecture texts. After six years, Hardy's father sent him to study with England's greatest architect of the day, Sir Arthur Bloomfield. Thomas seems to have worked none too hard, for he found time to lecture his classmates on poetry. But he absorbed enough of his profession to win a medal for an essay on brick work. At twenty-seven he was ready to set up business for himself; but he found it a dull livelihood at best. The towns-people and workmen, and the beauty of the old churches he was sent to restore in-terested him more than the actual prob-lems of mortar and wood. Someone has said that his chief achievement in the pro-fession was winning a wife.

He had already begun writing poetry, but no one would have it. It was not until his career as a novelist was finished that any was published. His work first saw print in an anonymous humorous sketch in a small magazine. Always shy about his own work, he sent the manuscript of his first novel to George Meredith. His dis-approval resulted in Hardy's destroying the book. His second he finally had the cour-age to publish, but the violently critical reviews were discouraging. Against the wishes of his fiancee, he de-termined to give up writing and concentrate on architecture. Such vows were short-lived! The next year *Under the Greenwood Tree* appeared and on the strength of its slim success, Hardy married. From then on annual and biennial novels poured from his busy pen. He returned to his old profession only long enough to build his own house in Dorchester. As Hardy's genius matured, his novels acquired wider reputation until with the publication of his two most famous stories, *Tess of the D'Urbervilles* and *Jude the Obscure,* a storm of abuse was heaped upon him. The Victorians resented, bitterly, his bold-ness in disclosing the hearts of men and women. Freed from all sentimental claptrap, realistic in an age when realism had to be plush covered for public consumption, Hardy's books rocked the smug and prudish Victorians. Hardy at last was completely tired of his long struggle; he vowed never to write fiction again and returned to his first interest, poetry. Belatedly the world realized his great gifts; he was showered with honors, the Order of Merit only one among them.

During the first World War the great gentleman served industriously as the local Justice of the Peace, the only service open to him because of his age. He died at the age of eighty-seven, one of the few great writers who from the beginning of their careers "saw life steadily and saw it whole."

JAMES HILTON (1900–)—"TO A LONDON THREE-YEAR-OLD"

In college at Cambridge, James Hilton was one of those singled out for a brilliant career and he has fulfilled his classmates' prediction. Graduating with honors in English, he began immediately to write novels, as well as magazine articles and reviews. His books sold slowly until 1933, when *Goodbye, Mr. Chips* was published in the *British Weekly*. The magazine had contracted for a long short story from Hilton for its Christmas edition. He had two weeks in which to write it. As the time grew short, Hilton, returning from a bicycle ride in search of inspiration, came home and dashed off the short novel in a few days. Mr. Chips, the shy, gentle little schoolmaster, and his wife Cathie, won the hearts of Britisher and American alike. After its brilliant success in America and on the screen, some of Hilton's earlier works won similar popularity. *Knight without Armor, Lost Horizon, We Are Not Alone,* and, most recently, *Random Harvest* have all become near-classics of the twentieth century. Recently, Hilton, a smallish dapper Englishman, has spent much time in Hollywood overseeing the filming of his novels. Stars of the film *Random Harvest* won the coveted "Oscar" award in 1942.

A. E. HOUSMAN (1859–1936)—"WHEN GREEN BUDS HANG," "LOVELIEST OF TREES"

Alfred Edward Housman has done for Shropshire what Thomas Hardy did for Wessex and Arnold Bennett for the pottery towns—he has pre-sented it to the world. Yet he did it quite unwillingly and with the utmost difficulty. According to his own confession, writing poetry was something of a fever, which he had strength to endure during just a few brief periods. He wrote almost continually from the time he was twenty, yet published only two slim volumes: *A Shropshire Lad* and *Last Poems,* both jewel-like in their perfection.

Housman's life was almost tragically lonely. His childhood in a large family was carefree and happy, but during his four years at Oxford something happened which made of him a melancholy, rigidly reserved, and deliberately lonely man. Perhaps it was his failure in an exam for honors, perhaps it was an unfortunate friendship; but in any case he left without a degree, refused to have anything to do with his six brothers and sisters, and went to work for ten years as a clerk in the patent office. In 1892 when he was named professor of Latin at University

College, Oxford, he at last wrote to his family again, but his new success gave him few friendships. He never married, seems never to have had any love affairs, never enjoyed the comradeship of society. He found interest enough in his work at Oxford and later at Cambridge. In 1933 his beautifully written critical essay, "The Name and Nature of Poetry," added the final touch to his already great fame, both as a translator from Latin and Greek and as a poet.

As a professor, the shy, thin-lipped recluse was sympathetic always to a stupid student but ruthless in his criticism of careless or incompetent work in other writers and critics. At his death he left orders that his brother Laurence, the dramatist, should destroy all writing that failed to meet his standards of excellence. Thus the twentieth century, century of carelessness and experimentation, has in Housman's work at least one slim, perfect sheaf of poetry and criticism.

HAROLD MONRO (1879–1932)—"REAL PROPERTY"

"Hardworking and lazy, generous and mean, a lover of freedom and a tyrant, a bohemian and a bourgeois" is a friend's description of the poet and poetry-popularizer, Harold Monro. Startling contrast seems the keynote of his personality and work. The son of a Scotch engineer and his practical wife, Monro had always more of the wild Celt in him than the thrifty Scot. At Cambridge his chief passion was horse-racing. Later, literature and literary acquaintances interested him far more than the mere earning of a living. Yet he could be practical and efficient when needed; he was successful as an officer in an anti-aircraft battery in World War I and at a clerical post in the War Office. Three times he attempted to found a successful poetry magazine and all three were financial failures for himself although they helped to secure recognition for unknown poets he defended. With the magazines, he attempted to run a bookshop in the slums of London to interest the poorer classes in poetry and the classics. He enthusiastically arranged for readings of poetry by himself and his poet friends at regular times in the bookshop, but the people of the slums remained indifferent to the lure of verse. Undaunted by his many failures he continued to publish poems and criticism. Possessing rare judgment in poetry, he was the first to recognize many now famous writers; and although he was of consequence as a poet himself, he was even more influential as a lover and popularizer of good modern poetry.

JOHN LLEWELLYN RHYS (–1942)—"ENGLAND IS MY VILLAGE"

John Llewellyn Rhys, Acting Flight Lieutenant in the Royal Air Force was killed in service on the fifth of August, 1942. The only biographical sketch yet published is that written by his wife as the preface to his book, *England Is My Village*. The son of a Welsh rector, John Rhys from childhood had two passions, flying and writing. In 1934 he won his flying license at Cardiff and rose rapidly in the R.A.F. Reserve. On sick leave in 1935 he published his first novel, *The Flying Shadow*. The next year while serving as an Acting Pilot Officer in the R.A.F. he snatched time to write *The World Owes Me a Living*. The tempo of his flying duties increased; but on leave, on week-end liberties, and after flying routines he continued to work at his hobby; his style gained clarity and simplicity as the need for hurry grew. In the meantime a young girl pilot, also a fledgling writer, had read *The Flying Shadow* and written enthusiastically to its author. The two met and flew, wrote and talked together; they were married in 1939. She knew and accepted the fact that he believed, as he had written, that death was not the extinction but the achievement of life itself. It is she who could write late in 1942 that the wonder was not that they had had so little time together but that they had had so much.

JOHN MILLINGTON SYNGE (1871–1909)—"PRELUDE"

Although William Butler Yeats is called the popularizer of Irish literature, he was helped by other distinguished writers. John Millington Synge was one of the most brilliant and most sincere. Like Yeats he was born and bred in Ireland. When he was nineteen, he went to Germany to study the violin, then on to Italy and then to France where he decided to change his career to literary criticism. Quiet and abstemious, he studied and wrote industriously in the noisy Latin quarter of Paris. His health had always been precarious and he seems to have realized that he had little time left to him.

His devotion to the Irish cause and his best writing came after his meeting Yeats in 1891 who suggested that he spend some time on the Aran Islands to find untouched Irish legends and people. In the next eleven years, he lived in various country districts of Ireland making himself at home with humble folk and learning to know the country. It was during this period that he made his reputation as a dramatist. His now most famous play, *The Playboy of the Western World,* was greeted on the Abbey Theater stage with custard pies and hisses. In poetry he fought against sentimentalism and strove for humanness by the use of bitter realism. Literary critics grew increasingly conscious of his ability, but Synge's health failed rapidly. He was engaged to one of the leading actresses of the Abbey Theater who hardly saw him except as she sat by his hospital bed. His death in 1909 left a wide vacancy in the group of Irish writers fighting for recognition of Irish literary talent and Irish tradition.

WILLIAM BUTLER YEATS (1865–1939)—"THE LAKE ISLE OF INNISFREE"

Someone once wrote of Yeats that he fell in love with Ireland and with literature and the affair lasted his life. Ireland never had a greater nor a more sincere champion; nearly all his life was willingly spent there, and any stay in London found him lonesome for County Sligo. After grammar school, Yeats at eighteen began studying painting only to discover that he was a poet. Following a brief and not too successful fling in London literary society, he returned to Dublin to take a leading part, with Lady Gregory's aid, in the Celtic revival, the Irish literary renaissance. Together they founded the Irish Literary Theater (later called the Abbey Theater) and the Irish Academy. In 1917 Yeats married and settled in a tower on the seacoast of Ireland. He served in the Irish Senate for six years, but his heart was always in his poetry for which he won the Nobel Prize in 1923. His work seemed to gain force and power with each year until at his death at seventy-three the *New Republic* could write "he died like Shelley at the height of his powers with half his work unwritten."

OF LITERARY FORM AND STYLE

NEW TECHNIQUES IN THE ENGLISH STORY

Perhaps it is because of the war. Perhaps it is because American and English writers are finding warmer reading audiences in each other's countries and are more concerned with each other's work. At any rate, the prose styles of writers across the Atlantic are growing more and more alike. There was a time when it was easy to spot an English author in an American magazine. If the subject was serious, there was an unmistakable British aloofness and dignity of style. If the subject was light, the humor rode along on strings of too-too British jargon. But today English prose is being streamlined to suit new world tastes. Even the words of statesmen and churchmen have taken on simplicity and directness. And the new stories are crisp and skillfully told.

It may be fairly said that British short-story writers are adopting American techniques. In this one type of literature, America has always taken the lead. English readers and writers have liked our stories and studied them; and Great Britain is still following our methods. All recent stories, of course, concern the war. And because Great Britain is two years older in it than we are and because, moreover, she has been part of the battle-ground, her war stories ring true. There is no doubt that they are born of experience. Among them may be found the very best short fiction this war has produced. Especially outstanding are stories of the air. There are besides stories of the sea, and of British courage and resourcefulness at home in withstanding bombings and meeting almost tragic shortages of food and equipment.

The technique is usually terse, direct—and being British—unsentimental. If the story is not told in the first person, it is usually presented from the point of view of one character—limited in detail to what he sees, hears, feels, and does. Materials are selected sparely—just enough to suggest the story. There is little description, and that presented incidentally, merely as it registers in the mind or senses of the key character. The reader must guess the details of time, place, and situation as he reads. Characterization, too, comes indirectly. We judge the character—as we do a new acquaintance—by what he says and does. The method requires craftsmanship. When skillfully used it produces superb stories, with no waste lines. Among the finest of the sort are those in the volume by John Llewellyn Rhys, *England Is My Village*.

QUESTIONS IN APPRECIATION:

1. Who is the key-character in "England Is My Village"? Check the details of the story. Does the reader learn anything that is not experienced by this one character? Prove your answer by reference to various parts of the story.

2. Select the two passages which you consider the best examples of descriptive writing. Through whose eyes do we see the scenes? Under what circumstances? Which details seem especially significant?

3. How does the reader learn the answers to *When, Where,* and *What about?* Would you say the setting is presented directly or indirectly? Why? Instead of saying, "On the morning before the take-off, Robert's mind was preoccupied," how has the author conveyed that impression? Cite the passage. Instead of saying, "Robert was obviously nervous as he climbed aboard," how has the author given us that information? What are the advantages of this method of story-telling? Do you think it is a hard or an easy method to use? Discuss.

4. What details throughout the story make it seem true to life? Would you know, without being told, that the author was a flier? If so, how? How has the author kept the story from being sentimental? Do you think an Irish or French writer would have told the story in the same way? Discuss. To what extent does the story excite the interest and sympathy of the reader? Do you think the story would appeal to readers of any nationality? Why or why not?

LYRIC VERSE ON HOMELAND THEMES

As a background to the war writings there is a body of literature that expresses the present-day Englishman's delight in his homeland. Much of it is lyric verse. Some of the poems appeared early in the century, before war had become a threat; some came out during the first war or in the post-war days—a kind of "escape" from the disturbances of life; and some are being written now—reminders of what men are fighting for.

Its mood is usually quiet, conveying a pleasure in the little beauties of British landscape. Not much of the scenery in the British Isles is on the grand scale. Their mountains with us would rate as hills. But the little glens and coverts, the broad moors, the fields marked off in patterned squares by hedges—these have always been dear to the poet. And though he is proud of his cities and of the courage and stability that they typify, he usually walks their pavements cherishing some dream of country fields.

The lyric form is simple, in keeping with the homelike quality of the theme. The poet shows his skill in his economy of words. There is no padding, no over-dressing. Each word, however commonplace, has its poetic values. The style is clear. The imagery has the natural outdoor freshness that belongs with country scenes. And the swift, direct appeal of the verses lies in this freshness. There is the added charm of sincerity and simple loveliness.

QUESTIONS IN APPRECIATION:

1. Notice that although "When Green Buds Hang" is a spring poem, it does not mention the word *spring*. How do we learn the season of the year? In what unusual way does the poet say that flowers are blossoming in the fields? How has the poet managed to create for the reader an impression of being out of doors in early spring?

2. In "Loveliest of Trees" quote three unusual ways the poet has found to say that the cherry trees are in blossom. What unusual reason does the poet give for spending a spring day out of doors? Why do you think this brief poem has become a favorite with readers everywhere?

3. In "Real Property" how does the poet tell us that he is a city man? How do you think he could give such a good description of a wheat field? What feelings do we share with the author? What typically British qualities does the poem reveal?

4. How can you tell from "Weathers" that the poet knew the countryside well? He grew up in the southwest part of England. From the glimpses afforded by the poem, what kind of country do you think it was? What is the poetic effect of "Weathers" as you read it aloud? How has the poet secured two entirely different moods with the same stanza form? Study and discuss.

5. In "The South Country" how has the poet suggested the industrial and commercial aspect of the Midlands? the rocky bleakness of the North? the rugged character of the West? Quote details. How has he given emphasis to the different charms of the South Country? Which lines from the poem do you like best? Why?

6. Which one of the first four lines of "Prelude" gives the stanza that "lift" that makes it poetry? What do you think is the most poetic expression in the second stanza? Review your definition of lyric poetry (see the *Appendix*). What qualities make these eight simple lines a true lyric? What qualities must a man have to write such a poem?

7. Study the rhythmic pattern of "The Little Waves of Breffny." Are

31

all the feet made up of two syllables? Can you tell what gives the poem its Irish lilt? How should "wind" in the sixth line be pronounced? How can you tell? Notice the effective use of verbal forms—like *"shining to the sea"* and *"rambling* through my heart." Point out at least six other verbs or verbals that are used with descriptive force in the poem. What Irish qualities do you detect in the mood and imagery of the poem?

8. Though few of Yeats's readers have ever been to Innisfree, his lyric about the lake isle has become a general favorite. Why do you think this is so? Would you call it a typically Irish poem? Why or why not? Point out, if you can, some points of similarity between it and "The Little Waves of Breffny." What are the most important differences between the two poems? Read the lines that are most suggestive of the poet's mood. How would you define that mood? In what respects is that mood representative of Irish poetry?

9. What details in the first three stanzas of "To a London Three-Year-Old" seem especially suggestive of normal city life? What expressions in the description indicate the fact that Hilton is fond of London? Where does he express his pride in England and Englishmen? Is it a justifiable pride? Why or why not?

10. What poetic form did Brooke choose for his tribute to England? Why is it an especially suitable form? What thought is developed in the first eight lines? What larger thought is developed in the last six lines? Does it rise to a climax in the last line? What is the most significant piece of imagery in the poem? How does the poem make the reader feel? In what respects is it a true *lyric?*

FOR FURTHER READING

BELLOC, HILAIRE, *Cromwell; Selected Essays; Collected Poems*
BRIDGES, ROBERT, *October and Other Poems*
BROOKE, RUPERT, *Collected Poems*
COYLE, KATHLEEN, *The Magical Realm*
DAVIES, W. H., *The Poems of William H. Davies*
DE LA MARE, WALTER, *Come Hither; Peacock Pie; Collected Poems, 1941*
GRAVES, ROBERT, *Country Sentiment*
HARDY, THOMAS, *Collected Poems*
HILTON, JAMES, *Good-bye, Mr. Chips; Random Harvest*
HODGSON, RALPH, *Poems*
HOUSMAN, A. E., *A Shropshire Lad; More Poems*
MASEFIELD, JOHN, *The Collected Poems of John Masefield*
MONRO, HAROLD, *Real Property; The Earth for Sale*
RHYS, JOHN LLEWELLYN, *England Is My Village*
SYNGE, JOHN MILLINGTON, *The Playboy of the Western World* (drama);
    Riders to the Sea (drama)
YEATS, WILLIAM BUTLER, *Last Poems and Plays; Selected Poems*

H

British character is sturdy but infinitely varied.
It respects the significance of human personality.

A CONSECRATION

JOHN MASEFIELD

Not of the princes and prelates with periwigged charioteers
Riding triumphantly laurelled to lap the fat of the years,—
Rather the scorned—the rejected—the men hemmed in with
    the spears;

The men of the tattered battalion which fights till it dies,
5 Dazed with the dust of the battle, the din and the cries.
The men with the broken heads and the blood running into
    their eyes.

Not the be-medalled Commander, beloved of the throne,
Riding cock-horse to parade when the bugles are blown.
But the lads who carried the koppie and cannot be known.

10 Not the ruler for me, but the ranker, the tramp of the road,
The slave with the sack on his shoulders pricked on with the
    goad,
The man with too weighty a burden, too weary a load.

The sailor, the stoker of steamers, the man with the clout,
The chantyman bent at the halliards putting a tune to the
    shout,
15 The drowsy man at the wheel and the tired look-out.

Others may sing of the wine and the wealth and the mirth,

    9. KOPPIE—A word used in South Africa to mean kop, or small hill. The
reference is to the Boer War—"the men who won the hill."
    13. CLOUT—Loin cloth.
    14. CHANTYMAN—The sailor who leads in the singing as the men work at
the halliards (sails).

33

The portly presence of potentates goodly in girth;—
Mine be the dirt and the dross, the dust and scum of the
    earth!

Theirs be the music, the color, the glory, the gold;
20 Mine be a handful of ashes, a mouthful of mold.
Of the maimed, of the halt and the blind in the rain and the
    cold—
Of these shall my songs be fashioned, my tales be told.

FOR INTERPRETATION

1. Writers commonly speak of a "dedication" of their works to some
one they wish to honor. What added meaning is there in the word "consecration"? Why do you think Masefield has used it as the title for his
poem?

2. Read the poem through carefully. For what sort of people is Masefield *not* writing? List them, either in your words or the poet's.

3. To what kind of men does he consecrate his work? What are some
of the occupations to which Masefield especially refers? What stories or
circumstances are suggested by the following expressions: (*a*) "The men
hemmed in with the spears"; (*b*) "The men of the tattered battalion
which fights till it dies"; (*c*) "The lads who carried the koppie"; (*d*) "The
man with too heavy a burden"; (*e*) "The man with the clout." Are there
still "slaves with a sack on the shoulders"? If so, where?

4. From what you know of Masefield's poetry, would you say that he
has kept the promise made in this *consecration?* Discuss.

ROUNDING THE HORN

JOHN MASEFIELD

In his long poem *Dauber,* Masefield tells the story of one of the men
he might have had in mind when he wrote "A Consecration." The
"Dauber" was a poor artist who wanted to be able to paint ships and sea
and sky truly. And so he shipped as a hand on a sailing vessel. He was
in every way unfitted for the work of a sailor and did his jobs badly.
The other seamen had no understanding of his real talent, thought him
"queer," and made his life a torment.

The stanzas quoted below are from the passage in which the ship makes
the perilous passage around Cape Horn at the tip of South America. Even

a seasoned, skillful sailor finds it a hazardous task to handle a sail out on
a yard arm in the teeth of an Antarctic gale. Consider the plight of the
Dauber——

THEN came the cry of "Call all hands on deck!"
The Dauber knew its meaning; it was come:
Cape Horn, that tramples beauty into wreck,
And crumples steel and smites the strong man dumb.
5   Down clattered flying kites and staysails; some
Sang out in quick, high calls: the fair-leads skirled,
And from the southwest came the end of the world . . .

"Lay out!" the Bosun yelled. The Dauber laid
Out on the yard, gripping the yard, and feeling
10 Sick at the mighty space of air displayed
Below his feet, where mewing birds were wheeling.
A giddy fear was on him; he was reeling.
He bit his lip half through, clutching the jack.
A cold sweat glued the shirt upon his back.

15 The yard was shaking, for a brace was loose.
He felt that he would fall; he clutched, he bent,
Clammy with natural terror to the shoes
While idiotic promptings came and went.
Snow fluttered on a wind-flaw and was spent;
20 He saw the water darken. Someone yelled,
"Frap it; don't stay to furl! Hold on!" He held.

Darkness came down—half darkness—in a whirl;
The sky went out, the waters disappeared.
He felt a shocking pressure of blowing hurl
25 The ship upon her side. The darkness speared
At her with wind; she staggered, she careered;
Then down she lay. The Dauber felt her go,
He saw her yard tilt downwards. Then the snow

---

5. KITES—Light, lofty sails for use in light breezes.
6. FAIR-LEADS—Blocks or rings which serve as guides for running rigging.
9. YARD—A long spar which supports the sail.
21. FRAP IT—Bind it tightly together.

Whirled all about—dense, multitudinous, cold—
30   Mixed with the wind's one devilish thrust and shriek,
Which whiffled out men's tears, defeated, took hold,
Flattening the flying drift against the cheek.
The yards buckled and bent, man could not speak.
The ship lay on her broadside; the wind's sound
35   Had devilish malice at having got her downed.

How long the gale had blown he could not tell,
Only the world had changed, his life had died.
A moment now was everlasting hell.
Nature an onslaught from the weather side,
40   A withering rush of death, a frost that cried,
Shrieked, till he withered at the heart; a hail
Plastered his oilskins with an icy mail. . . .

[When the gale has subsided somewhat, the bosun mate takes charge of
clearing away the masts, spars, and sails that have been broken or torn;
and so the men are again ordered into the rigging. The sea is still churn-
ing in the wind and the cold is bitter.]

"Up!" yelled the Bosun; "up and clear the wreck!"
The Dauber followed where he led; below
45   He caught one giddy glimpsing of the deck
Filled with white water, as though heaped with snow.
He saw the streamers of the rigging blow

Straight out like pennons from the splintered mast,
Then, all sense dimmed, all was an icy blast.

50 Roaring from nether hell and filled with ice,
Roaring and crashing on the jerking stage,
An utter bridle given to utter vice,
Limitless power mad with endless rage
Withering the soul; a minute seemed an age.
55 He clutched and hacked at ropes, at rags of sail,
Thinking that comfort was a fairy tale,

Told long ago—long, long ago—long since
Heard of in other lives—imagined, dreamed—
There where the basest beggar was a prince.
60 To him in torment where the tempest screamed,
Comfort and warmth and ease no longer seemed
Things that a man could know; soul, body, brain,
Knew nothing but the wind, the cold, the pain.

52. AN UTTER BRIDLE GIVEN TO UTTER VICE—That is, there was no restraint
whatever on the wind.

FOR INTERPRETATION

1. With what lines in the first stanza does Masefield suggest the fear
that all seamen have of Cape Horn? Why is it so difficult to "round the
Horn"?

2. What preparation did the crew make for taking the ship around?
Why? What was the Dauber's assignment? How did he feel about it?
What made his job extra hard and extra dangerous? Explain what was
meant by the command, "Frap it; don't stay to furl!"

3. Quote the lines with which Masefield describes the blow of the storm
that struck the ship as it turned. Quote the lines that tell how the ship
responded to the force of the storm. Quote the lines that describe the
effect of the storm on the men.

4. Which stanza tells of the Dauber's sensations during the gale?
What is the most vivid impression created by the stanza—of what sensation?

5. Did the Bosun climb up into the rigging with the men? How can
you tell? With what words does the poet indicate the strength of the
wind? What was the effect of the wind and cold on the Dauber? Which
lines do you think best describe his feelings? What are the feelings of the
reader as he reads this last stanza?

AN IRISH AIRMAN FORESEES HIS DEATH

WILLIAM BUTLER YEATS

I KNOW that I shall meet my fate
Somewhere among the clouds above;
Those that I fight I do not hate,
Those that I guard I do not love;
5   My country is Kiltartan Cross,
My countrymen Kiltartan's poor,
No likely end could bring them loss
Or leave them happier than before.
Nor law, nor duty bade me fight,
10   Nor public men, nor cheering crowds,
A lonely impulse of delight
Drove to this tumult in the clouds;
I balanced all, brought all to mind,
The years to come seemed waste of breath,
15   A waste of breath the years behind
In balance with this life, this death.

FOR INTERPRETATION

1. Who is speaking in the poem? How old is he?
2. What does he think will be the outcome of his fighting? What lines tell us? How does he feel about his job of fighter-flying—does he hate it? fear it? enjoy it? How can you tell?
3. What reasons does he give for being a fighter in the air force—is it for love of country? for revenge? for fame? for some other reason?
4. Do you think the airman is pretending his indifference to ordinary motives? Or is he telling the truth? Discuss. Which do you think is the braver man—the Dauber or the Irish airman? Discuss.

TO THE FOUR COURTS, PLEASE

JAMES STEPHENS

MG   THE driver rubbed at his nettly chin
With a huge, loose forefinger, crooked and black,

And his wobbly, violet lips sucked in,
And puffed out again and hung down slack:
5   One fang shone through his lop-sided smile,
In his little pouched eye flickered years of guile.

MB   And the horse, poor beast, it was ribbed and forked,
And its ears hung down, and its eyes were old,
And its knees were knuckly, and as we talked
10   It swung the stiff neck that could scarcely hold
Its big, skinny head up—then I stepped in,
And the driver climbed to his seat with a grin.

U   God help the horse and the driver too,
And the people and beasts who have never a friend,
MG1 15   For the driver easily might have been you,
MB1   And the horse be me by a different end.
D   And nobody knows how their days will cease,
L   And the poor, when they're old, have little of peace.

FOR INTERPRETATION

1. What details in "To the Four Courts, Please" let the reader know that the driver is poor? Would he come properly under the poor-but-honest rating? How can you tell? What kind of conveyance is he driving? Is there anything attractive about him or his equipment? Why did the poet hire him? Explain.

2. What kind of person was the poet? Was he fastidious? friendly? proud? self-centered? imaginative? sympathetic? How do you judge?

3. Explain the title of the poem.

AN OLD WOMAN OF THE ROADS

PADRAIC COLUM

In Ireland, old women beggars are not uncommon sights. Alone in the world and destitute, unable to work, they prefer the uncertain fortune of begging to accepting the "charity" of the poorhouse. A poet meeting such a forlorn creature on the road might well wonder what she was thinking.

LG O, TO have a little house!
    To own the hearth and stool and all!
    The heaped-up sods upon the fire,
    The pile of turf against the wall!

   5 To have a clock with weights and chains
    And pendulum swinging up and down!
    A dresser filled with shining delph,
    Speckled and white and blue and brown!

LG1 I could be busy all the day
   10 Clearing and sweeping hearth and floor,
    And fixing on their shelf again
    My white and blue and speckled store!

LG2 I could be quiet there at night
    Beside the fire and by myself,
   15 Sure of a bed and loath to leave
    The ticking clock and the shining delph!

DG1 Och! but I'm weary of mist and dark,
    And roads where there's never a house nor bush,
    And tired I am of bog and road,
   20 And the crying wind and the lonesome hush!

3. THE HEAPED-UP SODS—Peat, the common fuel of Ireland.

LG   And I am praying to God on high,
              And I am praying Him night and day,
              For a little house—a house of my own—
              Out of the wind's and the rain's way.

FOR INTERPRETATION

1. Describe the cottage of which the old woman dreams. What are its furnishings? How do house and furniture compare with most people's dream houses? Discuss. Why would the old woman consider a hearth and stool so important? What kind of fuel would she burn? What most of all would the house mean to her?

2. Which do you think is the more pathetic figure, the old woman of the roads, or the cabby in "To the Four Courts, Please"?

GUNGA DIN

RUDYARD KIPLING

A number of British soldiers lie sprawled about their quarters, smoking and exchanging yarns. One of their number who has seen service in India is speaking.

        You may talk o' gin and beer
        When you're quartered safe out 'ere,
        An' you're sent to penny-fights an' Aldershot it;
        But when it comes to slaughter
5   You will do your work on water,
        An' you'll lick the bloomin' boots of 'im that's got it.
        Now in Injia's sunny clime,
        Where I used to spend my time
        A-servin' of 'Er Majesty the Queen,
10   Of all them blackfaced crew
        The finest man I knew
        Was our regimental *bhisti*, Gunga Din.
          He was "Din! Din! Din!
          You limping lump o' brick-dust, Gunga Din!

2. QUARTERED SAFE OUT 'ERE—Quartered at Aldershot, near London.
3. PENNY-FIGHTS—Sham battles.
12. *Bhisti*—Water-carrier.

41

15   Hi! *slippy hitherao!*
      Water! get it! *Panee lao!*
      You squidgy-nosed old idol, Gunga Din."

       The uniform 'e wore
       Was nothin' much before,
20   An' rather less than 'arf o' that be'ind,
       For a piece o' twisty rag
       An' a goatskin water-bag
       Was all the field-equipment 'e could find.
       When the sweatin' troop-train lay
25   In a sidin' through the day,
       Where the 'eat would make your bloomin' eyebrows
         crawl,
       We shouted *"Harry By!"*
       Till our throats were brick-dry,
       Then wopped 'im cause 'e couldn't serve us all.
30   It was "Din! Din! Din!
       You 'eathen, where the mischief 'ave you been?
       You put some *juldee* in it
       Or I'll *marrow* you this minute
       If you don't fill up my helmet, Gunga Din!"

35   'E would dot an' carry one
       Till the longest day was done;
       An' 'e didn't seem to know the use o' fear.
       If we charged or broke or cut,
       You could bet your bloomin' nut,
40   'E'd be waitin' fifty paces right flank rear.
       With 'is *mussick* on 'is back
       'E would skip with our attack,
       An' watch us till the bugles made "Retire,"
       An' for all 'is dirty 'ide
45   'E was white, clear white, inside
       When 'e went to tend the wounded under fire!

15. *Slippy hitherao*—Slide here quickly.
16. *Panee lao*—Bring water swiftly.
27. *Harry By!*—O, brother!
32. *Juldee*—Speed.
33. *Marrow*—Hit.
41. *Mussick*—Water bag made of skin.

It was "Din! Din! Din!"
With the bullets kickin' dust-spots on the green,
When the cartridges ran out,
50   You could hear the front-files shout,
"Hi! ammunition-mules an' Gunga Din!"

I shan't forgit the night
When I dropped be'ind the fight
With a bullet where my belt-plate should 'a' been.
55   I was chokin', mad with thirst,
An' the man that spied me first
Was our good old grinnin', gruntin' Gunga Din.
'E lifted up my 'ead,
An' he plugged me where I bled,
60   An' 'e guv me 'arf-a-pint o' water—green;
It was crawlin' and it stunk,
But of all the drinks I've drunk,
I'm gratefullest to one from Gunga Din.
It was "Din! Din! Din!
65   'Ere's a beggar with a bullet through 'is spleen,
'E's chawin' up the ground,
An' 'e's kickin' all around:
For Gawd's sake git the water, Gunga Din!"

'E carried me away
70   To where a *dooli* lay,
An' a bullet come an' drilled the beggar clean.
'E put me safe inside,
An' just before 'e died:
"I hope you liked your drink," sez Gunga Din.
75   So I'll meet 'im later on
At the place where 'e is gone—
Where it's always double drill and no canteen;
'E'll be squattin' on the coals,
Givin' drink to poor damned souls,
80   An' I'll get a swig in hell from Gunga Din!
Yes, Din! Din! Din!
You Lazarushian-leather Gunga Din!

70. *Dooli*—A litter for the wounded.
82. LAZARUSHIAN—From Lazarus, a kindly beggar.

Though I've belted you and flayed you,
By the livin' Gawd that made you,
85   You're a better man than I am, Gunga Din!

FOR INTERPRETATION

1. What had the soldiers been talking about when the Tommy back from India remembered Gunga Din? Express the thought of the first six lines in simple English. Who are meant by the "black-faced crew" of line 10? What was Gunga Din's job? How do you account for the way the soldiers talked to him? Did they really like him? Or wasn't it till afterwards that they realized his worth? Can one judge men's affections by the names they call each other? or the tones in which they say things? Discuss.

2. What did Gunga Din look like? Why was he so important to the regiment? How do you know that he more than did his duty? What was the extra service he gave along with his job? "The finest man I knew" is the comment "Tommy" makes about Gunga Din. What qualities of character in Gunga Din excite the admiration of men of every race? Enumerate them and in each case, prove that Gunga had that quality. Do you agree with the thought expressed by "Tommy" in the last two lines of the poem? Why or why not?

HE FELL AMONG THIEVES

HENRY NEWBOLT

The situation in "He Fell Among Thieves" is something like that in Kipling's well-known poem, "The Ballad of East and West." Only this time the young Englishman has pursued and killed the thieves and then fallen into the hands of more outlaws in their own territory.

MB1   "Ye have robbed," said he, "ye have slaughter'd and made an end,
         Take your ill-got plunder, and bury the dead:
         What will ye more of your guest and sometime friend?"
D   "Blood for our blood," they said.

MB1 5 He laugh'd: "If one may settle the score for five,
         I am ready; but let the reckoning stand till day:

44

I have loved the sunlight as dearly as any alive."

D   "You shall die at dawn," said they.

M   He flung his empty revolver down the slope,
10   He climb'd alone to the Eastward edge of the trees:
       All night long in a dream untroubled of hope
          He brooded, clasping his knees.

       He did not hear the monotonous roar that fills
          The ravine where the Yassin river sullenly flows;
15   He did not see the starlight on the Laspur hills,
          Or the far Afghan snows.

L   He saw the April noon on his books aglow,
          The wisteria trailing in at the window wide;
       He heard his father's voice from the terrace below
20   Calling him down to ride.

G   He saw the little gray church across the park,
          The mounds that hid the loved and honor'd dead:
       The Norman arch, the chancel softly dark,
          The brasses black and red.

B1 25 He saw the School Close, sunny and green,
          The runner beside him, the stand by the parapet
             wall,
       The distant tape, and the crowd roaring between,
          His own name over all.

B2   He saw the dark wainscot and the timber'd roof,
30   The long tables, and the faces merry and keen;
       The College Eight and their trainer dining aloof,
          The Dons on the dais serene.

B3   He watched the liner's stem ploughing the foam,
          He felt her trembling speed and the thrash of her
             screw;
35   He heard the passengers' voices talking of home,
          He saw the flag she flew.

M   And now it was dawn. He rose strong on his feet,
          And strode to his ruined camp below the wood;
          He drank the breath of the morning cool and sweet:
  40   His murderers around him stood.

          Light on the Laspur hills was broadening fast,
          The blood-red snow peaks chill'd to dazzling white;
          He turn'd and saw the golden circle at last,
          Cut by the Eastern height.

U 45   "O glorious Life, Who dwellest in earth and sun,
          I have lived, I praise and adore Thee."
B1   A sword swept.
L   Over the pass the voices one by one
          Faded, and the hill slept.

FOR INTERPRETATION

1. Who speaks the first three lines of the poem? What had the thieves done besides steal? What indicates that the speaker had once been on friendly terms with the men? Who makes the reply? What does their answer mean?

2. How many outlaws has the Englishman killed? Why is he now helpless? What time of day is it that the conversation takes place? What request does the Englishman make and why? What line tells that the request is granted?

3. Why did the young man throw his revolver away? Why did he climb to the *"Eastward* edge of the trees"? Explain the significance of the line, "in a dream *untroubled* of hope." Do you think the mind is more at ease when one realizes that there is no hope? Discuss.

4. Describe the immediate scene that surrounds him. What are the scenes that the Englishman sees during the night? Where are they? What impression do you get of his boyhood home? What kind of record did he make in school? in college? Where do you think the liner was going? What was "the flag she flew"? Why do you think the flag is mentioned especially? What do you learn about the young man himself from the thoughts he entertained on his last night alive? What might some men have been thinking in such a situation?

5. Describe how he meets the dawn. What is the significance of his prayer? What adjectives best describe his character? Which of these qualities are typical of Englishmen at their best? Discuss. What action is indicated by the last two lines of the poem? What is the final feeling left with the reader?

REMINISCENCES OF CONRAD

JOHN GALSWORTHY

Joseph Conrad was British only by adoption. But he was a real personality; and at the time of his death in 1924 an appraisal of the man and his works was written by a fellow writer, the top-ranking novelist of the times—John Galsworthy.

MANY writers knew my dead friend, and will write of him better than I; but no other writer knew him quite so long, or knew him both as sailor and novelist.

It was in March, 1893, that I first met Conrad on board the English sailing ship *Torrens* in Adelaide Harbor. He was superintending the stowage of cargo. Very dark he looked in the burning sunlight—tanned, with a peaked brown beard, almost black hair, and dark brown eyes, over which the lids were deeply folded. He was thin, not tall, his arms very long, his shoulders broad, his head set rather forward. He spoke to me with a strong foreign accent. He seemed to me strange on an English ship. For fifty-six days I sailed in his company.

The chief mate bears the main burden of a sailing ship. All the first night he was fighting a fire in the hold. None of us seventeen passengers knew of it till long after. It was he who had most truck with the tail of that hurricane off the Leeuwin, and later with another storm. He was a good seaman, watchful of the weather, quick in handling the ship; considerate with the apprentices—we had a long, unhappy Belgian youth among them, who took unhandily to the sea and dreaded going aloft; Conrad compassionately spared him all he could. With the crew he was popular; they were individuals to him, not a mere gang; and long after he would talk of this or that among them, especially of old Andy, the sailmaker: "I likéd that old fellow, you know." He was friendly with the young second mate, a cheerful, capable young seaman, very English; and respectful, if faintly ironic, with his whiskered, stout old English captain. I, supposed to be studying navigation for the Admiralty Bar, would every day work out the position of the ship with the captain. On one side of the saloon table we would sit and check our observations with those of Conrad, who from the other side of the table would look at us a little quizzically. For Conrad had commanded ships, and his subordinate position on the *Torrens* was only due to the fact that he was then still convalescent from the Congo experience which had nearly killed him. Many evening watches in fine weather we spent on the poop. Ever the great teller of a tale, he had already nearly twenty years of tales to tell. Tales of ships and storms, of Polish revolution, of his youthful Carlist gun-running adventure, of the Malay seas, and the Congo; and of men and men: all to a listener who had the insatiability of a twenty-five-year-old.

When, seven or eight years later, Conrad, though then in his best period and long acclaimed a great writer by the few, was struggling, year in year out, to keep a roof over him amidst the apathy of the many who afterwards fell over each other to read him in his worst period, I remember urging him to raise the wind [1] by tale-telling in public. He wouldn't and he was right. Still, so incomparable a *raconteur* must have made a success, even though his audience might have missed many words owing to his strange yet fascinating accent.

---

[1] TO RAISE THE WIND, etc.—To build up a public following by lecturing—telling stories of his experiences at sea.

On that ship he talked of life, not literature; and I remember feeling that he outweighed for me all the other experiences of that voyage. Fascination was Conrad's great characteristic—the fascination of vivid expressiveness and zest, of his deeply affectionate heart, and his far-ranging subtle mind. . . .

Between his voyages in the last days of his sailor's life Conrad used to stay at rooms in Gillingham Street, near Victoria Station. It was there that he read so prodigiously, and there that he suffered from bouts of that lingering Congo fever which dogged his health and fastened a deep, fitful gloom over his spirit. In a letter to me he once said: "I don't say anything of actual bodily pain, for, God is my witness, I care for that less than nothing." He was, indeed, truly stoical, and his naturally buoyant spirit reacted with extreme suddenness. But all the years I knew him—thirty-one—he had to fight for decent health. Such words as "I have been abominably ill—abominably is the right word," occur again and again in his letters, and his creative achievement in a language not native to him, in face of these constant bouts of illness, approaches the marvelous.

It was the sea that, in my view, gave Conrad to the English language. A fortunate accident—for he knew French better than English at that time. He started his manhood, as it were, at Marseilles. In a letter to me (1905) he says: "In Marseilles I did begin life thirty-one years ago. It's the place where the puppy opened his eyes." He was ever more at home with French literature than with English, spoke that language with less accent, liked Frenchmen, and better understood their clearer thoughts. And yet, perhaps, not quite an accident; for after all he had the roving quality which has made the English the great sea nation of the world; and, I suppose, instinct led him to seek in English ships the fullest field of expression for his nature. England, too, was to him the romantic country; it had been enshrined for him, as a boy in Poland, by Charles Dickens, Captain Marryat, Captain Cook, and Franklin, the Arctic explorer. He always spoke of Dickens with the affection we have for the writers who captivate our youth.

No one, I take it, ever read the earliest Conrad without the bewildered fascination of one opening eyes on a new world; without, in fact, the feeling he himself describes in that passage of *Youth,* where he wakes up in an open boat in his first Eastern port, and sees "the East looking at him." I doubt if he will ever be surpassed as a creator of what we Westerners term "exotic atmosphere." The Malay coasts and rivers of *Almayer's Folly, An Outcast of the Islands* and the first pages of *The Rescue;* the Congo of *Heart of Darkness;* the Central Southern America of *Nostromo,* with many other land and seascapes, are bits of atmospheric painting *in excelsis.* Only one expression adequately described the sensations of us who read *Almayer's Folly* in 1894. We rubbed our eyes. Conrad was critically accepted from the very start; he never published a book that did not rouse a chorus of praise; but it was twenty years before he was welcomed by the public with sufficient warmth to give him a decent income.

Chance, in 1914—an indifferent Conrad—at last brought him fortune. From that year on to the end his books sold well; yet with the exception of *The Secret Sharer* and some parts of *Victory,* none of his work in that late period was up to his own exalted mark. Was it natural that popular success should have coincided with the lesser excellence? Or was it simply an example of how long the strange takes to pierce the pickled hide of the reader of fiction? Or, still more simply, the undeniable fact that the reading public is more easily reached than it used to be? . . .

A sailor and an artist, he had little sense of money. He was not of those who can budget exactly and keep within it; and anyway he had too little, however neatly budgeted. It is true that his dramatic instinct and his subtlety would take a sort of pleasure in plotting against the lack of money, but it was at best a lugubrious amusement for one who had to whip his brain along when he was tired, when he was ill, when he was almost desperate. Letter after letter, talk after talk, unfolded to me the travail of those years. He needed to be the Stoic he really was.

I used to stay with him a good deal from 1895–1905, first at Stanford in Essex and then at Stanford in Kent. He was indefatigably good to me while my own puppy's eyes were opening to literature, and I was still in the early stages of that struggle with his craft which a writer worth his salt never quite abandons.

His affectionate interest was always wholly generous. In his letters to me, two to three hundred, there is not a sentence which breaks, or even jars, the feeling that he cared that one should do good work. There is some valuable criticism, but never any impatience, and no stinting of appreciation or encouragement. He never went back on friendship. The word "loyalty" has been much used by those who write or speak of him. It has been well used. He was always loyal to what he had at heart—to his philosophy, to his work, and to his friends; he was loyal even to his dislikes (not few) and to his scorn. People talk of Conrad as an aristocrat; I think it rather a silly word to apply to him. His mother's family, the Bebrowskis, were Polish land-owners; the Korzeniowskis, too, his father's family, came, I think, of landowning stock, but the word aristocrat is much too dry to fit Conrad; he had no touch with "ruling," no feeling for it, except, maybe, such as is necessary to sail a ship; he was first and last the rover and the artist, with such a first-hand knowledge of men and things that he was habitually impatient with labels and pigeon-holes, with cheap theorizing and word debauchery. He stared life very much in the face, and distrusted those who didn't. Above all, he had the keen humor which spiflicates all class and catalogs, and all ideals and aspirations that are not grounded in the simplest springs of human nature. He laughed at the clichés of so-called civilization. His sense of humor, in-deed, was far greater than one might think from his work. He had an almost ferocious enjoyment of the absurd. Writing seemed to dry or sardonize his humor. But in conversation his sense of fun was much more vivid; it would leap up in the midst of gloom or worry, and take charge with a shout.

Conrad had six country homes after his marriage, besides two temporary abodes. He wrote jestingly to my wife: "Houses are naturally rebellious and inimical to man." And, perhaps, having lived so much on ships, he really had a feeling of that sort. He certainly grew tired of them after a time.

I best remember Pent Farm at Stanford in Kent—that little, very old, charming, if inconvenient farmhouse, with its great barn beyond the yard, under the lee of the almost overhanging Pent. It was a friendly dwelling where you had to mind your head in connection with beams; and from whose windows you watched ducks and cats and lambs in the meadows beyond. He liked those quiet fields and that sheltering hill. Though he was not what we should call a "lover of nature" in the sense of one who spends long hours lost in the life of birds and flowers, of animals and trees, he could be vividly impressed by the charm and the variety of such things. He was fond, too, of Hudson's books; and no lover of Hudson's work is insensible to nature.

In Conrad's study at the Pent we burned together many midnight candles, much tobacco. In that house were written some of the *Youth* volume, *Lord Jim,* most of the *Typhoon* volume, *Nostromo, The Mirror of the Sea, The Secret Agent,* and other of Conrad's best work. Save that the story *Youth* was written just before, at Stanford in Essex, the "Pent" may be said to synchronize with Conrad's best period. Kent was undoubtedly the county of his adoption, and this was the first of his four Kentish homes.

Many might suppose that Conrad would naturally settle by the sea. He never did. He had seen too much of it; like the sailor who when he turns into his bunk takes care that no sea air shall come in, he lived always well inland. The sea was no favorite with one too familiar with its moods. He disliked being labeled a novelist of the sea. He wrote of the sea, as perhaps no one, not even Herman Melville, has written; but dominant in all his writing of the sea is the note of struggle and escape. His hero is not the sea, but man in conflict with that cruel and treacherous element. Ships he loved, but the sea—no. Not that he ever abused it, or talked of it with aversion; he accepted it as he accepted all the inscrutable remorselessness of Nature. It was man's job to confront Nature with a loyal and steady heart—that was Conrad's creed, his contribution to the dignity of life. Is there a better? First and last he was interested in men, fascinated by the terrific spectacle of their struggles in a cosmos about which he had no illusions. He was sardonic, but he had none of the cynicism characteristic of small, cold-hearted beings. . . .

In later years, when his enemy, gout, often attacked his writing hand, he was obliged to resort a good deal to dictation of first drafts. I cannot but believe that his work suffered from that necessity. But there were other and increasing handicaps—the war, which he felt keenly, and those constant bouts of ill-health which dragged at his marvelous natural vitality. I think I never saw Conrad quite in repose. His hands, his feet, his knees, his lips—sensitive, expressive, and ironical—something was always in motion, the dynamo never quite at rest within him. His mind was extraordinarily active and his memory for impressions and people most retentive, so that he stored with wonderful accuracy all the observations of his dark-brown eyes, which were so piercing and yet could be so soft. He had the precious faculty of interest in detail. To that we owe his pictures of scenes and life long past—their compelling verisimilitude, the intensely vivid variety of their composition. The storehouse of his subconscious self was probably as interesting and comprehensive a museum as any in the world. It is from the material in our subconscious minds that we create. Conrad's eyes never ceased snapshotting, and the millions of photographs they took were laid away by him to draw on. Besides, he was not hampered in his natural watchfulness by the preoccupation of an egoistic personality. He was not an egoist; he had far too much curiosity and genuine interest in things and people to be that. I don't mean to say that he had not an interest in himself and a belief in his own powers. His allusions to his work are generally disparaging; but at heart he knew the value of his gifts; and he liked appreciation, especially from those (not many) in whose judgment he had faith. He received more praise, probably, than any other writer of our time; but he never suffered from that *parvenu* disease, swelled head; and "I," "I," "I," played no part in his talk. . . .

"Genius" has somewhere been defined as the power to make much out of little. In *Nostromo* Conrad made a continent out of just a sailor's glimpse of a South American port, some twenty years before. In *The Secret Agent* he created an underworld out of probably as little actual experience. On the other hand, we have in *Youth* and *Heart of Darkness* the raw material of his own life transmuted into the gold of fine art. People, and there are such, who think that writers like Conrad, if there be any, can shake things from their sleeve, would be staggered if they could have watched the pain and stress of his writing life. In his last letter to me but one, February, 1924, he says: "However, I have begun to work a little—on my runaway novel. I call it 'runaway' because I've been after it for two years (*The Rover* is a mere interlude) without being able to overtake it. The end seems as far as ever! It's like a chase in a nightmare—weird and exhausting. Your news that you have finished a novel brings me a bit of comfort. So there are novels that *can* be finished—then why not mine? Of course I see 'fiction' advertised in the papers—

heaps of it. But published announcements seem to me mere phantasms. . . . I don't believe in their reality." There are dozens of such allusions to almost despairing efforts in his letters. He must, like all good workmen, have had his hours of compensation; but if ever a man worked in the sweat of spirit and body it was Conrad. That is what makes his great achievement so inspiring. He hung on to his job through every kind of weather, mostly foul. He never shirked. In an age more and more mechanical, more and more given to short cuts and the line of least resistance, the example of his life's work shines out; its instinctive fidelity, his artist's desire to make the best thing he could. Fidelity! Yes, that is the word which best sums up his life and work.

The last time I saw Conrad—about a year ago—I wasn't very well, and he came and sat in my bedroom, full of affectionate solicitude. It seems, still, hardly believable that I shall not see him again. His wife tells me that a sort of homing instinct was on him in the last month of his life, that he seemed sometimes to wish to drop everything and go back to Poland. Birth calling to Death—no more than that, perhaps, for he loved England, the home of his wandering, of his work, of his last long landfall.

If to a man's deserts is measured out the quality of his rest, Conrad shall sleep well.   *1924*

DID YOU READ WITH UNDERSTANDING?

1. In what two-fold way was Galsworthy acquainted with Conrad? How did that make him especially well qualified to write about Conrad?

2. What kind of sailor was Conrad? Why did he make a good officer? How would he have treated a man like the Dauber in Masefield's poem? How can you tell? How was Conrad different from most sailors? What evidence did he give in 1893 that he would make a good writer?

3. What nationality was Conrad by birth? What would be his "native" tongue? What other language did he speak better than English? Why did he write his books in English? For what reasons does Galsworthy think English a suitable choice for him? How many of the English authors, favorites of Conrad, have you read? How many books or stories by Conrad have you read? How would you describe his English style?

4. What were the outstanding *human* traits of Conrad? What qualities gave individuality to the man?

5. Where did Conrad do his best writing? What does Galsworthy consider his best works? Did Conrad like the sea? Why could he write of it so well? Did Conrad write easily? What made him a great writer?

VICTORIA REGINA

LAURENCE HOUSMAN

In 1935 Mr. Laurence Housman, British novelist and playwright, gave to the modern world one of its great historical dramas, *Victoria Regina*. At first the play was denied presentation by the British censor because "the person of Victoria was too sacred for stage presentation." Under King Edward VIII, however, the play was produced, and permission was given for American production. The role of Victoria was made famous through the superb acting of Helen Hayes.

Mr. Housman, in his introduction to the published text of the play, makes the point that England has had two great queens, Elizabeth and Victoria, both so great that they gave their names to the age in which they reigned. We already know the tremendous significance of the Elizabethan Age and Mr. Housman gives us in the play much of the color and flavor as well as the historical development of the Victorian Era. The play covers the life of Victoria from her childhood as the princess to the Diamond Jubilee of 1897, when the entire Empire paid homage to the Queen.

Five selected scenes from the play follow, with introductory and connecting narrative so that the reader may follow the action of the entire play and at the same time enjoy the original text of a few outstanding episodes.

OPENING EPISODES OF THE PLAY

The opening scenes of the play take place in the year 1837. The first episode gives a vivid picture of the tutorial education of the princess, and lets the reader know that the King is seriously ill. In the event of his death Victoria, only eighteen years of age, will become queen. Scene 2 depicts the announcement of her accession to the throne as made by Lord Conyngham and the Archbishop of Canterbury. In this scene and in the one that follows, Victoria shows unquestionably that she intends to be sovereign, even excluding the anxious minstrations of her mother, the Duchess of Kent. Victoria's concluding line is, "So. Now I am Queen. And my reign has really begun—Poor Mama!" The third scene is presented below.

SUITABLE SUITORS

1838

THE QUEEN *is still in mourning* [1] *but she does not mourn. Animated and happy, she sits listening to what, in earlier youth, she was never allowed to hear—the conversation of a gentleman of breeding, worldly, witty, and to a certain extent wise. This she thoroughly enjoys. And* LORD MELBOURNE, *her Prime Minister, enjoys talking to her. She is not clever; she cannot say clever things; but the mingled strain of artlessness and self-possession, of dignity and simplicity, which he finds in his Royal Mistress's character—a character which he is artfully molding, not so much to his own ends as his own convenience—attracts and delights him. They are now on such intimate terms that* THE QUEEN, *when he comes for an audience, does not keep him long standing. They are seated now; and as an indication of their pleasant relations,* THE QUEEN *is going on with her wool-work.*

Victoria. How do you begin the day, Lord Melbourne?

Melbourne. Begin it, Ma'am?

Victoria. Yes. What do you do first—you, who have so many things to do in the day? I find it difficult to know myself where to begin.

Melbourne. Well, starting at the very beginning, Ma'am, I breakfast—if I may be allowed to say so—in bed.

Victoria. Oh! I should never have thought of that!

Melbourne. Try it, Ma'am, try it! It makes an invaluable break between sleeping and waking. Sleeping is one thing:

[1] IN MOURNING—For the death of her uncle, the former King.

56

it takes time. Waking is another: it takes more time. Working is another: and takes more time than all the others put together.

Victoria. And after breakfast, what then?

Melbourne. Well, let me think! . . . First, I rise, Ma'am. Over that I need not go into details.

Victoria. No?

Melbourne. Or—would you like me to, Ma'am?

Victoria. [*A little disappointed.*] No, oh, no. You rise?

Melbourne. I rise from my bed. Then I ride in the park; when I come home I write. So I begin with the three R's.

Victoria. But "write" begins with a *W*.

Melbourne. I am corrected, Ma'am. "Write" *does* begin with a W. Your Majesty is right, as usual.

Victoria. [*Laughing.*] Oh! you are funny, Lord Melbourne.

Melbourne. Funny?

Victoria. So witty, I mean. You always say something amusing. Yes; please go on!

Melbourne. That, Ma'am is all the beginning of my day. When that is done, the day is half over.

Victoria. And when do you say your prayers, Lord Melbourne?

Melbourne. My prayers? Oh, I say them whenever I have time for them.

Victoria. [*A little shocked.*] But—Lord Melbourne!

Melbourne. As often, and as long as possible.

Victoria. That seems to me a little irregular.

Melbourne. Did your Majesty never hear the story of the holy monk [2] who had a Vision vouchsafed to him: a Vision of—well, of a very high character? And just as the Vision appeared, the chapel-bell began ringing. Duty—discipline—required the monk to leave the seraphic Vision and go into chapel with the rest: a function which, in these circumstances, was so like praying to the Vision behind its back, that it seemed almost foolish. It was a hard thing to do; but the monk did it. In great anguish of spirit, he left the Vision to itself, and went and did his duty. The service seemed intolerably long; he was dying to get back to his Vision. At last he was able to do so. The Vision was still there; and as he fell down before it in renewed adoration, the Vision made this remark; "If you had not answered that bell,

---

[2] THE STORY OF THE HOLY MONK—The story Lord Melbourne refers to is told by Longfellow as "The Legend Beautiful" in his *Tales of a Wayside Inn.*

I should not have stayed"—or words to that effect. Ma'am, my position as Prime Minister is very similar to that of the pious monk. I am constantly having to leave the vision to answer the *bell*.

Victoria. I thought, Lord Melbourne, that visions were rather superstitious things.

Melbourne. They are, Ma'am. In these days they are! Do your best to avoid them. And so, Ma'am, with your Majesty's permission, let me, for the moment, leave visions and come down to facts, and the affairs of state. There are certain things which will have soon to be decided, and one or two in which delay— delay of preparation at all events—is inadvisable.

Victoria. Oh, yes; there are many, I'm sure.

Melbourne. There is one especially, which your Majesty graciously deigned to mention the other day. You then said, Ma'am—with a courage which I thought remarkable in one so young—"Some day we must marry" . . . Has your Majesty given that matter any further thought?

Victoria. Oh, yes, Lord Melbourne, I have thought of it a great deal.

Melbourne. Is your Majesty prepared yet to take me into your Majesty's gracious confidence?

Victoria. You mean?

Melbourne. As to the possible recipient of so overwhelming an honor.

Victoria. Oh, I have not thought of any person—in particular. I mean, I have made no decision.

Melbourne. I am relieved to hear it, Ma'am. Then your Majesty has still an open mind!

Victoria. An open mind? Oh, *of course,* I shall make my own choice, Lord Melbourne.

Melbourne. Why, of course, Ma'am. I would not suggest otherwise, for a moment.

Victoria. But there are certain things as to which I am quite resolved.

Melbourne. As for instance?

Victoria. My marriage, Lord Melbourne, must be a marriage of affection.

Melbourne. That, I am sure, Ma'am, can be arranged without difficulty.

Victoria. Someone, I mean, whose character I can respect: one whom I can love and look up to.

Melbourne. Look up to?

Victoria. Yes, Lord Melbourne, it may sound strange to you; but I must have as my husband one whom I can eventually look up to—when I have trained him for the position he will have to occupy.

Melbourne. Oh, quite so, quite so. I trust that such a person will be found. And as your Majesty has owned to an open mind on the subject, I have here with me a list of—of possibles.

Victoria. Oh, Lord Melbourne, how interesting! . . . How many?

Melbourne. Well, at present, Ma'am, only five. But more are coming.

Victoria. Coming?

Melbourne. That is, I am making inquiries about them.

Victoria. What kind of inquiries?

Melbourne. All kinds of inquiries, Ma'am: my bounden duty. I would not wish to present your Majesty with one to whom there could be any possible objection.

Victoria. And you have already found *five!* Lord Melbourne, how clever of you!

Melbourne. "Possibles," I said. The inquiry is still going on; I am making it now. After inquiry of your Majesty, possibly there will be only one left.

Victoria. I would like to see your list, Lord Melbourne.

Melbourne. If your Majesty will pardon me a moment. When I have fully explained the considerations which guided me in my selection, I will submit my list for your Majesty's judgment, and (as I hope) approval.

Victoria. I cannot approve all five!

Melbourne. Just as a preliminary, Ma'am, why not? From five in the running select your favorite—the winner.

Victoria. Perhaps I shall not choose one for a long time. But go on; I am quite interested and excited.

Melbourne. The conditions, Ma'am, for a suitable consort to your Majesty's throne are necessarily special and particular—I might even say, peculiar. He must, of course, be of royal blood; on the other hand, he must not be the direct or likely heir of any foreign king or reigning prince.

Victoria. But why not, Lord Melbourne?

Melbourne. Political complication might arise, Ma'am. The crown of Hanover has passed from your Majesty to another, because of the law which limits the succession to males only: a circumstance which I regard as fortunate. We want no more crowns of Hanover; the country is better without them. To proceed, then: he must be a prince of some royal house, not too petty, not too important. We must avoid entangling alliances. He must also be of the Protestant faith. He must be sufficiently young to be a suitable life-partner to your Majesty. He must know, or be capable of learning the English language; capable also of adapting himself to English customs, habits, and prejudices. The last is the most difficult of all, since the English have a prejudice against foreigners.

Victoria. But, Lord Melbourne, that makes it impossible!

Melbourne. No, Ma'am. It only rather restricts the choice. Someone must be found who, once naturalized, is able to share the prejudice. I've known it done. Your Majesty's cousin, Prince George of Cambridge, for instance, is rapidly acquiring a thoroughly British outlook. In another five years or so he will have learned to dislike foreigners as much as we do.

Victoria. But do *you* dislike foreigners, Lord Melbourne?

Melbourne. No, Ma'am, no: of course not! But sometimes, for political reasons, one has to pretend to.

Victoria. Well, and what more?

Melbourne. It would be well, Ma'am, if he had some means of his own; though they need not be large. Parliament will provide whatever addition is necessary. He must have presence suited to his station; also a certain amount of brain, but not too much. He must not expect to interfere in politics.

Victoria. Indeed, no! I should never allow it.

Melbourne. Finally he must have health, and a sound constitution; he must—that is to say—come of good stock. And that, Ma'am, has been our main difficulty. Good stock, in the royal families of Europe, is rare.

Victoria. Please explain, for I don't quite understand. "Good stock"—I thought that meant cattle.

Melbourne. It does, Ma'am, in certain connections. But it also means—what comes from father to son. You find it referred to in the Second Commandment where we are told that the sins

60

of the fathers are visited on the children; also their virtues. In certain royal lines the sins and the virtues have been mixed; and one has to be careful that they shall not be more mixed. For that reason the marriage of royal cousins is generally inadvisable.

Victoria. Oh.

Melbourne. Generally, I say. In the case of a certain branch of your Majesty's family connections it is unfortunately true in a rather special degree. For that reason, in the list I am about to submit, I have not included—though it was suggested to me—two of your Majesty's cousins, who might otherwise have been desirable candidates—their Serene Highnesses Prince Ernest and Prince Albert of Saxe-Coburg Gotha.[3]

Victoria. But they both looked quite strong and healthy when I last saw them two years ago.

Melbourne. Apparently, Ma'am. But appearances are sometimes deceptive. It is, of course, a delicate—even a painful subject. But, acting under medical advice, and with a due sense of my responsibility, I have not included either of those young Princes in the list which I have now the honor to present to

your Majesty. [*He rises, and puts the list into her hand: hurriedly she glances down the names.*]

Victoria. Oh, but do I know any of them?

[3] The Saxe-Coburg cousins belonged to a line in which profuse bleeding was hereditary.

Melbourne. Your Majesty knows one of them very well.

Victoria. Oh—I didn't see. But Prince George is my cousin too.

Melbourne. By another branch, your Majesty. There is not there the same objection.

Victoria. Oh, but I couldn't marry my Cousin George! He is so—so——

Melbourne. Nobody wishes to decide your Majesty's choice. There are others

Victoria. But, as I say, I don't know any of them.

Melbourne. That, Ma'am, can easily be remedied. You ask them to your Court in turn, saying nothing. And you let them go away again—saying nothing; or you *do* say something; and then—either they stay, or they come again.

Victoria. But it is for me to decide, is it not?

Melbourne. It is for your Majesty to decide. Your Majesty need not marry at all.

Victoria. Oh, but I must marry. Mama always said so.

Melbourne. So I have been told. But in so important a matter, even devoted filial affection should not be allowed to influence your *choice*. I have merely indicated, Ma'am, that were any attempt to be made to influence your choice in a certain direction, that choice—for reasons already given, I should have to oppose.

Victoria. Lord Melbourne, I should not allow any opposition in a matter of that kind. It would not influence me for a moment.

Melbourne. No?

Victoria. Indeed, rather the other way.

Melbourne. I see. I understand, Ma'am. I sympathize. I shall say no more. I will only commend the matter to your Majesty's good sense—and conscience.

Victoria. Oh, how kind you always are to me, Lord Melbourne! What a lot you are teaching me!

Melbourne. What a lot you are teaching *me*. I have served under older sovereigns—under two. But I have never served under one who listened to advice so wisely or so well.

Victoria. [*Rising.*] Good-bye, Lord Melbourne. Will you keep the list, or shall I?

Melbourne. By your leave, Ma'am; let what I have said be either remembered or forgotten. [*He tears the list and throws it into the fireplace.*] The choice must be your own.

Victoria. Yes; but you haven't yet shown me—any portraits.
Melbourne. Portraits, Ma'am? Why portraits?
Victoria. I can't decide about anyone—till I know what they are like. It wouldn't be fair to them—or to me.
Melbourne. But your Majesty can send for them, and see.
Victoria. Oh, no. I'm not going to send for any, if I don't like the look of them.
Melbourne. Portraits are sometimes deceptive, Ma'am.
Victoria. Yes; I saw a portrait of my Cousin George of Cambridge the other day: quite handsome he looked.
Melbourne. I can get their portraits, Ma'am, if you wish. But court painters, like Prime Ministers, know their duty; and they only do what is expected of them. If they can't do that, they have to go.
Victoria. [*Going toward a table, on which stands a framed portrait.*] Here is a portrait that was sent to Mama, the other day—of my cousin, Prince Albert.
Melbourne. [*Who has followed to the table.*] Oh! Ah! Yes. H'm.
Victoria. Surely *he must* have grown very handsome! It would not be possible for a court painter to imagine anyone like that.
Melbourne. You never know, Ma'am, you never know. Imagination sometimes goes a long way. Well, the list having gone, am I now to make a collection of portraits for your Majesty?
Victoria. Oh, no, Lord Melbourne. I wasn't speaking seriously when I said that.
Melbourne. No more was I, Ma'am. But I do ask your Majesty to think seriously. The future welfare of this country is now in this little hand. [*He stoops and kisses it.*]
Victoria. Indeed, Lord Melbourne, I pay great attention to everything that you say. And I shall continue to take your advice, whenever I find it—possible. Good-bye.
[LORD MELBOURNE *bows himself out. She goes and takes up the portrait and kisses it.*]
Albert . . . Albert . . . Albert . . . will you marry me?

CONTINUING THE STORY

In the succeeding scene we discover the British minister of the Court of Saxe-Coburg Gotha in conference with the Prime Minister,

Lord Melbourne, in an attempt to arrange a marriage between Victoria and Prince Ernest, only legal son of the Duke of Saxe-Coburg Gotha. It is revealed that Prince Albert is not his son, hence a marriage with him will be most unwelcome. However, it also means that Albert is free from the bleeding taint that marked the Duke's family.

As the play moves on, we see Victoria neatly reversing the tables and disposing of her mother's constant presence and officiousness. In the eyes of all her court she is truly a queen. Even on the point of arranging her marriage Victoria decides—and proposes—to Albert! Her arrangements for the wedding, honeymoon, and political position of Albert, as Prince Consort, quite overwhelm him. It is obvious, however, that Victoria's wilfulness is tempered by genuine love for him.

LEADING STRINGS

1841

THE QUEEN (*it is still in the early days of her marriage*) *sits writing in one of the private apartments at Windsor. She looks at the clock which has just struck, and speaks to a lady-in-waiting, who stands at attention in the background.*

The Queen. Will you, please, go and send the Prince to me? It is ten o'clock; he ought to be here.

[*The Lady curtsies and goes.* THE QUEEN *takes up a small framed portrait, gazes upon it fondly, and resumes her writing. A stage-minute later (that is to say, ten seconds)* PRINCE ALBERT *enters: he carries a small nosegay, which he deposits with courtly grace in front of her. She lays down her pen, and, taking up the flowers to smell, says, correctively but not severely.*]

Ah! I was wondering when these would come.

Albert. [*Still very foreign in his pronunciation.*] You did not think that I had forgotten?

The Queen. No, I only thought you were a little late; as you are.

Albert. Just one minute. I do not yet quite know, to realize, how long at Windsor, it shall take to get from one place to another.

The Queen. It is all very grand and large, is it not? But that is what we—in our position—have to put up with.

Albert. Would it not be rather nice to make one corner of it our own?

The Queen. How do you mean—our own? It is *all* ours.

Albert. More private: where no one can come but ourselves. I mean—during the day.

The Queen. But we are quite private enough here, are we not?

Albert. No. At any moment someone comes and knocks; one of your ladies, or secretaries. I mean a room—a suite all private to itself—where, when you have seen your ministers, and all the rest, we can go in together, and not be disturbed by anyone: where it is known that—except on something emergent—no one shall come.

The Queen. Yes. Ah! yes.

Albert. Where, by ourselves, you could sing to me, and I could play to you, and read to you.

The Queen. Yes, Albert, that is just what I should love. I will have it all arranged for.

Albert. Will you not let me do it—my own way?

The Queen. You think I shall not do it as you wish, Albert?

Albert. Not so at all. But this I would just like to do—myself. At present it seems there is so little I *may* do.

The Queen. But you do a great deal, dearest, everything that I *want* you to do.

Albert. [*Sadly.*] Yes. And that is all.

The Queen. Is that not enough? . . . What is the matter?

Albert. I could wish that you wanted me to do a little more, Vicky—in my own way.

The Queen. But what else *can* you do?

Albert. Who knows—till you have let me try? There are so many things here that want doing badly.

The Queen. What sort of things?

Albert. Almost everything. The service—the ménage here is more than one hundred years old. We are still in the Middle Ages—almost.

The Queen. But that is so interesting!

Albert. And so wasteful.

The Queen. Wasteful? Why?

Albert. I will give you just an instance. The other day, for curiosity, I asked to be told the scale on which things for the commissariat are ordered—daily, weekly, monthly; the meat,

the wine, and all the rest of it. My dear, it is more like the provisioning of an army than of a single establishment.

The Queen. But this is Windsor.

Albert. It is a dozen Windsors—the Windsors of four reigns at least all rolled into one. One of the things I discovered was that anything once ordered always goes on being ordered. The thing is sent in and paid for, but it is not used.

The Queen. Then where does it go?

Albert. Where? You may well ask.

The Queen. Then I shall look into it at once, and have it altered.

Albert. Why not let *me* do it?

The Queen. You, Albert? But you do not understand our English ways.

Albert. But it is I who have discovered it.

The Queen. Yes. How did you? Did you go into the kitchens, Albert?

Albert. No; and I did not disguise myself either. I went to the controller's office, to the desk of the head accountant, and asked if I might see the books. I was told no, impossible. I went and took them down from the shelf, and looked at them myself. I have been doing that now for a week.

The Queen. Behind my back; without asking me?

Albert. Behind your back, *weibchen.* And now, to your face, I tell it. Here you are, the Queen of England, and being cheated by your own servants. Let me give you just one or two instances. You have in your stables twice so many horses than you can use. Who uses them? They have become the perquisite of your head-stableman. He hires them out.

The Queen. My horses hired! How improper! How abominable!

Albert. Yes.

The Queen. And how dishonest!

Albert. They do not think so. Custom has sanctioned it. They are quite open about it, when it is found out; and when you alter it, as it should be altered, they will consider themselves defrauded.

The Queen. Then they shall! But how extraordinary that such a thing should ever have been allowed!

Albert. I will give you one other instance—very funny. I found there was in the provision list, every month, forty pounds' weight of tallow candles. It surprised me to find that tallow candles were used here at all. I inquired; they were not. The tallow candles just come in to be looked at, and go out again. They are one of the kitchen perquisites.

The Queen. [*Scandalized.*] Really!

Albert. And how did they come in the first place? Thirty years ago, old King George, your grandpapa, had a cold in his nose; and tallows were ordered for it. In those days that was the cure. So the tallow has been on order ever since, though the nose that it was ordered to soothe has been twenty-one years in the grave.

The Queen. But forty pounds, Albert!

Albert. Yes, my dear, for the nose of a King—forty pounds; anything less than that would not have looked well in the accounts.

The Queen. And you have found all this out, Albert, by yourself?

Albert. Yes. With a lot of black faces looking on—while I did so.

The Queen. I think you should have come to me first, before doing so.

Albert. Why?

The Queen. For permission; that you might have my authority.

Albert. No, Vicky, I am not going to ask your permission for everything.

The Queen. Do you mean that?

Albert. Very much so, I mean it.

The Queen. Albert, is this going to be the first time that you disobey me?

Albert. Perhaps it should have come earlier. It will not be the last.

The Queen. Albert! You forget yourself!

Albert. I think, sometimes, that *you* forget *me*: that I am not your lover only, for you to play with and fondle. I am your husband too.

The Queen. And am not I—a good wife?

Albert. You are all that is kind; and I am grateful. But am I always to be a stranger in this country of yours?

The Queen. Oh, do not say that; you hurt me! But it takes time. You see, Albert, dear, you are so good—so serious about things—that you find it difficult to understand people—*other* people, I mean, who are different.

Albert. Goodness should not prevent understanding, Vicky.

The Queen. But it does, dearest! It makes you judge people too strictly.

Albert. But do I?

The Queen. Of course you do! And in a way, I like it—because it shows me *you*. But sometimes it is rather inconvenient, you know.

Albert. For instance?

The Queen. Well, don't you remember, the other night, when Uncle Augustus came in after dinner, having dined elsewhere. And of course, he *had* dined as *usual;* and so—almost at once you sent one of your gentlemen, with your compliments, to tell him that his carriage was waiting.

Albert. How did you know?

The Queen. He wrote to me the next day: such an explosive letter, saying such things about you, that I couldn't possibly let you read it. . . . So you see, dear——

Albert. Do you wish that I had let him stay?

68

The Queen. I wish that you had left it to me, Albert; for I had already decided what to do.

Albert. And what had you decided?

The Queen. I was going to bring the Court to an end by retiring early. Then all would have gone off quite naturally, and no one would have noticed. It would have been better, dearest.

Albert. And suppose the incident had been repeated?

The Queen. Well, Albert, after all he is an old man; and we can't expect to alter him now.

Albert. But we do expect your Court to alter, from what it has been, do we not? From what I have heard, there is already quite a great difference.

The Queen. Oh, yes; and it is nearly all your doing, Albert. And I would not have it otherwise, except for my Uncle, for whom we must make allowance.

Albert. Even your Uncles should be made to respect you.

The Queen. But they do, I am sure.

Albert. It was not respectful for him to come as he came the other night.

The Queen. It would not have been, had he quite realized— had he known——

Albert. How drunk he was?

The Queen. Albert, he *is* my Uncle. Please don't use such a common expression about one of *us.*

Albert. Is it too common—that word—said in English? Forgive me; I will say it in German.

The Queen. No, Albert. I wish you to talk English still, till you are more used to it. [*He moves away from her, controlling himself by an effort. She goes after him.*]

Of course, dearest, I love to hear you speak your own language, *sometimes.* It is so much more yourself. But till you know it better, you must, please, still speak English. And it is the same about English ways and customs—you must get to know them better, and be more like the rest of us.

Albert. You wish me to become English?

The Queen. Why, of course. *I* am English; so my husband must be English, too.

Albert. For that one should have begun earlier.

The Queen. I married you as soon as ever I could, Albert.

Albert. Ah, *weibchen!* So long as you do not repent of it.

The Queen. You are happy, Albert?

Albert. I will be more than happy, so long as—serving you—I am able to make a life worth living. But you must let me serve you—not feel myself useless.

The Queen. Useless!

Albert. Sometimes I feel that I am put—not quite in the corner, but on the shelf, just a little.

The Queen. Who does that?

Albert. You, my dear.

The Queen. But I—I worship you, Albert.

Albert. Too much! Let me come down to earth a little, now and then. Give my hands and my brain something to do, so that I may be able to respect myself. Am I only your plaything?

The Queen. Albert!

Albert. All day you work for hours with ministers and secretaries. And while they are with you, I may not come in. At the end of it I see you worn out from doing it all alone; but I may not help you. You do not even speak! Sometimes there are things that are still doubtful—how to decide; and I may not advise you. You do not ask me, or tell me anything!

The Queen. But Albert! Albert! You do not understand! The English are so jealous; they don't know you as I know you. They still look upon you as a foreigner, and are suspicious, for fear I should let you—advise me.

Albert. Am I *never* to help, or advise you—never? From your life's work am I always to be shut out?

The Queen. But you do help me—so much!

Albert. Let me help you *now.*

The Queen. How?

Albert. Let me see some of those papers that you spend so long over. I could read them for you, and make a few notes. That would save you time.

The Queen. Oh, but I must see everything *myself.* That is what I am here for.

Albert. Do you suppose your ministers show you everything?

The Queen. Why, of course!

Albert. Impossible. Government is not as simple as all that. They themselves have to rely upon others for much that has to be done; even in things for which they are responsible. Cannot you rely upon me . . . a little?

The Queen. Albert, dearest, you distress me! In every way that is possible, I do already rely on you; and always, in everything that I have had to decide *for* you, I have only done it for your good.

Albert. Yes, you even chose my secretary for me.

The Queen. Why of course, Albert! How could *you* know—coming here a stranger—who would be the best?

Albert. [*Continuing.*] Who reports to you—regularly, I believe.

The Queen. Surely you don't mind my knowing?

Albert. I would prefer to tell you myself what I do. In future I mean to.

The Queen. Why, of course. I always wish to hear everything.

Albert. Yes. The other day I made an engagement. You cancelled it.

The Queen. Yes, Albert. I had very good reason for doing so.

Albert. No doubt. You did not speak to me about it.

The Queen. But that was to spare your feelings.

Albert. But my secretary knew. When I questioned him why one engagement entered into my diary for this week had been struck out, he said he had done so under instruction.

The Queen. Yes, Albert.

Albert. From *you.*

The Queen. You were going to dine, he told me, with a foreign minister. It would have been in the papers. My government did not wish that, just now, any member of the royal family should pay him such a compliment.

Albert. You see, I am told nothing of your relations with foreign countries. I see only what appears in the newspapers. . . . Not only do you not give me your confidence, but you have me watched. Tomorrow I am going to choose another secretary—for myself.

The Queen. Albert, you are making a great mistake!

Albert. Repairing one. I ought to have done this before.

The Queen. You are not to do it, Albert. . . . I say you are not to.

Albert. Then, for the present, I leave you. [*He turns to go.*]

The Queen. Where are you going?

Albert. In here, to my own room, to write letters—alone.
[*He goes in, and closes the door. We hear the key turn in
the lock.* THE QUEEN *also hears it, and starts to her feet.
Very angry, but a little frightened, she pauses, then advances resolutely to the door, and tries it. The door does
not yield. She beats upon it violently with her hand,
pauses, then beats again.*]

The Queen. Open the door! Albert, open the door!

Albert. [*From within.*] Who is that speaking?

The Queen. Her Majesty, the Queen!

Albert. Her Majesty, the Queen, must wait.

[THE QUEEN *stands, hardly believing her ears. She stands
for a long time. Her eyes turn to the door questioning it
about this unbelievable situation, which (for such a thing
has never happened before) she cannot yet understand. For
a moment, foolish, fiery resolution takes hold of her: she
crosses the room and lays her hand upon the bell-rope. Ye
gods! What is her little Majesty going to do now? But
fundamental common sense comes to her rescue; and with
common sense comes, also, understanding. Timidly now,*

biting her lips, trying to keep back the tears, she crosses again, and stands irresolutely at the door. In a very different way now, her hand advances, she knocks softly, pauses, and knocks again. And as she listens the beloved voice speaks again from within.]

Albert. Who is there?

[*There is a pause. The tears come rushing; her voice trembles as she speaks.*]

The Queen. Your wife, Albert! Your poor unhappy little wife!

[*The door opens.* ALBERT *appears. She flings herself into his arms.*]

Oh, Albert! Albert! Albert!

Albert. Hush, hush, *weibchen!* Don't cry! Don't cry! It's all right.

[*But she does cry. How long does not matter, for it is doing her good.*]

CONTINUING THE STORY

In a series of episodes which follow we note that the marriage of Victoria and Albert is both successful and happy. By his knowledge of psychology and his adroit handling of different situations Albert gradually assumes his rightful, though politically unwelcome, place as Victoria's adviser. Through his influence the Queen becomes a patron of the arts. Financial arrangements at Buckingham Palace and Windsor Castle are greatly improved. Victoria's pride and sometimes arbitrary attitudes are toned down. She learns to face difficult situations, often precipitated by her own quick temper and jealous disposition, frankly and fearlessly.

Six children have been born to the Queen and Prince Albert. Albert Edward, the eldest, begins at eight years of age his arduous task of learning to become King in the years to come.

A succession of the great personages of the era move through the scenes of the play. Macaulay, eminent historian, discusses history and the Indian question with the Queen. Prime Minister, Lord John Russell, forces the resignation of Lord Palmerston as Secretary of State for Foreign Affairs. Such personages as Tennyson, Disraeli, and Dr. Stanley, later Dean of the Abbey, are in favor with the Queen.

It is 1861. The Civil War in America is something of a problem to Queen Victoria. The "Trent Affair" almost involves England. By sheer diplomacy Prince Albert is able to avoid an open break. The effort, however, is the "last straw," and his health breaks. His death occurs soon afterward.

BEREAVEMENT

1861

In the deepest of widow's weeds, THE QUEEN *sits nursing a pet dog; and in the wistful gaze of the dumb beast she finds comfort, and a sympathy which she is less ready to accept when it is offered her by mere humans. She sits at her writing-table, having interrupted for a few moments the correspondence which she is conducting on black-edged notepaper of the deepest dye.*

The Queen. Yes, you understand, don't you?—a little. No, you don't, you don't, doggie! but you try to. That's the best you can do for me. It's all that anyone can do now. Nobody can really understand. . . . And now you must get down, dear; I must go on with my writing.

[*She puts the dog gently down, and returns sadly to her correspondence. A* GENTLEMAN USHER *enters, and stands waiting for permission to speak.*]

The Queen. [*After a pause.*] Yes?
Usher. Mrs. Gladstone, your Majesty.

The Queen. Oh, yes. Let her come in. And while she *is* here, I do not wish to see anyone.

[*The* USHER *bows, and goes.* THE QUEEN *takes up a portrait from the writing-table, and gazes at it fondly.*]

The Queen. Oh! Albert! Albert!

[*The door opens; the* USHER *enters, followed by* MRS. GLAD-STONE.]

Usher. Mrs. Gladstone, your Majesty.

The Queen. Dear Mrs. Gladstone, how good of you to come, so soon!

Mrs. Gladstone. Directly—when I got your Majesty's command. I was so grateful that your Majesty wished it.

The Queen. There are very few I wish to see, now, Mrs. Gladstone; but you were one. You have always been so kind to me.

Mrs. Gladstone. The kindness has been your Majesty's.

The Queen. You have come to see an unhappy woman, the joy of whose life is over.

Mrs. Gladstone. Oh, I understand how your Majesty must feel! And I won't talk about time making any difference. But memories will. Your Majesty will find a great comfort in memories,—presently.

The Queen. They are a great pain to me. Almost more than I can bear.

Mrs. Gladstone. Yes, of course. But you would not be without them. They are already, Ma'am, are they not, the nearest to comfort—of anything?

The Queen. That is quite true, Mrs. Gladstone—quite true. Do, please, sit down! No; sit near me. . . . You also, at some time, must have known great sorrow.

Mrs. Gladstone. Yes, Ma'am; few of us can miss having it at some time in our lives.

The Queen. What has been your greatest sorrow, Mrs. Glad-stone?

Mrs. Gladstone. My sister, Ma'am, my only sister. She was my closest and dearest friend.

The Queen. How long is it since you lost her?

Mrs. Gladstone. Four years, Ma'am.

The Queen. Does it seem long?

Mrs. Gladstone. No, Ma'am; she is still so much alive to

me. At first she seemed dead—gone, utterly. She doesn't now.
So much comes back; every day—new memories. Your Majesty
will find that, too; I am sure.

The Queen. Thank you, Mrs. Gladstone; I hope so, too.
But already I remember so much. I don't think there can be
anything I have forgotten. As I read his diaries, and his dear
letters, everything seems like yesterday.

Mrs. Gladstone. Yes: when we have loved much, time seems
hardly to mean anything.

The Queen. You say the very thing I have been trying to
say to myself, Mrs. Gladstone,—and to believe. It's a comfort
to hear someone else saying it. . . . And, of course, now, *he*
remembers everything too. So, in memory, we are together—
still.

Mrs. Gladstone. Yes, Ma'am; and of one so really good as
he was, what lovely and comforting memories you must have
always with you.

The Queen. Yes, always; just as *he* was always with me.
In all our married life, we were hardly ever apart; during
twenty-two years only a few weeks. At first he was not with
me so constantly—during the day, I mean. I had not found
out then how much more he was fit to be King than I was to
be Queen. And people were jealous and afraid—even my own
ministers—lest he should have too much influence over me.
And, just at first, sometimes we differed, he and I; but he was
always right—always right! And before long, I found that I
could do nothing safely without him. And there he was, always
at my side—helping, advising, directing, guiding—often saving
me from making mistakes; and my ministers also. As time
went on, they also learned to listen to him, and wished him to be
present in all our consultations; all except just a few—Lord
Palmerston sometimes. But even he has written and spoken
to me, very kindly and feelingly, about what we owed to his
great wisdom and foresight. The very last thing he did has,
perhaps, saved us from war with America. Will people ever
know what this country owes to him? He ought to have been
King: he was—almost; for I decided nothing till he had advised
me about it. And now he is gone—I am alone; and though
people don't know it, a new reign has begun—a Queen without
her King! Oh, what shall I do? What shall I do without him?

Mrs. Gladstone. Is it not possible, Ma'am—your son, the Prince, now being of age—that he may be of some help to your Majesty?

The Queen. [*With some asperity.*] No! Indeed, no, Mrs. Gladstone! He has not either his father's mind, nor his father's character. I cannot allow him to take any part, at present, in my responsible work of government.

Mrs. Gladstone. But he must do so some day, your Majesty; and it is a work for which he will need training.

The Queen. I have to hope, Mrs. Gladstone, that it will not have to be yet—not till he is a good deal older, and more—settled. At present, he is far too much the man of pleasure, and amusement. He is devoted to me, of course; as I am also to him. But he makes me very anxious.

Mrs. Gladstone. I think he has a very kind heart, your Majesty. Wherever he goes, he attracts and wins people.

The Queen. Yes; and not always of the best kind. Attracting people is sometimes his great temptation, and he does not feel—no, he does not *feel* his father's death as he ought to do. . . . Just think! Only a fortnight after, I found him—*smoking!* It was a great shock to me; his father having always forbidden it. *He* never smoked—never felt the need of it. So why should Bertie?

Mrs. Gladstone. But so many more do so now, Ma'am. It has become very much more common.

The Queen. Yes, "common"! that is the word for it. How much the world is changing—from what *he* would have wished! But *I* shall never change—anything.

Mrs. Gladstone. To be faithful in all one's thoughts and wishes, is a great help, Ma'am, is it not? It makes one feel nearer.

The Queen. Dear Mrs. Gladstone, you do say such nice things! I wish we could have talked longer; it would have done me good, I'm sure. But even now the affairs of my government have to go on; and I as the head of it. And I believe that already I have an appointment, and that one of my ministers is waiting to see me. So now I must say good-bye to you. Thank you for coming. You must come again—soon.

[*And as* MRS. GLADSTONE *curtsies over the hand offered her,* THE QUEEN *bends down and kisses her.*]

Mrs. Gladstone. Oh, yes, Ma'am, your Majesty has only to send for me. I wish—we all wish—that we could do anything that might be of use or comfort to your Majesty. But even love feels helpless sometimes.

The Queen. It is the only thing that can help now—that has helped me at all. . . . Good-bye!

[MRS. GLADSTONE *makes her last curtsy, and retires.* THE QUEEN *goes to the window, and stands looking out for a while; then, returning to the writing-table, she rings a bell. The* GENTLEMAN *enters.*]

The Queen. If Lord Palmerston is here, I am now ready to see him.

Usher. Lord Palmerston *is* here, your Majesty.

The Queen. Very well. Ask him to come in.

[*The* USHER *retires, and reappears, followed by* LORD PALM-ERSTON.]

Usher. Lord Palmerston, your Majesty.

The Queen. Good morning, Lord Palmerston. You wrote that you wished to see me today, if possible.

Lord Palmerston. I thank your Majesty for so graciously making the appointment. May I express the hope that your Majesty is now better?

The Queen. I am quite well, thank you, Lord Palmerston. You have come about something that requires my immediate attention, I believe?

Lord Palmerston. I have, Ma'am, unfortunately. I would have been glad to have spared your Majesty, could it have allowed of postponement.

The Queen. Oh, no, please. I wish everything to go on as usual.

Lord Palmerston. Today, Ma'am, is the thirtieth of December; and the New Year's Honors still await your Majesty's approval and confirmation. Tomorrow they must go to the press, for next day's publication.

The Queen. Yes, of course. It would not do for there to be any delay in the usual announcements. . . . You have them with you?

Lord Palmerston. I have, Ma'am. Lord Granville has communicated to me your Majesty's wish that Mr. Dilke should

78

be made a Baronet, and that Mr. Bowring should be made a Companion of the Bath. Both those things will be done accordingly. But there are also three other persons, whose names I have for some time wished to submit to your Majesty for the dignity of Baronet; and, if your Majesty should be graciously pleased to approve of them, the list would stand as follows: Mr. Dilke [THE QUEEN *bows her assent*], Mr. William Browne, of Liverpool.

The Queen. Who is he?

Lord Palmerston. A very wealthy and distinguished merchant, Ma'am, who has lately made a magnificent present of a public library to his fellow-citizens. . . . Mr. Thomas David Lloyd, a well-known and respectable gentleman of high standing, in the County of Carnarvon; and Mr. Matthew Rich, to whom the government is under great obligation for political services—he having vacated his seat for Richmond, Yorkshire, to enable your Majesty's Solicitor-General to be elected in his place.

The Queen. Have they all sufficient means, Lord Palmerston, to support the dignity in a becoming manner?

Lord Palmerston. Oh, yes, your Majesty; they are all men of wealth—great wealth, most of them.

The Queen. Then we approve.

Lord Palmerston. I thank your Majesty.

The Queen. Is there anything else?

Lord Palmerston. Nothing, Ma'am, that cannot conveniently wait for a later occasion.

The Queen. [*Rising.*] Very well, Lord Palmerston. Then, for the present, that will do.

Lord Palmerston. May I, with your Majesty's gracious permission, be allowed, before I withdraw, to express a fervent hope that the intensity of your Majesty's grief may not lead your Majesty to neglect the preservation of your health, which is so necessary for the care and welfare of your Majesty's children, and hardly less for that of your Majesty's devotedly attached and affectionate subjects, of whom, Ma'am, I am ever one.

The Queen. Thank you, Lord Palmerston. I am keeping quite well. Good-bye.

[THE QUEEN *inclines her head, but does not offer her hand.*
LORD PALMERSTON *bows and retires.* THE QUEEN *sits
down again, and with her eyes fixed upon the portrait,
speaks.*]

Oh, Albert! Albert! Albert! Why did you leave me? How
can I bear to go on living, and doing all this—*alone!*

CONTINUING THE STORY

In the episodes which follow we see Victoria growing older, and
we feel the devotion of her subjects and her ministers. We are conscious of the deepening influence of Prince Albert on her own personality and in her acts as Queen. We see her still frankly facing her
problems, seeking advice when puzzled, yet never failing to make up
her own mind in characteristic fashion. Even those who love her
are amused at her whims, foibles, and stubbornness. But it is affectionate amusement, not derision.

THE BLUE RIBBON

1887

*Monsieur Benjamin Constant's portrait of the Queen, sitting
crowned and enthroned in a soft cascade of sunlight, is so well
known that the fact of its back being now to the spectator hardly
matters.* MONSIEUR CONSTANT *has himself arranged it in the
best light available; but the windows of Windsor Castle do not
give quite the light that he would wish. Still, though the opportunity for favorable display is not all that the artist could desire, the honor conferred by the royal command more than
compensates.* MONSIEUR CONSTANT, *ceremonially arrayed, flut-
ters in front of his masterpiece; and the* COURT OFFICIAL *who
has charge of him, stands quietly looking on, admiring the gestures with which, almost as much as with words, the distinguished
visitor conducts his conversation.*

Court Official. I hope the light is as you wish, Monsieur?

Constant. The light? Oh, yes, as you cannot change the
windows—it must do!

Court Official. We can, if you like, Monsieur, have the windows closed, and the chandeliers lighted.

Constant. Ah, no, no, no, no, no! That might make my collars to look untrue. And my collars are very actually chosen.

[The COURT OFFICIAL *realizes, after a moment, that it is his picture, not his clothes, that* MONSIEUR CONSTANT *is referring to. He turns to study it with the respect due to its vast size.]*

Court Official. It is a remarkable picture, Monsieur Constant.

Constant. [*With proud humility.*] Of so remarkable a personage, it would be difficult *not.*

Court Official. In Paris—it has been popular?

Constant. Popular? *Ma foi! mais oui!* [1] It has struck the conscience of the whole nation. They look: "Ah! a Queen!" they say. "Why have we not still Kings and Queens?" Our government was quite glad that I brought it away to Bond Street—to relieve the political situation.

Court Official. Dear me! And in Bond Street, also, it has been a great success?

Constant. Ah! If your Queen Victoria had not been popular before, this would have made her to be so!

Court Official. You had no sittings from Her Majesty, Monsieur? But you must surely have come over to England to paint the throne, and that background. The House of Lords, is it not?

Constant. Ah, yes; no! For that, photographs were sufficient. The rest—myself!

Court Official. Indeed? And the light—the effect of light coming down from above—that is wonderful!

Constant. The light? Ah! yes, the light! Ah! That is my *forte.* That is where I excel in my imagination.

Court Official. Remarkable! [*And then the* COURT OFFICIAL *has a duty to perform, which must be done delicately.*] Monsieur Constant, you have met royalty before?

Constant. Ah, no! In republican France, *hélas!* we do not have much opportunity for to meet royalty.

Court Official. I only asked because we have a certain etiquette —as to which I am sure you will find no difficulty. Our manners at Court are more like the French manners than the English.

Constant. More civilized, you would say?

Court Official. Well, in your country you have more ceremony —more grace: so you will understand. . . . When Her Majesty enters, she will only bow to you. When she leaves she may give you her hand. If, then, she raises it slightly, you will kiss it—

---

[1] *Ma foi! mais oui!—My faith! but yes!*—Equivalent to our "Oh, yes indeed!"

not otherwise. In conversing with Her Majesty, you will always say "Your Majesty" or "Ma'am"—pronounced so.

Constant. Ah! *Parfaitement! "Même"—toujours la même chose.*[2]

Court Official. Her Majesty may ask you questions. You will avoid, as far as possible, asking any questions in return. For instance, you must not say "Does Your Majesty also paint?" If Her Majesty wishes, she will inform you of the fact herself. If Her Majesty discusses art with you—as she may do—do not insist too much upon your own opinion; allow Her Majesty to have the last word, and to have it early, in any matter on which you find that you differ.

Constant. Mais oui, Monsieur, parfaitement![3]

Court Official. If anything Her Majesty says embarrasses you —I mean, if you feel embarrassed in stating your own view, then it will be always safe and correct for you to bow, saying nothing. And Her Majesty will herself change the conversation to some new subject.

Constant. That will be so? Ah!

Court Official. I tell you this, Monsieur Constant, so that you may feel more at ease. Seeing Her Majesty constantly, to us it has become second nature. To those who only attend Court rarely, it is more difficult.

Constant. Monsieur, I am extremely obliged.

[*Another* COURT OFFICIAL *of lower grade now enters and indicates with a half-bow that he is there to know that all is ready, and to make announcement. You see the words "Her Majesty" formed by his lips, but you do not hear them. He withdraws silently, closing the door.*]

Court Official. Her Majesty will be here in a few moments.

Constant. Ah, then allow me! [*Darting toward the picture, he draws a curtain across it.*]

Court Official. But why are you covering the picture, Monsieur?

Constant. So that when Her Majesty stands just where she should stand to see it, then I open—so!

Court Official. You must not expect Her Majesty to stand where you wish, Monsieur. She will stand where she herself wishes.

[2] AH!, etc.—*Oh, perfectly. "Même"—always the same thing.*
[3] *Mais oui, Monsieur, parfaitement!—Oh yes, Sir, perfectly!*

Constant. But to see the picture from where it should be seen!

Court Official. That Her Majesty will decide for herself, Monsieur.

Constant. Ah! *Si?* That is very English. Yes!

[*And now the door opens, and two Indian Attendants glide in, and stand motionless on either side. There is a pause; and then—small, short, stout, but with an amazing dignity which is almost grace,* THE QUEEN *enters. She moves forward, halts at a few paces from her visitor (who meanwhile has been repeatedly bowing) and, as the* COURT OFFICIAL *pronounces his name, she bows to him with that marvelous mixture of distance and courtesy which turns her widow's cap into a crown.*]

Court Official. Monsieur Benjamin Constant, your Majesty.

The Queen. I am very pleased to meet you, Monsieur Constant. You have come only recently from France?

Constant. I have had that honor, your Majesty—that pleasure.

The Queen. From Paris?

Constant. It is from Paris I come, your Majesty.

The Queen. It is your first visit to this country?

Constant. It is, Madame, it is.

The Queen. You live in Paris?

Constant. I live always in Paris; I work in Paris, Madame.

The Queen. It was very good of you to come, Monsieur. You are going to show me your picture.

Constant. Ah, yes! If your Majesty would condescend. Just three steps more away.

The Queen. But I always prefer to look at pictures closely, Monsieur, so as to see how they are done.

Constant. [*Resignedly.*] Ah, so!

The Queen. One has to look closely before one can be sure that they are good.

Constant. Ah, but of this picture—a subject so illustrious—I trust that your Majesty shall have no doubt.

[*He draws the curtain. There is a long pause.* THE QUEEN *looks at the picture with calm, dignified detachment.*]

The Queen. We are redder than that, Monsieur.

Constant. Ah! but does your Majesty's gracious complexion never vary—a leetle?

The Queen. Never as much as that, Monsieur.

Constant. Ah, *c'est dommage!* [4]

The Queen. A little more color, Monsieur, could easily be added.

Constant. But then, Madame, what will have to become of my collar-scheme—that is, my picture?

The Queen. But this is a portrait, Monsieur, of *Me*.

Constant. Yes, but of the imagination—all my own. I had no sittings from your Majesty.

The Queen. Now that you have seen me, you will be able to correct it.

Constant. Oh, but impossible!

[*The* Court Official *touches his arm, whereat he adds insinuatingly.*]

—unless your Majesty should graciously sit to me.

The Queen. I have not sat for my portrait, Monsieur, for many years.

---

[4] *Ah, c'est dommage!—Oh, that's too bad!*

84

Constant. But what a deprivation is not that, Madame, to artists, and to the whole world!

The Queen. There is something else, Monsieur Constant, which you must correct.

Constant. Comment? [5]

The Queen. The ribbon of the Garter—the blue; you have made it too light.

Constant. But permit me to explain, Madame! The light shining on it—so bright from above—the texture, the silk, the reflection—they do all make it lighter than would look otherwise.

The Queen. It is too light, Monsieur. I wear the Garter, so I know. Also, though you may not know it, I have practiced painting myself. I had two masters to teach me—Sir John Hayter, and Mr. Cope; both excellent artists. They taught me to be true to nature.

Constant. They painted your Majesty's portrait, ever?

The Queen. No. When I was studying with them, I had my portrait painted—in a group with my whole family—by Winterhalter. I will give orders that you shall be shown it before you go. Winterhalter was a great painter, was he not?

Constant. Winterhalter? Oh, Winterhalter was everything that the public wished him to be. He had a great name in his day. Now he is dead.

The Queen. Yes; more than twelve years ago. I remember sending a wreath to his funeral, and also a letter to his widow. The Prince and I had a great regard for him. There are few artists today like him.

Constant. Very, very few, Madame; or one never hears of them.

The Queen. No. . . . Your portrait of me has had a great success, Monsieur, I am told?

Constant. Un succès fou, [6] Madame. That is the only word for it.

The Queen. In Bond Street.

Constant. There; yes, Madame.

The Queen. Have you other pictures on exhibition as well?

Constant. By myself, no, Madame—not in the same room. We are alone together.

[5] *Comment—What? or What is it?*
[6] *Un succès fou—A complete success!*

The Queen. [*After a pause.*] You mean, my picture is alone?

Constant. [*Conscious that he stands corrected.*] Yes, I do mean that, your Majesty—that only.

The Queen. I think it was very clever of you to do it without sittings. I wish I could have given you a sitting—just one. But I never sit now. And I hope, Monsieur, that you will at once make those two corrections: a little more red in the face, and to the ribbon more blue.

Constant. The red—oh, yes, Madame if your Majesty orders it. But the blue—the blue, Madame, that—as the artist—I must be allowed to——

The Queen. Good-bye, Monsieur Constant. It has been a great pleasure to meet you. Thank you very much for bringing the picture. As a picture, I like it. As a portrait, you will now be able, by those alterations, to make it better, I hope. Good-bye.

[*She offers him her hand. He bends and kisses it. She goes to the door, turns, bows, and retires, followed by her attendants.*]

Constant. [*A little agitated.*] Did I right—to kiss?

Court Official. I think so.

Constant. Did she like the picture enough for me to kiss—you think?

Court Official. Oh, I think so, distinctly.

Constant. [*With an artist's grievance.*] Oh, but she did not understand! She did not understand!

Court Official. Her Majesty is accustomed to have her own opinion about things, Monsieur, and not to change it.

Constant. Ah! So English!

Court Official. And now—we have Her Majesty's permission—would you like to see the Winterhalter?

Constant. The Winterhalter? No! I know Winterhalter, and all about him—quite well. *Eau sucré*—that is what he is.

Court Official. Eau sacré. Holy water?

Constant. Holy? No, I did not say "holy"; not *sacré—sucré*: sugar—*and* water!

[*And then, once more, the* COURT OFFICIAL *of lower grade enters, and this time speaks audibly.*]

Second Court Official. Her Majesty requests that Monsieur Constant will wait a few moments. Her Majesty has something she wishes to send him.

[*Having delivered his message, the* COURT OFFICIAL *withdraws, leaving* MONSIEUR CONSTANT *in a twitter of excitement.*]

Constant. Ah! but that is—that is—very unexpected! What will it be, you think? Some honor for me? *Est-ce possible?* [7]

Court Official. Perhaps a souvenir, Monsieur. Probably a signed photograph.

Constant. [*His hopes dashed.*] Oh? . . . Well, so long as it is not a photograph of the Winterhalter, I do not mind. . . . But —redder? How am I to make that a redder face, and not spoil the collar-harmony of my picture?

Court Official. Don't, Monsieur. Her Majesty will not see it again.

Constant. Ah! Thank you; you are wise, and very kind.

[*Again the* SECOND COURT OFFICIAL *enters, bearing in his hand a small packet, which he presents to* MONSIEUR CONSTANT.]

Constant. [*His hopes rising again.*] Oh; but this is not a photograph. No, it is too small. It is an honor, surely, an order that she send me! [*He opens the packet, while he speaks.*] Hey? What for is this small piece of blue ribbon?

Court Official. There is a note pinned to it, I see.

Constant. Ah, yes! [*He unpins it, and reads.*] "You see, Monsieur, I am right." What this mean?—"You see, Monsieur, I am right"?

Court Official. [*After examination.*] That is the ribbon of the Garter, Monsieur; the blue about which you and Her Majesty did not quite agree. You are to see, she says, that she was *right*.

Constant. Oh! *Mais c'est incroyable!* [8] She do not understand!

Court Official. No, Monsieur, perhaps not. But here we don't say so.

Constant. Ah! This is England! I must go back to France! Monsieur, I have to tell you she is no artist. Oh, but a great Queen! A wonderful person! *Enfin!* . . .[9] This—I may keep? [*He holds up the piece of blue ribbon.*]

Court Official. Certainly, Monsieur.

Constant. [*His reward with him.*] Ah! This blue ribbon— for me! Always! *Merci!* [10]

[7] *Est-ce possible—Is it possible?*
[8] *Mais c'est incroyable—But it is unbelievable!*
[9] *Enfin!—At last!*
[10] *Merci!—Thank you!*

[And, with a flourish of satisfaction, he pockets the souvenir, which will always give point and corroboration to his story whenever he tells it; as he will do frequently, until one day it reaches ears that were waiting for it: and so—finds its place here.]

CONTINUING THE STORY

As the play nears its close we see an aged Queen Victoria, forced to walk with a cane, but mentally still a powerful influence. There is no question that she understands the problems of Empire, both domestic and colonial.

HAPPY AND GLORIOUS

JUNE 20, 1897

From that "great relief," confirmed by the voice of the electorate two years later, THE QUEEN passes serenely on to the culminating triumph of her reign. The Diamond Jubilee provides material for a tableau rather than a play; and it is as a tableau that we have here presented to us this gathering together, at Buckingham Palace, of more than fifty of the Queen's direct descendants, together with representatives of all the crowned heads of a Europe still at peace.

The Triumphal Procession is over, and the large upper chamber becomes filled with Royalty. Bonnets, costumes, uniforms mingle in a moving clash of colors; Orders sparkle, sword-chains clink, spurs jingle. Their owners step delicately, bowing their way from group to group; and—some now encountering for the first time— high form and ceremony are still the rule. But here and there Members of the Royal Family, meeting each other, exchange remarks of a familiar character, though sometimes in a foreign accent. And as all (except an Official or two) who thus mix and converse are Royal Highnesses—if nothing more—there is no need to trouble about names. Nobody today, except THE QUEEN herself (and perhaps the Heir-Apparent) is individually important. So, not as individuals but in the group, we listen to their ROYAL HIGHNESSES chatting among themselves over the events of the day, filling up time till the chief character makes her appearance.

Royal Highnesses. Well! So that's over! . . . How beautifully everything went! . . . Excellently! . . . Very well indeed! . . . Nothing could have been better! . . . I hope Mama enjoyed it as much as we did. . . . Oh, I'm sure she did. . . . What crowds! What cheering! And what perfect order! . . . Yes, the English are a wonderful people. . . . Have you seen Mama, since she got back? . . . Yes, I have just been with her. . . . How has she borne it? . . . Oh, she's all right. She will be up in a minute. They are getting her into her chair.

An Imperial Highness. My dear Uncle Bertie, congratulations! What a glorious landmark in the annals of your great nation!

His Royal Highness. Thank you. Yes, very satisfactory, I think. I am so glad that you were able to be present.

An Imperial Highness. Ach! I would not have missed it for anything!

His Royal Highness. [*To an* OFFICIAL.] Sir Arthur, will you please to give orders for the window to be ready?

[SIR ARTHUR *bows, and goes to give the order. Presently two Footmen enter, and undo the bolts of the center window. A Court Official enters, comes to His Royal Highness, bows, and makes a communication.*]

His Royal Highness. [*To* HIS IMPERIAL HIGHNESS.] Excuse me for one moment.

Sir Arthur. [*To the Footmen.*] Do not go; remain.

[*They stand to attention on either side of the window. And now, from the corridor outside, comes an approaching sound —a mingling of voices, footsteps, and a low rolling of wheels; and* THE QUEEN *enters, seated in her wheeled chair, accompanied by her two sons. The assembled family and the royal guests, with the formality befitting a great occasion, bow low upon her entrance. The word "Congratulations" emerges from the general hum of voices. Then expressions of affection take the place of ceremony.*]

A Royal Princess. Mama, dear, how are you?

The Queen. Very tired, my dear; but oh, so happy! . . . To think now that it is all over! . . . So glad that I had the strength for it!

Princess. And the courage, Mama, dear!

Another Princess. You were quite wonderful, Mama!

The Queen. Yes, so the Doctor tells me. He has just felt my

pulse and taken my temperature. And he says that he could not
have believed it possible. Oh, I'm—I'm so thankful!

His Royal Highness. So is everybody. And now, Mama, I
think you had better take a glass of wine. It will do you good.

The Queen. Thank you.

His Royal Highness. And may we also drink to your good
health, Mama?

The Queen. Certainly; why, yes, certainly! Please, all of
you! [*In the background Attendants have already begun serving
wine into glasses. A glass is brought to* THE QUEEN.]

The Queen. What is it?

His Royal Highness. Champagne, Mama.

The Queen. No, no; I will have sherry. [*So sherry is
brought.*] How long has it taken?

Princess. Nearly three hours, Mama.

The Queen. Oh, dear me! And it seems like yesterday and
tomorrow—almost! . . . Three hours!

His Royal Highness. Your Imperial and Royal Highnesses, I
have great pleasure in asking you to drink to the health of Her
Majesty, the Queen. May she continue long, in health and prosperity, to enjoy the love of her children and her people.

[*The health is drunk with decorous enthusiasm.* THE QUEEN
*sits bowing her acknowledgments to all the assembled Fam-
ily, with tears and smiles.*]

The Queen. Thank you! Oh, thank you!

Princess. Won't you go and rest now, Mama?

The Queen. Not yet. . . . That cheering that I hear means
that my dear people are expecting to see me again. I must try
not to disappoint them.

Princess. It would be nice if you could, Mama. You think
you can?

The Queen. Yes, but I can't get up. I must go as I am. Have
the windows opened.

[*The windows are opened by the Footmen; the cheering
swells.*]

The Queen. Yes, but over the balustrade, they will not be able
to see me. I must be raised. Tell them to bring in the sliding
dais.

His Royal Highness. It is already there in position, Mamma.

The Queen. Really! How thoughtful!

[*And so, when the window is opened, the sliding dais is let down from without into the window-frame. While this is being done with quiet efficiency by the well-trained footmen,* THE QUEEN *continues speaking.*]

Then, now, will you, Bertie, and some of the others go out, and let them know that I am coming? Not too many, just a few.

[*So six members of the Royal Family go out on to the balcony, and the cheering grows louder.* THE QUEEN, *seeing that the dais is now in position, makes a gesture of command, and the chair, slowly propelled, mounts the ramp prepared for it, and passes into the balcony. Immediately the cheering becomes tremendous, and would go on without abatement for much longer than exhausted old human nature can allow.* THE QUEEN *gives the signal for retirement; the chair is withdrawn, and backs into its former central position; and the Royal Family retire, bowing from the public gaze. The dais is lifted, the window is closed again.*]

The Queen. It's very gratifying, very, to find—after all these years—that they do appreciate all that I have tried to do for them —for their good, and for this great country of ours. We have been so near together today—they and I: all my dear people of

91

England, and Scotland—*and* Ireland, and the dear Colonies, and India. From all round the world I have had messages. Such loyalty—such devotion! Most extraordinary! Tell Mr. Chamberlain how very much I approve of all the arrangements he made for the proper representation of all parts of my Empire in the Procession. Everything so perfectly in order. Most gratifying! . . . Well, I must go now and rest, or I shall not be able to take my place at dinner tonight, and that would never do! . . . So happy! . . . As we were coming back you were in front, Bertie, so perhaps you didn't see—it was just by Hyde Park Corner, there was a great crowd there; and a lot of rough men—of course it ought not to have happened, but it didn't matter—broke right through the lines of the police and troops guarding the route; and they ran alongside the carriage, shouting and cheering me. And I heard them say: "Go it, Old Girl! You've done it well! You've done it well!" Of course, very unsuitable—the words; but so gratifying! And oh, I hope it's true! I hope it's true! . . . Hark! They are still cheering. . . . Albert! Ah! If only you could have been here!

[*And, having said her say, the great, wonderful, little old Lady gives the signal to her Attendants, and is wheeled slowly away.*]

DID YOU READ WITH UNDERSTANDING?

1. What is the meaning of the title, *Victoria Regina?* Why is it a particularly apt title?

2. Why is the play called a "dramatic biography"? Why does the author state in his preface that he has constructed the dialogue of the various episodes more on literary than theatrical lines?

3. To keep a correct mental background for the play, refresh your memories with the following dates and items of information about the Queen? (*a*) In what year was Victoria born? (*b*) How old was she when she married? (*c*) How long were she and Albert married before the Prince Consort died? (*d*) How many years was Victoria a widow? (*e*) When was the Diamond Jubilee celebrated? What event did it commemorate? (*f*) How many years longer did Victoria live? How old was she at her death? How many years had she reigned?

SUITABLE SUITORS:

1. What do we learn about Victoria in the italicized stage directions at the beginning of this scene?

92

2. What is the significance of the statement, "The Queen is still in mourning but she does not mourn"?

3. Why does the Prime Minister say, "I am constantly having to leave the vision to answer the bell"? Do you think Lord Melbourne is sincere in his application of the story to himself? Or does it merely serve as a pretty excuse? How do you judge?

4. Why does Victoria use the pronoun "we" instead of "I"?

5. Has Victoria "an open mind"? Explain.

6. What is evidently to be the role of Victoria's husband as she sees it? Explain.

7. What are the qualifications for Victoria's husband as stated by the Prime Minister?

8. How does Victoria regard her "Mama"? Quote lines to prove your point.

9. How "well" does Victoria take the advice of Lord Melbourne? How can you tell?

10. What is the significance of Victoria's concluding speech?

LEADING STRINGS:

1. What is evidently the official relationship between Victoria and Albert?

2. What is Albert's reaction to the situation? Quote lines to illustrate.

3. What kind of man does Albert seem to be?

4. Are your sympathies with Albert, or with Victoria? Why?

5. How does Albert show that he understands feminine psychology?

BEREAVEMENT:

1. How does the author make us aware of the genuine grief of Victoria?

2. Does Victoria seem to be *woman,* or *queen,* or both in this scene? Is Mrs. Gladstone able to give the Queen any comfort? What significant thing does she say about love? Can you explain her meaning?

3. What is Victoria's opinion of her son, the Prince of Wales? Was her judgment verified by history?

4. Is Victoria efficient as queen? Quote lines to prove your answer. How does she feel about her responsibilities?

5. What is the final impression left by the scene?

THE BLUE RIBBON:

1. "The Blue Ribbon" has some of the best humor of the play. Describe the various amusing features. Which situations are amusing? How much of the humor lies in the characters themselves? Discuss.

2. What do the suggestions of the court official show us about Victoria's character? Point out incidents later in the scene which prove that he understood the Queen well.

3. Does Queen Victoria have a sense of humor? Is she vain? Quote lines from the play to prove your answer.

4. Reading between the lines, what kind of artist do you think Winter-halter was? Did Monsieur Constant handle the situation tactfully? Discuss. Do you think the Court Official's instructions had proved helpful?

5. How might the artist have felt when he discovered the piece of blue ribbon? Why was he genuinely pleased? What double significance does the ribbon have?

HAPPY AND GLORIOUS:

1. What is the atmosphere of this scene? What is the feeling among the different members of the royal family? What is their attitude toward the Queen?

2. Why does Victoria refuse to rest? What does this show of her character?

3. Discuss Victoria's last speech. What impression is made by the closing lines?

4. Why do you suppose the author chose to end the play with this scene? Does the biography seem complete? Would a scene telling of Victoria's death have been a better ending for the play? Give reasons for your answer.

OVERVIEW:

1. Describe the character of the Queen as she appears in the earliest scenes. Describe her character in the two later scenes. What growth or development do you notice? What qualities persist throughout the play? What would you say were her outstanding characteristics?

2. What character stands second in importance to the Queen? What are the predominant qualities in this character? Do they influence the development of the play? If so, how?

3. In what respects does the play typify the character of England and the British? Discuss.

British character has a Celtic strain of fancy and sentiment.

A CLOAK WITH BEADS

JAMES MATTHEW BARRIE

As a background for the series of sketches of Scotch life which Barrie called *A Window in Thrums* he assumes the role of a school-teacher—a young man who has taken lodgings with Hendry Munn, a weaver, and Hendry's wife, Jess. The cottage is a poor affair with a thatched roof and dirt floor. It has a front room used only on rare occasions, and a large kitchen which really served as the living room. Jess was an invalid, who for years could go no farther than from her bed to a chair beside the window, and then only when supported by Hendry and their daughter Leeby. The schoolmaster had an attic room in the loft. Jess's window overlooked the brae, or hillslope, that led down to the town of Thrums. Here she sat and worked at sewing or cooking, at the same time keeping an eager eye on the comings and goings on the brae. In keeping with the folks of whom he writes, Barrie uses the Scotch dialect for his sketches.

On WEEK-DAYS the women who passed the window were meagerly dressed; mothers in draggled winsey gowns, carrying infants that were armfuls of grandeur. The Sabbath clothed every one in her best, and then the women went by with their hands spread out. When I was with Hendry, cloaks with beads were the fashion, and Jess sighed as she looked at them. They were known in Thrums as the Eleven and a Bits[1] (three-penny bits), that being their price at Kyowowy's on the square. Kyowowy means finicky, and applied to the draper by general consent. No doubt it was very characteristic to call the cloaks by their market value. In the glen my scholars still talk of their school books as the tupenny, the fowerpenny, the saxpenny. They finish their education with the tenpenny.

Jess's opportunity for handling the garments that others of her sex could finger in shops, was when she had guests to tea. Persons who merely dropped in and remained to tea, got their meal, as a rule, in the kitchen. They had nothing on that Jess could not easily take in as she talked to them. But when they came by special invitation, the meal was served in the room, the guests' things being left on the kitchen bed. Jess not being able to go ben the house,[2] had to be left with the things. When the time to go arrived, these were found on the bed, just as they had been placed there, but Jess could now tell Leeby whether they were imitation, why Bell Elshioner's feather went far round the bonnet, and Chirsty Lownie's reason for always holding her left arm fast against her side when she went abroad in the black jacket. Ever since My[3] Hobart's eleven and a bit was left on the kitchen bed, Jess had hungered for a cloak with beads. My's was the very marrow of the one T'nowhead's wife got in Dundee for ten-and-sixpence; indeed, we would have thought that 'Lisbeth's also came from Kyowowy's, had not Sanders Elshioner's sister seen her go into the Dundee shop with T'nowhead (who was loth), and hung about to discover what she was after.

Hendry was not quick at reading faces like Tammas Haggart, but the wistful look on Jess's face when there was talk of eleven and a bits had its meaning for him.

[1] ELEVEN AND A BITS—Eleven shillings, threepence—about three dollars in our money.

[2] BEN THE HOUSE—Going into the front room was called "going ben (within) the house," or simply "going ben." The front room had a wooden floor; a table with four books; six horsehair chairs, two of which could not be sat on; and two framed pictures.

[3] MY—A proper name, such as Mary.

"They're grand to look at, no doubt," I have heard him say to Jess, "but they're richt annoyin'. That new wife o' Peter Dickie's had ane on in the kirk⁴ last Sabbath, an' wi' her sittin' juist afore us I couldna listen to the sermon for tryin' to count the beads."

Hendry made his way into these gossips uninvited, for his opinions on dress were considered contemptible, though he was worth consulting on material. Jess and Leeby discussed many things in his presence, confident that his ears were not doing their work; but every now and then it was discovered that he had been hearkening greedily. If the subject was dress, he might then become a little irritating.

"Oh, they're grand," Jess admitted; "they set a body aff oncommon."

"They would be no use to you," said Hendry, "for ye canna wear them except ootside."

"A body doesna buy cloaks to be wearin' at them steady," retorted Jess.

"No, no, but you could never wear yours though ye had ane."

"I dinna want ane. They're far ower grand for the like o' me."

"They're no nae sic thing. Am thinkin' ye're juist as fit to wear an eleven and a bit as My Hobart."

"Weel, mebbe I am, but it's oot o' the question gettin' ane, they're sic a price."

"Ay, an' though we had the siller,⁵ it would surely be an awfu' like thing to buy a cloak 'at ye could never wear?"

"Ou, but I dinna want ane."

Jess spoke so mournfully that Hendry became enraged.

"It's most nichty," he said, "'at ye would gang an' set yer heart on sic a completely useless thing."

"I hinna set my heart on't."

"Dinna blether. Ye've been speakin' aboot thae eleven and a bits to Leeby, aff an' on, for twa month."

Then Hendry hobbled off to his loom, and Jess gave me a look which meant that men are trying at the best, once you are tied to them.

The cloaks continued to turn up in conversation, and Hendry poured scorn upon Jess's weakness, telling her she would be better

---

⁴ KIRK—Church.
⁵ THE SILLER—The silver—the money.

employed mending his trousers than brooding over an eleven and a bit that would have to spend its life in a drawer. An outsider would have thought that Hendry was positively cruel to Jess. He seemed to take a delight in finding that she had neglected to sew a button on his waistcoat. His real joy, however, was the knowledge that she sewed as no other woman in Thrums could sew. Jess had a genius for making new garments out of old ones, and Hendry never tired of gloating over her cleverness so long as she was not present. He was always athirst for fresh proofs of it, and these were forthcoming every day. Sparing were his words of praise to herself, but in the evening he generally had a smoke with me in the attic, and then the thought of Jess made him chuckle till his pipe went out. When he smoked he grunted as if in pain, though this really added to the enjoyment.

"It doesna matter," he would say to me, "what Jess turns her hand to, she can mak ony mortal thing. She doesna need nae teachin'; na, juist gie her a guid look at onything, be it clothes, or furniture, or in the bakin' line, it's all the same to her. She'll mak another exactly like it. Ye canna beat her. Her bannocks [6] is so superior 'at a Tilliedrum woman took to her bed after tastin' them, an' when the lawyer has company his wife gets Jess to mak some bannocks for her an' syne pretends they're her ain bakin'. Ay, there's a story aboot that. One day the auld doctor, him, 'at's deid, was at his tea at the lawyer's, an' says the guidwife, 'Try the cakes, Mr. Riach; they're my ain bakin'.' Weel, he was a fearsomely outspoken man, the doctor, an' nae suner had he the bannock atween his teeth, for he didna stop to swallow't, than he says, 'Mistress Geddie,' says he, 'I wasna born on a Sabbath. Na, na, you're no the first grand leddy 'at has gien me bannocks as their ain bakin' 'at was baked and fired by Jess Logan, her 'at's Hendry McQumpha's wife.' Ay, they say the lawyer's wife didna ken which wy to look, she was that mortified. It's juist the same wi' sewin'. There's wys o' ornamentin' christenen' robes an' the like 'at's kent to naebody but hersel'; an' as for stockin's, weel though I've seen her mak sae money, she amazes me yet. I mind o' a furry waistcoat I aince had. Weel, when it was fell dune, do you think she gae it awa to some gaen aboot body (vagrant)? Na, she made it into

[6] BANNOCKS—Oatmeal or barley cakes, baked on a griddle.

a richt neat coat to Jamie, wha was a bit laddie at the time.
When he grew out o' it, she made a slipbody o't for hersel'. Ay,
I dinna ken⁷ a' the different things it became, but the last time
I saw it was ben in the room, whaur she'd covered a footstool
wi' 't. Yes, Jess is the cleverest crittur I ever saw. Leeby's
handy, but she's no a patch on her mother."

I sometimes repeated these panegyrics to Jess. She merely
smiled, and said that men haver⁸ most terribly when they are
not at their work.

Hendry tried Jess sorely over the cloaks, and a time came
when, only by exasperating her, could he get her to reply to
his sallies.

"Wha wants an eleven an' a bit?" she retorted now and again.

"It's you 'at wants it," said Hendry promptly.

"Did I ever say I wanted ane? What use could I hae for 't?"

"That's the question," said Hendry. "Ye cann gang the length
o' the door, so ye would never be able to wear 't."

"Ay, weel," replied Jess, "I'll never hae the chance o' no bein'
able to wear 't, for, hoowever muckle I wanted it, I couldna
get it."

Jess's infatuation had in time the effect of making Hendry
uncomfortable. In the attic he delivered himself of such sentiments as these:

"There's nae understandin' a woman. There's Jess 'at hasna
her equal for cleverness in Thrums, man or woman, an' yet she's
fair skeered about thae cloaks. Aince a woman sets her mind
on something to wear, she's mair onreasonable than the stupidest
man. Ay, it micht mak them humble to see hoo foolish they are
syne. No, but it doesna do't.

"If it was a thing to be useful noo, I wouldna think the same
o't, but she could never wear't. She kens she could never wear't,
an' yet she's juist as keen to hae't.

"I dinna like to see her so wantin' a thing, an no able to
get it. But it's an awfu' sum, eleven an' a bit."

He tried to argue with her further.

"If ye had eleven an' a bit to fling away," he said, "ye dinna
mean to tell me 'at ye would buy a cloak instead o' cloth for a
gown, or a flannel for petticoats, or some useful thing?"

---

⁷ I DINNA KEN—I do not know.
⁸ HAVER—Babble, chatter.

"As sure as death," said Jess, with unwonted vehemence, "If a cloak I could get, a cloak I would buy."

Hendry came up to tell me what Jess had said.

"It's a michty infatooation," he said, "but it shows hoo her heart's set on thae cloaks."

"Aince ye had it," he argued with her, "ye would juist hae to lock it awa in the drawers. Ye would never even be seein' 't."

"Ay, would I," said Jess. "I would often tak it oot an' look at it. Ay, an' I would aye ken it was there."

"But naebody would ken ye had it but yersel'," said Hendry, who had a vague notion that this was a telling objection.

"Would they no?" answered Jess. "It would be a' through the toon afore nicht."

"Weel, all I can say," said Hendry, "is 'at ye're terrible foolish to tak the want o' sic a useless thing to heart."

"Am no takkin' 't to heart," retorted Jess, as usual.

Jess needed many things in her days that poverty kept from her to the end, and the cloak was merely a luxury. She would soon have let it slip by as something unattainable had not Hendry encouraged it to rankle in her mind. I cannot say when he first determined that Jess should have a cloak, come the money as it liked, for he was too ashamed of his weakness to admit his project to me. I remember, however, his saying to Jess one day:

"I'll warrant ye could mak a cloak yersel' the marrow o'[9] thae eleven and a bits, at half the price?"

"It would cost," said Jess, "sax an' saxpence,[10] exactly. The cloth would be five shillin's, an' the beads a shillin'. I have some braid 'at would do fine for the front, but the buttons would be saxpence."

"Ye're sure o' that?"

"I ken fine, for I got Leeby to price the things in the shop."

"Ay, but it maun be ill to shape the cloaks richt. There was a queer cut aboot that ane Peter Dickie's new wife had on."

"Queer cut or no queer cut," said Jess, "I took the shape o' My Hobart's ane the day she was here at her tea, an' I could mak' the identical o't for sax and sax."

"I dinna believe't," said Hendry, but when he and I were alone he told me: "There's no a doubt she could make it. Ye

[9] THE MARROW O'—The like of.
[10] SAX AND SAXPENCE—About a dollar and a half.

heard her say she had ta'en the shape? Ay, that shows she's rale set on a cloak."

Had Jess known that Hendry had been saving up for months to buy her material for a cloak, she would not have let him do it. She could not know, however, for all the time he was scraping together his pence he kept up a ring-ding-dang about her folly. Hendry gave Jess all the wages he weaved except three pence weekly, most of which went in tobacco and snuff. The dulse-man [11] had perhaps a halfpenny from him in the fortnight. I noticed that for a long time Hendry neither smoked nor snuffed, and I knew that for years he had carried a shilling in his snuff-mull. The remainder of the money he must have made by extra work at his loom by working harder, for he could scarcely have worked longer.

It was one day shortly before Jamie's return [12] to Thrums that Jess saw Hendry pass the house and go down the brae when he ought to have come in to his brose.[13] She sat at the window watching for him, and by and by he reappeared carrying a parcel.

"Whaur on earth hae ye been?" she asked, "an' what's that you're carryin'?"

"Did ye think it was an eleven and a bit?" said Hendry.

"No, I didna," answered Jess indignantly.

Then Hendry slowly undid the knots of the string with which the parcel was tied. He took off the brown paper.

"There's yer cloth," he said, "an' here's one an saxpence for the beads an' the buttons."

While Jess still stared he followed me ben the house.

"It's a terrible haver," [14] he said, apologetically, "but she had her heart on't."

---

[11] DULSEMAN—*Dulse* is the name for several coarse kinds of seaweed. The Scotch toasted it on hot tongs, and munched it instead of tobacco.

[12] JAMIE'S RETURN—Jamie, Jess and Hendry's son, was a barber in London.

[13] BROSE—Porridge made of oatmeal and hot water.

[14] HAVER—This time *haver* means folly or foolishness.

DID YOU READ WITH UNDERSTANDING?

Do not be concerned if you do not understand every Scotch expression. You will find as you read along that you get into the swing of it. Usually the context gives a clue to the meaning of the unfamiliar forms.

1. Why do you think the women of Thrums on the Sabbath "went by

101

with their hands spread out"? What would they be wearing that was out of the ordinary? What peculiar name was given to the little short beaded cloaks when they were fashionable? Why were they so called?

2. Why would such a cloak be useless to Jess? Why do you think she wanted one so badly? What satisfactions would she have from it? How could Hendry tell that she wanted one, when she denied it persistently?

3. Did Jess and Hendry show much affection for each other in their speech? How did the schoolmaster know that Hendry was fond of Jess? Was Jess equally fond of her husband? How can you tell?

4. What bits of detail in the sketch give the reader an idea of the extreme poverty in the home? Mention several. Were the family extremely unhappy? Or did they take their way of living as a matter of course? Or did they get considerable enjoyment out of life? Discuss.

5. Would Jess mind having to make her cloak? Or would she enjoy it all the more for that reason? Discuss.

6. What kind of man was Hendry? Describe him in your own words.

SILVER

WALTER DE LA MARE

D	SLOWLY, silently, now the moon
	Walks the night in her silvery shoon;
LG1	This way, and that, she peers, and sees
	Silver fruit upon silver trees;
MG1	5 One by one the casements catch
	Her beams beneath the silvery thatch;
B1	Couched in his kennel, like a log,
	With paws of silver sleeps the dog;
MG1	From their shadowy cote the white breasts peep
	10 Of doves in a silver-feathered sleep;
LG1	A harvest mouse goes scampering by,
	With silver claws and a silver eye;
LG	And moveless fish in the water gleam,
	By silver reeds in a silver stream.

FOR INTERPRETATION

1. Describe the picture suggested by the first six lines of the poem. If you were an artist, what sort of illustration would you make for those six

lines? Describe now a companion illustration for the rest of the poem.

2. Do you think the poet may have written the poem after being outside on a moonlight night? Or do you think he made it up in his imagination? Give the reasons for your answer.

3. What kind of place or scene is suggested by the details in the picture? What is there in the poem that suggests movement as well as moonlight? Discuss.

PIANO

D. H. LAWRENCE

SOFTLY, in the dusk, a woman is singing to me;
Taking me back down the vista of years, till I see
A child sitting under the piano, in the boom of the tingling strings
And pressing the small, poised feet of a mother who smiles as she sings.

5 In spite of myself, the insidious mastery of song
Betrays me back, till the heart of me weeps to belong
To the old Sunday evenings at home, with winter outside
And hymns in the cozy parlor, the tinkling piano our guide.

So now it is vain for the singer to burst into clamor
10 With the great black piano appassionato. The glamor
Of childish days is upon me, my manhood is cast
Down in the flood of remembrance, I weep like a child for the past.

FOR INTERPRETATION

Read the poem through carefully before answering the following questions.

1. Where is the poet, do you think, when the idea for this poem comes to him? Who else is present? Describe the situation.

2. A song carries his thoughts away from that moment to what other time and place? Describe the scene of his memory. Who is the child sitting under the piano?

3. What change in the setting is suggested by the first two lines of the third stanza? Does the change destroy the spell of his remembering? What lines give the answer?

4. What common human emotion does the poem portray?

THE ICE-CART

WILFRID WILSON GIBSON

B1   Perched on my city office-stool,
              I watched with envy, while a cool
              And lucky carter handled ice. . . .
L1   And I was wandering in a trice,
D   5   Far from the gray and grimy heat
              Of that intolerable street,
L1   O'er sapphire berg and emerald floe
              Beneath the still, cold ruby glow
              Of everlasting Polar night,
       10 Bewildered by the queer half-light,
M1   Until I stumbled, unawares,
              Upon a creek where big white bears
              Plunged headlong down with flourished heels,
              And floundered after shining seals
       15 Through shivering seas of blinding blue.
D1   And as I watched them, ere I knew,
              I'd stripped, and I was swimming, too,
              Among the seal-pack, young and hale,
              And thrusting on with threshing tail,
L   20 With twist and twirl and sudden leap
              Through crackling ice and salty deep—
              Diving and doubling with my kind,
              Until at last, we left behind
              Those big white, blundering bulks of death,
M1   25 And lay, at length, with panting breath
              Upon a far untraveled floe,
              Beneath a gentle drift of snow—
              Snow drifting gently, fine and white,
              Out of the endless Polar night,
       30 Falling and falling evermore

Upon that far untraveled shore,
Till I was buried fathoms deep
Beneath that cold, white drifting sleep—
L   Sleep drifting deep,
35 Deep drifting sleep. . . .

B   The carter cracked a sudden whip:
B1 I clutched my stool with startled grip,
Awakening to the grimy heat
Of that intolerable street.

FOR INTERPRETATION

1. Why might an office worker on a hot day envy the iceman? Might the iceman in turn envy the office worker? Why?

2. Describe the daydream inspired by the ice cakes. What do you see? feel? hear?

3. Which lines would have the most enticing appeal on a hot day in the city? Read them. What breaks the spell of the dream?

THE LANDSCAPE NEAR AN AERODROME

STEPHEN SPENDER

More beautiful and soft than any moth
With burring furred antennae feeling its huge path
Through dusk, the air-liner with shut-off engines
Glides over suburbs and the sleeves set trailing tall
5 To point the wind. Gently, broadly, she falls,
Scarcely disturbing charted currents of air.

Lulled by descent, the travelers across sea
And across feminine land indulging its easy limbs
In miles of softness, now let their eyes trained by watching
10 Penetrate through dusk the outskirts of this town
Here where industry shows a fraying edge.
Here they may see what is being done.

Beyond the winking masthead light
And the landing-ground, they observe the outposts
15 Of work: chimneys like lank black fingers
Or figures frightening and mad: and squat buildings
With their strange air behind trees, like women's faces
Shattered by grief. Here where few houses
Moan with faint light behind their blinds
20 They remark the unhomely sense of complaint, like a dog
Shut out and shivering at the foreign moon.

In the last sweep of love, they pass over fields
Behind the aerodrome, where boys play all day
Hacking dead grass: whose cries, like wild birds,
25 Settle upon the nearest roofs
But soon are hid under the loud city.

Then, as they land, they hear the tolling bell
Reaching across the landscape of hysteria
To where, larger than all the charcoaled batteries
30 And imaged towers against that dying sky,
Religion stands, the church blocking the sun.

FOR INTERPRETATION

1. What is the setting or viewpoint from which Mr. Spender has written his poem? Is he within or without the plane? What kind of plane is it? In what respect is it different from all the other planes you have read about in this modern unit? Is the plane landing or taking off?

2. What are the changes in landscape as the poem progresses? What time of day is it?

3. What is the attitude of the passengers within the plane? What is the usual attitude of passengers approaching a strange city? Does it differ much whether the approach is made by automobile or train or boat or plane? Discuss.

4. Explain the meaning of the following expressions:
   a. "The outskirts of this town *where industry shows a fraying edge.*"
   b. "Beyond the winking light . . . they observe *the outposts of work.*"
   c. "Here . . . they remark *the unhomely sense of complaint,* like a dog shut out and shivering at the foreign moon." (What other lines must be read with (c) to give it meaning?)

5. Describe the picture presented in the last five lines. What seems to be the attitude of the writer toward religion? How do you judge?

SHEEP

W. H. DAVIES

WHEN I was once in Baltimore,
   A man came up to me and cried,
"Come, I have eighteen hundred sheep,
   And we will sail on Tuesday's tide.

5   "If you will sail with me, young man,
   I'll pay you fifty shillings down;
These eighteen hundred sheep I take
   From Baltimore to Glasgow town."

He paid me fifty shillings down,
10   I sailed with eighteen hundred sheep;
We soon had cleared the harbor's mouth,
   We soon were in the salt sea deep.

The first night we were out at sea
   Those sheep were quiet in their mind;
15   The second night they cried with fear—
   They smelt no pastures in the wind.

They sniffed, poor things, for their green fields,
   They cried so loud I could not sleep;
For fifty thousand shillings down
20   I would not sail again with sheep.

FOR INTERPRETATION

Retell in simple prose the story of Mr. Davies' poem "Sheep." How long a sea-voyage do you think the young man had? How can you tell? What is there left for the reader to imagine between the first two and the last two lines of the last stanza? Discuss.

THE DONKEY

GILBERT KEITH CHESTERTON

WHEN fishes flew and forests walked
   And figs grew upon thorn,
Some moment when the moon was blood,
   Then surely I was born;

5   With monstrous head and sickening cry
   And ears like errant wings,
The devil's walking parody
   On all four-footed things.

The tattered outlaw of the earth,
10   Of ancient crooked will;
Starve, scourge, deride me: I am dumb,
   I keep my secret still.

Fools! For I also had my hour;
   One far fierce hour and sweet:
15   There was a shout about my ears,
   And palms before my feet.

FOR INTERPRETATION

1. What does the word *parody* mean? Why does the donkey consider
himself "the devil's walking *parody on all four-footed things*"? Mention

108

the things about himself that he dislikes. Does the world in general agree with this conception of the donkey? Discuss.

2. What is the donkey's secret source of consolation? Explain the significance of the *hour* to which the donkey refers. Why do you think that honor was conferred upon a donkey? Discuss.

THE RETURN

LORD DUNSANY

CAN you all hear me? I am speaking on the wireless. And I believe that I am in touch with you.

I thought that perhaps you might care to hear a ghost story. An actual personal experience, with nothing secondhand about it. A thing that occurred actually to myself, perhaps the most personal ghost story that any of you may have heard.

Well, to begin with, I was a long way away, when there came over me very suddenly an irresistible feeling to return to the old haunts that I had known a long while ago. I say "to begin with," for one must begin somewhere; and my long wanderings, and the remote parts to which I had come, are not much concerned with this tale. Sufficient that I turned at once for home, borne by a longing so strong that it seemed to leave me no choice, and I came in the course of time to that very village whose every chimney I knew. Every path I knew there too, and every little track running off from the paths the width of a single footstep, by which children ran to gardens of their own that they had found or made among weeds; but some of these paths had altered in the long time since I was there. It was a long, long time. The old public house was the same, the Green Man at the corner. And there I drifted, almost aimlessly, and yet with a feeling that there as much as anywhere I might find the life of the old village throbbing away. It was as I passed over the fields on the way to the Green Man that I first heard people talking about a ghost. I was passing a wheat field, over the stubble, brushing by a line of sheaves, when two men at work there, taking the sheaves away, began to talk of the ghost all of a sudden. "They say it comes every hundred years," said one. I knew at once they were speaking about a ghost.

"Yes," said the other, looking up at the leaves turning with the earliest touch of the autumn, "and it should be about the very day."

"It is," said the first; and I heard them say no more, and passed on feeling sure I should hear more at the inn. At the inn I knew none of them, not one; and where once I thought I did, it was only some old family likeness. So I sat all by myself in a corner beside a curtain and listened to what they said. And, just as I came in, their talk took the same turn as what I had heard in the wheat field. There was a ghost, it seemed, that came to that village once in a hundred years, and the hundred years were up. "Might be coming soon," said one, who looked like a gamekeeper.

"Aye, if there's any truth in it," said a farmer.

"True enough, by all accounts," said some.

"And there's been a look about the shadows lately," the keeper said, "like what my grandmother told me of."

"Your grandmother?" one of them asked.

"Yes, she saw it," he said.

"Must have been an old woman," said a man, looking round from the bar, on which he was leaning.

"Saw it as a child," said the keeper.

"I wouldn't walk near the stream tonight," said another, "not if any mist was rising. You'd meet it, all damp in the mist."

I sat there quietly in the shade of the curtain listening to all they said.

"Wonder where it comes from," said the farmer.

"Ah," they all said, and shook their heads, and no one even ventured to guess about that.

"Drifts over the fields where it used to walk, I expect, and up to the old house," said the bartender. "But as to where it comes from—ah."

And then their talk died away, as though it were somehow chilled by a draft blowing out of eternity. And when I saw I should get no more of this story from them I slipped quietly out of the room.

Two women were talking on a doorstep as I passed the next house; they seemed to be talking about the price of tea. And suddenly, I heard one say: "It will be about the hundred years."

"Aye," said the other one, "I shouldn't wonder." And one of

them went inside the house at that, and the other hurried away along the street, and I was all alone once more.

I passed a group of children in the road; and saw from a certain hush that came over their playing, and from the way that a few of them put their heads together and glanced up towards the old house, that they too were talking of the ghost. It left no doubt that that house was the seat of the mystery, and that there these ends of tales one heard in the village would be all gathered together. But when would it be? Was it the hundred years? It hardly seemed to me that it could be yet. The air seemed somehow not quite sufficiently haunted, though it hardly seems worth telling you so airy a fancy. Partly to see the old village again, and partly to get more facts, if I could, about this tale of the ghost, I hung about the village. I went to the village green. It delighted me to see the calm old space again—altered, but not out of knowledge; and there were geese on it, just as of old. And then a young man and a girl came by, going along a path that slanted across the green, the same path that there had been in my time. And by some strange chance they too, as soon as they came within hearing, began to speak of the end of the hundred years, and that visitor that all of them were expecting. Half believing and half wondering, they passed away out of hearing.

Oꞑe is moved by impulses more than by reason when one comes to old haunts that one knew. Had reason moved me alone, I should have gone at once to the old house on the hill beyond the village, and satisfied my curiosity there. But stronger than curiosity, stronger than any other emotion within me, I found the lure of the great willows, standing in their strange attitudes by the long-remembered stream. To them I went as evening began to draw in. A white mist rose as I came, and began to creep slowly through fields that sloped to the stream. I went with it, glad of its company, and loitered about those fields whose every boundary was unchanged by even a yard since the days when I knew them. And there the old haystacks stood, dark in the same corners, as though they had never been used since last I saw them; and the mist came up and touched them, and flowed about them, till they stood amongst it like islands. I seemed to know every one of them, not only by their positions, but by the size of them. You see, nothing could ever have happened

111

in the years since I was there to make each field give more hay, or any less, or to find a better place for the haystack to stand in each field. It was this that made me see, what I already profoundly felt, that I still had my share in this village. Much had changed, but the fundamental things were there as ever. Indeed it could not have been otherwise. And it made me feel more friendly with the mist, with which I was sauntering amongst these remembered nooks, to reflect that it was another of those things that would be in that valley always. Or if it wandered away in the warm weather, carried off by some stray wind, it would return like myself.

Couples walking late, or men traveling lonely, turned now away from the mist, as though they found something ominous in its waving and wandering whiteness; they turned suddenly for the uplands, and we were left quite alone. And I knew they were right to avoid the stream at this hour, for there was a most haunted feeling about it, and that feeling slowly increased as the evening grew stiller and later. Rooks passed, and all the singing birds were asleep. A few wild ducks came over, and circled once, and dropped past me down to their home in a patch of irises; they alone seeming unperturbed by whatever was making the mist so unmistakably eerie. And then a silence fell that nothing disturbed at all, and all the while the eeriness was increasing.

It was like that till the moon rose. But when the moon came huge and yellow and magical and very nearly full, almost with a leap over a ridge of the downland that showed just clear of the osiers,[1] I suddenly knew that the hundred years were up, and that whatever haunted the old house over the meadows, on the opposite side from the moon, would be now on its way if ever. So I left the stream at once and turned for the hill, to see what was to be seen. I went, all the way, over fields every one of which I had carried so long in my memory that I knew my way unmistakably. Sometimes they differed from the picture of them that I had treasured so long, but only by being a little duller, by shining a little less vividly, as must be the way with heavy solid earth when compared with an old memory. Voices were rising now in the village behind me, as though the large moon coming over the ridges, or the end of the hundred years,

[1] THE OSIERS—The willows.

had awoken all of a sudden uneasy apprehensions; and not only
human voices rose in a hum, but there came sharply through
them the outcry of dogs, which clearly shared the vague fear
that seemed haunting their masters. The sound of the voices
grew low as I moved away from them, but never ceased to fill
the night with fear. At what moment the hundred years would
end I knew not, but it seemed to me that as the moon rose higher
the very last hours of the century were falling away.

I crossed a road, and a couple walking down it paused suddenly and looked up to the old house on the hill. I saw the
shape of it, dark, with no windows lit, though now and then the
moon flashed curiously upon panes. And this bulk in the night,
with flashes upon the windows, I knew for the end of my journey.
In this house my life had begun, and to it I returned. It was
this house that had called me, through all the length of my
wanderings, and that I felt drawing me now, as the Pole draws
the needles of magnets. I paid no heed any more to that uneasy
hum that came quavering up from voices astir in the village,
but left them to whatever troubled them in the mist, and made
straight for that house. Far down below me now were the mist
and its fears, and the slope of the hill steepened. I swept up it;
and just as I came to the edge of the lawns I knew, as I know
no other lawns, I found a high wall before me. They had built
it since the days when I knew those lawns. There seemed something about the moon and about the hour that told me not to
loiter before this wall, and I pressed on to the house.

The lawns were the same as ever, and all the dew was glittering under the moon, and a hush was heavy upon them, and the
house was deep in sleep. Not a sound came from the black bulk
of the house, not a movement of door or window, though I had
returned to my home from so far and after so long. It stood
there black and silent, but the chill and the hush and the darkness of the house were to stop me no more than the wall. I had
come from so far to see those lawns again, and the old house standing amongst them. I went round to the door, and the glass which
there was in its panels stared blankly at me, with shutters behind them; and all the bolts were locked. There a dog saw me.
It had been lying down in a barrel, guarding the door, when it
suddenly saw me and howled. But still no sound or movement
came from the house.

I knew I was very near to the end of my long journey now, the old wainscot of oak on an upper landing, carved with the curious heads of ancient kings, dark with the years and darkening all the corridor, that ran to the door of a room that was once my nursery. I knew now that this carved oak was the end of my journey. I entered the house, and the dog howled once more. Before me, all in the dark, were the stairs I knew. I needed no light. I knew every turn of those stairs, and every step of them, and the very flight of the echoes that used to rise from the creak of each different board. I sped up them, and the dog was howling now with one long quivering howl. I came to the landing, and there was the old dark corridor, and there were the ancient heads with their curious faces that seemed to look at me with the first welcome I had had since my long journey began. The howling of the dog, which was louder now, seemed at last to disturb the house, for far away I heard the thudding of footsteps. And the steps were coming towards me.

Can you hear me? I feel that you can. I believe I am near you. A door opened some way off. The steps were nearer. A woman came along the corridor, holding a candle, walking slowly, and looking about her anxiously as she came. And just then clearly out of the tower of the old church of the village the notes of midnight floated over the mist; and it felt to me at that moment that the hundred years were over. And all of a sudden the woman holding the candle saw me. She seemed to see me more clearly than any had done in the village: I noticed that in her eyes as her mouth opened slowly. And then she screamed.

This is a personal experience. Nothing secondhand, as so often there is in such stories. I turned from the woman's white face to the dark of the old carved wainscot, whose every panel and every figure I knew; and sinking far into that venerable timber, sinking home to the deeps of the oak, I knew that *I* was the ghost.

DID YOU READ WITH UNDERSTANDING?

1. Does the story have a matter-of-fact beginning? Is the curiosity of the reader concerned with the narrator? Does the narrator tell more, or less, about himself than is usually told in stories of the first person?

2. Is there anything unusual about the changes that have taken place in the village since the narrator's last visit there? What is there significant in the fact that the speaker sees no familiar faces. How is our

interest aroused in the ghost? Do the actions of the visitor seem natural under the circumstances? Discuss. Do you wonder, as you read, at any of the things he does?

3. When you read the story for the first time, did you expect to see a ghost? Where? What kind? Did you guess the ending of the story before you came to it? If not, why not? If so, point out the clues that made you suspect it. Is the speaker surprised to find himself the ghost?

4. What hints stand out clearly on a second reading of the story? List several. How does the opening sentence of the story take on added meaning after one knows the ending? Explain. At what point in the story would the alert reader be most likely to guess the identity of the ghost?

THE MONKEY'S PAW

W. W. JACOBS

WITHOUT, the night was cold and wet, but in the small parlor of Lakesnam Villa the blinds were drawn and the fire burned brightly. Father and son were at chess, the former, who possessed ideas about the game involving radical changes, putting his king into such sharp and unnecessary perils that it even provoked comment from the white-haired old lady knitting placidly by the fire.

"Hark at the wind," said Mr. White, who, having seen a fatal mistake after it was too late, was amiably desirous of preventing his son from seeing it.

"I'm listening," said the latter, grimly surveying the board as he stretched out his hand. "Check."

"I should hardly think that he'd come tonight," said his father, with his hand poised over the board.

"Mate," replied the son.

"That's the worst of living so far out," bawled Mr. White, with sudden and unlooked-for violence; "of all the beastly, slushy, out-of-the-way places to live in, this is the worst. Pathway's a bog, and the road's a torrent. I don't know what people are thinking about. I suppose because only two houses on the road are let, they think it doesn't matter."

"Never mind, dear," said his wife soothingly; "perhaps you'll win the next one."

Mr. White looked up sharply, just in time to intercept a knowing glance between mother and son. The words died away on his lips, and he hid a guilty grin in his thin grey beard.

"There he is," said Herbert White, as the gate banged to loudly and heavy footsteps came toward the door.

The old man rose with hospitable haste, and opening the door, was heard condoling with the new arrival. The new arrival also condoled with himself, so that Mrs. White said, "Tut, tut!" and coughed gently as her husband entered the room, followed by a tall burly man, beady of eye and rubicund of visage.

"Sergeant-Major Morris," he said, introducing him.

The sergeant-major shook hands, and taking the proffered seat by the fire, watched contentedly while his host got out whisky and tumblers and stood a small copper kettle on the fire.

At the third glass his eyes got brighter, and he began to talk, the little family circle regarding with eager interest this visitor from distant parts, as he squared his broad shoulders in the chair and spoke of strange scenes and doughty deeds, of wars and plagues and strange peoples.

"Twenty-one years of it," said Mr. White, nodding at his wife and son. "When he went away he was a slip of a youth in the warehouse. Now look at him."

"He don't look to have taken much hard," said Mrs. White politely.

"I'd like to go to India myself," said the old man, "just to look round a bit, you know."

116

"Better where you are," said the sergeant-major, shaking his head. He put down the empty glass and, sighing softly, shook it again.

"I should like to see those old temples and fakirs and jugglers," said the old man. "What was that you started telling me the other day about a monkey's paw or something, Morris?"

"Nothing," said the soldier hastily. "Leastways, nothing worth hearing."

"Monkey's paw?" said Mrs. White curiously.

"Well, it's just a bit of what you might call magic, perhaps," said the sergeant-major off-handedly.

His three listeners leaned forward eagerly. The visitor absent-mindedly put his empty glass to his lips and then set it down again. His host filled it for him.

"To look at," said the sergeant-major, fumbling in his pocket, "it's just an ordinary little paw, dried to a mummy."

He took something out of his pocket and proffered it. Mrs. White drew back with a grimace, but her son, taking it, examined it curiously.

"And what is there special about it?" inquired Mr. White, as he took it from his son and, having examined it, placed it upon the table.

"It had a spell put on it by an old fakir," said the sergeant-major, "a very holy man. He wanted to show that fate ruled people's lives, and that those who interfered with it did so to their sorrow. He put a spell on it so that three separate men could each have three wishes from it."

His manner was so impressive that his hearers were conscious that their light laughter jarred somewhat.

"Well, why don't you have three, sir?" said Herbert White cleverly.

The soldier regarded him in the way that middle age is wont to regard presumptuous youth. "I have," he said quietly, and his blotchy face whitened.

"And did you really have the three wishes granted?" asked Mrs. White.

"I did," said the sergeant-major, and his glass tapped against his strong teeth.

"And has anybody else wished?" inquired the old lady.

"The first man had his three wishes, yes," was the reply. "I

117

don't know what the first two were, but the third was for death. That's how I got the paw."

His tones were so grave that a hush fell upon the group.

"If you've had your three wishes, it's no good to you now, then, Morris," said the old man at last. "Why do you keep it?"

The soldier shook his head. "Fancy, I suppose," he said slowly. "I did have some idea of selling it, but I don't think I will. It has caused enough mischief already. Besides, people won't buy. They think it's a fairy tale, some of them, and those who do think anything of it want to try it first and pay me afterward."

"If you could have another three wishes," said the old man, eyeing him keenly, "would you have them?"

"I don't know," said the other. "I don't know."

He took the paw, and dangling it between his front finger and thumb, suddenly threw it upon the fire. White, with a slight cry, stooped down and snatched it off.

"Better let it burn," said the soldier solemnly.

"If you don't want it, Morris," said the old man, "give it to me."

"I won't," said his friend doggedly. "I threw it on the fire. If you keep it, don't blame me for what happens. Pitch it on the fire again, like a sensible man."

The other shook his head and examined his new possession closely. "How do you do it?" he inquired.

"Hold it up in your right hand and wish aloud," said the sergeant-major, "but I warn you of the consequences."

"Sounds like the *Arabian Nights*," said Mrs. White, as she rose and began to set the supper. "Don't you think you might wish for four pairs of hands for me?"

Her husband drew the talisman from his pocket and then all three burst into laughter as the sergeant-major, with a look of alarm on his face, caught him by the arm.

"If you must wish," he said gruffly, "wish for something sensible."

Mr. White dropped it back into his pocket, and placing chairs, motioned his friend to the table. In the business of supper the talisman was partly forgotten, and afterward the three sat listening in an enthralled fashion to a second installment of the soldier's adventures in India.

"If the tale about the monkey paw is not more truthful than those he has been telling us," said Herbert, as the door closed behind their guest, just in time for him to catch the last train, "we shan't make much out of it."

"Did you give him anything for it, father?" inquired Mrs. White, regarding her husband closely.

"A trifle," said he, coloring slightly. "He didn't want it, but I made him take it. And he pressed me again to throw it away."

"Likely," said Herbert, with pretended horror. "Why, we're going to be rich, and famous, and happy. Wish to be an emperor, father, to begin with; then you can't be henpecked."

He darted round the table, pursued by the maligned Mrs. White armed with an antimacassar.[1]

Mr. White took the paw from his pocket and eyed it dubiously. "I don't know what to wish for, and that's a fact," he said slowly. "It seems to me I've got all I want."

"If you only cleared the house, you'd be quite happy, wouldn't you?" said Herbert, with his hand on his shoulder. "Well, wish for two hundred pounds, then; that'll just do it."

His father, smiling shamefacedly at his own credulity, held up the talisman, as his son, with a solemn face somewhat marred by a wink at his mother, sat down at the piano and struck a few impressive chords.

"I wish for two hundred pounds," said the old man distinctly.

A fine crash from the piano greeted the words, interrupted by a shuddering cry from the old man. His wife and son ran toward him.

"It moved," he cried, with a glance of disgust at the object as it lay on the floor. "As I wished it twisted in my hands like a snake."

"Well, I don't see the money," said his son, as he picked it up and placed it on the table, "and I bet I never shall."

"It must have been your fancy, father," said his wife, regarding him anxiously.

He shook his head. "Never mind, though; there's no harm done, but it gave me a shock all the same."

They sat down by the fire again while the two men finished their pipes. Outside, the wind was higher than ever, and the old man started nervously at the sound of a door banging up-

[1] ANTIMACASSAR—A tidy, or doily.

stairs. A silence unusual and depressing settled upon all three, which lasted until the old couple rose to retire for the night.

"I expect you'll find the cash tied up in a big bag in the middle of your bed," said Herbert, as he bade them good night, "and something horrible squatting up on top of the wardrobe watching you as you pocket your ill-gotten gains."

II

In the brightness of the wintry sun next morning as it streamed over the breakfast table Herbert laughed at his father's fears. There was an air of prosaic wholesomeness about the room which it had lacked on the previous night, and the dirty, shriveled little paw was pitched on the sideboard with a carelessness which betokened no great belief in its virtues.

"I suppose all old soldiers are the same," said Mrs. White. "The idea of our listening to such nonsense! How could wishes be granted in these days? And if they could, how could two hundred pounds hurt you, father?"

"Might drop on his head from the sky," said the frivolous Herbert.

"Morris said the things happened so naturally," said his father, "that you might if you so wished attribute it to coincidence."

"Well, don't break into the money before I come back," said Herbert, as he rose from the table. "I'm afraid it'll turn you into a mean, avaricious man, and we shall have to disown you."

His mother laughed, and following him to the door, watched him down the road, and returning to the breakfast table, was very happy at the expense of her husband's credulity. All of which did not prevent her from scurrying to the door at the postman's knock, nor prevent her from referring somewhat shortly to retired sergeant-majors of bibulous habits when she found that the post brought a tailor's bill.

"Herbert will have some more of his funny remarks, I expect, when he comes home," she said, as they sat at dinner.

"I dare say," said Mr. White, "but for all that, the thing moved in my hand; that I'll swear to."

"You thought it did," said the old lady soothingly.

"I say it did," replied the other. "There was no thought about it; I had just—What's the matter?"

His wife made no reply. She was watching the mysterious

movements of a man outside, who, peering in an undecided fashion at the house, appeared to be trying to make up his mind to enter. In mental connection with the two hundred pounds, she noticed that the stranger was well dressed and wore a silk hat of glossy newness. Three times he paused at the gate, and then walked on again. The fourth time he stood with his hand upon it, and then with sudden resolution flung it open and walked up the path. Mrs. White at the same moment placed her hands behind her, and hurriedly unfastening the strings of her apron, put that useful article of apparel beneath the cushion of her chair.

She brought the stranger, who seemed ill at ease, into the room. He gazed furtively at Mrs. White, and listened in a pre-occupied fashion as the old lady apologized for the appearance of the room, and her husband's coat, a garment which he usually reserved for the garden. She then waited as patiently as her sex would permit for him to broach his business, but he was at first strangely silent.

"I—was asked to call," he said at last, and stooped and picked a piece of cotton from his trousers. "I come from Maw and Meggins."

The old lady started. "Is anything the matter?" she asked breathlessly. "Has anything happened to Herbert? What is it? What is it?"

Her husband interposed. "There, there, mother," he said hastily. "Sit down, and don't jump to conclusions. You've not brought bad news, I'm sure, sir," and he eyed the other wistfully.

"I'm sorry—" began the visitor.

"Is he hurt?" demanded the mother.

The visitor bowed in assent. "Badly hurt," he said quietly, "but he is not in any pain."

"Oh, thank God!" said the old woman, clasping her hands. "Thank God for that! Thank——"

She broke off suddenly as the sinister meaning of the assurance dawned upon her and she saw the awful confirmation of her fears in the other's averted face. She caught her breath, and turning to her slow-witted husband, laid her trembling old hand upon his. There was a long silence.

"He was caught in the machinery," said the visitor at length, in a low voice.

"Caught in the machinery," repeated Mr. White, in a dazed fashion, "yes."

He sat staring blankly out at the window, and taking his wife's hand between his own, pressed it as he had been wont to do in their old courting days nearly forty years before.

"He was the only one left to us," he said, turning gently to the visitor. "It is hard."

The other coughed, and rising, walked slowly to the window. "The firm wished me to convey their sincere sympathy with you in your great loss," he said, without looking round. "I beg that you will understand I am only their servant and merely obeying orders."

There was no reply; the old woman's face was white, her eyes staring, and her breath inaudible; on the husband's face was a look such as his friend the sergeant might have carried into his first action.

"I was to say that Maw and Meggins disclaim all responsibility," continued the other. "They admit no liability at all, but in consideration of your son's services they wish to present you with a certain sum as compensation."

Mr. White dropped his wife's hand, and rising to his feet, gazed with a look of horror at his visitor. His dry lips shaped the words, "How much?"

"Two hundred pounds," was the answer.

Unconscious of his wife's shriek, the old man smiled faintly, put out his hands like a sightless man, and dropped, a senseless heap, to the floor.

III

In the huge new cemetery, some two miles distant, the old people buried their dead, and came back to a house steeped in shadow and silence. It was all over so quickly that at first they could hardly realize it, and remained in a state of expectation as though of something else to happen—something else which was to lighten this load, too heavy for old hearts to bear. But the days passed, and expectation gave place to resignation—the hopeless resignation of the old, sometimes miscalled apathy. Sometimes they hardly exchanged a word, for now they had nothing to talk about, and their days were long to weariness.

It was about a week after that that the old man, waking suddenly in the night, stretched out his hand and found himself alone. The room was in darkness, and the sound of subdued weeping came from the window. He raised himself in bed and listened.

"Come back," he said tenderly. "You will be cold."

"It is colder for my son," said the old woman, and wept afresh.

The sound of her sobs died away on his ears. The bed was warm, and his eyes heavy with sleep. He dozed fitfully, and then slept until a sudden wild cry from his wife awoke him with a start.

"The monkey's paw!" she cried wildly. "The monkey's paw!"

He started up in alarm. "Where? Where is it? What's the matter?"

She came stumbling across the room toward him. "I want it," she said quietly. "You've not destroyed it?"

"It's in the parlor, on the bracket," he replied, marveling. "Why?"

She cried and laughed together, and bending over, kissed his cheek.

"I only just thought of it," she said hysterically. "Why didn't I think of it before? Why didn't you think of it?"

"Think of what?" he questioned.

"The other two wishes," she replied rapidly. "We've only had one."

"Was not that enough?" he demanded fiercely.

"No," she cried triumphantly; "we'll have one more. Go down and get it quickly, and wish our boy alive again."

The man sat up in bed and flung the bed clothes from his quaking limbs. "You are mad!" he cried, aghast.

"Get it," she panted; "get it quickly, and wish—Oh, my boy, my boy!"

Her husband struck a match and lit the candle. "Get back to bed," he said unsteadily. "You don't know what you are saying."

"We had the first wish granted," said the old woman feverishly; "why not the second?"

"A coincidence," stammered the old man.

"Go and get it and wish," cried the old woman, and dragged him toward the door.

He went down in the darkness, and felt his way to the parlor, and then to the mantelpiece. The talisman was in its place, and

123

a horrible fear that the unspoken wish might bring his mutilated son before him ere he could escape from the room seized upon him, and he caught his breath as he found that he had lost the direction of the door. His brow cold with sweat, he felt his way round the table, and groped along the wall until he found himself in the small passage with the unwholesome thing in his hand.

Even his wife's face seemed changed as he entered the room. It was white and expectant, and to his fears seemed to have an unnatural look upon it. He was afraid of her.

"Wish!" she cried, in a strong voice.

"It is foolish and wicked," he faltered.

"Wish!" repeated his wife.

He raised his hand. "I wish my son alive again."

The talisman fell to the floor, and he regarded it shudderingly. Then he sank trembling into a chair as the old woman, with burning eyes, walked to the window and raised the blind.

He sat until he was chilled with the cold, glancing occasionally at the figure of the old woman peering through the window. The candle end, which had burnt below the rim of the china candlestick, was throwing pulsating shadows on the ceiling and walls, until, with a flicker larger than the rest, it expired. The old man, with an unspeakable sense of relief at the failure of the talisman, crept back to his bed, and a minute or two afterward the old woman came silently and apathetically beside him.

Neither spoke, but both lay silently listening to the ticking of the clock. A stair creaked, and a squeaky mouse scurried noisily through the wall. The darkness was oppressive, and after lying for some time screwing up his courage, the husband took the box of matches, and striking one, went downstairs for a candle.

At the foot of the stairs the match went out, and he paused to strike another, and at the same moment a knock, so quiet and stealthy as to be scarcely audible, sounded on the front door.

The matches fell from his hand. He stood motionless, his breath suspended until the knock was repeated. Then he turned and fled swiftly back to his room, and closed the door behind him. A third knock sounded through the house.

"*What's that?*" cried the old woman, starting up.

"A rat," said the old man, in shaking tones—"a rat. It passed me on the stairs."

His wife sat up in bed listening. A loud knock resounded through the house.

"It's Herbert!" she screamed. "It's Herbert!"

She ran to the door, but her husband was before her, and catching her by the arm, held her tightly.

"What are you going to do?" he whispered hoarsely.

"It's my boy; it's Herbert!" she cried, struggling mechanically. "I forgot it was two miles away. What are you holding me for? Let go. I must open the door."

"Don't let it in!" cried the old man, trembling.

"You're afraid of your own son," she cried, struggling. "Let me go. I'm coming, Herbert; I'm coming."

There was another knock, and another. The old woman with a sudden wrench broke free and ran from the room. Her husband followed to the landing, and called after her appealingly as she hurried downstairs. He heard the chain rattle back and the bottom bolt drawn slowly and stiffly from the socket. Then the old woman's voice, strained and panting.

"The bolt," she cried loudly. "Come down, I can't reach it."

But her husband was on his hands and knees groping wildly on the floor in search of the paw. If he could only find it before the thing outside got in. A perfect fusillade of knocks reverberated through the house, and he heard the scraping of a chair as his wife put it down in the passage against the door. He heard the creaking of the bolt as it came slowly back, and at the same moment, he found the monkey's paw, and frantically breathed his third and last wish.

The knocking ceased suddenly, although the echoes of it were still in the house. He heard the chair drawn back and the door opened. A cold wind rushed up the staircase, and a long loud wail of disappointment and misery from his wife gave him courage to run down to her side, and then to the gate beyond. The street lamp flickering opposite shone on a quiet and deserted road.

DID YOU READ WITH UNDERSTANDING?

1. What kind of home does the reader discover in the opening paragraphs of "The Monkey's Paw"? What small details make the setting seem very natural and matter of fact? Why did Mr. White speak with such sudden violence about the out-of-the-way place in which they lived? What little touches show the real affection in the home?

2. Is the reader inclined to believe the sergeant-major's story about the monkey's paw? Why or why not? Do you think the sergeant-major had come with the express purpose of selling the monkey's paw—or at least of looking for some gift in exchange for it? Discuss. Does he evidently fear the thing himself? What is there in his manner that might serve as a warning? Discuss. By what ruse does he try to absolve himself from the responsibility of passing on the monkey's paw?

3. What reason had the holy man given for casting a spell on the monkey's paw? What was the magic intended to prove? Why did Mr. White wish for so small a sum of money? What convinced him that there was evil in the monkey's paw? What was the first effect of the wish on the family? How does Mrs. White show that she half believes in the power of the monkey's paw? What had the soldier said about the way in which the wishes were fulfilled? How was Mr. White's first wish fulfilled? What transformation took place within the home?

4. Why was Mr. White so horrified at his wife's desire to wish their son alive again? Why did he make the wish? Why was he afraid to have his wife answer the knocks at the door? What do you think Mrs. White would have found if she had opened the door before her husband found the monkey's paw? Discuss. What was Mr. White's third and last wish? Was he right in making it? What would you have done? Discuss. Will the mother feel better or worse for this night's experience? Why? How about the father—will he feel better or worse? Why? Did the monkey's paw, in this case, prove the truth of the holy man's philosophy? Discuss.

British character is balanced with common sense and humor.

THE DISILLUSIONED

J. B. PRIESTLEY

It was our experience at the circus last Tuesday afternoon that compelled me to reflect upon this matter. Even the children were disappointed when we actually visited the circus. For weeks we had been staring at the colored bills, across which was pasted the startling slip: *For One Day Only.* There was the most artful crescendo of this bill-posting. Every day the children announced that they had seen new pictures of the circus and thereupon reported fresh wonders. Elephants and tigers and ponies and clowns and cowboys, all superb in the three-color process, claimed more and more space on our hoardings,[1] from which auctioneers and real estate agents and other dull fellows were banished. Nero and Heliogabalus [2] themselves, if they had caught a glimpse of our hoardings, would have decided to stay on in the town.

---

[1] HOARDINGS—Temporary screens of boards, hence billboards.
[2] NERO AND HELIOGABALUS (ELAGABALUS)—Dissolute Roman emperors who led especially spectacular lives.

Now I do not say that it was a bad little traveling circus, but I do say that it was certainly not the circus of the colored bills. There were no lions and tigers at all. Instead of a whole crazy regiment of clowns, there were only two, and they were rather dingy fellows. The cowboys turned out to be the men who had first shown us our seats, and though their hats and boots undoubtedly came from the Wild West, between these extremities all three of them were too homely for our taste. Where was the long procession of elephants, each of them as big as a house? There were only two elephants and they seemed quite small after those monsters of the hoardings. "I think they must be young elephants," said one of the children. "They're awfully small, aren't they?"

I do not say that our visit was a failure. (The two younger children have been circus ponies ever since and do nothing but trot round in circles.) But I do think it would have been a far greater success if we had never seen all those lying pictures. Our hopes were raised too high, so that disappointment was inevitable. The children naturally assumed they would see in reality all that the poster artists and the printers had contrived for them. They are still puzzled about it. They invent excuses for the proprietor. The other elephants must have gone for a walk or run after the missing lions and tigers. Forty clowns or so—and those that have the nicest costumes too—must not have been feeling very well. It is almost pathetic to hear them thus excusing the cunning old fabulist. These children are growing up in a world of artful advertisement. Only the other day, one of them, who can read quite nicely, chanced to see an advertisement of some domestic commodity and cried: "Mummie, it says it's the *best* in all the world. Why don't you *buy* some?" Here was this precious stuff, the best in the world, to be had for the asking, and we were stupidly doing nothing about it. Soon she will realize that the matter was not quite so urgent as she imagined. Even now she may be thinking in secret that perhaps the man who owned the circus and put out all those false pictures of it had simply taken her in. Disillusion is already dogging her footsteps.

This is, I understand, an age of disillusion. It is also an age in which the business of suggesting that many things are perfect has become a highly organized trade or profession. I suspect that there is some connection between these two facts. Consider our position. Men have always dreamed of perfection, but in past ages they did not think of perfection as existing at all in the ordinary world. It was always somewhere round the corner. If you could find your way into the Garden of the Hesperides, to the Isles of the Blest, to that secret Avalon where there is neither rain nor snow, then there you would come upon life made perfect. If you were a poet, a dreamer, an idealist, you found a quiet corner and thought about these beautiful places. If your wine was sourer than usual and your new tunic was shredding away, you shrugged your shoulders, then remembered that in the Hesperides or Avalon all the wine was unimaginably delicious and tunics lasted just as long as you wanted them to last. I do not doubt for a moment that in those days merchants concocted their fables and hucksters cried up their wares most monstrously. But there was certainly no elaborate machinery for pointing out that all manner of things were perfect. The whole world was not told to Drink Aristides' Wine and Never Have a Headache, that Trunk Hose From Richard Whittington's Wear For Ever. There was no large-scale attempt to introduce the Philosopher's Stone or the Fountain of Youth into every home. It was not generally understood that the payment of the first installment or even the filling in of a coupon would anchor the Isles of the Blest outside your front door.

Nowadays we do not believe that life that is all goodness, truth, and beauty is being lived somewhere beyond the nearest mountains or the western seas. All the enchanted islands have vanished. We have stopped singing about Dixie, which I take to be one—and apparently the last—of these ideal realms. But have we suddenly forgotten how to dream of perfection? I think not. There is no perfect life going on round the corner, but now, surely, it is even nearer than that. In front of me, at this moment, are two magazines, one English and the other American, the kind with shiny paper and expensive advertisements; and in the pages at the beginning and end of these magazines I find reports of life that has been made perfect.

I do not know where to begin. When I turn over these pages I am bewildered, mazed with good news. Reflect on the irritations, the boredoms, the long grinding tragedies, of this life of ours. Be brave for a moment and remember the dismal antics of our bodies; our fatty tissues and acids in the stomach, our gout and dyspepsia and startling blood pressures, our failing sight and thinning hair and rotting teeth. Keep steadily in mind the days when you have not been able to entertain yourself and the nights when you have not been able even to entertain your friends. Think how we suffer from clothes that do not fit, boots that wear out, raincoats that drink like sponges, tobacco that burns the tongue, cars that will not take hills in top-gear, mattresses that do nothing but sag, and trains that are always late. All these, from the huge miseries that come crashing into our lives like a rhinoceros to the little irritations that bite like mosquitoes, have disappeared. The people here know nothing about them. They are as gods. Look at the women—seven foot tall, beautifully slender, exquisitely gowned and hatted, their hair so cunningly and crisply waved! Look at the men—so ruddy of cheek and bright of eye, so broad and square in the shoulders, so astonishingly tailored and laundered! What domestic felicity they enjoy! "Welcome home!" they cry, for ever smiling and holding out their arms.

Examine the children—they are called "Kiddies" here—and notice their apple-cheeks, their sturdy limbs, their playfulness that never, never turns into naughtiness, into stamping and screaming. In winter they sit in front of bright fires (Coal, Gas, Electric) and listen happily to the World's Masterpieces of Music; they recline in chairs so marvelously sprung that they would never get up out of them if they did not know that upstairs were the most comfortable mattresses ever offered to the public and instant sleep induced by a cup of Whatisit. In summer they sprawl on gamboge sands by the side of a royal blue sea, in perpetual sunshine, and have to hand pipes that will not crack, the aristocrat of cigarettes, bottles of elixir (various brands); and the men look more god-like than ever, partly because their hair has been fixed for the day by a little cream; the women, fully protected against sunburn, are dazzlingly beautiful and gracious; and the kiddies, well stuffed with a miraculous breakfast food, are growing an inch a day—and all their clothes are growing with them. (Even the suitcases are quietly expanding in the box-room.) And winter or summer, their watches never go wrong and their shoes never pinch; they never worry or mope or quarrel; they never sicken and die. And this, we are told, is not Avalon but our own world.

Alas! we are forever discovering that it is not our own world, that try as we may—sending off at once, refusing all imitations, filling in coupons, paying first installments—we cannot reproduce the life of these people in the advertisements. There is always a catch. We are always being taken in. There are only two clowns and two elephants. Thus, living in an age of advertisement, we are perpetually disillusioned. The perfect life is spread before us every day, but it changes and withers at a touch—never a Snark, always a Boojum.

DID YOU READ WITH UNDERSTANDING?

1. Do you think the Priestley's experience with the over-advertised circus was an uncommon one? Or is it a habit of small circuses to exaggerate their wares? Why is such an experience bad for children?

2. Explain the meaning of the title. What do you think is the age of disillusionment, that is, the age at which people suffer the most disillusioning experiences? What are some of the disillusionments that most children have to face?

3. Are Mr. Priestley's comments on magazine advertising pretty fairly based on facts? What other advertising mediums are characterized by the same sort of "selling"? Is it good business to over-advertise? Why do so many firms do it? How can it be effectively discouraged?

4. What effect does the perfectionist type of advertising have on the general public? Discuss. Explain Mr. Priestley's statement, "Living in an age of advertisement, we are perpetually disillusioned."

THE OPEN WINDOW

"SAKI"

"My aunt will be down presently, Mr. Nuttel," said a very self-possessed young lady of fifteen; "in the meantime you must try and put up with me."

Framton Nuttel endeavored to say the correct something which should duly flatter the niece of the moment without unduly discounting the aunt that was to come. Privately he doubted more than ever whether these formal visits on a succession of total strangers would do much towards helping the nerve cure which he was supposed to be undergoing.

"I know how it will be," his sister had said when he was preparing to migrate to this rural retreat; "you will bury yourself down there and not speak to a living soul, and your nerves will be worse than ever from moping. I shall just give you letters of introduction to all the people I know there. Some of them, as far as I can remember, were quite nice."

Framton wondered whether Mrs. Sappleton, the lady to whom he was presenting one of the letters of introduction, came into the nice division.

"Do you know many of the people round here?" asked the niece, when she judged that they had had sufficient silent communion.

"Hardly a soul," said Framton. "My sister was staying here, at the rectory, you know, some four years ago, and she gave me letters of introduction to some of the people here."

He made the last statement in a tone of distinct regret.

"Then you know practically nothing about my aunt?" pursued the self-possessed young lady.

"Only her name and address," admitted the caller. He was wondering whether Mrs. Sappleton was in the married or widowed state. An undefinable something about the room seemed to suggest masculine habitation.

"Her great tragedy happened just three years ago," said the child; "that would be since your sister's time."

"Her tragedy?" asked Framton; somehow in this restful country spot tragedies seemed out of place.

"You may wonder why we keep that window wide open on an October afternoon," said the niece, indicating a large French window that opened onto a lawn.

"It is quite warm for the time of the year," said Framton; "but has that window got anything to do with the tragedy?"

"Out through that window, three years ago to a day, her husband and her two young brothers went off for their day's shooting. They never came back. In crossing the moor to their favorite snipe-shooting ground they were all three engulfed in a treacherous piece of bog. It had been that dreadful wet sum-

mer, you know, and places that were safe in other years gave
way suddenly without warning. Their bodies were never recovered. That was the dreadful part of it." Here the child's
voice lost its self-possessed note and became falteringly human.
"Poor aunt always thinks that they will come back some day,
they and the little brown spaniel that was lost with them, and
walk in at that window just as they used to do. That is why the
window is kept open every evening till it is quite dusk. Poor
dear aunt, she has often told me how they went out, her husband
with his white waterproof coat over his arm, and Ronnie, her
youngest brother, singing, 'Bertie, why do you bound?' as he
always did to tease her, because she said it got on her nerves.
Do you know, sometimes on still, quiet evenings like this, I almost get a creepy feeling that they will all walk in through that
window——"

She broke off with a little shudder. It was a relief to Framton
when the aunt bustled into the room with a whirl of apologies
for being late in making her appearance.

"I hope Vera has been amusing you?" she said.

"She has been very interesting," said Framton.

"I hope you don't mind the open window," said Mrs. Sappleton
briskly; "my husband and brothers will be home directly from
shooting, and they always come in this way. They've been out
for snipe in the marshes today, so they'll make a fine mess over
my poor carpets. So like you men-folk, isn't it?"

She rattled on cheerfully about the shooting and the scarcity
of birds, and the prospects for duck in the winter. To Framton
it was all purely horrible. He made a desperate but only par-
tially successful effort to turn the talk on to a less ghastly topic;
he was conscious that his hostess was giving him only a fragment
of her attention, and her eyes were constantly straying past him
to the open window and the lawn beyond. It was certainly an
unfortunate coincidence that he should have paid his visit on this
tragic anniversary.

"The doctors agree in ordering me complete rest, an absence
of mental excitement, and avoidance of anything in the nature of
violent physical exercise," announced Framton, who labored
under the tolerably wide-spread delusion that total strangers and
chance acquaintances are hungry for the least detail of one's ail-

ments and infirmities, their cause and cure. "On the matter of diet they are not so much in agreement," he continued.

"No?" said Mrs. Sappleton, in a voice which only replaced a yawn at the last moment. Then she suddenly brightened into alert attention—but not to what Framton was saying.

"Here they are at last!" she cried. "Just in time for tea, and don't they look as if they were muddy up to the eyes!"

Framton shivered slightly and turned towards the niece with a look intended to convey sympathetic comprehension. The child was staring out through the open window with dazed horror in her eyes. In a chill shock of nameless fear Framton swung round in his seat and looked in the same direction.

In the deepening twilight three figures were walking across the lawn towards the window; they all carried guns under their arms, and one of them was additionally burdened with a white coat hung over his shoulders. A tired brown spaniel kept close at their heels. Noiselessly they neared the house, and then a hoarse young voice chanted out of the dusk: "I said, Bertie, why do you bound?"

Framton grabbed wildly at his stick and hat; the hall door, the gravel drive, and the front gate were dimly noted stages in his headlong retreat. A cyclist coming along the road had to run into the hedge to avoid imminent collision.

"Here we are, my dear," said the bearer of the white mackintosh, coming in through the window; "fairly muddy, but most of it's dry. Who was that who bolted out as we came up?"

"A most extraordinary man, a Mr. Nuttel," said Mrs. Sappleton; "could only talk about his illnesses, and dashed off without a word of good-bye or apology when you arrived. One would think he had seen a ghost."

"I expect it was the spaniel," said the niece calmly; "he told me he had a horror of dogs. He was once hunted into a cemetery somewhere on the banks of the Ganges by a pack of pariah dogs, and had to spend the night in a newly dug grave with the creatures snarling and grinning and foaming just above him. Enough to make any one lose their nerve."

Romance at short notice was her speciality.

DID YOU READ WITH UNDERSTANDING?

1. Notice that the setting of "The Open Window" is definitely English. The formal call still was a common feature of British life—at least until the second World War broke. Why is Mr. Nuttel staying at the country rectory? Why is he calling on an utter stranger? How does the young niece make sure that it will be safe to "rib" him with a yarn?

2. Is the reader, like Mr. Nuttel, inclined to swallow the girl's tale? Why or why not? What convincing bit of acting does the girl do to help deceive her victim? What is there about Mrs. Sappleton's manner to alarm her guest? What is the real reason for her attitude? Even if the niece had not been the one to welcome Mr. Nuttel, do you think he and his hostess would have enjoyed the call? Why or why not?

3. What did you, at your first reading, think when the three men and the dog appeared at the open window? What final touch completely unmanned Mr. Nuttel? How did the niece explain the young man's dashing off? Do you think the last sentence of the story is necessary? Why or why not? Is fifteen an age when a girl or boy would be likely to play such a trick? Discuss.

ALL YANKEES ARE LIARS

ERIC KNIGHT

You can always tell the Irish,
You can always tell the Dutch.
You can always tell a Yankee;
But you cannot tell him much.

MR. SMITH was pleased with The Spread Eagle.[1] He was pleased with Polkingthorpe Brig. The village was off the beaten track—the truly rural sort of English village the American always wants to see.

The inn was low and rambling, with great sloping roofs. Over the door swung the sign—a darksome bird in a weather-beaten setting.

Everything justified his decision to take this bicycle trip up into the north—the mullioned windows, the roaring fire, the Yorkshire accents of the men who shuffled over the sanded stone floor of the low-ceilinged room as they played darts. Mr. Smith was almost beginning to understand what they were talking

[1] THE SPREAD EAGLE—The name of the inn where Mr. Smith was staying.

136

about. During his excellent high tea he had sorted out the four
men playing darts. One was Saw Cooper, a farmer; a small old
man was referred to as Sam; a young, bright-faced lad who
played darts left-handed was Gollicker Pearson; and the fourth,
a huge man, was just called Ian.

Mr. Smith watched them play, listening to the endless thwock
of the darts in the cork board as he finished his meal. The barmaid, plump, corn-haired, came toward him, her apron rustling
stiffly.

"Would there be owt else?"

"No. It was a very good meal." Mr. Smith smiled. He
wanted to make the girl talk some more. "Er—what do they do
for fun in this place of an evening?"

"Foon?" she repeated. "Well, they sit here—or o' Sat'day
neights lots o' fowk goa ovver to Wuxley to t' pictures." She
waited. "They gate Boock D'Arcy i' T' Singing Cowboy," she
added suggestively.

Mr. Smith had already become acquainted with British cinemas
in small towns. Also, he was a Southern Californian, and had
that familiarity with movies that belongs to all Southern Cali-
fornians. He had no inclination to go four miles to see a last
year's Class B Western. "No. I think I'll have another ale and
sit here," he said.

"If tha'll sit ovver by t' fire, Ah'll bring it to thee theer. Then
Ah can clean oop here."

Mr. Smith sat on the bench by the generous fire and nursed
his ale. The dart game came to an end with Saw Cooper losing
and paying for the round. The men brought their mugs to the
fire. Mr. Smith shifted politely. The men, in the presence of a
stranger, grew quiet. Mr. Smith decided to put them at ease.

"Pretty chilly for an October evening, isn't it?"

The men considered the remark, as if looking at both sides of
it. Finally Saw Cooper spoke.

"Aye," he said.

The others nodded. There was silence, and the five regarded
the fire. Then, suddenly, young Gollicker smiled.

"Tha shouldn't heed t' cowd, being a Yankee," he said.

"Ah, but I'm not a Yankee," Mr. Smith said.

They stared at him in disbelief.

"Yankees," explained Mr. Smith, "come from New England."

They looked from Mr. Smith to one another. The big man named Ian took a deep breath.

"Yankees," he said, "coom fro' t' United States."

"Well, yes. New England is a part of the United States," Mr. Smith said. "But it's thousands of miles away from where I live. In fact, believe it or not, I should think you're closer to the Yankees than I am. You see, the United States is a big country. In the part where the Yankees come from, it gets very cold in the winter. Where I am—in Southern California—it never snows. Why, I've never known it to snow there in all my life."

"No snow?" Gollicker breathed.

Mr. Smith smiled. For, after all, he was a Southern Californian—and they were discussing climate. "No snow," he said. "In wintertime we have a bit of a rainy season, but after February it clears, and then it doesn't even rain for nine months—not a drop."

"Noa rain for a nine month—noan at all?" Saw Cooper asked.

"Not a drop. Day after day, the sun comes out, clear skies, never a drop of rain for nine months. Never!"

"Whet do ye graw theer, lad?" Saw asked, slyly.

"Lots of things. Truck, vegetables, oranges—all kinds of things."

There was a silence again. Big Ian took a breath.

"Orinjis," he said, and then took another breath, "graw i' Spain."

He looked at Mr. Smith so emphatically that Mr. Smith nodded.

"Oh, yes," he said. "They grow in Spain, too, I understand."

"Orinjis," Ian repeated, "graw i' Spain."

That seemed to settle the question. They all looked in the fire in silence. Saw Cooper sniffed.

"Whet else graws theer?"

"Well, I have a ranch there; we grow alfalfa."

"Whet's that off to be?"

"Alfalfa? We use it for hay. It's a desert plant originally, but it thrives in California. We get eight cuttings a year."

"Eight cuttings o' hay a year?"

"Eight cuttings a year."

The little man, Sam, spoke for the first time: "Mister, if it doan't rain for a nine month, how can ye get eight cuttings o' hay a year?"

"Oh, that's easy," Mr. Smith said. "We irrigate the land." He went into a short but conclusive description of irrigating.

"Heh," Saw Cooper said. "Wheer's this here watter coom fro'?"

"In the San Fernando Valley we buy it from the water company, just like you do in your homes."

"Wheer do they get it?"

"From reservoirs."

"If it doan't rain, where's t' reservoys get t' watter?"

"Oh, we pipe it down from five hundred miles north. It rains a lot up there."

"And ye sprinkle t' farming land out o' t' watter tap. How mony acres hesta?"

"It isn't like sprinkling from the tap, of course. I used that to illustrate. The pipes are large—we have fourteen-inch valves on our pipes. We flood the land—cover it right over with water."

Saw looked in the fire. "Does corn graw theer?"

"Well, generally our land is too valuable to put into corn. But it will grow corn [2] fourteen feet high."

They made noises in their throats and shifted their feet.

"Fohteen foot," Saw breathed. "Eigh, ba gum!"

"Mister," Sam said, "once Ah were oop to see t' Firth o' Forth brig. Ah suppose they hev bigger brigs i' Yankeeland?"

Mr. Smith should have touched on the new Oakland bridge, but then, he was a *Southern* Californian.

"We have bridges, but they're building vehicular tunnels under the rivers now."

"Whet for?"

"Well, there's so much motor traffic."

"How mony moatorcars goa through 'em?"

Mr. Smith lit his pipe happily. They seemed quite interested in America.

"I couldn't say. The way they turn 'em out, I should say there's hundreds of thousands."

"How fast do they turn 'em out?" Gollicker asked.

---

[2] CORN—In European usage *corn* means any small grain, especially wheat. What we call *corn* an Englishman calls *maize*.

"I don't know. I think they roll out finished at the rate of one every couple of minutes."

"And they goa i' tunnels, not i' brigs?" Sam commented.

"Oh, we have some bridges."

"Big uns, Ah suppose."

"Well," Mr. Smith said modestly, thinking of the Pulaski Skyway coming into New York, "we have some that go right over entire towns. You're practically on one bridge for miles."

Saw Cooper spat in the fire. "How mony fowk is there in all America?"

Mr. Smith didn't know, but he felt expansive. And after all, there was South America too.

"A quarter of a billion, I should say," he hazarded.

"A quarter of a billion," they repeated. Then they stared at Mr. Smith, and he became aware of their disbelief.

"Wait a moment," he said. "I think a billion is different in America from here. It's a thousand million in America and a million million here, isn't it?"

"A billion," said Ian slowly, "is a billion."

The others nodded, and then Ian stood. The others rose too.

"Oh—er—wait a minute. Won't you all have a drink with me?" Mr. Smith invited.

"Us is off to play darts for a round—us four," Ian said, meaningly.

The other three laughed.

"Ah knew them theer brigs o' thine'd hev to be big," Saw Cooper said as a parting shot as he swung over the bench, "that's so's they'd be able to goa ovver wheat what graws fohteen foot high when ye sprinkle it fro' t' watter tap."

He grinned at the others in victory.

"I didn't say wheat; I said corn," Mr. Smith protested.

"Same thing," Saw snapped.

"It isn't. Wheat grows in an ear. Corn grows on a cob; it has broad long leaves."

"Heh! That's maize," Saw said.

Big Ian stepped between Saw Cooper and Mr. Smith.

"Now, lad," he said flatly, "tha said corn, and Ah heeard thee. Thee and thy orinjis, and farming out o' t' watter tap, and brigs ovver cities, and it nivver rains, and denying th' art a Yankee,

140

and a billion is a billion and yet it ain't. Tha's tripped thysen oop a dozen times, it seems to me. Now, hesta owt to say?"

Mr. Smith looked at Big Ian, standing belligerently with legs widespread and his thumbs in the waistband of his corduroy trousers. He looked round and saw everyone in the inn waiting, silent.

Then a curious thing happened. In that minute the smell of soft-coal smoke and pig-twist tobacco and ale was gone, and instead Mr. Smith was smelling the mixed odor of sun-baked land and citrus blossom and jasmine and eucalyptus trees, just as you smell it in the cool darkness coming across the San Fernando Valley. And he was homesick. Suddenly it felt unreal that he should be so far from home, sitting in an English inn with these men about him. He looked up at the faces, forbidding in their expression of disapproval. And he began to laugh.

It was all so unreal that he laughed until he cried. Every time he looked up he saw the faces, now even more comical in their bewilderment than they had been in their disapproval. They stared at him, and then Big Ian began to laugh.

"Eigh, Ah'll be jiggered!" he roared. "Drat ma buttons if Ah won't!"

It was Mr. Smith's turn to be puzzled now.

Big Ian roared, and suddenly slapped Mr. Smith on the back so heartily that his chin flew up in the air and then banged back on his chest. The others looked on in amazement.

"Why, whet's oop, Ian?" Saw asked.

"Why, ye gowks!" Ian roared. "He's laughing at ye! He's been heving us on! Sitting theer for an hour, keeping his mug straight and telling us the tale! And us swallering it, thinking he was serious!"

"But," Mr. Smith said—"but you don't——"

"Nay, now no moar on it!" Ian roared. "Ye've codded us for fair, and done it champion! Lewk at owd Sam's face!"

The others regarded Ian and scratched their heads and grinned sheepishly, and finally looked at Mr. Smith in admiration.

"But—" Mr. Smith began again.

"Nay, now, ye copped us nappin," Ian said, "and here's ma hand on it. Soa we'll hev noa moar—onless ye'd like to tell us whet Yankeeland's rightly like."

141

Mr. Smith drew a deep breath. "Well, what would you like to hear about?"

"About cowboys," young Gollicker breathed. "Werta ivver a cowboy?"

For a moment Mr. Smith stood on a brink, and then an imp pushed him over.

"Of course I've been a cowboy—naturally," Mr. Smith said. "What would you like to hear about it?"

"Wait a minute," Gollicker said. They all adjusted themselves on the bench. "Now," he went on, "tell us about a roundup— tha knaws, 'Ah'm yeading for t' last roundup,' like they sings."

Mr. Smith held his mental breath and plunged.

"Ah," he said. "A roundup and the life of a cowboy. Up at the crack of dawn, mates, and down to the corral. There you rope your horse——"

"A mustang?" Gollicker asked.

"A mustang," Mr. Smith agreed.

"A wild one off'n the prairies, happen?"

"Indeed a wild one from off the prairies," Mr. Smith agreed. "I see you know America yourself."

Gollicker grinned modestly. "Doan't let me interrupt, measter," he apologized.

Mr. Smith drew another breath. He saw he was up against at least one expert, so he made it very good. Inwardly he thanked fate for what he had hitherto regarded as two entirely misspent weeks on a Nevada dude ranch. He gave them, in more senses than one, a moving picture of the cowboy's life.

When he was done, Gollicker sighed and Big Ian nodded.

"Now," Sam said, "how about them bloody buffalo?"

"Ah, the buffalo," Mr. Smith said. "The thundering herd! The bison! For a while there was a danger—or thought to be— that the herds were dying out. But now, I am glad to say—and no doubt you are just as glad to hear—the herds are increasing, and ere long, again the crack of a rifle will bring down a bull in full gallop."

"But how about them bloody Indians?" Saw put in.

Mr. Smith considered the Indians at the station in Santa Fe. They didn't seem at all satisfactory. But he was inspired. He drew himself up.

"You will pardon me if I do not speak of that," he said. "We

142

have not too much love for the paleface who stole our lands. I say 'we,' for my mother was Yellow Blanket, a princess of the Blackfoot tribe. Therefore, let us not speak of the white man and the red man."

He stared into the fire—majestically, he hoped.

"Now, see what tha's done?" Ian said to Saw. "Happen it'll learn thee to keep thy yapper shut once in a while. . . . Tha maun excuse him, measter. Tell us about gangsters instead. Didta ivver run into any gangsters?"

"Run into them? Why, how could you help it?" Mr. Smith asked.

Swiftly and graphically he painted for them an America in which here was the town where the bullets of the gangs cracked day and night. Here was the last street, and on it the last house, and beyond that was the trackless prairie where the buffalo thundered, the cowboy rode and the Indian ever lurked.

As he finished, he looked up. Everyone in the inn was listening. Men had gathered behind him silently. At the bar, the maid leaned on her elbows, entranced.

"Ah, I talk too much," Mr. Smith said.

"Nay, goa on, lad," they said. "Goa on."

"Well, it's dry work. How about a drink?"

"Champion," said Saw.

"Owd on," Big Ian said. "Us'll play darts for a round."

"Now, Ian, if the lad wants to buy——"

"Ah said," Ian repeated, "us'll play darts—ony body that wishes to be in on t'round. And t' loser will pay."

Mr. Smith paid anyhow, for the dart game was trickier than he had thought, and they all seemed to be experts.

He was getting very much better when the barmaid called: "Time, gentlemen, please."

Mr. Smith was sorry. It had been a good evening. They all said good night cheerfully. Big Ian shook him by the hand.

"Well, soa long, lad. We had a champion time. But Ah just want to say, tha didn't fool me when tha were kidding us at first. Tha sees, for one thing, us goas to t' pictures and so us knaws whet America's really like. And then Ah'd allus heeard tell that all Yankees were liars."

"Yes," Mr. Smith said, regarding his conscience, "I did tell some lies."

"Aye, but Ah suppose it's a way ye Yankees hev," Ian said. "But it's all right as long as tha told us t' trewth finally."

DID YOU READ WITH UNDERSTANDING?

1. In what part of England is Yorkshire? Where apparently do Yorkshiremen get their information about America? In how many different ways is the name "Yankee" used? In its original sense to whom does the term "Yankee" apply? What does it mean to a Southerner? to a baseball fan? to a foreigner? What did the term mean as Mr. Smith used it? as the Yorkshiremen used it? Was Mr. Smith speaking the truth when he said that the Yorkshiremen were closer to the Yankees than a Californian would be? Check on a map.

2. Is Mr. Smith sticking pretty close to the truth in the information about his ranch? about California weather? irrigation? American bridges and tunnels? When does he make his first misstatement? Why? When does he begin to lie? Why? When did Mr. Smith's audience begin to disbelieve his statements? Why?

3. What was the implication behind Ian's remark, "Us is off to play darts for a round—*us four*"? What made Mr. Smith laugh? Why did the men think he was laughing? Why were they not displeased? How did Mr. Smith earn the privilege of buying the drinks for the crowd? Explain.

4. What made this a happy evening for Mr. Smith? for the Yorkshiremen? In what respects was the attitude of the Yorkshiremen like that of human beings in general? Discuss.

EXTENDED ACTIVITIES

BRITISH CHARACTER IS STURDY BUT INFINITELY VARIED

HOW LITERATURE REFLECTS THE TIMES

One effect of the two wars is that it has made England more conscious than ever before of the multitudes of personalities that make up the British Empire. Theoretically, England has always been convinced of the importance of the individual. The doctrine is part of her inheritance from the free-spirited Saxons and Norsemen. In the last twenty years the sweep of Fascist and Nazi philosophies through continental Europe has intensified British faith in the fundamental concept of her own government—*that the state exists to protect and serve the individual.* Progress in English history has been slowly in the direction of that ideal. The greatest changes in twentieth century life—aside from those growing out of the wars—have been made in the interests of social reform. England has been ahead of America in the matter of providing for old age pensions, unemployment insurance, and other measures of social security. For more than a century, attention has been focused on the under-privileged, under-nourished poor of factory towns and city slums.

Literature, as a matter of course, has shown a corresponding interest in all manner of men. Back in the nineteenth century Thomas Hood and Mrs. Browning and Charles Dickens had started it. Poems like "The Song of the Shirt" and "The Cry of the Children" were appeals to the sentiments of the public in behalf of the workers. They, along with novels like *Oliver Twist,* had started the first wave of reform in factories, public institutions, charity schools, and the like. The writer of the twentieth century has used a different approach. He makes his appeal from the individual side. Without comment or moral he pictures one old woman, homeless and friendless; a decrepit cabby and a horse; a park bench tramp; an Irish maid-servant. The sketchy portraits make a wordless appeal.

But not all interest in the individual is on behalf of the wretched. It is equally true that the strong and the young and the great have personal values. They interest the artist because of the soul and personality peculiar to each. And so Laurence Housman can write a human drama about a queen; and poets find inspiration in men who are brave and fine, or brave and selfish, or rich but cowardly. It is true that recent literature represents all classes of people and almost invariably from a personal point of view.

One other point should be made. With the simultaneous development of world communication by radio and the shortening of time and space by mechanized speed on water, land, and air, and with both developments

145

intensified by the needs of war, Great Britain has really got acquainted with the peoples of her Empire. Through her literature move the figures of Anzac and Bushman, Hindu and Arab, and all the representatives of lands or tribes that owe allegiance to the crown. From every part of the homeland and colonies, writers are depicting native people as well as native scenes. And so today, more than ever before, British literature presents a mingled personnel. It reveals the sturdiness of the dominant English, the sentiment and fancy of the Scotch and Irish, the melody of the Welsh, the color and mystery of men from far possessions. Thus in multiple variety, the personalities of a great commonwealth speak from the pages of its literature.

FOR ACQUAINTANCE WITH AUTHORS

JAMES MATTHEW BARRIE (1860–1937)—"A CLOAK WITH BEADS"

"Nothing that happens after we are twelve matters very much," wrote Barrie; true to his own words even as a spry little old man, knighted and famous, James Barrie kept much of the curiosity and awareness of a twelve-year-old. The list of Barrie's successes is long, but *Peter Pan,* the story of and for ageless twelve-year-olds, will last as long as any of them.

At twelve Barrie had no thought of the fame that was to be his. His mother, a superior woman, made him a writer and a man of culture—with little help from young James. At the Dumfries Academy in Scotland he played a good game of cricket, wrote up the accounts of the matches for the local newspaper and now and again inclosed a letter to the editor on the desirability of longer vacations. That was the sum total of his scholastic and literary achievements. At the University of Edinburgh he received his M.A., and entered immediately into journalism. In London he did free-lance, anonymous work which was slow in catching hold until he began a series of essays and short stories on his own native village which he called "Thrums." His most successful novel, *The Little Minister,* was published in 1891; from then on he was one of England's leading writers. Early in the nineteen hundreds he tried his now experienced hand—again successfully—at drama. Three of his plays, *Quality Street, The Admirable Crichton,* and *Peter Pan* are still performed. At the end of his career, Barrie was one of the literary deities of the early twentieth century.

GILBERT KEITH CHESTERTON (1874–1936)—"THE DONKEY"

Gilbert Keith Chesterton, often known by his initials, G. K. C., was an impressive personality. His frame was huge, and he enjoyed a rough unkempt appearance. He started out to be an artist, but some early art criticisms were so well liked and he had such a good time doing them, that he decided to make his living as a journalist and writer. He became an established essayist, poet, journalist, critic, and lecturer. He was one of those Englishmen that must come over once in a while to tell what is wrong with America. And how Americans love it! He had a fund of wit and was as clever with his tongue as with his pen.

Chesterton died suddenly of a heart attack in June, 1936.

One of his most popular works is the collection of detective stories entitled, *The Innocence of Father Brown.* There are a number of volumes of light essays to his credit: *Tremendous Trifles, Generally Speaking,* and *Come to Think of It.* His serious criticisms appear in studies of Dickens and Browning in the *English Men of Letters* series, and in *The Victorian Age in Literature.*

PADRAIC COLUM (1881–   )—"AN OLD WOMAN OF THE ROADS"

As Irish as his own name, Padraic Colum belongs with those most closely associated with the Irish revival: Yeats, Synge, Stephens, and Lady Gregory. Colum lived all his early life in Ireland, in the legend-filled house of his grandmother. The Abbey Theater produced his first play when he was only twenty. A few years later he founded with James Stephens the *Irish Review,* and many of his poems first appeared in it. In 1923 he was asked by the Hawaiian government to survey their traditions and legends to help them accumulate a body of national literature much as he had done for Ireland. Today Colum lives in New York with his wife who is a well-known American literary critic.

W. H. DAVIES (1870–1940)—"SHEEP"

A thief, beggar, and "bum" by choice, William Henry Davies lived his life on the dusty fringes of polite society until he was past thirty. Born in Wales, he early learned petty thievery and truancy, and after a rudimentary education was apprenticed to a picture-frame maker. Thoroughly indifferent to his trade, Davies on the private income of two shillings a week left him by his grandmother managed to get passage on a boat to America. He landed in New York with ten dollars, met one of the big bosses of the hoboes and for six years earned his bread through begging, courted prison sentences through the cold winter months, and saw America by train-jumping. When he felt nostalgia for England, he hopped a cattle boat.

News of the Klondike gold found a ready recruit in the "super-tramp," but the haphazard course of Davies' life was abruptly ended when he fell while boarding a train in Canada on his way to Alaska. The amputation of his leg, besides sobering his views of life, showed him his latent writing talent. He went to London where he lived in the cheapest rooms he could find, peddled from door to door to earn enough to buy paper and food, wrote in public libraries and at last with the utmost difficulty had *The Soul's Destroyer* printed. With grave audacity he sent the cheap little book to possible purchasers, George Bernard Shaw among them. Strangely enough, several of the readers saw the genius in his book. Shaw was impressed enough to write letters of introduction for Davies which brought his name before the public. Another critic lent him a cottage. The one-time tramp settled down to a pleasant life in the country, where he published his very successful *Autobiography of a Super-Tramp* and good humoredly suffered the adulation of an admiring public.

WALTER DE LA MARE (1873–   )—"SILVER"

"A shadowy Pied Piper," de la Mare has been called. Surely he turns as bewitching a tune with his delicate rhythms as the Piper ever blew, and his following is equally devoted and blind. In the prosaic post of bookkeeper for the Standard Oil Company, de la Mare took refuge in long hair, velvet coat, and his writing world of fantasy. For several years he published verse in magazines under the pseudonym of Walter Ramal and drudged daily over figures as Walter de la Mare. In 1908 a government grant and pension won him release from his desk; the success of his poems, appealing as they do to the child in every adult, gradually lessened the necessity for book reviewing which he detested. His novel, *Memoirs of a Midget*, has been equally popular, and today he ranks as one of the better known twentieth century English poets.

LORD DUNSANY (EDWARD J. PLUNKETT) (1878–   )—"THE RETURN"

Master of "the mysterious kingdom where geography ends and fairyland begins," Lord Dunsany looks the well-contented squire he prefers to be. A soldier and sportsman first, Dunsany vows that only three percent of his life belongs to writing. Dunsany's chosen field is the short play; his first, "The Glittering Gates," the story of two dead burglars who jimmied the gates of heaven, packed the Abbey Theater in Dublin.

Dunsany saw service in the Boer War, the first World War, and has recently returned from the Nazi occupied Greece of the Second War. Of his experiences during the first World War Lord Dunsany, six feet four and correspondingly burly, wrote, "Our trenches were only six feet deep; I shall never fear publicity again." Lord Dunsany writes to please himself; his field is a limited one, but the public's approval demonstrates that he has pleased others than himself. His plays have been produced in Moscow, England, Ireland, and America.

JOHN GALSWORTHY (1867–1933)—"REMINISCENCES OF CONRAD"

The Galsworthys have been in Devonshire, England, "since the flood— of Saxons, at all events," as the writer once put it. John was born at Coombe, in Surrey in 1867, and his works are typical of good English birth and breeding.

After his schooling at Harrow and Oxford, he made an attempt at the practice of law, his father's profession. But it proved uncongenial. "I read," he said, "in various chambers, practiced almost not at all, and disliked my profession thoroughly." His father's wealth and generosity enabled the young man to close his office and go vagabonding. He traveled for two years, visiting most of the out-of-the-way places of the world. On one of his voyages he made the acquaintance of Joseph Conrad, then still a sailor. John Galsworthy encouraged Conrad to begin writing, but apparently thought nothing of becoming a writer himself.

It was the girl he was later to marry that encouraged him to write. Though one had little different to offer the world, he said, one might try writing "to please her of whom one was fond." In the next two years he wrote nine tales, all of which he later characterized as "very bad." But the start had been made. From that time there was a steady succession of novels, essays, and plays.

The most notable work is the history of three generations of the Forsyte family, the nucleus of which has been gathered into one thick volume, *The Forsyte Saga*. However, later volumes carried on the history until in *Swan Song* the centralizing character, Soames Forsyte, died. It is a most unusual cycle of fiction, for the settings of the books are contemporaneous with John Galsworthy's life, from the mid-Victorian days of his youth until well into the post-World War I period. The chief characters are from the social class that he knew best—the upper middle class. In 1906, Mr. Galsworthy became very much interested in the stage, and for the next twelve years wrote chiefly plays. About two thirds of his work are novels and dramas; the rest are short stories, sketches, essays, and a few poems.

WILFRID WILSON GIBSON (1878–   )—"THE ICE-CART"

From a home in the spare country of Northumberland, Wilfrid Gibson made his way as a young man to London. Though he had had little education, he was eager to write. Before he was thirty he has tasted some success, and with the years he has gained mastery in his writing. He has written of the shepherds of the north country, of the city people with whom he works, and of soldiers and battles. He has an easy lyric style and a bright imagination. Poor health kept him from serving in World War I, but his war poetry is convincingly right in thought and feeling.

LAURENCE HOUSMAN (1865–   )—"VICTORIA REGINA"

Younger brother of the poet-professor, A. E. Housman, Laurence Housman suddenly won popular approval with his play *Victoria Regina*. Before Helen Hayes raised his name in theater lights, Housman had enjoyed the praise of a scholarly few for his play cycle of the life of St. Francis, and the curiosity of an inquisitive few who wondered over the identity of *An Englishwoman's Love Letters*. In addition he had written three novels which he admits he liked better than did the public. Today readers are growing more familiar with his work, and perhaps one day his fame will equal that of his illustrious brother.

Laurence began as an art student, but after six unfruitful years, turned to writing fairy tales and legends, and even a few poems which he also illustrated. The anonymous *Love Letters*, his next attempt, were attributed to everyone from Queen Victoria downwards. They did not, he confesses, enhance his reputation. His entrance into writing for the "uncommercial" stage, as he calls it, marked his entrance into literary fame. He has been called "England's most censored playwright," a rakish title he enjoys as much as anyone. Thirty-two of his plays have been censored because they represented either Biblical personages or living members of the royal family.

W. W. JACOBS (1863–   )—"THE MONKEY'S PAW"

It is hard to imagine anyone less likely to write a spine-chilling horror story than William Jacobs. Primarily a humorist and a spinner of sea yarns, Jacobs is smallish and quiet, the father of five and a writer through hard and diligent work. He began humbly enough as a clerk in the Savings Bank Department of the General Post Office, writing now and then, usually quite apathetically, for his own amusement. The success of his first book, *Many Cargoes*, surprised him most of all; he gave up his prosaic job with elation and set out on a writing career. If he had written nothing but "The Monkey's Paw," guaranteed to send shivers up the stiffest spine, his name would be assured of fame.

RUDYARD KIPLING (1865–1936)—"GUNGA DIN"

Belligerent champion of God and of Britain, Rudyard Kipling was a slight bespectacled little man, looking not much like the fierce imperialist he was. Even the great Elizabeth had no more devoted patriot writer in Raleigh, Spenser, or Shakespeare than had Victoria in Rudyard Kipling— though his outspoken exposure of wrongs was sometimes misunderstood. For nearly fifty-four years he wrote pro- lifically in his own chosen field, and English life and letters are the richer for it.

Rudyard was born in Bombay, India, of English parents; learned Hindustani as soon as English, and listened wide-eyed to the tales of his "ayah." At six he was sent back to England to be educated, first in grammar school and then at the United Service College, "Westward Ho." Neither studies nor athletics interested him par- ticularly and at seventeen when he was given the choice of returning to India or continuing at a university, he set out once more for India. At Lahore he wangled a job as reporter on the newspaper; his in- defatigable industry, his zest for a good story, and his own twinkling eyes and quick smile won him readers and friends. As fillers for the paper he would write rollicking sketches of three British Tommies in India or human verses in cockney dialect. Letters came from all over India asking that the poems and stories be published. *Departmental Ditties* and *Plain Tales from the Hills* were the result. Kipling's popularity in India led him to want to try his hand in England. A period of travel to Japan and America followed and then came the *Jungle Books* and *Captains Courageous*. In 1901 the publication of *Kim* saw him truly famous. He retired to a large country estate in Sussex, settled down to politics, and the celebrating of England and her glory. In 1907 he won the Nobel Prize and all England rejoiced. During the first World War he lost his only son; yet he bravely con- tinued his lecturing and writing for the Allied cause. Mr. Kipling died when just past seventy, beloved by a truly tremendous reading public.

ERIC KNIGHT (1897–1943)—"ALL YANKEES ARE LIARS"

"A stubborn lot, these British, but there is no dry rot here, no jingoism or exultation," wrote Eric Knight after a visit to England shortly before his death. His description might well apply to himself, British by birth but American by adoption. Only stubbornness and an immense ambition can explain his own career. As a boy Knight had as rough a childhood as one can imagine. His father, a diamond merchant, died when Eric was two; his mother, twenty-four and pretty, went to Russia as the governess to Princess Xenia's children, leaving her own with various unenthusiastic relatives in England. Eric was shoved from one to another until the age of twelve when he kept himself by work in a series of mills and a glass-blowing factory. The children were finally reunited with their mother in New York when Eric was fifteen.

There was little enough money and the boy was delighted to get a job as copy boy on the *Philadelphia Press*. In his spare time he was soon writing feature articles for a syndicate bureau to earn enough to go to school again. This time he tried art work, but the first World War interrupted his studies and as a private in the Canadian Light Infantry he saw service in France. In 1919 he returned to journalism; tried his hand as a foreign correspondent; traveled in Central America and Europe; and in 1934 won success with *The Happy Land,* a novel of Yorkshire suffering after the war from "the fearful narcotic of idle men on the dole." His second novel, *This Above All,* a story of World War II, enjoyed a brilliant success; Eric Knight had at last "arrived." With his American wife, Jere, herself a would-be writer, he settled in a rickety house in Pennsylvania, raised pigs, chickens, ducks, geese, and potatoes, and thought up more scrapes for Sam Small to fly into. The peaceful interlude ended abruptly with the entrance of the United States into war. Captain—and soon Major—Knight was assigned to special service; on January 15, 1943, the transport plane in which he was traveling crashed in Dutch Guiana.

D. H. LAWRENCE (1885–1930)—"PIANO"

David Lawrence's forty-four years of life were filled with hectic activity and furious writing, filled too with a violent and never-realized search for health and happiness. His early life was made miserable by the drunkenness and brutality of his father. His mother, to whom David was devoted, had been a former schoolteacher and she did what she could for the five children. David early learned to shift for himself. He finally won a teaching certificate from the Nottingham Training School and secured a teaching post but found little contentment in it. The editor of *The English Review* read the manuscript of his first novel and suggested that Lawrence try to have it published. Just as the book appeared, he received word of the death of his mother. He resigned his teaching job, took the fifty pounds realized from the sale of his first book, and set out for Europe. On the way he met his future wife, a German woman. After the outbreak of the war, Lawrence found life increasingly difficult; his German wife Frieda and his own German travels made him open to suspicion and the two were evacuated from the English seacoast to the interior.

The years left him after the war were spent in a ceaseless search for a climate helpful to his tubercular condition. By now his reputation as an author was made. His *Poems* in 1913 and his novel, *Sons and Lovers,* had been the most popular. Restlessly, he and his wife traveled to Europe, Italy, Sicily, and Australia, finally stopping at Taos, New Mexico, where David painted and wrote until his death.

JOHN MASEFIELD (1878–   )—"A CONSECRATION," "ROUNDING THE HORN"

John Masefield's life has been as colorful and as varied as his poetry. He has known the sea and the fields, laborers and statesmen, hospital ships and country estates, nonentity and fame. Today he is Poet Laureate of England, holder of the Order of Merit, the most coveted honor England can bestow; member of the British Council of World War II, and the acknowledged dean of English letters. And he remains the gentle, quiet, courteous Englishman who won sympathy as a mill hand in a carpet factory in Yonkers, New York.

Masefield's early life was colored by his experiences sailing before the mast on a windjammer. His formal schooling ended at thirteen when he was placed by his guardian on the training ship *Convoy.* From then on, life and the sea took over his education. On one voyage when he was to join his ship at New York, he decided to give up sea-faring and earn a living in America. For three years he worked at odd jobs: in a bakery, a livery stable, and finally in a carpet factory. He began to read widely and try his hand at writing. Although as a boy he had made a few juvenile attempts at poetry, he had not felt the urge to write until one Sunday afternoon in a Yonkers rooming house he read Chaucer's *Canterbury Tales.* It was Chaucer who unlocked his genius and became his model.

In 1897 he returned to London, his mind set on a career in letters. For five years he struggled with editors and at last was named literary editor of the *Manchester Guardian.* His volume, *Salt Water Ballads,* was successful. His rapid, racy style, the humble origin of his characters, the brisk pattern of his rhythms made him a popular writer. During World War I he served on a hospital ship in Gallipoli. After the war his reputation as England's most popular poet was secure. He has since tried his hand at plays and nautical history, but always his first interest lies in the actualities of living and in people—all those "hemmed in by the spears" of life. His most recent work is his autobiography.

HENRY NEWBOLT (1862–1938)—"HE FELL AMONG THIEVES"

From editor of a college magazine to President of the English Association in England is a long journey, but Henry Newbolt managed it in about forty-five years. On the way he acquired an excellent reputation as a naval historian, as an editor, and as a poet of the conventional upper classes. At Oxford on a scholarship, he prepared for the bar, and, after passing his examinations, worked as a lawyer for twelve years with neither conspicuous success nor delight. His hobby of verse-writing pleased him more. One day while working in the British Museum reading room, Newbolt met Laurence Binyon, the poet, and the two had many a lunch and afternoon chat together. Binyon encouraged the other's literary attempts and in 1900 John Murray invited Newbolt to edit his magazine, *The Monthly Review.* During his four years as editor, Newbolt polished his style and gained confidence. He also published *The Year of Trafalgar* which established his reputation as a naval historian. Meanwhile, his hesitantly brought-forth volumes of poetry, full of English patriotism and bluff heartiness, had won many a reader. In 1919 he was named Chairman of the Committee on English in national education and knighted. In 1928 he was given the post of President of the English Association.

J. B. PRIESTLEY (1894–   )—"THE DISILLUSIONED"

To an already established reputation as a writer, John Boynton Priestley has recently added the distinction of being called "the unofficial voice of the common people of Britain" for his war time broadcasts. A prolific —and an excellent—writer, Priestley helped earn his way at Cambridge by contributing to magazines and newspapers. His college career followed service in the infantry during World War I. Since 1919 he has written essays, a short history of the English novel, several best-selling novels, and some seventeen plays. In 1937 three of his plays were running at once in London. Unusually enough, his war experiences seem to have touched him lightly. His "long, hearty, sentimental" novels are devoid of the topics usually favored by writers of 1919–1939. Prodigious in activity as in creative work, Priestley has traveled and lectured in the United States, tried his hand successfully in the films, and written long, vituperative—and always clever—criticisms of all that has met with his displeasure. Five feet nine and weighing two hundred pounds, Priestley relaxes by playing at theatricals with his brood of six children.

"SAKI" (H. H. MUNRO) (1870–1916)—"THE OPEN WINDOW"

Perhaps the best tribute to H. H. Munro who took the pseudonym "Saki" was written by Christopher Morley: "The empty glass we turn down for him is the fragile hollow-stemmed goblet meant for the dryest champagne; it is of the finest." "Saki" was the real H. H. Munro hidden for many years behind competent journalism and staid editorials until released in *Reginald,* his first collection of short stories. The sharp dryness of his wit, the glorious fun of his situations, and the inanity of his people made Saki the pet of many a reader of short stories. His fantasia of England under the Hohenzollerns, *When William Came,* caused nearly as much stir as Orson Welles's invasion from Mars of a later date. Saki's growing fame was cut short by his enlistment in the British forces in 1915. Refusing any offer of a commission, he served as a corporal in France and was killed in battle.

STEPHEN SPENDER (1909–   )—"THE LANDSCAPE NEAR AN AERODROME"

Stephen Spender is one of the "new" English poets. Like all the young and earnest poets of preceding generations, he is determined to do battle against conventional poetry and politics. He painted and wrote as a child, tried Oxford in his youth, but rebelled against its staidness and left without a degree. From the age of seventeen he supported himself by printing chemists' labels on his own hand press until his poetry brought him a livable income. Since Oxford he has traveled widely; his politics and philosophy are individualistic and left-wing. During the recent Civil War in Spain he translated from Loyalist poets and German radicals. At the outbreak of the second World War he was editor of the magazine *Horizon* and was well on the way to success as a critic and poet.

JAMES STEPHENS (1882–   )—"TO THE FOUR COURTS, PLEASE"

Under five feet tall, bald, and with the face of an elf, James Stephens is one of the most picturesque and one of the most beloved of the Irish group of writers. His heavy Irish brogue, his keen sense of humor, and his rich store of Irish verse and story from which he can recite extemporaneously for hours make him a welcome member of any gathering.

Stephens was born in Dublin into near poverty. He grew up in the slums, educated himself, and learned stenography. Befriended by George Russell, another of the Irish writers, his work was entirely unknown until the publication of his book, *Crock of Gold.* Since then he has become famous for his creation of almost a new mythology from Irish legend and superstition as well as his devotion to the humbler characters of Irish life.

WILLIAM BUTLER YEATS (1865–1939)—"AN IRISH AIRMAN FORESEES HIS DEATH"

A story of William Butler Yeats's life has already been told in the EXTENDED ACTIVITIES for Unit I–I.

OF LITERARY FORM AND STYLE

CHARACTER STUDY IN PROSE AND IN VERSE

The present interest in people as persons finds expression both in prose and in verse. It is reflected, for example, in the present emphasis on biography, and in the technique of the modern biographer. The writer is no longer concerned merely with a recording of dates and events in the life of his subject; he is trying to reproduce or recreate a man or woman. He shows us the familiar human traits in his subject—apparently inconsequential details that nevertheless let us see a personality, not a figurehead. Lytton Strachey has done outstanding work in the new approach to biography; and even "occasional" selections like Galsworthy's appraisal of Conrad put the emphasis on individual values.

Similarly, in fiction, characterization is of first importance. We become interested in the thing that happens because we are interested in the person it happens to. It follows, as a matter of course, that a person of any sort, age, or condition becomes a proper subject for literature. The man of a park bench, a farmer, a child—it does not matter who the subject is so long as values are being interpreted in human souls.

This is as true for verse as it is for prose. The poet often seems to be following the technique of the story writer in selecting themes and characters. Apparently a walk down a city street can furnish subjects for a dozen lyrics—the homeless flower vender, the cabby, the office boy, the clerk, the man of important business. Any one character can by a turn of the head or a tone of voice impress his personality or his circumstances on a poet. Then there emerges—usually in objective strokes—a sketch that recreates him for the reader, and with a rush of sympathetic insight. James Stephens, Padraic Colum, W. W. Gibson—these are some of the poets who are helping us see how everybody else is living. John Masefield, especially in his earliest works, declared himself the champion of the working man—the man of the crowd. His sailors and men of the streets ring true, for Masefield has rubbed elbows with them. William Butler Yeats more often was inspired by the dreamer, the poet, the artist. Kipling and Newbolt show us the men of romance and adventure, but in completely human guise. Even poetry about the war is reduced to the terms of the men who fight in it. No more striking repudiation of Nazi doctrines of totalitarianism need to be sought than the insistence with which English—along with American—writers continue to *individualize* their literature.

QUESTIONS IN APPRECIATION:

Character Studies in Poetry

1. What tendency in twentieth century literature does "A Consecration" exemplify? How? What attitude toward other people is built up by the poem? Explain. List several picturesque ways Masefield has found to describe people. What is the general rhythmic effect of the poem? Describe briefly its poetic form.

2. Notice how in the passage "Rounding the Horn," the form of the poem seems completely subordinated to the *action* and *sensation* of the experience. How has the poet secured this effect? Notice that the stanzas rhyme, but that the reader is hardly conscious of the fact. Why? How has Masefield given the impression of motion? of cold? of danger? of storm? Does the reader have a personal or impersonal interest in the

storm? Why? Does one learn anything about the personality or character of the Dauber from this short selection? Discuss.

3. In Yeats's poem, what Irish characteristics do you find in the airman who talks of death? Where do you think Yeats got the inspiration for this lyric? Do you think the form of the poem suitable to its subject? Why or why not? Does the reader's interest center in the *flight* or in the *airman?* Why? Do you like the poem? Why or why not?

4. In "To the Four Courts, Please" can you see a picture of the cabby and his horse? Without looking at the poem, describe both horse and driver. Have some one jot down the details of your description; then check back with the poem. Have you put in any details that James Stephens did not mention? If so, what suggested them? If you had been in the author's place would you have chosen this horse and driver? Why or why not? What effect or impression does the poet create in the first ten lines? in lines 11–12? in the whole poem? Why do you think the poet added the last stanza?

5. What kind of words has the poet used in "An Old Woman of the Roads"? What kind of stanzas? Why? What bits of detail make the picture of such a humble house seem attractive? Which lines of the poem suggest the worst hardships in the lot of the beggar? How would most people feel about seeing a dirty old woman on the road? How does the poet make us feel about this old woman?

6. In what kind of speech is the story of Gunga Din told? Why? What details or incidents make the poem sound true to life—true to soldier life in general, true to British type soldier, true to military service in India? What features in the description make Gunga Din sound like a real person? Do you think the soldier is sincere in his admiration for Gunga Din? Is he a bit sentimental about the matter? Why might he be? How would you describe the poetic form of "Gunga Din"? Why do you think the selection has proved popular as a dramatic reading?

7. Where is the setting of "He Fell Among Thieves" laid? Which stanza tells us exactly? Does the reader *sense* the place even earlier? What is the difference in rank and breeding between this soldier and the man who told the story of "Gunga Din"? How does the reader sense the difference at once? In what respects is the author's technique in telling the story of the poem like the technique of modern short story writers? How does the young man show himself true to British traditions? Can one form an adequate opinion of British character from knowledge of a single personality? Do you find any traits in common in these various characters—the Dauber, the Irish airman, the British soldier who told of Gunga Din, the British soldier who "fell among thieves"? Which one do you admire most?

Character Study in Prose

1. Part of the equipment of a successful biographer must be a real appreciation born of familiarity with the subject. This familiarity may

be the result of study, or of personal acquaintance, or both. In what respects was Galsworthy especially well equipped to write about Conrad?

2. What information that Galsworthy gives arouses the most genuine interest in Conrad as a personality? Mention several incidents or instances. To what extent does Galsworthy deepen one's appreciation of Conrad's works? Why are we inclined to respect the opinions of John Galsworthy?

3. In what respects does Galsworthy prove himself a good writer? Point out two or three passages that you think are especially well done.

BIOGRAPHY IN DRAMA

The appearance in 1935 of Laurence Housman's *Victoria Regina* marked the advent of something new in drama. The idea of basing a play upon the life of a significant character was not new; but the way in which Housman treated his subject and the dramatic form in which he presented it were certainly different. Instead of dividing his play into three or five acts, the author developed one sequence of separate scenes —some long, some short, their only dramatic unity resting in the portrayal of the character who *is* the play.

In form, then, *Victoria Regina* is like a pageant. It gives a panoramic picture of one of the longest and most brilliant reigns in history. But in effect it is much more human and more closely knit than a pageant. It is a personal document, not an historical one. The playwright has taken the Victoria of public record and made her flesh and blood. He has done it faithfully and sympathetically. It is true that he displays her shortcomings along with her virtues. He shows us that she had no humor; that she was arrogant by birth and breeding; that she was stubborn and spoiled, as queens are likely to be. But he shows us too that she was a great and good woman. We are willing to concede more readily her virtues because Mr. Housman has not glossed over her faults.

The play is significantly English. In a sense Victoria stands for the personality of the English people. She was the kind of queen they could understand and give their devotion to. They liked her dignity, her forthright manner of attacking a problem, her respect for tradition, but also her readiness to act and decide for herself. They liked her pride in the Empire and her pride in herself as its queen. They agreed with her that the English were always right; that they had a sort of regal responsibility to look after the other peoples of the earth. But they liked Victoria, too, because she was womanly; because she had been in love, because she sometimes made mistakes, because she loved her children while understanding their faults, because she had grieved deeply, because she did not flinch from duty. All these phases of her personality, Mr. Housman has presented in the scenes of his play. And the attention of the reader is swept along, not by the action of a drama in the ordinary sense, but by their absorption in the character being unfolded before them.

Technically, it required careful planning to meet the demands of many detached scenes spread over a period of sixty years. Yet on the stage, the episodes follow smoothly. Modern stage devices, together with alternation of shallow and deep stage sets make possible an almost continuous performance with few long waits. Important transitions from scene to scene must be made by the principal character as she progresses through the years from a slim girl of eighteen to a plump and finally chair-bound woman in her eighties. Helen Hayes, who carried the role on the American stage, made the changes subtly and persuasively.

The play is different in one other respect—in that though it acts well, it is also good reading. The stage directions are worded informally and seem as much a part of the text as the descriptions in a story. And the lines read well. There is dignity of expression because of the ceremony attached to royalty—especially in the sedate court of Victoria. And yet Mr. Housman has made the words sound real. If he felt himself something of an experimenter in doing the play, he must be pleased with the success which *Victoria Regina* has met on the stage, on the screen, and in the hands of the reader.

QUESTIONS IN APPRECIATION:

1. How does the opening stage direction help set the mood for the scene, "Suitable Suitors"? When the scene is presented on the stage, what purpose would such directions serve? Discuss.

2. What do you think are the traits of Victoria which the author wanted this scene to emphasize? What are the devices by which he brings out those traits? Is the reader—or the audience—sure at the end of the scene that Lord Melbourne is "molding Victoria's character to suit his own convenience"? Or does he merely *think* he is? How do you judge?

3. "Leading Strings" is one of the episodes in which Victoria is not the dominant character. How has the author contrived to reveal the exceptional qualities of Prince Albert? In a play of this type each episode must carry the play forward. Does the audience feel at the close of the scene that Albert has made progress in his desire to command the respect as well as the love of his wife? that he is going to be allowed to use some of his ability? that the young people are going to reach a real understanding of each other? How has the author managed to make this a scene of character *development,* not merely character *portrayal?* Discuss. What is the effect of the closing stage direction? What good does it do when the episode is dramatized?

4. The episode, "Bereavement," is divided into two interviews. Do the interviews serve different purposes—that is, do they show different aspects of the Queen's personality? What growth or change do you note in the character of the Queen since the preceding episode? Which character usually speaks the last line of any scene? It usually concerns what person? What effect does it leave with the audience or reader?

5. In the episode, "The Blue Ribbon," are the sympathies of the audience with the painter or with the Queen? Why? What kind of amusement does the audience feel? Does the audience agree with the painter in his characterization of the Queen at the close of the scene? How has the author contrived to give the whole episode a touch of comedy? Discuss. What secret—denied to the audience—does the reader of the play share with its author, as the scene is ended?

6. What is the general effect to be achieved by the last scene? Why would it be difficult to handle on the stage? Why are the stage directions especially important here? Why does the author not specify who makes the various speeches in the general conversation? In what respect is the last line of the play in harmony with the theme that runs throughout? Explain.

7. Does the play present any one *motif* as the most important influence in shaping the personality of the Queen? Discuss. In the scenes presented here, what seems to be the unifying element? What is the predominating attitude of other people—audience included—toward the Queen? Do you find any one speech in the play that seems to express it? Discuss. Why is *Victoria Regina* properly described as *biography* as well as *drama?* What circumstances would make Mr. Housman's task both delicate and difficult? What evidence is there that he accomplished it extraordinarily well? Discuss.

ROMANCE AND FANTASY IN MODERN LITERATURE

The average Englishman prides himself on being a man without sentiment. The Nordic strain in his blood holds stern check on his emotions—or at least on show of them. The regimented systems of schools like Eton and Harrow and the colleges of Oxford and Cambridge have been designed to turn out wooden-faced men drilled to stand up under punishment without a whimper, to accept joy or despair without the flicker of an eyelash. Sentiment they have labeled weak, or cheap. To play the game, to be sporting in any emergency, to keep the old heart under—that has been the English ideal for generations. This restraint of feeling, of course, has been communicated to English literature. The lyric verse, you may have noted, is marked by a certain reserve. It just does not—ever—"tear a passion to tatters."

But no Englishman is a pure-bred Nordic; and therefore English literature, though basically matter-of-fact, is shot through with threads of romance and fancy. There is a sparkle born of the Celtic strain in the British pattern. Some of this sparkle came with the Normans from France; the rest has trickled in from Scotland, Ireland, and Wales.

Now the Scotchman the world may think to be a dour fellow, flinty and harsh as his stony land. Not so!—say the Scotch writers. Think of the pure sentiment of the Scotch songs of other centuries—"Annie Laurie" or "Comin' through the Rye." And of the modern writers, there are James Barrie, and Ian MacLaren, and J. J. Bell, and Harry Lauder, each in his own way repeating the lesson one should learn from Burns—that the Scotchman, beneath a rugged face, shields a remarkably soft heart. He is capable of lifelong devotion to a friend or a sweetheart or a cause. He can make and hide a sacrifice. He is still held by a three-fold loyalty—to family, country, and God. Scotch literature, whether in prose or verse circles around those three themes. There is almost always poverty in the Scotch scene; and so there is frugality and pride of soul. But there is faithfulness to wife and child. There is reverence, and scholarship; and sometimes—in literature, at least, there is an outburst of real romance—the grand imaginings of a Stevenson or the whimsy of a puckish Barrie. That's Scotland.

And what of the Welsh? The men of Wales are the music makers of the kingdom. Fond of their own land, clinging stubbornly to their own tongue, a Welshman seldom bares his heart in English. He "writes his name in music." It is doubtful if there ever was a Welshman without a musical ear. By nature, not by the book, the Welsh are singers and players and composers. Some of the most beloved of the American composers have been of Welsh descent. And in their own strange speech, they are poets; but theirs is not a melody that English *words* can trace.

Then there are the Irish—the Irish whose land is a strange mingling of beauty and despair. It is a land of sunshine and mist and rain and wind. It has its own blue waters, but it faces west to a grey Atlantic. It has mountains of a sort, and glens, and green green fields, and flowers of an almost tropic brightness born of the damp sea air. But there are also the bad lands—the bogs, treacherous and unprofitable. Peat for fuel, moss—little else comes from the great central marshes. And so there is great poverty, with homes more humble than those of the Scotch poor, and with less general education. And yet the Irishman is the most sentimental and imaginative poet of all Britain. Perhaps it is because, with more than half his land being uninhabitable, he lavishes more affection on the rest; perhaps, because poverty has led him to build a dream-world of escape. But probably it is mostly because the Irish Celt is by nature warmhearted and more than half a believer in fairies and "banshees." There is a mystic, almost superstitious flavor to Irish literature—that touch of "something more than meets the eye." Drama and story and verse all show it. There has been a great deal of modern Irish literature, *good* literature. Splendid poets like Yeats and Synge and George Russell (A. E.) have been interested not only in verse but in Irish traditions. They have turned part of their genius toward the drama, writing plays and helping establish a good native theater. Thus Ireland holds a high place in creative literature and has been especially influential in giving British art an aura of fancy and sentiment.

From these and from other sources, English literature has caught some romantic coloring. Sometimes the influence is direct, as when we find the mystic element of Irish plays taking hold of a London public, or when the enthusiasm for Barrie set the world reading his *Little Minister* and *Peter Pan*. But a good deal of it has been indirect, through propinquity and intermarriage. Almost every Englishman has some Celtic blood in his veins—sometimes enough to help him create fantasy; always enough to make him appreciate it when somebody else has created it. And so the fantastic or the delicately imaginative has its place in modern British literature. And so, too, we sometimes see into the heart of the writer.

QUESTIONS IN APPRECIATION:

"A Cloak with Beads"

1. What does the reader learn from "A Cloak with Beads" about the nature of the Scotch people? Does Barrie's sketch sound as if he were exaggerating the poverty of the home? Or does it sound as if his picture were taken from life? Discuss. Does Barrie seem to be idealizing his characters, or do they seem lifelike? Why?

2. How does the picture of Scotch homelife in this sketch compare with pictures presented in other Scotch selections? (Keep this selection in mind for comparison with the scenes from Burns's poem, "The Cotter's Saturday Night.") In what respects is the family life presented in this selection somewhat like family life anywhere? What characteristic sidelights on human nature does it furnish? Mention two or three examples.

3. How does "A Cloak with Beads" prove that the Scotch are a people of sentiment?

Poems of Fancy and Sentiment

1. Could a scholar without imagination have written "Silver"? Discuss. The poem has fourteen lines. How do you know that it is not a sonnet?

2. How does the form of "Piano" differ from the form of "Silver"? Does the form in this case suit the subject? Or do you think some other form might have been used to advantage? Does the poem create a very real sense of emotional experience? Or is it vague and unsubstantial? Discuss. What are its most effective lines? Would you describe this as a poem of fancy? or of sentiment? or of both? Why?

3. What rhythmic effect is suggested by the short rhymed lines of "The Ice-Cart"? Which lines have a soft dreamy effect? What gives them their special sound and movement? Must the imagination of the reader match that of the poet if one is to enjoy a lyric like "The Ice-Cart"? Discuss.

4. In what respects is "The Landscape Near an Aerodrome" like a sequence taken with a motion picture camera? Point out the words that suggest movement. Point out at least four illustrations of the fact that it is not the scenes described which are unusual in this poem, but the

poet's imaginative interpretation of them. Does the unrhymed verse seem especially suitable to the subject and mood of this poem? Discuss. Why does the approach to a city by air offer better inspiration for a lyric poem than an approach to the same city by automobile?

5. The poem "Sheep" is written in very simple words. Why does it make a strong impression upon the reader? Most of the poem is a mere recital of facts. Explain why, in this instance, it requires more imagination to *read* the poem than it did to write it. How does the reader know, nevertheless, that the poet is an imaginative man?

6. What kind of imagination does Mr. Chesterton show in "The Donkey"? How has he used it? What do you suppose gave him the idea for this lyric? Why are these lines on a humble, even ludicrous, subject properly called *poetry?* Discuss.

"The Return"

1. Why is it necessary for one to read Lord Dunsany's story twice in order to appreciate it fully? What features does one enjoy especially on the second reading? Explain.

2. On first reading does the story have an eerie atmosphere? Or does the manner of the narrator give it a casual, natural tone? Explain. How does the author indicate that there was a ghostliness about the air of the village on that evening?

3. How does the author evade having his ghost make difficult explanations as to where he is now or what he has been doing for the last one hundred years? What is the effect of having the next-to-the-last paragraph begin with "Can you hear me? I feel that you can"?

4. Do you consider this a good ghost story? Why or why not?

"The Monkey's Paw"

1. In his story, "The Monkey's Paw," Mr. Jacobs has given a fantastic theme the semblance of fact by keeping the background commonplace and the characters true to life. Point out several instances in which the Whites talk and act just like any ordinary family. Does the sergeant-major act like an ordinary retired soldier? Could the death of Herbert possibly have been a coincidence? Discuss.

2. What evidence is there that there is something supernatural about the monkey's paw? Is the reader inclined to believe in the strange power of the paw? Why or why not? Is there a possible rational explanation for the whole affair? Discuss.

3. With what details has the author built up a feeling of eeriness and horror? How does the reader feel when Mrs. White opens the door upon an empty street?

4. How do you think Edgar Allan Poe would have told the story of the monkey's paw? Discuss. What modern story-techniques do you discover in Mr. Jacobs' story?

THE SALT OF COMMON SENSE AND HUMOR

We have said that normally the Englishman makes little show of his emotions, that by temperament he is matter of fact. In his prose literature this quality is predominant. The British novelist does especially well with realistic fiction. His people attack their problems with a prosaic determination that rises sometimes to a heroism of patience and endurance. The novels of Thomas Hardy written in the closing years of the nineteenth century brought men close to the lives of country people. The stories are told with an almost ruthless realism, pointing the way to such contemporary novelists as Somerset Maugham. Arnold Bennett, also, picked his characters from the country districts—from the pottery towns —and painted them with sober, down-to-earth exactness.

The greatest of the twentieth century novelists has proved to be John Galsworthy, who created in his *Forsyte Saga* a family as British in thought and action as may be found in all the rounds of empire. A wealthy middle class family whose focal center is London, the Forsytes— father, son, daughter, grandchild, unto the third and fourth generations —represent the mind and will of Britain through a period of fifty years or more. It may be regretted that Galsworthy did not live to show us the descendants of Soames and Jolyon in the crisis of England's latest and greatest war. But the *Saga* itself and the succeeding Forsyte volumes mark the opening decades of the century truly and significantly.

So many recent writers deal with contemporary themes that complete enumeration is impossible. Before we make note of representative names, one other trend in prose should be noted—the appearance of a salty, wholesome humor. In the last ten years particularly, men have learned that the Englishman can laugh, and that he knows how to make other folks laugh. The fun in recent fiction and drama furnishes a good balance to basic British sobriety and Celtic romance. A rapid survey will glance at writers in a number of fields, both fiction and non-fiction.

Among the novelists there is Hugh Walpole with his stories of cathedral towns; Conrad, whom we have already noted as the superb artist of the sea, but who gives his novels the stamp of truth; Sir Arthur Conan Doyle—often the romanticist, but one who made the rationalizing detective and the commonplace scene a "must" in detective fiction; his successors—E. Phillips Oppenheim and G. K. Chesterton—both masters of detective fiction; the ladies—E. M. Delafield and Miss Sackville-West and Virginia Woolf. Geoffrey Household has written one blood-thrilling romance in the realistic manner—*Rogue Male*, one of the best pieces of present-war fiction; James Hilton may repeat the success of *Good-bye, Mr. Chips* with his *Random Harvest;* and Howard Spring has written a splendid English story in *Fame Is the Spur.*

Among the humorists, P. G. Wodehouse has held first place—at least among American readers. Jeeves, the butler extraordinary, is his favorite character whose exploits, with those of his master, have enlivened scores of stories, some of them book length. Eric Knight is also a ruling favorite—one who knows his Yorkshiremen and who likes, above all things, to show what happens when Yank and Britisher meet. And H. H. Munro (Saki) does a roguish mixing of humor and fantasy. On the stage, the plays of J. B. Priestley and A. A. Milne have given the bow to comedy, though both writers have proved themselves good craftsmen in any kind of writing.

Speaking of the stage, one does not forget the witty, exhilarating plays that shocked the opening years of the century—the satiric sallies of George Bernard Shaw—still challenging, still rare entertainment. And among the younger craftsmen of the stage is Noel Coward, always an artist and brilliantly contemporary.

Even such a hasty sweep of the field reveals a well-balanced diet on the tables of contemporary English prose. The reader may choose at will from romance, fancy, sentiment, humor, or sober common sense.

QUESTIONS IN APPRECIATION:

"The Disillusioned"

1. A good introduction to an essay or discussion-type article should challenge the reader's immediate attention, be familiar enough in subject to be understandable to most readers, *or* be unusual enough to excite curiosity, and finally be sensibly related to the material that follows. Has Mr. Priestley provided a good introduction to his essay?

2. Why would it be a bad policy to exaggerate statements or to over-draw one's illustrations in a discussion of this type? Has Mr. Priestley exaggerated or overdrawn his material? Discuss.

3. Is his subject one that is likely to interest most people? Why or why not? What is his attitude in developing it—one of mild but slightly humorous protest? one of aggrieved disgust? one of irony? of anger? of tolerance? Discuss. Is the reader amused? annoyed? disturbed? bored? aroused? indifferent? interested? entertained? Why?

"The Open Window"

1. A second reading of "The Open Window" shows how carefully the author built his story so as to make it sound plausible. Mention several touches that make the situation just right for the girl to play her hoax. Does the fact that Mr. Nuttel is recovering from a nervous disorder have any bearing on the plot? Discuss.

2. How does "The Open Window" compare with the usual American short story in technique, characterization, and general interest? In what respects may it be considered a typically *English* story?

"All Yankees Are Liars"

1. Consider the four-line jingle at the beginning of the story. Does it really fit the facts of the story? Why do you think Mr. Knight quoted it? Read the biographical sketch of Mr. Knight. Why is he well quali-

fied to speak of English-American relations and mutual misconceptions?

2. Do you like the four short descriptive paragraphs with which the story opens? Why or why not? Why is it possible for the author to develop the rest of the story almost entirely by conversation?

3. What is the central idea around which this story is built? Do you believe that just this same sort of conversation could take place between an American and some country Englishmen? Why or why not?

4. What kind of humor do you find in the story? Discuss.

FOR FURTHER READING

BARRIE, JAMES M., *The Little Minister; Sentimental Tommy; Margaret Ogilvy; Representative Plays; A Window in Thrums*

BELL, J. J., *Oh, Christina!; Wee MacGreegor*

BENNETT, ARNOLD, *Clayhanger; Tales of the Five Towns*

CHESTERTON, G. K., *As I Was Saying; The Innocence of Father Brown; The Wisdom of Father Brown*

CONRAD, JOSEPH, *Mirror of the Sea; Lord Jim; Youth; Nostromo; Victory; Personal Record; Typhoon*

DUNSANY, LORD, *Alexander and Other Plays; The Gods of the Mountain*

GALSWORTHY, JOHN, *The Forsyte Saga; The Freelands; Caravan; Candelabra; Strife; Justice; The Silver Box*

GREGORY, LADY ISABELLA, *Seven Short Plays*

HARDY, THOMAS, *The Return of the Native; Collected Poems; Wessex Tales; Life's Little Ironies*

HOUSMAN, LAURENCE, *Victoria Regina*

JACOBS, W. W., *Many Cargoes*

KIPLING, RUDYARD, *Kim; The Light That Failed; Actions and Reactions; Something of Myself for My Friends, Known and Unknown*

KNIGHT, ERIC, *Sam Small Flies Again*

LAUDER, HARRY, *Roamin' in the Gloamin'*

LEACOCK, STEPHEN, *Essays and Literary Studies*

LLEWELLYN, RICHARD, *How Green Is My Valley*

MACLAREN, IAN, *Beside the Bonnie Briar Bush; In the Days of Auld Lang Syne*

MILNE, A. A., *The Dover Road; The Truth about Blayds* (drama)

MUNRO, H. H., *The Complete Short Stories of "Saki"*

PRIESTLEY, J. B., *The Good Companions; The Balconinny; English Journey*

SAYERS, DOROTHY L., *Murder Must Advertise*

SHAW, GEORGE BERNARD, *Pygmalion; Arms and the Man*

SNAITH, J. C., *The Sailor*

STEPHENS, JAMES, *The Crock of Gold*

WODEHOUSE, P. G., *Brinkley Manor*

WOOLF, VIRGINIA, *The Death of the Moth; Flush*

Englishmen are true to traditions of courage and right.
Twentieth-century Britishers have faced the test of two wars.

FOR ALL WE HAVE AND ARE

RUDYARD KIPLING

Written at the outbreak of the first World War, these lines sound as
appropriate to the second World War as if Kipling had written them in the
perilous summer of 1940, when Prime Minister Churchill quoted them
and Englishmen gave *all that they had* to keep *all that they are.*

U   For all we have and are,
         For all our children's fate,
         Stand up and take the war.
         The Hun is at the gate!

D   5   Our world has passed away
         In wantonness o'erthrown.
         There is nothing left today
         But steel and fire and stone!

B1   Though all we knew depart,
    10   The old Commandments stand:—
U   "In courage keep your heart,
         In strength lift up your hand."

M   Once more we hear the word
         That sickened earth of old:—
M1   15   "No law except the Sword
         Unsheathed and uncontrolled."
         Once more it knits mankind,
         Once more the nations go
         To meet and break and bind
    20   A crazed and driven foe.

4. HUN—In the first World War, the Germans were called "Huns" because
the destructiveness of their march through neutral Belgium was considered
comparable to the savagery of the Huns that invaded Europe beginning with
the fourth century.

G   Comfort, content, delight,
                     The ages' slow-bought gain,
                     They shriveled in a night.
                     Only ourselves remain
     25   To face the naked days
                     In silent fortitude,
                     Through perils and dismays
                     Renewed and re-renewed.
B1   Though all we made depart,
     30   The old Commandments stand:—
U   "In patience keep your heart,
                     In strength lift up your hand."

L   No easy hope or lies
                     Shall bring us to our goal,
MD   35   But iron sacrifice
                     Of body, will, and soul.
M   There is but one task for all—
L   One life for each to give.
M1   What stands if Freedom fall?
L1   40   Who dies if England live?

FOR INTERPRETATION

1. What acts of aggression on the part of Germany drew England into the first World War? Where do you think the German armies were when Kipling wrote, "The Hun is at the gate"? What acts of destruction inspired him to write lines 5 and 6?

2. Have Englishmen in both wars lived up to the ideal expressed in lines 9–12? Discuss, using definite illustrations.

3. Show how lines 15–20 may be applied to World War II. Why did lines 21–32 seem particularly appropriate to England in the summer of 1940? If you are not sure of the answer, read the selection, "The War of the Unknown Warriors," further on in this section.

4. To what nations in 1943 might lines 33–38 apply? If the word "Freedom" were repeated instead of "England" in the last line, how broad might be the application of the poem in the second World War years? Discuss.

5. How do you account for the astonishing aptness of the poem to situations in 1914 and 1940–1943? Discuss.

DREAMERS

SIEGFRIED SASSOON

D   SOLDIERS are citizens of death's gray land,
        Drawing no dividend from time's tomorrows.
        In the great hour of destiny they stand,
        Each with his feuds, and jealousies, and sorrows.
B 5 Soldiers are sworn to action; they must win
        Some flaming, fatal climax with their lives.
L   Soldiers are dreamers; when the guns begin
        They think of firelit homes, clean beds, and wives.

D   I see them in foul dug-outs, gnawed by rats,
    10 And in the ruined trenches, lashed with rain,
B1   Dreaming of things they did with balls and bats,
        And mocked by hopeless longing to regain
        Bank-holidays, and picture shows, and spats,
        And going to the office in the train.

FOR INTERPRETATION

1. What does the first line of the poem say about the lot of a soldier? In what sense is it true? What is the meaning of the second line? What is the aim or purpose of the soldier as Sassoon sees it?

2. When do soldiers become dreamers? Why? What do they dream about? Why these particular things?

APOLOGIA PRO POEMATE MEO

WILFRED OWEN

B1   I TOO saw God through mud—
D   The mud that cracked on cheeks when wretches
          smiled.
M   War brought more glory to their eyes than blood,
L   And gave their laughs more glee than shakes a child.

TITLE—*In Defense of My Poem.* The war poems of Wilfred Owen were grim, filled with the horrible realities of war. To the suggestion that he might show some of the lighter phases of soldier life, "Apologia Pro Poemate Meo" seems a sardonic answer.

LG 5 Merry it was to laugh there—
          Where death becomes absurd and life absurder.
B   For power was on us as we slashed bones bare
          Not to feel sickness or remorse of murder.

B1   I too have dropped off fear—
D 10   Behind the barrage, dead as my platoon;
L   And sailed my spirit surging, light and clear,
          Past the entanglement where hopes lay strewn;

B1   And witnessed exultation—
D   Faces that used to curse me, scowl for scowl,
L 15   Shine and light up with passion of oblation—
          Seraphic for an hour; though they were foul.

B1   I have made fellowships—
          Untold of happy lovers in old song.
MG   For love is not the binding of fair lips
     20   With the soft silk of eyes that look and long,

L   By Joy, whose ribbon slips:
B   But wound with war's hard wire whose stakes are
            strong;
D   Bound with the bandage of the arm that drips;
MB   Knit in the welding of the rifle-thong.

B1 25 I have perceived much beauty
D   In the hoarse oaths that kept our courage straight;
L   Heard music in the silentness of duty;
          Found peace where shell-storms spouted reddest
            spate.

D   Nevertheless, except you share
     30   With them in hell the sorrowful dark of hell,
          Whose world is but the trembling of a flare,
          And heaven but as the highway for a shell,

B1   You shall not hear their mirth:
          You shall not come to think them well content

35   By any jest of mine.

U   These men are worth

Your tears; you are not worth their merriment.

FOR INTERPRETATION

1. Read the poem through carefully, keeping the title in mind. What do you think was the author's purpose in writing the poem?

2. Explain the chief differences between the way the first World War was fought and the way the second World War has been fought. Where did Englishmen do most of their fighting in the first war? Under what conditions? For how long a time? In what respects is Mr. Owen's poem definitely a poem of the first war? Which lines or expressions seem particularly applicable to 1914–1918?

3. What psychological effects of war does the poem cite? Do you think army men of today have had something of the same experience? What kind of fellowships has the soldier known? What does he say are the most binding ties of love? Why and how could there be beauty in the oaths of battle?

4. To whom do you think the poet is speaking in the last two stanzas? What kind of *mirth* is born in battle? Who alone can understand that mirth? What do you think is the meaning of the last three lines of the poem? How does the poet's purpose in writing the poem help you to understand the closing lines?

5. Is the war-psychology of this poem similar to or different from that of Siegfried Sassoon's poem? Do the poems have similar or different effects upon the reader? Explain.

HATE NOT, FEAR NOT

ROBERT GRAVES

Even in the first World War there was acknowledgment of the paradox that good soldiers do not hate the men they kill. "Hate Not, Fear Not" and the two lyrics which follow it—all written at the time of the first war—express thoughts insistently pressing in upon those engaged in the second.

B   KILL if you must, but never hate:

L   Man is but grass and hate is blight,

B   The sun will scorch you soon or late,

G   Die wholesome then, since you must fight.

D   5   Hate is a fear, and fear is rot
             That cankers root and fruit alike;
U   Fight cleanly then, hate not, fear not,
             Strike with no madness when you strike.

D   Fever and fear distract the world,
B   10   But calm be you though madmen shout;
             Through blazing fires of battle hurled,
U   Hate not, strike, fear not, stare Death out!

THE MAN HE KILLED

THOMAS HARDY

    "HAD he and I but met
      By some old ancient inn,
  We should have set us down to wet
      Right many a nipperkin!

5   "But ranged as infantry,
      And staring face to face,
  I shot at him as he at me,
      And killed him in his place.

    "I shot him dead because—
10   Because he was my foe,

Just so: my foe of course he was;
That's clear enough; although

"He thought he'd 'list, perhaps,
Off-hand like—just as I—
15   Was out of work—had sold his traps—
No other reason why.

"Yes; quaint and curious war is!
You shoot a fellow down
You'd treat, if met where any bar is,
20   Or help to half a-crown."

I DID NOT LOSE MY HEART

A. E. HOUSMAN

I DID not lose my heart in summer's even
When roses to the moonrise burst apart:
When plumes were under heel and lead was flying,
In blood and smoke and flame I lost my heart.

5   I lost it to a soldier and a foeman,
A chap that did not kill me, but he tried;
That took the saber straight and took it striking,
And laughed and kissed his hand to me and died.

FOR INTERPRETATION

1. Do you think it is possible for man to kill "without hate"? Discuss. The second line of Mr. Graves's poem says, "Man is but grass, and hate is blight." Does the blight strike the man who hates, or his enemy? Discuss. How can a man die "wholesome" in the midst of the fight? What poem written by a soldier in the second war expresses something of this same thought? Which do you think would be harder to conquer in battle, *hate* or *fear*? Why?

2. Who is speaking in Hardy's poem, "The Man He Killed"? In your own words give a review of what he says. For most of the wars of the world do you think that the thought of these stanzas has been true—that

the soldiers have no private grudges, that meeting under any other circumstances they might even be friends? Discuss. If that thought is true, is there in it any kernel of hope for the abolishment of wars? Explain. Under what circumstances may it not be true? Explain.

3. What kind of man is speaking in the lyric by Mr. Housman? How does he differ from Mr. Hardy's soldier? In what respects are the two men alike? What kind of man was his foeman? How can you tell? What would have happened if these two men had met in peace times? How does *this* soldier feel about the man *he* killed? Is this poetic exaggeration, or may the thought be true? Discuss.

4. Which two of the three lyrics credit the enemy with a spirit as free from personal hate as their own? How do all three of the lyrics indicate a tendency toward human understanding and world fellowship? Should that spirit be encouraged? If so, how?

HERE DEAD WE LIE

A. E. HOUSMAN

HERE dead we lie because we did not choose
To live and shame the land from which we sprung.
Life, to be sure, is nothing much to lose;
But young men think it is, and we were young.

FOR INTERPRETATION

Who is speaking in the poem? What gives the lines a special pathos? What attitude toward war on the part of the young men do the lines imply? What attitude toward life on the part of the poet?

PEACE

WALTER DE LA MARE

NIGHT arches England, and the winds are still;
Jasmine and honeysuckle steep the air;
Softly the stars that are all Europe's fill
Her heaven-wide dark with radiancy fair;

174

5   That shadowed moon now waxing in the west,
     Stirs not a rumor in her tranquil seas;
     Mysterious sleep has lulled her heart to rest,
     Deep even as theirs beneath her churchyard trees.

     Secure, serene; dumb now the nighthawk's threat;
10   The gun's low thunder drumming o'er the tide;
     The anguish pulsing in her stricken side . . .
     All is at peace. Ah, never, heart, forget
     For this her youngest, best, and bravest died,
     These bright dews once were mixed with blood and sweat.

8. BENEATH HER CHURCHYARD TREES—In England the churchyards are cemeteries.

FOR INTERPRETATION

1. How soon after the 1918 Armistice do you think the sonnet "Peace" was written? Why? At what time of year? How can you tell? What is the significance of the expression, "the stars *that are all Europe's*"? Had England seen more of the stars than Europe during the war years?

2. What is meant by "*theirs* beneath the churchyard trees" in line 8? In what sense is the word "dumb" used in line 9? To what does it apply besides to the "nignthawk's threat"? What does "this" in the thirteenth line refer to? What thought does the peace of the evening bring to the poet? Did England forget? Discuss.

AFTERMATH

SIEGFRIED SASSOON

DB1   *Have you forgotten yet?* . . .
  B   For the world's events have rumbled on since those
          gagged days,
       Like traffic checked a while at the crossing of city
          ways:
DB1   And the haunted gap in your mind has filled with
          thoughts that flow
     5 Like clouds in the lit heavens of life; and you're a
          man reprieved to go,

		Taking your peaceful share of Time, with joy to spare.
DB		*But the past is just the same,—and War's a bloody game. . . .*
DB1		*Have you forgotten yet? . . .*
U		*Look down, and swear by the slain of the War that you'll never forget.*

M	10	Do you remember the dark months you held the sector at Mametz,—
		The nights you watched and wired and dug and piled sand-bags on parapets?
D		Do you remember the rats; and the stench
		Of corpses rotting in front of the front-line trench,—
L		And dawn coming, dirty-white, and chill with a hopeless rain?
DB1	15	Do you ever stop and ask, "Is it all going to happen again?"

L		Do you remember that hour of din before the attack,—
B		And the anger, the blind compassion that seized and shook you then
		As you peered at the doomed and haggard faces of your men?
D		Do you remember the stretcher-cases lurching back
	20	With dying eyes and lolling heads, those ashen-gray Masks of the lads who once were keen and gay?

DB1		*Have you forgotten yet? . . .*
U		*Look up, and swear by the green of the Spring that you'll never forget.*

FOR INTERPRETATION

1. How long after the Armistice do you think this poem was written—sooner or later than the sonnet by de la Mare? How do you judge? Why would Sassoon not be likely to *forget?* Discuss.

2. Why does the poet fill in his picture of war experiences with such sharply distressing details? What does he fear will happen? Were his fears realized? Explain. Why is it necessary in peace to be mindful of war?

176

3. What does the word "Aftermath" mean? Explain why it is an appropriate title for the poem.

A SERGEANT'S PRAYER

HUGH BRODIE

MB1   ALMIGHTY and all present Power,
Short is the prayer I make to Thee,
I do not ask in battle hour
For any shield to cover me.

U 5   The vast unalterable way,
From which the stars do not depart
MB1   May not be turned aside to stay
The bullet flying to my heart.

        I ask no help to strike my foe,
  10   I seek no petty victory here,
The enemy I hate, I know,
To Thee is also dear.

        But this I pray, be at my side
When death is drawing through the sky.
U 15 Almighty God who also died
MB1   Teach me the way that I should die.

FOR INTERPRETATION

1. We hear a good deal these days about the place of prayer in the lives of men in the service. What are we likely to think such men would pray for? What does this sergeant *not* pray for? Why not?

2. What is his prayer? Does he seem to think that he can or will escape death? Did he? (See biographical note.)

3. What lines in the poem express the faith that the workings of Eternal Providence are greater than the destinies of individual men? Which lines in the poem indicate the fact that religion is a source of courage to men of faith?

177

THE WAR OF THE UNKNOWN WARRIORS

WINSTON CHURCHILL

In July 1940 the world was shaking a sober head over the plight of Britain. With the fall of France, Germany was supreme in western Europe. The Pétain government on July 5th broke off diplomatic relations with Great Britain. England, it seemed, stood alone. Invasion by Germany was to be expected at any moment. And certainly there would be an air blitz. Probably a few people outside the island believed that there was a chance for it to survive. But the British were not dismayed. Typical of their attitude of assured resistance was their Prime Minister, Winston Churchill. On July 14th, he delivered to the nation one of his heartening radio addresses—the now famous speech, "The War of the Unknown Warriors."

DURING the last fortnight the British Navy, in addition to blockading what is left of the German Fleet and chasing the Italian Fleet, has had imposed upon it the sad duty of putting effectually out of action for the duration of the war the capital ships of the French Navy.[1] These, under the Armistice terms,

---

[1] THE CAPITAL SHIPS OF THE FRENCH NAVY—When the French ships in an African port had refused to surrender, British guns were trained upon them, against sailors who a few days before had been companions in arms with English seamen.

signed in the railway coach at Compiègne, would have been placed within the power of Nazi Germany. The transference of these ships to Hitler would have endangered the security of both Great Britain and the United States. We therefore had no choice but to act as we did, and to act forthwith. Our painful task is now complete. Although the unfinished battleship, the *Jean Bart,* still rests in a Moroccan harbor and there are a number of French warships at Toulon and in various French ports all over the world, these are not in a condition or a character to derange our preponderance of naval power. As long, therefore, as they make no attempt to return to ports controlled by Germany or Italy, we shall not molest them in any way. That melancholy phase in our relations with France has, so far as we are concerned, come to an end.

Let us think rather of the future. Today is the fourteenth of July, the national festival of France. A year ago in Paris I watched the stately parade down the Champs Elysées of the French Army and the French Empire. Who can foresee what the course of other years will bring? Faith is given to us to help and comfort us when we stand in awe before the unfurling scroll of human destiny. And I proclaim my faith that some of us will live to see a fourteenth of July when a liberated France will once again rejoice in her greatness and in her glory, and once again stand forward as the champion of the freedom and the rights of man. When the day dawns, as dawn it will, the soul of France will turn with comprehension and with kindness to those Frenchmen and Frenchwomen, wherever they may be, who in the darkest hour did not despair of the Republic.

In the meantime, we shall not waste our breath nor cumber our thought with reproaches. When you have a friend and comrade at whose side you have faced tremendous struggles, and your friend is smitten down by a stunning blow, it may be necessary to make sure that the weapon that has fallen from his hands shall not be added to the resources of your common enemy. But you need not bear malice because of your friend's cries of delirium and gestures of agony. You must not add to his pain; you must work for his recovery. The association of interest between Britain and France remains. The cause remains. Duty inescapable remains. So long as our pathway to victory is not impeded, we are ready to discharge such offices of good will toward the French Government as may be possible, and to foster the trade and help the administration of those parts of the great French Empire which are now cut off from captive France, but which maintain their freedom. Subject to the iron demands of the war which we are waging against Hitler and all his works, we shall try so to conduct ourselves that every true French heart will beat and glow at the way we carry on the struggle; and that not only France, but all the oppressed countries in Europe may feel that each British victory is a step towards the liberation of the Continent from the foulest thralldom into which it has ever been cast.

All goes to show that the war will be long and hard. No one can tell where it will spread. One thing is certain: the peoples of Europe will not be ruled for long by the Nazi Gestapo, nor will the world yield itself to Hitler's gospel of hatred, appetite and domination.

And now it has come to us to stand alone in the breach, and face the worst that the tyrant's might and enmity can do. Bearing ourselves humbly before God, but conscious that we serve an unfolding purpose, we are ready to defend our native land against the invasion by which it is threatened. We are fighting *by* ourselves alone; but we are not fighting *for* ourselves alone. Here in this strong City of Refuge which enshrines the title-deeds of human progress and is of deep consequence to Christian civilization; here, girt about by the seas and oceans where the Navy reigns; shielded from above by the prowess and devotion of our airmen—we await undismayed the impending assault. Perhaps it will come tonight. Perhaps it will come next week. Perhaps it will never come. We must show ourselves equally capable of meeting a sudden violent shock or—what is perhaps a harder test—a prolonged vigil. But be the ordeal sharp or long, or both, we shall seek no terms, we shall tolerate no parley; we may show mercy—we shall ask for none.

I can easily understand how sympathetic onlookers across the Atlantic, or anxious friends in the yet-unravished countries of Europe, who cannot measure our resources or our resolve, may have feared for our survival when they saw so many States and kingdoms torn to pieces in a few weeks or even days by the monstrous force of the Nazi war machine. But Hitler has not yet been withstood by a great nation with a will power the equal of his own. Many of these countries have been poisoned by intrigue before they were struck down by violence. They have been rotted from within before they were smitten from without. How else can you explain what has happened to France?—to the French Army, to the French people, to the leaders of the French people?

But here, in our Island, we are in good health and in good heart. We have seen how Hitler prepared in scientific detail the plans for destroying the neighbor countries of Germany. He had his plans for Poland and his plans for Norway. He had his plans for Denmark. He had his plans all worked out for the doom of the peaceful, trustful Dutch; and, of course, for the Belgians. We have seen how the French were undermined and overthrown. We may therefore be sure that there *is* a plan—perhaps built up over years—for destroying Great Britain, which after all has the honor to be his main and foremost enemy. All I can say is that any plan for invading Britain which Hitler made two months ago must have had to be entirely recast in order to meet our new position. Two months ago—nay, one month ago—our first and main effort was to keep our best Army in France. All our regular troops, all our output of munitions, and a very large part of our Air Force, had to be sent to France and maintained in action there. But now we have it all at home. Never before in the last war—or in this—have we had in this Island an Army comparable in quality, equipment or numbers to that which stands here on guard tonight. We have a million and a half men in the British Army under arms tonight, and every week of June and July has seen their organization, their defenses and their striking power advance by leaps and bounds. No praise is too high for the officers and men—aye, and civilians—who have made this immense transformation in so short a time. Behind these soldiers of the regular Army, as a means of destruction for parachutists, airborne invaders, and any traitors that may be found in our midst (but I do not believe there are many—woe betide them, they will get short shrift)—behind the regular Army we have more than a million of the Local Defense Volunteers, or, as they are much better called, the "Home Guard." These officers and men, a large proportion of whom have been through the last war, have the strongest desire to attack and come to close quarters with the enemy wherever he may appear. Should the invader come to Britain, there will be no placid lying down of the people in submission before him, as we have seen, alas, in other countries. We shall defend every village, every town, and every city. The vast mass of London itself, fought street by street, could easily devour an entire hostile army; and we would rather see London laid in ruins and ashes than that it should be tamely and abjectly enslaved. I am bound to state these facts, because it is necessary to inform our people of our intentions, and thus to reassure them.

This has been a great week for the Royal Air Force, and for the Fighter Command. They have shot down more than five to one of the German aircraft which have tried to molest our convoys in the Channel, or have ventured to cross the British coast line. These are, of course, only the preliminary encounters to the great air battles which lie ahead. But I know of no reason why we should be discontented with the results so far achieved; although, of course, we hope to improve upon them as the fighting becomes more widespread and comes more inland. Around all lies the power of the Royal Navy. With over a thousand armed ships under the White Ensign, patrolling the seas, the Navy, which is capable of transferring its force very readily to the protection of any part of the British Empire which may be threatened, is capable also of keeping open communication with the New World, from whom, as the struggle deepens, increasing aid will come. Is it not remarkable that after ten months of unlimited U-boat and air attack upon our commerce, our food reserves are higher than they have ever been, and we have a substantially larger tonnage under our own flag, apart from great numbers of foreign ships in our control, than we had at the beginning of the war?

Why do I dwell on all this? Not, surely, to induce any slackening of effort or vigilance. On the contrary. These must be redoubled, and we must prepare not only for the summer, but for the winter; not only for 1941, but for 1942; when the war will, I trust, take a different form on the defensive, in which it has hitherto been bound. I dwell on these elements in our strength, on these resources which we have mobilized and control —I dwell on them because it is right to show that the good cause *can* command the means of survival; and that while we toil through the dark valley we can see the sunlight on the uplands beyond.

I stand at the head of a Government representing all Parties in the State—all creeds, all classes, every recognizable section of opinion. We are ranged beneath the Crown of our ancient monarchy. We are supported by a free Parliament and a free Press; but there is one bond which unites us all and sustains us in the public regard—namely (as is increasingly becoming known), that we are prepared to proceed to all extremities, to endure them and to enforce them; *that* is our bond of union in His Majesty's Government tonight. Thus only, in times like these, can nations preserve their freedom; and thus only can they uphold the cause entrusted to their care.

But all depends now upon the whole life-strength of the British race in every part of the world and of all our associated peoples and of all our well-wishers in every land, doing their utmost night and day, giving all, daring all, enduring all—to the utmost—to the end. This is no war of chieftains or of princes, of dynasties or national ambition; it is a war of peoples and of causes. There are vast numbers, not only in this Island but in every land, who will render faithful service in this war, but whose names will never be known, whose deeds will never be recorded. This is a War of the Unknown Warriors; but let all strive without failing in faith or in duty, and the dark curse of Hitler will be lifted from our age.

DID YOU READ WITH UNDERSTANDING?

1. Review briefly the events of the war from September 1939 to July 14, 1940. What Armistice is referred to in the first paragraph? Why were the British-French relationships an especially painful subject at this time? Why was July 14 an especially significant day? What hope does Churchill express for the future of France?

2. What does Mr. Churchill predict as to the length and scope of the war? Explain his statement, "We are fighting *by* ourselves alone, but not *for* ourselves alone." What is the "strong City of Refuge" to which he refers? In what sense is it a shrine of liberty and civilization?

3. What are the exact dangers which England sees ahead of her? List the means of defense which Mr. Churchill says are available. How did those resources compare with the material resources of the enemy at that time? What advantages other than material resources did England possess? Discuss.

4. Which of the threatened dangers became reality for England within the next six months? Does this speech help to explain why the Nazis were not able to crush England as they had crushed France? Discuss.

5. To whom does the Prime Minister make his appeal in the speech? How only can freedom survive? Explain whom he means by the "Unknown Warriors." How does this speech—and the subsequent events of the war—illustrate the fact that the British have held true to traditions of *courage* and *right*? Discuss.

THE BEACHES OF DUNKIRK

"BARTIMEUS"

THE yacht-club telephone rang and the elderly steward, unaccustomed to the sound of it, laid down his paper, removed his spectacles, and picked up the receiver. A man's voice spoke authoritatively for about a minute.

The steward said nothing. He was an old Navy man and had been a pensioner for a quarter of a century, but he recognized the note in the speaker's voice. He waited till the end of the message.

"Aye, aye, sir," he said, and then added, "there's only the one yacht here now, sir. The *Wanderer*. Motor yacht, forty feet long. There's no crew, sir. Owner's fighting in France. There's a young lady on board at this moment . . ."

The voice interrupted him. He listened, turning the spectacles over in his knotted fingers, staring into vacancy.

"Aye, aye, sir. I'll do what I can. Old Navy man myself. They said I was too old to fight . . ."

There was no answer. "Hullo, sir?" Silence. He replaced the receiver.

The *Wanderer* was lying at her buoy and there was no sign of the girl. He untied the dinghy lying at the jetty and rowed alongside. At the sound of the oars as he boated them the girl's head and shoulders appeared above the companionway. She was flushed and had a scrubbing brush in her hand.

"They want her, miss," he said simply. "They rung up from the Admiralty. Proceed to Ramsgate for orders. They're taking every craft on the South Coast."

She brushed a lock of hair back from her damp forehead with

her forearm. "I'm single-handed," she said. "Can you run the engine if I steer?"

"You, miss?" He hadn't thought of that.

"She's full up with petrol. There's water, too, and some stuff in tins to eat. Bring some bread."

"You know what it's for, don't you, miss? They won't let a woman——"

"They needn't know," was the girl's answer. She stood motionless, thinking. The ebb tide running past the strakes of the dinghy[1] made a little chuckling noise in the stillness.

"Bring a couple of shrapnel helmets . . . get them from the A.R.P. people. . . . What about Johnnie?"

"Johnnie?" He turned that over in his mind. Johnnie was simple but he was useful in a boat. Ashore he just sat and played with pebbles, but put him in a boat and he was all there. The club employed him to ferry people to their yachts and for attending to the moorings and odd jobs like scraping and painting. He didn't speak very plain, but after all it wasn't talk they wanted on the beaches of Dunkirk. Another aspect of the situation occurred to him. She seemed to take it for granted he was coming. "What about the club, miss? I'm the caretaker *and* steward."

She had emerged from her reverie. "The club? What does the club matter?"

He grinned, showing tobacco-stained fangs. "You've said it, miss. Give me half an hour."

When he was halfway across to the jetty she hailed him again. Her clear voice was like a boy's.

"Johnnie will want a shrapnel helmet too."

He nodded; she went below and fell to mopping up the mess on the cabin floor. She had decided to give the boat a scrub-out because it occupied her mind, which, having had no word from France for three weeks, was inclined to imagine things. This was where they had spent the happiest hours of his leave. The happiest hours of their lives. And now for all she knew he was waiting on those hellish beaches, one of all those thousands of exhausted men, waiting under shell and machine-gun fire for succor from England. She flung the mop and scrubber into the bucket and jerked open a drawer. There was all his old kit: gray

---

[1] STRAKES OF THE DINGHY—The planks running from stem to stern of the skiff attached to the yacht.

185

flannel trousers, sweater, an old shooting jacket, a yellow muffler. She would push her hair up under the shrapnel helmet. . . . His pipes stuck in a rack over his bunk caught her eye. That would be the finishing touch. Keep one of those in her mouth when they got to Ramsgate, and talk gruff. She selected a blackened bulldog and experimented in front of the glass. It tasted utterly foul.

Coming down channel they overtook a convoy of motor yachts and followed them. She had the chart open in front of her but the daylight was fading and there were no lights anywhere she could recognize. She had never entered Ramsgate from seaward. Only from the railway station, once as a child, carrying her doll and a spade and bucket, in charge of her nurse.

She listened to the drone of the engine with satisfaction. Old Ferris had been a mechanician when he served in the Navy. It wasn't so good at the start but he was enjoying himself down in the engine room now he had picked up the hang of the thing. Every now and again he put his head out of the hatch with his spectacles on the end of his nose. "Running as sweet as a nut, miss," he announced.

"Bravo," she answered back.

Johnnie sat in the bows staring at the evening star. She tried to remember why she had brought Johnnie. He worshiped her like a dog, but that wasn't the reason. It was because she felt she had no right to take an able-bodied man from his work in England; and on the spur of the moment she could think of nobody on the spot who was as handy in the boat. He and she used to take Johnnie away for the week end sometimes. Johnnie washed up and looked after the boat when they went ashore. . . . She was one of the few people who understood what he said. He turned his head and smiled at her at that moment. It was the slow confiding smile of a child. He hadn't the remotest idea where he was going. He didn't care. He just trusted her. She felt a swift pang of compunction, and stifled it, giving him back his smile. Reassured, he resumed his contemplation of the star.

She climbed ashore in the dusk, the awful pipe clenched between her teeth, and was confronted by a man in the uniform of a lieutenant commander.

"What ship?"

"*Wanderer*." Nobody had ever called the *Wanderer* a ship before. He would have liked that.

"What is she?"

"Forty-foot motor cruiser."

"Armed?"

She shook her head. Other owners of yachts were crowding round asking for orders.

He glanced at her shrapnel helmet.

"Well, you'd better collect some rifles and life belts. First-aid outfit too, if you haven't got it."

"Then what?" She stuck her hands in her trouser pockets, making her voice as gruff and laconic as possible.

"La Panne. Time it so as to get there in the dawn. Take off all you've got room for each trip and transfer them to something bigger. Stick it as long as you can, and good luck." He indicated a gap in the barbed wire where she supposed there were rifles and life belts obtainable and dismissed her from his mind.

She went back to the edge of the jetty and hailed old Ferris. The harbor was crammed with the dim forms of boats maneuvering for berths alongside. Beside her on the pierhead was a soldier with a Bren gun mounted on a tripod.

"Ferris," she called down to the *Wanderer*. "Come ashore with me and collect some rifles and life belts." The soldier sidled up beside her.

"Here, Skipper," he muttered, "Rifles ain't no use. Take me and this Bren gun. Wait till it's dark and I'll slip down and come along with you. They won't miss me till I'm back."

She grinned delightedly. He would know about rifles, too. She had never fired one in her life. "All right," she whispered. "What's your name?"

"Tanner's the name, Skipper. You're a sport." She felt a bit of a sport.

The sky line was like the edge of the Pit. To the westward the oil tanks of Dunkirk were a sullen blaze that every now and again leaped upwards like the eruption of a volcano as a shell burst in the flaming inferno. Fires glowed dully along the coast, and shore batteries blinked white flashes that reached the ear as dull reverberations like distant thunder. The searchlights wheeled about the low-lying clouds into which tracer shells were soaring.

They had solved the problem of navigating to La Panne by following a paddle steamer that had half a dozen lifeboats in tow. The whole night was full of the sound of motorboats' exhausts.

There was a young moon peeping in and out of the drifting clouds and it revealed the indistinct lines of little craft far and wide, heading in the same direction.

Johnnie sat entranced by the spectacle, crowing huskily at intervals. Tanner, having mounted his Bren gun in the stern, gave her a relief at the wheel. He said it was much the same as driving a car. She practiced loading the rifle under his tuition. Old Ferris visited them at intervals, calling her "Skipper." It didn't matter what Johnnie called her because nobody could understand what he said.

"You're a bit young for this game, eh, Skipper?" asked Tanner. "How old are you?"

"About a hundred," she replied with a gruff laugh. And in that moment, before the dawn of hell's delight, she felt it.

The dawn came slowly, revealing the small craft of the south coast of England covering the Channel like water beetles on the surface of a pool. Pleasure steamers and yachts, barges, scoots, wherries, lifeboats, motorboats, rowing boats, and canoes. . . . Fishermen, yachtsmen, longshoremen, men who had never been afloat in their lives, millionaires and the very poor, elderly men and lads in their teens, answering in a headlong rush the appeal for boats. Boats for the beaches and the last of the Expeditionary Force.

Somehow she hadn't thought about the dead. Her thoughts were entirely occupied with the living. It wasn't until Johnnie began making queer noises of distress and pointing down into the shallow water that she saw them—the men who had been machine-gunned in the shallows, wading out into the water to reach security. They were still there, some floating, some submerged; in an odd way they seemed to convey resentment at the disturbance of their oblivion by the passing keels.

She called Johnnie to her side. "Take the lead line and sound over the bows. Call the soundings. Nothing else matters. Do you understand, Johnnie? Nothing else matters. I am here."

He made guttural noises, pointing at Tanner, who was blazing away with the Bren gun at a Heinkel overhead that had bombed a trawler astern of them. She held him with her eyes. "Nothing else matters, do you understand?" He picked up the lead line and went forward obediently. She put her lips to the voice pipe. "Go very slow, Ferris."

"Go very slow," repeated the old man.

She crept inshore. The beach was pitted with shell craters out of which men came running, wading out into the water to meet them. From the sand dunes more men stumbled, helping the wounded. The whole foreshore was alive with men and boats, and the smoke from the Dunkirk fires flowed over them like a dark river.

At three and a half feet she would stop. It was the least they could float in. She listened to the strange cries Johnnie emitted as he hauled in the dripping lead line, understanding them perfectly.

Presently, her mouth to the voice pipe, she gave the order to stop. Tanner was having trouble with the Bren gun and swearing in a ceaseless flow of incomprehensible blasphemy. Old Ferris, complete in shrapnel helmet and life belt, climbed out of his hatch and came towards her, lighting his pipe.

"They said I was too old to fight, but——"

"Get back. We're in four feet. I must keep working the engines." A bomb burst among the men wading towards them. She shut her eyes for a moment. "Keep on sounding, Johnnie. What water have you got?"

"Fraghgaph-ah-ah," crowed Johnnie.

"Good boy. Keep it going."

The Bren gun broke out afresh. Tanner, having cleared the jamb, opened fire again, chanting oaths like a denunciatory psalm. "Slow astern, Ferris."

Another cluster of men wading to their armpits had reached them.

Johnnie looked back at her and pointed at their sun-scorched, puffing faces. No doubt existed in his mind that it was all something to do with his lead-line achievements. He was delighted. Somewhere out of sight a German field-gun battery opened fire, the shells whistling viciously overhead.

She searched every face as they came splashing and gasping towards her and somehow contrived to hoist each other inboard. She took sixty or seventy at a trip and transferred them to the nearest vessel lying out in the deep water; she had hitherto believed that the utmost capacity of the *Wanderer* was a dozen. Backwards and forwards they went under exploding bombs, under machine-gun fire and whining shells. Tanner ran out of ammunition and they went alongside a destroyer where he got another case and a spare barrel for the Bren gun. She lost all count of time, all fear, all feeling. Sometimes she interrogated weary men: Had they seen his unit? Had they ever heard his name? They shook their heads and begged for water. She had none left.

Then suddenly it seemed that the beaches were empty. Unknown to her the men were being marched westward to Dunkirk where the French and British destroyers were crowding alongside the mole and embarking troops in thousands under shellfire. Except for a few scattered units moving west the beaches were empty. The task was done; but where was he—where was he?

The Bren gun had been silent for a long time but she hadn't noticed. Now, turning to look seaward, she saw Tanner lying beside it with his knees screwed up into his belly. She ran aft and knelt beside him.

His eyes sought hers out of his gray face. "I bought it, Skipper. Sorry. . . . Got a drop of water?"

She raised his head and held it against her breast. "There isn't any water left."

His eyes were suddenly puzzled. . . . He moved his head sideways a little and then smiled, and died, ineffably content.

They followed a big gray coaster back to Dover. Old Ferris got a spare red ensign out of the locker and tucked Tanner up in it. He didn't mind Tanner's being killed, having been disposed to regard him jealously as an intruder into a nice little family party. Moreover he disapproved of his language. He walked forward to the wheelhouse. She was moving the spokes of the wheel slowly between her blistered hands. Her shrapnel helmet lay on the chart beside the valiant briar pipe. She was aware of the old man beside her and of having reached the end of her tether at one and the same moment.

Old Ferris kicked Johnnie, asleep at her feet into wakefulness. "Take the wheel," he said gruffly, and held her as she pitched, sobbing and exhausted, into his arms.

They berthed alongside the Admiralty pier and she climbed ashore to find someone who could give them fuel and water. The quays were thronged with troops in thousands being fed and sorted out into units and entrained. A hospital ship was evacuating wounded into fleets of ambulances. She stepped aside to give room to the bearers of a stretcher and glanced at the face on the pillow.

He had a bandage round his head and opened his eyes suddenly on her face.

"I've been looking for you," she announced in a calm matter-of-fact tone. She felt no emotion whatever.

He smiled. "Well, here I am," he said.

DID YOU READ WITH UNDERSTANDING?

1. How much information about time, place, conditions, and characters is furnished in the first six paragraphs? Mention any specific items. How does the title of the story help furnish the setting? What casual touch indicates that since the war, there has been little to do at the boat club? How has the author suggested the urgency of the telephone message? What do you think the voice at the other end of the wire said?

2. How do you think the girl knew, without being told, what the boat was wanted for? Is there any indication that she anticipated a call for the boat to help in evacuation? Discuss. What is the significance of the statement that "having had no word from France in three weeks, she was inclined to imagine things"? What kind of word had she expected? What things would she imagine? Why would the authorities not want a girl to help in the undertaking? Why was this girl determined to go? What would make it fairly easy for her to pass for a boy? Why would they need shrapnel helmets?

3. Why was it fortunate that the girl ran into Tanner at Ramsgate? What kind of gun do you think a "Bren gun" is? How can you tell? What kept Tanner from discovering that his skipper was a girl? How was the girl able to steer for a strange harbor at night?

4. What *Pit* is meant in the sentence that announces their arrival at Dunkirk—"The sky line was like the edge of the Pit"? How do you think it looked, literally? Why were the small boats needed at Dunkirk? What made their task dangerous? What made it gruesome? What qualities would a girl need if she were to stick it out? Was each member of her crew useful? Explain. How many soldiers do you think the *Wanderer* helped rescue? How can you estimate it?

5. What was the girl looking for when she "searched every face as they came splashing toward her"? What was the sign that their job was done? What had happened to Tanner? What did he mean when he said, "I *bought* it, Skipper"? Discuss. Do you think he knew before he died that his skipper was a girl? Why did he die *content*?

6. How were they able to find their way back to Dover? What indicates the success of the whole evacuation project? Mention specific details. What one detail made it more than a success to the girl? Do the last three sentences of the story seem true to life? Discuss.

Englishmen are realizing the need for international understanding and fellowship.

MY AMERICA

LORD TWEEDSMUIR

As Governor-General of Canada, Lord Tweedsmuir had excellent opportunity to get acquainted officially with the United States; but his interest in America was of much older standing. It began, he tells us, in his boyhood. He proves in the following selection that he understands us and that he really likes us.

I FIRST discovered America through books. Not the tales of Indians and the Wild West which entranced my boyhood; those seemed to belong to no particular quarter of the globe, but to an indefinable land of romance, and I was not cognizant of any nation behind them. But when I became interested in literature I came strongly under the spell of New England. Its culture seemed to me to include what was best in Europe's, winnowed and clarified. Perhaps it was especially fitted to attract youth, for it was not too difficult or too recondite, but followed the "main march of the human affections," and it had the morning freshness of a young people. Its cheerfulness atoned for its occasional bleakness and anemia. Lowell was the kind of critic I wanted, learned, rational, never freakish, always intelligible. Emerson's gnomic wisdom [1] was a sound manual for adolescence, and of Thoreau I became—and for long remained—an ardent disciple. To a Scot of my upbringing there was something congenial in the simplicity, the mild austerity, and the girded discipline of the New England tradition. I felt that it had been derived from the same sources as our own.

Then, while I was at Oxford, I read Colonel Henderson's *Stonewall Jackson* and became a student of the American Civil War. I cannot say what especially attracted me to that campaign; partly, no doubt, the romance of it, the chivalry and the supreme heroism; partly its extraordinary technical interest, both military and political; but chiefly, I think, because I fell in love with the protagonists.[2] I had found the kind of man that I could whole-heartedly admire. Since those days, my study of the Civil War has continued, I have visited most of its battlefields, I have followed the trail of its great marches, I have read widely in its literature; indeed, my memory has become so stored with its details that I have often found myself able to tell the descendants of its leaders facts about their forebears of which they had never heard.

My interest soon extended from the soldiers to the civilians, and I acquired a new admiration for Abraham Lincoln. Then it was enlarged to include the rest of America's history—the first settlements, the crossing of the Appalachians, the Revolution, the building of the West. Soon America, instead of being the unstoried land which it appears to most English travelers, became for me the home of a long tradition and studded with sacred places. I dare to say that no American was ever more thrilled by the prospect of seeing Westminster Abbey and the Tower, Winchester and Oxford, than I was by the thought of Valley Forge and the Shenandoah and the Wilderness.

I came first into the United States by way of Canada—a good way to enter, for English eyes are already habituated to the shagginess of the landscape and can begin to realize its beauties. My first reflection was that no one had told me how lovely the country was. I mean *lovely*, not vast and magnificent. I am not

---

[1] GNOMIC WISDOM—Wisdom expressed in terse, proverb-like sentences.
[2] PROTAGONISTS—Leaders.

thinking of the Grand Canyon and the Yosemite and the Pacific Coast, but of the ordinary rural landscape. There is much of the land which I have not seen, but in the East and the South and the Northwest I have collected a gallery of delectable pictures. I think of the farms which are clearings in the Vermont and New Hampshire hills, the flowery summer meadows, the lush cow-pastures with an occasional stump to remind one that it is old forest land, the quiet lakes and the singing streams, the friendly accessible mountains; the little country towns of Massachusetts and Connecticut with their village greens and elms and two-century-old churches and courthouses; the secret glens of the Adirondacks and the mountain meadows of the Blue Ridge; the long-settled champaign ³ of Maryland and Pennsylvania; Virginian manors more Old-England perhaps than anything we have at home; the exquisite links with the past like much of Boston and Charleston and all of Annapolis; the sunburnt aromatic ranges of Montana and Wyoming; the Pacific shores where from snow mountains fishable streams descend through some of the noblest timber on earth to an enchanted sea.

It is a country most of which I feel to be in a special sense "habitable," designed for homes, adapted to human uses, a friendly land. I like, too, the way in which the nomenclature reflects its history, its racial varieties, its odd cultural mixtures, the grandiose and the homespun rubbing shoulders. That is how places should be named. I have no objection to Mechanicville and Higginsville and Utica and Syracuse. They are a legitimate part of the record. And behind are the hoar-ancient memorials of the first dwellers, names like symphonies—Susquehanna, Ticonderoga, Shenandoah, Wyoming.

America is, no doubt, a vast country, though it can be comfortably put inside Canada. But it is not in every part a country of wide horizons. Dwellers on the Blue Ridge, on the prairies, and on the western ranges may indeed live habitually with huge spaces of land and sky, but most of America, and some of its most famous parts, is pockety, snug and cozy, a sanctuary rather than a watch-tower. To people so domiciled its vastness must be like the mathematician's space-time, a concept apprehended by the mind and not a percept of the eye. "The largeness of Nature

---

³ CHAMPAIGN—Plain; stretch of flat open country.

and of this nation were monstrous without a corresponding largeness and generosity of the spirit of the citizen." That is one of
Walt Whitman's best-known sayings, but let us remember that
the bigness of their country is for most Americans something to
be learned and imaginatively understood, and not a natural deduction from cohabiting with physical immensities.

Racially they are the most variegated people on earth. The
preponderance of the Anglo-Saxon stock disappeared in the Civil
War. Look today at any list of names in a society or a profession and you will find that, except in the navy, the bulk are from
the continent of Europe. In his day Matthew Arnold thought
that the chief source of the strength of the American people lay
in their homogeneity and the absence of sharply defined classes,
which made revolution unthinkable. Other observers, like Henry
James, have deplored the lack of such homogeneity and wished
for their country the "close and complete consciousness of the
Scots." (I pause to note that I cannot imagine a more nightmare conception. What would happen to the world if a hundred
and thirty million Scotsmen, with their tight, compact nationalism, were living in the same country?) I am inclined to query
the alleged absence of classes, for I have never been in any part
of the United States where class distinctions did not hold. There
is an easy friendliness of manner which conceals a strong class
pride, and the basis of that pride is not always, or oftenest, plutocratic.[4] Apart from the social snobbery of the big cities, there
seems to be everywhere an innocent love of grades and distinctions which is enough to make a communist weep. I have known
places in the South where there was a magnificent aristocratic
egalitarianism.[5] Inside a charmed circle all were equal. The
village postmistress, having had the right kind of great-great-
grandmother, was an honored member of society, while the immi-
grant millionaire, who had built himself a palace, might as well
have been dead. And this is true not only of the New England
F. F. M.'s [6] and the Virginian F. F. V.'s,[7] the districts with long
traditions, but of the raw little townships in the Middle West.
They, too, have their "best" people who had ancestors, though
the family tree may only have sprouted for two generations.

---

[4] PLUTOCRATIC—Based on wealth.

[5] EGALITARIANISM—Equalitarianism, or the doctrine that all are equal.

[6] F. F. M.—First Families of the Mayflower.

[7] F. F. V.—First Families of Virginia.

No country can show such a wide range of type and character, and I am so constituted that in nearly all I find something to interest and attract me. This is more than a temperamental bias, for I am very ready to give reasons for my liking. I am as much alive as anyone to the weak and ugly things in American life: areas, both urban and rural, where the human economy has gone rotten; the melting-pot which does not always melt; the eternal colored problem; a constitutional machine which I cannot think adequately represents the efficient good sense of the American people; a brand of journalism which fatigues with its ruthless snappiness and uses a speech so disintegrated that it is incapable of expressing any serious thought or emotion; the imbecile patter of high-pressure salesmanship; an academic jargon, used chiefly by psychologists and sociologists, which is hideous and almost meaningless. Honest Americans do not deny these blemishes; indeed they are apt to exaggerate them, for they are by far the sternest critics of their own country. For myself, I would make a double plea in extenuation. These are defects from which today no nation is exempt, for they are the fruits of a mechanical civilization, which perhaps are more patent in America, since everything there is on a large scale. Again, you can set an achievement very much the same in kind against nearly every failure. If her historic apparatus of government is cranky, she is capable of meeting the "instant need of things" with brilliant improvisations. Against economic plague spots she can set great experiments in charity; against journalistic baby-talk a standard of popular writing in her best papers which is a model of idiom and perspicuity; against catch-penny trade methods many solidly founded, perfectly organized commercial enterprises; against the jargon of the half-educated professor much noble English prose in the great tradition. That is why it is so foolish to generalize about America. You no sooner construct a rule than it is shattered by the exceptions.

As I have said, I have a liking for almost every kind of American (except the kind who decry their country). I have even a sneaking fondness for George Babbitt,[8] which I fancy is shared by his creator. But there are two types which I value especially, and which I have never met elsewhere in quite the same form.

[8] GEORGE BABBITT—The principal character in Sinclair Lewis' novel *Babbitt*, a self-satisfied American business man from a typical Middle West city.

One is the pioneer. No doubt the physical frontier of the United States is now closed, but the pioneer still lives, though the day of the covered wagon is over. I have met him in the New England hills, where he is grave, sardonic, deliberate in speech; in the South, where he has a ready smile and a soft, caressing way of talking; in the ranges of the West, the cowpuncher with his gentle voice and his clear, friendly eyes which have not been dulled by reading print—the real thing, far removed from the vulgarities of film and fiction. At his best, I think, I have found him as a newcomer in Canada, where he is pushing north into districts like the Peace River, pioneering in the old sense. By what signs is he to be known? Principally by the fact that he is wholly secure, that he possesses his soul, that he is the true philosopher. He is one of the few aristocrats left in the world. He has a right sense of the values of life, because his cosmos embraces both nature and man. I think he is the most steadfast human being now alive.

The other type is at the opposite end of the social scale, the creature of a complex society who at the same time is not dominated by it, but, while reaping its benefits, stands a little aloof. In the older countries culture, as a rule, leaves some irregularity like an excrescence in a shapely tree-trunk, some irrational bias, some petulance or prejudice. You have to go to America, I think, for the wholly civilized man who has not lost his natural vigor or agreeable idiosyncrasies, but who sees life in its true proportions and has a fine balance of mind and spirit. It is a character hard to define, but anyone with a wide American acquaintance will know what I mean. They are people in whom education has not stunted any natural growth or fostered any abnormality. They are Greek in their justness of outlook, but Northern in their gusto. Their eyes are shrewd and candid, but always friendly. As examples I would cite, among friends who are dead, the names of Robert Bacon, Walter Page, Newton Baker, and Dwight Morrow.

But I am less concerned with special types than with the American people as a whole. Let me try to set down certain qualities which seem to me to flourish more lustily in the United States than elsewhere. Again, let me repeat, I speak of America only as I know it; an observer with a different experience might not agree with my conclusions.

First I would select what, for want of a better word, I should call homeliness. It is significant that the ordinary dwelling, though it be only a shack in the woods, is called not a house, but a home. This means that the family, the ultimate social unit, is given its proper status as the foundation of society. Even among the richer classes I seem to find a certain pleasing domesticity. English people of the same rank are separated by layers of servants from the basic work of the household, and know very little about it. In America the kitchen is not too far away from the drawing-room, and it is recognized, as Heraclitus [9] said, that the gods may dwell there. But I am thinking chiefly of the ordinary folk, especially those of narrow means. It is often said that Americans are a nomad race, and it is true that they are very ready to shift their camp; but the camp, however bare, is always a home. The cohesion of the family is close, even when its members are scattered. This is due partly to the tradition of the first settlers, a handful in an unknown land; partly to the history of the frontier, where the hearth-fire burnt brighter when all around was cold and darkness. The later immigrants from Europe, feeling at last secure, were able for the first time to establish a family base, and they cherished it zealously. This ardent domesticity has had its bad effects on American literature, inducing a sentimentality which makes a too crude frontal attack on the emotions, and which has produced as a reaction a not less sentimental "toughness." But as a social cement it is beyond price. There have been many to laugh at the dullness and pettiness of the "small town." From what I know of small-town life elsewhere, I suspect obtuseness in the satirists.

Second, I would choose the sincere and widespread friendliness of the people. Americans are interested in the human race, and in each other. Deriving doubtless from the old frontier days, there is a general helpfulness which I have not found in the same degree elsewhere. A homesteader in Dakota will accompany a traveler for miles to set him on the right road. The neighbors will rally round one of their number in distress with the loyalty of a Highland clan. This friendliness is not a self-conscious duty so much as an instinct. A squatter in a cabin will share his scanty provender and never dream that he is doing anything unusual.

[9] HERACLITUS—Greek philosopher of about 500 B.C.

American hospitality, long as I have enjoyed it, still leaves me breathless. The lavishness with which a busy man will give up precious time to entertain a stranger to whom he is in no way bound remains for me one of the wonders of the world. No doubt this friendliness, since it is an established custom, has its fake side. The endless brotherhoods and sodalities into which people brigade themselves encourage a geniality which is more a mannerism than an index of character, a tiresome, noisy, back-slapping heartiness. But that is the exception, not the rule. Americans like company, but though they are gregarious they do not lose themselves in the crowd. Waves of mass emotion may sweep the country, but they are transient things and do not submerge for long the stubborn rock of individualism. That is to say, people can be led, but they will not be driven. Their love of human companionship is based not on self-distrust, but on a genuine liking for their kind. With them the sense of a common humanity is a warm and constant instinct and not a doctrine of the schools or a slogan of the hustings.

Lastly—and this may seem a paradox—I maintain that they are fundamentally modest. Their interest in others is a proof of it; the Aristotelian Magnificent Man was interested in nobody but himself. As a nation they are said to be sensitive to criticism; that surely is modesty, for the truly arrogant care nothing for the opinion of other people. Above all they can laugh at themselves, which is not possible for the immodest. They are their own shrewdest and most ribald critics. It is charged against them that they are inclined to boast unduly about those achievements and about the greatness of their country, but a smug glorying in them is found only in the American of the caricaturist. They rejoice in showing their marvels to a visitor with the gusto of children exhibiting their toys to a stranger, an innocent desire, without any unfriendly gloating, to make others partakers in their satisfaction. If now and then they are guilty of bombast, it is surely a venial fault. The excited American talks of his land very much, I suspect, as the Elizabethans in their cups talked of England. The foreigner who strayed into the Mermaid Tavern must often have listened to heroics which upset his temper.

The native genius, in humor, and in many of the public and private relations of life, is for overstatement, a high-colored, imaginative, paradoxical extravagance. The British gift is for understatement. Both are legitimate figures of speech. They serve the same purpose, for they call attention to a fact by startling the hearer, since manifestly they are not the plain truth. Personally I delight in both mannerisms and would not for the world have their possessors reject them. They serve the same purpose in another and subtler sense, for they can be used to bring novel and terrible things within the pale of homely experience. I remember on the Western Front in 1918 that two divisions, British and American, aligned side by side, suffered a heavy shelling. An American sergeant described it in racy and imaginative speech which would have been appropriate to the Day of Judgment. A British sergeant merely observed that "Kaiser 'ad been a bit 'asty." Each had a twinkle in his eye; each in his national idiom was making frightfulness endurable by domesticating it.

The United States is the richest, and, both actually and potentially, the most powerful state on the globe. She has much, I believe, to give to the world; indeed, to her hands is chiefly entrusted the shaping of the future. If democracy in the broadest and truest sense is to survive, it will be mainly because of her guardianship. For, with all her imperfections, she has a clearer view than any other people of the democratic fundamentals.

She starts from the right basis, for she combines a firm grip on the past with a quick sense of present needs and a bold outlook on the future. This she owes to her history; the combination of the British tradition with the necessities of a new land; the New England township and the Virginian manor *plus* the frontier. Much of that tradition was relinquished as irrelevant to her needs, but much remains: a talent for law which is not incompatible with a lawless practice; respect for a certain type of excellence in character which has made her great men uncommonly like our own; a disposition to compromise, but only after a good deal of arguing; an intense dislike of dictation. To these instincts the long frontier struggles added courage in the face of novelties, adaptability, enterprise, a doggedness which was never lumpish, but alert and expectant.

This is the historic basis of America's democracy, and today she is the chief exponent of a creed which I believe on the whole

to be the best in this imperfect world. She is the chief exponent
for two reasons. The first is her size; she exhibits its technique
in large type, so that he who runs may read. More important,
she exhibits it in its most intelligible form, so that its constitu-
ents are obvious. Democracy has become with many an unpleas-
ing parrot-cry, and, as I have urged elsewhere in this book, it is
well to be clear what it means. It is primarily a spiritual testament, from which certain political and economic orders naturally
follow. But the essence is the testament; the orders may change
while the testament stands. This testament, this ideal of citi-
zenship, she owes to no one teacher. There was a time when I
fervently admired Alexander Hamilton and could not away with
Jefferson; the latter only began to interest me, I think, after I
had seen the University of Virginia, which he created. But I
deprecate partisanship in those ultimate matters. The democratic testament derives from Hamilton as well as from Jefferson.

It has two main characteristics. The first is that the ordinary
man believes in himself and his ability, along with his fellows, to
govern his country. It is when a people loses its self-confidence
that it surrenders its soul to a dictator or an oligarchy. In Mr.
Walter Lippmann's tremendous metaphor, it welcomes manacles
to prevent its hands shaking. The second is the belief, which is
fundamental also in Christianity, of the worth of every human
soul—the worth, not the equality. This is partly an honest emotion, and partly a reasoned principle—that something may be
made out of anybody, and that there is something likeable about
everybody if you look for it—or, in canonical words, that ultimately there is nothing common or unclean.

The democratic testament is one lesson that America has to
teach the world. A second is a new reading of nationalism.
Some day and somehow the peoples must discover a way to
brigade themselves for peace. Now, there are on the globe only
two proven large-scale organizations of social units, the United
States and the British Empire. The latter is not for export, and
could not be duplicated; its strength depends upon a thousand-
year-old monarchy and a store of unformulated traditions. But
the United States was the conscious work of men's hands, and a
task which has once been performed can be performed again.
She is the supreme example of a federation in being, a federation

which recognizes the rights and individuality of the parts, but accepts the overriding interests of the whole. To achieve this compromise she fought a desperate war. If the world is ever to have prosperity and peace, there must be some kind of federation —I will not say of democracies, but of states which accept the reign of Law. In such a task she seems to me to be the predestined leader. Vigorous as her patriotism is, she has escaped the jealous, barricadoed nationalism of the Old World. Disraeli, so often a prophet in spite of himself, in 1863, at a critical moment of the Civil War, spoke memorable words:

> "There is a grave misapprehension, both in the ranks of Her Majesty's Government and of Her Majesty's Opposition, as to what constitutes the true meaning of the American democracy. The American democracy is not made up of the scum of the great industrial cities of the United States, nor of an exhausted middle class that speculates in stocks and calls that progress. The American democracy is made up of something far more stable, that may ultimately decide the fate of the two Americas and of 'Europe.'"

For forty years I have regarded America not only with a student's interest in a fascinating problem, but with the affection of one to whom she has become almost a second motherland. Among her citizens I count many of my closest friends; I have known all her presidents, save one, since Theodore Roosevelt, and all her ambassadors to the Court of Saint James since John Hay; for five years I have been her neighbor in Canada. But I am not blind to the grave problems which confront her. Democracy, after all, is a negative thing. It provides a fair field for the Good Life, but it is not in itself the Good Life. In these days when lovers of freedom may have to fight for their cause, the hope is that the ideal of the Good Life, in which alone freedom has any meaning, will acquire a stronger potency. It is the task of civilization to raise every citizen above want, but in so doing to permit a free development and avoid the slavery of the beehive and the antheap. A humane economic policy must not be allowed to diminish the stature of man's spirit. It is because I believe that in the American people the two impulses are of equal strength that I see her in the vanguard of that slow upward trend, undulant or spiral, which today is our modest definition of progress. Her major prophet is still Whitman. "Everything comes out of the dirt—everything; everything comes out of the people, everyday people, the people as you find them and leave them; people, people, just people!"

It is only out of the dirt that things grow.

DID YOU READ WITH UNDERSTANDING?

1. What were the first books that really interested John Buchan in America? Are you familiar with the works of those same authors? How much of their prose have you read? How does the author account for his interest in the American Civil War? Was he better informed about the War than most Americans are? Prove your answer. Why was he interested in visiting Valley Forge, the Shenandoah, and the Wilderness? What is the historical significance of the three names?

2. What was the author's first impression of American landscape? In what respects would it be an advantage to come into America first from eastern Canada? How many parts of the United States has the author visited? How does his first-hand information about our country compare with your own? What are the things that the author has enjoyed most in the American landscape? Explain his statement that most of the country seems to be, in a special sense "habitable." Why does he find American place names commendable? Illustrate.

3. What physical features does the author find to offset America's vastness? Explain the meaning of the following sentence: "The bigness of their country is for most Americans something to be learned and imaginatively understood, not a natural deduction from cohabiting with physical immensities." Find another sentence in the same paragraph that says the same thing with different words.

4. What are the racial characteristics of Americans? What is the meaning of *homogeneity?* Are we homogeneous or not? What destroyed the early preponderance of Anglo-Saxon stock? How do you think that came about? Discuss. Did Lord Tweedsmuir think it would be a good thing for Americans to have the close nationalism of the Scotch? Why or why not? What kind of class consciousness did the author find in America? What are the qualities that he enjoys most in Americans? Do you think that the characteristics he mentions really are typical of the people of the United States? Discuss. What kind of American does he not like? What two types does he like best of all?

5. What are our most serious faults as Lord Tweedsmuir saw them? Do you agree with him? Discuss. What are the opposite qualities of American and British humor? Why does the author say that these two opposite tendencies achieve the same effect?

6. What part must America play in the world of the future? Why? What important basic difference is there between English and American democracy? Why can the British type not be copied? Explain. What

are the two fundamental principles of the democratic idea? Explain
why one of them is the outcome of Christian philosophy.

7. Express in your own words the tribute which Lord Tweedsmuir has
paid America in his closing paragraph.

8. To what extent do you agree with Lord Tweedsmuir in his appraisal
of America—the country, her people, their government, and their responsibility for future progress of the human race? Discuss.

From IF JUDGMENT COMES

ALFRED NOYES

THE name of "War"
Is but a name today, a cheating cloak
For murder of the helpless multitude,
By monsters in high places. If the Right
5   Is Right, and worthy of honor among men
As Right, for ever, this crime must be brought home.
If not, the lesser murderers who die
Ten deaths a week, may with a dirty laugh
Wipe out the name of Justice.
10   There is no room
For "reparations" now. Who can repay
Those little children dead? What gold, what gear,
What boundary lines; what landmark re-removed?
Better that not one word of all these things
15   Be breathed on earth, and this one crime brought home;
That, in the sight of all men, for all time,
This crime be marked as crime, and men believe
Once more in Justice; men believe once more
In Right, believe no grasp of the machine
20   Seized by whatever cunning, can endow
The criminal with a power above the law
To order deaths by myriads, and to write
His name in "history," one of its "Great Men."

If others be found guilty, on your side,
25   *Or ours—or ours—*then, in the name of God

And Truth, the world must see this crime brought home.
This is no war for blind material things.
This war is fought along a world-wide front
Within the mind of man; and there can be
30   No victory now but on that field of thought.
Bombs, aeroplanes, and cannon fight as well
For falsehood as for truth. They are neutrals all.
Thought only can decide; and, on that field,
This world crime must be marked as crime for ever,
35   And ended, or man's world itself will end.

.   .   .   .

When man put out the lantern of the law
How many lights were quenched, the wide world round?
The ships were shadows, and on every sea
They hurried to dark harbors. Europe blacked
40   Her street-lamps, and the friendly window-lights
Were doubly blinded, even those lights of home.

Then, in that night, what hideous masquerade
Emerged from obscene kennels? Lust was there
Whinnying, "I am young, rose-breasted Joy";
45   And Hate was there, proclaiming, "I am Love";
And crapulous Vice and Madness, crowned with straw
Clamored, *Bow down and worship. We are New!*
Then Lie with drunken naked Lie linked hands,
And through the crumbling arches of the State
50   Danced on the graves of all those quiet dead
Who once had dared to dream that truth was true;
And lying statesmen, pandering to their hour,
Flattered the mode, and joined the dance of Death,
And Art and Letters mocked at their own toils,
55   And violently ran down their easier way
To Chaos and Corruption.

                                    Man had quenched
With his own hand, all lights that he could reach,
But not the stars in heaven, and not Thy Light,
60   O Liberty, nor Thine, whose unseen fire
Still burns on earth, the unfaltering altar-flame
Which tells of things eternal, worlds elsewhere.
Long has one cry come quivering through the dark:

206

A hundred times in this, our modern world,
65 *Millions have reeled upon the brink of war*
    By one man's evil will.
    Who shall deliver us from the cold machine
    That eats up millions by the will of one?
    Where is the true democracy?
70   Tonight
    There comes an answering voice from the New World:
    Christ never died for governments or laws.
    He did not die to build a nation up.
    He died for Men, the separate souls of Men.

FOR INTERPRETATION

1. Do you think Mr. Noyes's poem has been written for the first or the second World War? Cite lines to prove your answer. About what year do you think it was written? What kind of warfare, specifically, does it seem to protest?

2. Why does he say that *today* the "name of war is but a cloak for murder of the helpless multitude"? Has the same thing been true of wars in the past? Explain. Who do you think are "the lesser murderers" of line 7?

3. What kind of wrongs can the payment of "reparations" never repay? Explain. What specific *crime* do you think is being referred to in line 15 and following? Who do you think is the criminal of line 21? How has he "ordered death by myriads"?

4. Do you think that the poet would now say that there is guilt on *our* side and on *his?* Discuss.

5. Read carefully lines 27–30. Express the thought in simple prose. Study the next five lines. Express the thought in your own words.

6. Quote the lines in which the poet describes the black-outs of war. What crimes follow in the dark of the black-out? Are lines 42–56 literal or symbolic in their application? Explain. What single word may be used to name the thing suggested by the line, "Then Lie with drunken naked Lie linked hands"? Who are the dead "who once had dreamed that truth was true"?

7. What lights does the poet say man has not put out? What do you think is the burning, "still unfaltering altar-flame" on earth? What is the cry of the world? Why do you think the poet says the answer comes from the *New World?* What is the hope implied in the answer? Discuss. How do you think the poet feels about the hope for the world in 1943?

8. Do you think Mr. Noyes had a specific purpose in writing the poem? If so, what was it? Formulate a sentence which seems to you to express the theme of the poem.

THE END OF AN AGE

H. G. WELLS

The following selection is the first chapter from Mr. Wells's book, *The New World Order*, which came out in 1941. In "The End of an Age," the author gives a concise, factual account of the conditions which led up to the two world conflicts of the twentieth century. It is significant in these days when people everywhere are thinking about what will come "after the War." Any intelligent plan for a new world order must take into consideration the *old order* and why it has failed.

IN THIS small book I want to set down as compactly, clearly, and usefully as possible the gist of what I have learned about war and peace in the course of my life. I am not going to write peace propaganda here. I am going to strip down to their framework certain general ideas and realities of primary importance, and so prepare a nucleus of useful knowledge for those who have to go on with this business of making a world peace. I am not going to persuade people to say "Yes, yes," for a world peace; already we have had far too much abolition of war by making declarations and signing resolutions; everybody wants peace or pretends to want peace, and there is no need to add even a sentence more to the vast volume of such ineffective stuff. I am simply attempting to state the things we *must* do and the price we *must* pay for world peace if we really intend to achieve it.

Until the Great War, the first World War, I did not bother very much about war and peace. Since then I have almost specialized upon this problem. It is not very easy to recall former states of mind out of which, day by day and year by year, one has grown, but I think that in the decades before 1914 not only I but most of my generation—in the British Empire, America, France, and indeed throughout most of the civilized world— thought that war was dying out.

So it seemed to us. It was an agreeable and therefore a readily acceptable idea. We imagined the Franco-German War of 1870–1 and the Russo-Turkish War of 1877–8 were the final conflicts between great powers, that now there was a Balance of Power sufficiently stable to make further major warfare impracticable. A Triple Alliance faced a Dual Alliance and neither had much reason for attacking the other. We believed war was shrinking to mere expeditionary affairs on the outskirts of our civilization, a sort of frontier police business. Habits of tolerant intercourse, it seemed, were being strengthened every year that the peace of the powers remained unbroken.

There was indeed a mild armament race going on; mild by our present standards of equipment; the armament industry was a growing and enterprising one; but we did not see the full implication of that; we preferred to believe that the increasing general good sense would be strong enough to prevent these multiplying guns from actually going off and hitting anything. And we smiled indulgently at uniforms and parades and army maneuvers. They were the time-honored toys and regalia of kings and emperors. They were part of the display side of life and would never get to actual destruction and killing. I do not think that exaggerates the easy complacency of, let us say, 1895, forty-five years ago. It was a complacency that lasted with most of us up to 1914. In 1914 hardly anyone in Europe or America below the age of fifty had seen anything of war in his own country.

The world before 1900 seemed to be drifting steadily towards a tacit but practical unification. One could travel without a passport over the larger part of Europe; the Postal Union delivered one's letters uncensored and safely from Chile to China; money, based essentially on gold, fluctuated only very slightly; and the sprawling British Empire still maintained a tradition of free trade, equal treatment, and open-handedness to all comers round and about the planet. In the United States you could go for days and never see a military uniform. Compared with today that was, upon the surface at any rate, an age of easy-going safety and good humor. Particularly for the North Americans and the Europeans.

But apart from that steady, ominous growth of the armament industry there were other and deeper forces at work that were preparing trouble. The Foreign Offices of the various sovereign states had not forgotten the competitive traditions of the eighteenth century. The admirals and generals were contemplating with something between hostility and fascination the huger weapons the steel industry was gently pressing into their hands. Germany did not share the self-complacency of the English-speaking world; she wanted a place in the sun; there was increasing friction about the partition of the raw-material regions of Africa; the British suffered from chronic Russophobia [1] with regard to their vast appropriations in the East, and set themselves to nurse Japan into a modernized imperialist power; and also they "remembered Majuba"; [2] the United States were irritated by the disorder of Cuba and felt that the weak, extended Spanish possessions would be all the better for a change of management. So the game of Power Politics went on, but it went on upon the margins of the prevailing peace. There were several wars and changes of boundaries, but they involved no fundamental disturbance of the general civilized life; they did not seem to threaten its broadening tolerations and understandings in any fundamental fashion. Economic stresses and social trouble stirred and muttered beneath the orderly surfaces of political life, but threatened no convulsion. The idea of altogether eliminating war, of clearing what was left of it away, was in the air, but it was free from any sense of urgency. The Hague Tribunal [3] was established and there was a steady dissemination of the conceptions of arbitration and international law. It really seemed to many that the peoples of the earth were settling down in their

---

[1] RUSSOPHOBIA—Fear of Russia.

[2] MAJUBA—Majuba Hill in South Africa, the scene of a British defeat in 1881.

[3] HAGUE TRIBUNAL—The Permanent Court of Arbitration, created by the International Convention for the Pacific Settlement of International Disputes, adopted by the International Peace Conference of 1899.

various territories to a litigious [4] rather than a belligerent order. If there was much social injustice, it was being mitigated more and more by a quickening sense of social decency. Acquisitiveness conducted itself with decorum, and public-spiritedness was in fashion. Some of it was quite honest public-spiritedness.

In those days, and they are hardly more than half a lifetime behind us, no one thought of any sort of world administration. That patchwork of great powers and small powers seemed the most reasonable and practicable method of running the business of mankind. Communications were far too difficult for any sort of centralized world controls. *Around the World in Eighty Days,* when it was published seventy years ago, seemed an extravagant fantasy. It was a world without telephone or radio, with nothing swifter than a railway train or more destructive than the earlier types of H. E. shell. They were marvels. It was far more convenient to administer that world of the Balance of Power in separate national areas and, since there were such limited facilities for peoples to get at one another and do one another mischiefs, there seemed no harm in ardent patriotism and the complete independence of separate sovereign states.

Economic life was largely directed by irresponsible private businesses [5] and private finance, which, because of their private ownership, were able to spread out their unifying transactions in a network that paid little attention to frontiers and national, racial, or religious sentimentality. "Business" was much more of a world commonwealth than the political organizations. There were many people, especially in America, who imagined that "Business" might ultimately unify the world and governments sink into subordination to its network.

Nowadays we can be wise after the event and we can see that below this fair surface of things, disruptive forces were steadily gathering strength. But these disruptive forces played a comparatively small role in the world spectacle of half a century ago, when the ideas of that older generation, which still dominates our political life and the political education of its successors, were formed. It is from the conflict of those balance-of-

[4] LITIGIOUS—Legal; open to settlement by process of law.
[5] IRRESPONSIBLE PRIVATE BUSINESSES—That is, business enterprises not responsible to any one government; international organizations without governmental control.

power and private-enterprise ideas, half a century old, with these ever growing disruptive forces, that one of the main stresses of our time arises. These ideas worked fairly well in their period and it is still with extreme reluctance that our rulers, teachers, politicians, face the necessity for a profound mental adaptation of their views, methods, and interpretations to these disruptive forces that once seemed so negligible and which are now shattering their old order completely.

It was because of this belief in a growing good will among nations, because of the general satisfaction with things as they were, that the German declarations of war in 1914 aroused such a storm of indignation throughout the entire comfortable world. It was felt that the German Kaiser had broken the tranquility of the world club, wantonly and needlessly. The war was fought "against the Hohenzollerns." They were to be expelled from the club, certain punitive fines were to be paid, and all would be well. That was the British idea of 1914. This out-of-date war business was then to be cleared up once for all by a mutual guarantee by all the more respectable members of the club through a League of Nations. There was no apprehension of any deeper operating causes in that great convulsion on the part of the worthy elder statesmen who made the peace. And so Versailles and its codicils.

For twenty years the disruptive forces have gone on growing beneath the surface of that genteel and shallow settlement, and for twenty years there has been no resolute attack upon the riddles with which their growth confronts us. For all that period the League of Nations has been the opiate of liberal thought in the world.

Today there is war to get rid of Adolf Hitler, who has now taken the part of the Hohenzollerns in the drama. He too has outraged the club rules and he too is to be expelled. The war, the Chamberlain-Hitler War,[6] is being waged so far by the British Empire in quite the old spirit. It has learned nothing and forgotten nothing. There is the same resolute disregard of any more fundamental problem.

Still the minds of our comfortable and influential ruling-class people refuse to accept the plain intimation that their time is

---

[6] CHAMBERLAIN-HITLER WAR—This discussion was written while Chamberlain was still Prime Minister of England.

over, that the Balance of Power and uncontrolled business methods cannot continue, and that Hitler, like the Hohenzollerns, is a mere offensive pustule [7] on the face of a deeply ailing world. To get rid of him and his Nazis will be no more a cure for the world's ills than scraping will heal measles. The disease will manifest itself in some new eruption. It is the system of nationalist individualism and unco-ordinated enterprise that is the world's disease, and it is the whole system that has to go. It has to be reconditioned down to its foundations or replaced. It cannot hope to "muddle through" amiably, wastefully, and dangerously a second time.

World peace means all that much revolution. More and more of us begin to realize that it cannot mean less.

The first thing, therefore, that has to be done in thinking out the primary problems of a world peace is to realize this: that we are living in the end of a definite period of history, the period of the sovereign states. As we used to say in the eighties with ever increasing truth: "We are in an age of transition." Now we get some measure of the acuteness of the transition. It is a phase of human life which may lead, as I am trying to show, either to a *new way of living* for our species or else to a longer or briefer *dégringolade* [8] of violence, misery, destruction, death, and the extinction of mankind. These are not rhetorical phrases I am using here; I mean exactly what I say: the disastrous extinction of mankind.

That is the issue before us. It is no small affair of parlor politics we have to consider. As I write, in this moment, thousands of people are being killed, wounded, hunted, tormented, ill-treated, delivered up to the most intolerable and hopeless anxiety, and destroyed morally and mentally, and there is nothing in sight at present to arrest this spreading process and prevent its reaching you and yours. It is coming for you and yours now at a great pace. Plainly in so far as we are rational foreseeing creatures there is nothing for any of us now but to make this world-peace problem the ruling interest and direction of our lives. If we run away from it, it will pursue and get us. We have to face it. We have to solve it or be destroyed by it. It is as urgent and comprehensive as that.

---

[7] PUSTULE—Pimple.
[8] *Dégringolade*—A tumbling down; decline, or fall.

DID YOU READ WITH UNDERSTANDING?

1. How does Mr. Wells declare his intentions in the first paragraph—that is, what is to be the purpose of his book? What is he *not* trying to do? What do you consider the most important statement in the first paragraph? Quote it.

2. Describe briefly the *surface state of affairs* in the world from 1895 to 1900. What did people think about war? What important "symptom" did men overlook? Explain briefly the theory of "The Balance of Power." What were the Triple Alliance and the Dual Alliance? What agency for arbitrating international affairs had been established?

3. Mention the most uneasy forces that were working *beneath the surface;* for example, what European power was most dissatisfied with its status? What political distrusts flourished? Why did Great Britain encourage the growth of power in Japan? Explain why *international business,* even when privately owned, may prove a disrupting force in world affairs. Name some business firms—English or American—that have great world-wide organizations. To what extent were the causes of the first World War economic? To what extent have the causes of the second World War been economic? Explain.

4. What old habits of thinking does Mr. Wells say persist in circles of government and business? Is that condition as acute today as it was in 1940–41 when Mr. Wells wrote his book? Discuss. What are some of the old conceptions of politics, business, world organization, which the author thinks must go if civilization is to survive? Explain why world peace cannot be secured merely by disposing of the instigators and leaders of the present disturbance.

5. Do you agree with Mr. Wells in his statement that if some satisfactory new order for the world cannot be found, the future will result in the "disastrous extinction of mankind"? What do you consider the most significant statement in the last paragraph of the selection? Quote it.

6. The last chapter of *The New World Order* lists the author's suggestions for the bases of a lasting peace. You will find the chapter stimulating reading, and good for an extra-credit report and class discussion.

From THE WIND IS RISING

H. M. TOMLINSON

"Alas, yes! a whole world to remake. . . . For all is wrong and out of joint: the inward spiritual, and the outward economical. . . . As indeed . . . it is an old truth that wherever huge physical evil is, there as the parent and origin of it, has moral evil to a proportionate extent been."

Mr. Tomlinson has used these words from Carlyle's *The French Revolution* as preface to *The Wind Is Rising*, a thoughtful study of England and the present war. The chapters are a dozen dated essays extending from "Omens" (August 1939) through "The Battle of London" (September 1940) down to "A Year of It" (August 1941).

For a year England alone had been defending herself from the threat of invasion and the very possible reality of annihilation by air. And then, as Mr. Tomlinson puts it, "The *Mayflower* sailed east." America, not yet in the war, had nevertheless proposed to furnish lend-lease assistance. It was the first tangible evidence to England that the two English-speaking democracies might work together to extricate the world from the physical evil that had befallen it. His closing paragraphs, written in August 1941, are especially significant. To make connection with the earlier paragraphs a few selected sentences will suffice——

"A year ago we were alone. Aid was out of sight. Yet somehow aid has come, decisive as judgment. Whence came it? Well, whence come fellowship and generosity? Is there not a deal to be said after all in favor of simple faith? Sympathy had a chance to flow freely. A word did it." Mr. Tomlinson then continues——

THE ART of diplomacy, hitherto, has been devoted to the ancient game of crabbing. It studied to increase the odds. Its part in affairs has been a fastidious endeavor to check the vulgar circulation of life about the globe. For the advantage of human intercourse, it believed inhumanity to be highly beneficial. Now we have seen with what ease an enlightened statesman [1] can liberate the instinctive trust and good will of his fellows. It is with relief we see it is not more dead lumber we need piled up between us, but less. Since light is released, and we view each other better, let us make no mistake about it, as we did in 1919,[2] nor allow our politicals to make it.

In that year a door for the deliverance of men, found not without cost and difficulty, was opened, but at once shut. It was, in fact, slammed. The echoing finality in its bang depressed us into apathy. We retired, petulant and rather abusive, each to his old national designs within the jealous bounds of privilege. The consequence of that folly is our present preoccupation. Men perish daily, and in hosts, because of it. And it would be gentlemanly not to regard death and mutilation as an historical abstraction, distant, dry and innocuous, and no more disfiguring our own doorstep than the drainage of plague in Thibet. Blood can be

[1] ENLIGHTENED STATESMAN—President Roosevelt, who spoke the word that promised aid. [2] IN 1919—In drawing up the terms of the Versailles Treaty.

seen issuing, the desolation stinks, and the cries of personal agony are heard. Do not doubt that this infection, this poison from decaying life and labor, will enter our abodes and touch our bones. The fault will spread to its origin. Each one of us is answerable, and should accept. We had forgotten that democracy means us. Each is responsible for all. Cowardice in government is our own. The wheel comes full circle; and the wages of cynical indifference is death.

Another chance for us is here, after twenty wasted years, and this time it arises in urgency out of the tumult. That means, I suppose, it is a last chance, for one can but guess the date of another is in the Ides of March. If we lose it, then we are lost; it is as well to be plain, while there is time to save ourselves. The separating ocean is this day our communication, part of a common order, kept by two ensigns with one purpose, the safety of peaceful men. That is a rational act, when it benefits everybody but evil-doers. Exclusive privilege kept by guns is as spurious as plenary inspiration, but an agreed protection of commerce on international highways is as ordinary and necessary as a policeman on patrol; and is there no reason to safeguard our inheritance of the things of the spirit? But whether it be shop or temple, or both, if our peoples are of one mind about it, then their purpose is unassailable by any conspiracy of envy. And battle is but transient.

It has been my own emotion, so I suppose other travelers have felt it, but the sight of the American emblem in strange waters has always affected me as if it were next to my own flag. Do we not know, though we grudge admitting it, that this war, with its corrosion by substantial and mental filth from Shanghai to Bordeaux, would never have begun had others been aware that American and British ships, as sure as sun-up, would have orders for common action should any power hoist the skull and cross-bones? Of course we know it. Then why not admit it? Is not taking care that peace be kept an object suitable for intelligent men? Predatory rulers hungry for more control do not hesitate to take it, when confident they can hold it. What is the use of friendly peoples having a better ability, if they fear to use it till the ability is lost? The truth is, except to the atrabilious,[3] that by not doing what easily we could have done, we have allowed

[3] ATRABILIOUS—Melancholy.

the wilderness and pestilence to invade civilization and destroy culture over half the earth. Casuists could raise well-informed and intricate answers to that, and they will, for no man enjoys taking blame for what is bestial, but the direct minds of ploughman and mechanic, better used to observing cause and effect, will own to it that what we asked for we have.

What we have, what we see, is the murder of the life we knew. Let us keep the original salt in words for this. But there is far worse in it than murder. The very memory of what was good flies in the wind with the dust that was habitations and orchards, and the desert replaces the university. Even language decays. Men fear to use the right words, so the rot in the tongue speaks with the authority of disease, and names as Order the obliteration of the humanities. I know this European reality is unbelievable, because I am a witness, and it tangles and dismays all I had supposed was established by ancient law and custom as proper to man's sight and understanding. You know how the vagaries of a portentous dream make no sense, for though it appears to have formation and logic, the thing seen is outside space and time, with a significance somber and dubious.

The sights of this war are the same. You must doze off in a London shelter on a raid night to know that we are the shadows, and circumstance phantasmal. You arouse, puzzled by impossible chiaroscuro [4] in a confined space, smelling the smell of the grave, unbending with difficulty to overcome what perhaps is rigor mortis, while hearing the blaring of Tartarus.[5] The profile of a stranger, a kneeling girl—when did she descend to join us?—shows dimly, and she is laughing quietly. You hear her telling someone unseen that she woke, put up her hand, and felt the earth close to her nose. Did he hear her scream? She thought she was buried alive.

A man mutters. There is a space of silence, until come another series of volcanic bursts. The grave shudders. The girl still kneels, apparently in a shroud, and she is still laughing quietly, to herself now, or else sobbing, maybe both. The bass of the man mumbles, "Forget it." "I can't," she whispers, "I want to, can you find this pin at my throat?"

To make sure you are not underground for ever, you crawl up, and out. It is not easy. There is brilliant light without, but it is intermittent, alternating with blindness, and the tortuous upward way by which you arrived leaves you uncertain of direction. This is what used to be the open air. Here you are again. Nothing can be made of it. Uncertain lights disclose momentary shapes you do not recognize. You stand amid flashes from nowhere, as if numerous metallic doors were opening continuously to release a subterranean incandescence, and were thundering back on their hinges to be at once burst open again. It is London and its guns. A red glare far away holds in one area a tier of clouds. There is a groaning out of night that increases to an overwhelming roar. You have no time to dive underground, but the bombs erupt some streets away. You thought it was your knees that shook, and do not blame yourself, but it was only the earth in repugnance.

The first sight of the scene under the sun next morning rebukes you. Then it was but a nightmare? No. It is advisable not to go into that doubt. Explore it, and you may uncover enough to perplex views that you had supposed would abide all questions. There was a shipping parish I knew, and its past, somehow, was mine. I had felt myself actual there with the adventurous days of the great trading companies, the frigates and the clippers. I

[4] CHIAROSCURO—A picture in lights and shades.
[5] THE BLARING OF TARTARUS—The combined noises of an air attack—motors, bombs, sirens, and the like. The Greeks believed Tartarus was the place of punishment for the dead.

went into that place recently, having a doubt. Home and school had been there; but soon I saw I need not look for them. These my familiar ways? I was appalled. "And the places that knew him, shall know him no more." But how if he remain, and the places not? What then? It is a reversal of the natural. Or perhaps centuries had trafficked past while I was quiet, and I was only a ghost returned to wander among the relics of a forgotten life. Here I could see that the work of mortals, and the things they love, cannot be kept by affection. The dust will have them. There must be more ghosts in London than ever, now, wandering unseen and alone, seeking what they knew, but will never find.

It will not bear thinking about, not yet. Dolors must ease, and the mind be at rest. Reconciliation takes time. Meanwhile, as a beginning, I am trying to be a forgiving man. It is necessary to forgive before we begin to think anew, and there is much to forgive. For one thing, one hard to forgive, do you see the reason why so much of Europe is ashes and shambles? The reason is simple. It has nothing to do with politics, imperialism, economic necessity, living space, nor any of the muddles which fine theories declare land us in conflict; nothing at all. It is simply because in all European communities except one there was no will to war. That is the reason. Our fault was that we were peaceable; and worse, that we let it be known. Our enemy's confidence that he could take what he wanted came not of his strength. It came of his knowledge that his neighbors were so humane that they shrank from violence. He thereupon made greater uproar with his ironmongery to shock them. He saw they were reluctant to fight. They had had enough of that—too much of it; and he invested in Europe's horror of more dead bodies.

His neighbors, for their part, persuaded themselves that it was safe to dismiss as an orgy of self-indulgence this new outbreak of German glory. It would pass with exhaustion. They hoped, therefore, they believed, that those melancholic processional hordes with banners, trumpets and drums meant no more than that the Germans across the road were enjoying themselves in the way Germans oddly prefer. Most of us had weakened, too, in an old faith, had all but lost it, though Thor lived on. We had forgotten that god,[6] with the rest of divinity. Hitler knew that he and his like had caught everybody else at a juncture in human

---

[6] WE HAD FORGOTTEN THAT GOD—Thor, in Teutonic mythology, was the thunderer, the god of war.

progress when we were irresolute while considering what we had better do with our earth, so vastly improved by new knowledge, yet worsened for men. While we hesitated, with more concern for welfare than for war, the Nazis struck; their tribes erupted, and smoke was billowing from their line of march. It is hard to forgive murder and destruction made the easier through using the natural trust men have that decent instincts are shared by all.

The pattern in events is emerging. This war, we see now, transcends the defense of democratic institutions. It is above self-interest and national interest. It has no concern with frontiers. All social, economic and political divisions, the miserable signs of personal and national ascendancy, have vanished since it is manhood itself that is threatened. Monarchs, hierarchs, presidents and premiers come down in it to the same choice as the nobodies. Their souls are no more valuable, and that is the simple value which must be defended or go. This challenge is to manhood. This war is the last phase of the war which began in 1914, and is for mastership or fellowship, as was prophesied long ago.

Who is for the fellowship? Whether or not our earth, when this tribulation is past, will become the place which the dreams of good men have told us it could be, at least here we are, free to make it so, if we will it, free to decide whether we shall be subject to the gun, instead of keeping to the order to which men have attained, and to pursue our quest of the city not made with hands.

All the doors of the mind are open. There is no return. It is too late for regrets, reproaches, recriminations and recourse to precedent. The past has lost arguments, claims and privileges. We have no power to go back. There is no authority now but the trifling voice of conscience. And what is conscience, without fealty to our neighbor? The Chinaman dying in his unseen mountain, the Russian peasant on his prairie, watching his home burn, are our neighbors, and to be aware of that, in full understanding that one's own body is hurt, is a release of the spirit with greater power for good than is in all the systems of politics. We have lived a century, and witnessed its events, since last August.

DID YOU READ WITH UNDERSTANDING?

1. What was the "door for the deliverance of men" that was opened and shut in 1919? Explain. What are the results of having "slammed

the door"? What first-hand experiences account for the author's distressing vividness of detail in the second paragraph? Death, he says, is the wages of *what?*

2. What does he mean when he says that now we are facing our *last chance?* Explain the reference to the Ides of March. What are the two "ensigns" referred to in the third paragraph? Notice how the fourth paragraph develops this same thought.

3. What is the difference between "exclusive privilege kept by guns" and "agreed protection of commerce on international highways"? Discuss. What two motives for Anglo-American cooperation are implied by the words, "whether it be *shop* or *temple"?*

4. Who does the author say is responsible for the destruction of culture in Europe? Does he consider England blameless? Discuss.

5. Describe the scene inside an air-raid shelter during a night raid. Describe the raid as it appears to one above the ground. What changes have the raids made in the permanent landscape of England? What place, dear to the author, has been destroyed?

6. What is the task the author sets himself as he looks ahead to the end of the war? Why is it a hard task? What does he say made it possible for Germany to attack so destructively? Has America, since his writing, suffered a somewhat similar experience for the same reason?

7. For what purpose does he believe this war is being fought? Do you agree with his opinion? Why or why not? What opportunity does he say is ours? Who are our neighbors in the enterprise? In what respects was the year from August 1940 to August 1941 the most difficult period England had ever experienced?

8. Does Mr. Tomlinson seem to face the issues of the war squarely? Is he pessimistic or hopeful of the outcome? Discuss. To what extent do you agree with his conclusions? Discuss.

RECESSIONAL

RUDYARD KIPLING

Written just before the end of the nineteenth century at the time England, at the height of power, was celebrating a Diamond Jubilee for Queen Victoria—Kipling's "Recessional" has nevertheless a deep significance today. Some of the things the hymn foresees have already come to pass. Others may yet be fulfilled—and they are not happy predictions. But it is still not too late for English-speaking nations to remember the conditions under which any people may remain great. The thinking people of Britain today breathe Kipling's invocation with renewed sincerity—

"Lord God of Hosts, be with us yet,
Lest we forget—lest we forget!"

GOD of our fathers, known of old,
  Lord of our far-flung battle-line,
Beneath whose awful hand we hold
  Dominion over palm and pine—
5 Lord God of Hosts, be with us yet,
  Lest we forget—lest we forget!

The tumult and the shouting dies;
  The Captains and the Kings depart
Still stands Thine ancient sacrifice,
10 An humble and a contrite heart.
Lord God of Hosts, be with us yet,
  Lest we forget—lest we forget!

Far-called our navies melt away;
  On dune and headland sinks the fire;
15 Lo, all our pomp of yesterday
  Is one with Nineveh and Tyre!
Judge of the nations, spare us yet,
  Lest we forget—lest we forget!

If, drunk with sight of power, we loose
20 Wild tongues that have not Thee in awe,
Such boasting as the gentiles use
  Or lesser breeds without the Law—
Lord God of Hosts, be with us yet,
  Lest we forget—lest we forget!

25 For heathen heart that puts her trust
  In reeking tube and iron shard,
All valiant dust that builds on dust,
  And guarding calls not Thee to guard,
For frantic boast and foolish word—
30 Thy mercy on Thy people, Lord!

10. AN HUMBLE AND A CONTRITE HEART—See Psalms 51:17.
16. NINEVEH AND TYRE—Nineveh was the capital of ancient Assyria. Tyre
was a wealthy and powerful city of the ancient Phoenicians.
21. GENTILES—Here used in its original sense of "outsider"; the implication
being that the nation itself is guilty of the boasting which it ascribes to other
nations.
26. REEKING TUBE—Smoking tub barrel.
26. IRON SHARD—Shell fragment.

FOR INTERPRETATION

1. What two expressions from the first stanza of "Recessional" suggest the extent of Britain's empire? Who, does the poet say, is the actual ruler? What do you think Kipling fears his country may *forget*? See if the succeeding stanzas help suggest an answer.

2. What particular *tumult* and *shouting* is being referred to in the second stanza? What general meaning may be attached to lines 7 and 8? Explain the significance of the next two lines. They are a reference to what part of what book?

3. At the time of the Jubilee, signal fires were lighted on the headlands all around Great Britain so that the island was encircled with a symbolic ring of flame. At the time of the "Recessional" the fires are pictured as dying down. At the same time the fleets and armies that had come from all parts of the world are returning to their stations and the visiting dignitaries are leaving. What do Nineveh and Tyre (l. 16) represent? What positions did they once hold? What happened to them? What connection does the poet imply between England and these ancient capitals? What sort of omen does the poet attach to the dying of the headland fires? Why?

4. What danger lurks in overconfidence? Do you think the danger is as great to nations as to individuals? Suggest some illustrations from recent history. With what words does the poet warn against overconfidence? The Jews prided themselves on being the Lord's "Chosen People." Outsiders, or "gentiles" were considered with contempt. Has there been a similar attitude on the part of the English toward the rest of the world? on the part, in fact, of white men in general? What warning is implied throughout the fourth stanza?

5. May a "Christian" people have a *heathen* heart? Discuss. Great nations have a tendency to trust in what? Of whom has England considered herself the guardian? On whom does she need to depend for her own protection? For what national sins does she need forgiveness? What is the poet's closing prayer?

6. With what feelings do you think Kipling saw England drawn into the first World War? What personal loss did he suffer in it? With what feelings would Kipling have watched the progress of the second War— if he were alive? Is it of any advantage for a man to have prophetic foresight? Discuss. Selections in this third group of contemporary literature disclose the fact that many men, especially writers, foresee issues clearly. How can men in general learn to profit by such vision? Or must civilization forever plunge down hill, after reaching the summit, forever disregarding the prophets? Discuss.

EXTENDED ACTIVITIES

ENGLISHMEN ARE TRUE TO TRADITIONS OF COURAGE AND RIGHT

HOW LITERATURE REFLECTS THE TIMES

MODERN BRITISHERS HAVE FACED THE TEST OF TWO WARS

Although the death of Queen Victoria in 1901 marked the end of an age—an age of glory for the old Empire—there was some carry-over into the next reign. As Prince of Wales, Edward had made himself acquainted with every part of the domain; as king, he continued to build up good will not only in British territory but with all the important nations of the world. But rumors of unrest were stirring, and four years after the accession of George V (1910) the impossible had happened—Europe was at war. Germany's violation of Belgium in 1914 was the signal for England to take up arms. And British troops from all over the world took the field.

The first World War left deeper scars in Europe than most Americans realize. For England the war had meant four bitter years of trench warfare on the Continent, of open fighting in the Near East, of struggles against submarines, and a first taste of aerial combat. It was four times as long a stretch of active engagement as America suffered; it was much closer home, and it was on a much larger scale. For four years England was drained of her young men. Month after month these endured bombardment, living in mud and filth. They accepted bloodshed and death as their daily lot. The war in France was a prolonged misery never to be erased from the minds and souls of those who suffered it. And of course thousands upon thousands died. Acres of white crosses marked the fields of Flanders and France. When the war was won for England, it was because "her youngest, best, and bravest died."

The conflict etched itself deep in the literature, especially in the poetry. Some of the young men, like Wilfred Owen and Rupert Brooke, wrote a few deathless lyrics—and died. Some, like Sassoon, brought their hurt and bitterness back to a land that seemed to forget at what cost peace had been won. Much of England's best verse in the ten years following the Armistice was a protest against the post-war reaction of gaiety and unconcern. Fiction, too, presented a generation of "flappers" and "lounge lizards." Galsworthy's later novels, for example, like *The White Monkey* and *The Silver Spoon,* show a generation that seems pretty thin stock in contrast with the older Forsytes.

But the peace proved only an interlude. By 1939, England was in it again—this time for her very life. The fears of her writers had been realized. Ruling statesmen saw it almost too late. But the British heritage is strong. The carelessness and sophistication of the post-war years were surface matters. Young men again proved themselves indomitable fighters, this time in a frenzied mechanized fighting removed from trench and dug-out to the "footless halls of air." Again from every part of the Empire came reinforcements while Great Britain defended her homeland and carried on active warfare on far-spread fronts.

Since 1939 practically everything in English literature has been concerned with the war. There is literature of all types—stories, novels, articles, sketches, biographies—and of course, poems. The war stories are particularly good, in the new terse style. The themes involve problems of the home-front—ration books, evacuees, lack of help, defense work— and all the acute situations of actual warfare. The settings may be in bomb shelters or army camps, aboard mine-sweeper or submarine, or— more often than not—above the clouds. Non-fiction includes everything from sketch to book-length on the war itself, on pre-war causes, and post-war plans. Some of the literature will live. Today we are too close to judge with assurance. But the conflict cuts deep into the tissue of English life. When the scars have healed, England hopes they will mark an operation that has really cured some of the ills of mankind.

FOR ACQUAINTANCE WITH AUTHORS

"BARTIMEUS" (LEWIS A. D. RICCI) (1886–   )—"THE BEACHES OF DUNKIRK"

Under the pen name of Bartimeus, the name of the blind beggar who sat by the gate of Jericho, a former captain in the Royal Navy has written stories of the heroism of this war and the first. Since he was fifteen, Captain Ritchie, as he now spells his name, has known little but England's ships and her seamen. After two years on the training ship *Britannia,* he put to sea as a midshipman. During the first war he served under Jellicoe in the Grand Fleet against Germany and was made a Chevalier of the Legion of Honor. Years later, following fever, he lost the sight of one eye and was transferred to the accountancy branch of the Navy. It is in this branch as Paymaster that he has watched this war. He feels it his job "to publish abroad the virtues, the valor, and the peculiarities of a class of men deeply desirous of remaining out of the limelight," and he has accomplished his job with rare humor and sympathy.

HUGH BRODIE (D. 1943)—"A SERGEANT'S PRAYER"

A member of the Royal Australian Air Force and a former student at Melbourne University, Hugh Brodie was reported missing in action early in 1943.

WINSTON LEONARD SPENCER CHURCHILL (1874–   )—"THE WAR OF THE UNKNOWN WARRIORS"

The most important man in England during the trying period that followed the fall of France was the new Prime Minister, Winston Churchill. Succeeding Neville Chamberlain at a time when the country seemed on the brink of disaster, Churchill accepted the challenge and set to work with astonishing zest. He was well equipped for the task. He comes of an illustrious British family, the House of Marlborough. His father, Lord Henry Randolph Churchill, himself a statesman and writer, had married an American girl; and Winston combines a certain Yankee vigor and forthrightness with good English sense and stability. He was educated at two good schools. Then at the age of twenty-one he entered the army. During the Boer War, from 1899 until 1902, he was a press correspondent in Africa. When he entered politics it was as a Liberal; but the Cabinet he organized in 1940 was Conservative. He has a natural aptness with words. Since he has assumed office, his words have been a power in England—in fact, in the world. He has supplemented his speeches with energetic, well-directed action, and is proving a capable, intelligent leader.

He is the author of a number of books. His collected speeches are of special interest to Americans. *While England Slept* contains his speeches on national defense and foreign policy from 1932 to 1938; *Blood, Sweat, and Tears* is a collection dating from May 1938 to February, 1941; and *The Unrelenting Struggle* brings the story up to date.

WALTER DE LA MARE (1873–   )—"PEACE"

For the story of Walter de la Mare's life, see the EXTENDED ACTIVITIES for Unit I-II.

ROBERT GRAVES (1895–   )—"HATE NOT, FEAR NOT"

Encouraged by his superior officer, Siegfried Sassoon, Robert Graves first wrote poetry seriously during his period of service with the Royal Welsh Fusiliers in World War I. Wounded late in 1917, he returned to England, determined on a career and free of all his early boyish indifference. The war had come just as he was about to enter Oxford, but he decided he would win a degree anyway. It was 1926 before he finished at St. John's College and none of the years had been easy. Gradually, his name won attention in magazines and bookstalls; his verse gained depth and power. Before the Spanish Civil War he conducted the Seizen Press on the island of Majorca, bringing out his own work and that of other left-wing moderns. In 1934 he won the Hawthornden and James Tait Black prizes for his historical novel of Roman civilization, *I, Claudius*. Like many other modern writers he has been profoundly discouraged by the outbreak of the second World War, convinced for the time being of "the certainty of the despair of life."

THOMAS HARDY (1840–1928)—"THE MAN HE KILLED"

The story of Thomas Hardy's life is told in the EXTENDED ACTIVITIES of Unit I-I.

A. E. HOUSMAN (1859–1936)—"HERE DEAD WE LIE," "I DID NOT LOSE MY HEART"

The story of A. E. Housman's life is told in the EXTENDED ACTIVITIES of Unit I-I.

RUDYARD KIPLING (1865–1936)—"FOR ALL WE HAVE AND ARE," "RECESSIONAL"

A biography of Rudyard Kipling may be found in the EXTENDED ACTIVITIES of Unit I-II.

ALFRED NOYES (1880–   )—"IF JUDGMENT COMES"

Today Alfred Noyes is more often taken for a prosperous business man than a poet, perhaps because he has never known the years of hardship and failure that are common to most poets. His first published poem, "Drake," appeared serially in a British magazine and was awaited as eagerly as a popular novel. All his succeeding work was enthusiastically welcomed because he writes for the ordinary lover of poetry, simple narratives in steady, insistent, musical rhythms. His *Tales of the Mermaid Tavern,* personalized stories of the Elizabethans, enjoyed a wide sale. For several years he lectured at Harvard and Princeton, resigning to take a post in the British  Foreign Office during the World War I. Since the war his work has been colored by his conversion to Catholicism with the result that he has added theological discussion, history, and biography to the long list of his works.

WILFRED OWEN (1893–1918)—"APOLOGIA PRO POEMATE MEO"

Wilfred Owen was shot as he crossed the Sambre Canal at the head of his company one week before the armistice of World War I. He was twenty-five years old, and virtually unknown at his death. He belongs with the brave company of Marlowe, Keats, Brooke, and Synge who died before their best work had even been dreamed.

Wilfred Owen was a poet from childhood, a dreamy precocious child who worshiped the cult of Keats. He enlisted immediately after the outbreak of the war and served in the front lines until his health failed. Transferred to a hospital in Edinburgh, he met Siegfried Sassoon who encouraged him and helped him find a market for his verse, which like Sassoon's was preoccupied with the horror and futility of war. Just as his work began to acquire some reputation, he was sent back again to the front lines where he won the Military Cross for gallantry under fire before his death. Sassoon supervised the editing of his volume of poems which appeared in 1920—poems which though often fragmentary had as their single theme Owen's bitterness toward war and its evils.

SIEGFRIED SASSOON (1886–   )—"DREAMERS," "AFTERMATH"

Sassoon is one of the few war poets of World War I fortunate to live through that violent debacle in which the best of England's young men were lost. Since then, he has never ceased to write with brutal realism

of war. At Cambridge in the early nineteen-hundreds Sassoon was more interested in poetry, hunting, and tennis than in studies; and was "sent down" before graduation. He had already published a volume of verse reminiscent in style of Masefield's early work but lacking in power and genuineness. The war made of him a pacifist and a true poet. After his enlistment and commission he served four years, was wounded twice, won the Military Cross, and emerged a captain. Utter desolation was his only personal reaction. In 1917 when he was invalided home, he threw his Military Cross in the sea and announced publicly that he would serve no longer. Already his vicious war poetry had caused some stir in England; military authorities declared him temporarily insane, sent him to Palestine, and in a few months Sassoon returned to France again.

After the war and its subsequent glorifying of peace, Sassoon's bitter exposure of the horror of trench warfare was accepted. In 1928 he published anonymously the *Memoirs of a Fox-Hunting Man,* which was eventually recognized as his own fictionalized autobiography. Sassoon's literary violence is in contrast to his own peaceable, friendly nature; he lives quietly with his wife in Wiltshire, enjoys his writing successes and turns to reading and music for recreation.

H. M. TOMLINSON (1873–   )—"THE WIND IS RISING"

Propinquity to ships does not always make a sailor. Henry Major Tomlinson was born near the docks of London, and had his first job in a shipping office on the wharves; but it was not until he was a newspaper man that he went on his first voyage. Since that first trip up the Amazon, which he described in *The Sea and the Jungle,* he has visited other far-away places.

"I had been scribbling since a child and judiciously burning it all," he has written; and in 1904, tiring of the routine of his shipping-office job,

he exchanged it for a position on *The Morning Leader,* a newspaper to which he had been contributing articles. When that paper merged with *The Daily News,* Tomlinson continued with the second daily. The paper sent him on his voyage up the Amazon, and in 1914 sent him as war correspondent to France and Belgium. From 1915 to 1917 he was Official Staff Correspondent, attached to headquarters of the British Armies in France. Tomlinson said that "war was no inspiration, only horror"; however, out of his experiences have grown two books, *Waiting for Daylight,* and the novel, *All Our Yesterdays.* A second book of travels is *Tidemarks,* in which he has recorded a trip through the Malay Archipelago. In the opening years of the second World War he wrote the essays which form the chapters of *The Wind Is Rising.* Of his success, Mr. Tomlinson has admitted modestly, "It's all so accidental. It just happened in spite of me."

LORD TWEEDSMUIR (JOHN BUCHAN) (1875–1940)—"MY AMERICA"

Typical of the restless energy symbolic of the twentieth century, John Buchan's life was crowded with politics, writing, big business, and statesmanship. From a boyhood which he boasted was "one of the idlest on record" he plunged into Oxford scholastic life, won prizes for his verse and essays, honors for his scholarship, and was elected President of the Union in his last year. He was soon successful as a lawyer, but one profession seemed never enough for him. He tried his hand at editorial writing, became a partner in a publishing house and then in his spare moments dashed off some glorious adventure stories, *Thirty-Nine Steps* and *Prester John* among them. His position as Director of the huge Reuter Press Agency was still not enough; during World War I he became Director of Information in England, a job which furnished the source material for his later history of the war. From 1927 almost to his death he was equally active in Parliament and literature. His public life left him only brief periods for writing, but he turned out a vast amount of copy, his biographies of Caesar and Cromwell among the best. His final achievement came in 1935 when he was named Governor-General of Canada and elected to the peerage.

H. G. WELLS (1866–   )—"THE END OF AN AGE"

Perhaps the most significant illustration of Wells's power as a writer lies in the national panic caused by Orson Welles's dramatization of H. G.'s book, *The War of the Worlds,* in 1938. Or perhaps it lies in the sale of two million copies of his four-volume *Outline of History.* Or perhaps in the fact that although a writer in the Victorian Age, he has managed to retain an enthusiastic audience well into the twentieth century. In any case, the taut little Englishman with the bright eyes and twitchy moustache

who described himself in his mock obituary as "one of the most prolific literary hacks of his time" has a prodigious number of well-thumbed volumes to his credit.

The son of a professional cricketer and a lady's maid, Wells has never forgotten his origin; he writes of and champions the lower middle class. All his schooling he acquired through his own diligence. At the Midhurst Grammar School his scholarship was such that the master wanted to make him his assistant. At London University he took honors in biology and might have remained a working scientist had his health not collapsed while writing a biology textbook. During his convalescence he tried journalism and his fingers have been smudged with printer's ink ever since.

Since 1895 he has published something better than a book a year. His first books were fascinating pseudo-scientific stories like *The Time Machine* and *In the Days of the Comet*. Their success led him to try more serious fiction—realistic novels with a social slant like *Tono-Bungay* and *Ann Veronica*. More recently someone has said that "he has set up shop as a prophet" and the result is a series of novels advertising his social and political theories. Since the beginning of the second World War he has become a thorough pessimist, but mercurial as is his temperament and his skill, the post-war period may find him writing any one of a dozen things.

OF LITERARY FORM AND STYLE

A SAMPLING OF WAR LITERATURE—MODERN STYLE

In presenting selections of literature representative of the second World War, on the field and at home, it is possible only to indicate current trends in form and style.

The verse shows, on the whole, no striking differences in form from the poetry of the first World War which has been discussed briefly in the section "How Literature Reflects the Times." But there is considerable difference in detail and also in attitude or point of view. There is less of protest against the misery of war. The misery is there; but they accept it with a feeling of consecration to duty and compelling necessity. It is a high type of courage to which Hugh Brodie gives expression in "A Sergeant's Prayer"——

> "The vast unalterable way
> From which the stars do not depart
> May not be turned aside to stay
> The bullet flying to my heart."

There is a realization of eternal values that are at stake. There is no bravado. Often there is no personal hate for the enemy. There is, instead, a determination to do a job that has to be done. Personal issues are submerged in a crisis of human destinies. The poets are expressing this spirit of devotion.

Of material for fiction there is no lack. Finding a suitable plot is the last thing to trouble the story-writer. With melodrama—in the flesh—the order for living, all the writer needs is the time and the knack of putting it down. The human angle of civilian bombing, the *comraderie* of air-raid shelters, the quiet British efficiency that turned Dunkirk from catastrophe to heroic miracle—here is material for thousands of tales. Some of them are getting written. The style of telling is usually swift, convincing narrative. It sounds true because it is. And the writer trims down his words because the story itself is so big.

One of the great factors in English morale is her faith in the leadership of Winston Churchill and his staff. The personality of the man is one to inspire confidence. He is a thinker, a speaker, and a doer. Much of the non-fiction prose is colored by his personality—either in his own picturesque words or in lifelike representations of him. Philip Guedalla has written a recent biography of Mr. Churchill; but the power and force of the Prime Minister are easily apparent even in short selections from his own work. His radio broadcasts were of immeasurable value in building up British morale in the summer and fall of 1940. As his biographer has said, he told the British people what they already believed and thus made them believe it all the more firmly. He has been peculiarly the spokesman of his nation.

QUESTIONS IN APPRECIATION:

War Poetry

1. Does "For All We Have and Are" sound like other Kipling poems that you know? Why or why not? Is it a poem likely to give a lift to national morale? Discuss. Which lines make a good war slogan? Why? Why do you think Kipling has used short words and short, hard lines? To what extent do you think the poem representative of English philosophy and personality?

2. How can you tell that "Dreamers" is a sonnet? (See *Appendix*.) Is the subject appropriate for the sonnet form? Why or why not? Which do you think is the most poetically significant line of the sonnet? Why? Can you tell why it is effective in this particular to have the closing lines mention such inconsequential things as *spats*, and *going to the office in the train?* Discuss.

3. What is there unusual about the form of "Apologia Pro Poemate Meo"? Describe the stanza pattern Owen has used. What is its poetic effect? To what poem of this section does it offer the sharpest contrast in mood? How do you account for the differences between the two

lyrics? How does the poem make the reader feel about war? With what thoughts or details has the poet secured this effect?

4. Which of the three lyrics "Hate Not, Fear Not," "The Man He Killed," and "I Did Not Lose My Heart" expresses an abstract principle, abstractly? Which one suggests a similar principle by relating a single incident and its *emotional effect?* Which one relates an incident illustrative of the same thought, with the speaker pondering about it *in his own mind?* Which one of the three poems makes the strongest appeal to you? Why? Which one do you think is most *poetic?* Discuss.

5. Does "Here Dead We Lie," brief as it is, create a definite poetic mood? How does it make the reader feel? Do you think it is more or less effective than other poems in the group as the expression of an attitude about war? Discuss. What special name is given to a four-line poem? Check with "Poetic Forms" in the *Appendix* if you do not know.

6. In what two-fold sense does the subject "peace" apply in the sonnet by de la Mare? Quote lines which suggest the cost at which peace was obtained. How has the poet achieved the effect of climax in the closing lines of the sonnet? Why was the sonnet a good form to use for this lyric? How does this peace-time poem differ in thought, attitude, and mood from the war-time poems you have just been reading?

7. Show how "Aftermath" develops, in a different way, the same theme as de la Mare's "Peace." Would you say one poem is more effective than the other? Or are they both effective, but in different ways?

8. Why is the simple stanza form of "A Sergeant's Prayer" appropriate to the thought of the poem? Which lines of the poem show dignity and strength? What is the poetic effect of the last stanza?

"The War of the Unknown Warriors"

1. What was the occasion and what was the purpose of Mr. Churchill's speech? Show how his opening sentences are fitted to the day itself and to recent events.

2. What in his speech would especially appeal to Britishers within the island? What would appeal to Englishmen in the Dominions and Colonies? What sort of impression would such a speech be likely to make in the United States? Why?

3. Why is Mr. Churchill's address easy to understand? What makes it impressive? Why may this radio address be considered a piece of English *literature?* Discuss.

"The Beaches of Dunkirk"

1. Is the story-telling technique in "The Beaches of Dunkirk" somewhat similar to that used in "England Is My Village"? Discuss. Is the story told entirely from the point of view of one character? Explain.

2. Is the girl the principal character? How do you judge? Why is she not given a name? Would you have been more interested in the story

if she and her soldier in France had been given names? Why or why not? Why are we not given more information about her?

3. Notice how the author has speeded up the action of the story by passing from one scene to another (for instance, from the club house to the dock) without transition sentences. Point out another instance of the sort. Is there any resulting difficulty in following the story? What other devices give the story rapid action? Point out at least two examples of what you consider good writing.

4. What do you think was the author's purpose in telling this particular story? Express its theme in a single sentence. Does the story sound as if it might be true? Why or why not?

CURRENT NON-FICTION IS WORLD-MINDED

It is not enough to say that current non-fiction in Britain is serious minded. It is world-minded. The best writers in England are concerned immediately with the war. Again England is within the theater of operations; for a time, even, she had the center of the stage. In the previous war, for four years she heard the continuous rumble of guns across the channel. This time her home ground has taken a terrific strafing. She has had enough of the bombings to know what modern war means in terms of civilian slaughter. And knowing, she is concerned as never before to do the right things to stop it and if possible to prevent its coming again. She has learned from experience that it is not enough after the fighting to let the victor take care of himself. No, somehow the winner has to help make things right for the world. It is no easy task, men admit; and so they are trying first to get acquainted with the world.

A look at recent magazine material and at the lists of non-fiction (and incidentally good *non*-fiction tops the best-seller records today) indicates, first of all that England and America are really getting together. And that it is not just in military action but in actual understanding and good will. There are many contributing factors. For one thing, England's prime minister is an Anglo-American. From his American mother he has inherited a Yankee forthrightness that suits us well. He is a good talker, and he includes us in his circle of listeners. He does it in neighborly fashion, and what is unusual with Britishers, he does it without condescension. There are other men who do almost equally well as ambassadors of good will. Lord Tweedsmuir, the late Governor-General of Canada was one of them. He was moved by a genuine interest in the United States. He got acquainted with us. He actually read our histories; and then he came to see us, not once, but many times. Out of solid understanding were born respect and liking. In his autobiography he is generous in his appreciation of his neighbor across the border.

Before the 1939 outbreak, most good British writers got to the United States at least once, if not for any other reason, to supervise the Hollywood filmings of their smash hits. In more ways than one, the movie industry has become an internationalizing influence. And so writers like

James Hilton and Noel Coward and Jan Struther and P. G. Wodehouse came to America. They lived with us. They got acquainted; and of course they liked us. Jan Struther writes a poem, "Traveling America," that points out comfortable kinships in landscape between us and the homeland, that finds something different, too,—strange, and large, and moving. J. B. Priestley shows to us the magic of our own Southwest. Yes, England has discovered America. Misconceptions are fading. Some day the enlightened Britisher will write about us for his hometown folks and even in Yorkshire men will believe that oranges grow in California.

In all seriousness, thoughtful Britishers realize that not only must English and Americans surrender mutual suspicions and distrusts, but that together they must attempt the task of underwriting the needs of the world. And they are agreed that no materialistic approach is going to work. Unless men are moved by a faith in certain eternal values and are ready to put those values into practice, civilization is doomed. The principles of Christian philosophy are being invoked by statesmen and teachers and scientists. The Church itself is taking a leading part in the studies that would establish the bases for some kind of lasting peace. The war was scarcely a year old when there was held the Malvern conference of the World Federation of Churches in the interests of post-war guidance. Sir William Temple, Archbishop of Canterbury, is directing an intelligent movement worldwide in its ramifications. His own writings on the subject—as in his little book, *The Hope of the New World*—are fair and liberal and clearly conceived.

Men like H. G. Wells who write rapidly from a rich background of experience or like H. M. Tomlinson who write thoughtfully from an equally full experience are united in their concern. They show no disposition to shield England or to shift the blame for the state of the world on to foreign shoulders. They look at facts; they tell the truth; and they fasten their hope on the innate decency and active faith of the common man. Without apology they appeal to religion. When man forgets, he makes a mess of his universe. The scholar and philosopher in this hour make no prouder plea than the prayer of Kipling's "Recessional." This World War has been a humbling experience. It has made Great Britain really aware of the world.

QUESTIONS IN APPRECIATION:

"My America"

1. What kind of background made it possible for Lord Tweedsmuir, an Englishman, to write authoritatively about America? Explain.

2. Why is his essay easy to follow? His vocabulary is scholarly; yet the selection is not difficult reading. Why not? What method does he use most often to prove his points or to explain his meaning? Point out at least one example.

3. What makes "My America" exceedingly interesting reading? Do you think most Americans would be inclined to agree with Lord Tweedsmuir?

Why? Do you think the author was an able psychologist? Why or why not? Does the article sound sincere? logical? unbiased? Discuss.

4. In what respects may "My America" be described as a piece of *constructive* writing? What effect may it be expected to have on readers on this side of the Atlantic? Would it be a good thing to have the essay widely read in England also? Why or why not?

"If Judgment Comes"

1. Notice the strength of expression in the selection from "If Judgment Comes." Compare it, for example, with the poem by the same author in the preceding group of selections. How has Mr. Noyes made this poem *strong?* Point out several methods. Consider the poetic form, the kind of words, the type of sentences, the kind of imagery, and so on.

2. Why is this a poem to make people *think?* Is the poet fundamentally true in the picture he draws of war? of its menace? of its causes? Does he suggest a hope? What impression does he leave with the reader?

3. How does the poet show that he is taking a world-wide, not a nationalistic, view of the problems involved in war? Is he looking for a world solution? From what force does he think it can come? Discuss.

"The End of an Age"

1. Which of the following attributes do you consider essential in a *helpful* discussion of public affairs—clearness, open-mindedness, reliability of factual background, sincerity of purpose, intelligence, human understanding? Name the attributes in the order of their relative importance. Which of the qualities you have listed as *essential* do you discover in Mr. Wells's essay, "The End of an Age"? Explain.

2. What kind of literary style do you think is most suitable for the type of essay you have just been reading? Has Mr. Wells used a suitable style? Explain why you think he has, or has not, as the case may be.

3. What attitude on the part of a writer is most likely to command the respectful attention of his readers—a white-hot enthusiasm for his subject; an antagonistic attitude toward existing affairs or toward men holding opposite views; a tolerant impersonal viewpoint? Why? How would you describe the attitude of Mr. Wells in "The End of an Age"?

4. Did you find Mr. Wells's essay interesting? informative? stimulating? worthwhile? Why or why not? Discuss.

"The Wind Is Rising"

1. What are some of the most apparent points of differences in style between the selection from *The Wind Is Rising* and Mr. Wells's discussion, "The End of an Age"? Do you think the selections were intended to reach the same types of readers? to serve the same, or similar, or different purposes? Discuss.

2. What is there about Mr. Tomlinson's essay that calls for careful reading? What is there about it that *repays* careful reading? Discuss.

3. Review the account of Mr. Tomlinson's life. Why is he well equipped to discuss world affairs? Point out passages in the essay that indicate that the author is (*a*) well read in history, (*b*) well read in literature, (*c*) well informed on present-day affairs.

4. The author has a genius for saying things in a way that should be remembered. Select for discussion and memorization the four sentences that seem to you the best examples of the expression of significant truths in thought-compelling words.

5. The author has been described as "one of the two greatest essayists in England today." So far as you can judge, would you agree with that opinion? How would you rank him in ability with other writers of any kind of prose? Discuss.

6. To what extent do you think Mr. Tomlinson's opinions reflect the views of Great Britain in general? Discuss.

"*Recessional*"

1. What indicates that "Recessional" is a prayer? At what time in the service is the *recessional* hymn sung? Why is the thought of this poem more appropriate for a *re*cessional than for a *pro*cessional hymn—especially for the recessional of the Jubilee ceremonies? Are you familiar with the music that has been composed for the hymn? If so, do you think that in this instance words and music have been well mated?

2. Point out words, phrases, and sentences that give the poem a Scriptural tone. Why are these expressions appropriate? What is the meaning of *awful*, as it is used in line 3? What other words are used with unusual significance in the poem? What are the three special petitions that the poet makes in his prayer?

3. How do you think the "Recessional" compares in power and appropriateness with other patriotic poems of England? of other countries? Discuss. How do you think it ranks with the other works by Kipling? Does it have significance to Americans as well as to Britishers? Explain.

FOR FURTHER READING

ANGELL, NORMAN, *Let the People Know*
"BARTIMEUS" (Lewis A. D. Ricci) *Action Stations*
BUCHAN, JOHN, *Pilgrim's Way*
JAMESON, STORM, (ed.), *Challenge to Death; London Calling*
KIPLING, RUDYARD, *Barrack-Room Ballads; The Five Nations*
LASKI, HAROLD J., *The Revolution of Our Time*
MASEFIELD, JOHN, *In the Mill*
NEVINS, ALLAN AND BREBNER, J. B., *The Making of Modern Britain*
NOYES, ALFRED, *If Judgment Comes; Poems of the New World*
SASSOON, SIEGFRIED, *Counter-Attack; Picture Show*
STRUTHER, JAN, *Mrs. Miniver*
TEMPLE, WILLIAM, *The Hope of a New World*
WELLS, H. G., *The New World Order*

THE FOUNDATION PERIODS
449-1492

"PILGRIMS EVERY ONE"

The Anglo-Saxons contributed a language and the beginnings of a literature.

ANGLO-SAXON ENGLAND

(449–1066)

History rides the decks of ships. The first chapter in the story of our own country was written in the year 1492 when three sailing vessels pointed their prows westward from Spain. And the language in which that history would be written was determined in 1620 when the *Mayflower* dropped anchor in a bay off Plymouth Rock.

Similarly the basic language and culture of England had been settled a thousand years earlier by men who came in boats—in small open boats—crossing from the dark forests of northern Europe to beach on the sands of Britain. The men who surged ashore were warriors, tall and blond and strong. They had come for conquest and a new homeland. Before their onslaughts the native Britons rallied for a brief resistance under their great hero, King Arthur. But at his death the kingdom fell apart. Britons who survived fled into Wales or over into Ireland. The newcomers made themselves at home in the land.

They called themselves—depending upon the part of the continent from which they had come—Angles, or Saxons, or Jutes. But they were all related, and they spoke a common language which came to be called *Anglo-Saxon*. It was a *Germanic* (or *Teutonic*) speech—the parent-tongue of modern English, Norwegian, Swedish, and German. One of the tribes gave its name to the country—"Angle-lond." Eventually they were all calling themselves "Anglisc-men."

These newcomers were heathens, worshiping old Norse gods and believing in demons and dragons. The people of southern Europe counted them barbarians. But they brought to Britain an oral literature—battle songs, old charms, tales of heroes and their deeds. From the remnants of this literature, we learn what kind of men they were and how they lived. They were a serious folk—fighters and sailors. The sea was for them a highway, carrying their curve-stemmed boats on ventures of plunder and conquest. They were not so good at tilling the soil. The earliest shadows of feudalism lay over their patchwork of common farming lands; for to work the land effectively seemed to call for a government based on kinship and personal allegiance. The leaders drew followers or "thanes" around them, who in turn watched over the peasants and slaves. Each little realm had its "Witan," or King's Council, and its Assembly. Wessex, Northumbria, and Kent emerged as the most powerful kingdoms. Tithes or taxes were demanded of the peasants—so many loaves, so much cheese, butter, and fish. Tiny huts of wattle clustered around the larger wood or stone hall of the lord. These great halls were high and drafty. Heat came from an open fire in the center of the dining hall. Tapestries for warmth covered the mud-chinked walls, but wind and smoke swirled through or about them. Ale and mead—a potent liquor brewed from honey—were their drinks; and pork, eels, dark bread, and cheese their staple foods. Men ate and drank heartily; and as the drinking horn passed from mouth to mouth, the men boasted or listened to marvelous tales recited by the "scops," or gleemen.

If Christian missionaries had reached Britain in earlier times—as tradition indicates—their work had been obliterated by the pagan Saxons. But in 597 Pope Gregory sent Augustine on a special mission to "Anglelond." The country was ripe for conversion, and shire by shire was won over to Christianity. Monasteries were established, becoming centers of learning as well as of faith. The monks adapted the Latin alphabet to Anglo-Saxon uses, and for the first time old songs and legends got written down. No one can tell to what extent the monks exerted a pious censorship over their pagan materials, but we believe that a good many changes occurred as the old tales became manuscript copies.

The greatest single piece of Anglo-Saxon literature is the long poem *Beowulf*. The story had its origin on the mainland before the first invasion of Britain. It was one of the oral sagas that came with the men in their open boats, and generations passed before it was written down. The monks who recorded the version that has come down to us omitted all references to pagan gods. But the dragons and monsters remained. So did the pictures of the fierce fighting men who believed in them,—all enriched with details about their feasts, their armor, their weapons, and their way of thinking. The poem is written in unrhymed verse that echoes the surge and thunder of the sea. Its most compelling interest lies in the character of Beowulf, because he shows the qualities that the pagan Saxons admired. His chief physical characteristic was strength. His greatest moral quality was courage; but he was also modest, loyal, just, and kind.

As old, perhaps, as *Beowulf* are some surviving lyrics—charms to be sung at planting time or harvest, and riddles sung in the mead halls to test the wits of the warriors. Some few longer poems describe the fortunes and wanderings of the minstrels. In all these fragments there is a certain rough beauty, especially in the descriptions of sea and storm and wind and wave.

From the seventh century on, the influences of Christianity become apparent in the literature. Most of the writing was religious. A favorite form was the Scriptural "paraphrase"—a retelling of Bible stories in unrhymed verse. There were also hymns, saints' legends, and histories or chronicles of the times. Thanks to the industry and scholarship of a church scholar, the Venerable Bede, we have a valuable source book of early

English history in his Latin work, *An Ecclesiastical History of the English People.*

And then, when England was settling back under the civilizing influence of Christianity—then, in the last half of the eighth century, came another heathen horde—the Danes. They burst upon northern England, plundering and burning as they swept through Northumbria. Most of the monasteries were destroyed, and priceless manuscripts lost forever. The monks were killed or dispersed. The Danes pushed southward across the Thames, and within a century threatened to overrun all England.

But the ninth century brought a deliverer—Alfred, the truly Great. He burned the slim, black-flagged boats of fresh invaders; he pushed the established Danes back into stonier, remoter territory. He united the Saxons for common defense and rolled back the tide of conquest. When he had forced the Danes to a peace, he turned his attention to the education of his people. To his capital at Winchester he invited scholars and teachers. He stressed the importance of a native language and literature. He wanted books written, not in Latin, but in Anglo-Saxon. He himself undertook the translation of Bede's *Ecclesiastical History* into Saxon. And he caused the chronicles kept at Winchester to be brought up to date and expanded. This work became the basis for the oldest history in the native tongue—*The Anglo-Saxon Chronicle.*

In the century following Alfred's death, Saxons were again pitted against Danes, and petty kingdoms fought for power. Literature declined and learning came to a standstill. The eleventh century was a dark one for England. Her peace was threatened from another quarter. Edward the Confessor, a Saxon king, had been brought up in Normandy (now northern France) and he welcomed to his court certain powerful Normans. It was a fatal foothold. Now when Danish revolts flamed in the north, French attacks stabbed at the south. When Edward's successor, Harold, came to the throne, the situation was past help. Undermanned and poorly armed, Harold moved to meet Duke William of Normandy, whom Edward—it was said—had invited to be the next king of England. At Hastings from dawn till twilight on a day in 1066, Harold's band stood against the long-range bows of the French. Then Harold fell wounded, and the army broke. William of Normandy became William the Conqueror of England.

The sovereignty of the Anglo-Saxon was gone forever; but to the land of England he had given a name, a language, a literature; and he was to mingle his blood with the conquering French, bequeathing to later-day Englishmen a strain of simple, sturdy strength. The modern Britisher is still glad to claim part of his heritage from these Nordic forefathers.

BEOWULF

TRANSLATED BY J. DUNCAN SPAETH

The epic, *Beowulf,* takes its name from its hero, a thane or warrior of Hygelac, king of the Geats, who lived in Sweden. Hrothgar, king of the Spear-Danes and friend of Beowulf's father, was in trouble. His mead-hall, Heorot, was being attacked nightly by a man-eating monster named Grendel. Beowulf came to the rescue with a picked band of "shoulder-companions." Single-handed the hero met and killed Grendel, and then Grendel's mother, the horrible "mere-wyf." Beowulf and his men returned to the land of the Geats, where Beowulf later became king. He ruled his people well, defending them from their enemies and dealing justly with his subjects. After a long reign he died a heroic death and was given a hero's funeral. His body was burned on a promontory overlooking the sea, and a great memorial mound and beacon was built in his honor.

Like most epics, *Beowulf* has an elaborate beginning which does honor, not only to the hero but to his famous ancestors. But the reader is most interested in the parts of the poem that deal with the "superman" himself. The first of the selections which follow describes Beowulf and his com-

panions as they arrive at the land of the Danes. The next passages tell
about Beowulf's preparations for his fight with Grendel and about the
fight itself. The scenes of ceremonial welcome and feasting have been
omitted.

BEOWULF'S ARRIVAL AT THE HALL AND THE MANNER OF HIS RECEPTION

THE street was stone-paved; straight it led
To the goal of their journey. Glistened their byrnies
Stout and strong-linked; sang the rings
Of their iron mail as they marched along,
5   In armor and helmet right up to the hall.
Sea-voyage-sated, they set their shields,
Their linden-woods broad, along the wall.
As they bent to the bench, their byrnies clattered.
They stacked their spears that stood in a row,
10 Ashwood tipped with iron above;
Well-equipped was the warlike band.
A stately Dane the strangers addressed,
Asked who they were and whence they had come:
"Whence do ye bear your burnished shields,
15 Your visored helmets and harness gray
Your heap of spear-shafts? A servant of Hrothgar's
His herald, am I. Hardier strangers,
Nobler in mien, have I never seen.
'Tis clear you come to the court of Hrothgar,
20 Not outlaws and beggars, but bent on adventure."
To him gave answer the hero brave,
The lord of the Weders these words returned,
Bold 'neath his helmet: "We are Hygelac's men,
His board-companions. I am Beowulf called.
25 Ready am I the ruler to answer,
To say to thy lord, the son of Healfdene,
Why we have come his court to seek,
If he will graciously grant us a hearing."

2. BYRNIES—Body armors of chain-mail.

BEOWULF'S WATCH IN HEOROT

THE best of kings
Had placed in the hall, so heroes report,

A watch against Grendel, to guard his house,
Deliverance bring to the land of the Danes.
5   But the lord of the Jutes joyfully trusted
In the might of his arm and the mercy of God.
Off he stripped his iron byrnie,
Helmet from head, and handed his sword,
Choicest of blades, to his body-thane,
10   And bade him keep the battle armor.
Then made his boast once more the warrior,
Beowulf the bold, ere his bed he sought,
Summoned his spirit; "Not second to Grendel
In combat I count me and courage of war.
15   But not with the sword will I slay this foeman,
Though light were the task to take his life.
Nothing at all does he know of such fighting.
Of hewing of shields, though shrewd be his malice
Ill deeds to contrive. We two in the night
20   Shall do without swords, if he dare to meet me
In hand to hand battle. May the holy Lord
To one or the other award the victory,
As it seems to Him right, Ruler all-wise."
Then he sought his bed. The bolster received
25   The head of the hero. In the hall about him,
Stretched in sleep, his sailormen lay.
Not one of them thought he would ever return
Home to his country, nor hoped to see
His people again, and the place of his birth.
30   They had heard of too many men of the Danes
O'ertaken suddenly, slain without warning,
In the royal hall.

9. BODY-THANE—Body-servant.

BEOWULF'S FIGHT WITH GRENDEL

Now Grendel came, from his crags of mist
Across the moor; he was curst of God.
The murderous prowler meant to surprise
In the high-built hall his human prey.
5   He stalked 'neath the clouds, till steep before him
The house of revelry rose in his path,

The gold-hall of heroes, the gaily adorned.
Hrothgar's home he had hunted full often,
But never before had he found to receive him
10 So hardy a hero, such hall-guards there.
Close to the building crept the slayer,
Doomed to misery. The door gave way,
Though fastened with bolts, when his fist fell on it.
Maddened he broke through the breach he had made;
15 Swoln with anger and eager to slay,
The ravening fiend o'er the bright-paved floor
Furious ran, while flashed from his eyes
An ugly glare like embers aglow.
He saw in the hall, all huddled together,
20 The heroes asleep. Then laughed in his heart
The hideous fiend; he hoped ere dawn
To sunder body from soul of each;
He looked to appease his lust of blood,
Glut his maw with the men he would slay.
25 But Wyrd had otherwise willed his doom;
Never again should he get a victim
After that night. Narrowly watched
Hygelac's thane how the horrible slayer
Forward should charge in fierce attack.
30 Nor was the monster minded to wait:
Sudden he sprang on a sleeping thane,
Ere he could stir, he slit him open;
Bit through the bone-joints, gulped the blood,
Greedily bolted the body piecemeal.
35 Soon he had swallowed the slain man wholly,
Hands and feet. Then forward he hastened,
Sprang at the hero, and seized him at rest;
Fiercely clutched him with fiendish claw.
But quickly Beowulf caught his forearm,
40 And threw himself on it with all his weight.
Straight discovered that crafty plotter,
That never in all mid earth had he met
In any man a mightier grip.
Gone was his courage, and craven fear
45 Sat in his heart, yet helped him no sooner.
Fain would he hide in his hole in the fenland,

His devil's den. A different welcome
From former days he found that night!
Now Hygelac's thane, the hardy, remembered
50   His evening's boast, and bounding up,
Grendel he clenched, and cracked his fingers;
The monster tried flight, but the man pursued;
The ravager hoped to wrench himself free,
And gain the fen, for he felt his fingers
55   Helpless and limp in the hold of his foe.
'Twas a sorry visit the man-devourer
Made to the Hall of the Hart that night.
Dread was the din, the Danes were frighted
By the uproar wild of the ale-spilling fray.
60   The hardiest blenched as the hall-foes wrestled
In terrible rage. The rafters groaned;
'Twas wonder great that the wine-hall stood
Firm 'gainst the fighters' furious onslaught,
Nor fell to the ground, that glorious building.
65   With bands of iron 'twas braced and stiffened
Within and without. But off from the sill
Many a mead-bench mounted with gold
Was wrung where they wrestled in wrath together.
The Scylding nobles never imagined
70   That open attack, or treacherous cunning,
Could wreck or ruin their royal hall,
The lofty and antlered, unless the flames
Should some day swallow it up in smoke.
The din was renewed, the noise redoubled;
75   Each man of the Danes was mute with dread,
That heard from the wall the horrible wail,
The gruesome song of the godless foe,
His howl of defeat, as the fiend of hell
Bemoaned his hurt. The man held fast;
80   Greatest he was in grip of strength,
Of all that dwelt upon earth that day.

THE DEFEAT OF GRENDEL

LOATH in his heart was the hero-deliverer
To let escape his slaughterous guest.
Of little use that life he deemed

To human kind. The comrades of Beowulf
5   Unsheathed their weapons to ward their leader,
Eagerly brandished their ancient blades,
The life of their peerless lord to defend.
Little they deemed, those dauntless warriors,
As they leaped to the fray, those lusty fighters,
10 Laying on boldly to left and to right,
Eager to slay, that no sword upon earth
No keenest weapon could wound that monster:
Point would not pierce, he was proof against iron;
'Gainst victory-blades the devourer was charmed.
15 But a woeful end awaited the wretch,
That very day he was doomed to depart,
And fare afar to the fiends' domain.
Now Grendel found, who in former days
So many a warrior had wantonly slain,
20 In brutish lust, abandoned of God,
That the frame of his body was breaking at last.
Keen in courage, the kinsman of Hygelac
Held him grimly gripped in his hands.
Loath was each to the other alive.
25 The grisly monster got his death-wound:
A huge split opened under his shoulder;
Crunched the socket, cracked the sinews.
Glory great was given to Beowulf.
But Grendel escaped with his gaping wound,
30 O'er the dreary moor his dark den sought,
Crawled to his lair. 'Twas clear to him then,
The count of his hours to end had come,
Done were his days. The Danes were glad,
The hard fight was over, they had their desire.
35 Cleared was the hall, 'twas cleansed by the hero
With keen heart and courage, who came from afar.
The deed of renown he had done that night.
His boast to the Danes he bravely fulfilled;
From lingering woe delivered them all:
40 From heavy sorrow they suffered in heart;
From dire distress they endured so long;
From toil and from trouble. This token they saw:
The hero had laid the hand of Grendel

Both arm and claws, the whole forequarter
45 With clutches huge, 'neath the high-peaked roof.

FOR INTERPRETATION

BEOWULF'S ARRIVAL AT HEOROT:

1. How do we learn that Beowulf and his men came by boat?
2. "Well-equipped was the war-like band," says the poet. Briefly describe their equipment.
3. What made the Dane who greeted them think that the men did not come as beggars, but that they were bent on adventure?
4. How did Beowulf's reply indicate his character?

BEOWULF'S WATCH IN HEOROT:

1. What is surprising about Beowulf's preparations to meet Grendel? Does he depend upon anything besides his own strength?
2. In what spirit did Beowulf's men prepare for the night? Why?

THE FIGHT:

1. What clues does the poem give to the appearance of Grendel? To his size and form? Does he seem to be like a man in any respects? How is he different?
2. What was Beowulf's strategy? How did he hope to overcome the monster?
3. What details in the description indicate the fierceness of the fight? Who besides Beowulf's men heard the struggle?

THE DEFEAT OF GRENDEL:

1. How did Beowulf's men try to help their leader? With what result?
2. What would have happened if Beowulf had planned to kill Grendel with a sword? Why?
3. What caused the death of Grendel? What trophy remained from the fight?
4. What lines express the joy of the Danes at the defeat of Grendel?

THE PLOUGHMAN'S CHARM

TRANSLATED BY J. DUNCAN SPAETH

Many of the lines of the ploughman's charm must have been part of an old heathen incantation. The name "Erce" in the first line was probably another name for "Nerthus," or Mother Earth in the Germanic mythology.

By adding the name of the Lord to the song, the monks believed that they
had made it a Christian prayer which might properly be sung at ploughing
time.

G1   *Here is the remedy how thou mayest cure thy land if it
refuses to bear, or if aught untoward hath befallen it by way
of witchcraft or sorcery. Strew seed on the body of the
plough and repeat these words:——*

U   Erce, Erce, Erce, Mother of Earth,
        May the Almighty, Lord Everlasting,
        Grant thee fields, green and fertile,
        Grant thee fields, fruitful and growing,
  5 Hosts of Spear-shafts, shining harvests,
        Harvest of Barley the broad,
        Harvest of Wheat the white,
        All the heaping harvests of earth!
        May the Almighty Lord Everlasting,
 10 And his holy saints in heaven above,
        From fiend and foe defend this land,
        Keep it from blight and coming of harm,
        From spell of witches wickedly spread!
        Now I pray the Almighty who made this world,
 15 That malice of man, or mouth of woman
        Never may weaken the words I have spoken.

G1   *Start the plough, and when the first furrow is turned,
say:——*

U   Hail to thee Earth, Mother of men!
        Grow and be great in God's embrace,
        Filled with fruit for the food of men!

G1   *Knead a loaf of bread with milk and holy water, lay it under the first furrow and say:——*

U 20 Field be full of food for men,
        Blossom bright, for blessed thou art
        In the name of the Holy who made the Heavens,
        Created the earth whereon we live.
        God who gavest this ground
 25 Grant us growth and increase
        Let each seed that is sown, sprout and be useful.

FOR INTERPRETATION

1. Which lines in the song seem to have been added by the Christian monk who wrote it down? By the omission of certain lines, can you make it read like a pagan charm? Try it.

2. What indications do you find that the Anglo-Saxon Christians mixed some superstition with their religion?

3. What new glimpses of Anglo-Saxon life do you catch from reading this poem? What are the most important differences between it and the scenes from the poem *Beowulf?* Discuss.

RIDDLES

TRANSLATED BY J. DUNCAN SPAETH

Part of the entertainment at old English feasts was the singing and guessing of riddles. The scop would sing the words while he strummed an accompaniment on his harp-like instrument. Sometimes the answer was shouted before he had finished the song. Sometimes he had to sing a hard one over and over, before the right answer came. See if you can guess the answers to these three riddles.

RIDDLE I

THERE's a troop of tiny folk traveling swift,
Brought by the breeze o'er the brink of the hill,
Buzzing black-coated bold little people,——
Noisy musicians; well-known is their song.
5   They scour the thickets, but sometimes invade
The rooms of the town. Now tell me their names.

RIDDLE II

I'M PRIZED by men, in the meadows I'm found,
Gathered on hill-sides, and hunted in groves;
From dale and from down, by day I am brought.
Airy wings carry me, cunningly store me,
5   Hoarding me safe. Yet soon men take me;
Drained into vats, I'm dangerous grown.
I tie up my victim, and trip him, and throw him;
Often I floor a foolish old churl.
Who wrestles with me, and rashly would measure

248

10 His strength against mine, will straightway find himself
    Flung to the ground, flat on his back,
    Unless he leave his folly in time,
    Put from his senses and power of speech,
    Robbed of his might, bereft of his mind,
15 Of his hands and feet. Now find me my name,
    Who can bind and enslave men so upon earth,
    And bring fools low in broad daylight.

RIDDLE III

    I WAR with the wind, with the waves I wrestle;
    I must battle with both when the bottom I seek,
    My strange habitation by surges o'er-roofed.
    I am strong in the strife, while still I remain;
5   As soon as I stir, they are stronger than I.
    They wrench and they wrest, till I run from my foes;
    What was put in my keeping they carry away.
    If my back be not broken, I baffle them still;
    The rocks are my helpers, when hard I am pressed;
10 Grimly I grip them. Guess what I'm called.

FOR INTERPRETATION

RIDDLE I:

1. What clues does the poem furnish as to the size, number, habits, and appearance of the subjects of this first riddle?

2. Are you helped in choosing your answer by the things the poet does *not* say about his subject? Discuss.

3. Put down on a slip of paper the names of two or three things that might be the answer to this riddle.

RIDDLE II:

1. Who is speaking in this second riddle?

2. To what do the "airy wings" of line 4 refer?

3. What is the meaning of the words "I'm dangerous grown" in line 6?

4. At what point did you guess the answer?

5. Explain in your own words the meaning of the last nine lines.

RIDDLE III:

1. Notice how each succeeding line of this riddle carries us closer to the answer. Explain in your own words the meaning of the third line.

2. Explain the meaning of lines 4 and 5.

3. At what point did you guess the answer? Check your answers with those given in the EXTENDED ACTIVITIES section.

NORTHUMBRIAN HYMN

CAEDMON

TRANSLATED BY J. DUNCAN SPAETH

Caedmon's hymn in praise of "the Lord of Heaven" is the first English poem of whose authorship we can be sure. In his *Ecclesiastical History* the holy Father Bede tells the story of how Caedmon, a humble servant in the abbey at Whitby, learned that he had the gift of song. He was very shy and would leave the table rather than try to take his turn at singing. But one night he dreamed that One appeared to him, saying "Sing, Caedmon, some song for Me." Caedmon protested that he could not sing; but the request was repeated, with the direction that he should "sing the beginning of all created things." The next morning Caedmon told his dream to the Abbess. She had the story of the Creation read to Caedmon; and presently, he had turned the story into English verse.

Bede wrote down the following nine lines as the first hymn that Caedmon sang in answer to his vision. It is believed that the song was composed in the year 670.

> Now hymn we aloud the Lord of Heaven,
> Praise His wisdom and wonderful power,
> The glorious works of the great Creator,
> How the Father Eternal founded this world.
> 5   First he set for the sons of men,
> Heaven to roof them. The Holy Ruler,
> The King of mankind, then cast the foundations
> Of earth in the midst, and made thereafter
> Land for the living, the Lord Almighty.

FOR INTERPRETATION

1. What meaning does the word *hymn* have in the first line of the song?
2. According to Caedmon, what were the first three steps in the creation of the world? Does his order agree with that of the creation as told in the book of *Genesis?* Discuss.
3. Does Caedmon's wording sound Biblical or original? Discuss.

From THE ANGLO-SAXON CHRONICLE

ALFRED AND OTHERS

Although the year 449 has been established as the date for the beginnings of English literature, the records of English history go back to a somewhat earlier date. When in 55 B.C., Julius Caesar and his Roman legions conquered Britain, they found the land inhabited by Celts who had originally come out of eastern Europe. It is through Caesar's reports that we have our first written accounts of Britain.

During the four hundred and fifty-odd years that Rome claimed Britain as a colony, the land enjoyed a kind of Latin civilization. London was built and excellent roads were laid. Many of the Britons were educated in Roman speech and manners. It is probable that in the last century of the occupation many of them were Christianized, for Rome had already accepted the new religion officially. Under Roman supervision, the Britons had their own kings. To protect them and their lands from the savage Picts, who lived in what is now Scotland, the Romans built a great wall across the center of the island and stationed garrisons along it.

By the fifth century, Rome's power was waning. The soldiers in her armies of occupation all over the world were called home. The Britons, deserted by their conquerors were helpless. Tribes from Scotland first swarmed over the wall, plundering and killing. The Britons tried to get help from German tribes across the sea, with results which are recorded in the early entries of *The Anglo-Saxon Chronicle*.

The events related for the years 449 and 455 are especially interesting. It was at this time or a generation later that the real King Arthur must have lived—a king strong enough to unite the Britons and defeat the Saxons. But treachery in his household resulted in another invitation to the followers of Hengist and Horsa to fight against him, and the fate of the Britons in their own land was sealed. The country reverted to an almost barbaric heathendom under the Anglo-Saxon-Jutish victors.

Anno 409.[1] This year the Goths took the city of Rome by storm, and after this the Romans never ruled in Britain; and this was about eleven hundred and ten years after it [2] had been built. Altogether they ruled in Britain four hundred and seventy years since Caius Julius [3] first sought the land.

Anno 418. This year the Romans collected all the Treasures that were in Britain, and some they hid in the earth, so that no one has since been able to find them; and some they carried with them into Gaul.

Anno 443. This year the Britons sent over sea to Rome, and begged for help against the Picts; but they had none, because they were themselves warring against Attila, king of the Huns. And then they sent to the Angles and entreated the like of the Athelings [4] of the Angles.

Anno 449. This year Martianus and Valentinus succeeded to the empire,[5] and reigned seven years. And in their days Hengist and Horsa,[6] invited by Vortigern, king of the Britons, landed in Britain, on the shore which is called Wippidsfleet; at first in aid of the Britons, but afterwards they fought against them. King Vortigern gave them land in the southeast of this country, on condition that they should fight against the Picts, and had the victory wheresoever they came. They then sent to the Angles; desired a larger force to be sent, and caused them to be told the worthlessness of the Britons, and the excellencies of the land. Then they soon sent thither a larger force in aid of the others. At that time there came men from three tribes in Germany; from the Old-Saxons, from the Angles, from the Jutes. From the Jutes came the Kentish-men and the Wight-warians, that is, the tribe

---

[1] *Anno 409*—In the year 409. The dates of the various entries correspond fairly accurately with the known dates of Roman history. The Goths attacked Rome in 408 and sacked the city in 410 A.D.

[2] IT—Rome.

[3] CAIUS JULIUS—Julius Caesar.

[4] ATHELINGS—Princes.

[5] EMPIRE—The Roman Empire.

[6] HENGIST AND HORSA—Hengist, a king of the Jutes, and Horsa his brother landed at Ebbsfleet in 449 and eventually established the kingdom of Kent.

which now dwells in Wight, and that race among the West-Saxons which is still called the race of Jutes. From the Old-Saxons came the men of Essex and Sussex and Wessex. From Anglia, which has ever since remained waste betwixt the Jutes and Saxons, came the men of East Anglia, Middle Anglia, Mercia, and all Northhumbria. Their leaders were two brothers, Hengist and Horsa: they were the sons of Wihtgils; Wihtgils son of Witta, Witta of Wecta, Wecta of Woden: from this Woden sprang all our royal families, and those of the South-humbrians also.

Anno 455. This year [7] Hengist and Horsa fought against King Vortigern at the place which is called Ægels-threp and his brother Horsa was there slain, and after that Hengist obtained the kingdom, and Æsc his son.

[7] THIS YEAR—It is presumably after these events that Arthur arose and established his kingdom for a time.

DID YOU READ WITH UNDERSTANDING?

1. What historical event marked the end of Roman rule in Britain?

2. Was the Roman withdrawal from Britain immediate, or did it cover a period of some years? How can you tell?

3. What seems to have been the attitude of the Britons toward their former conquerors, the Romans? Discuss.

4. Tell in your own words why the Angles first came to Britain, and what they did after they arrived. What opinion did they form of the Britons?

5. Question for discussion: Why, since the Britons were the first historic inhabitants of the island, do histories of English literature always begin with the Anglo-Saxons instead of with the earlier Britons?

EXTENDED ACTIVITIES

THE ANGLO-SAXONS CONTRIBUTED A LANGUAGE AND THE BEGINNINGS OF A LITERATURE

HISTORY IN BRIEF

	Romano-Britons	Angles Saxons Jutes	"Anglisc-men"	Danes or Vikings	Normans	Events in America
400-499 A.D. (5th Century)	Rome's control declines	Northern pagans conquer Britain				
500-599 A.D. (6th Century)						
600-699 A.D. (7th Century)			Christianity spreads throughout the land			
700-799 A.D. (8th Century)						
800-899 A.D. (9th Century)			Alfred the Great	Attempted invasion partially repulsed by Alfred and successors		
900-999 A.D. (10th Century)			Canute the Dane defeats Saxon armies and names himself king			
1000-1099 A.D. (11th Century)					Norman influence under Edward the Confessor. William of Normandy becomes King of England 1066 A.D.	Leif Erikson believed to have visited America about 1000 A.D.

FOR ACQUAINTANCE WITH AUTHORS

CAEDMON (D. 680)—"NORTHUMBRIAN HYMN"

Our knowledge of the unlearned herdsman, turned suddenly poet through divine inspiration, comes only through Bede's report of him in the *Ecclesiastical History*. After his revelation he was associated with the monastery at Whitby in northeastern England where, it is said, he would turn into verse the holy stories related to him by the monks.

BEDE (673–735)—"ECCLESIASTICAL HISTORY OF THE ENGLISH PEOPLE"

All but seven years of Bede's sixty-two were spent within the large monasteries of Wearmouth and Jarrow in Northumbria. His life, exclusively devoted to the Church, was saintly and scholarly enough to win for him the title of "venerable." At thirty he entered the priesthood and from then on, in addition to the religious and farming duties required of the monks, he taught, studied, and wrote. Science, history, theology, Greek, Latin, Hebrew, medicine, and astronomy—all interested this competent scholar of the eighth century. His *Ecclesiastical History,* written at the request of the King of Northumbria, is his chief contribution today. In his own time his writings and teaching spread the fame of the twin monasteries, and monks came from all England to hear him. Men spoke not only of his wisdom and his scholarship, but of his piety, humility, and gentleness—virtues often lacking in the Anglo-Saxon England of the eighth century.

ALFRED (848–900)—"THE ANGLO-SAXON CHRONICLE"

As the fourth son of King Aethelwulf, there seemed little chance that the precocious young Alfred would ever be king; but at twenty-two he was riding at the head of the English armies in their furious struggle against the Danes. For the next fourteen years the battles raged. At last in 896 the defeat of the Danes was accomplished and Alfred turned from his reform of the army and navy to the reconstruction of the monasteries, economic reform, and even the importation of scholars from the continent. One of his greatest contributions was his translation of Biblical stories into the people's Saxon tongue. Throughout the former centuries Latin had been the language of the priests, the only chroniclers of the history of the times and often the only people who could write. Alfred's translation of stories into the vernacular marks the emergence of the language we know as English, and of the record of a land and its people that we know as "English literature."

"My will was to live worthily as long as I lived and after my life to leave to them that should come after, my memory in good works," wrote Alfred of his own life. No other person perhaps, surely no other king, ever lived more worthily or left a greater store of memory in good works.

OF LITERARY FORM AND STYLE

THE ANGLO-SAXON LANGUAGE

Before one can appreciate the form of early English poetry, one must understand something about the language in which it was written. At first glance a passage in Anglo-Saxon looks altogether strange——

Da com on more   under mist hleothum
Grendel gongan.   Godes yrre baer.

But if we place the modern words beneath the old, a surprising likeness appears:

Da   com   on   more   under   mist   hleothum
There came on, over (the) moor under misty clouds

Grendel gongan. Godes   yrre   baer.
Grendel going.   God's   ire,   (he) bore.
(wrath)

One reason that certain surviving words look very different is that Anglo-Saxon was an *inflected* language. The same word might have several spellings to indicate different uses. Thus *gethoht* is merely the participle of *thoht*, or *thought*. It is true that many of the old words have disappeared entirely and that some survive only in certain poetic or old-fashioned expressions; but it is also true that most of our short, everyday words are direct descendants of this early English speech.

An important characteristic of the Germanic languages is that they form new words by joining two or more old words. The Anglo-Saxon word for *vocabulary* was *word-hoard;* for *drowning* was *sea-death*. Often these compounds were poetically imaginative expressions such as *World-father* for *Creator*, and *foamy-necked floaters* for *boats*. Modern English has kept this capacity for forming compounds; but it is usually more convenient for us to make new words by using Greek or Latin stems, prefixes, and suffixes. And so though we have expressions like *schoolhouse, playwright*, and *moving van*, we also say *depend* (not *under-hang*) and submarine (not *under-sea-boat*). As we follow the history of England and her literature, we shall trace the changes that have made the English language expand into a richly varied and expressive speech.

THE FORM OF ANGLO-SAXON POETRY

As you have read the selections from *Beowulf* and from other early English verse, you have noticed that the lines do not rhyme. Nor is there the smooth, measured rhythm which we find in most modern poetry. Yet there is a marked poetic effect. A little study discloses the use of certain definite devices which gave Anglo-Saxon poetry its movement and harmony.

Briefly, the poems were written in lines that contained four accents, with a pause in the middle of the line. Moreover, the important accented syllables began with the same letter. Here are two typical lines from *Beowulf*:

Gren'del gong'an.   God'es yr're baer.
(Grendel going. God's ire, (he) bore.)

Flo'ta fam'ig-heals   fu'gel geli'cost.
(Foamy-necked floaters, like unto fowls)

Dr. Spaeth describes the unit of old English verse as "a line of four beats, divided into two halves by a pause, but linked together by alliteration." The alliteration might consist of three or four accented syllables beginning with the same sound, or it might have two pairs of alliterating words, as in the line——

*H*ilde-*w*aepnum and *h*eapo-*w*aedum
(*B*rave *w*eapons and *b*attle-*w*eeds)

The translations of the selections which you have read have imitated carefully the important features of the original poems. You will notice that each line has four major accents, that there is a slight pause in the middle of each line, and that every line is marked by alliteration——

*F*irm 'gainst the *f*ighter's *f*urious onslaught.

or

There was *w*oe on the *w*aters; the *w*aves spat gore.

It has been said that the Anglo-Saxon lacked the sentiment and lively fancy of the earlier Britons, the Celts. But it would be wrong for us to suppose that he was without imagination. A review of the poems you have just been reading will show his fondness for figures of speech, especially for metaphor and personification. The use of metaphorical compounds like "whale-road" for *sea,* "bone-case" for *skeleton,* or "linden-wood" for *shield* is so characteristic that it is recognized as a particular figure of speech and called a *kenning.* And notice the picturesque use of personification in the second and third riddles. In fact, the use of strongly figurative language is one of the important features of early English poetry. Modern translators are careful to preserve the imaginative spirit of the original as well as its alliterative, rhythmic dress.

TYPES OF ANGLO-SAXON POETRY

The Epic

Beowulf is a true folk epic (see the *Appendix* for definitions). It is legendary in subject and heroic in style. It grew up through many centuries and was preserved by recitation from one generation to the next. The author who first wrote it down is unknown; and that is perhaps just as well, for the poem does not reflect the genius of a single man but rather the ideals and culture of a people. Its form, which follows the typical pattern of Anglo-Saxon verse, gives it the strength and dignity that characterizes any true epic. It is the only genuine *folk* epic in the English tongue.

QUESTIONS IN APPRECIATION:

1. Explain why the subject matter of the poem *Beowulf* may be truly described as legendary. What incidents from the poem do you think may have had their basis in fact?

2. Do you think that the heroic feats ascribed to Beowulf indicate a childish attitude of mind on the part of the Anglo-Saxons? Or do men of all ages enjoy hearing or reading about the deeds of "supermen"? Discuss.

3. The true folk epic always contains some supernatural characters. What are the supernatural elements in *Beowulf?* Do you think that those who first told the stories believed that there were monsters and dragons for men to fight? Or do you think that these creatures may have been used as symbols of different forces of nature which man had to overcome? Discuss.

4. By example, show the Anglo-Saxon's fondness for figures of speech. Choose at least five illustrations.

5. Choose two lines which illustrate devices which gave Anglo-Saxon poetry its movement and harmony.

6. How does the form of the poem compare in poetic effect with any unrhymed modern poem which you know—such a poem as "Lancelot and Elaine" or the *Song of Hiawatha?* Does the form of the poem seem to fit the subject matter? Discuss.

Lyric Verse

As we study Anglo-Saxon literature, we must remember that we are making our judgments on a few sample writings that remain from an apparently rich original store. We shall never know how many valuable manuscripts were destroyed during the ninth century when the Danes plundered Northumbria and burned the monasteries. Fortunately one complete copy of *Beowulf* escaped. Of other poetry we have only fragments.

Such fragments seem to show that there was little difference in form between Anglo-Saxon lyrics and the longer poems. There is merely a difference in length and, of course, in subject. Lyric poetry used the same kind of line and accent, the same alliteration, and the same figures of speech. In almost no instance was there any use of rhyme.

Short poems composed by the minstrels tell of their wanderings. Some of the scops traveled far, and their songs name interesting persons and places. Such songs, and the riddles and charms probably were composed in the pre-Christian period. Later lyrics are chiefly hymns. In all these lyrics, as in the longer poems, vividness of impression and poetic vigor are outstanding characteristics. There was nothing soft nor gentle nor romantic about Anglo-Saxon verse.

QUESTIONS IN APPRECIATION:

1. Charms and incantations are often crude jingles. What qualities in "The Ploughman's Charm" lift it to the level of artistic poetry? Illustrate your points by quoting lines from the poem.

2. If a composer were to write a musical setting for the charm, describe the kind of music that you think would be most appropriate. What instruments should be used? Why?

3. Check your answers to the riddles. The answer to the first one is probably *gnats*—certainly insects of some sort, and no mention is made of bite or sting. The answer to the second is *honey-mead,* the strong liquor

brewed from honey; and to the third, an *anchor*. Had you guessed the correct answers?

4. Which of the riddles has a touch of humor? Which one do you think shows the strongest poetic imagination? Be prepared to defend your choice by quoting lines from the riddle.

5. By example from the charm and from the riddles, show that Anglo-Saxon lyric poetry used the same figures of speech used in narrative poetry.

6. According to Bede's story, Caedmon was only a herdsman who could neither read nor write. How can you account for his excellent poetic vocabulary and style? What features of Anglo-Saxon life might tend to make even an uneducated man a good poet? Discuss.

OUR FIRST ENGLISH HISTORIES

Thanks to the work of Bede and Alfred, England has a record of her national growth almost from the very beginning. Both men were devoted to learning and teaching, and both recognized the importance of preserving accurate records for the generations which should follow them.

Even though Bede's *Ecclesiastical History of the English People* was written in Latin, it holds an important place in our literature as the source from which many later writers drew their information. For it, Bede had gathered his information from every known source; then he sifted, sorted, and arranged. Finally he was ready to write. Going back to the times of Romanized Britain, he pieced together traditions and facts. He was careful to tell us when his information had been gained by hearsay. But many documents which have since been lost or destroyed were available to him. We are greatly in debt to him for the care and diligence with which he compiled his *History*.

By all odds the most important work in Anglo-Saxon prose was *The Anglo-Saxon Chronicle,* or *Chronicles.* More than one chronicle manuscript has come down to us. It is likely that such chronicles had been started before the time of Alfred, but that he saw the value of their records and worked to organize and preserve them. The work of bringing the record up to date was probably given over to monks laboring under his direction, but it is thought that Alfred himself wrote the accounts of events during his reign. The actual range of history covered is from the year 60 B.C. to 1154 A.D.

Since the chronicles were kept by so many different scribes over so long a stretch of time, the separate entries differ greatly in style of writing, in interest, and in content. Those that cover the period of the Roman occupancy of Britain are like a calendar of important events retold in simple chronological order. Bede's *Ecclesiastical History* was probably the chief source of information for this section and for the early years of the Anglo-Saxon period. Then monastery records became available. There are periods when the facts related are few and uninteresting—obituaries of kings or churchmen, dates of battles without comment or detail. But there are other passages which give full, well-written accounts of important history. In the later centuries, the chronicles sometimes included a song or a ballad. The finest piece of verse that they hold is "The Battle of Brunanburh"—a stirring war ballad written in the Saxon's most vigorous style. *The Anglo-Saxon Chronicle* is an historical record which no other nation can equal.

QUESTIONS IN APPRECIATION:

1. Do you think that the five entries from *The Anglo-Saxon Chronicle* were actually written in the years assigned to them? Why or why not?

2. The selections as you have read them have been modernized in spelling and vocabulary, but the general style is that of the original. From the following list select at least three adjectives to describe that style: *elaborate, ornate, simple, extravagant, direct, narrative, descriptive, impassioned, forceful, involved.*

3. It has been said that the early histories are important as sources of information for later works of literature. What writers or works with which you are familiar have made use of the information contained in these five selections? Discuss.

FOR FURTHER READING

BEATY, JOHN, *Swords in the Dawn*
BISHOP, FARNHAM AND BRODEUR, ARTHUR G., *The Altar of the Legion*
BULWER-LYTTON, EDWARD GEORGE, *Harold, The Last of the Saxon Kings*
CLEMENS, SAMUEL L., *A Connecticut Yankee in King Arthur's Court*
CRUSE, AMY, *The Golden Road in English Literature*
DOYLE, SIR ARTHUR CONAN, *The Last Galley*
KINGSLEY, CHARLES, *Hereward the Wake*
KIPLING, RUDYARD, *Puck of Pook's Hill*
MILLAY, EDNA ST. VINCENT, *The King's Henchman*
PYLE, HOWARD, *The Story of King Arthur and His Knights*
QUENNEL, MARJORIE AND CHARLES H. B., *Everyday Life in Roman Britain*
TAPPAN, EVA M., *In the Days of Alfred the Great*

H·II

MEDIEVAL ENGLAND

(1066-1492)

The year of the defeat of the Saxons—1066—is as unforgettable in English history as is 1492 in American. Followers of Harold thought that the Battle of Hastings had sounded the death knell for Angle-lond. Instead it was the first step in the making of a new and better England. The Saxons did not die. They lived to mingle with the Norman-French and add their impress to every aspect of the new life.

But the first years were dark ones. With the thoroughness of a modern dictator the conquering William had sent Saxon earls scurrying and had given their lands to his Norman friends. Norman churchmen supplanted English bishops, and the whole direction of affairs passed into the hands of the newcomers. William's strong government was made possible largely by the feudal system which he enforced. Under this system, all the land belonged to the king, who then portioned it out to individual lords in return for each man's promise of personal loyalty, of furnishing a unit of fighting men, and of paying a certain sum of money. Each lord in turn exacted military service, labor, taxes, and produce from those under him. The serfs were virtual slaves, bound to the land and sold with it. The Anglo-Saxons, dispossessed of their land, found themselves under-vassals or serfs to Norman over-lords.

As may be supposed, this subjugation of a people was not accomplished quickly nor easily. For a hundred years there was strife and bickering. The Saxons grudged every foot of the land they surrendered, every feudal tie that knit them into vassalage. They took orders sullenly in French and carried them out in muttered Anglo-Saxon. The outcome was that, all unconsciously, over a period of two or three generations, French and "Anglisc" were knit into one speech.

Fiction and ballad have mourned the fate of the losing Saxon. True, the Saxons had certain great virtues. They were strong, brave, usually honorable, and certainly freedom-loving. But they were not organizers. They could not learn to unite for common good. They were slow and stubborn. And so in the end they had lost.

The Normans, on the other hand,—originally Norsemen who had settled in France—had profited from their contacts with a Celtic-Latin people. They had intermarried with the French and had adopted French manners and speech. They had become a lively, ambitious people with a

261

talent for government. They were also witty, keen, romantic, artistic. Without their leavening influence, England could not have become one of the great nations of the earth.

And the Saxons were not wholly losers, even in government. Their unquenchable devotion to justice and freedom gave the finally united nation strength to wring from King John in 1215 the Magna Carta—the written charter of English liberties. The charter assured fundamental rights and privileges. No free man could be imprisoned or punished except by the lawful judgment of his equals. Thus was established the right to trial by jury. The king was forbidden to seize property left by a noble when he died. All fines were to be fixed by law. There could be no extra assessment of taxes without consent of the council. In effect the charter abolished the most serious abuses of personal rights.

Another victory for lovers of freedom was won in 1265 when for the first time Parliament sat, not with just the clergy and the nobility, but with representatives from the common people—an assembly which was to become the English House of Commons. For the first time, the great middle class had a voice in national affairs.

By the thirteenth century, life had fallen into a pattern full of color and vitality. Along with feudalism the Normans had introduced the romantic institution of chivalry, and England was gay with knights and squires and pages and heralds. The system was really a program of education for young noblemen, carrying them from kindergarten years through "college" training and internship. Not that they actually went to school. Little boys from wealthy homes were placed as pages in the castles of high-ranking friends or kinsmen. The duties of a page ranged from those of errand boy to personal valet. At the same time the boy was receiving instruction in manners and soldiery—occasionally also in reading, languages, and arts. If he proved courteous and obedient, he became a squire, serving the lord of the castle at home and on the field, although not with sword and armor. After seven years as a squire, the young man who had shown himself brave, loyal, and Christian was knighted by his lord. As full-fledged knight he was ready to do battle for his patron, to serve the Church, to defend his king, and to sing praises and win honors for his lady. The system produced a select body of well-trained, well-equipped gentlemen-soldiers; but it placed undue emphasis on manners and physical strength. If a knight could excel at jousting, it did not matter whether or not he could read. It was not until changing methods of warfare made heavy armor impractical that the institution broke down.

Knighthood and the Crusades had given medieval England a worldwide outlook. The Anglo-Saxon had been an "isolationist," content to stick to his island and let the rest of the world look after itself. The Normans were easy cosmopolitans. They liked travel. Crusades and pilgrimages now had made them familiar not only with Europe but with Asia. They brought back to England tales of adventures in Rome or

Jerusalem, descriptions of Saracen mosques, curious costumes, snatches of foreign speech and song. They became acquainted on their trips to Rome with Italian art and literature, then in its glory. Returning to England they carried with them the first quickening influence of the Renaissance—that revival of intellectual and artistic interests which was to sweep all Europe.

The problems of French inheritance left by the death of William the Conqueror plagued his descendants until the fourteenth century, when the Hundred Years' War forced a settlement. The Norman kings had owned vast holdings in France, which they found it difficult to control. The French kings were jealous of the rich returns yielded to their English cousins. The Hundred Years' War was fought over these holdings. It produced a wave of English patriotism, a number of spectacular battles, and a new weapon—the longbow, which made knights in armor useless and led to the breakdown of chivalry. The war also cost England all her French territory and brought to the island the Black Death which, in 1349, destroyed one-third of the population. The returned soldiers were discontented; taxes were exorbitant; there was murmuring against the Church. The general unrest culminated in the Peasants' Revolt—an unsuccessful attempt to abolish serfdom. Quarrels over the kingship brought about civil war between the royal houses of Lancaster and York. The thirty years' dispute was known as the War of the Roses because each family had a rose as its device. Henry Tudor, who belonged to neither house, ended the dispute by defeating both claimants and taking the throne for himself as Henry VII.

In the meantime, the new importance of weaving made it possible for commoners to leave the manors and find work in the crowded towns. Burroughs and cities grew boisterous. Tax collectors were stoned off the streets and the towns maintained a bustling, noisy democracy. Democracy it was, for the entire populace met in mass meeting to elect their sheriffs and portmen. As far as possible the town governments ignored the crown, the clergy, and the barons. Country fairs were held annually. People flocked to them, spending days and nights on the highways crowded with merchants and packmen. Wines and silks and trinkets found their way from the continent to the fairs and thence to the villages. Nearly every house had its lower floor open to the street like a booth, where youngsters sold the family wares. These were troublous, bubbling times when anything could happen—and did!

Middle English literature presents a bright panorama of all these changing scenes. The Normans, loving music, had filled England with song. Lyric poetry became really singable with French rhymes and pretty, graceful forms. The use of rhymes increased the popularity of the ballads making them easy to remember and easy to sing. In them the common man—unable, though he was, to read or write—could set forth his mind and heart. The ballads praised good Robin Hood or denounced the tyrant John; they retold old legends, fearful superstitions, gruesome tragedies—stories of every possible theme. And in the telling they reflected the shifting fears and passions of the folk who made them up—their humor, their hatred of injustice, their respect for religion but their distrust of a greedy abbot, their wishful thinking which could transform an outlaw into a romantic helper of the poor. Springing up all over England throughout this medieval period, the ballads lived on the lips of the people until a much later period began to write them down.

For the educated few there were long romances, some in prose and some in verse. Those most popular in England had to do with the adventures of King Arthur and his followers, retold as if Arthur had lived in the days of chivalry and as if his soldiers had been knights. The metrical romances—as the tales in rhyme were called—glorified the famous characters of history and literature, re-created in a setting of medieval splendor.

A full-face portrait of this hearty, pageant-loving England is presented in one fourteenth-century work—*The Canterbury Tales* of Geoffrey Chaucer. The glimpses we catch of the author himself show him a gentleman and a poet. He was a traveler. He knew the continent, and he knew his England. He must have been a good mixer. He could fraternize with an easy-going churchman or talk books with a scholar from Florence. He knew people—good and bad—and he put a picture gallery of characters from his own day into the Prologue of his *Tales*.

The Canterbury Tales is not Chaucer's only contribution to literature, but it is his most interesting one. His work includes poems in all the fashions of his time. He had a light touch with lyrics. He wrote other long poems more melodious than his masterpiece. But it is through the *Tales* and their "Prologue" that readers of succeeding centuries have been able to live again, for a space, in this "England that was merry"—the lusty, singing England of the not-too-dark Middle Ages.

Fourteenth-century England was vividly portrayed by Geoffrey Chaucer.

From THE CANTERBURY TALES

SELECTIONS FROM "THE PROLOGUE"

GEOFFREY CHAUCER

Chaucer's masterpiece, *The Canterbury Tales,* is essentially a collection of stories in verse. The poet used an old device of having a group of travelers entertain themselves with the stories, told as they rode along. His characters were pilgrims going to the shrine of Thomas à Becket in Canterbury. Twenty-nine of them had met by chance at the Tabard Inn, across the Thames from London. The innkeeper, a jolly fellow, decides to make the pilgrimage also. It is he who proposes that each pilgrim tell two stories on the way to Canterbury and two more on the return—the one who tells the best tale to be treated to a dinner at the Tabard.

The plan thus called for over a hundred stories. Chaucer finished twenty-four—most of them rollicking narratives in rhymed verse. They are knit together by comments and conversation among the pilgrims.

Entertaining as the stories are, it is Chaucer's characterizations of the travelers that make *The Canterbury Tales* a remarkable work. "The Prologue" which introduces the company is a great piece of realistic writing. Chaucer describes each person, apparently impartially, just as he appeared, with careful attention to details of dress and mannerisms. But behind each picture we catch the poet's own shrewd appraisal of character. And the whole is enlivened with sparkles of humor. As we meet the pilgrims one by one, we feel that we are getting acquainted with Old England and finding that her people were not too different from men and women today. We feel, too, that we are learning to know the author—a quiet little man, keen and observant, with a kindly twinkle in his eye.

To get the "feel" of Chaucer's verse, one should read it in the original. However, six hundred years have made enough changes in spelling and pronunciation to puzzle the general reader; and so first acquaintance had best come through a modernized version. As a sample of the original, the first eighteeen lines are presented in Middle English, with a parallel reading in modern English. To get the effect of Chaucer's pronunciation, the final *e*'s should be pronounced and the vowels should be given the sounds they have in most European languages. Long $\bar{a}$ is *ah;* $\bar{e}$ is $\bar{a}$; $\bar{\imath}$ is *ee;* $\bar{oo}$ is $\bar{o}$; *ee* is $\bar{a}$; *ou* or *ow* is $\bar{oo}$. Final $\ddot{e}$ is pronounced like the final *a* in *Virginia.*

The modern version here presented keeps very close to the original in wording and imitates the free, easy style of Chaucer's verse.

OPENING LINES OF "THE PROLOGUE"

Wʜᴀɴ that Aprillë with his shourës sōōtë
The droghte of Marche hath percëd to the rōōtë,
And bathëd every veyne in swich licour,
Of which vertu engendrëd is the flour;

5   Whan Zephirus eek with his swetë brēēth
Inspirëd hath in every holt and hēēth
The tendrë croppës, and the yongë sonnë
Hath in the Ram his halfë course y-ronnë,
And smalë fowlës maken melodyë,

10   That slepen al the nyght with open yë,
So priketh hem nature in hir coragës:
Than longen folk to goon on pilgrymagës,
And palmers for to seken straungë strondës,
To fernë halwës couthe in sondry londës:

15   And specially, from every shirës endë
Of Engelond, to Caunterbury they wendë,
The holy, blisful martir for to sekë,
That hem hath holpen whan that they were sēēke.

A MODERN ENGLISH TRANSLATION

WHEN April with his gentle showers
Has pierced to the roots the March-dry bowers,
And swelled each vein with those fresh juices
Whose power the coming flower produces,
5 When the West Wind, too, with his sweet breath
Has called to life in wood and heath
The tender shoots; when the new young sun
Has half his course through Ram's sign run,
And the little birds make melody—
10 That sleep all night with open e'e
(So Nature stirs within each heart)—
Folks long some pilgrimage to start,
And Palmers wish to seek strange strands—
The distant shrines of various lands;
15 And specially from each shire's end
Of England to Canterbury they wend,
The holy martyr seeking still
Who helps them ever when they are ill.

It happ'ed in that season one fine day
20 In Southwerk at the Tabard, where I lay
Ready my pilgrimage to make
To Canterbury for devoutness' sake,
At night there came to that hotel
Full nine and twenty others as well
25 Of different folks who by chance had come
Together—pilgrims every one,
Who wished to Canterbury to ride.
The rooms and stables were good and wide,
And we were made easy with the best.
30 And before the sun had gone to rest,
I had spoken with them, one by one,
And a place in their company had won,

---

8. HALF HIS COURSE THROUGH RAM'S SIGN—People of the Middle Ages
were familiar with all the signs of the zodiac. This was a common way of
indicating early April—about April 11th.

13. PALMERS—Pilgrims returned from the Holy Land, carrying palm leaves
as evidence of their journey.

17. HOLY MARTYR—Thomas à Becket. It was believed that miraculous cures
might be had at his tomb.

Making our plans right early to rise
To take our way as I'll now advise.

35 But first, while I have time and space
Before farther in this tale I pace,
I think it a reasonable ambition
To describe to you the whole condition
Of each of them, as they seemed to me,
40 And who they were, and of what degree,
And even the clothes they were riding in;
And with a knight I will now begin.

THE KNIGHT

A KNIGHT there was, and he a worthy man
Who from the time that he first began
To ride abroad loved chivalry,
Truth, honor, freedom, and courtesy.
5 Right worthy was he in his liege-lord's war;
Besides he had ridden (no other so far)
Both in Christendom and in heathen lands,
And everywhere honored his true worth stands.

[Here follow sixteen lines which name the different places where the
Knight had fought—in Africa, Lithuania, Prussia, Russia, Granada, and
the like. He had been in fifteen "mortal battles" and in three tournaments,
each time slaying his foe.]

And always he had highest praise
10 For being modest and wise in his ways,

And in his bearing as meek as a maid;
He never a word of discourtesy said
In all of his life to any poor wight;
He was truly a perfect, well-bred knight.
15 I'll tell you now of his dress and array—
His horses were good; he himself was not gay.
He wore a short coat of cloth rather coarse
All stained by covering of chain-mail, perforce,
For he'd just returned from an expedition
20 And had set out at once upon this mission.

WITH him was his son, a gay young SQUIRE,
A lover, who to knighthood himself did aspire,
With locks crisp and curly as if laid in press.
Some twenty years old he would be, I guess.
5 In stature he seemed of the average length,
And wonderfully nimble; and great was his strength.
He had been quite some time with the Military
In Flanders and Artoys and French Picardy,
And borne himself well e'en in that little space
10 In the hope to stand high in his lady-love's grace.

3. AS IF LAID IN PRESS—Men as well as women used various devices for putting a curl in naturally straight hair. Older men curled and waved their beards.

Embroidered he was, like a meadow, I've said,
All covered with flowers, the white and the red.
Singing he was, or piping all day,
And he was as fresh as the blithe month of May.
15 Short was his cloak, with sleeves long and wide.
Well sat he his horse, and could expertly ride.
He could make little songs and also compose;
He could joust, draw, and write, and dance on his toes.
So hotly he loved that at night—'tis his tale—
20 He slept nevermore than the true nightingale.
He was courteous, humble, willingly able,
And he carved for his father when seated at table.

And there was a NUN, A PRIORESS.
Her smiling was very simple and coy,
Her strongest oath, just, "By St. Loy!"
Her name was Madame Eglantine.
5 Right well she sang the service divine—
Though through her nose—quite resonantly;
And French she spoke most properly—
In the style of Stratford-on-the-Bowe,
For French of Paris she did not know.

10 At meals she was well-bred, withal;
No morsel from her lips did fall,
Nor dipped she her fingers in sauce too deep.
Each mouthful she carried, careful, to keep
From dropping a portion upon her breast.
15 She wanted her manners to be the best.
She wiped her upper lip so clean
No grease upon the cup was seen
After her turn at the common draught.
Politely she reached for the meat she sought;
20 Her etiquette truly was of the best.
She was pleasant, cheerful; and for the rest,
Was careful to note the rules of Court
And follow them always. That was her forte.
She wished to be worthy and held in esteem.
25 Her conscience was overly tender, I ween.
Her heart was kind, moved to compassion
If a mouse were hurt in any fashion—
If trapped or killed or maimed or bled.
Some little dogs—her pets—she fed
30 With meat or milk or fine white bread,
And sore she wept if one was dead;
And if one was beaten with a stick,
Her tender heart made Madame sick.
Her wimple was pleated, neat, precise;
35 Her nose was straight; eyes, glass-grey, nice.
Her mouth was tiny, soft, and red,
And truly she boasted a wide forehead—
Almost a span broad, I surmise;
Not any dimension was undersize.
40 Her cloak was perfection, I was aware.
A coral bracelet her arm did bear—
A rosary trimmed with beads of green,
Holding a locket of golden sheen
Engraved with, first, a capital *A,*
45 Then in Latin, the motto, "Love conquers alway."
One other Nun kept her company—
Her chaplain; and her priests were three.

---

34. HER WIMPLE—The veil of her habit, worn over the head and around
the neck and chin.

A HABERDASHER, a CARPENTER,
A WEAVER, DYER, UPHOLSTERER—
These rode with us, in the livery
Of one great Guild, their fraternity.
5   Their equipment was all fresh and new;
No brass-tipped knives, but silver true;
Of silver also, hand-wrought and bright,
Were girdles and purses—a goodly sight.
Each seemed a worthy citizen
10   To grace the dais at Guild-hall then,
Or even—so wise each separate man—
To be safely chosen as Alderman;
Each boasted income and property, too,
And a wife to enjoy the special to-do—
15   To be called "Madame" at Court or Hall,
To march the first at Church festival
And wear a mantle with a train
Borne by a page with great disdain.

They brought a cook along with them
20   To cook their chickens—with food a gem!
Boiled marrow-bones and spicy tarts,
And choosing ale were his special arts.
He could roast and boil and broil and fry,
Make soups and broths and bake a pie.
25   (Only it seemed a shame to me

He had a great sore below his knee.)
But his blanc-mange was surely a treat!

27. BLANC-MANGE—A highly regarded delicacy of minced capon, cream, sugar, and flour.

THE GOOD WYF OF BATH

THERE was a WIFE from the town of Bath
Who was somewhat deaf—no cause to laugh.
A cloth-maker, she, and proud her vaunt,
Better than weavers of Ypres and Gaunt.
5   In all the parish no other could go
Ahead of her with the offering—or lo,
If any did, so angry was she
She lost every shred of her charity.
Her dress-up kerchiefs were fine and sound;
10   They weighed, I venture, a full ten pound
What she wore on Sundays upon her head.
Her stockings were scarlet, fine and red,
And fastened straight; shoes soft and new.
Bold was her face; blond, red of hue.
15   She was a great woman all her life,
And five times had she been a wife.
Thrice had she gone to Jerusalem,
And many a foreign stream did she stem.

4. YPRES AND GAUNT (GHENT)—Two cities in West Flanders, famed for their fine weaving.

At Rome she stopped, and at Bologne,
20   At St. James in Galicia, and at Cologne.
She knew all the sights along the way.
Her mouth was gap-toothed, I really must say.
Upon a nag she easily sat,
Properly veiled; and she wore a hat
25   Broad as a shield, or target round;
Her riding skirts just cleared the ground,
And on her feet great spurs did clatter.
In company she could laugh and chatter.
Love-charms she had at her finger-tips,—
30   She knew that game from heart to lips.

19. AT BOLOGNE—The Cathedral at Bologne contained a famous image of the Virgin.
20. AT ST. JAMES—A famous shrine in Spain.
20. AT COLOGNE—The bones of the three Wise Men were supposed to rest in Cologne.

A CLERK from Oxford came also,
Devoted to logic—a scholar, you know.
Lean as a rake was the fellow's horse,
Nor was he fat himself, of course.
5   No, he looked hollow, hungrily;
Threadbare his coat was, certainly.

He had not taken a situation
In church or office for his vocation.
He'd rather have beside his bed
10   A score of books, bound black and red,
Of Aristotle's philosophy
Than robes or riches or fiddle or fee.
And though he might study alchemy
Little gold in his coffers could there be.
15   All he could borrow from his friends
He spent on books, and made amends
By praying daily, earnestly
For the souls of the lenders, gratefully.
To study he gave most care and heed;
20   No word he spoke, more than was need,
But what he said was well expressed
In words, short, quick, precisely addressed.
Toward moralizing he leaned in speech,
And glad would he learn, and gladly teach.

11. OF ARISTOTLE'S PHILOSOPHY—Aristotle was a Greek philosopher of the fourth century B.C. His works throughout the Middle Ages were considered the ground-work of all philosophical and scientific knowledge.

13. THOUGH HE MIGHT STUDY ALCHEMY—Chaucer used the phrase "although he was a *philosopher*"—but philosophy at that time was seriously concerned with alchemy, or the search for a process of turning base metals to gold.

WITH him [the Summoner] there rode a PARDON-SELLER
From Rouncival, a story-teller
And bosom friend, come straight from Rome.
Together they sang a true love poem,
5   "Oh hither, come hither, my love to me";
No trumpet blast could louder be.
The Pardoner's hair hung yellow as wax
But smooth and straight like a hank of flax;
In little strands drooped the locks of his head—
10   The few he had—o'er his shoulders spread;

1. WITH HIM—Chaucer has just been describing a particularly repellent Summoner, who was employed to call people to the church courts.

1. PARDON-SELLER—It was the practice at the time for men to buy from such persons as this Pardoner, *pardons* signed by the Pope for sins already committed or *indulgences* which guaranteed forgiveness for sins one expected to commit. Chaucer's Pardoner made a side-line of exhibiting and sometimes selling "relics"—bits of cloth which he professed to have come from the Virgin's veil or from Peter's ship, and so on.

And thinly it lay, separate hair by hair.
No hood for his fancy would he wear,
Instead in his wallet 'twas packed away;
He rode in the fashion of the day—

THE PARDONER

15   Hair loose, uncovered, except for a cap.
His eyes shone bright like a rabbit's or rat.
An image of Christ was sewed to his cap.
His wallet he carried upon his lap,
Brimful of pardons from the Pope.
20   His voice was reedy, thin as a goat's.
No beard he had, nor ever would,
His face as hairless as polished wood.
But in his business from South to North
No better pardoner e'er went forth.
25   His satchel carried a pillow-slip
From the veil of Mary; and from the ship
Of Peter, he had a piece of sail;
A cross of brass, all full of stones,
And in a glass some old pig's bones.
30   With these "relics," when he found
A country parson upon his round,

29. PIG'S BONES—Bones which the Pardoner claimed were those of some
saint.

276

He made more money a single day
Than the parson earned for two months' pay.
Thus with his tricks and flattery,
35 He fooled parson and people royally.
But truly, spite of song and jest,
Among many churchmen, he rated best—
He could read the Scripture and tell a story,
And best of all sing the offertory;
40 For he knew when that song had been sung
He then could use his oily tongue
To tease the money from every purse;
So gaily he sang—for better, for worse.

THE POOR PARSON

THERE was one good religious man,
And very poor his parish ran;
But he was rich in thought and work.
A learned man, he did not shirk,
5 But Christ's whole truth would boldly preach
And all the parish devoutly teach.

1. ONE GOOD RELIGIOUS MAN—*The Canterbury Tales* was written, of course, before the Reformation, so that the only Christian Church was the Catholic Church, which had become a powerful and wealthy institution. In his description of the Parish Priest—sometimes called the "Poor Parson"—Chaucer gives evidence that not all men connected with the Church were worldly and self seeking. The qualities which he ascribes to this country priest are those that have characterized the "good man of religion" through all the centuries, in every sect or denomination.

And he was kind and diligent,
And in adversity, content;
And this he proved on many a date.
10 He loathed to excommunicate
For unpaid tithes, but rather he
Would pay the poor parishioner's fee
From his own pocket or his share,
For little he used for his own care.

15 Wide was his parish, with houses scattered,
But thunder and rainstorm never mattered;
In trouble, sickness, he called on each one—
The farthest, the poorest, or greatest. 'Twas done
All afoot, with a staff in his hand.
20 This noble example he gave to his land—
That first he labored and then he taught.
And from the Gospel this truth he caught
And added his own figure, too,—
If gold should rust, what would iron do?
25 If the priest be faulty in whom we trust,
What wonder if the layman rust?
And shame 'twould be for a priest to keep
Himself more dirty than his sheep.
The parson should always example give
30 By holiness how his people should live.

He did not seek a softer living
But stayed at home, in service, giving.
No wolf to this parish harm could carry;
Here toiled a shepherd and no mercenary.
35 Though he was holy and righteous within,
He scorned no person who foundered in sin.
Not over bearing nor harsh nor proud,
He was kind and forgiving; and allowed
That by example he must try
40 To lead folks to that heaven on high.

10–11. TO EXCOMMUNICATE FOR UNPAID TITHES—If a man could not pay
his fees to the Church, he was denied all its privileges, civil as well as religious
—he could not be granted the right to legal marriage, nor baptism for his
children, nor burial in consecrated ground.

But any stubborn sinner he
Reproved, whatever his degree,
And showed each error, plainly, true.
No better priest I ever knew.
45 He cared no whit for pomp and wealth,
Nor shaped his doctrines to his health,
But Christ's own gospel taught, to wit,
And first himself he followed it.

[The other characters introduced in the "Prologue" include a Yeoman (who rode with the Knight), a Monk, a Friar, a Merchant, a Lawyer, a Franklin (or Country Squire), a Sailor, a Physician, a Plowman (brother of the Poor Parson), a Bailiff, a Miller, a Steward for a group of lawyers, and a Summoner to Ecclesiastical Courts. The last 144 lines introduce the jolly host of the Tabard Inn, who proposes the story-telling contest and who decides to join the pilgrims and act as master of ceremonies on the journey.]

FOR INTERPRETATION

OPENING LINES:

1. How many signs of spring does Chaucer enumerate in the first ten lines of "The Prologue"? What springtime habit of the birds is Chaucer referring to in line 10?

2. What is the usual effect of spring upon people? How did the coming of spring affect people in medieval times? What did it make them want to do?

3. Why did people like to go to Canterbury?

4. What do lines 30–34 tell you about Chaucer himself? What kind of man was he?

THE KNIGHT:

1. Chaucer's description of the Knight is quite matter of fact. He was a gentleman and a soldier by profession. In what respects is this knight like those you have met in books of fiction like *Ivanhoe* or in romantic poems like *The Idylls of the King?* In what, if any, respects is he different? Discuss.

2. There is no hint of sarcasm in Chaucer's description of the Knight. For what qualities does the poet respect the man? Does the Knight possess the same characteristics that men admire in a hero today? Discuss.

THE SQUIRE:

1. The Squire was in training to become a knight like his father. Do you think he will make a good knight? Why or why not?

2. The Squire was the youngest member of the party. How does he show his youthfulness?

3. Make a list of his accomplishments. What marks him as a well-educated man? Consult Chaucer's biographical sketch to see why the poet could write so understandingly of the Squire.

4. Do you find any places where Chaucer seems to be smiling at the young man? Do you think Chaucer liked him or not? Discuss.

THE NUN:

1. What impression do you get of the Nun in the first four lines? Is that impression strengthened or changed by the next five lines? Explain.

2. What customs in eating and drinking in medieval times made it not easy to be mannerly and neat at the table? Do you think Chaucer's comments on the table manners of Madame Eglantine are given in complete seriousness? Or are they over-emphasized? Discuss.

3. In what kind of good works might you expect a nun to be engaged? What evidence does Chaucer offer in proof of the tender heart and good conscience of this nun?

4. Was Madame Eglantine nice looking? Discuss. Do the details of her dress indicate anything of her character? Discuss.

5. Is your final impression of the nun about the same as your first impression? Discuss.

THE TRADESMEN AND THEIR COOK:

1. What indicates that the tradesmen were prosperous and socially important? What feature of medieval life dignified their professions? Explain.

2. What characteristics did their wives have in common with many modern wives? Discuss.

3. For centuries the most important table items for the English were, literally, meat and drink. How does the description of the Cook bear out this fact?

4. Why do you think Chaucer throws in the note about the sore on the Cook's shin?

THE WOMAN FROM BATH:

1. From the first eight lines, what impression do you get of the Wife of Bath? What details in the rest of the description strengthen that impression?

2. If a descendant resembling her were living today, what would her occupation very likely be? Discuss.

3. What details indicate that this woman had plenty of money?

4. What kind of husbands do you think she had had? Remember that divorce was practically unknown.

5. Do you think she would be good company on the pilgrimage? Dis-

cuss. How do you think she would get along with Madame Eglantine? Discuss.

THE CLERK FROM OXFORD:

1. Chaucer was himself a bookish man. Do you think he approves or disapproves of the Oxford scholar? Prove your answer.
2. Point out, if you can, any lines in which Chaucer seems to be laughing a little at the Clerk.
3. What is the highest praise he gives to the Clerk?

THE SELLER OF PARDONS:

1. What lines give you the first hint of Chaucer's attitude toward the Pardoner? Does he approve or disapprove of the man? How can you tell?
2. Does the appearance of the Pardoner seem in keeping with his business? Discuss.
3. What song did the Pardoner like to sing best of all? Why?

THE PARISH PRIEST:

1. What lines tell you at once that Chaucer admires the Parish Priest?
2. In what important respects did he differ from other churchmen of his day?
3. Make a list of at least five characteristics of this priest that men hope to find in any minister or priest. Do you think that such ministers have always been rare? Discuss.
4. What important differences in character do you find between the Parish Priest and the Pardoner? Discuss.

OVER-ALL:

1. Which characters in this group does Chaucer seem to admire? Which characters seem the most unpleasant?
2. Which descriptions are touched with humor? Is Chaucer's humor always disapproving? Discuss.
3. What impression do you get of Chaucer himself from his descriptions of the Canterbury pilgrims? Discuss.
4. How do these selections from "The Prologue" indicate that life in Medieval England was (a) often gay? (b) quite prosperous? (c) inseparably interwoven with, or dominated by, the Church? (d) very different from life in Anglo-Saxon England?

Lyrics and ballads became popular.

A HYMN TO THE VIRGIN

ANONYMOUS C. 1300

Very early in France, poets had made use of rhyme in the invention of graceful, unusual verse forms. The Normans introduced these fashions into English poetry. An example of the ingenuity of Middle English poets is to be seen in "A Hymn to the Virgin" composed by some unknown singer early in the fourteenth century.

You will notice that the English lines when read alone have their own rhyming pattern and express their own thought completely. But inserted among them are lines of a Latin poem that also rhymes, and that dovetails perfectly into the thought of the English verses.

Although most of the English words can be recognized, and the Latin lines are easy, a parallel translation is provided. Try reading the original verses aloud. Even though you do not know Latin, some of the words will have meaning for you. Remember that the final *ë* of the English words is like the final *a* in our word *Virginia.*

<table>
<tr>
<td>

OF ON that is so fayr and
bright
Velut maris stella

</td>
<td>

OF ONE that is so fair and
bright
Like a star of the sea

</td>
</tr>
</table>

282

Brighter than the day is
   light,
Parens et puella:
5 Ic crie to the, thou see
   to me,
Levedy, preye thi Sone
   for me,
Tam pia,
That ic mote come to thee
Maria.

Brighter than the day is
   light,
Both parent and maiden:
I cry to thee, thou see to
   me,
Lady, pray thy Son for
   me,
So Holy
That I might come to thee
Mary!

10 Al this world was for-lorë

Eva peccatrice,
Tyl our Lord was y-borë
De te genetricë.

With *avë* it went away

15 Thuster nuth and comz
   the day
Salutis
The wellë springeth ut of
   the,
Virtutis.

All this world was forlorn
   (or lost)
Through Eve, a sinner,
Till our Lord was born
*Through thee, Ma-
   donna.*

With rejoicing it went
   away

Dark night and comes the
   day
Of salvation;
The well springeth out of
   thee,
*Of thy power (or
   goodness).*

Levedy, flour of allë thing,
20 *Rosa sinë spina,*
Thu bere Jhesu, hevenë
   king
Gratia divina:
Of alle thu ber'st the pris,

Levedy, quene of paradys
25 *Electa:*
Maydë mildë, moder *es*

Effecta.

Lady, flower of all things,
Rose without thorn,
Thou bore Jesus, heavenly
   king
By grace divine,
Of all thou borest the
   prize,

Lady, queen of Paradise
O Chosen One
Maiden mild, Mother *art
   thou
Become.*

FOR INTERPRETATION

1. What lines in the first stanza describe the Virgin Mary? What request does the poet make of Mary?

2. What belief common to all Christians is expressed in the second stanza?

3. Show how the thought of the Latin lines in each stanza dovetails with the thought of the English lines.

PRAISE OF WOMEN

ROBERT MANNYNG

The better acquainted one becomes with writers of long ago the more clearly one sees the changelessness of human nature. Fashions in dress and speech may vary with the years, but the desires of a man's heart are the same in any century. We may smile at Robert Mannyng's spelling of "woman's," but most men will agree that he is entirely right in the value he places upon a "gode womman."

No THYNG ys to man so dere	NOTHING is to man so dear
As wommanys love in gode manere.	As woman's love in good manner.
A gode womman is mannys blys,	A good woman is man's bliss,
There her love right and stedfast ys.	Where her love right and steadfast is.
5 There ys no solas under hevene	There is no solace under heaven
Of alle that a man may nevene	Of all that a man may name
That shulde a man so moche glew	That should a man so much gladden
As a gode womman that loveth true.	As a good woman that loveth true.
Ne derer is none in Goddis hurde	No dearer is any in God's herd
10 Than a chaste womman with lovely worde.	Than a chaste woman with loving word.

284

1. How many times does the author express in slightly different words the central thought of the poem? Select the two lines in which you think he has given best expression to his theme.

2. What is the author's chief requirement for a *good* woman? Do you think of other qualities that he might have added? If so, name them.

3. Subject for discussion: Would the average man's definition of a good woman today be the same as Robert Mannyng's definition?

EARLY ENGLISH AND SCOTTISH BALLADS

From the twelfth century on, ballads were made up and sung the length and breadth of the British Isles. The use of rhyme introduced by the Normans made the ballad an easy form to memorize, and the wide variety of subject matter appealed to the common folk. Since the ballads were distinctly *oral* literature, their language changed with place and time. Had twelfth century ballads found their way into printed form at the time they were being sung, they would be in a language even more difficult for us to read than Chaucer's Midland dialect. However, it was not until the eighteenth century that any one found the ballads interesting enough to collect and publish. By that time they had taken on a fairly modern form. The *language* had changed with the speech of the generations that preserved it. The ballads do reflect dialectal differences, many of which still exist in the British Isles. And as one might expect from the casual way they were composed, there are mistakes in grammar and flaws in rhyme and rhythm.

To read a ballad well, one should get the "feel" of the movement, and then shape pronunciation and accent to fit that rhythm. Remember that these stories were really sung, often to the movement of a creaking saddle or to the stamping of feet and clapping of hands. A certain sing-song effect is therefore not inappropriate.

THE RIDDLING KNIGHT

In imagination can you picture a gathering of English farm folks on a holiday? Perhaps it is a harvest festival, or a wedding party, or a christening. Everyone has eaten plenty of good food. Cups of ale are going the rounds; and some one starts to sing. The first line gives the clue—it is the popular ballad of "The Riddling Knight," and the whole company swings in on the refrain. Hands begin to clap in time to the rhythm; feet are stomping. One group may begin to dance. As the singer carries on the story, the crowd choruses the refrains, breaking in after each line. It does not matter that the lines of the chorus make no particular sense— everyone is having a part in the singing. Everyone is having a hilarious time.

I

MGI	THERE were three sisters fair and bright,
G	*Jennifer, Gentle and Rosemary,* ·
MGI	And they three loved one valiant knight—
G	*As the dow flies over the mulberry-tree.*

II

DGI	5	The eldest sister let him in,
		And barr'd the door with a silver pin.

III

MGI	The second sister made his bed,
	And placed soft pillows under his head.

IV

LGI		The youngest sister that same night
	10	Was resolved for to wed wi' this valiant knight.

V

BI	"And if you can answer questions three,
	O then, fair maid, I'll marry wi' thee.

VI

B	'O what is louder nor a horn,
	Or what is sharper nor a thorn?

2. Lines 2 and 4 are to be repeated in each stanza.
4. DOW—Dove.
6. PIN—Bolt.
13. NOR—Than.

VII

15 'Or what is heavier nor the lead,
    Or what is better nor the bread?

VIII

'Or what is longer nor the way,
Or what is deeper nor the sea?' "—

IX

LG1 "O shame is louder nor a horn,
20 And hunger is sharper nor a thorn.

X

"O sin is heavier nor the lead,
The blessing's better nor the bread.

XI

"O the wind is longer nor the way
And love is deeper nor the sea."

XII

B1 25 "You have answer'd aright my questions three
U   *Jennifer, Gentle and Rosemary;*
B1   And now, fair maid, I'll marry wi' thee,
U   *As the dow flies over the mulberry-tree."*

17. WAY—Road.

FOR INTERPRETATION

1. Which line of the refrain contributes to the meaning of the first stanza? Does it add anything to the sense of the succeeding stanzas? Discuss. Which line of the refrain seems not at all to fit the meanings of the story-lines? How do you account for such a line? Discuss.

2. How must the name "Rosemary" be pronounced throughout the ballad? How must "sea" be pronounced in stanzas VIII and XI?

3. Could you guess the answers to any of the riddles? Could there be other possible answers to the riddles? If so, suggest some.

4. Which maiden did the knight marry?

287

ROBIN HOOD AND ALLAN-A-DALE

No one needs an introduction to Robin Hood and his gay minstrel, Allan-a-Dale. The ballad which tells how Robin helped Allan win his bride is a very old one. It was just such ballads as this that were being sung in Chaucer's day. Perhaps one of the pilgrims caroled it on the way to Canterbury.

M
　　COME listen to me, you gallants so free,
　　　　All you that love mirth for to hear,
　　And I will tell you of a bold outlàw,
　　　　That lived in Nottinghamshire.

5　As Robin Hood in the forest stood,
　　　　All under the greenwood tree,
　　There he was aware of a brave young man,
　　　　As fine as fine might be.

　　The youngster was clad in scarlet red,
10　　In scarlet fine and gay;
　　And he did frisk it over the plain,
　　　　And chaunted a roundelay.

288

As Robin Hood next morning stood
Amongst the leaves so gay,
15   There did he espy the same young man
Come drooping along the way.

The scarlet he wore the day before
It was clean cast away;
And at every step he fetched a sigh,
MB1   20   "Alas! and a well-a-day!"

M   Then steppèd forth brave Little John,
And Midge, the miller's son;
Which made the young man bend his bow,
When as he see them come.

MB1   25   "Stand off! stand off!" the young man said,
"What is your will with me?"
DB1   "You must come before our master straight,
Under yon greenwood tree."

M   And when he came bold Robin before,
30   Robin asked him courteously,
B1   "O, hast thou any money to spare,
For my merry men and me?"

MB1   "I have no money," the young man said,
"But five shillings and a ring;
35   And that I have kept this seven long years,
To have at my wedding.

"Yesterday I should have married a maid,
But she was from me ta'en,
And chosen to be an old knight's delight,
40   Whereby my poor heart is slain."

B1   "What is thy name?" then said Robin Hood,
"Come tell me, without any fail."
MB1   "By the faith of my body," then said the young
man,
"My name it is Allan-a-Dale."

B1 45 "What wilt thou give me," said Robin Hood,
          "In ready gold or fee,
       To help thee to thy true love again,
          And deliver her unto thee?"

MB1   "I have no money," then quoth the young man,
      50   "No ready gold nor fee,
          But I will swear upon a book
             Thy true servant for to be."

           "How many miles is it to thy true love?
              Come tell me without guile."
      55   "By the faith of my body," then said the young
              man,
           "It is but five little mile."

M   Then Robin he hasted over the plain,
              He did neither stint nor lin,
           Until he came unto the church
      60   Where Allan should keep his weddin'.

DB1   "What hast thou here?" the bishop then said,
              "I prithee now tell unto me."
B1   "I am a bold harper," quoth Robin Hood,
              "And the best in the north country."

DB1 65 "O welcome, O welcome," the bishop he said,
              "That music best pleaseth me."
B1   "You shall have no music," quoth Robin Hood,
              "Till the bride and bridegroom I see."

M   With that came in a wealthy knight,
      70   Which was both grave and old;
           And after him a finikin lass,
              Did shine like the glistering gold.

B1   "This is not a fit match," quoth Robin Hood,
              "That you do seem to make here;

58. LIN—Stop.

75 For since we are come into the church,
  The bride shall chuse her own dear."

M Then Robin Hood put his horn to his mouth
  And blew blasts two and three;
  When four-and-twenty yeomen bold
80 Came leaping over the lea.

  And when they came into the churchyard,
   Marching all in a row,
  The first man was Allan-a-Dale,
   To give bold Robin his bow.

B1 85 "This is thy true love," Robin he said,
   "Young Allan, as I hear say;
  And you shall be married this same time,
   Before we depart away."

DB1 "That shall not be," the bishop he cried,
90 "For thy word shall not stand;
  They shall be three times askèd in the church,
   As the law is of our land."

M Robin Hood pulled off the bishop's coat,
   And put it upon Little John;
B1 95 "By the faith of my body," then Robin said,
   "This cloth doth make thee a man."

M When Little John went into the quire,
   The people began to laugh;
  He asked them seven times into church,
100 Lest three times should not be enough.

MB2 "Who gives me this maid?" said Little John,
B1 Quoth Robin Hood, "That do I;
  And he that takes her from Allan-a-Dale,
   Full dearly he shall her buy."

97. QUIRE—The part of the chancel in which the choir sits.

U   105   And then having ended this merry wedding,
The bride looked like a queen;
And so they returned to the merry greenwood,
Amongst the leaves so green.

FOR INTERPRETATION

1. Why was Allan-a-Dale "frisking" it over the plain the first time that Robin saw him? Why did Allan come "drooping along the way" the next morning?

2. What made Robin think Allan might have money to spare? What reward does Robin agree to accept for helping Allan marry his sweetheart?

3. How did Robin get into the church at the time of the wedding?

4. What objection did the bishop make to the change in bridegroom? What formalities used to precede the marriage ceremony? How did Robin Hood meet the objection of the bishop? Who performed the wedding service?

5. Why do you think there was no opposition on the part of the guests?

6. What line tells us that the bride was well pleased?

7. Do you know the name of a song often sung at weddings which was composed for Allan-a-Dale's wedding in the opera, *Robin Hood?*

THE LOWLANDS O' HOLLAND

Tragedies of the sea were all too common to folks of the British Isles. England and Scotland have been, from earliest times, the homeland of sailors. And with small boats and stormy seas, there were hundreds of sailors who never returned. Some of their stories were told in ballads like the following, which, surviving in fragmentary or altered form, leave us guessing about what really happened.

I

LG   "My love has built a bonny ship, and set her on the sea,
With seven score good mariners to bear her company;
There's three score is sunk, and three score dead at sea,
And the Lowlands o' Holland has twin'd my love and
me.

II

5   "My love he built another ship, and set her on the main,
And nane but twenty mariners for to bring her hame;

4. TWIN'D—Parted.

But the weary wind began to rise, and the sea began to
rout,
My love then and his bonny ship turn'd withershins
about.

III

"Then shall neither coif come on my head nor comb
come in my hair;
10   Then shall neither coal nor candle-light shine in my
bower mair;
Nor will I love another one until the day I die,
Sin' the Lowlands o' Holland has twin'd my love and
me."—

IV

DG   "O haud your tongue, my daughter dear, be still and be
content;
There are mair lads in Galloway, ye neen nae sair
lament."—
LG   15   "O there is none in Gallow, there's none at a' for me,
For I never loved a love but one, and he's drown'd in
the sea."

8. WITHERSHINS ABOUT—Around against the sun; here apparently "upside
down."
9. COIF—A close-fitting cap.
14. GALLOWAY—A district in Southwestern Scotland, along the coast.
14. YE NEEN NAE SAIR LAMENT—You need not weep so sorely.

FOR INTERPRETATION

1. How many men sailed with the first ship? What do *you* think happened to it? If only three score of the men were drowned (sunk), what
do you think happened to the other three score "dead at sea"? Discuss.
2. What do you think "The Lowlands o' Holland" refers to? Why?
3. Where do you think the sailor built his second ship? Why would it
be hard to bring her home with only twenty mariners? What happened to
the second ship? How do you think the girl learned of the tragedy?
4. What signs of mourning does the girl vow to show? Does the mother
approve? What consolation does she offer? How does the girl reply?
5. Do you think the girl will keep her vows? Discuss.
6. How does the reader know that this is a Scotch ballad? How should
the word *die* be pronounced in line 11?

EXTENDED ACTIVITIES

CONQUERING NORMANS ADDED COLOR AND FRESHNESS AND VARIETY

≻ I·II ≺

HISTORY IN BRIEF

	Normans	Angevins or Plantaganets	The House of Lancaster	The House of York	The Tudors	Events in America
1000-1099 (11th Century)	William, the Conqueror William II					
1100-1199 (12th Century)	Henry I (Charter of Liberties) Stephen	Henry II Richard, the Lion-Hearted				
		—CRUSADES—				
1200-1299 (13th Century)		John I (Magna Carta 1215) Henry III (House of Commons 1265)				
1300-1399 (14th Century)		Edward I, II, III (Hundred Years' War) Richard II (deposed)				
1400-1499 (15th Century)			Henry IV, V, VI (Wars of the Roses) (End of Hundred Years' War)	Edward IV, V Richard III	Henry VII (End of Wars of the Roses) (Caxton's printing press set up)	Columbus discovers America, 1492

FOR ACQUAINTANCE WITH AUTHORS

ROBERT MANNYNG (1264-1340)—"PRAISE OF WOMEN"

Robert Mannyng, a monk who wrote for the "solace and amusement of the unlearned when they sit together in fellowship," was one of the first writers to deliberately address his work to the lower, uneducated classes. In simple poetry he retold Bible legends, interspersing religious instruction with moral teachings. He wrote also a number of pleasing lyrics, of which his "Praise of Women" is best known.

GEOFFREY CHAUCER (1340–1400)—"THE CANTERBURY TALES"

Chaucer, were he to return today, would be highly amused at the aura of literary sanctity surrounding himself and his *Canterbury Tales*. He would be, perhaps, a bit shamefaced at being called the "Father of English Poetry," a title too dignified and prim for the man who delighted in poking fun at all humanity—himself included. Yet he would have enjoyed the irony of it; he who probably expected to be remembered for his faithful service to three kings, for his competent handling of his post as Comptroller of Customs, perhaps for some of his translations of Italian and French literature. Instead, history has glorified him as the author of a group of stories he composed for his own and his friends' amusement—*The Canterbury Tales*.

We know little of Chaucer's life except that he was a busy man of affairs, happy now and then at "having balanced his ledgers and gone back to his books." His father was a wine merchant, rather well-to-do; and as was the custom his son was placed as a page in the home of a nobleman. As a young squire, Chaucer saw service in the army of Edward III in France, was captured and later released through ransom paid by the king. It seems likely that his career as a secret agent and diplomat had already begun; from then on his public life is highlighted by confidential diplomatic missions to France and Italy. During his stays in England he served as a sort of ceremonial functionary in court; his fortunes, politically and privately, depending upon those of the powerful John of Gaunt, his patron.

Although he began his hobby of writing by imitating French and Italian poets, his interest in men and life led him to describe the people around him. His accuracy was such that today, after six centuries, the prioress almost fingers the amulet on her rosary and the moonstruck squire lifts huge sighs to heaven and his lady. His accurate and sensitive description has led critics to say that Chaucer was a novelist when there were no novels.

OF LITERARY FORM AND STYLE

THE EMERGENCE OF MODERN ENGLISH

From the scholar's point of view, one of the most important effects of the Norman Conquest was the modification of the Anglo-Saxon language into modern English. Two different kinds of changes took place, one having to do with the word-store or vocabulary, the other having to do with grammatical structure.

The first change was really the case of one language absorbing another. The original Anglo-Saxon, like a small, tough sponge, soaked up a sea of French words, expanding enormously in the process. Numerically and expressively the stock of words was multiplied. For we do not today use two words of the same original meaning in exactly the same way. For example, *house* from the Saxon indicates an ordinary dwelling; but *mansion* and *manse* from the French *maison* indicate special kinds of houses. Usually the Anglo-Saxon words are the ones with the humble or common meaning, and the Norman-French have become the dress-up or specialized words.

The Norman-French was a *Romance* language—that is, it was a modification of the Latin which had been spoken by the Roman soldiers who conquered Gaul. Thus English received through it a great store of Latin derivatives. Another fund of Latin words kept coming into English use directly, through the studies of churchmen and scholars. Today, for example, we make use of the Anglo-Saxon word *red,* the Norman-French word *rouge,* and words like *ruby* and *rubicund* directly from the Latin.

The absorption of French and Latin words into English gave our language the capacity to make thousands of new words by using prefixes and suffixes. At the same time it retained the picturesque, though sometimes cumbersome, knack of making compounds. The blend of Teutonic and Romance characteristics has resulted in giving modern English the most flexible and expressive vocabulary of all the living languages.

The second change that took place was a remarkable simplification of English grammar. Both Latin and Anglo-Saxon were highly inflected languages—that is, the various uses of words were indicated by changes in form of the words themselves. In learning a new language these inflections are the most difficult to master. And so when Saxon and Norman got to talking together, they picked up each other's words and let the inflected endings go. The resulting simplification of inflections was further aided by the adoption of a simple or normal sentence order and by the substitution of natural gender for the confusing system of grammatical gender. The student who has wrestled with the scrambled arrangement of a sentence in any foreign tongue will appreciate this modification.

With a greatly increased vocabulary and a greatly simplified grammatical structure, a vital, flexible language emerged during the Middle English period. And the popularity of such great literary works as *The Canterbury Tales* helped to stabilize that language.

QUESTIONS IN APPRECIATION:

1. Read carefully the first eighteen lines of Chaucer's "Prologue" in the Middle English version. Is your first impression that there are many or few words in it unknown in modern English?

2. What are the modern forms for the following words: shoures, droghte, perced, rote, licour, eek, fowles, slepen, ye, seken?

3. *Couthe* meant *known;* what modern word meaning *unknown* or *strange* uses this form? *Halwes* meant *shrines* or *holy places;* what modern word does it suggest? *Corages* meant *hearts;* do you think our word *courage* may have come from it? Check your answer by looking up *courage* in a large dictionary.

4. In the two lyrics, "Hymn to the Virgin" and "Praise of Women" is it peculiarities of spelling or the use of words unknown to us that makes the language seem queer? Is there any likeness between the word *levedy* and our word *lady?* Do you think of a modern word for *gladness* that is something like *glew?* Name any words in these two poems which bear no slightest resemblance to words of corresponding meaning in modern English.

5. Is the sentence order in "Praise of Women" like the sentence order in modern English? Is the meaning of the poem easy or difficult to get?

ENGLISH LITERATURE TAKES ON FRILLS

In the eleventh and twelfth centuries English literature went into retirement as if it were mourning the passing of Anglo-Saxon supremacy. The truth is that Saxon literature had gone into a decline even before the Battle of Hastings and that during the first century after the Conquest, the Normans were clinging to their French. Then suddenly, about the beginning of the thirteenth century, the new English language began making her literary debut—and all dressed up in the latest French modes. Her verses were flounced with rhyme and refrain. Even the materials were new; for now instead of only religious themes, there were love songs, nature poetry, tales of chivalry, books of travel, snatches of satire —writings of almost every sort.

Ballads, already mentioned, were being sung the length and breadth of the nation. And there were pretty little lyrics of carefully planned pattern. Even history was told in rhyme, Layamon's *Brut,* for example, tracing the history of England from Roman times to the days of Chaucer, and all in jingling verse. Such works were called "riming chronicles." There were also long *metrical romances* which retold stories about Britain, France, ancient Rome, and Troy. The Emperor Charlemagne and King Arthur were popular subjects for these rhymed romances. One of the best known among them is "Sir Gawayne and the Grene Knight"—an adventurous tale in which Gawayne proves himself faultless in five virtues: purity, compassion, fellowship, courtesy, and frankness.

With the Church holding a predominant place in medieval life, there was naturally a religious flavor in much of the writing, and some of the poetry was definitely religious in purpose. Perhaps the most important single poem aside from *The Canterbury Tales* was a long religious allegory, *The Vision of Piers, the Plowman,* attributed to William Langland

(1332–1400), a poor clerk of the Church. One day as he slept beside a stream he dreamed of Peter, the plowman, who was to come to remedy all abuses. The poem was told and retold, written and rewritten until no one is sure how much of it is Langland's work. However, it does give a picture of fourteenth-century England viewed by an ordinary citizen who writes of the horror of the Black Death, berates lazy workmen, mourns the corruption of the law courts, and looks forward to the second coming of Christ.

The field of prose literature likewise shows a surprising variety of forms and subject matter. During the Middle English period appeared the very important translation of the New Testament from Latin into English by John Wyclif. This was the first attempt at a translation of the Bible into the speech of the common people. In the fourteenth century there appeared also a remarkable work of truth and fiction, *The Voyage and Travaile of Sir John Mandeville.* It was evidently a translation from the Latin or French of an earlier collection from tales of famous travelers. There are hearsay accounts of prodigious wonders, but the unknown English translator (Mandeville was apparently a penname) only vouches for the truth of the accounts about places he has seen himself. These descriptions are sober enough, and he further proves his wisdom by advancing a very good argument that the earth is round—this, in 1356.

In the fifteenth century came Thomas Malory's *Le Morte d'Arthur,* a prose compilation of the stories of King Arthur. From all sources Malory took the legends and stories surrounding the British hero and wove them into a long narrative romance. What Chaucer had done for English poetry, Malory did for English prose. His graceful style and the highly romantic flavor of his tales have made his book a favorite in his day. It has remained a valuable source book for poets and artists.

Books had begun to be entertaining, and by the time William Caxton had set up his printing press in 1476, there was splendid material for him to work on. Caxton had learned the art of printing in Cologne. When he set up his own press in England, among the first books he published were Malory's *Le Morte d'Arthur,* Chaucer's *The Canterbury Tales,* and Wyclif's *Bible.* And this, in brief, was the status of English literature at the time that Columbus set out on his epoch-making voyage.

QUESTIONS IN APPRECIATION:

1. What important differences in *form* do you notice between the Anglo-Saxon lyrics, such as the Riddles, and the two Middle English lyrics? What differences in *poetic effect?* Discuss.

2. How do the ballads reflect the spirit of Medieval England? Discuss.

3. Read the definition of a ballad presented in the *Appendix.* Point out the respects in which "Robin Hood and Allan-a-Dale" is a typical folk ballad.

4. What important differences in *form* do you notice between the

298

Beowulf translation and the selections from *The Canterbury Tales?*
What differences in poetic effect? Why? Discuss.
  5. From any of the selections from Middle English literature, point out
     evidence that:
     a. The Normans were a musical people.
     b. That they had brought a livelier spirit into English life.
     c. That England had acquired a knowledge of, and interest in, the
          world at large.
     d. That English literature was, in general, expanded and improved
          under Norman influence.

TALES ON THE WAY TO CANTERBURY

Just as "The Prologue" to *The Canterbury Tales* presents a typical cross-
section of Middle English *life*, so do the *Tales* themselves provide a taste
of Middle English literature and learning. For Chaucer varied his stories
and the style of their telling to suit each narrator. The Knight told a
long leisurely love story—a typical *metrical romance*. It was really a tale
of ancient Thebes and Athens, but in the Knight's telling it took on the
background of chivalry, with knights and ladies and tournaments in regular medieval style. The Prioress told a Church legend of a pathetic child
martyr, that made the company weep. Her Priest told a gaily elaborated
version of the fable of the cock and the fox. In this merry tale, the cock
Chanticleer and his favorite hen Pertelote are presented as man and wife
with astonishingly lifelike traits. Chanticleer is pompous, long-winded,
full of learning (he quotes Cato and Cicero, and even a line from Robert
Mannyng's "Praise of Women"); but throws his judgment to the winds
when Pertelote looks at him sidewise and hints that he's a coward.
Chaucer thoroughly enjoyed himself in telling this one.
The scholarly clerk tells very soberly the bookish tale of patient
Griselda—the meek and loyal wife who accepted without reproach the
cruelest testing by her husband. And Chaucer tacks on a very matter-of-
fact epilogue beginning thus—or in words to this effect—

> "Griselda is dead and so is her patience
> And both lie buried in Italy;
> And now let me tell the world—
> Let no wedded man be so rash as to try
> *His* wife's patience in the hope to find
> A modern Griselda. He won't!"

The garrulous Wife of Bath, after an introduction three times as long
as her story, tells a fairy tale built around a solution to the question of
what every woman wants more than anything else—to be boss over her
husband.
One might go on at length. The Pardoner told a clever allegory of
Death and three roisterers; the Monk started a cycle of tragedies so depressing that he was stopped in full flight and not allowed to continue.

Chaucer began a rhymed tale of Sir Thopas in such wretched doggerel that the Host stops him, saying that if he is no better poet than that, he had better not try any verse! Chaucer accordingly is one of the two characters to tell his story in prose.

But space will not allow a review of all the stories. In their diversity they reflect the multiple interests of medieval life. And in their telling Chaucer shows his familiarity with the languages and literatures of Greece, Rome, Italy, and France. His own side-remarks and those which he puts into the mouths of the other pilgrims furnish further insight into his understanding of human nature and his appreciation of men with all their faults and follies.

Each member of the class should read at least one of the *Tales* and prepare a report to present orally. There are a number of good modern versions of *The Canterbury Tales* available; and a good language student should not find it too difficult to read one story in the original. Tales which are suitable for retelling are those of the Knight, the Clerk, the Pardoner, the Wife of Bath, the Nun's Priest, and the Prioress.

FOR FURTHER READING

BELLOC, HILAIRE, *William the Conqueror*
DAVIS, WILLIAM STEARNS, *Life on a Medieval Barony*
DOYLE, SIR ARTHUR CONAN, *The White Company*
HALL, MAUDE M., *Ballads and Other Narrative Poems*
HILL, WILLIAM ERNEST (translator), *The Canterbury Tales*
LAMB, HAROLD, *The Crusades*
MACKINTOSH, ELIZABETH, *Richard of Bordeaux*
NICOLSON, J. U. (translator), *The Canterbury Tales*
NOYES, ALFRED, *Sherwood*
PYLE, HOWARD, *Men of Iron; The Merry Adventures of Robin Hood*
QUENNELL, MARJORIE AND CHARLES H. B., *The History of Everyday Things in Britain* (1066–1799)
QUILLER-COUCH, SIR ARTHUR, *The Oxford Book of Ballads*
SCOTT, SIR WALTER, *Ivanhoe; The Talisman*
SEDGWICK, HENRY DWIGHT, *Dan Chaucer*
STEVENSON, ROBERT LOUIS, *The Black Arrow*
STUART, DOROTHY M., *The Men and Women of Plantagenet England*
TAPPAN, EVA MARCH, *When Knights Were Bold*
TENNYSON, ALFRED, *The Idylls of the King*

THE AGE OF ELIZABETH
1492-1620

"THE PLAY'S THE THING"

Macbeth

III

A new spirit had grown out of the activities of the Renaissance.

ELIZABETHAN ENGLAND

(1492–1620)

During the closing years of the fifteenth century the yeast of the Renaissance had started working in England. "Renaissance"—rebirth— the word itself holds a whisper of glory—was the term given to a great intellectual movement which spread over Europe during the fifteenth and sixteenth centuries. The world actually was being reborn, under the very noses of inquisitive Englishmen. Madly they set out to explore the result—on the seas, in books, in painting, in music, sculpture, and art. The richness of Italian culture overflowed into Europe and England. Men began to look at art—not because it could decorate their churches, but because it was beautiful. They discovered that literature dealt with life. They began to see that great ideals, noble impulses, however long ago expressed, never really die but come to life again for every generation that stops to ponder them.

Even the boundaries of the old world cracked under the impetus of this tidal wave. A Genoese voyager—one Christopher Columbus—had sailed for the West and found new lands. Were these shores the fringes of the Eastern Indies? Perhaps. At any rate, there was no dropping-off-place, no Edge-of-the-World to fear.

As the great intellectual movement rolled northward it worked in different ways in different countries. In England the movement showed itself especially in new directions in scholarship and in an outpouring of literary works. Printing presses rolled. Schools and universities were flooded with students. There was a reaching out for new knowledge, new experiences. Life, it seemed, could be touched with wonder.

The revival of learning was, however, only one phase of the great change in life which took place during this period in England. In every department the old was being superseded by the new. The Tudor kings had reached the throne—keen, shrewd, close-fisted business men. In 1509 came Henry VIII, eighteen years of age, handsome and clear-eyed, expert at shooting and tennis, fond of music and books. England swelled with pride. To be English, to speak English, to love England suddenly became important.

Everywhere were signs of economic progress; the new aristocracy of trade had coins to jingle in their leather bags. Their wives could flaunt damask and silk and velvet as well as the lord's lady. Towns and cities pushed their way across manor lands; streets echoed to galloping horses, to merchants' vans and the closed chairs of noblemen. In the new wealth and new glory only the Church failed to prosper. In Germany, Martin Luther preached openly against the abuses of the Church—and the Protestant Reformation had begun in Europe. Word of the out-spoken young priest found approval in England. At the same time, Henry VIII, grown tired of his Spanish wife who was years older than he, met the fair Anne Boleyn, a girl of sixteen and lady-in-waiting to the queen. Henry, with the earnestness he applied to all endeavor, set out in pursuit. Since divorce was not permitted by the Roman Catholic Church, and since divorce was essential to Henry's interests, he precipitated a quarrel with the Pope and made Protestantism the state religion. Henry was now, in 1534, Supreme Head of the English Church; in his stout capable hand he held more power than any ruler before him.

With his new title Henry ordered the destruction of the monasteries and the filling of the royal coffers with their wealth and property. Not since the invasion of the Danes had there been such pillaging and wanton destruction of priceless relics and manuscripts. The glass of the Lincoln Cathedral was used as a mark for crossbow practice and few remonstrated. As far as literature is concerned, one of the great results of the Reformation in England was a renewed interest in the Bible which led to attempts to make a new translation of it. The translation of the New Testament which John Wyclif had made was in a language which men no longer generally understood. In 1526 William Tyndale had begun a translation of the Old Testament which was distinguished for its simplicity, vigor, and clarity. After his death his work was continued by Miles Coverdale; and in 1538, Old and New Testament were put together to form the Great Bible. Coming as it did with Henry's break with the Church of Rome, the Tyndale-Coverdale translation enjoyed wide circulation throughout the land.

With his art of maintaining popularity and his shrewd eye for a good servant, Henry made Parliament his ally and not his check-rein. He waxed fat and irritable, but his subjects, still worshipful, prayed that he might be spared until the young prince Edward, his only son, could take the throne. Edward, the son of Henry and his third wife, Jane Seymour, was nine when his father died, a pale-faced, intelligent child. Under his regents, Protestantism was strengthened during his six years as king. As he lay dying, Protestants and Catholics elbowed for position; once more the succession was in dispute.

To the throne came Mary, crabbed and sour at thirty-seven, daughter of Henry and his first wife, Catherine of Aragon. Mary was a devout Catholic; England held its breath in trepidation. Its fears were realized; Catholic counselors appeared and persecutions of loyal Protestants began. Certain that all evils were the result of England's falling from faith, Mary burned at the stake in five years more victims than Henry in thirty-eight.

As long as she was physically able, she pursued her obstinate course of persecutions, trials, and force-fed religion. The bells that tolled her death pealed more joy than sorrow.

To England's throne in 1588 climbed Elizabeth—a very Queen of England. Tall and straight, the daughter of Anne Boleyn and Henry was twenty-five, red-haired, long nosed, and sharp tongued. She was not, as her subjects later insisted, a Heaven-descended goddess but the last of the Tudors with their greatness and their faults. Her coarse jests and ready wit, her physical endurance and her keen mind brought back the image of Henry VIII in all his glory. She inherited an empty treasury, a disbanded army, wasted navy, and untried counselors in addition to her own personal problem of choosing—or evading—a husband. With flirtation as one of her powerful weapons, Elizabeth set out to restore English pride and English position.

Forty-five years she reigned and the brew of English pride bubbled over in a froth of gold. Under her rule the monarchy became established and the authority of the central government made itself felt in every corner of the land. The Protestant church was restored, but the Catholics were left in peace. With affairs abroad Elizabeth also dealt deftly. Both France and Spain would have welcomed an alliance with England, but knowing that favors to one would mean war with the other, Elizabeth kept a middle ground and favored neither.

Mary, Queen of Scotland, one-time Queen of France, and now claimant to the English throne through her grandmother who was a daughter of Henry VII, threatened Elizabeth's security. Graciously lovely at nineteen, Catholic, and rich in foreign influence, Mary was unwelcome at Elizabeth's court where she had fled from Scotland. Political expediency favored her death, but Elizabeth kept her prisoner for twenty years before she sent her to the guillotine on a charge of plotting against the Queen's life. The tragic Queen of Scots moved all who met her to pity, but her death brought unity and strength to England. Under condemnation of death Mary had appealed to Philip of Spain to avenge her and to secure the throne for her son. At her death, Philip assembled a large fleet and army which set out in 1488. Elizabeth made hasty preparations for invasion, but the smaller English fleet under Sir Francis Drake attacked the enemy spread out in a seven-mile crescent across the English Channel. Of the hundred and fifty vessels in the Spanish Armada, less than a third escaped. Although the victory was due as much to weather conditions favoring the attackers as to their skill and daring, the victory was nonetheless a tremendous one. It marked England's emergence as a world power, and patriotic enthusiasm ran high. Pride in the British navy has ever since been traditional.

Elizabeth's reign was distinguished also for her policies of trade extension and of colonization. Men set out to hunt fabulous silver mines in America and rivers whose waters rolled over precious stones. Large merchant companies such as the Hudson Bay Company and the East India

Company were chartered to trade with Russia and the Far East. Men like Sir Walter Raleigh and Sir Humphrey Gilbert made attempts to settle colonies in America. Manufacturing received promotion and encouragement. Agriculture was studied and improved. The great middle class came into a position of economic and political power. The standard of living generally was rising, and people as a whole were enjoying more of the material comforts of life. Beauty and enjoyment rather than defense determined the domestic architecture. Cheerless, windowless manor houses gave place to many-windowed country houses whose diamond panes caught the English sunlight. Gold and silver tableware gleamed from the heavy polished tables. Bejeweled ladies stiff in hooped-out gowns flirted with gentlemen in ruffs and broidered doublets, gay hose and pointed shoes. Traveling theatrical companies paraded their comedy before the well-fed nobles and wealthy merchants. Madrigals and ballads hung sweetly over the perfumed air. The floors might be filthy under the fresh strewn rushes; the gutters might run with garbage and mud but the times were spacious and bright. Even the yeoman's lot improved; he, too, discarded his straw pallet for a feather tick, his wooden trenchar for plates and tankards of pewter. He ate better and wined better and laughed at the latest ribald comedies.

About herself, Elizabeth gathered a brilliant court. Gentlemen adventurers and scholars enlivened the palace. She gave a gracious nod to writers; and straightway pens began to flow. Explorers, courtiers, men-in-waiting, soldiers—everyone turned out lyrics when on leave between battles and voyages. Men who had tried their fortunes around the world came home to tell strange wonders. And other men wrote exuberant accounts of their achievements. There were statesmen and orators who held audiences spellbound by their eloquence.

But the great Queen also liked to laugh. And so to London came actors and playmakers. The English stage became a shining road to glory. Comedies, tragedies, blood-and-thunder dramas, masques, romances, chronicles walked their dreams across its boards. And to this busy life of the London theaters came, late in the sixteenth century, young William Shakespeare, destined to be supreme in his own day and for centuries to come.

The new spirit was the inspiration of great prose as well as of poetry and drama. It animated cold intellectual natures like that of Sir Francis Bacon who declared, "I have taken all knowledge to be my province." It was the inspiration of great translations, notably the King James Version of the Bible begun under Elizabeth though not completed until 1611 under James I.

Scan the names of those who wrote their books and dedicated them to bright Queen Bess—Sidney and Spenser and Lyly; Raleigh, Bacon, Marlowe, Shakespeare, Jonson—never again in so short a space of time was any country to produce such a roll of honor.

Renaissance exuberance found expression in an outburst of lyric verse.

From THE FAERIE QUEENE

EDMUND SPENSER

The Faerie Queene is really a long poem composed of many shorter poems, or *cantos*, which in turn are built up of scores of narrative incidents. Spenser completed only about one-fourth of his original plan, and yet the poem as it stands is one of the longest in our language. It was intended to be an allegory—that is, an imaginative story in which the characters and events are symbolic of certain ideas or truths. For example, in the stanzas which are quoted below, the Red Cross Knight represents *Holiness* and Una represents *Truth*. The whole first book of *The Faerie Queene* has to do with their adventures together—the general thought being that if Holiness (or Religion) is to count for anything in the world, it must be united with Truth.

As Book I opens, we learn that the Red Cross Knight has been commissioned by Queene Gloriana to ride with Una to rescue her parents who are kept captive by a huge dragon. The Knight is clad in the armor of the *Christian faith*. They encounter many trials and hardships brought about by such enemies as Duessa (Falsehood), Archimago (Hypocrisy), and Sansfoy (Faithlessness). However, the Book ends with victory over the dragon and the betrothal of the two lovers.

The stanzas quoted below describe Una and the Knight at the opening of their quest. And in illustration of the kind of allegory running through the whole, there are three stanzas which tell of Una's adventures with a savage lion.

Spenser purposely made use of old-fashioned words and spellings to give his poem an air of antiquity.

A GENTLE Knight was pricking on the plaine,
Yecladd in mightie armes and silver shielde,
Wherein old dints of deepe wounds did remaine,
The cruell markes of many a bloudy fielde;
5 Yet armes till that time did he never wield:
His angry steede did chide his foming bitt,
As much disdayning to the curbe to yield:
Full jolly knight he seemed, and faire did sitt,
  As one for knightly giusts and fierce encounters fitt.

10 But on his brest a bloudie Crosse he bore,
The deare remembrance of his dying Lord,
For whose sweete sake that glorious badge he wore,
And dead as living ever him ador'd:
Upon his shield the like was also scor'd,
15 For soveraine hope, which in his helpe he had:
Right faithfull true he was in deede and word,
But of his cheere did seeme too solemne sad;
  Yet nothing did he dread, but ever was ydrad.

Upon a great adventure he was bond,
20 That greatest Gloriana to him gave,
The greatest Glorious Queene of Faerie lond,
To winne him worshipe, and her grace to have,
Which of all earthly things he most did crave;

11. HIS DYING LORD—The reference is to Christ.
15. FOR SOVERAINE HOPE . . . HE HAD—The Knight hoped to have Divine help in fulfilling his mission.
18. YDRAD—Dreaded, or feared. Like *yclad*, in the first stanza, the form is in imitation of the old past participles.
20. GLORIANA—Queene of the Fairy Court, symbolizes *Glory* in the allegory and is also understood to represent Queen Elizabeth.

And ever as he rode, his hart did earne
25   To prove his puissance in battell brave
Upon his foe, and his new force to learne;
Upon his foe, a Dragon horrible and stearne.

A lovely Ladie rode him faire beside,
Upon a lowly Asse more white then snow,
30   Yet she much whiter, but the same did hide
Under a vele, that wimpled was full low,
And over all a blacke stole she did throw,
As one that inly mournd: so was she sad,
And heavie sat upon her palfrey slow;
35   Seemed in heart some hidden care she had,
And by her in a line a milke white lamb she lad.

[In company with the Lady Una, the Red Cross Knight meets and slays the dragon, Error. Later in their journey the Knight is tricked by a dream into believing that Una is false to him, and he forsakes her. Una, distressed, wanders on alone and lost.]

One day nigh wearie of the yrkesome way,
From her unhastie beast she did alight,
And on the grass her daintie limbs did lay
40   In secret shadow, farre from all mens sight:
From her faire head her fillet she undight,
And laid her stole aside. Her angel's face
As the great eye of heaven shynèd bright,
And made a sunshine in the shadie place;
45   Did never mortall eye behold such heavenly grace.

It fortuned out of the thickest wood
A ramping Lyon rushèd suddainly,
Hunting full greedy after salvage blood;
Soone as the royall virgin he did spy,
50   With gaping mouth at her ran greedily,
To have at once devourd her tender corse:

25. PUISSANCE—Power, force.
31. VELE—A veil, or head-covering, pleated (wimpled) like those worn by nuns.
36. IN A LINE . . . SHE LAD—She led a lamb by a leash.

But to the pray when as he drew more ny,
His bloody rage asswagèd with remorse,
And with the sight amazd, forgat his furious forse.

55 Instead thereof he kist her wearie feet,
And lickt her lilly hands with fawning tong,
As he her wrongèd innocence did weet.
O how can beautie maister the most strong
And simple truth subdue avenging wrong?
60 Whose yeelded pride and proud submission,
Still dreading death, when she had markèd long,
Her hart gan melt in great compassion,
And drizling teares did shed for pure affection.

[The Lion accompanies Una as her protector. Una and the Knight are at length reunited. After many, many adventures, the final dragon is slain and Una and the Red Cross Knight are betrothed.]

53. HIS BLOODY RAGE . . . REMORSE—Una's beauty, innocence, and helplessness turn the Lion's rage into pity.
57. WEET—Know, or understand.
60–61. WHOSE YEELDED PRIDE . . . STILL DREADING DEATH—*Whose* refers to the Lion. Una still feared the beast would kill her.

FOR INTERPRETATION

1. Describe in your own words the picture you form of the Red Cross Knight after reading the first stanza. Explain the allegorical meaning implied by the fact that his armor showed the dints of battle, though he had never been armed before.
2. What did the symbol which the Knight wore on his breast signify? Describe the Knight's countenance, or expression.
3. What was the "great adventure" on which the Knight was bound?
4. In your own words, describe the dress and appearance of the Lady Una. Why did she wear a black cloak, as if in mourning?
5. If you were an illustrator about to make a picture of Una, which stanza would you try to portray—the fourth or fifth? Why?
6. What poetic idea does the incident of Una and the Lion mean to represent? Which lines express that thought? Do you believe that there really is truth in the thought? Discuss.
7. In terms of Spenser's allegory, why is it necessary for Una and the Red Cross Knight to be reunited?

From AMORETTI

EDMUND SPENSER

Edmund Spenser called the group of sonnets which he wrote for the Irish girl he was to marry "Amoretti"—that is, "Little Loves," or "Cupids." They were like valentines; and like most of the Elizabethan love lyrics, they were filled with poetic exaggeration and very elaborate figures of speech. Sonnets xv and xxxvii are good ones to remember because they illustrate the musical quality of Spenser's verse and because they are typical Elizabethan sonnets.

The first sonnet refers indirectly to the thriving, world-wide commerce that had sprung up. The second one was inspired by the golden net which his Irish Elizabeth wore over her blond tresses.

XV

YE TRADEFUL merchants that with weary toil
Do seek most precious things to make your gain,
And both the Indias of their treasures spoil,
What needeth you to seek so far in vain?
5 For lo, my love doth in herself contain
All this world's riches that may far be found:
If sapphires, lo, her eyes be sapphires plain;
If rubies, lo, her lips be rubies sound;
If pearls, her teeth be pearls, both pure and round;
10 If ivory, her forehead ivory ween;
If gold, her locks are finest gold on ground;
If silver, her fair hands are silver sheen.
But that which fairest is, but few behold—
Her mind adorned with virtues manifold.

3. BOTH THE INDIAS—East and West Indies—the latter having been so named by explorers who thought they had found a western route to India.

XXXVII

What guile is this, that those her golden tresses
She doth attire under a net of gold,
And with sly skill so cunningly them dresses
That which is gold or hair may scarce be told?
5 Is it that men's frail eyes, which gaze too bold,
She may entangle in that golden snare,

And, being caught, may craftily enfold
Their weaker hearts, which are not well aware?
Take heed, therefore, mine eyes, how ye do stare
10 Henceforth too rashly on that guileful net,
In which if ever ye entrappèd are,
Out of her bands ye by no means shall get.
Fondness it were for any, being free,
To covet fetters, though they golden be!

13. FONDNESS—Foolishness, folly.

FOR INTERPRETATION

1. To whom is Sonnet xv addressed? What question does the poet ask?
2. Poetic exaggeration is called "hyberbole." What excellent example of hyberbole do you find in the sonnet?
3. Explain the six metaphors that follow.
4. What synonym of common use would you substitute for "guile" in the first line of Sonnet xxxvii?
5. What subtle compliment does the poet pay to the lady's hair?
6. What advice or warning does he give to himself?
7. Do the two poems give you similar pictures of the lady? Discuss.

HARK, HARK! THE LARK

WILLIAM SHAKESPEARE

Far, far better known than the play in which it appears is this nine-line serenade from *Cymbeline*. Has ever there been conceived a lovelier morning song to waken a lady?

HARK, hark! the lark at heaven's gate sings;
    And Phoebus 'gins arise,
His steeds to water at those springs
    On chaliced flowers that lies;
5 And winking Mary-buds begin
    To ope their golden eyes.
With every thing that pretty is,
    My lady sweet, arise,
    Arise, arise!

310

FOR INTERPRETATION

1. The English skylark sings as it flies, dropping down its song from great height. How does Shakespeare say this same thing in poetry?
2. Explain the reference to Phoebus and his steeds in lines 2–4. What are the "springs" that lie on "chaliced flowers"?
3. What other bits of dawn are suggested besides the singing of the lark and the rising of the sun?
4. Many lovely musical settings have been composed for this lyric. Why do you think it should inspire so many musicians? Discuss. Name at least one composer who has written a score for the song.

SONNETS

WILLIAM SHAKESPEARE

For purely poetic expression of thoughts, nothing can quite equal Shakespeare's sonnets. Lyrics by other poets of his day sparkled with "conceits" and glittering extravagances. His are rich and deep with unforgettable beauty. We do not know who was the lady or who was the friend that inspired the sonnets; but their affection survives "death's dateless night" in immortal lines.

XVIII

SHALL I compare thee to a summer's day?
Thou art more lovely and more temperate:
Rough winds do shake the darling buds of May,
And summer's lease hath all too short a date;
5   Sometimes too hot the eye of heaven shines,
And often is his gold complexion dimmed;
And every fair from fair sometime declines,
By chance or Nature's changing course untrimmed.
But thy eternal summer shall not fade
10   Nor lose possession of that fair thou ow'st;
Nor shall Death brag thou wander'st in his shade,
When in eternal lines to time thou grow'st:

7–8. AND EVERY FAIR . . . COURSE UNTRIMMED—Everything that is lovely must lose its beauty through age or accident.
12. WHEN IN ETERNAL LINES TO TIME THOU GROW'ST—The beauty of the lady will live forever in the lines of the sonnet she inspired.

So long as men can breathe or eyes can see,
So long lives this, and this gives life to thee.

XXIX

When in disgrace with fortune and men's eyes
I all alone beweep my outcast state,
And trouble deaf heaven with my bootless cries,
And look upon myself, and curse my fate;
5 Wishing me like to one more rich in hope,
Featured like him, like him with friends possest,
Desiring this man's art, and that man's scope,
With what I most enjoy contented least;
Yet in these thoughts myself almost despising,
10 Haply I think on Thee—and then my state,
Like to the lark at break of day arising
From sullen earth, sings hymns at heaven's gate;
For thy sweet love remembered such wealth brings
That then I scorn to change my state with kings.

XXX

When to the sessions of sweet silent thought
I summon up remembrance of things past,
I sigh the lack of many a thing I sought,
And with old woes new wail my dear time's waste;
5 Then can I drown an eye, unused to flow,
For precious friends hid in death's dateless night,
And weep afresh love's long-since-canceled woe,
And moan the expense of many a vanished sight.
Then can I grieve at grievances foregone,
10 And heartily from woe to woe tell o'er
The sad account of fore-bemoanèd moan
Which I new pay as if not paid before;
But if the while I think on thee, dear friend,
All losses are restored, and sorrows end.

10. TELL—Count, or add up.

LXXIII

That time of year thou may'st in me behold
When yellow leaves, or none, or few, do hang

Upon those boughs which shake against the cold,
Bare ruined choirs, where late the sweet birds sang.
5 In me thou see'st the twilight of such day
As after sunset fadeth in the west;
Which by and by black night doth take away,
Death's second self, that seals up all in rest.
In me thou see'st the glowing of such fire
10 That on the ashes of his youth doth lie,
As the death-bed whereon it must expire,
Consumed with that which it was nourished by.
This thou perceiv'st, which makes thy love more strong
To love that well which thou must leave ere long.

4. CHOIR—That part of the church where the choir sits; sometimes called the choir-*loft*.
12. CONSUMED WITH THAT WHICH IT WAS NOURISHED BY—A fire is finally choked by the ashes of the fuel that fed it.

CXVI

Let me not to the marriage of true minds
Admit impediments. Love is not love
Which alters when it alteration finds,
Or bends with the remover to remove:
5 O, no! it is an ever-fixèd mark,
That looks on tempests and is never shaken;
It is the star to every wand'ring bark,
Whose worth's unknown, although his height be taken.
Love's not Time's fool, though rosy lips and cheeks
10 Within his bending sickle's compass come;
Love alters not with his brief hours and weeks,
. But bears it out even to the edge of doom.
If this be error and upon me proved,
I never writ, nor no man ever loved.

9. LOVE'S NOT TIME'S FOOL—Love is not the victim of Time; love does not vanish as the beloved grows older.

FOR INTERPRETATION

SONNET XVIII:

1. What occasional discomforts of summer does the poet mention in lines 1–6?

2. Tell in your own words the meaning of lines 9–12.

3. In the last line of the poem, to what does *this* refer?

4. Express in a single sentence the theme (central thought) of the sonnet.

SONNET XXIX:

1. Choose a single word—a noun or an adjective—to indicate the state of mind described in the first two lines of the sonnet.

2. In simple, common words describe the various kinds of human behavior suggested in lines 3–8.

3. What thought has power to break the mood described in the first eight lines? Find lines in the first part of the sonnet that are in exact contrast to line 12, and to lines 13 and 14.

SONNET XXX:

1. Quote the lines from the sonnet which express the following ideas: (*a*) pensive recollection; (*b*) regret for unfulfilled desires or hopes; (*c*) regret for lost years; (*d*) regret for departed friends; (*e*) regret for old heartaches; (*f*) regret for past injuries.

2. Explain the meaning of lines 10–12.

3. What solace can the poet find for his sorrows?

4. Would you say that sonnets XXIX and XXX are based on the same theme or on similar themes? Discuss.

SONNET LXXIII:

1. Quote the lines with which the poet compares the present stage of his life to autumn.

2. What is the second figure of speech with which the poet suggests his age? Quote the lines that express it.

3. Point out and explain the third metaphor on the same subject. Which of the three metaphors seems to you most suitable? most beautifully expressed?

4. How old was Shakespeare when he died? When do you think this sonnet was written?

5. What conclusion does the poet draw or point out from these thoughts on the autumn of his life? To whom do you think this sonnet was written? Why? Who do you think is meant by *thou* in the last two lines?

SONNET CXVI:

1. What is an *impediment?* Express the thought of the first sentence in simple prose.

2. What things does the poet say have no power to destroy true love?

3. How does he suggest the *constancy* of real love? Quote the lines. How long will love prove true?

4. What does Shakespeare stake in proof of the truth of his statements? Do you think he is right? Discuss.

CHERRY-RIPE

THOMAS CAMPION

In the days of good Queen Bess every one who could wield a pen tried his hand—at one time or another—at writing love songs. The most admired verses were light, pretty, musical, and usually built around some clever fancy. "Cherry-Ripe" by Thomas Campion is merely one example of hundreds and hundreds of such lyrics. Here the poet's "conceit" —as elaborate metaphors were called—pictures his lady's lips as cherries ripe for picking, but not to be touched until she gives her consent. Notice how cleverly the idea is carried out through the three stanzas.

THERE is a garden in her face
    Where roses and white lilies grow;
A heavenly paradise is that place,
    Wherein all pleasant fruits do flow;
5   There cherries grow. that none may buy,
    Till "Cherry-Ripe" themselves do cry.

Those cherries fairly do enclose
    Of orient pearl a double row,
Which when her lovely laughter shows,
10   They look like rose-buds fill'd with snow.
Yet them no peer nor prince may buy,
    Till "Cherry-Ripe" themselves do cry.

Her eyes like angels watch them still;
    Her brows like bended bows do stand,

315

15   Threat'ning with piercing frowns to kill
       All that attempt with eye or hand
       Those sacred cherries to come nigh,
       Till "Cherry-Ripe" themselves do cry!

FOR INTERPRETATION

1. What are the "roses and white lilies" of line 2? How will one "buy" the cherries?
2. Explain the metaphor of the first four lines in the second stanza.
3. What good example of hyperbole do you find in the poem?
4. Point out the similarities in thought and in style of expression that may be found between "Cherry-Ripe" and Spenser's "Amoretti."

TO CELIA

BEN JONSON

The thought that beauty never really dies has been the theme of poets all through the centuries. As one instance, consider the English song which we know as "Drink to Me Only with Thine Eyes." The words we sing were written more than three hundred years ago to some lovely English lady. The music that is linked with Jonson's verses is also old— an English air of forgotten authorship.

    DRINK to me only with thine eyes,
       And I will pledge with mine;
    Or leave a kiss within the cup
       And I'll not look for wine.
5   The thirst that from the soul doth rise
       Doth ask a drink divine:
    But might I of Jove's nectar sup,
       I would not change for thine.

    I sent thee late a rosy wreath,
10   Not so much honoring thee
    As giving it the hope that there
       It could not withered be;

7. JOVE'S NECTAR—The nectar drunk by Jupiter and the other Olympian gods was believed to make them immortal.

316

But thou thereon didst only breathe
And send'st it back to me;
15   Since when it grows, and smells, I swear
Not of itself, but thee!

FOR INTERPRETATION

1. The metaphors in the first stanza of "To Celia" are based upon what social custom? Explain the poet's meaning in the first four lines of the stanza. Does the last half of the stanza continue with the same metaphor? Explain.

2. Ben Jonson, who was a scholar as well as a poet, had part of his inspiration for "To Celia" from two lines in ancient Greek—lines that read in English—

> "I send thee myrrh, not that thou mayest be
> By it perfumed, but it perfumed by thee."

In the second stanza does Jonson merely repeat the thought of the Greek poet, or does he enlarge upon it? Explain your answer.

3. Why do you think "To Celia" is still a favorite song, not only in England, but through the world? Discuss.

HYMN TO DIANA

BEN JONSON

In his "Hymn to Diana," Ben Jonson is again keeping alive some of the poetic ideas of the beauty-loving ancient world. The moon was pictured by the earliest Greeks as a silver chariot driven by the sister of Phoebus Apollo. The moon-goddess had several names—Cynthia, Phoebe, Diana. And when she was thought of also as a huntress—for like her brother, she carried a bow and quiver—she was known as Artemis. Diana was unmarried and was the patron deity of all maidens.

QUEEN and Huntress, chaste and fair,
Now the sun is laid to sleep,
Seated in thy silver chair
State in wonted manner keep;
5   Hesperus entreats thy light,
Goddess excellently bright.

5. HESPERUS—Star of the West—the evening star.

Earth, let not thy envious shade
Dare itself to interpose;
Cynthia's shining orb was made
10   Heaven to clear when day did close;
Bless us then with wishèd sight,
Goddess excellently bright.

Lay thy bow of pearl apart
And thy crystal-shining quiver;
15   Give unto the flying hart
Space to breathe, how short soever;
Thou that mak'st day of night,
Goddess excellently bright.

FOR INTERPRETATION

1. Point out the lines or phrases in the poem which refer to Diana as goddess of the *moon;* as goddess of the *hunt;* as a *maiden goddess.*

2. To what natural phenomenon does the poet refer in the first two lines of the second stanza? Why was Diana's work as goddess of the moon especially important to the Greeks?

3. Does "Hymn to Diana" seem to you as musical as "To Celia"? Why do you suppose it has not become a familiar song as the other lyric has?

A LAMENT

PSALM 137—KING JAMES VERSION

Tribulation and exile are no new experiences to the Jewish nation. Their history is a succession of dramatic rises and falls. About six hundred years before the birth of Christ, the Hebrews suffered bitter defeat at the hands of Nebuchadnezzar. Their city of Jerusalem was destroyed, the Temple pillaged, and all their princes, scholars, and leaders led into captivity in Babylon. Their literature for the next half century reflects the shame and sorrow of exile.

Early in the period of their captivity, some unknown poet wrote the Psalm from which the following "Lament" has been taken. Of particular interest to us is the exquisite translation from an ancient language into our own English. The scholars of King James have kept the dignity and music of Hebrew poetry as well as the feeling of desperate grief.

B		BY THE rivers of Babylon,
		There we sat down,
U		Yea, we wept when we remembered Zion.
G		We hanged our harps upon the willows
	5	In the midst thereof.
		For there they that carried us away captive
		Required of us a song;
		And they that wasted us
		Required of us mirth, saying
DB	10	"Sing us one of the songs of Zion."
LG		How shall we sing the Lord's song
		In a strange land?
G		If I forget thee, O Jerusalem,
		Let my right hand forget her cunning;
	15	If I do not remember thee,
		Let my tongue cleave to the roof of my mouth;
		If I prefer not Jerusalem
		Above my chief joy!

FOR INTERPRETATION

1. Babylon in the sixth century B.C. was a beautiful and luxurious city. What lines in the song suggest something of its beauty? What lines

319

suggest that the exiles might have found some compensating pleasures in the rich city? Discuss.

2. How did their captors make sport of the Hebrews?

3. What two names did the Hebrews have for their capital city? Why were their city and their religion bound so closely together?

4. What pledge did the Hebrews in exile make to themselves?

5. Which line of the psalm do you think expresses the deepest pathos?

THE GOODNESS AND MAJESTY OF GOD

From ISAIAH 40—KING JAMES VERSION

The Jews had been carried into captivity in 586 B.C. while Babylon was at the height of her power. By 546 B.C. a new king was aspiring to conquer the world—Cyrus the Great, who had already won the kingdoms of Persia and Medea. Hope revived in the Jewish exiles as Cyrus turned his attention toward Babylon.

The latter part of the book of *Isaiah* contains the writings of a young poet-prophet who foresaw that Cyrus would become God's instrument for the release of his people. In a magnificent ode on the greatness of

God, he asserts God's dominion over the peoples of the earth and predicts the Hebrews' deliverance from Babylon.

A part of the ode is presented below. Again we are amazed at the remarkable skill of translation which has done over the words of ancient Hebrew into English poetry.

U O ZION, that bringest good tidings, get thee up into the high mountain;
   O Jerusalem, that bringeth good tidings, lift up thy voice with strength;
   Lift it up, be not afraid; say unto the cities of Judah, "Behold your God!"

LG Behold, the Lord God will come with strong hand and his arm shall rule for him;

MG 5 Behold, his reward is with him, and his work before him.

MGI He shall feed his flock like a shepherd; he shall gather his lambs with his arm,
   And shall carry them in his bosom, and shall gently lead those that are with young.

LG To whom then will ye liken God? Or what likeness will ye compare unto him? . . .

B Have ye not known? Have ye not heard?

   10 Hath it not been told you from the beginning?
   Have ye not understood from the foundations of the earth?

U It is he that sitteth upon the circle of the earth,
   And the inhabitants thereof are as grasshoppers;
   That stretcheth out the heavens as a curtain,

   15 And spreadeth them out as a tent to dwell in.
   That bringeth princes to nothing;

1–3. O ZION, FF.—Jerusalem, the capital of the southern kingdom of Judah, was built upon a hill. Within the city walls rises Mount Zion, which became the site of the palace of King David, of the government buildings, and of the Temple. In these first three lines the poet-prophet is calling upon the city to lift up her head and rejoice that her glory is about to be restored.

8. TO WHOM THEN WILL YE LIKEN GOD?—The prophet is referring to the practices of heathen peoples, always close neighbors of the Hebrews, who made images of carved wood overlaid with gold and silver, setting them up as gods for worship. In the following lines he reminds the Hebrews that from the beginning there has been revealed to them the power and majesty of Jehovah— a God too great to be reproduced in stone or metal.

He maketh the judges of the earth as vanity.
Yea, they shall not be planted; yea, they shall not
    be sown;
Yea, their stock shall not take root in the earth;
20   And he also shall blow upon them, and they shall
    wither,
And the whirlwind shall take them away as stubble.

DB1   "To whom then will ye liken me, or shall I be equal?"
    saith the Holy One.
U   Lift up your eyes on high, and behold who hath
    created these things,
That bringeth out their host by number:
25   He calleth them all by names by the greatness of
    his might,
For that he is strong in power; not one faileth.

LG   Why sayest thou, O Israel, "My way is hid from the
    Lord
And my judgment is passed over from my God?"
G   Hast thou not known? Hast thou not heard that the
    everlasting God,
30   The Lord, the Creator of the ends of the earth, faint-
    eth not, neither is weary?
U   There is no searching of his understanding.
He giveth power to the faint;
And to them that have no might he increaseth
    strength.
Even the youths shall faint and be weary,
35   And the young men shall utterly fall:
But they that wait upon the Lord shall renew their
    strength;
They shall mount up with wings as eagles;
They shall run and not be weary;
And they shall walk and not faint.

---

23. THESE THINGS—The stars of heaven. Most ancient peoples were good
astronomers. Though they understood much about the movements of the
heavenly bodies, they were in awe of whatever power or force kept them in
their places. They marveled too at the number of stars and planets. Literally,
they cannot be counted—not even today.

FOR INTERPRETATION

1. What are the good tidings that Jerusalem may report to her people?
2. Who is to receive the reward that the Lord will bring? What will be the *work* before him? (l. 5)
3. Who are the flock referred to in lines 6 and 7?
4. Lines 12–26 is one of those passages so often found in the Old Testament in which are presented the Hebrew conceptions of God. As you read these lines bear in mind stories you have learned from the mythologies of ancient nations—the Greeks or the Norse, for instance—so that you may have some standard by which to judge the spiritual philosophy of the Jew.

    a. How does the poet suggest the all-powerful nature of God? Quote lines that tell what God can do.

    b. Quote lines that express belief that God controls the affairs of men. Quote lines that express belief that God controls the forces of nature.

    c. What line or lines suggest that the Hebrews had a dignified conception of geography? Compare with other primitive beliefs—those of the Romans, the Chinese, etc.

5. Why might the Jews of the day of Isaiah have believed (*a*) that their ways were "hidden from the Lord" (*b*) that he had passed final judgment upon them? What encouraging thought does the prophet leave with them?
6. Quote the lines that express the thought that God's will toward man is good. Upon what conditions rests God's willingness and power to help men?
7. The King James Version of the Bible appeared five years before the death of Shakespeare. Does the translation of this passage (*a*) suggest in any detail the life and thought of Elizabethan England? (*b*) present a narrow view of a philosophy peculiar to a single nation? (*c*) manifest a universal and timeless quality that is the property of all great literature? Discuss.

MAN'S DUTY TO MAN

From MATTHEW 5—KING JAMES VERSION

To the Jews in Old Testament times had been given the Ten Commandments as a guide for living in accordance with God's will. As the years went by, Jewish priests and scholars had added interpretations and amplifications until the books of the Law filled many scrolls. There were learned men whose lives were devoted to studying and explaining the Law. But they used long words and high-sounding sentences, and the common people were often confused.

Then came Jesus of Nazareth to teach people once more in simple words how God wanted them to live. The whole body of the Law he compressed into two simple commandments; and in his sermons about the countryside, he explained by homely illustrations how men could keep those commandments. The passage below is a selection from what is commonly known as "The Sermon on the Mount."

And He opened· his mouth and taught them, saying,

Ye are the salt of the earth: but if the salt have lost his savour,[1] wherewith shall it be salted? It is henceforth good for nothing, but to be cast out, and to be trodden under foot of men.

Ye are the light of the world. A city that is set on a hill cannot be hid. Neither do men light a candle, and put it under a bushel,[2] but on a candlestick: and it giveth light unto all that are in the house. Let your light so shine before men, that they may see your good works, and glorify your Father which is in heaven.

Ye have heard that it hath been said, "An eye for an eye,[3] and a tooth for a tooth": but I say unto you, that ye resist not evil; but whosoever shall smite thee upon the right cheek, turn to him the other also. And if any man will sue thee at the law and take away thy coat, let him have thy cloak also. And whosoever shall compel thee to go a mile,[4] go with him twain.

Give unto him that asketh of thee, and from him that would borrow of thee turn not thou away.

Ye have heard that it hath been said, "Thou shalt love thy neighbor, and hate thine enemy." But I say unto you, love your enemies, bless them that curse you, do good to them that hate you, and pray for them that despitefully use you, and persecute you; that ye may be the children of your Father which is in heaven; for he maketh his sun to rise on the evil and on the good, and sendeth rain on the just and on the unjust.

[1] HIS SAVOUR—Its flavor. The use of *his* is a survival from the old grammatical genders of the Anglo-Saxons.

[2] A BUSHEL—A bushel measure. We would say today, "under a basket."

[3] AN EYE FOR AN EYE—Under the earliest Jewish Law, a man was held exactly accountable for any injury he caused to another. If he knocked out a man's tooth, he must suffer the loss of his own tooth; if he took a man's life, he must forfeit his own life. It was the obligation of the injured man or his family to administer the punishment.

[4] COMPEL THEE TO GO A MILE—Remember that Palestine was at this time an "occupied country," and that whatever a Roman demanded of a Jew in the way of service—running an errand or carrying a bundle—he got, though usually grudgingly.

For if ye love them which love you, what reward have ye? Do not even the publicans [5] the same? And if ye salute your brethren only, what do ye more than others? Do not even the publicans so? Be ye therefore perfect, even as your Father which is in heaven is perfect.

[5] PUBLICANS—The publicans, or tax-collectors, were notoriously corrupt; hence their name became the synonym for *grasping selfishness*.

DID YOU READ WITH UNDERSTANDING?

1. What two important uses does table salt have? What would happen to our food if we used salt that had lost its saltiness? What kind of people are the *salt of the earth?* What do they do in and for the world? What might tempt them to lose their *saltiness?* How can they guard against it? Discuss.

2. What kind of people are the *light of the world?* Do you think that people who are good at heart are sometimes guilty of *hiding their light?* Why do people, especially young people, sometimes pretend to be worse than they are? What is the harm in that kind of pretending? Is the person who takes pride in his own goodness living up to the command given in the last sentence of the second paragraph? Is it possible for any one to *let his light shine* without being disliked by others? Discuss.

3. Do you think that between individuals the policy of *not resisting evil* would really work? Think carefully before you answer. For example, what happens whenever a fellow strikes back? Can a person keep from hitting back and still not be a sissy? What would happen if a man *ordered* you to do a favor for him and you did twice as much as he asked you to do? Discuss.

4. Do you think that Jesus meant that people should not resist evil of any kind? Think again. What kind of evil is He talking about here? Were there some kinds of evil that He himself resisted? What evil did He not resist? Why not?

5. Do you think that the policy of non-resistance could really work between nations? Discuss.

6. Bearing in mind the points covered by questions 3–5, try to draw some general conclusions as to what paragraph 3 means and what it does not mean.

7. A question that has bothered many a soldier in World War II— perhaps in other wars—is this: *Is it possible to fight for what I believe to be right and still not hate my enemy?* How would you answer the question?

8. Do you think that leaders in public affairs are showing a greater or less degree of concern about applying the teachings of Jesus of Nazareth to the solution of today's problems? What kinds of philosophy, for instance, are underlying plans for a post-war world? Discuss.

OF STUDIES

FRANCIS BACON

"Why do I have to go to school?" is a question that comes up every so
often in the average American home. "What good are these things?"—
with a contemptuous gesture toward a stack of textbooks—"what good
is studying going to do me anyway?"

Well, Francis Bacon, who lived in the days of Shakespeare, has an
answer to such questions. Even though it was written three centuries
ago, it is still a good answer. Briefly, he says that studies add to our
profit, to our appearance or personality, and to our fun. Of course,
it doesn't take much talking to prove the first point. Some studies are
necessary to prepare us to earn a living. And yes, studies do help one
"shine" in society. But the high school boy who feels "fed up" with
school may balk a bit at the third reason. Yet Bacon considered it so
important that he named it first. And isn't he right? Suppose for a
moment that you had never gone to school. Suppose you could not read
or write. Think of the pleasures you would have to miss. Yes, Bacon
is wise to begin by saying, "Studies serve for delight." He is right about
most of the other things, too.

STUDIES serve for delight, for ornament, and for ability. Their
chief use for delight is in privateness and retiring; for ornament, is in discourse; and for ability, is in the judgment and
disposition of business. For expert men [1] can execute and perhaps judge of particulars, one by one; but the general counsels,

[1] EXPERT MEN—Specialists who lack general information or culture.

and the plots and marshaling of affairs, come best from those that are learned. To spend too much time in studies is sloth; to use them too much for ornament is affectation; to make judgment wholly by their rules is the humor [2] of a scholar. They perfect nature, and are perfected by experience; for natural abilities are like natural plants, that need proyning [3] by study; and studies themselves do give forth directions too much at large, except they be bounded in by experience. Crafty men [4] contemn studies; simple men admire them; and wise men use them: for they teach not their own use; but that [5] is a wisdom without them and above them, won by observation. Read not to contradict and confute; nor to believe and take for granted; nor to find talk and discourse; but to weigh and consider. Some books are to be tasted, others to be swallowed, and some few to be chewed and digested: that is, some books are to be read only in parts; others to be read, but not curiously; [6] and some few to be read wholly, and with diligence and attention. Some books also may be read by deputy,[7] and extracts made of them by others; but that would be only in the less important arguments, and the meaner sort of books; else distilled books are like common distilled waters, flashy [8] things. Reading maketh a full man; conference a ready man; [9] and writing an exact man. And therefore, if a man write little, he had need have a great memory; if he confer [10] little, he had need have a present wit; and if he read little, he had need have much cunning, to seem to know that he doth not. Histories make men wise; poets witty; the mathematics subtile; natural philosophy deep; moral grave; logic and rhetoric able to contend. *Abeunt studia in mores.*[11] Nay, there is no stond or impediment in the wit, but may be wrought out by fit studies: [12] like as diseases of the body may have appro-

[2] HUMOR—Peculiarity or tendency.
[3] PROYNING—Pruning.
[4] CRAFTY MEN—Laborers; workmen of various crafts or guilds.
[5] THAT—The knowledge of how to use one's learning.
[6] CURIOUSLY—With close attention.
[7] READ BY DEPUTY—"Read" through reviews or reports by others.
[8] FLASHY—Flat, tasteless.
[9] CONFERENCE A READY MAN—Conversation (or repartee) makes a man quick-witted.
[10] CONFER—Converse.
[11] *Abeunt studia in mores*—Studies pass into (or grow into) manners.
[12] NO STOND . . . WROUGHT OUT BY FIT STUDIES—No lack of mental ability but may be remedied by.

priate exercises. Bowling is good for the stone and reins; [13] shooting for the lungs and breast; gentle walking for the stomach; riding for the head; and the like. So if a man's wit be wandering, let him study the mathematics; for in demonstrations, if his wit be called away never so little, he must begin again: if his wit be not apt to distinguish or find differences, let him study the Schoolmen; [14] for they are *cymini sectores*: [15] if he be not apt to beat over matters, and to call one thing to prove and illustrate another, let him study the lawyers' case: so every defect of the mind may have a special receipt.

[13] STONE AND REINS—Gall-stones and similar affections.
[14] SCHOOLMEN—Theologians or philosophers.
[15] *Cymini sectores*—Hair-splitters or quibblers.

DID YOU READ WITH UNDERSTANDING?

Bacon must be read thoughtfully. He can pack a world of meaning into a single sentence. Before you try to answer the following questions, be sure that you have read the notes and that you have looked up any unfamiliar words.

1. Think over the opening sentence. Which studies that you are taking serve one or more of these uses of education? Are the *arts* subjects taken merely for pleasure? Are *industrial* courses taken just because of their vocational values? Discuss.

2. To *paraphrase* means to reword a passage without changing its meaning. As a test of your understanding of the essay, try paraphrasing any three of sentences 2 to 10.

3. Give some illustrations of the truth of the statement that the chief use of studies "for delight is in privateness and retiring." Is it true, for instance, that an uneducated person is more at a loss for entertainment when he is alone than when he is with others? Discuss.

4. Apply Bacon's advice that one should *weigh and consider* one's reading to the last part of the essay. That is, do you think that a man lacking a logical mind can develop one by studying geometry? Or that a slow-witted person can become a clever conversationalist through much practice? Do modern psychologists believe that the different faculties of the mind can be developed by various mental exercises? Discuss.

5. *For Extra Credit*: Choose any sentence, or part of a sentence, that expresses what seems to you a particularly important truth, and using it as a text, either (*a*) prepare an oral development of it to present before the class, or (*b*) expand it into a written paragraph of at least 100 words.

EXTENDED ACTIVITIES

A NEW SPIRIT HAD GROWN OUT OF THE ACTIVITIES
OF THE RENAISSANCE

HISTORY IN BRIEF

	The Tudors	The Stuarts	Events in America
1500-1599 (16th Century)	Henry VIII (1509-1547) (The Reformation in England) (First Complete English Bible) Edward VI (1547-1553) Mary (1553-1558) Elizabeth (1558-1603) (Defeat of the Spanish Armada) (Shakespeare born 1564)		Pacific Ocean discovered by Balboa, 1513 Hudson Bay discovered by Sebastian Cabot, 1519 The Mississippi River discovered by De Soto in 1528 Sir Francis Drake claims for England territory between 38°-42° N Sir Humphrey Gilbert claims Newfoundland, 1583 Sir Walter Raleigh's settlement of Roanoke, 1585
1600-1699 (17th Century)		James I (1603-1625) (Shakespeare dies 1616)	Jamestown settled, 1607 Lake Champlain discovered, 1609 Hudson River discovered, 1609 Sailing of the *Mayflower*, 1620

FOR ACQUAINTANCE WITH AUTHORS

EDMUND SPENSER (1552–1599)—"THE FAERIE QUEENE," "AMORETTI"

Edmund Spenser had all the attributes of a successful courtier but never attained the success. The son of a cloth maker, he worked his way through Cambridge by serving as a sizar or waiter. Soon after he left college he published "The Shepherd's Calendar," a long poem in allegorical form about the then popular shepherds and shepherdesses. The poem brought him immediate success. He hoped for a court appointment but none came. It is said that a tactless doggerel verse about one of the Queen's suitors led to his banishment from court and to an administrative post in Ireland. Whenever possible he turned to writing as an escape from the duties he detested. During his ten years in Ireland he wrote his best work, *The Faerie Queene*, which although presented by Sir Walter Raleigh to the Queen and popular with the reading public, failed to bring him either a new job or the Queen's smile. Disappointed once more, Spenser returned to Ireland where he lived in Kilcoman Castle, an estate that had been seized by the English from an Irish lord. Soon afterwards, during an insurrection of the natives, his castle was burned. He, his wife and four children, were forced to flee to England. Bitter and broken in health, Spenser lived only a few weeks longer.

There could hardly be found a greater contrast than that between Chaucer and Spenser although the two were the leading figures of early English poetry and Spenser was devoted to Chaucer's work. He lacked Chaucer's love of people and his sympathetic sense of humor. Spenser was the first of the "escapist" school of literature. He preferred the pageantry of life as he liked to dream it—all the edges softened and blurred with color, beauty, and the delicacy of rhyme.

WILLIAM SHAKESPEARE (1564–1616)—"HARK, HARK! THE LARK," SONNETS XVIII, XXIX, XXX, LXXIII, CXVI

Of William Shakespeare, the greatest figure in English literature, a more complete account will be given in the next section on Elizabethan drama. Although he is best known as a dramatist, his poetry alone would have made him famous. In addition to two long narrative poems, *Venus and Adonis* and *The Rape of Lucrece,* he wrote one hundred fifty-four sonnets, exquisitely beautiful in their expression and deeply thoughtful in their content.

His songs are bits of charming lyrical verse found in many of his dramas. All of his poetry reflects his love of nature and his keen observance of human characteristics. Nothing was too trivial to be overlooked by his keen intellect. His poetry reaches a state of perfection in its naturalness of setting that no other writer has ever equalled.

THOMAS CAMPION (1567–1620)—"CHERRY-RIPE"

Thomas Campion is one of many in the company of distinguished professional men who composed poetry for amusement. After a thorough college education, he practiced law for a time in London but soon entered medical training. In the French expedition in 1591, Campion served under Lord Essex as a surgeon, then returned to London to become a successful physician. His first volume of poems in Latin were popular and from them he turned to songs, masques, and poems in English. His masques, half poetry and half music, embellished with elaborate costuming and "machinery," were often performed at court.

BEN JONSON (1573–1637)—"TO CELIA," "HYMN TO DIANA"

Like Shakespeare, Jonson is better known as a dramatist, yet he ranks with the great lyric poets of the period. In his own time he was highly regarded as a poet and scholar, and on the accession of James I in 1603 he was named the first Poet Laureate.

FRANCIS BACON (1561–1625)—"OF STUDIES"

Were one to read the works of Francis Bacon without knowing anything of his life and personality, one might well ask, "What manner of man is this?" The mirror of his works reflects the portrait of a courtier —brilliant, keen, clear-headed, cold, unscrupulous, and hard. It is not a flattering picture, not one that you would like for yourself; yet one suspects that Bacon was not ill-pleased with his life. His was a time of intrigue and craft—and the stakes were high! Because of his brilliance he "got along." The fact that he came near losing his head as well as his fortune was one of the chances of the game.

Born the son of the Lord Keeper of the Seal, Francis Bacon found the finest educational facilities of the age open to him. There was private instruction under tutors, followed by college work at Cambridge, and travel with study abroad. We see him in his early teens disgusted with Cambridge because he found his instructors stupid and their methods antiquated. Generations later the world was to acknowledge the correctness of the boy's insistence that knowledge is drawn not from the works of dead philosophers but from observation and experimentation.

Bacon was not only intelligent and studious, but also ambitious. Finding himself without income at the death of his father, the eighteen-year-old youth turned to the practice of law for his living and his rise was rapid. Within ten years he was Counsel-Extraordinary to Elizabeth. After the Queen's death in 1603, Bacon's rise was even more rapid. He was at once knighted by James I. In succeeding years he rose from post to post, until in 1621 he became Lord High Chancellor of England. In the meantime he had married a rich London heiress, and taken his place in the House of Lords. An eloquent speaker, he drew throngs of listeners whenever he made an address. In 1621 then, Sir Francis Bacon, Baron Verulan, Viscount St. Albans (for these were his titles) appeared one of the wealthiest and most influential men in England. His ascent had been gradual; his fall was disastrously swift.

That very year he was accused of having accepted bribes. Bacon made a complete confession, exonerating his associates—some of them of higher rank than himself. Punishment was severe but left him his life. He was fined nearly $200,000; he was barred from ever again holding public office; he was denied admittance to Court and to Parliament; he was committed to imprisonment in the Tower. The intervention of the king made his prison term a short one and part of his fine was restored to him; but Bacon never again entered public life.

From his nineteenth year Bacon had been writing more or less steadily —chiefly scientific, political, and economic discussions in Latin and English. Now he gave himself over to scientific studies. It is a matter of common knowledge that he contracted the bronchitis which caused his death while he was trying an initial experiment in the modern principle of cold storage. He wanted to see whether packing a chicken with snow would preserve it.

His works have impressive titles, many of them in Latin. *The Advancement of Learning* and the *Novum Organum* are particularly interesting to the student of philosophy and science; but the general reader knows only his essays in which his changing views of life and morality keep pace with the record of his career.

OF LITERARY FORM AND STYLE

ENGLISH POETRY AWAKENS TO THE RENAISSANCE

An Out-Pouring of Lyric Verse

During the period of the Renaissance in Italy, art of every sort had been enriched. Even as early as the fourteenth century, Englishmen had been aware of the new Italian poetry. Chaucer had come back to England to pour into native verse some of the zest for living that he had discovered in Italian literature. The new vitality spread from narrative verse to other forms. All sorts of lyrics developed. So many men were writing poetry that several collections of verse were made—one of the earliest and best being Tottel's *Miscellany,* published in 1557. The anthology preserved for leisure reading hundreds of pretty verses that were being recited and sung about the court or passed in manuscript from hand to hand.

As one studies such verses and those that followed in the next half century, one notes a general similarity in subject matter and style.

In the first place, most of the lyrics were love poems—very extravagant love poems. With few variations each poet sang to some lady or to a succession of ladies—embroideries of the theme used by Sir Philip Sidney in one of his songs to "Stella":

> "To you, to you, all song of praise is due,
> Only in you my song begins and endeth."

The stanzas would tell over, one by one, the superlative charms of the beloved—her eyes, her hair, her lips, her finger-tips, her feet. After reading a score or so addressed to Celias and Julias and Stellas, we can quite appreciate Shakespeare's sketch of the lover, "sighing like a furnace and penning sonnets to his mistress's eyebrows."

In the second place, the lyrics were deliberately romantic and impractical. Marlowe's "The Passionate Shepherd to His Love" is a fair illustration. Promising all sorts of fanciful delights, the shepherd begs, "Come live with me and be my love." His allurements read like this—

> "And I will make thee a bed of roses
> And a thousand fragrant posies,
> A cap of flowers and a kirtle
> Embroidered all with leaves of myrtle."

It is surprising that Sir Walter Raleigh paused long enough from his romancing about the New World, America, to pen a realistic reply to the shepherd in which he points out that "flowers do fade" and that if put to proof "gowns and shoes and beds of *roses*" would be pretty poor substitutes for the real thing. But Raleigh's matter-of-factness in this instance was an exception to the usual flood of romantic imagery.

A third characteristic was the use of elaborate figures of speech. Often the writer built a whole poem upon one metaphor or "conceit," which he developed with elaborate detail. So fanciful and exaggerated were the figures of speech that any verse collection of the period might well bear the sub-title—as one did—of "A Gallant Galaxy of Daintie Devyses."

The Sonnet Comes to England

The two names that appeared most often in Tottel's *Miscellany* were those of Sir Thomas Wyatt and the Earl of Surrey—two young gentlemen about the court. Besides writing songs in the usual form, they began experimenting with the fascinating new Italian pattern, the sonnet. Wyatt wrote a number of English sonnets using the Italian rhyming scheme. Then Surrey invented a scheme that rhymed more easily in English—a sonnet variation that became exceedingly popular. Most of the Elizabethans, including Shakespeare, used Surrey's adaptation, so that we now speak of it as the "Elizabethan" or "Shakespearean sonnet." For an exact description of the two forms, see the section on "Types of Poetry" in the *Appendix* of this book.

It became the fashion for men to write not just one sonnet, but a whole series, or *cycle* of sonnets. Most of them featured a love theme, and were dedicated to some lady.

Elizabethan Songs

The name *lyric* implies that the form must be musical. Originally all lyrics were composed as songs. And in sixteenth-century England, with the exception of the sonnets, almost all lyrics were of the song type. They actually had been written to be sung; and music, through the succeeding centuries has helped them fulfill their destinies. As we shall see later, the richest poetic contribution of the age was its drama. Most of the playwrights were poets, good poets. They used a sonorous unrhymed verse for the action of their plays, but throughout the scenes they interspersed songs to be sung to the accompaniment of different stringed instruments. The most gifted inventor of such song-gems was Shakespeare. His comedies sparkle with the loveliness of lyrics like, "Hark, Hark! the Lark," "Who Is Sylvia?", and "Under the Greenwood Tree." Even in the lightest of his songs there is a richness of imagination that rises above the mere prettiness of most Elizabethan verse. Their singing lines have tempted great musicians from every nation to compose settings for them, so that as songs they still delight the world.

The Musical Quality of Spenser's Verse

A poet who took particular delight in the musical quality of words was Edmund Spenser. All his poems—his descriptive nature pieces, his sonnets, his longer lyrics, his *Faerie Queene*—all are marked by unusually harmonious melody. For his great allegory he invented a pleasing stanza form that has been named for him, the "Spenserian stanza" (see *Appendix*). Spenser enjoyed also the romantic fancy that graced the poetry of his day, using it lavishly in all his works. He is like certain modern painters who are not concerned with making a lifelike picture, but rather with suggesting a mood. And so we find in his verse woods where grow all manner of trees from every clime and season; or meadows where at one time his nymphs may pick violets and roses, lilies and primroses. Those who like the land of make-believe set to tinkling melodies will enjoy the graceful imaginings of Edmund Spenser.

QUESTIONS IN APPRECIATION:

"The Faerie Queene"

1. Copy one of the stanzas from *The Faerie Queene;* indicate the rhyming scheme, and underline the rhyming words. Mark the accented syllables and indicate the number of feet to a line. Check your results with the pattern of the Spenserian stanza as described in the *Appendix*.

2. Spenser employs all the poetic devices of *alliteration, onomatopeia,* and *assonance.* From the stanzas of *The Faerie Queene* point out at least one example of each.

3. Which of the stanzas seems to you to sound most musical? Which words or devices make it so?

4. What kind of poems do you think would sound well if written in the Spenserian stanza? For what kinds of poems—or for poems on what kinds of subjects—would the Spenserian stanza not be suitable? Discuss.

5. Do the descriptions of the Red Cross Knight and Una seem to you to be *realistic* or *idealistic?* Discuss. Is the incident of Una and the Lion *romantic* or *true to life?* Discuss.

6. Be prepared to defend one of the following statements in an oral or written discussion: *Spenser's poetry is similar to Chaucer's* or *Spenser's poetry is entirely different from Chaucer's.*

Sonnets and Other Lyrics

1. Study the rhythm and rhyming schemes for the sonnets by Spenser and by Shakespeare. Does the pattern of Spenser's sonnets correspond to

one of the sonnet patterns described in the *Appendix?* If so, which kind? If not, point out the variations. In the same manner check the pattern of Shakespeare's sonnets.

2. Point out other poetic devices besides rhyme and rhythm with which Spenser ornamented his sonnets.

3. What "conceit" does Spenser use in Sonnet xv? In Sonnet xxxvii? In what respects are these two sonnets characteristic of Elizabethan lyrics?

4. From the five sonnets by Shakespeare make a list of at least ten effective figures of speech. Make a similar list of the two most poetically expressive word-combinations from each sonnet.

5. Be prepared to point out several differences in style between Spenser's sonnets and Shakespeare's.

6. Review the definition of lyric poetry in the *Appendix.* In what respects is "Hark, Hark! the Lark" a true lyric?

7. Point out the respects in which Thomas Campion's "Cherry-Ripe" is truly representative of Elizabethan lyrics.

8. Would you say that Ben Jonson's verses "To Celia" and "Hymn to Diana" are typical of Elizabethan lyric poetry? Discuss.

THE FIRST EDITION OF THE WORLD'S ALL-TIME BEST SELLER

In the year 1611, eight years after the death of Elizabeth, but while England still surged ahead with the impetus of her reign, there came from the press the first edition of the book that was to become the most widely owned and read volume in the English tongue—the King James Version of the Bible. As in the case of most great achievements, there was a long history of earlier effort, some of which has already been briefly mentioned.

In the generations before Chaucer, there had been no English Bible. Churches used a Latin translation called the "Vulgate," and most of the Church services were in the same tongue so that they had little meaning for the average man. It will be remembered that during Chaucer's lifetime lived John Wyclif, who believed that men should be able to read or listen to the Scriptures in their own tongue. To make such a thing possible, he set about translating the Vulgate into English, and succeeded in completing his work on the New Testament. The work had to be carried on by stealth and the first manuscripts were all hand-written, but a beginning had been made.

In 1500, more than a century after the death of Wyclif, it was still against the law for any one to have an English Bible in his possession. But another fearless reformer was at work—William Tyndale. Tyndale made a translation of the New Testament, and began a translation of the Old Testament. But his religious enemies caught up with him. In 1536 he was strangled to death and his body burned. His work was continued by Miles Coverdale, and in 1538, just two years after the death of Tyn-

dale, Old and New Testament were put together to form the *Great Bible.*
Amazingly the book was printed in England. Not only was it not suppressed; it was ordered into every church in the land. A dramatic change
had taken place in English history. Henry VIII had broken with the
Church of Rome.

In the next seventy-five years rapid changes were occurring in the
English language, and by 1600 there was felt the need for a revision of
England's most widely read book. King James I shortly after his accession appointed forty-seven scholars to complete the English Bible. The
work was in progress for several years, and the translators made use of
the best contributions of other scholars from Wyclif on. Their text was
chiefly that of the Tyndale-Coverdale version, but they checked also with
original sources. The result was a translation which for poetic beauty
and power has never been surpassed. It is still the best loved book in
the English language. In recent years, several good modern translations
have been made; but for devotional reading, ministers and laymen alike
turn to the King James Version.

For convenience in study and reference, scholars had divided the Bible
into numbered verses. These artificial divisions hide to some extent the
various types of literature which the books of the Bible present. For
that reason certain modern editions have made use of the King James
text, but spaced the selections so that the reader may readily recognize
their literary forms. Thus the books of *Psalms* look in truth like a collection of poetry or songs; *Chronicles* and *Kings* and *Samuel* are very
apparently books of history; *Romans* and *Hebrews* appear as letters, and
so on.

One thing should be said of the seventeenth century language in which
the Bible is expressed. The distinction was still made between the singular and plural forms of the second personal pronoun. And these pronoun
forms were declined. That is, the nominative singular form was *thou,* the
nominative plural *ye;* the objective singular was *thee,* the objective plural
you; the singular possessives were *thy* and *thine,* the plural possessives
your and *yours.* These distinctions were made in the everyday speech
of the time, and they are still made in poetic and devotional language.
Notice the careful discrimination of form in the following passages:

Singular: *Thou* art my God, and I will praise *Thee.*
          Thine is the kingdom and the power and the glory.
Plural: No doubt, *ye* are the people, and wisdom shall die with *you.*
          If *ye* know how to give good gifts unto *your* children, how much
           more will *your* heavenly Father give the Holy Spirit to them
           that ask it.

QUESTIONS IN APPRECIATION:

1. If you are at all familiar with the *Psalms,* you will know that Hebrew
poetry followed some very definite patterns, many of which can be shown
in translation. In the "Lament" from Psalm 137 show how the repeti-

tion of words and phrases has been used as a *poetic device*. What keeps the repetition from becoming monotonous? Do you know of other selections from the *Psalms* which illustrate the use of the same device? If so, quote them.

2. For many years the only music used in churches was the singing of Psalms or other Scriptural selections. Even today many of our best loved anthems and religious solos are musical settings of parts of the Bible. The "lyrics" are the words of the King James Version. What do these facts prove about the *literary quality* of the English translation? What important poetic quality must any passage have if it is to be set to music? Discuss.

3. Do you think it would be possible to compose a musical setting for Psalm 137? If so, what kind of music would you suggest? Discuss.

4. List the different kinds of poetic devices (see the *Appendix*) which are apparent in the translation of Isaiah's ode. Are they the same devices that were used in the 137th Psalm? Are there any new ones?

5. The ode contains many striking figures of speech. Does the credit for such imagery belong to the original Hebrew poet or to the translator? Discuss.

6. For many generations the Bible was one of a very small collection of books to be found in every home. It was read from cover to cover, and long passages from it were memorized. It is said for this reason to have had more influence on English style of expression than any other book. Can you name any writer—English or American—whose style of writing in prose or poetry sounds *Biblical?* What qualities of expression will you look for? In what phase of modern life is the influence of King James's English still felt? Why?

7. What differences in form are apparent between the selection from the "Sermon on the Mount" and the two selections from the Old Testament?

8. What similarities do you notice in the manner of expression of the "Sermon" and of the Old Testament selections? Which of these similarities do you think are traceable to the original writers? Which do you think are the result of their being translated at the same period of time by one group of translators?

9. Be prepared to give the reason for the use of each *thou, thee, thy, thine,* and *ye* that appear in the three selections. Why do we also find the forms *you* and *your?* Do you think you would like the sound of these passages as well if we substituted the modern forms throughout? Discuss.

ENGLISH PROSE TAKES ON FORM AND STYLE

In the widespread quickening of literary power under Elizabeth, prose expression had a share. Up to this time, most scholarly works had been written in Latin. A few writers continued to present their studies in that classic tongue; but scores of others were glad to set down in simple

English the results of their research in fields of history, travel, navigation, biography, and the like. So many were the good books to appear that we can only glance at some representative titles.

Two English clergymen, Richard Hakluyt and Samuel Purchas, became interested in England's achievements in exploration. They made careful study of the records of men like Drake and Frobisher, checking dates and names and places. Hakluyt published his findings in a three-volume work, *Principal Navigations, Voyages and Discoveries of the English Nation,* issued in 1589, 1598, and 1600. Purchas continued the undertaking after Hakluyt's death with two volumes, *Purchas, His Pilgrimage* in 1613 and *Hakluytus Posthumous, or Purchas, His Pilgrims* in 1625. The books are of interest because they have furnished later writers with accurate information about early English "sea-dogs."

Sir Walter Raleigh and Captain John Smith wrote first-hand accounts of their experiences in the New World, but they were so eager to dazzle the reader with American splendors that their pages were misleading. For some generations certain Englishmen entertained visions of an American paradise drawn from the accounts in Raleigh's *Discovery of Guiana* or Smith's *Virginia, New England, and the Summer Isles.* While he was in prison, awaiting execution, Sir Walter wrote an ambitious but also untrustworthy *History of the World.* It does conclude with a courageous and moving address to Death.

The fervent patriotism of the times aroused an interest in British history. As early as 1578 Holinshed published his *Chronicles of England, Ireland and Scotland,* an important work because it gave Shakespeare the material for *Macbeth* and for his English historical plays. William Camden did a careful piece of historical research which resulted in *Britannia*—an orderly chronicle of English history—and in the *Annals of Queen Elizabeth,* a good dependable story of the times. A man who was himself an exile during the religious persecutions of Elizabeth's half-sister Mary, returned to England after Mary's death to write the stories of Christian martyrs in England and Scotland. The book first appeared in Latin; but the author, John Foxe, later translated it into English. Known as Foxe's *Book of Martyrs,* it was a favorite of the early Puritans and one of the first books brought to America. John Knox, a great religious reformer, wrote *The History of the Reformation in Scotland,* now chiefly famous for its pages about Elizabeth's tragic cousin, Mary Queen of Scots.

Biography of course, stands out in all great histories; and the period shows an interest in the lives of great men of all times. One exceedingly popular book was Thomas North's excellent translation of Plutarch's *Parallel Lives of Greek and Roman Heroes.* This work also furnished Shakespeare with the material for some of his tragedies—notably for *Julius Caesar* and *Antony and Cleopatra.*

The books noted above were written, on the whole, in a simple, direct narrative style. Even after three hundred years they tell their stories well. Another fashion of prose writing was, however, developed by a small group of romancers. John Lyly, who was also a poet and a play-wright, wrote a book called *Euphues* which purported to be the account of the experiences of an Athenian youth visiting in England. The ro-mance was written in a "prettified," high-flown style which later led to the coining of the word *euphuism* to indicate an artificially elegant mode of literary expression. Another English gentleman, Sir Philip Sidney, wrote a *euphuistic* prose romance, *Arcadia*. Both books, much admired in their day, are now all but forgotten. It is the substantial studies in history, travel, and biography that still find readers.

THE ENGLISH ESSAY MAKES ITS BOW

The most important development in literary prose was the appearance of a form new to English writers—the *essay*. It was Francis Bacon who made the introduction. Over in France a brilliant writer, Michel de Montaigne, had been writing down brief impressions of men and human affairs and publishing them as "Essais." Montaigne died in 1592. Five years later, Bacon who knew and admired the work of the Frenchman, published ten short prose reflections and called them "Essays." And so the English term was born. Bacon had not rated his papers highly, and he was surprised at their success. His long, serious studies had all been written in Latin; but the essays proved he had a brilliant command of English and an almost poetic prose style. In 1612 he released a second edition, containing twenty-eight additional papers; and in 1625, his final edition, numbering fifty-eight.

Bacon's English is marked by short, pithy sentences; or by longer sentences that break easily into parallel parts. He never loses his way grammatically; and his fondness for balanced structure—phrase with phrase or clause with clause—gives his prose a definite rhythm. It reads well aloud. And it is packed with thought. The best known of all the essays, "Of Studies," appeared in the first edition of his papers. It shows forth his wit, his eloquence, and his intellectual interests. The essays added to the second edition while he was rising rapidly to power have a worldly-wise point of view and are coldly calculating in thought. The last twenty, written during retirement after his public disgrace, have a sober moral tone.

The essays reflect to some extent the thoughts and attitudes of the days of Elizabeth and of her successor, James I. More particularly they reflect the man who wrote them—a man described by a later poet as "the wisest, brightest, meanest of all time."

QUESTIONS IN APPRECIATION:

1. Discuss: English prose of the later sixteenth century reflects the strong spirit of nationalism in Elizabethan England.

2. If you are not sure of the meaning of the term *parallel structure*, look it up in a rhetoric or composition book. Point out at least five striking examples of parallel structure in the essay, "Of Studies."

3. If a man were to reproduce the thought of "Of Studies" clearly in modern English do you think his discussion would be longer or shorter than Bacon's? Why?

4. Although Bacon was a prose writer and Shakespeare a poet, do you see any points of resemblance in the styles of the two men? Discuss. Do you think Bacon could have written poetry, or dramas, if he had tried? Why or why not?

5. Select from Bacon's essay at least four sentences for memorization. Be sure to choose sentences that express a significant thought exceptionally well.

FOR FURTHER READING

ASCH, SHOLEM, *The Nazarene*

BATES, ERNEST SUTHERLAND (ed.), *The Bible, Designed to Be Read as Living Literature*

DAVIS, WILLIAM STEARNS, *Life in Elizabethan Days*

DOUGLAS, LLOYD C., *The Robe*

GOUDGE, ELIZABETH, *Towers in the Mist*

KINGSLEY, CHARLES, *Westward, Ho!*

MAJOR, CHARLES, *When Knighthood Was in Flower; Dorothy Vernon of Haddon Hall*

NEALE, JOHN ERNEST, *Queen Elizabeth*

NOYES, ALFRED, *Tales of the Mermaid Tavern*

PALGRAVE, FRANCIS TURNER (ed.), *The Golden Treasury* (see sonnets by Shakespeare, Book I)

QUILLER-COUCH, SIR ARTHUR, *The Oxford Book of English Verse* (1400–1900)

READE, CHARLES, *The Cloister and the Hearth*

SCOTT, SIR WALTER, *Kenilworth*

SICHEL, EDITH, *The Renaissance*

STRACHEY, LYTTON, *Elizabeth and Essex*

II-II

EARLY ENGLISH DRAMA

(1000–1620)

English drama may be said to have begun with a simple people's delight in the candle-lighted, purple-stoled processions which enriched the mass on certain feast days. Then later, the Church presented tableaux of Bible stories for the instruction of a flock who watched in wide-eyed wonder. The tableaux gradually developed into dramatic scenes with acting and speaking. Those who came to the country fairs at Easter week stayed on to attend the church services, elaborate with songs and tableaux performed by the young priests. By 1100 the "Miracles" as they came to be called were almost a part of the yearly church program. On feast days the crowds forced the tableaux to retire to the church yards where the audience grew more jovial and less pious. Although the Pope in 1210 issued an edict forbidding the appearance of priests on the stage, the people continued to expect their pageants on holy days. Groups of tradesmen known as "guilds" became responsible for play-acting. Each craft might enact a scene in the cycle which represented the story of Noah and the flood, or the Nativity. The strictly Biblical subject matter was sometimes supplemented by stories from the lives of the great saints and martyrs of the Church.

The now boisterous audience grew more demanding. Elements of humor were introduced by actors with a gift for pantomime. Noah's wife developed character; stubbornly she refused to leave dry ground and had to be forced into the ark; always she made Noah's life miserable by her querulous scolding. Holiday crowds swarmed over the church yards and into the fields; and to accommodate their audience, the guilds developed a system of high-wheeled carts that moved from one street to another, stopping to present their scene of the cycle. City traffic had to be routed to the corners where the wagons stopped. On the feast of Corpus Christi villagers came for the day, more to be amused than to be religiously instructed although they loved the familiarity of the old stories done, as it were, in color.

Allegorical figures were sometimes introduced to explain and "point" the moral of the tale. Finally, the stories departed entirely from their Biblical foundation and told of ordinary man and his struggle for salvation. Saintly characters wore gilt hair and beards; souls were dressed in black or white coats depending on their destination; angels won admiring gasps from the audience with gold skins, and wings that flapped. By popular acclaim the "star" came to be not Man but the Devil, as stormy a villain as ever strode the boards, dressed in black or red, sometimes breathing smoke from his mouth, and often endowed with a long and agile tail. At his heels came Vice, in fool's clothes, whose duty it was to tease audience and Devil alike. Ultimately both were swept back by the Virtues into a gaping hell-mouth—smoky and sulphurous and, if it were an elaborate production, belching red flames at intervals.

The best known and one of the more sedate of the "Moralities," as later scholars called these plays, was *Everyman*. The leading character, Everyman, starts out in life accompanied by a number of friends including Beauty, Strength, Discretion, Friendship, Kindred, and Riches. In the course of life he meets other characters such as Good Works, Repentance, and Mercy. There are bouts with Vice and Evil. Finally he is summoned by the character Death. His companions such as Kindred, Riches, and Strength now leave him, and Good Deeds alone is willing to go with him on the journey to which Death beckons.

Henry VIII and Mary often watched another sort of play, an "Interlude," or short entertainment given between the courses of a state banquet. Here real people and life situations were represented, but the outcome was still predetermined: "Good" always triumphed.

The Elizabethan drama which was to flower at the end of the sixteenth century owes much to its humble origin before the altar of a flourishing Church. The Miracle and Mystery plays gave it dramatic sense, a salting of humor, and a spark of English life. The Morality play freed the actor from a Biblical story whose outlines his audience already knew. The Interludes encouraged an author's imagination, dealt with men who were men, and came close to life itself.

Towards the close of the fifteenth century drama left the maternal admonition of the Church to become a prodigal and wastrel—disowned by its creator and arrogant at her condemnation. During the first fifty years of the sixteenth century the Renaissance brought to England the wonder of the Greek and Roman drama. Avid young writers copied Greek and Roman style, plot and form. The public now met drama in which the good did not always triumph and in which the story held all the shining newness of a bright shilling.

Strolling players armed with scripts and gay costumes set up their temporary stage in the quadrangular court of an inn. Rushes were strewn on the wooden scaffolding; juniper was burned in the yard to purify the air. At three o'clock the flag was run up to announce the beginning of the performance, trumpets blared, and the townsfolk flocked to the innyard. The common folk stood on the ground; the gentry, the burghers, and the dignitaries of the town occupied the galleries. Here the leading lady—whose chin often bristled with a new beard—squeaked her alarm at pasteboard dragons; here armies had it out with wooden swords; here groundlings drank ale, cracked nuts, jeered the villain, and hailed the hero.

True British drama, forerunner of present day drama, is often said to have been born in 1550 when a schoolmaster wrote a crude comedy entitled *Ralph Roister Doister*—as good a warning of the evils of poor punctuation as has ever been written. For the first time the characters are avowedly English although the plot shows some Greek and Roman influence. In 1561 came the first English tragedy, *Gorboduc,* modeled after the Roman dramatist Seneca and written in blank verse; and in 1566 appeared another farcical comedy, *Gammer Gurton's Needle,* written by a bishop.

Interior of the Fortune Theater, London, built in 1599

The culmination toward which the English drama had been developing for centuries came in the days of Elizabeth. Plays were as popular in Elizabeth's time as the movies are in our own. Nowhere, of course, was the popularity of the play more to be marked than in London, where it early attracted the displeasure of the Puritans who were strong enough in 1574 to secure the enactment of an Order of the Common Council in Restraint of Dramatic Exhibitions. This order led to the building of the first playhouse, called *The Theater,* which was erected by James Burbage in 1576 on a site just north of the city limits where the Order did not apply. For a model he seems to have taken the innyard. It seems probable that the interior of *The Theater* was circular. In this open space, which was called the *pit* or *yard*, on the hard-packed earth stood the "groundlings"—apprentices, serving men, soldiers, colliers, tinkers, and the like. About the inside walls on the three sides parallel and opposite to the stage were galleries, probably three tiers, after the fashion of the innyards. The best seats were in the galleries. Here sat the "gallery-commoners"—the merchants and gentry. As the picture of *The Fortune* shows, there was also a gallery over the rear stage. This was the "Lords roome." In the "Lords roome" sat the more aristocratic patrons of the play, both men and women, the latter carefully masked. On the very edge of the stage itself sat the swaggering gallants of the day.

The stage was a raised platform projecting out into the pit. Over the "stage forward" was a "shadow or cover" supported by posts. At the rear and under the "Lords roome" was a kind of recess which might be cut off from the stage forward by a curtain or "arras." Rising above the gallery was a tower which was used for three purposes. Here was flown a flag giving the name of the theater, as *The Theater, The Swan,* or *The Globe.* On days when plays were to be given a second flag announcing the fact was also hung out. From this tower also the trumpeter sounded the three blasts which announced that the play was about to begin.

There was no scenery such as we know on the Elizabethan stage. It is possible that the curtain or arras at the rear sometimes bore a crude painted picture. It is probable, however, that the setting was generally indicated by no more than a placard or piece of cloth bearing a legend, such as *Macbeth's Castle,* or *A heath.* Although there was little or no scenery, considerable use was made of *properties.* A picture of *The Swan* shows a bench or settle on the stage, and other articles of furniture no doubt were used when required. A document of the time mentions "engines, weapons, and powder used in plays."

One peculiarity of the Elizabethan stage was the absence of actresses. Women's parts were taken by boys, especially trained. This accounts for the fact that Shakespeare frequently has his women characters impersonate men and for the further fact that in all the plays men predominate. Elizabethan actors made little or no attempt to dress according to the time and setting of the play. "Costume," says one writer, "was a means of indicating rank and office more than time or place; it was meant to reveal the characters rather than the setting of the story." The Elizabethan age delighted in extravagant display, especially in clothes.

The actor's life was a strenuous one. Professor Adams in his *A Life of William Shakespeare* writes, "Elizabethan troupes . . . not only performed as a rule every week day, and often on Sundays, but also changed their plays from day to day in a most astonishing fashion. The forenoons of the actors were commonly spent in rehearsals. The afternoons, of course, were occupied with performances before the public, lasting from two or three o'clock until five or six. As to the evenings, not a small share of the time surely had to be devoted to learning new, or refreshing the memory on old plays."

In the reading of Elizabethan plays we are likely to overlook one of the chief attractions for the audience—the songs and incidental music. Elizabethans were fond of music. And the groundlings and gallants also loved "sound and fury" for its own sake. They liked hurly-burly and commotion. The reader should note the frequency of trumpet calls and fanfares, and other appeals to the ear indicated in the stage directions by *Flourish, Cry within, Thunder and lightning, Drum, Flourish and shout,* and the like. The frequency of *Alarums* in battle scenes no doubt served both to keep the audience on the alert and to stimulate its imagination.

The audience itself was a turbulent and unruly one. Expressions of approval and disapproval were common through applause, noisy laughter, loud spitting, and a whole series of rude guffaws and curses. If the nobles were bored by the play, they interrupted or mimicked the actors or even jumped to the stage and engaged in combat with them.

By 1616 there were in London at least seven well-established theaters in which plays were regularly given, not to mention certain great inns, such as the Boar's Head, where plays evidently continued.

So great was the demand for plays that not only professional literary men, but scholars and courtiers as well, tried their hand at playmaking. The first men who had taken up dramatic writing as a profession were the so-called "University Wits," so named since they were all University men, who, instead of going into the church or teaching, turned to writing to earn their living. The most conspicuous of the "University Wits" was Christopher Marlowe, who, before his death at twenty-nine produced four remarkable dramas. Associated with Marlowe are the names of a number of other dramatists, all of whom worked feverishly, often in collaboration, to produce the greatest possible number of dramatic novelties for the stage. In their search for material, they ransacked the past. History, classic myth, legend, medieval romance, and folk tale were all grist to the mill. The situation much resembled that of our own day in which to meet the insatiable demand for movies the literature of the past has been freely used.

Then at the close of the sixteenth century came young William Shakespeare, destined to become the greatest dramatist of England, if not of all time. Shakespeare invariably made use of old material. In fact, he began his distinguished career as a re-vamper of old plays. His originality consisted in the treatment of his borrowed material. Though he never ceased to turn to old plays and old stories for plots of his own, we should remember Lowell's comment on Chaucer that if a man discover a process for converting a lump of lead into gold, we should not complain, when he hands us the gold, that he stole the lead.

From DOCTOR FAUSTUS

CHRISTOPHER MARLOWE

In the year 1587—the year that brought Shakespeare to London—Christopher Marlowe's first play, *Tamburlaine,* had been produced and had proved to be a hit. Within a year Marlowe had written another successful tragedy—this one based upon the German legend of Doctor Faustus. Theatrical London was full of praise for the young author, particularly for the poetic form and imaginative power of his plays. A few selections from *Doctor Faustus* will suffice to show the poetic possibilities in Marlowe's unrhymed verse form, and also his skill in using it.

Traditionally Faustus was a German professor filled with a thirst for knowledge and dissatisfied with his studies in Theology, Medicine, Philosophy, and Law at the University of Wittenberg. He therefore determined to make a league with the devil—Lucifer (or Satan) to provide him with supernatural powers for twenty-four years, at the end of which time Faust was to surrender himself, body and soul. Lucifer assigned Mephistophilis, one of his evil spirits, to be special companion and helper to the professor. When Faust speaks the first lines quoted below, he has talked with Mephistophilis and made up his mind to accept the terms, but he has not yet signed the compact.

[*Doctor Faustus* speaking, as he contemplates the power that will be his when he has bound his bargain with Lucifer and been given Mephistophilis as his servant—]

HAD I as many souls as there be stars,
I'd give them all for Mephistophilis.

346

By him I'll be great emperor of the world,
And make a bridge thorough the moving air,
5 To pass the ocean with a band of men:
I'll join the hills that bind the Afric shore,
And make that [country] continent to Spain,
And both contributory to my crown.
The Emperor shall not live but by my leave,
10 Nor any potentate of Germany.
Now that I have obtain'd what I desire,
I'll live in speculation of this art
Till Mephistophilis return again.

[*Mephistophilis* speaking, in reply to Faustus' questions about hell and about how Mephisto happens to be out of it, attending upon Faustus—]

Why, this is hell, nor am I out of it:
15 Think'st thou that I, that saw the face of God,
And tasted the eternal joys of heaven,
Am not tormented with ten thousand hells,
In being deprived of everlasting bliss? . . .
Hell hath no limits, nor is circumscrib'd
20 In one self-place; but where we are is hell,
And where hell is, there must we ever be:
And to be short, when all the world dissolves,
And every creature shall be purified,
All places shall be hell that are not heaven.

[*Faustus* speaking, after Mephistophilis has brought Helen of Troy back from the Land of the Shades—]

25 Was this the face that launch'd a thousand ships,
And burnt the topless towers of Ilium?
Sweet Helen, make me immortal with a kiss.—
Her lips suck forth my soul: see, where it flies.
Come, Helen, come, give me my soul again.
30 Here will I dwell, for heaven is in these lips,
And all is dross that is not Helena. . . .
O, thou art fairer than the evening air
Clad in the beauty of a thousand stars;

20. WE—Spirits of evil. According to tradition, the angels that fought with Lucifer against God were banished from heaven and became devils or evil spirits.
26. ILIUM—Troy. When Paris, Prince of Troy, stole Helen from King Menelaus, the other Greeks united, formed a great fleet and with Menelaus laid siege to Troy. After ten years of fighting the city was destroyed.

Brighter art thou than flaming Jupiter
35 When he appear'd to hapless Semele;
More lovely than the monarch of the sky
In wanton Arethusa's azured arms!

[*Chorus* speaking, after Faustus—offstage—has been torn asunder by demons—]

Cut is the branch that might have grown full straight,
And burnèd is Apollo's laurel-bough,
40 That sometimes grew within this learnèd man.
Faustus is gone. . . .
Terminat hora diem; terminat auctor opus.
(The hour ends the day; the actor ends the work.)

34–5. FLAMING JUPITER . . . HAPLESS SEMELE—Semele was one of the mortals beloved by Jupiter. Once when especially pleased with her, he promised to grant any request she should make. Her request was that he should appear before her in the full regalia that he wore on Mount Olympus as king of the gods. Knowing she had expressed a fatal wish, Jupiter tried to dissuade her; but Semele was insistent. When Jupiter appeared before her in crown and robes and weapons, she was consumed by the lightning from his thunderbolts.
36. MONARCH OF THE SKY—Probably Apollo, god of the sun.
37. ARETHUSA—Arethusa was the name of a fountain which is supposed to have had its source in southern Greece, to have flowed underground and under the sea, and to have welled up in Sicily. Arethusa was originally a nymph who was transformed by Diana into a fountain so that she might escape from a pursuing river god. In these two lines, the poet probably means only the beauty of the sun as it is seen through the leaping spray of the fountain.
39. APOLLO'S LAUREL-BOUGH—The laurel, signifying honorable achievement, was sacred to Apollo, the patron of the arts and sciences.

FOR INTERPRETATION

1. Does it seem to be knowledge or power that Faustus wants from Mephistophilis? What are some of the things he plans to do?
2. Why do you think *through* is spelled *thorough* in line 4? What do you think is the meaning of *continent* in line 7?
3. How does Marlowe reflect the spirit of his times in lines 1–13?
4. How does Mephistophilis define hell? Why is his definition a surprising one? Do you think many people of his day would have accepted it? Discuss. What does it reveal to you about Marlowe himself?
5. How does Marlowe suggest the loveliness of Helen of Troy? Which of his three similes seems to you the most expressive?
6. Explain the meaning of lines 38–40. How do they apply to Doctor Faustus? Why do they also apply to Christopher Marlowe?
7. Have you heard any of these lines quoted before? If so, which ones? Which lines do you think particularly worthy of remembering?

MACBETH

WILLIAM SHAKESPEARE

Macbeth is thought to have been written and first staged shortly after the coming of James I to the throne of England, and the association of the play with the king has interesting aspects. First, in Shakespeare's day the person of the monarch was a matter of great interest among Englishmen, and there must have been a great deal of curiosity about James and about the country from which he came. Shakespeare, who was a practical playwright, must have recognized what we should call the advertising value of a play dealing with Scottish affairs. Secondly, the play's indubitable allusions to James himself must have been highly gratifying to that monarch, whose colossal vanity has become a legend of later times. Thirdly, both James and the public, for the most part, believed in the existence of witches. They were doubtless awed by the witches in *Macbeth*, and it is not difficult to understand how the witch scenes might have struck them as among the most remarkable things in the play.

For the facts of his story, Shakespeare went to the *Chronicles of England, Ireland, and Scotland,* compiled by Raphael Holinshed. According to the *Chronicles,* there was about the year 1050 a Scottish king, Macbeth, who with the aid of his wife did murder a king. However, the facts which Shakespeare took from Holinshed he rearranged to suit his purpose, treating them not as a historian but as a dramatist.

DRAMATIS PERSONÆ

DUNCAN, *King of Scotland*

MALCOLM ⎫ *his sons*
DONALBAIN ⎭

MACBETH ⎱ *generals of the*
BANQUO ⎰ *King's army*

MACDUFF ⎤
LENNOX |
ROSS | *noblemen of*
MENTEITH | *Scotland*
ANGUS |
CAITHNESS ⎦

FLEANCE, *son to* BANQUO

SIWARD, *Earl of Northumberland, general of the English forces*

Young SIWARD, *his son*

SEYTON, *an officer attending on* MACBETH

Boy, *son to* MACDUFF
An English Doctor
A Scotch Doctor
A Sergeant
A Porter
An Old Man

LADY MACBETH
LADY MACDUFF
Gentlewoman *attending on*
LADY MACBETH

HECATE
Three Witches
Apparitions

Lords, Gentlemen, Officers, Soldiers, Murderers, Attendants, and Messengers

SCENE: *Scotland; England*

ACT I

SCENE 1. *A desert place.*

Thunder and lightning. Enter three Witches.

1 Witch. When shall we three meet again
In thunder, lightning, or in rain?
2 Witch. When the hurlyburly's done,
When the battle's lost and won.
5   *3 Witch.* That will be ere the set of sun.
1 Witch. Where the place?
2 Witch.   Upon the heath.

WITCHES—The general run of people in Shakespeare's day believed in the existence of witches. *Macbeth* was probably first staged in 1606. The student should remember that as late as 1692, twenty persons were executed in Salem Village, Massachusetts, for "witchcraft."
    3. HURLYBURLY—Tumult. The tumult of the battle.
    4. BATTLE—The battle being fought under the leadership of Macbeth and Banquo against the enemies of Duncan. See Scene 2.

3 Witch.   There to meet with Macbeth.
1 Witch.   I come, Graymalkin!
2 Witch.   Paddock calls:—Anon!
10   *All.*   Fair is foul, and foul is fair;
Hover through the fog and filthy air.

[Exeunt.

8. GRAYMALKIN—Gray cat, old cat.
9. PADDOCK—Toad. It was believed that the "familiar spirits" who controlled witches or gave them their power often accompanied them in the form of cats and toads. The implication is that the witches are obeying their familiar spirits who now summon them away.
9. ANON—Immediately. This is the answer of the witch to the call.
11. HOVER—Probably the meaning is, "Let us be off through the fog and filthy air." What does the word "hover" suggest as to the manner in which the witches made their departure?

SCENE 2.   *A camp near Forres.*

Alarum within. Enter DUNCAN, MALCOLM, DONALBAIN,
LENNOX, *with* Attendants, *meeting a bleeding* Sergeant.

Duncan.   What bloody man is that?   He can report,
As seemeth by his plight, of the revolt
The newest state.
Malcolm.   This is the sergeant
Who like a good and hardy soldier fought
5 'Gainst my captivity.   Hail, brave friend!
Say to the king the knowledge of the broil
As thou didst leave it.
Sergeant.   Doubtful it stood,
As two spent swimmers that do cling together
And choke their art.   The merciless Macdonwald—
10 Worthy to be a rebel, for to that
The multiplying villainies of nature
Do swarm upon him—from the western isles
Of kerns and gallowglasses is supplied;

3. NEWEST STATE—Latest news.
9. CHOKE THEIR ART—Prevent each other from swimming.
10. WORTHY TO BE A REBEL—Fit only to be a rebel.
10. FOR TO THAT—For to that end, because.
11. MULTIPLYING VILLAINIES OF NATURE DO SWARM UPON HIM—The reference is to the fact that Macdonwald had uttered "manie slanderous words" and "railing taunts" against Duncan.
12. WESTERN ISLES—Ireland and the islands west of Scotland.
13. KERNS AND GALLOWGLASSES—Light-armed and heavy-armed footsoldiers.

351

And fortune, on his damned quarrel smiling,
15 Show'd like a rebel's whore: but all's too weak;
For brave Macbeth—well he deserves that name—
Disdaining fortune, with his brandish'd steel,
Which smok'd with bloody execution,
Like valour's minion carv'd out his passage
20 Till he fac'd the slave;
Which ne'er shook hands, nor bade farewell to him,
Till he unseam'd him from the nave to th' chaps,
And fix'd his head upon our battlements.
    Duncan. O valiant cousin! worthy gentleman!
25   *Sergeant.* As whence the sun 'gins his reflection
Shipwrecking storms and direful thunders break,
So from that spring whence comfort seem'd to come
Discomfort swells. Mark, king of Scotland, mark:
No sooner justice had, with valour arm'd,
30 Compell'd these skipping kerns to trust their heels,
But the Norweyan lord, surveying vantage,
With furbish'd arms and new supplies of men,
Began a fresh assault.
    Duncan.   Dismay'd not this
Our captains, Macbeth and Banquo?
    Sergeant.   Yes;
35 As sparrows eagles, or the hare the lion.
If I say sooth, I must report they were
As cannons overcharg'd with double cracks;
So they doubly redoubled strokes upon the foe:
Except they meant to bathe in reeking wounds,

14. DAMNED—Doomed.   19. MINION—Darling, favorite.
21. WHICH—Who. Refers to Macbeth.
22. FROM THE NAVE TO TH' CHAPS—From the navel to the jaws.
24. COUSIN—Macbeth and Duncan were first cousins.
25. 'GINS HIS REFLECTION—Begins his return. The allusion is to the return
of the sun at the spring equinox, a time of storms. Note the pun on the
word "spring" in the third line below. The meaning is that, as the spring is
a source not only of gladness but of storms as well, so the course of the battle
is a cause for joy—the joy at Macbeth's victory, and a cause also for alarm—
alarm at the fresh assault begun by the Norweyan lord.
31. NORWEYAN—Norwegian.
31. SURVEYING VANTAGE—Seeing his opportunity.
32. FURBISH'D—Bright, untarnished, shining.
35. AS SPARROWS EAGLES—That is, as much as sparrows might dismay eagles.
36. SAY SOOTH—Speak truth.   37. CRACKS—Charges of powder.

40 Or memorize another Golgotha,
   I cannot tell—
   But I am faint, my gashes cry for help.
   Duncan. So well thy words become thee as thy wounds;
   They smack of honour both. Go get him surgeons.

                                    [*Exit* Sergeant, *attended.*

                     Enter Ross.

45 Who comes here?
   Malcolm.   The worthy thane of Ross.
   Lennox. What a haste looks through his eyes! So should he
        look
   That seems to speak things strange.
   Ross.   God save the king!
   Duncan. Whence cam'st thou, worthy thane?
   Ross.   From Fife, great king;
   Where the Norweyan banners flout the sky
50 And fan our people cold.
   Norway himself, with terrible numbers,
   Assisted by that most disloyal traitor,
   The thane of Cawdor, began a dismal conflict;
   Till that Bellona's bridegroom, lapp'd in proof,
55 Confronted him with self-comparisons,
   Point against point, rebellious arm 'gainst arm,
   Curbing his lavish spirit; and, to conclude,
   The victory fell on us.
   Duncan.   Great happiness!
   Ross.   That now

39–41. EXCEPT THEY MEANT . . . I CANNOT TELL—The Sergeant's meaning is:
So fierce was their attack that I cannot tell what they meant unless it was
to "bathe" in blood or make the place as memorable as another Golgotha.
Golgotha is "the place of the skull," the scene of the crucifixion of Christ.
See *Matthew* 27:33 and *Mark* 15:22.
   45. THANE—A nobleman.
   49. FLOUT—Mock.
   50. COLD—Cold with terror.
   51. NORWAY HIMSELF—The king of Norway: Sueno or Sweno.
   54. BELLONA—The old Roman goddess of war. Bellona's bridegroom is, of
course, Macbeth.
   54. LAPP'D IN PROOF—Clad in impenetrable armor.
   55. CONFRONTED HIM WITH SELF-COMPARISONS—Matched himself against him.
   57. CURBING HIS LAVISH SPIRIT—Checking his unrestrained daring.
   58. THAT NOW—So that now. Note that Duncan's speech "Great happiness!" is an exclamation of pleasure and interrupts the speech of Ross. Ross
says: The victory fell on us so that now Sweno . . . craves composition.

Sweno, the Norway's king, craves composition;
60 Nor would we deign him burial of his men
Till he disbursed, at Saint Colme's inch,
Ten thousand dollars to our general use.
Duncan. No more that thane of cawdor shall deceive
Our bosom interest. Go pronounce his present death,
65 And with his former title greet Macbeth.
Ross. I'll see it done.
Duncan. What he hath lost, noble Macbeth hath won.

                                     [*Exeunt.*

59. COMPOSITION—Terms of peace.
61. SAINT COLME'S INCH—The island of Inchcolm in the Firth of Forth. On this island was the monastery of St. Columba. "Inch" means island, so that "Saint Colme's inch" means St. Columba's Island.
62. DOLLARS—This word, of course, is not used in a modern sense. It was applied in Shakespeare's time to both the German *thaler* and the Spanish *piece of eight.*
64. DECEIVE OUR BOSOM INTEREST—Enjoy our confidence in order to betray it.
64. PRONOUNCE HIS PRESENT DEATH—Sentence him to instant death.

SCENE 3. *A heath near Forres.*

Thunder. Enter the three Witches.

1 Witch. Where hast thou been, sister?
2 Witch. Killing swine.
3 Witch. Sister, where thou?
1 Witch. A sailor's wife had chestnuts in her lap,
5 And munch'd, and munch'd, and munch'd. "Give me,"
      quoth I:
"Aroint thee, witch!" the rump-fed ronyon cries.
Her husband's to Aleppo gone, master o' the Tiger:
But in a sieve I'll thither sail,

2. KILLING SWINE—In Shakespeare's day an animal dying from no apparent cause was popularly believed to have been bewitched.
6. AROINT THEE—Away with you! An expression which was supposed to be especially effective against witches, spirits, and the like.
6. RUMP-FED—Fat.
6. RONYON—An abusive term for a woman.
7. ALEPPO—An ancient city of Syria. In Shakespeare's day it was a great commercial center.
7. TIGER—In a popular book of the day there was a long and interesting account of a trip in the Orient made by a merchant who sailed out in a ship called the *Tyger.* Shakespeare no doubt had read this account and took the name of his ship from it.
8. SIEVE—Witches were believed to go to sea in sieves.

And, like a rat without a tail,
10 I'll do, I'll do, and I'll do.
   2 Witch.   I'll give thee a wind.
   1 Witch.   Thou 'rt kind.
   3 Witch.   And I another.
   1 Witch.   I myself have all the other;
15 And the very ports they blow,
All the quarters that they know
I' the shipman's card.
I'll drain him dry as hay.
Sleep shall neither night nor day
20 Hang upon his pent-house lid;
He shall live a man forbid:
Weary se'nnights nine times nine
Shall he dwindle, peak, and pine:
Though his bark cannot be lost,
25 Yet it shall be tempest-tost.
Look what I have.
   2 Witch.   Show me, show me.
   1 Witch.   Here I have a pilot's thumb,
Wreck'd as homeward he did come   [*Drum within.*
30   *3 Witch.*   A drum, a drum!
Macbeth doth come.
   All.   The weird sisters, hand in hand,
Posters of the sea and land,
Thus do go about, about:

9. WITHOUT A TAIL—Whenever a witch assumed the form of an animal, one might know it by the fact that there would be some defect about the latter—as the "rat without a tail."
10. I'LL DO—That is, the witch in form of a rat will work the ship some ill, possibly gnawing a hole in the ship's bottom so that it will leak.
11. GIVE THEE A WIND—Witches were believed to sell winds to sailors. Here the 2nd and 3rd Witches each offer to give the 1st Witch a wind to keep her in her nefarious business.
17. SHIPMAN'S CARD—The mariner's chart or compass.
20. PENT-HOUSE LID—Eyelid. The resemblance of the eyebrow to a pent-house is the reason for this figure.
21. FORBID—Under a curse or ban.
22. SE'NNIGHTS NINE TIMES NINE—81 weeks.
23. DWINDLE, PEAK, AND PINE—Grow thin and waste away. Wasting or consumptive diseases were generally believed to be the work of witches.
33. POSTERS—Swift travellers. Compare with our expression "post-haste."
34. THUS DO GO ABOUT—That is, join hands and dance about in a ring. The witches go about three times for each "to make up nine." Numbers, especially odd numbers, and in particular three and nine, were formerly believed to have magical properties.

35 Thrice to thine, and thrice to mine,
And thrice again, to make up nine.
Peace! the charm's wound up.

Enter MACBETH *and* BANQUO

Macbeth. So foul and fair a day I have not seen.
Banquo. How far is 't call'd to Forres? What are these
40 So wither'd, and so wild in their attire,
That look not like th' inhabitants o' the earth,
And yet are on 't? Live you? or are you aught
That man may question? You seem to understand me,
By each at once her choppy finger laying
45 Upon her skinny lips: you should be women,
And yet your beards forbid me to interpret
That you are so.
    Macbeth. Speak, if you can: what are you?
    1 Witch. All hail, Macbeth! hail to thee, thane of Glamis!
    2 Witch. All hail, Macbeth! hail to thee, thane of Cawdor!
50   *3 Witch.* All hail, Macbeth, that shall be king hereafter!
    Banquo. Good sir, why do you start, and seem to fear
Things that do sound so fair?—I' the name of truth,
Are ye fantastical, or that indeed
Which outwardly ye show? My noble partner
55 You greet with present grace and great prediction
Of noble having and of royal hope,
That he seems rapt withal; to me you speak not.
If you can look into the seeds of time,
And say which grain will grow and which will not,

38. FOUL AND FAIR—Where have the words appeared before?
44. CHOPPY—Chapped.
52. I' THE NAME OF TRUTH—Banquo is now addressing the witches.
53. FANTASTICAL—Creatures of the fancy or imagination.
55. PRESENT GRACE—This goes with "noble having" in the line below, and "great prediction" goes with "royal hope," so that the meaning is "present grace of noble having" and "great prediction of royal hope." The first expression refers to the greeting of the first two witches who greet Macbeth by the noble titles he at present has. The second expression refers to the greeting of the third witch who hails Macbeth with the prophecy, or prediction, that he shall be king.
57. RAPT WITHAL—As if in a trance with it (your greeting).
58. LOOK INTO THE SEEDS OF TIME—Foretell the future.

60 Speak, then, to me, who neither beg nor fear
Your favours nor your hate.
 1 Witch. Hail!
 2 Witch. Hail!
 3 Witch. Hail!
65 *1 Witch.* Lesser than Macbeth, and greater.
 2 Witch. Not so happy, yet much happier.
 3 Witch. Thou shalt get kings, though thou be none:
So all hail, Macbeth and Banquo!
 1 Witch. Banquo and Macbeth, all hail!
70 *Macbeth.* Stay, you imperfect speakers, tell me more:
By Sinel's death I know I am thane of Glamis;
But how of Cawdor? the thane of Cawdor lives,
A prosperous gentleman, and to be king
Stands not within the prospect of belief
75 No more than to be Cawdor. Say from whence
You owe this strange intelligence? or why
Upon this blasted heath you stop our way
With such prophetic greeting? Speak, I charge you.
       [Witches *vanish.*
 Banquo. The earth hath bubbles as the water has,
80 And these are of them. Whither are they vanish'd?
 Macbeth. Into the air; and what seem'd corporal melted
As breath into the wind. Would they had stay'd!
 Banquo. Were such things here as we do speak about?
Or have we eaten on the insane root
85 That takes the reason prisoner?
 Macbeth. Your children shall be kings.
 Banquo.   You shall be king.
 Macbeth. And thane of Cawdor too: went it not so?
 Banquo. To th' selfsame tune and words. Who's here?

67. GET—Beget.
70. IMPERFECT—Unfinished. That is, who have not told all.
71. SINEL—Macbeth's father.
74. STANDS NOT WITHIN THE PROSPECT OF BELIEF—That is, seems an unbelievable thing.
79. THE EARTH HATH BUBBLES—To Banquo the witches are of no significance. He neither fears them nor attaches any importance to their words—they are as bubbles.
81. CORPORAL—Corporeal, having a body, having substance.
84. INSANE ROOT—It was the belief of the time that there were certain herbs and roots which, when eaten, produced madness.

Enter Ross *and* Angus.

Ross. The king hath happily receiv'd, Macbeth,
90 The news of thy success; and, when he reads
Thy personal venture in the rebels' fight,
His wonders and his praises do contend
Which should be thine or his; silenc'd with that,
In viewing o'er the rest o' the selfsame day,
95 He finds thee in the stout Norweyan ranks,
Nothing afeard of what thyself didst make,
Strange images of death. As thick as hail
Came post with post; and every one did bear
Thy praises in his kingdom's great defence,
100 And pour'd them down before him.
    Angus.   We are sent
To give thee from our royal master thanks;
Only to herald thee into his sight,
Not pay thee.
    Ross. And, for an earnest of a greater honour,
105 He bade me, from him, call thee thane of Cawdor;
In which addition, hail, most worthy thane!
For it is thine.
    Banquo. [*Aside.*]   What, can the devil speak true?
    Macbeth. The thane of Cawdor lives; why do you dress me
In borrow'd robes?
    Angus.   Who was the thane lives yet;
110 But under heavy judgment bears that life
Which he deserves to lose. Whether he was combin'd
With those of Norway, or did line the rebel
With hidden help and vantage, or that with both

91. PERSONAL VENTURE—That is, the risk Macbeth took in person in seeking
out and fighting Macdonwald.
92. HIS WONDERS AND HIS PRAISES DO CONTEND WHICH SHOULD BE THINE OR
HIS—"Thine" goes with "praises," and "his" with "wonders." The meaning
is: He is struck speechless (silenced with that) between trying to express his
own wonder and your praises at the same time.
97. STRANGE IMAGES OF DEATH—Death as represented, or imaged, in those
slain by Macbeth. The meaning is that Macbeth himself did not fear the
fate which he saw overtake others at his hand.
98. POST WITH POST—Messenger after messenger.
104. EARNEST—Promise.
106. ADDITION—That is, title added to your name.
112. LINE—Strengthen, reinforce.

He labour'd in his country's wreck, I know not;
115 But treasons capital, confess'd and prov'd,
Have overthrown him.
Macbeth. [*Aside.*]   Glamis, and thane of Cawdor!
The greatest is behind. [*To* Ross *and* ANGUS.]   Thanks for
    Your pains.
[*To* BANQUO.]   Do you not hope your children shall be kings,
When those that gave the thane of Cawdor to me
120 Promis'd no less to them?
Banquo.   That trusted home
Might yet enkindle you unto the crown,
Besides the thane of Cawdor. But 'tis strange;
And oftentimes, to win us to our harm,
The instruments of darkness tell us truths,
125 Win us with honest trifles, to betray 's
In deepest consequence.
Cousins, a word, I pray you.
Macbeth.   [*Aside.*]   Two truths are told,
As happy prologues to the swelling act
Of the imperial theme.—I thank you, gentlemen.—
130 [*Aside.*]   This supernatural soliciting
Cannot be ill; cannot be good. If ill,
Why hath it given me earnest of success,

114. LABOUR'D IN HIS COUNTRY'S WRECK—Strove to bring about his country's downfall.
115. TREASONS CAPITAL—Acts of treason punishable by death.
117. THE GREATEST IS BEHIND—The greatest honor is yet to come.
120. THAT TRUSTED HOME—The prophecy of the witches taken too seriously.
121. ENKINDLE YOU UNTO THE CROWN—Incite you to obtain the crown.
122–126. BUT 'TIS STRANGE; AND OFTENTIMES . . . DEEPEST CONSEQUENCE—Banquo's meaning is that when men enter upon evil doing they are often so deceived by their initial good fortune that they cannot be convinced that they will come to grief in the end.
127. COUSINS—A form of address applied to a distant relative, or sometimes by one nobleman to another. Banquo here speaks apart to Ross and Angus, leaving Macbeth free to speak his long *Aside.*
128. HAPPY PROLOGUES . . . IMPERIAL THEME—This figure is taken from the stage. A prologue is a part delivered before a play by way of introduction or preface to the play. By the "two truths" Macbeth has reference to the fact that the greetings of the first two witches, who hailed him as "thane of Glamis" and "thane of Cawdor," have come true. "Happy" means favorable or propitious. "Swelling" means glorious. "Imperial" means kingly. Macbeth's imagination has caught fire. He conceives of what has happened as a promising prologue to a glorious drama which is about to begin.
130. SOLICITING—Prompting, incitement. 132. EARNEST—Promise.

Commencing in a truth? I am thane of Cawdor:
If good, why do I yield to that suggestion
135 Whose horrid image doth unfix my hair
And make my seated heart knock at my ribs,
Against the use of nature? Present fears
Are less than horrible imaginings.
My thought, whose murder yet is but fantastical,
140 Shakes so my single state of man that function
Is smother'd in surmise, and nothing is
But what is not.
 Banquo. Look, how our partner's rapt.
 Macbeth. [*Aside.*] If chance will have me king, why,
  chance may crown me,
Without my stir.
 Banquo. New honours come upon him,
145 Like our strange garments, cleave not to their mould
But with the aid of use.
 Macbeth. [*Aside.*] Come what come may,
Time and the hour runs through the roughest day.
 Banquo. Worthy Macbeth, we stay upon your leisure.
 Macbeth. Give me your favour. My dull brain was wrought
150 With things forgotten. Kind gentlemen, your pains
Are register'd where every day I turn
The leaf to read them. Let us toward the king.
 [*To* BANQUO.] Think upon what hath chanc'd; and, at more
  time,

134. SUGGESTION—That is, the thought of murdering Duncan.
135. IMAGE—Macbeth has a vivid imagination. He can see the deed as done.
135. UNFIX MY HAIR—Make it stand on end.
139. WHOSE MURDER YET IS BUT FANTASTICAL—In which the murder is now
only an imagined deed.
140. MY SINGLE STATE OF MAN—My whole being.
141. FUNCTION IS SMOTHER'D IN SURMISE—Power to do the deed is paralyzed
by the horror which thinking about it arouses.
141. NOTHING IS BUT WHAT IS NOT—That is, the only realities to Macbeth
are the devisings of his heated imagination.
147. TIME AND THE HOUR—The meaning is that by biding one's time and
seizing favorable opportunity, one can overcome the greatest of difficulties.
149. GIVE ME YOUR FAVOUR—Pardon me.
149. WROUGHT—Moved. Macbeth pretends that he has been lost in thought,
trying to recall some forgotten matter.
151. WHERE EVERY DAY . . . TO READ THEM—That is, in his memory.
152. LET US TOWARD THE KING—This part of the speech is addressed to
Banquo.
153. CHANC'D—Happened. Macbeth here has reference to the meeting with
the witches.

The interim having weigh'd it, let us speak
155 Our free hearts each to other.
   Banquo.   Very gladly.
   Macbeth.   Till then, enough. Come, friends. [*Exeunt.*

154. THE INTERIM HAVING WEIGH'D IT—In the meanwhile having thought it over.

SCENE 4. *Forres. The palace.*

Flourish. Enter DUNCAN, MALCOLM, DONALBAIN, LENNOX, *and* Attendants.

   Duncan. Is execution done on Cawdor? Are not
Those in commission yet return'd?
   Malcolm.   My liege,
They are not yet come back. But I have spoke
With one that saw him die; who did report
5 That very frankly he confess'd his treasons,
Implor'd your highness' pardon, and set forth
A deep repentance. Nothing in his life
Became him like the leaving it; he died
As one that had been studied in his death
10 To throw away the dearest thing he ow'd,
As 'twere a careless trifle.
   Duncan.   There's no art
To find the mind's construction in the face;
He was a gentleman on whom I built
An absolute trust.

Enter MACBETH, BANQUO, ROSS, *and* ANGUS.

                  O worthiest cousin!
15 The sin of my ingratitude even now
Was heavy on me. Thou art so far before,
That swiftest wing of recompense is slow

2. THOSE IN COMMISSION—Those commissioned, or charged to see the execution done on Cawdor.
9. AS ONE THAT HAD BEEN STUDIED—As an actor who had studied it as a "part" until he had become perfect in it.
10. OW'D—Owned.
11. CARELESS—Uncared for.
11-12. THERE'S NO ART . . . IN THE FACE—There is no way to read a man's character in his face.
14. WORTHIEST COUSIN—Macbeth.

To overtake thee. Would thou hadst less deserv'd,
That the proportion both of thanks and payment
20 Might have been mine! Only I have left to say,
More is thy due than more than all can pay.
    Macbeth. The service and the loyalty I owe,
In doing it, pays itself. Your highness' part
Is to receive our duties; and our duties
25 Are to your throne and state children and servants;
Which do but what they should, by doing everything
Safe toward your love and honour.
    Duncan.   Welcome hither:
I have begun to plant thee, and will labour
To make thee full of growing. Noble Banquo,
30 That hast no less deserv'd, nor must be known
No less to have done so, let me infold thee
And hold thee to my heart.
    Banquo.   There if I grow,
The harvest is your own.
    Duncan.   My plenteous joys,
Wanton in fulness, seek to hide themselves
35 In drops of sorrow. Sons, kinsmen, thanes,
And you whose places are the nearest, know,
We will establish our estate upon
Our eldest, Malcolm, whom we name hereafter
The Prince of Cumberland; which honour must

19-20. THAT THE PROPORTION . . . MIGHT HAVE BEEN MINE—That is, that I
might have been able to reward you both in honors and gratitude in proportion to your deserts.
    27. SAFE TOWARD YOUR LOVE AND HONOUR—That is, which will make you
loved and honored.   34. WANTON—Unrestrained.
    35. DROPS OF SORROW—Tears. The meaning is: My joys are so great that
they bring tears to my eyes.
    39. PRINCE OF CUMBERLAND—The crown of Scotland was elective rather
than hereditary, which means that the king's eldest son did not succeed to
the throne by right of birth. The final choice of their king lay with the
thanes, and they might set aside an immediate heir in favor of one whom
they thought more competent. Both Duncan and Macbeth were sons of two
daughters of the old King Malcolm, so that Macbeth had some claim to the
throne.
    39-42. WHICH HONOUR . . . ON ALL DESERVERS—Duncan's meaning is that
Malcolm shall not be the only one to enjoy honor, but that all who have deserved it (especially Banquo and Macbeth) shall be held in high esteem according to their merits. This speech must have irritated Macbeth, for to Malcolm
goes the very substantial honor of being named Duncan's successor, while
Macbeth who feels himself better fitted to be king must be content with
nothing more substantial than high esteem.

40 Not unaccompanied invest him only,
But signs of nobleness, like stars, shall shine
On all deservers. From hence to Inverness,
And bind us further to you.
    Macbeth. The rest is labour, which is not us'd for you.
45 I'll be myself the harbinger, and make joyful
The hearing of my wife with your approach;
So humbly take my leave.
    Duncan.   My worthy Cawdor!
    Macbeth. [*Aside.*] The Prince of Cumberland! that is a step
On which I must fall down, or else o'erleap,
50 For in my way it lies. Stars, hide your fires;
Let not light see my black and deep desires;
The eye wink at the hand; yet let that be
Which the eye fears, when it is done, to see.   [*Exit.*
    Duncan. True, worthy Banquo; he is full so valiant,
55 And in his commendations I am fed;
It is a banquet to me. Let's after him,
Whose care is gone before to bid us welcome.
It is a peerless kinsman.   [*Flourish. Exeunt.*

42. INVERNESS—Macbeth's castle.
44. THE REST IS LABOUR, WHICH IS NOT US'D FOR YOU—Macbeth's meaning
is that the rest which is not spent in Duncan's service is labor. Is he sincere?
45. HARBINGER—Forerunner. An officer whose duty it was to go ahead and
make provision for the king and his retinue. The connection between this
and the preceding line lies in Macbeth's implication that he will employ his
"rest" in Duncan's service and carry the news to Inverness.
52. WINK AT—Pretend not to see.
54. TRUE, WORTHY BANQUO; HE IS FULL SO VALIANT—The "he" in this speech
refers to Macbeth. While Macbeth has been speaking his *Aside* Banquo has
been speaking in praise of Macbeth to Duncan. Duncan is confirming some
remark of Banquo's with the words: "(That is) true, worthy Banquo."
58. IT—Refers to Macbeth, who was Duncan's kinsman.

SCENE 5. *Inverness.* MACBETH'S *castle.*

Enter LADY MACBETH, *alone, with a letter.*

Lady Macbeth. [*Reads.*] They met me in the day of success;
and I have learn'd by the perfect'st report, they have more in

1. THEY—The witches.
2. BY THE PERFECT'ST REPORT—From the most reliable source. Macbeth
may be making reference here to the fact that one of the prophecies has
actually come true, or it may be that he has been making some inquiry into
the power of the witches and is convinced that they actually have more than
mortal knowledge.

them than mortal knowledge. When I burn'd in desire to question them further, they made themselves air, into which they
5 vanish'd. Whiles I stood rapt in the wonder of it, came missives
from the King, who all-hail'd me "Thane of Cawdor"; by which
title, before, these weird sisters saluted me, and referr'd me to the
coming on of time, with "Hail, king that shalt be!" This have I
thought good to deliver thee, my dearest partner of greatness, that
10 thou mightst not lose the dues of rejoicing, by being ignorant of
what greatness is promis'd thee. Lay it to thy heart, and farewell.

Glamis thou art, and Cawdor, and shalt be
What thou art promis'd. Yet do I fear thy nature;
It is too full o' the milk of human kindness
15 To catch the nearest way. Thou wouldst be great;
Art not without ambition, but without
The illness should attend it. What thou wouldst highly,
That wouldst thou holily; wouldst not play false,
And yet wouldst wrongly win. Thou 'ldst have, great Glamis,
20 That which cries, "Thus thou must do," if thou have it;
And that which rather thou dost fear to do
Than wishest should be undone. Hie thee hither,
That I may pour my spirits in thine ear,
And chastise with the valour of my tongue
25 All that impedes thee from the golden round
Which fate and metaphysical aid doth seem
To have thee crown'd withal.

9. DELIVER THEE—Communicate to you.
10. LOSE THE DUES OF REJOICING—That is, that you might not lose any of
the rejoicing which is your due.
15. NEAREST WAY—The murder of Duncan.
17. ILLNESS—Wickedness, unscrupulousness.
17-18. WHAT THOU WOULDST HIGHLY, THAT WOULDST THOU HOLILY—Whatever great honors you wish, you prefer to come by them legitimately.
18-19. WOULDST NOT PLAY FALSE, AND YET WOULDST WRONGLY WIN—You will
not play false, yet you covet a thing which can be won only by dishonest
means. There is perhaps the further meaning here: Although you will not
play false yourself, you have no scruples about accepting a result brought
about dishonestly, like one who will not steal yet will not hesitate to keep a
sum of money which he has found even though he knows the loser.
21. AND THAT—The full sense is: And you would also have that, etc.
21. THAT WHICH—That is, the crown. The meaning is: You would have
the crown, which cries, "Thus (murder Duncan) thou must do, if you
have me."
25. GOLDEN ROUND—The crown.
26. METAPHYSICAL—Supernatural.

Enter a Messenger.

What is your tidings?

Messenger. The king comes here to-night.

Lady Macbeth.   Thou 'rt mad to say it!

Is not thy master with him? who, were 't so,

30 Would have inform'd for preparation.

Messenger. So please you, it is true; our thane is coming.

One of my fellows had the speed of him,

Who, almost dead for breath, had scarcely more

Than would make up his message.

Lady Macbeth.   Give him tending;

35 He brings great news.   [*Exit* Messenger.

The raven himself is hoarse

That croaks the fatal entrance of Duncan

Under my battlements. Come, you spirits

That tend on mortal thoughts, unsex me here;

And fill me from the crown to the toe top-full

40 Of direst cruelty! make thick my blood;

Stop up th' access and passage to remorse,

That no compunctious visitings of nature

Shake my fell purpose, nor keep peace between

The effect and it! Come to my woman's breasts,

45 And take my milk for gall, you murd'ring ministers,

Wherever in your sightless substances

You wait on nature's mischief! Come, thick night,

And pall thee in the dunnest smoke of hell,

32. HAD THE SPEED OF HIM—Outdistanced him.

35–37. THE RAVEN HIMSELF . . . UNDER MY BATTLEMENTS—The raven formerly enjoyed the reputation of being a bird of ill omen. Lady Macbeth means that the raven that croaks at the entrance of Duncan into Macbeth's castle must croak himself hoarse if his croaking is to be proportionate to the evil which will befall Duncan.

38. MORTAL—Deadly, murderous.

38. UNSEX—Divest me of the tender and merciful nature which is woman's.

40. MAKE THICK MY BLOOD—According to the physiology of Shakespeare's day, "spirits" passed along the blood. Lady Macbeth asks that her blood may become thick to stop the passage of remorse (the "spirit" of pity) so that it may not find access (entrance) into her heart.

42. COMPUNCTIOUS VISITINGS OF NATURE—Natural feelings of compunction.

43. FELL—Fierce, cruel.

43–44. NOR KEEP PEACE BETWEEN THE EFFECT AND IT—Come as a peacemaker between the purpose and the effect, or execution.

45. TAKE MY MILK FOR GALL—Turn my milk into gall.

46. SIGHTLESS—Invisible.

48. PALL—Wrap.

That my keen knife see not the wound it makes,
50 Nor heaven peep through the blanket of the dark.
To cry, "Hold, hold!"

Enter MACBETH.

Great Glamis! worthy Cawdor!

Greater than both, by the all-hail hereafter!
Thy letters have transported me beyond
This ignorant present, and I feel now
55 The future in the instant.

   Macbeth.   My dearest love,
Duncan comes here to-night.

    Lady Macbeth.   And when goes hence?

    Macbeth. To-morrow, as he purposes.

    Lady Macbeth.   O, never
Shall sun that morrow see!
Your face, my thane, is as a book where men
60 May read strange matters. To beguile the time,
Look like the time; bear welcome in your eye,
Your hand, your tongue; look like the innocent flower
But be the serpent under 't. He that's coming
Must be provided for; and you shall put
65 This night's great business into my dispatch,
Which shall to all our nights and days to come
Give solely sovereign sway and masterdom.

    Macbeth. We will speak further.

    Lady Macbeth.   Only look up clear;
To alter favour ever is to fear.
70 Leave all the rest to me.   *[Exeunt.*

---

52. THE ALL-HAIL HEREAFTER—The reference is to the greeting of the third witch: "All hail, Macbeth, that shalt be king hereafter."

60. TO BEGUILE THE TIME, LOOK LIKE THE TIME—"Time" here means the occasion, which is one for display of hospitality. The lines following make Lady Macbeth's meaning clear—to deceive those present at the "time," behave in the manner the "time" requires.

65. DISPATCH—Management.

66. WHICH—Modifies "great business."

66–67. SHALL TO ALL OUR NIGHTS AND DAYS . . . SWAY AND MASTERDOM—That is, shall give us the kingdom and make us masters of the situation henceforth.

68–69. ONLY LOOK UP CLEAR; TO ALTER FAVOUR EVER IS TO FEAR—That is, do not let your face betray us, to change countenance (alter favour) is to show signs of fear.

367

SCENE 6. *Before* MACBETH'S *castle.*

Hautboys and torches. Enter DUNCAN, MALCOLM, DONALBAIN,
BANQUO, LENNOX, MACDUFF, ROSS, ANGUS, *and* Attendants.

Duncan. This castle hath a pleasant seat; the air
Nimbly and sweetly recommends itself
Unto our gentle senses.
   Banquo.   This guest of summer,
The temple-haunting martlet, does approve,
5 By his lov'd mansionry, that the heaven's breath
Smells wooingly here; no jutty, frieze,
Buttress, nor coign of vantage, but this bird
Hath made his pendent bed and procreant cradle.
Where they most breed and haunt, I have observ'd
10 The air is delicate.

Enter LADY MACBETH.

Duncan.   See, see, our honour'd hostess!
The love that follows us sometime is our trouble,
Which still we thank as love. Herein I teach you
How you shall bid God 'ild us for your pains,
And thank us for your trouble.
   Lady Macbeth.   All our service
15 In every point twice done and then done double
Were poor and single business to contend

Hautboys (hō'boi)—High-pitched musical instruments, sounded to announce
the entrance of important persons, usually royalty.
    1. SEAT—Site, situation.
    4. TEMPLE-HAUNTING MARTLET—An allusion possibly to the martin, which
nests in church towers.
    4. APPROVE—Prove.
    5. MANSIONRY—Building, nest.
    6. JUTTY—Projection.
    7. COIGN OF VANTAGE—Convenient corner or nook.
    8. PENDENT—An allusion possibly to the way in which the nest built on
some slight "jutty" projected out or over-hung the edge.
    8. PROCREANT CRADLE—Cradle for bringing forth young.
    11–12. THE LOVE THAT FOLLOWS US . . . WE THANK AS LOVE—Duncan means
that the love which others have for us (follows us) sometimes puts us to
trouble, yet we are grateful for it.
    12–14. HEREIN . . . YOUR TROUBLE—The meaning is: Since, therefore, it is
our love which puts you to your pains and trouble now, you may ask God
to reward us for causing you the trouble of entertaining us.
    16. SINGLE BUSINESS TO CONTEND—That is, a weak repayment for those
honors, etc.

Against those honours deep and broad wherewith
Your majesty loads our house: for those of old,
And the late dignities heap'd up to them,
20 We rest your hermits.
    Duncan.   Where's the thane of Cawdor?
We cours'd him at the heels, and had a purpose
To be his purveyor: but he rides well,
And his great love, sharp as his spur, hath holp him
To his home before us. Fair and noble hostess,
25 We are your guest to-night.

    Lady Macbeth.   Your servants ever
Have theirs, themselves, and what is theirs, in compt,
To make their audit at your highness' pleasure,
Still to return your own.
    Duncan.   Give me your hand;
Conduct me to mine host. We love him highly,
30 And shall continue our graces towards him.
By your leave, hostess.   *[Exeunt.*

20. WE REST YOUR HERMITS—We remain, so to speak, your beadsmen. The
meaning is made clear by the definition of beadsman—one who having received alms from another is bound to pray for his benefactor.
21. COURS'D—Pursued, followed closely.   22. PURVEYOR—Forerunner.
26–27. IN COMPT, TO MAKE THEIR AUDIT—Subject to account, against the day
it shall please you to make their audit (call them to account).

SCENE 7. MACBETH'S *castle.*

Hautboys and torches. Enter a Sewer, *and divers* Servants *with dishes and service, over the stage. Then enter* MACBETH.

Macbeth. If it were done when 'tis done, then 'twere well
It were done quickly. If th' assassination
Could trammel up the consequence, and catch
With his surcease success; that but this blow
5   Might be the be-all and the end-all here,
But here, upon this bank and shoal of time,
We'd jump the life to come. But in these cases
We still have judgment here, that we but teach
Bloody instructions, which, being taught, return
10 To plague th' inventor. This even-handed justice
Commends th' ingredients of our poison'd chalice
To our own lips. He's here in double trust:
First, as I am his kinsman and his subject,
Strong both against the deed; then, as his host,
15 Who should against his murderer shut the door,
Not bear the knife myself. Besides, this Duncan
Hath borne his faculties so meek, hath been

SEWER—A servant, or officer of the household, who carried in and arranged dishes for a banquet. These servants pass over the stage to the banquet hall. Macbeth has left the table, much perturbed by the fears and imaginings which he voices in his soliloquy.
   1. IF IT WERE DONE WHEN 'TIS DONE—That is, if the deed when done only ended the matter, and there were no consequences.
   3. TRAMMEL UP—Prevent. To trammel up means literally to catch as in a net—to tangle up, and thus prevent the consequences from following.
   4. AND CATCH WITH HIS (ITS) SURCEASE SUCCESS—That is, bring success with its cessation. Macbeth uses the term surcease, or cessation, to describe such a deed as he has described above—that is over when it is done, and has no consequences—a "be-all and end-all."
   4. THAT BUT—If only.
   6. BUT HERE—Only here.
   6. UPON THIS BANK AND SHOAL OF TIME—Upon this earth.
   7. JUMP THE LIFE TO COME—Risk or chance what will happen in the life to come.
   8. HAVE JUDGMENT HERE—Meet retribution here.
   8. THAT—So that; and that judgment is that.
   8–10. WE BUT TEACH BLOODY INSTRUCTIONS . . . PLAGUE TH' INVENTOR—That is, all we do is to teach others by example what they shall do to us.
   11. COMMENDS—Delivers.
   11. CHALICE—Cup. Pricks of conscience caused Macbeth ever to fear, lest he should be served of the same cup, as he had ministered to his predecessor.
   17. BORNE HIS FACULTIES SO MEEK—Exercised his powers in so mild a manner.

So clear in his great office, that his virtues
Will plead like angels, trumpet-tongu'd, against
20 The deep damnation of his taking-off;
And pity, like a naked new-born babe
Striding the blast, or heaven's cherubim hors'd
Upon the sightless couriers of the air,
Shall blow the horrid deed in every eye,
25 That tears shall drown the wind. I have no spur
To prick the sides of my intent, but only
Vaulting ambition, which o'erleaps itself
And falls on th' other.

Enter LADY MACBETH.

How now! what news?
Lady Macbeth. He has almost supp'd. Why have you
    left the chamber?
30 *Macbeth.* Hath he ask'd for me?
Lady Macbeth.   Know you not he has?
Macbeth. We will proceed no further in this business:
He hath honour'd me of late; and I have bought
Golden opinions from all sorts of people,
Which would be worn now in their newest gloss
35 Not cast aside so soon.
    Lady Macbeth.   Was the hope drunk
Wherein you dress'd yourself? hath it slept since?
And wakes it now, to look so green and pale
At what it did so freely? From this time

18. So CLEAR IN HIS GREAT OFFICE—So free from fault as a king.
21–22. LIKE A NAKED NEW-BORN BABE—See *Psalm* 18:10. "And he rode
upon a cherub, and did fly: yea, he did fly upon the wings of the wind."
23. SIGHTLESS COURIERS OF THE AIR—The invisible winds.
27–28. VAULTING AMBITION, WHICH O'ERLEAPS ITSELF AND FALLS ON TH' OTHER
—The image is that of a horseman who has put his horse over (vaulted) an
obstacle only to fall on the other side.
32–35. I HAVE BOUGHT . . . NOT CAST ASIDE SO SOON—The meaning is that
Macbeth's deeds have earned him the great esteem of all classes and that he
feels he should enjoy that esteem rather than lose it by murdering Duncan.
35–38. WAS THE HOPE DRUNK . . . AT WHAT IT DID SO FREELY—The meaning
is: Was the hope (that is, the hope of being able to murder Duncan) like that
of a drunken man, who while he is drunk plans and dares great things, but
who when he wakes green and pale from his debauch finds himself without
the daring which drink gave him?
39. FROM THIS TIME SUCH I ACCOUNT THY LOVE—Lady Macbeth means that
henceforth she will regard his love for her as nothing more than the maudlin
protestation of a drunken man.

Such I account thy love. Art thou afeard
40 To be the same in thine own act and valour
As thou art in desire? Wouldst thou have that
Which thou esteem'st the ornament of life,
And live a coward in thine own esteem,
Letting "I dare not" wait upon "I would,"
45 Like the poor cat i' the adage?
    Macbeth.   Prithee, peace:
I dare do all that may become a man;
Who dares do more is none.
    Lady Macbeth.   What beast was 't, then,
That made you break this enterprise to me?
When you durst do it, then you were a man;
50 And, to be more than what you were, you would
Be so much more the man. Nor time nor place
Did then adhere, and yet you would make both:
They have made themselves, and that their fitness now
Does unmake you. I have given suck, and know
55 How tender 'tis to love the babe that milks me;
I would, while it was smiling in my face,
Have pluck'd my nipple from his boneless gums,
And dash'd the brains out, had I so sworn as you
Have done to this.
    Macbeth.   If we should fail?
    Lady Macbeth.   We fail.
60 But screw your courage to the sticking-place,

42. ORNAMENT—Crown.
45. THE ADAGE—The proverb alluded to is: "The cat would eat fish, but she will not wet her feet."
47. BEAST—Lady Macbeth uses this term in contrast with "man" used by Macbeth in the speech above.
48. BREAK THIS ENTERPRISE—Propose the murder of Duncan. This line indicates to some students of the play that the "enterprise" originated with Macbeth. Others think that the enterprise really originated with her under the inspiration of Macbeth's letter, and that she can believe, or say at least, that she has only followed him.
52. ADHERE—Agree, that is, present themselves opportunely together. The meaning of the passage is: When you first proposed to murder Duncan, you were held back only by want of a good opportunity. You were so hot to do it then that you were all for creating such an opportunity. Now that opportunity (time and place) has presented itself you are unnerved by it.
60. SCREW YOUR COURAGE TO THE STICKING-PLACE—The allusion is to screwing up the strings of a musical instrument to their proper degree of tension, "when the peg remains fast in its 'sticking place.'"

And we'll not fail.   When Duncan is asleep—
Whereto the rather shall his day's hard journey
Soundly invite him—his two chamberlains
Will I with wine and wassail so convince,
65 That memory, the warder of the brain,
Shall be a fume, and the receipt of reason
A limbeck only.   When in swinish sleep
Their drenched natures lie as in a death,
What cannot you and I perform upon
70 Th' unguarded Duncan? what not put upon
His spongy officers, who shall bear the guilt
Of our great quell?
    Macbeth.   Bring forth men-children only;
For thy undaunted mettle should compose
Nothing but males.   Will it not be receiv'd,
75 When we have mark'd with blood those sleepy two
Of his own chamber and us'd their very daggers,
That they have done 't?
    Lady Macbeth.   Who dares receive it other,
As we shall make our griefs and clamour roar
Upon his death?
    Macbeth.   I am settled, and bend up
80 Each corporal agent to this terrible feat.
Away, and mock the time with fairest show;
False face must hide what the false heart doth know.
                              [*Exeunt.*

---

62. THE RATHER—The more quickly.
64. WASSAIL—Revelry.
64. CONVINCE—Overcome.
65-67. THE WARDER OF THE BRAIN . . . A LIMBECK ONLY—According to the anatomy of Shakespeare's day, the brain was believed to be divided into three ventricles, or cavities.   The memory was thought to be situated in the one at the base of the brain where the spinal cord enters.   In this position the memory served, like the warder or sentinel of a castle, to warn the reason against attack.   "When the memory is converted by intoxication into a mere fume, then it fills the brain itself, the receipt or receptacle of reason, which thus becomes like an alembic"—a vessel used in distilling into which the vapor, or fume, rises.
71. SPONGY—Drunken.
72. QUELL—Murder, slaying.
74. RECEIV'D—Thought.
77. OTHER—Otherwise.
79-80. BEND UP EACH CORPORAL AGENT—Bring to bear each physical power.

ACT II

SCENE I. *Inverness. Court of* MACBETH'S *castle.*

Enter BANQUO, *and* FLEANCE *with a torch before him.*

Banquo. How goes the night, boy?
Fleance. The moon is down; I have not heard the clock.
Banquo. And she goes down at twelve.
Fleance.   I take 't, 'tis later, sir.
Banquo. Hold, take my sword. There's husbandry in heaven;
5 Their candles are all out. Take thee that too.
A heavy summons lies like lead upon me,
And yet I would not sleep. Merciful powers,
Restrain in me the cursèd thoughts that nature
Gives way to in repose!

Enter MACBETH, *and a* Servant *with a torch.*

               Give me my sword.
10 Who's there?
Macbeth. A friend.
Banquo. What, sir, not yet at rest? The king's a-bed:
He hath been in unusual pleasure, and
Sent forth great largess to your offices:
15 This diamond he greets your wife withal,
By the name of most kind hostess; and shut up
In measureless content.
Macbeth.   Being unprepar'd,
Our will became the servant to defect;

4. HUSBANDRY—Economy, thrift.
5. CANDLES—The stars.
5. TAKE THEE THAT TOO—Banquo hands Fleance some weapon.
8. THE CURSÈD THOUGHTS THAT NATURE GIVES WAY TO IN REPOSE—The dreams of the weird sisters which Banquo mentions in a speech below.
9. GIVE ME MY SWORD—Hearing footsteps approaching, Banquo calls for his sword.
14. LARGESS TO YOUR OFFICES—Gifts for your household officers or servants.
16–17. SHUT UP IN MEASURELESS CONTENT—Probably means "as one whose satisfaction is complete."
17–19. BEING UNPREPAR'D . . . HAVE WROUGHT—The meaning is: Not being prepared for the king's coming, our natural desire (will) to receive him with the ceremony and hospitality due him has been thwarted by our not having had sufficient time to make adequate preparation.

Which else should free have wrought.

Banquo.   All's well.
20 I dreamt last night of the three weird sisters:
To you they have show'd some truth.

Macbeth.   I think not of them;
Yet, when we can entreat an hour to serve,
We would spend it in some words upon that business,
If you would grant the time.

Banquo.   At your kind'st leisure.
25 *Macbeth.* If you shall cleave to my consent, when 't is,
It shall make honour for you.

Banquo.   So I lose none
In seeking to augment it, but still keep
My bosom franchis'd, and allegiance clear,
I shall be counsell'd.

Macbeth.   Good repose the while!
30 *Banquo.* Thanks, sir: the like to you!

[*Exeunt* Banquo *and* Fleance
Macbeth. Go bid thy mistress, when my drink is ready,
She strike upon the bell. Get thee to bed.   [*Exit* Servant.
Is this a dagger which I see before me,
The handle toward my hand? Come, let me clutch thee.
35 I have thee not, and yet I see thee still.
Art thou not, fatal vision, sensible
To feeling as to sight? or art thou but
A dagger of the mind, a false creation,
Proceeding from the heat-oppressed brain?
40 I see thee yet, in form as palpable
As this which now I draw.
Thou marshall'st me the way that I was going;

22. Entreat an hour to serve—That is, find an hour convenient to the
purpose.
25–26. Cleave to my consent . . . honour for you—The meaning is: If
you shall consent to my plan, when I unfold it to you, it will bring you honor.
26. So—Provided that.
26. None—That is, no honor.
28. Bosom franchis'd—That is, free from dishonor.
28. Allegiance clear—Loyalty to the king untarnished.
29. Counsell'd—I shall listen to your plan.
32. *Exit* Servant—Macbeth is now left alone in the darkness.
36–37. Sensible to feeling—Perceptible to feeling or to the touch.
40. Palpable—Capable of being touched.
42. Marshall'st me—The dagger seems to move farther from him, leading
him on.

And such an instrument I was to use.
Mine eyes are made the fools o' the other senses,
45 Or else worth all the rest; I see thee still;
And on thy blade and dudgeon gouts of blood,
Which was not so before. There's no such thing:
It is the bloody business which informs
Thus to mine eyes. Now o'er the one half-world
50 Nature seems dead, and wicked dreams abuse
The curtain'd sleep; witchcraft celebrates
Pale Hecate's offerings; and wither'd murder,
Alarum'd by his sentinel, the wolf,
Whose howl 's his watch, thus with his stealthy pace,
55 With Tarquin's ravishing strides, towards his design
Moves like a ghost. Thou sure and firm-set earth,
Hear not my steps, which way they walk, for fear
Thy very stones prate of my whereabout,
And take the present horror from the time,
60 Which now suits with it. Whiles I threat, he lives:
Words to the heat of deeds too cold breath gives.

[*A bell rings.*

44–45. THE FOOLS O' THE OTHER SENSES, OR ELSE WORTH ALL THE REST—Either
his eyes are made the fools of his imagination, since he sees what is not, or
else they are worth more, since they can see what he cannot clutch with
his hand.
46. DUDGEON—Haft or hilt.
46. GOUTS—Drops, smears.
48. INFORMS—Takes form.
51. CURTAIN'D SLEEP—The Elizabethan bed was hung about with curtains.
51–52. WITCHCRAFT CELEBRATES PALE HECATE'S OFFERINGS—Performs the rites
dedicated or offered to Hecate. In Greek mythology Hecate was queen of
Hades, or the underworld. The modern pronunciation is hĕk'a-tē. Shakespeare employs it as if it were a word of two syllables, possibly hĕk'āte.
54. WHOSE HOWL 'S HIS WATCH—The "his" refers to murder, that is, the
murderer. The allusion is to the watch who used to go about the city and
cry out the hour, as, "Twelve o'clock and all's well." The wolf is thought
of here as the murder's watch, whose howl means: "Now is the time for
your deed and all's well."
55. WITH TARQUIN'S RAVISHING STRIDES—The murderer is pictured as approaching his victim with the stealthy strides of Tarquin. Tarquin was a
Roman king whose assault on Lucrece, a Roman matron, so aroused the
people that as a result the kingdom was destroyed and a republic established.
58. PRATE—Cry out.
59–60. AND TAKE THE PRESENT HORROR . . . SUITS WITH IT—That is, And
break the silence that adds such horror to the night and makes it the more
suitable for the murder.
61. WORDS TO THE HEAT OF DEEDS TOO COLD BREATH GIVES—That is, when
the time requires action, talking about what one is going to do accomplishes
nothing.

I go, and it is done; the bell invites me.
Hear it not, Duncan; for it is a knell
That summons thee to heaven or to hell.   [*Exit.*

62. THE BELL—The bell which Lady Macbeth was to ring when Macbeth's drink was ready. It probably was intended also to signify that Duncan and his grooms were asleep and that the daggers were laid ready for the murder.

SCENE 2. *The same.*

Enter LADY MACBETH.

Lady Macbeth. That which hath made them drunk hath
    made me bold;
What hath quench'd them hath given me fire. Hark! Peace!
It was the owl that shriek'd, the fatal bellman,
Which gives the stern'st good-night. He is about it.
5 The doors are open; and the surfeited grooms
Do mock their charge with snores. I have drugg'd their possets,
That death and nature do contend about them,
Whether they live or die.
    Macbeth. [*Within.*]   Who's there? what, ho!
    Lady Macbeth. Alack, I am afraid they have awak'd,
10 And 'tis not done. Th' attempt and not the deed
Confounds us. Hark! I laid their daggers ready;
He could not miss 'em. Had he not resembled
My father as he slept, I had done 't.

Enter MACBETH.

                                        My husband!
    Macbeth. I have done the deed. Didst thou not hear a noise?

2. QUENCH'D THEM—Put them to sleep. Lady Macbeth refers to the grooms whose drinks she has drugged.
3. OWL—Commonly supposed to be a bird of ill omen.
3. FATAL BELLMAN—It was the custom to have a bellman, or crier, warn the prisoners in Newgate Prison who were to be executed on the day following.
4. HE—Macbeth.
5. SURFEITED—Glutted with food and drink.
6. MOCK THEIR CHARGE—Set at naught their responsibility.
6. POSSETS—A drink made of "hot milk poured on ale or sack, having sugar, grated bisket, and eggs, with other ingredients boiled in it, which all goes to curd." It seems to have been drunk before retiring to induce sleep.
7. THAT—So that.
11. CONFOUNDS—Ruins. That is, to make an unsuccessful attempt will bring ruin.
12. HAD HE NOT RESEMBLED—"He" refers to Duncan.

15   *Lady Macbeth.*   I heard the owl scream and the crickets
Did not you speak?
    Macbeth.   When?
    Lady Macbeth.   Now.
    Macbeth.   As I descended?
    Lady Macbeth. Ay.
    Macbeth. Hark!
Who lies i' the second chamber?
    Lady Macbeth.   Donalbain.
20   *Macbeth.* This is a sorry sight.   [*Looking on his hands.*

    Lady Macbeth.   A foolish thought, to say a sorry sight.
    Macbeth.   There's one did laugh in 's sleep, and one cried
       "Murder!"
That they did wake each other: I stood and heard them;
But they did say their prayers, and address'd them
25 Again to sleep.
    Lady Macbeth.   There are two lodg'd together.
    Macbeth.   One cried "God bless us!" and "Amen" the
       other,

20. SORRY—Woeful, wretched.
22. THERE'S ONE—One of those in the second chamber.
25. THERE ARE TWO LODG'D TOGETHER—Two in the second chamber—probably
Malcolm and Donalbain.

As they had seen me with these hangman's hands:
Listening their fear, I could not say "Amen,"
When they did say "God bless us!"

30   *Lady Macbeth.*   Consider it not so deeply.

Macbeth.   But wherefore could not I pronounce "Amen"?
I had most need of blessing, and "Amen"
Stuck in my throat.

Lady Macbeth.   These deeds must not be thought
After these ways: so, it will make us mad.

35   *Macbeth.*   Methought I heard a voice cry "Sleep no more!
Macbeth does murder sleep,"—the innocent sleep,
Sleep that knits up the ravell'd sleave of care,
The death of each day's life, sore labour's bath,
Balm of hurt minds, great nature's second course,

40   Chief nourisher in life's feast,—

Lady Macbeth.   What do you mean?

Macbeth.   Still it cried "Sleep no more!" to all the house:
"Glamis hath murder'd sleep, and therefore Cawdor
Shall sleep no more; Macbeth shall sleep no more!"

Lady Macbeth.   Who was it that thus cried? Why,
          worthy thane,

45   You do unbend your noble strength, to think
So brainsickly of things. Go get some water,
And wash this filthy witness from your hand.
Why did you bring these daggers from the place?
They must lie there; go carry them, and smear

50   The sleepy grooms with blood.

Macbeth.   I'll go no more:
I am afraid to think what I have done;
Look on 't again I dare not.

Lady Macbeth.   Infirm of purpose!
Give me the daggers: the sleeping and the dead
Are but as pictures; 'tis the eye of childhood

55   That fears a painted devil. If he do bleed,

27. As—As if.
27. HANGMAN'S—Executioner's.
37. RAVELL'D SLEAVE—Floss silk, sometimes called sleave-silk. A "ravell'd sleave" means a tangled skein of silk.
39. SECOND COURSE—The meat course, or chief course at a banquet.
45. UNBEND—Relax, that is, lose your self-control or constancy.
55. PAINTED DEVIL—The picture of a devil. Lady Macbeth implies that there is nothing to fear from the sight of the murdered Duncan.

I'll gild the faces of the grooms withal;
For it must seem their guilt. [*Exit. Knocking within.*
Macbeth. Whence is that knocking?
How is 't with me, when every noise appals me?
What hands are here? Ha! they pluck out mine eyes!
60 Will all great Neptune's ocean wash this blood
Clean from my hand? No; this my hand will rather
The multitudinous seas incarnadine,
Making the green one red.

Re-enter LADY MACBETH.

Lady Macbeth. My hands are of your colour, but I shame
65 To wear a heart so white. [*Knocking within.*] I hear a
knocking
At the south entry: retire we to our chamber.
A little water clears us of this deed.
How easy is it, then! Your constancy
Hath left you unattended. [*Knocking within.*] Hark!
more knocking.
70 Get on your night-gown, lest occasion call us,
And show us to be watchers. Be not lost
So poorly in your thoughts.
Macbeth. To know my deed, 'twere best not know myself.
[*Knocking within.*
Wake Duncan with thy knocking! I would thou couldst!
[*Exeunt.*

56. GILD—Make red.
57. GUILT—Note the pun or "gild" and "guilt"—a rather ghastly play on
words.
59. WHAT HANDS ARE HERE?—Macbeth speaks as if he now saw the blood
on his hands for the first time.
60. NEPTUNE—Roman god of the sea.
62. MULTITUDINOUS—Is this an effective word to image forth the vastness
of the sea?
62. INCARNADINE—Make red.
68. YOUR CONSTANCY HATH LEFT YOU UNATTENDED—Your firmness has deserted you.
70. NIGHT-GOWN—Dressing-gown.
70–71. LEST OCCASION CALL US, AND SHOW US TO BE WATCHERS—Lady Macbeth admonishes Macbeth to put on his dressing gown so that if the occasion
(the knocking) demands them, it will not appear that they have been up.
73. TO KNOW MY DEED, 'TWERE BEST NOT KNOW MYSELF—Lady Macbeth
has urged Macbeth that he cease being "lost so poorly" in his thoughts—in
other words, that he be his natural self. His reply means: If to be myself
means to realize what I have done, it were best that I should never come
back to myself.

SCENE 3. *The Same.*

Enter a PORTER. *Knocking within.*

Porter. Here's a knocking indeed! If a man were porter of
hell-gate, he should have old turning the key. [*Knocking.*]
Knock, knock, knock! Who's there, i' the name of Beelzebub?
Here's a farmer, that hang'd himself on the expectation of
5 plenty. Come in time; have napkins enough about you; here
you'll sweat for 't. [*Knocking.*] Knock, knock! Who's there, in
the other devil's name? Faith, here's an equivocator that could
swear in both the scales against either scale; who committed
treason enough for God's sake, yet could not equivocate to
10 heaven. O, come in, equivocator. [*Knocking.*] Knock, knock,
knock! Who's there? Faith, here's an English tailor come
hither for stealing out of a French hose. Come in, tailor; here
you may roast your goose. [*Knocking.*] Knock, knock; never at
quiet! What are you? But this place is too cold for hell. I'll
15 devil-porter it no further: I had thought to have let in some of
all professions, that go the primrose way to the everlasting bon-
fire. [*Knocking.*] Anon, anon! I pray you, remember the porter.
                                                            [*Opens the gate.*

Enter MACDUFF *and* LENNOX.

Macduff. Was it so late, friend, ere you went to bed,
That you do lie so late?

PORTER—The Porter, who has had his share of the night's wassail is
drunk. He imagines that he is porter at hell-gate, and that the knocking is
that of damned souls seeking entrance. He fumbles at the lock, as the
knocking is repeated.
   2. HAVE OLD—Grow old; have one's fill of turning the key.
   3. BEELZEBUB—Prince of devils.
   4-5. ON THE EXPECTATION OF PLENTY—The farmer had expected a good
yield, or a good price for his crop, and being disappointed had hanged himself.
   5. NAPKINS—Handkerchiefs to wipe away the sweat.
   7. EQUIVOCATOR—One who swore falsely. There is an allusion here to a
matter familiar to Shakespeare's audience.
   9. EQUIVOCATE TO HEAVEN—Get himself into heaven through equivocation.
   12. STEALING OUT OF A FRENCH HOSE—An allusion to the practice commonly
charged in those days against tailors, that they stole part of the cloth brought
to them to be made up. As used here, "hose" means trousers, or breeches.
   13. GOOSE—A tailor's goose is a heavy pressing iron. It got its name from
the fact that the handle somewhat resembled the neck of a goose. A pun on
"goose" is intended.   16. PRIMROSE WAY—Easy way.
   17. ANON, ANON—The customary reply of porters or waiters to their patrons.
It means immediately or at once.
   17. REMEMBER THE PORTER—Remember to tip him.

20   *Porter.* Faith, sir, we were carousing till the second cock.

     Macduff. I believe drink gave thee the lie last night.

     Porter. That it did, sir, i' the very throat on me: but I requited him for his lie; and, I think, being too strong for him, though he took up my legs sometime, yet I made a shift to cast

25 him.

     Macduff. Is thy master stirring?

Enter MACBETH.

Our knocking has awak'ed him; here he comes.

     Lennox. Good morrow, noble sir.

     Macbeth.   Good morrow, both.

     Macduff. Is the king stirring, worthy thane?

     Macbeth.   Not yet.

30   *Macduff.* He did command me to call timely on him.

I have almost slipp'd the hour.

     Macbeth.   I'll bring you to him.

     Macduff. I know this is a joyful trouble to you;

But yet 'tis one.

     Macbeth. The labour we delight in physics pain.

35 This is the door.

     Macduff.   I'll make so bold to call,

For 'tis my limited service.   [*Exit.*

     Lennox. Goes the king hence to-day?

     Macbeth.   He does;—he did appoint so.

     Lennox. The night has been unruly: where we lay,

Our chimneys were blown down; and, as they say,

40 Lamentings heard i' the air, strange screams of death,

And, prophesying with accents terrible

Of dire combustion and confus'd events

     20. SECOND COCK—About 3 A.M.

     21. LIE—Note the puns on "lie."

     24. CAST—To throw as in wrestling. The Porter speaks as if he had been wrestling with drink which as he says "took up my legs sometime." There is a pun intended here, "cast" being used also in the sense of to cast up or vomit.

     30. TIMELY—Early.

     34. PHYSICS—Heals, or cures.

     36. MY LIMITED SERVICE—Appointed service.

     38. THE NIGHT HAS BEEN UNRULY—It was formerly a general belief that a great calamity in human affairs was foreshadowed by unusual disturbance in the world of nature.

     42. COMBUSTION—Conflagration, fire. Probably used figuratively for tumult or disturbance.

New hatch'd to th' woeful time, the obscure bird
Clamour'd the livelong night: some say, the earth
45 Was feverous and did shake.
    Macbeth.   'T was a rough night.
    Lennox. My young remembrance cannot parallel
A fellow to it.

Re-enter MACDUFF.

    Macduff. O horror, horror, horror! tongue nor heart
Cannot conceive nor name thee!
    Macbeth.⎫
            ⎬What's the matter?
    Lennox.⎭
50   *Macduff.* Confusion now hath made his masterpiece!
Most sacrilegious murder hath broke ope
The Lord's anointed temple, and stole thence
The life o' the building.
    Macbeth.   What is 't you say? the life?
    Lennox. Mean you his majesty?
55   *Macduff.* Approach the chamber, and destroy your sight
With a new Gorgon. Do not bid me speak;
See, and then speak yourselves.
[Exeunt MACBETH and LENNOX.
Awake, awake!
Ring the alarum-bell. Murder and treason!
Banquo and Donalbain! Malcolm! awake!
60 Shake off this downy sleep, death's counterfeit,
And look on death itself! Up, up, and see
The great doom's image! Malcolm! Banquo!

---

43. EVENTS NEW HATCH'D TO TH' WOEFUL TIME—Events born to, that is,
in keeping with the woeful time.
43. OBSCURE—Loving the darkness. The allusion is to the owl, which was
regarded as a bird of ill omen.
46-47. CANNOT PARALLEL A FELLOW—Cannot call up its equal.
50. CONFUSION—Destruction.
51. SACRILEGIOUS—Note the pronunciation of this word: săk rĭ lē'jŭs. Do
not confuse the last three syllables with "religious."
52. ANOINTED TEMPLE—See *I Samuel*, 24:10 where the king is referred to as
"the Lord's anointed," and *II Corinthians*, 6:16 where the Christian is called
"the temple of the living God."
56. GORGON—The reference is to Medusa, a character in Greek mythology
whose appearance was so terrible that whoever looked at her was turned
to stone.
62. GREAT DOOM'S IMAGE—A sight as terrible as the Last Judgment.

As from your graves rise up, and walk like sprites,
To countenance this horror. Ring the bell.   [*Bell rings.*

Enter LADY MACBETH.

65 *Lady Macbeth.* What's the business,
That such a hideous trumpet calls to parley
The sleepers of the house? Speak, speak!
  Macduff.   O gentle lady,
'Tis not for you to hear what I can speak:
The repetition, in a woman's ear,
70 Would murder as it fell.

Enter BANQUO.

                    O Banquo, Banquo,
Our royal master's murder'd!
  Lady Macbeth.   Woe, alas!
What, in our house?
  Banquo.   Too cruel anywhere.
Dear Duff, I prithee, contradict thyself,
And say it is not so.

Re-enter MACBETH *and* LENNOX, *with* Ross.

75 *Macbeth.* Had I but died an hour before this chance,
I had liv'd a blessed time; for, from this instant,
There's nothing serious in mortality.
All is but toys; renown and grace is dead;
The wine of life is drawn, and the mere lees
80 Is left this vault to brag of.

Enter MALCOLM *and* DONALBAIN.

  Donalbain. What is amiss?
  Macbeth.   You are, and do not know 't:
The spring, the head, the fountain of your blood

63. SPRITES—Spirits. The figure of the Judgment Day is continued.
64. COUNTENANCE—Be in keeping with.
66. PARLEY—Conference.
75. CHANCE—Unfortunate event.
77. MORTALITY—Life. There is nothing worthwhile in life.
78. GRACE—Good opinion, esteem.
79. LEES—Dregs.
80. VAULT—Macbeth has in mind a vault or storage place for wine. By
"this vault" he means, of course, himself.

Is stopp'd; the very source of it is stopp'd.

Macduff.   Your royal father's murder'd.

Malcolm.   O! by whom?

85   *Lennox.*   Those of his chamber, as it seem'd, had done 't:
Their hands and faces were all badg'd with blood;
So were their daggers, which unwip'd we found
Upon their pillows:
They star'd, and were distracted; no man's life
90   Was to be trusted with them.

Macbeth.   O, yet I do repent me of my fury,
That I did kill them.

Macduff.   Wherefore did you so?

Macbeth.   Who can be wise, amaz'd, temperate and furious,
95   Loyal and neutral, in a moment? No man.
The expedition of my violent love
Outrun the pauser, reason. Here lay Duncan,
His silver skin lac'd with his golden blood;
And his gash'd stabs look'd like a breach in nature
For ruin's wasteful entrance; there, the murderers,
100   Steep'd in the colours of their trade, their daggers
Unmannerly breech'd with gore. Who could refrain,
That had a heart to love, and in that heart
Courage to make 's love known?

Lady Macbeth.   Help me hence, ho!

Macduff.   Look to the lady.

Malcolm.   [*Aside to* DONALBAIN.]   Why do we hold our
        tongues,
105   That most may claim this argument for ours?

Donalbain.   [*Aside to* MALCOLM.]   What should be spoken
        here, where our fate,
Hid in an auger-hole, may rush, and seize us?
Let's away.
Our tears are not yet brew'd.

86. BADG'D—Marked, smeared.
94. EXPEDITION—Haste.
96. PAUSER, REASON—Reason which makes one stop (pause) to think before
he acts.
101. BREECH'D—Covered.
103. MAKE 'S—Make his.
105. ARGUMENT—Matter in hand, that is, the murder of Duncan, their
father.
107. HID IN AN AUGER-HOLE—Where no place is so small, not even an auger-
hole, but that our fate may lurk therein.

Malcolm. [*Aside to* DONALBAIN.]   Nor our strong sorrow
110 Upon the foot of motion.
    Banquo.   Look to the lady;
                    [LADY MACBETH *is carried out.*
And when we have our naked frailties hid,
That suffer in exposure, let us meet
And question this most bloody piece of work,
To know it further.   Fears and scruples shake us:
115 In the great hand of God I stand, and thence
Against the undivulg'd pretence I fight
Of treasonous malice.
    Macduff.   And so do I.
    All.   So all.
    Macbeth.   Let's briefly put on manly readiness,
And meet i' the hall together.
    All.   Well contented.
         [*Exeunt all but* MALCOLM *and* DONALBAIN.
120   *Malcolm.*   What will you do?   Let's not consort with them:
To show an unfelt sorrow is an office
Which the false man does easy.   I'll to England.
    Donalbain.   To Ireland I; our separated fortune
Shall keep us both the safer.   Where we are,
125 There's daggers in men's smiles; the near in blood,
The nearer bloody.
    Malcolm.   This murderous shaft that's shot

109–110. NOR OUR STRONG SORROW UPON THE FOOT OF MOTION—Donalbain has just said "Our tears are not yet brew'd" and Malcolm continues with a remark which means: And our great grief has not yet been given expression. The emotion of fear, for the time, supplants that of grief.
111. NAKED FRAILTIES—Banquo and the others have rushed forth half-dressed.
116. UNDIVULG'D PRETENCE—The not-yet-known design or purpose. Banquo means that he stands ready to fight against whatever treasonable purpose is to be found behind the murder.
118. BRIEFLY—Quickly.
118. MANLY READINESS—Armor. The implication is that being armed they will feel more ready to act like men.
119. WELL CONTENTED—Agreed.
121. OFFICE—Action, "duty."
125–126. THE NEAR IN BLOOD, THE NEARER BLOODY—The meaning is that being sons of Duncan, the nearer in blood or relationship, the nearer they are to death.
126–128. THE MURDEROUS SHAFT . . . AVOID THE AIM—Whoever killed our father is not yet done, for we stand yet between the murderer and the throne. We must away to avoid being struck by the same arrow.

Hath not yet lighted; and our safest way
Is to avoid the aim.   Therefore, to horse;
And let us not be dainty of leave-taking,
130 But shift away.   There's warrant in that theft
Which steals itself, when there's no mercy left.   [*Exeunt.*

130. SHIFT AWAY—Steal away.
130. WARRANT—Justification. The meaning is that there can be no blame
or discourtesy in stealing away without taking leave from a place where they
can expect no mercy.

SCENE 4. *Outside* MACBETH'S *castle.*

Enter Ross *and an* Old Man.

Old Man.   Threescore-and-ten I can remember well;
Within the volume of which time I have seen
Hours dreadful and things strange; but this sore night
Hath trifl'd former knowings.
   Ross.   Ah, good father,
5 Thou see'st the heavens, as troubl'd with man's act,
Threatens his bloody stage; by th' clock 'tis day,
And yet dark night strangles the travelling lamp.
Is 't night's predominance, or the day's shame
That darkness does the face of earth entomb,
10 When living light should kiss it?
   Old Man.   'Tis unnatural,
Even like the deed that's done.   On Tuesday last,
A falcon, tow'ring in her pride of place,
Was by a mousing owl hawk'd at and kill'd.
   Ross.   And Duncan's horses—a thing most strange and
      certain—
15 Beauteous and swift, the minions of their race,
Turn'd wild in nature, broke their stalls, flung out,

4. HATH TRIFL'D FORMER KNOWINGS—Had made former experiences seem
trifling.
4. GOOD FATHER—An expression commonly used in addressing old men.
6. BLOODY STAGE—The earth. The figure is from the theatre, the meaning
being: The heavens displeased at man's act threatens to destroy the bloody
stage altogether.
7. TRAVELLING LAMP—Sun.
10. UNNATURAL—Monstrous, abnormal, not according to nature.
12. TOW'RING—Soaring. The term was used to designate the soaring of the
falcon to the "place" from which it swooped down upon its prey.
13. MOUSING—An owl which was accustomed to attack nothing more
vicious than mere mice.
15. MINIONS—Most favored, best cared for.

Contending 'gainst obedience, as they would make
War with mankind.
Old Man.   'Tis said they eat each other.
Ross. They did so, to th' amazement of mine eyes,
20 That look'd upon 't.

Enter MACDUFF.

Here comes the good Macduff.
How goes the world, sir, now?
Macduff.   Why, see you not?
Ross. Is 't known who did this more than bloody deed?
Macduff. Those that Macbeth hath slain.
Ross.   Alas, the day!
What good could they pretend?
Macduff.   They were suborn'd.
25 Malcolm and Donalbain, the King's two sons,
Are stol'n away and fled; which puts upon them
Suspicion of the deed.
Ross.   'Gainst nature still!
Thriftless ambition, that will ravin up
Thine own life's means! Then 'tis most like
30 The sovereignty will fall upon Macbeth.
Macduff. He is already nam'd; and gone to Scone
To be invested.
Ross.   Where is Duncan's body?
Macduff. Carried to Colmekill,
The sacred storehouse of his predecessors,
35 And guardian of their bones.
Ross.   Will you to Scone?
Macduff. No, cousin, I'll to Fife.
Ross.   Well, I will thither.

18. EAT—The past tense of eat, commonly pronounced ĕt in British usage, where we should say āte.
24. PRETEND—Expect to derive from the deed.
24. SUBORN'D—Bribed.
27. STILL—This word is used frequently in the play and each time means "always."
28. RAVIN UP—Devour utterly.
31. SCONE (skoon)—The ancient royal city of Scotland and place of coronation of the Scottish kings.
33. COLMEKILL—St. Colum's or St. Columba's cell. The island of Iona, where the tombs of the ancient kings may still be seen.
36. FIFE—Macduff's home. Macduff was Thane of Fife.
36. THITHER—To Scone.

Macduff. Well, may you see things well done there,—adieu!—
Lest our old robes sit easier than our new!
   Ross. Farewell, father.
40   *Old Man.* God's benison go with you; and with those
That would make good of bad, and friends of foes!   [*Exeunt.*

38. LEST OUR OLD ROBES SIT EASIER THAN OUR NEW—Lest the new order of
things be worse than the old.
40. BENISON—Blessing.

ACT III

SCENE I. *Forres. The palace.*

Enter BANQUO.

Banquo. Thou hast it now: king, Cawdor, Glamis, all,
As the weird women promis'd, and, I fear,
Thou play'dst most foully for 't; yet it was said
It should not stand in thy posterity,
5 But that myself should be the root and father
Of many kings. If there come truth from them,
As upon thee, Macbeth, their speeches shine,
Why, by the verities on thee made good,
May they not be my oracles as well,
10 And set me up in hope? But hush! no more.

Sennet sounded. Enter MACBETH, *as king;* LADY MACBETH, *as
   queen;* LENNOX, ROSS, Lords, Ladies, *and* Attendants.

   Macbeth. Here's our chief guest.
   Lady Macbeth.   If he had been forgotten,
It had been as a gap in our great feast,
And all-thing unbecoming.
   Macbeth. To-night we hold a solemn supper, sir,
15 And I'll request your presence.
   Banquo.   Let your highness
Command upon me; to the which my duties

4. IT SHOULD NOT STAND IN THY POSTERITY—See the prophecy of the third
witch, Act I, Scene 3.
9. MY ORACLES—Prophets of the truth.
Sennet—A sound of trumpets.
13. ALL-THING—Altogether.
14. SOLEMN—Formal.

Are with a most indissoluble tie
For ever knit.
    Macbeth. Ride you this afternoon?
    Banquo.   Ay, my good lord.
20   *Macbeth.* We should have else desir'd your good advice,
Which still hath been both grave and prosperous,
In this day's council; but we'll take to-morrow.
Is 't far you ride?
    Banquo. As far, my lord, as will fill up the time
25 'Twixt this and supper. Go not my horse the better,
I must become a borrower of the night
For a dark hour or twain.
    Macbeth.   Fail not our feast.
    Banquo. My lord, I will not.
    Macbeth. We hear, our bloody cousins are bestow'd
30 In England and in Ireland, not confessing
Their cruel parricide, filling their hearers
With strange invention: but of that to-morrow,
When therewithal we shall have cause of state
Craving us jointly. Hie you to horse; adieu,
35 Till you return at night. Goes Fleance with you?
    Banquo. Ay, my good lord: our time does call upon 's.
    Macbeth. I wish your horses swift and sure of foot;
And so I do commend you to their backs.
Farewell.   [*Exit* BANQUO.
40 Let every man be master of his time
Till seven at night; to make society
The sweeter welcome, we will keep ourself
Till supper-time alone: while then, God be with you!
    [*Exeunt all but* MACBETH, *and an* Attendant.

21. GRAVE AND PROSPEROUS—Worth paying attention to and invariably turning out well.
22. WE'LL TAKE TO-MORROW—We'll let the matter go until to-morrow.
29. BLOODY COUSINS—Donalbain and Malcolm.　29. BESTOW'D—Lodged.
31. PARRICIDE—Murder of a parent.
32. INVENTION—Falsehood.
33. THEREWITHAL—In addition to the matter of what shall be done about Donalbain and Malcolm.
33–34. CAUSE OF STATE CRAVING US JOINTLY—Affairs of state which demand our joint attention.
36. UPON 's—Upon us. That is, it is already the time we agreed upon to ride out.
40. BE MASTER OF HIS TIME—Do as he wishes.
43. WHILE—Until.

Sirrah, a word with you: attend those men
45 Our pleasure?
  Attendant. They are, my lord, without the palace-gate.
  Macbeth. Bring them before us.   [*Exit* Attendant.
                                    To be thus is nothing,
But to be safely thus. Our fears in Banquo
Stick deep; and in his royalty of nature
50 Reigns that which would be fear'd. 'Tis much he dares;
And, to that dauntless temper of his mind,
He hath a wisdom that doth guide his valour
To act in safety. There is none but he
Whose being I do fear; and, under him,
55 My Genius is rebuk'd, as, it is said,
Mark Antony's was by Cæsar. He chid the sisters,
When first they put the name of king upon me,
And bade them speak to him; then prophet-like
They hail'd him father to a line of kings.
60 Upon my head they plac'd a fruitless crown,
And put a barren sceptre in my gripe,
Thence to be wrench'd with an unlineal hand,
No son of mine succeeding. If 't be so,
For Banquo's issue have I fil'd my mind;
65 For them the gracious Duncan have I murder'd;
Put rancours in the vessel of my peace `
Only for them; and mine eternal jewel
Given to the common enemy of man,
To make them kings, the seed of Banquo, kings!
70 Rather than so, come, fate, into the list,
And champion me to th' utterance!—Who's there?

44. SIRRAH—A form commonly used in addressing a servant or an inferior.
44. ATTEND—Wait.
44. THOSE MEN—The murderers who soon come upon the scene.
47. TO BE THUS—To be king.
51. TO—In addition to.
55–56. MY GENIUS . . . BY CÆSAR—Genius here means guarding spirit.
The allusion is to a passage in North's *Plutarch* in *The Life of Marcus Antonius*.
It is related that Antonius was once told by a soothsayer that his
fortune was inferior to Octavius Cæsar's.
62. UNLINEAL HAND—By one not descended from me. The following line
makes the meaning clear.   64. FIL'D—Defiled.
66. RANCOURS IN THE VESSEL—Bitterness in the cup.
67. MINE ETERNAL JEWEL—My immortal soul.
68. COMMON ENEMY—Satan.
71. CHAMPION ME TO TH' UTTERANCE—Fight with me to the death.

Re-enter Attendant, *with two* Murderers.

Now go to th' door, and stay there till we call.—

> [*Exit* Attendant.

Was it not yesterday we spoke together?
   1 Murderer. It was, so please your highness.
   Macbeth.   Well then, now.
75 Have you consider'd of my speeches? Know
That it was he, in the times past, which held you
So under fortune; which you thought had been
Our innocent self. This I made good to you
In our last conference, pass'd in probation with you,
80 How you were borne in hand, how cross'd, the instruments,
Who wrought with them, and all things else that might
To half a soul and to a notion craz'd
Say, "Thus did Banquo."
   1 Murderer.   You made it known to us.
   Macbeth. I did so, and went further, which is now
85 Our point of second meeting. Do you find
Your patience so predominant in your nature
That you can let this go? Are you so gospell'd,
To pray for this good man and for his issue,
Whose heavy hand hath bow'd you to the grave
90 And beggar'd yours for ever?
   1 Murderer.   We are men, my liege.
   Macbeth. Ay, in the catalogue ye go for men;
As hounds and greyhounds, mongrels, spaniels, curs,
Shoughs, water-rugs, and demi-wolves, are clept
All by the name of dogs; the valued file
95 Distinguishes the swift, the slow, the subtle,

76-77. HELD YOU SO UNDER FORTUNE—Kept you from being rewarded according to your merits. Macbeth has chosen to do the murder two disgruntled soldiers whom he incites against Banquo by telling them that their misfortunes are the result of Banquo's injustice.

79. PASS'D IN PROBATION WITH YOU—Went over point by point with you, giving you proof in each instance.

80. BORNE IN HAND—Deluded with false hopes or promises.

82. NOTION—Mind, understanding.

87. GOSPELL'D—So filled with the lesson of the gospel which says, "Pray for them which despitefully use you, and persecute you." See *Matthew* 5:44.

93. SHOUGHS, WATER-RUGS, DEMI-WOLVES—Breeds of dogs.

93. CLEPT—Called.

94. VALUED FILE—The list which sets down the values of each dog. This expression is used in contrast to "catalogue" in the first line of the speech.

The housekeeper, the hunter, every one
According to the gift which bounteous nature
Hath in him clos'd; whereby he does receive
Particular addition, from the bill
100 That writes them all alike; and so of men.
Now, if you have a station in the file,
Not i' the worst rank of manhood, say 't;
And I will put that business in your bosoms,
Whose execution takes your enemy off,
105 Grapples you to the heart and love of us,
Who wear our health but sickly in his life,
Which in his death were perfect.
    2 Murderer.   I am one, my liege,
Whom the vile blows and buffets of the world
Hath so incens'd, that I am reckless what
110 I do to spite the world.
    1 Murderer.   And I another
So weary with disasters, tugg'd with fortune,
That I would set my life on any chance,
To mend it, or be rid on 't.
    Macbeth.   Both of you
Know Banquo was your enemy.
    Both Murderers.   True, my lord.
115   *Macbeth.* So is he mine; and in such bloody distance,
That every minute of his being thrusts
Against my near'st of life; and though I could
With barefac'd power sweep him from my sight
And bid my will avouch it, yet I must not,

96. HOUSEKEEPER—Watchdog.
99. PARTICULAR ADDITION—His own distinctive attribute; his rank.
99. BILL—The catalogue or general list.
101. STATION IN THE FILE—If you have that which distinguishes you from the common run of men.
105. GRAPPLES YOU—Fastens you.
106. WEAR OUR HEALTH BUT SICKLY IN HIS LIFE—Find our well-being impaired or in danger while he is alive.
111. TUGG'D WITH FORTUNE—Buffeted about by fortune.
115. BLOODY DISTANCE—The figure is from duelling. Macbeth speaks of Banquo as one who stands within duelling distance—that is, so close that he (Banquo) can with a single thrust at any minute pierce Macbeth's "near'st of life" (vitals).
119. AVOUCH IT—Give no explanation to the kingdom other than that it is my will or desire.

120 For certain friends that are both his and mine,
    Whose loves I may not drop, but wail his fall
    Who I myself struck down; and thence it is,
    That I to your assistance do make love,
    Masking the business from the common eye
125 For sundry weighty reasons.
        2 Murderer.   We shall, my lord,
    Perform what you command us.
        1 Murderer.   Though our lives—
    Macbeth. Your spirits shine through you. Within this hour
        at most
    I will advise you where to plant yourselves;
    Acquaint you with the perfect spy o' the time,
130 The moment on 't; for 't must be done to-night,
    And something from the palace; always thought
    That I require a clearness; and with him—
    To leave no rubs nor botches in the work—
    Fleance his son, that keeps him company,
135 Whose absence is no less material to me
    Than is his father's, must embrace the fate
    Of that dark hour. Resolve yourselves apart;
    I'll come to you anon.
        Both Murderers.   We are resolv'd, my lord.
        Macbeth. I'll call upon you straight: abide within.
                                                    [*Exeunt* Murderers.
140 It is concluded. Banquo, thy soul's flight,
    If it find heaven, must find it out to-night.   [*Exit.*

---

121. BUT WAIL—Instead of sweeping Banquo from my sight myself, I must bewail (publicly) his murder.

126. THOUGH OUR LIVES—Though our lives answer for it.

129. ACQUAINT YOU WITH THE PERFECT SPY O' THE TIME—This probably means: Let you know by means of a perfect spy (the third murderer) when to strike.

131. SOMETHING—At some distance.

131. ALWAYS THOUGHT—It being always remembered that I must be kept clear of suspicion.

133. TO LEAVE NO RUBS NOR BOTCHES—To leave no rough spots, or flaws, and botches such as betray poor workmanship. The expression is parenthetical.

137. RESOLVE YOURSELVES—Make up your minds.

Scene 2. *The palace.*

Enter Lady Macbeth *and a* Servant.

Lady Macbeth. Is Banquo gone from court?
Servant. Ay, madam, but returns again to-night.
Lady Macbeth. Say to the king, I would attend his leisure
For a few words.
Servant. Madam, I will.
Lady Macbeth. Nought's had, all's spent,
5 Where our desire is got without content.
'Tis safer to be that which we destroy
Than by destruction dwell in doubtful joy.

Enter Macbeth.

How now, my lord! why do you keep alone,
Of sorriest fancies your companions making;
10 Using those thoughts which should indeed have died
With them they think on? Things without all remedy
Should be without regard; what's done is done.
Macbeth. We have scotch'd the snake, not kill'd it:
She'll close and be herself, whilst our poor malice
15 Remains in danger of her former tooth.
But let the frame of things disjoint, both the worlds suffer,
Ere we will eat our meal in fear, and sleep
In the affliction of these terrible dreams
That shake us nightly. Better be with the dead,
20 Whom we, to gain our peace, have sent to peace,
Than on the torture of the mind to lie
In restless ecstasy. Duncan is in his grave;
After life's fitful fever he sleeps well;
Treason has done his worst: nor steel, nor poison,

5. Content—Happiness, peace of mind.
10. Using—Cherishing, constantly thinking.
11. Things without all remedy should be without regard—What cannot be remedied should be ignored.
13. Scotch'd—Cut, slashed.
14. She'll close and be herself—Grow together again and be as formerly.
16. The frame of things—The universe. The meaning of the lines is: Let the universe fall apart and heaven and earth perish before we will eat our meal in fear, etc.
21. On the torture of the mind to lie—The figure alludes to the rack, an instrument of torture employed in the Middle Ages.
22. Ecstasy—Frenzy.

25 Malice domestic, foreign levy, nothing,
Can touch him further.
    Lady Macbeth.   Come on;
Gentle my lord, sleek o'er your rugged looks;
Be bright and jovial among your guests to-night.
    Macbeth. So shall I, love; and so, I pray, be you.
30 Let your remembrance apply to Banquo;
Present him eminence, both with eye and tongue:
Unsafe the while, that we
Must lave our honours in these flattering streams,
And make our faces vizards to our hearts,
35 Disguising what they are.
    Lady Macbeth.   You must leave this.
    Macbeth. O, full of scorpions is my mind, dear wife!
Thou know'st that Banquo and his Fleance lives.
    Lady Macbeth. But in them nature's copy 's not eterne.
    Macbeth. There's comfort yet; they are assailable;
40 Then be thou jocund; ere the bat hath flown
His cloister'd flight; ere to black Hecate's summons
The shard-borne beetle with his drowsy hums
Hath rung night's yawning peal, there shall be done
A deed of dreadful note.
    Lady Macbeth.   What's to be done?

25. MALICE DOMESTIC—Rebellion, such as that raised by Macdonwald. See Act I, Scene 2.

25. FOREIGN LEVY—War from without, such as the attack of Norway. See Act I, Scene 2.

27. GENTLE MY LORD—My gentle lord.

30. REMEMBRANCE APPLY TO—Remember to be gracious to him.

31. PRESENT HIM EMINENCE—Treat him as eminent, make much of him.

33. LAVE OUR HONOURS IN THESE FLATTERING STREAMS—Wash, for the purpose of keeping unsoiled, our honors in these streams of flattery. The meaning is: We are not safe so long as we are dependent upon the support which can be gained only through flattery.

34. VIZARDS—Masks.

38. NATURE'S COPY 'S NOT ETERNE—They will not live forever. The allusion in the figure is to a form of land tenure known as "copyhold." Copyhold did not give perpetual title to the holder.

39. ASSAILABLE—They may be destroyed. Macbeth interprets Lady Macbeth's remark in a way she probably did not intend it—that Banquo and Fleance can be murdered if necessary.

40–41. HATH FLOWN HIS CLOISTER'D FLIGHT—Has left the cloisters where perhaps he has hung all day; *i.e.* before nightfall.

42. SHARD-BORNE—Borne through the air on its hard, scaly wings which are like broken pieces, or shards, of pottery.

43. YAWNING PEAL—Summons to sleep. The entire clause means before bedtime.

45 *Macbeth.* Be innocent of the knowledge, dearest chuck,
Till thou applaud the deed. Come, seeling night,
Scarf up the tender eye of pitiful day,
And with thy bloody and invisible hand
Cancel and tear to pieces that great bond
50 Which keeps me pale! Light thickens, and the crow
Makes wing to th' rooky wood:
Good things of day begin to droop and drowse,
Whiles night's black agents to their preys do rouse.
Thou marvell'st at my words, but hold thee still;
55 Things bad begun make strong themselves by ill.
So, prithee, go with me.   [*Exeunt.*

45. CHUCK—Also chick, a term of endearment.
46. SEELING NIGHT—A technical term from falconry, designating a method
of closing the eyes of a hawk. Here "seeling night" means night which
closes the eyes.
47. SCARF UP—Blindfold.
49. THAT GREAT BOND—The prophecy of the third witch. The allusion
is probably to the "bond of destiny" which guarantees to Banquo's heirs
succession to the throne.
51. ROOKY—Rook-haunted, black, dismal.

SCENE 3. *A park near the palace.*

Enter three Murderers.

1 Murderer. But who did bid thee join with us?
3 Murderer.   Macbeth.
2 Murderer. He needs not our mistrust; since he delivers
Our offices, and what we have to do
To the direction just.
1 Murderer.   Then stand with us.
5 The west yet glimmers with some streaks of day:
Now spurs the lated traveller apace
To gain the timely inn; and near approaches
The subject of our watch.
3 Murderer.   Hark! I hear horses.
Banquo. [*Within.*] Give us a light there, ho!

2. HE—The Third Murderer.
2. NEEDS NOT OUR MISTRUST—We need not mistrust him.
2-4. DELIVERS OUR OFFICES . . . DIRECTION JUST—Tells us exactly what we
are to do even as we heard it from Macbeth.
6. LATED—Belated.
7. TO GAIN THE TIMELY INN—To reach the inn in good time, that is,
before dark.

2 Murderer.   Then 'tis he: the rest
10 That are within the note of expectation
Already are i' the court.

1 Murderer.   His horses go about.

3 Murderer. Almost a mile; but he does usually,
So all men do, from hence to th' palace gate
Make it their walk.

Enter BANQUO, *and* FLEANCE *with a torch.*

2 Murderer.   A light, a light!

3 Murderer.   'Tis he.

15 *1 Murderer.* Stand to 't.

Banquo. It will be rain to-night.

1 Murderer.   Let it come down.

[*They set upon* BANQUO.

Banquo. O, treachery! Fly, good Fleance, fly, fly, fly!
Thou mayst revenge. O slave!   [*Dies.* FLEANCE *escapes.*

3 Murderer. Who did strike out the light?

1 Murderer.   Was 't not the way?

20 *3 Murderer.* There's but one down; the son is fled.

2 Murderer.   We have lost
Best half of our affair.

1 Murderer. Well, let's away, and say how much is done.

[*Exeunt.*

9–11. THEN 'TIS HE: THE REST . . . ARE I' THE COURT—It is Banquo, since
all others who are expected are already within the court of the castle.

11. HIS HORSES GO ABOUT—Banquo's servants lead the horses along the road
which evidently approaches the castle by a circuitous path. Banquo and
Fleance dismount and approach the castle by a footpath.

15. STAND TO 'T—Get ready. The remark is directed to the other murderers. It was the part of the First Murderer to strike down Banquo's light,
and his remark means: Make ready, I am going to strike down the light.

16. LET IT COME DOWN—The blow. Here is a play on words.

SCENE 4. *Hall in the palace.*

A banquet prepared. Enter MACBETH, LADY MACBETH, ROSS,
LENNOX, LORDS, *and* Attendants.

Macbeth. You know your own degrees; sit down: at first
And last the hearty welcome.

1. DEGREES—Degrees of rank. It being a state, or formal, banquet, the
guests would sit according to rank.

Lords.   Thanks to your majesty.

Macbeth.   Ourself will mingle with society,
And play the humble host.

5 Our hostess keeps her state, but in best time
We will require her welcome.

    Lady Macbeth.   Pronounce it for me, sir, to all our friends,
For my heart speaks they are welcome.

First Murderer *appears at the door.*

    Macbeth.   See, they encounter thee with their hearts' thanks.
10 Both sides are even: here I'll sit i' the midst.
Be large in mirth; anon we'll drink a measure
The table round.—[*Goes to the door.*] There's blood upon thy
    face.

    Murderer.   'Tis Banquo's then.

    Macbeth.   'Tis better thee without than he within.
15 Is he dispatch'd?

    Murderer.   My lord, his throat is cut; that I did for him.

    Macbeth.   Thou are the best o' the cut-throats; yet he's good
That did the like for Fleance: if thou didst it,
Thou art the nonpareil.

    Murderer.   Most royal sir,
20 Fleance is scap'd.

    Macbeth.   Then comes my fit again: I had else been perfect,
Whole as the marble, founded as the rock;
As broad and general as the casing air;
But now I am cabin'd, cribb'd, confin'd, bound in

5. HOSTESS KEEPS HER STATE—Lady Macbeth sits in her chair of state
on a dais at the upper end of the hall, while Macbeth "mingles with" his
guests—that is, sits at table with them. He has not yet sat down, but
lingers near the door, expecting the Murderer.

6. REQUIRE HER WELCOME—Ask her to give you welcome.

9. SEE, THEY ENCOUNTER THEE WITH THEIR HEARTS' THANKS—This is addressed to Lady Macbeth, and refers to the manifestations of thanks returned
by the guests.

10. THE MIDST—The chair which Macbeth chooses was evidently at mid
table.

11. LARGE—Unrestrained.   11. ANON—Soon.

14. 'TIS BETTER THEE WITHOUT THAN HE WITHIN—It is better on your face
than in his veins.

19. NONPAREIL—One without an equal.

23. AS BROAD AND GENERAL AS THE CASING AIR—As unrestrained and unconfined as the air which envelops the earth but is itself boundless.

24. CABIN'D, CRIBB'D—Shut up, hampered.

25 To saucy doubts and fears.   But Banquo's safe?
   Murderer.   Ay, my good lord; safe in a ditch he bides,
   With twenty trenchèd gashes on his head,
   The least a death to nature.
   Macbeth.   Thanks for that.
   There the grown serpent lies; the worm that's fled
30 Hath nature that in time will venom breed,
   No teeth for th' present.   Get thee gone; to-morrow
   We'll hear ourselves again.   [*Exit* Murderer.
   Lady Macbeth.   My royal lord,
   You do not give the cheer: the feast is sold
   That is not often vouch'd, while 'tis a-making,
35 'Tis given with welcome.   To feed were best at home;
   From thence the sauce to meat is ceremony;
   Meeting were bare without it.

   Enter the Ghost *of* BANQUO, *and sits in* MACBETH's *place.*

   Macbeth.   Sweet remembrancer!
   Now, good digestion wait on appetite,
   And health on both!
   Lennox.   May 't please your highness sit.
40 *Macbeth.*   Here had we now our country's honour roof'd,
   Were the grac'd person of our Banquo present;
   Who may I rather challenge for unkindness
   Than pity for mischance.
   Ross.   His absence, sir,

   25. To saucy doubts—By insolent doubts.
   27. Trenchèd—Deep-cut.   29. Worm—The young serpent—Fleance.
   32. Hear ourselves—Hear one another.
   33-35. The feast is sold . . . best at home—The meaning is: The feast
   which is not often vouched (proclaimed by the host as a thing he does out of
   pleasure) is like a meal which one buys, where there is no sentiment connected
   with the eating at all.   While the feast is on (a-making), the host must make
   it clear that his guests are welcome.   If the purpose of a banquet is merely
   to eat, then according to Lady Macbeth, it were best to eat at home.
   36-37. From thence . . . without it—That which makes eating away
   from home enjoyable is the ceremony, or attention paid to one.   Mere meeting and eating together without the ceremony is no delight.
   37. Remembrancer—One who reminds another.   He is addressing Lady
   Macbeth.   He has not yet seen the ghost.
   40. Our country's honour roof'd—All the worthy men of our country
   under one roof.   The meaning of the lines is: Here we should have our
   country's honor roof'd if only the gracious person of our Banquo were present.
   42. Who may . . . for mischance—Whose absence is due, I hope, to unkindness rather than to mischance or accident.

Lays blame upon his promise. Please 't your highness
45 To grace us with your royal company.
    Macbeth. The table's full!
    Lennox.   Here is a place reserv'd, sir.
    Macbeth. Where?
    Lennox. Here, my good lord. What is 't that moves your
      highness?
    Macbeth. Which of you have done this?
    Lords.   What, my good lord?
50   *Macbeth.* Thou canst not say I did it: never shake
Thy gory locks at me.
    Ross. Gentlemen, rise; his highness is not well.
    Lady Macbeth. Sit, worthy friends: my lord is often thus,
And hath been from his youth: pray you, keep seat;
55 The fit is momentary; upon a thought
He will again be well. If much you note him,
You will offend him, and extend his passion.
Feed, and regard him not. [*Aside to* MACBETH.] Are you a
    man?
    Macbeth. Ay, and a bold one, that dare look on that
60 Which might appal the devil.
    Lady Macbeth. [*Aside to* MACBETH.] O proper stuff!
This is the very painting of your fear;
This is the air-drawn dagger which, you said,
Led you to Duncan. O, these flaws and starts,
Impostors to true fear, would well become
65 A woman's story at a winter's fire,
Authoriz'd by her grandam. Shame itself!
Why do you make such faces? When all's done,
You look but on a stool.
    Macbeth. Prithee, see there! Behold! look! lo! how say you?

44. LAYS BLAME UPON HIS PROMISE—Makes him guilty of an unkindness, since he promised to be present.
    50. THOU—This speech is addressed to the ghost of Banquo.
    55. UPON A THOUGHT—In a moment.
    58. *Aside to* MACBETH—Lady Macbeth has left her seat and come down to Macbeth.
    60. O PROPER STUFF!—Nonsense!
    63. FLAWS—A sudden squall of wind, hence in this case, an outburst of feeling or "nerves."
    63. STARTS—Alarms. Compare with our word "startle."
    64. IMPOSTORS TO—Mere allusions when compared to.

70 Why, what care I?   If thou canst nod, speak too.
    If charnel-houses and our graves must send
    Those that we bury back, our monuments
    Shall be the maws of kites.   [Ghost *vanishes.*
       Lady Macbeth.   [*Aside to* MACBETH.]   What, quite un-
          mann'd in folly?
       Macbeth.   If I stand here, I saw him!
       Lady Macbeth.   [*Aside to* MACBETH.]   Fie, for shame!
75   *Macbeth.*   Blood hath been shed ere now, i' the olden time,
    Ere humane statute purg'd the gentle weal;
    Ay, and since too, murders have been perform'd
    Too terrible for the ear.   The time has been,
    That, when the brains were out, the man would die,
80 And there an end; but now they rise again,
    With twenty mortal murders on their crowns,
    And push us from our stools: this is more strange
    Than such a murder is.
       Lady Macbeth.   My worthy lord,
    Your noble friends do lack you.
       Macbeth.   I do forget.
85 Do not muse at me, my most worthy friends;
    I have a strange infirmity, which is nothing
    To those that know me. . Come, love and health to all;
    Then I'll sit down.   Give me some wine, fill full.

Re-enter the Ghost.

    I drink to th' general joy o' the whole table,
90 And to our dear friend Banquo, whom we miss;

70. WHY, WHAT CARE I?—This and the following three lines are addressed
to the ghost.
    71. CHARNEL-HOUSES—Sepulchers.
    72. MONUMENTS—Tombs.
    73. MAWS—Stomachs.   The meaning is: If the dead may return from
ordinary graves, it were better to be left unburied to be devoured by the kites
(a kind of hawk).
    76. ERE HUMANE STATUTE PURG'D THE GENTLE WEAL—Before humane laws
protecting human life made the commonwealth gentle.   Macbeth refers to
days before stable government protected life.
    81. WITH TWENTY MORTAL MURDERS—The allusion is to Banquo whom the
murderer described as "safe in a ditch . . . with twenty trenched gashes in
his head, the least a death to nature."
    84. LACK—Miss, or perceive your absence.
    85. MUSE—Wonder.

Would he were here! to all and him we thirst,
And all to all.
    Lords.   Our duties, and the pledge.
    Macbeth. Avaunt! and quit my sight! let the earth hide
    thee!
Thy bones are marrowless, thy blood is cold;
95 Thou hast no speculation in those eyes
Which thou dost glare with!

    Lady Macbeth.   Think of this, good peers,
But as a thing of custom: 'tis no other;
Only it spoils the pleasure of the time.
    Macbeth. What man dare, I dare:
100 Approach thou like the rugged Russian bear,
The arm'd rhinoceros, or the Hyrcan tiger;
Take any shape but that, and my firm nerves
Shall never tremble: or be alive again,
And dare me to the desert with thy sword;
105 If trembling I inhabit then, protest me

    93. AVAUNT!—Macbeth now sees the ghost.
    95. SPECULATION—Power of sight.
    101. HYRCAN—Hyrcanian. Hyrcania, a region south of the Caspian Sea,
mentioned in books of the time as the home of the tiger.
    105. IF TREMBLING I INHABIT THEN—If trembling with fear I then stay in
my castle.   105. PROTEST—Declare, call.

The baby of a girl. Hence, horrible shadow!
Unreal mockery, hence!   [Ghost *vanishes.*
                          Why, so: being gone,
I am a man again. Pray you, sit still.
Lady Macbeth. You have displac'd the mirth, broke the good
     meeting,
110 With most admir'd disorder.
     Macbeth.   Can such things be,
And overcome us like a summer's cloud,
Without our special wonder? You make me strange
Even to the disposition that I owe,
When now I think you can behold such sights,
115 And keep the natural ruby of your cheeks,
When mine is blanch'd with fear.
     Ross.   What sights, my lord?
Lady Macbeth. I pray you, speak not; he grows worse and
     worse;
Question enrages him. At once, good-night.
Stand not upon the order of your going,
120 But go at once.
     Lennox.   Good-night; and better health
Attend his majesty!
     Lady Macbeth. A kind good-night to all!
          [*Exeunt all but* MACBETH *and* LADY MACBETH.
Macbeth. It will have blood; they say blood will have blood.
Stones have been known to move and trees to speak;

108. SIT STILL—What were Macbeth's guests doing?   110. ADMIR'D—Strange.
   111. AND OVERCOME . . . WITHOUT OUR SPECIAL WONDER—Pass over us like a
summer's cloud to which we pay no attention.
   112. YOU MAKE ME . . . THAT I OWE—Macbeth has always possessed (owed)
a brave and undaunted spirit (disposition). He says in effect to Lady Macbeth
who shows no signs of fear, not having seen the ghost, "Your fearlessness makes
me hardly know myself, so that I wonder if I am he who has never been afraid
of anything."
   119. STAND NOT UPON THE ORDER OF YOUR GOING—This being a formal, or
state, banquet, the guests were seated according to rank. Lady Macbeth,
wishing to have the guests depart as quickly as possible before Macbeth
says that which will betray him, calls out to them to depart without regard
to rank or precedence.
   122. IT WILL HAVE BLOOD—"It" refers to the murder rather than to the
ghost. The sense is that the deed cries for vengeance.
   122–123. THEY SAY . . . TO SPEAK—Old wives' tales of astonishing and supernatural means by which murders came to light, when the murderer thought
himself safe, were common enough in Shakespeare's day.

Augures and understood relations have
125 By magot-pies and choughs and rooks brought forth
The secret'st man of blood. What is the night?
   Lady Macbeth. Almost at odds with morning, which is which.
   Macbeth. How say'st thou, that Macduff denies his person
At our great bidding?
   Lady Macbeth.   Did you send to him, sir?
130   *Macbeth.* I hear it by the way, but I will send.
There's not a one of them but in his house
I keep a servant fee'd. I will to-morrow,
And betimes I will, to the weird sisters:
More shall they speak; for now I am bent to know,
135 By the worst means, the worst. For mine own good
All causes shall give way: I am in blood
Stepp'd in so far that, should I wade no more,
Returning were as tedious as go o'er:
Strange things I have in head that will to hand,
140 Which must be acted ere they may be scann'd.
   Lady Macbeth. You lack the season of all natures, sleep.
   Macbeth. Come, we'll to sleep. My strange and self-abuse
Is the initiate fear that wants hard use:
We are yet but young in deed.   *[Exeunt.*

124. AUGURES—Divinations.
124. UNDERSTOOD RELATIONS—Relationships revealed by those who understand how to trace them.
125. MAGOT-PIES AND CHOUGHS—Magpies and jackdaws.
126. THE SECRET'ST MAN OF BLOOD—The murderer who supposed his secret unknown to any but himself. The sense of the whole passage is that the most carefully covered murders have been disclosed by divinations made upon magpies, etc., by those who have understood how to trace the relationship between the bird examined and the murder.
128. DENIES HIS PERSON—Macduff refused to attend the banquet.
130. I HEAR IT BY THE WAY—I hear it indirectly.
132. I KEEP A SERVANT FEE'D—Macbeth pays a servant in each of the houses of his great subjects to report to him what may be said there about him. He had not received any refusal from Macduff; he had heard through a spy in Macduff's castle what the attitude of the latter was toward him.
136. ALL CAUSES—Every other consideration.
139. WILL TO HAND—Press to be done.
140. SCANN'D—Examined carefully. The implication is that the things Macbeth had in mind doing are of such dreadful nature that it were best to do them first, for thinking about them too much would cause him to refrain.
141. SEASON—Preservation—that which keeps things fresh and wholesome.
142-143. MY STRANGE . . . HARD USE—The sense is as follows: Macbeth says that his self-delusion is but the result of the fear which the beginner (initiate fear) naturally has, and that it will disappear with hard use—that is, when he has become hardened and accustomed to killing.

SCENE 5. *A heath.*

Thunder. Enter the three *Witches, meeting* HECATE.

1 Witch. Why, how now, Hecate! you look angerly.
Hecate. Have I not reason, beldams as you are,
Saucy and overbold? How did you dare
To trade and traffic with Macbeth
5 In riddles and affairs of death;
And I, the mistress of your charms,
The close contriver of all harms,
Was never call'd to bear my part,
Or show the glory of our art?
10 And, which is worse, all you have done
Hath been but for a wayward son,
Spiteful and wrathful; who, as others do,
Loves for his own ends, not for you.
But make amends now: get you gone,
15 And at the pit of Acheron
Meet me i' the morning; thither he
Will come to know his destiny.
Your vessels and your spells provide,
Your charms, and every thing beside.
20 I am for th' air; this night I'll spend
Unto a dismal and a fatal end:
Great business must be wrought ere noon:
Upon the corner of the moon
There hangs a vaporous drop profound;
25 I'll catch it ere it come to ground:
And that distill'd by magic sleights
Shall raise such artificial sprites
As by the strength of their illusion

1. HECATE—See note lines 51–52, Act II, Sc. 1.
2. BELDAMS—Hags.
5. RIDDLES—In prophecies which have a double or equivocal meaning.
7. CLOSE—Secret.
15. ACHERON—Acheron was the name of a river in Hades. Here "the pit of Acheron" is used to designate the entrance to the infernal regions, or "hell-mouth."
24. VAPOROUS DROP—There was a belief among the ancients in "a foam which the moon was supposed to shed on particular herbs or other objects, when strongly solicited by enchantment."
24. PROFOUND—Full of magic qualities.
27. SPRITES—Spirits.

Shall draw him on to his confusion.
30 He shall spurn fate, scorn death, and bear
His hopes 'bove wisdom, grace, and fear;
And you all know security
Is mortals' chiefest enemy.   [*Music, and a Song.*
Hark! I am call'd; my little spirit, see,
35 Sits in a foggy cloud, and stays for me.   [*Exit.*
    [*Sing within:* "Come away, come away," etc.]
    1 Witch. Come, let's make haste; she'll soon be back
    again.   [*Exeunt.*

32. SECURITY—Over-confidence.

SCENE 6. *Forres. The palace.*

Enter LENNOX *and another* LORD.

Lennox. My former speeches have but hit your thoughts,
Which can interpret farther: only, I say
Things have been strangely borne. The gracious Duncan
Was pitied of Macbeth: marry, he was dead:
5 And the right-valiant Banquo walk'd too late;
Whom, you may say, if 't please you, Fleance kill'd,
For Fleance fled: men must not walk too late.
Who cannot want the thought, how monstrous
It was for Malcolm and for Donalbain
10 To kill their gracious father? damned fact!
How it did grieve Macbeth! did he not straight,
In pious rage, the two delinquents tear,
That were the slaves of drink and thralls of sleep?
Was not that nobly done? Ay, and wisely too;
15 For 't would have anger'd any heart alive
To hear the men deny 't. So that, I say,
He has borne all things well; and I do think

1. FORMER SPEECHES—Lennox and the Lord to whom he is now speaking
have talked about the happenings at Macbeth's castle on some former occasion. Lennox makes no direct accusations. He has probably spoken on the
former occasion much as he does now—simply stating facts and leaving it to
the other to "interpret farther," or in other words, to draw his own conclusions.
    3. BORNE—Managed, carried on. 4. MARRY—A mild oath or expletive.
    8. WHO CANNOT WANT THE THOUGHT—Who can fail to think.
    10. FACT—Deed, especially an evil deed.
    12. TWO DELINQUENTS—Duncan's two grooms.

That, had he Duncan's sons under his key—
As, an 't please heaven, he shall not—they should find
20 What 'twere to kill a father; so should Fleance.
But, peace! for from broad words, and 'cause he fail'd
His presence at the tyrant's feast, I hear,
Macduff lives in disgrace. Sir, can you tell
Where he bestows himself?
  Lord.   The son of Duncan,
25 From whom this tyrant holds the due of birth,
Lives in the English court; and is receiv'd
Of the most pious Edward with such grace
That the malevolence of fortune nothing
Takes from his high respect. Thither Macduff
30 Is gone to pray the holy king, upon his aid
To wake Northumberland and warlike Siward;
That by the help of these, with Him above
To ratify the work, we may again
Give to our tables meat, sleep to our nights;
35 Free from our feasts and banquets bloody knives,
Do faithful homage and receive free honours;
All which we pine for now; and this report
Hath so exasperate the king, that he
Prepares for some attempt of war.
  Lennox.   Sent he to Macduff?
40 *Lord.* He did: and with an absolute "Sir, not I,"
The cloudy messenger turns me his back,
And hums, as who should say, "You'll rue the time
That clogs me with this answer."

19. AN 'T—If it.
21. FROM BROAD WORDS—On account of plain speaking.
24. BESTOWS—Keeps himself, lodges.
24–25. THE SON OF DUNCAN . . . DUE OF BIRTH—Malcolm. "Holds" means
withholds. "Due of birth" means the crown.
27. MOST PIOUS EDWARD—Edward the confessor, king of England 1042–
1066.
28–29. THAT THE MALEVOLENCE . . . HIGH RESPECT—That his misfortune
has not made him the less respected.
31. NORTHUMBERLAND AND WARLIKE SIWARD—Holinshed says, "Malcolme
purchased such favour at King Edward's hands that old Siward earle of Northumberland was appointed with ten thousand men to go with him into Scotland."
40. WITH AN ABSOLUTE "SIR, NOT I"—This was Macduff's reply to the messenger who brought Macbeth's command.
41. CLOUDY—Sullen, frowning.
41. TURNS ME HIS BACK—Turns his back (on Macduff).

Lennox.   And that well might
Advise him to a caution, to hold what distance
45 His wisdom can provide. Some holy angel
Fly to the court of England and unfold
His message ere he come; that a swift blessing
May soon return to this our suffering country
Under a hand accurs'd!
Lord.   I'll send my prayers with him.
                                    [*Exeunt.*

43. Clogs—Burdens. The messenger hates to bear the answer to Macbeth
so goes with heavy feet.
44. Advise him to a caution—Advise Macduff to be cautious.
44. To hold what distance—To keep what distance from Macbeth.
47. His—Macduff's.

ACT IV

Scene i. *A cavern. In the middle, a boiling cauldron.*

Thunder. Enter the three Witches.

1 Witch. Thrice the brinded cat hath mew'd.
2 Witch. Thrice, and once the hedge-pig whin'd.
3 Witch. Harpier cries; 'tis time, 'tis time.
1 Witch. Round about the cauldron go;
5 In the poison'd entrails throw.
Toad, that under cold stone
Days and nights has thirty-one
Swelter'd venom sleeping got,
Boil thou first i' the charmed pot.
10 *All.* Double, double toil and trouble;

1. Brinded cat—Brindled or streaked cat. This is the graymalkin of
Act I, Scene 1, the "familiar" of the first Witch.
2. Thrice, and once—Odd numbers were thought to possess magical
properties. The "thrice" is a repetition of the "thrice" in the first line.
The "once" applies to the hedge-pig, which is the familiar of the second
Witch.
3. Harpier—The familiar of the third Witch.
3. 'Tis time—That is, to begin the preparations ordered by Hecate. See
Act III, Scene 5.
5. Poison'd entrails—Probably the entrails of some person who has been
murdered by poison. Note that the ingredients of this "hell-broth" are chosen
for their hideous and diabolical significance. Most of them reflect some dark
superstition of Shakespeare's day.
6–8. Toad . . . sleeping got—It was the common belief that toads were
poisonous. "Swelter'd venom" means poison sweated out.

Fire burn and cauldron bubble.

   2 Witch.   Fillet of a fenny snake,
In the cauldron boil and bake;
Eye of newt and toe of frog,

15 Wool of bat and tongue of dog,
Adder's fork and blind-worm's sting,
Lizard's leg and howlet's wing,
For a charm of powerful trouble,
Like a hell-broth boil and bubble.

20   *All.*   Double, double toil and trouble;
Fire burn and cauldron bubble.

   3 Witch.   Scale of dragon, tooth of wolf,
Witches' mummy, maw and gulf
Of the ravin'd salt-sea shark;

25 Root of hemlock digg'd i' the dark,
Liver of blaspheming Jew,
Gall of goat, and slips of yew
Sliver'd in the moon's eclipse,
Nose of Turk and Tartar's lips,

30 Finger of birth-strangled babe
Ditch-deliver'd by a drab,
Make the gruel thick and slab:
Add thereto a tiger's chaudron,

12. FILLET OF A FENNY SNAKE—Slice of a marsh snake.
14. NEWT—Salamander. It was believed that the salamander possessed magic properties, and that it could live in fire.
16. FORK—Forked tongue.
16. BLIND-WORM—The slow-worm, formerly believed to be venomous.
17. HOWLET—Owlet. The owl was regarded as a bird of ill omen.
23. MUMMY—In Shakespeare's day a balm for cuts and bruises was made from Egyptian mummies. It was the curious belief that in a mummy might be found the "balsam" by which the body heals a cut or bruise. A witch's mummy might be supposed to retain the evil power which the witch in life possessed.
23. MAW AND GULF—Stomach and gullet.
24. RAVIN'D—Glutted with food, presumably human flesh, for the shark has an old reputation for being a man-eater.
25. HEMLOCK—The poisonous herb of this name.
26. BLASPHEMING—So called, because not Christian.
27. GOAT—In the Bible the goat represents the wicked, as in the expression to "separate the sheep from the goats."
27. YEW—Cuttings from the yew tree, formerly believed to be poisonous.
28. MOON'S ECLIPSE—Generally held to be a time of ill omen.
29. TURK AND TARTAR—Non-Christian and infidels.
30. BIRTH-STRANGLED—Hence unchristened.
32. SLAB—Slimy.
33. CHAUDRON—Entrails.

411

For th' ingredients of our cauldron.

35   *All.* Double, double toil and trouble;
Fire burn and cauldron bubble.

  2 Witch. Cool it with a baboon's blood,
Then the charm is firm and good.

Enter HECATE *to the other three* Witches.

  Hecate. O, well done! I command your pains;
40 And every one shall share i' th' gains:
And now about the cauldron sing,
Like elves and fairies in a ring,
Enchanting all that you put in.

                    [*Music, and a Song,* "Black spirits," etc.

                              [*Exit* HECATE.

  2 Witch. By the pricking of my thumbs,
45 Something wicked this way comes:
Open, locks,
Whoever knocks!

Enter MACBETH.

  Macbeth. How now, you secret, black, and midnight hags!
What is 't you do?

  All.   A deed without a name.

50   *Macbeth.* I conjure you, by that which you profess,
Howe'er you come to know it, answer me:
Though you untie the winds and let them fight
Against the churches; though the yesty waves
Confound and swallow navigation up;
55 Though bladed corn be lodg'd, and trees blown down;
Though castles topple on their warders' heads;
Though palaces and pyramids do slope
Their heads to their foundations; though the treasure
Of nature's germens tumble all together,

---

    44. PRICKING—Prickling. The witch interprets the prickling sensation in her thumb as a sign.
    53. YESTY—Foamy, frothy.
    55. BLADED—In the blade. Corn, of course, means grain, not corn in the sense in which Americans think of the word.
    55. LODG'D—Laid flat by the wind.
    59. GERMENS—Seeds.

60 Even till destruction sicken; answer me
To what I ask you.
    1 Witch.   Speak.
    2 Witch.   Demand.
    3 Witch.   We'll answer.
    1 Witch. Say, if thou 'dst rather hear it from our mouths,
Or from our masters?
    Macbeth.   Call 'em, let me see 'em.
    1 Witch. Pour in sow's blood, that hath eaten
65 Her nine farrow; grease that's sweaten
From the murderer's gibbet throw
Into the flame.
    All.   Come, high or low;
Thyself and office deftly show!

Thunder. First Apparition, *an armed Head.*

    Macbeth. Tell me, thou unknown power,—
    1 Witch.   He knows thy thought:
70 Hear his speech, but say thou nought.
    1 Apparition. Macbeth! Macbeth! Macbeth! beware Macduff;
Beware the thane of Fife.—Dismiss me: enough.   [*Descends.*
    Macbeth. Whate'er thou art, for thy good caution, thanks;
Thou hast harp'd my fear aright: but one word more,—
75   *1 Witch.* He will not be commanded: here's another,
More potent than the first.

Thunder. Second Apparition, *a bloody Child.*

    2 Apparition. Macbeth! Macbeth! Macbeth!
    Macbeth. Had I three ears, I'd hear thee.

65. NINE FARROW—Litter of nine pigs.
65. SWEATEN—Sweated.
66. GIBBET—Gallows.
67. COME, HIGH OR LOW—The witches with these words summon or call up the apparitions which are to give answer to Macbeth.
68. OFFICE—Function. The meaning is: Give your message.
An Armed Head—This is a representation of Macbeth's own head. Macbeth addressing it as "unknown power" fails to recognize what it really is.
74. HARP'D MY FEAR ARIGHT—Struck the note of my fear.
A bloody Child—This represents Macduff as a child.
78. HAD I THREE EARS, I'D HEAR THEE—Had I three ears, I should listen with them all. Three is probably used because the apparition had called his name three times.

2 Apparition.   Be bloody, bold, and resolute; laugh to scorn

80 The power of man, for none of woman born
Shall harm Macbeth.   [*Descends.*

Macbeth.   Then live, Macduff: what need I fear of thee?
But yet I'll make assurance double sure,
And take a bond of fate: thou shalt not live;

85 That I may tell pale-hearted fear it lies,
And sleep in spite of thunder.

Thunder.   Third Apparition, *a Child crowned, with a tree in his hand.*

What is this,
That rises like the issue of a king,
And wears upon his baby brow the round
And top of sovereignty?

All.   Listen, but speak not to 't.

90 *3 Apparition.*   Be lion-mettl'd, proud; and take no care
Who chafes, who frets, or where conspirers are:
Macbeth shall never vanquish'd be until
Great Birnam wood to high Dunsinane hill
Shall come against him.   [*Descends.*

Macbeth.   That will never be:

95 Who can impress the forest; bid the tree
Unfix his earth-bound root? Sweet bodements! good!
Rebellion's head, rise never till the wood
Of Birnam rise, and our high-plac'd Macbeth
Shall live the lease of nature, pay his breath

100 To time and mortal custom. Yet my heart

---

83. MAKE ASSURANCE DOUBLE SURE—Macbeth trusts the prophecy implicitly, yet he intends to make doubly sure by killing Macduff.

84. TAKE A BOND OF FATE—Macbeth means that he will, in effect, by killing Macduff make fate give a guarantee or bond that he need fear no man.

A Child crowned, with a tree in his hand—This represents Malcolm, the rightful king.   88. ROUND—The crown.

89. TOP OF SOVEREIGNTY—The symbol of kingly power.

93. UNTIL GREAT BIRNAM WOOD . . . AGAINST HIM—Until Birnam wood shall move to Dunsinane hill—a seeming impossibility.

95. IMPRESS—To press, to force to serve as soldiers.

96. SWEET BODEMENTS—Fair prophecies.

99. LIVE THE LEASE OF NATURE—Live until he dies a natural death.

99. PAY HIS BREATH TO TIME AND MORTAL CUSTOM—Live a normal length of life and die a natural death.

Throbs to know one thing: tell me, if your art
Can tell so much: shall Banquo's issue ever
Reign in this kingdom?
All.   Seek to know no more.
Macbeth.   I will be satisfied: deny me this,
105 And an eternal curse fall on you!   Let me know:
Why sinks that cauldron? and what noise is this?
                                                    [*Hautboys.*

1 Witch. Show!
2 Witch. Show!
3 Witch. Show!
110   *All.* Show his eyes, and grieve his heart;
Come like shadows, so depart!

A *show of eight* Kings, *the last with a glass in his hand;*
Banquo's Ghost *following.*

Macbeth.   Thou art too like the spirit of Banquo; down!
Thy crown does sear mine eyeballs.   And thy hair,
Thou other gold-bound brow, is like the first:
115 A third is like the former.   Filthy hags!
Why do you show me this?   A fourth!   Start, eyes!
What, will the line stretch out to th' crack of doom?
Another yet!   A seventh!   I'll see no more:
And yet the eighth appears, who bears a glass
120 Which shows me many more; and some I see
That twofold balls and treble sceptres carry:

A show—A parade or pompous line.
Eight KINGS—These are the eight Stuart kings of Scotland, Robert II,
Robert III, and the six Jameses, the last of whom, James VI, was also
James I of England and was on the throne when this play was given. James
saw this play and this direct reference to him must have pleased his colossal
vanity.   The Stuart kings were believed to have been Banquo's descendants.
      There was a legend that Fleance fled into Wales, that he married a daughter
of the Prince of Wales, and that his son became Lord High Steward of
Scotland.   From this office he took the name Walter Stewart (stuart), founding the House of Stuart from which came the Stuart kings.
      112. SPIRIT OF BANQUO—The ghost of Banquo.   That is, the first king
resembles Banquo. Macbeth remarks each king in turn.
      119. GLASS—A mirror.   A mirror or looking-glass was used in Shake-
speare's day in making divinations and foretelling future events.
      121. THAT TWOFOLD BALLS AND TREBLE SCEPTRES CARRY—Another reference
to James I of England.   The "twofold balls" refer probably to the two
crowns united by James—those of England and Scotland; the "treble sceptres"
to the kingdoms of England, Scotland, and Ireland.

Horrible sight! Now I see 'tis true;
For the bloodbolter'd Banquo smiles upon me,
And points at them for his. [*Apparitions vanish.*] What, is
    this so?

125   *1 Witch.* Ay, sir, all this is so; but why
Stands Macbeth thus amazedly?
Come, sisters, cheer we up his sprites,
And show the best of our delights:
I'll charm the air to give a sound,
130 While you perform your antic round;
That this great king may kindly say
Our duties did his welcome pay.
    [*Music. The* Witches *dance, and vanish with* HECATE.
    Macbeth. Where are they? Gone? Let this pernicious
  hour
Stand aye accursed in the calendar!
135 Come in, without there!

Enter LENNOX.

Lennox.   What's your grace's will?
Macbeth. Saw you the weird sisters?
Lennox.   No, my lord.
Macbeth. Came they not by you?
Lennox.   No, indeed, my lord.
Macbeth. Infected be the air whereon they ride,
And damn'd all those that trust them! I did hear
140 The galloping of horse: who was 't came by?
Lennox. 'Tis two or three, my lord, that bring you word
Macduff is fled to England.
Macbeth.   Fled to England!
Lennox. Ay, my good lord.
Macbeth. [*Aside.*] Time, thou anticipat'st my dread exploits:
145 The flighty purpose never is o'ertook
Unless the deed go with it: from this moment

123. BLOODBOLTER'D—His hair matted with blood.
127. SPRITES—Spirits.
130. ANTIC ROUND—Grotesque dance.
134. AYE—Forever.
135. WITHOUT THERE—That is, without the "pit of Acheron" or cave where
Macbeth met the witches.
144. ANTICIPAT'ST—Dost prevent. 145. FLIGHTY—Fleeting, swift.

416

The very firstlings of my heart shall be
The firstlings of my hand.   And even now,
To crown my thoughts with acts, be it thought and done:
150 The castle of Macduff I will surprise;
Seize upon Fife; give to the edge o' the sword
His wife, his babes, and all unfortunate souls
That trace him in his line.   No boasting like a fool;
This deed I'll do before this purpose cool:
155 But no more sights.   Where are these gentlemen?
Come, bring me where they are.   [*Exeunt.*

148. THE VERY FIRSTLINGS . . . OF MY HAND—I shall no sooner think of a
thing than I shall do it.

SCENE 2.   *Fife.*   MACDUFF'S *castle.*

Enter LADY MACDUFF, *her* SON, *and* ROSS.

Lady Macduff.   What had he done, to make him fly the land?
Ross.   You must have patience, madam.
Lady Macduff.   He had none;
His flight was madness: when our actions do not,
Our fears do make us traitors.
     Ross.   You know not
5 Whether it was his wisdom or his fear.
     Lady Macduff.   Wisdom! to leave his wife, to leave his babes,
His mansion, and his titles, in a place
From whence himself does fly!   He loves us not;
He wants the natural touch: for the poor wren,
10 The most diminutive of birds, will fight,
Her young ones in her nest, against the owl.
All is the fear and nothing is the love;
As little is the wisdom, where the flight
So runs against all reason.
     Ross.   My dearest coz,

1. WHAT HAD HE DONE—Lady Macduff thinks that Macduff must have committed some act of treason or rebellion.   She cannot understand why else
one should be obliged to take flight.
     7. TITLES—Property, possessions.
     9. WANTS THE NATURAL TOUCH—Lacks the natural feeling or instinct which
makes the wren protect its young.
     11. HER YOUNG ONES IN HER NEST—Her young ones being in the nest.
     12. ALL IS THE FEAR—Do you think Shakespeare intends this impression
that Macduff fled for fear of his life?   Can you justify his leaving his family
behind?   14. Coz—Cousin.

¹⁵ I pray you, school yourself; but, for your husband,
He is noble, wise, judicious, and best knows
The fits o' the season. I dare not speak much further:
But cruel are the times when we are traitors
And do not know ourselves; when we hold rumour

²⁰ From what we fear, yet know not what we fear,
But float upon a wild and violent sea
Each way and move. I take my leave of you;
Shall not be long but I'll be here again.
Things at the worst will cease, or else climb upward
²⁵ To what they were before. My pretty cousin,
Blessing upon you!
  Lady Macduff. Father'd he is, and yet he's fatherless.
  Ross. I am so much a fool, should I stay longer,
It would be my disgrace and your discomfort.
³⁰ I take my leave at once.   [*Exit.*
  Lady Macduff. Sirrah, your father's dead:

17. FITS O' THE SEASON—The turn which things are taking.
19. DO NOT KNOW OURSELVES—Do not know that we are traitors.
19–22. WHEN WE HOLD RUMOUR . . . EACH WAY AND MOVE—The meaning is:
When having done nothing wrong, yet we fear, because we hear rumors
that we are held as having done wrong. In such a case we "float . . . each
way and move," that is, like a storm-tossed ship we can take no sure course
for we know not what is the right thing to do or what is the wrong.
25. MY PRETTY COUSIN—This is addressed to Macduff's boy.
29. MY DISGRACE AND YOUR DISCOMFORT—Disgrace myself by weeping and
distress you.
30. SIRRAH—This term was also used in addressing children.

And what will you do now? How will you live?

Son. As birds do, mother.

Lady Macduff.   What, with worms and flies?

Son. With what I get, I mean; and so do they.

Lady Macduff. Poor bird! thou'dst never fear the net nor lime,

35 The pitfall nor the gin.

Son. Why should I, mother? Poor birds they are not set for.

My father is not dead, for all your saying.

Lady Macduff. Yes, he is dead: how wilt thou do for a father?

Son. Nay, how will you do for a husband?

40 *Lady Macduff.* Why, I can buy me twenty at any market.

Son. Then you'll buy 'em to sell again.

Lady Macduff. Thou speak'st with all thy wit; and yet i' faith,

With wit enough for thee.

Son. Was my father a traitor, mother?

45 *Lady Macduff.* Ay, that he was.

Son. What is a traitor?

Lady Macduff. Why, one that swears and lies.

Son. And be all traitors that do so?

Lady Macduff. Every one that does so is a traitor, and must be hang'd.

50 *Son.* And must they all be hang'd that swear and lie?

Lady Macduff. Every one.

Son. Who must hang them?

Lady Macduff. Why, the honest men.

Son. Then the liars and swearers are fools; for there are liars

55 and swearers enow to beat the honest men and hang up them.

Lady Macduff. Now, God help thee, poor monkey! But how wilt thou do for a father?

---

34. LIME—Bird-lime, a sticky substance smeared on twigs to catch birds.

35. PITFALL NOR THE GIN—Trap nor snare. All these were common devices for catching small birds, which in Shakespeare's time were still used in pies and other dishes.

42. WIT—Understanding.

47. SWEARS AND LIES—Swears allegiance falsely.

50. THAT SWEAR AND LIE—The boy takes the expression literally.

419

Son. If he were dead, you'd weep for him; if you would not,
it were a good sign that I should quickly have a new father.
60 *Lady Macduff.* Poor prattler, how thou talk'st!

Enter a Messenger.

Messenger. Bless you, fair dame! I am not to you known,
Though in your state of honour I am perfect.
I doubt some danger does approach you nearly:
If you will take a homely man's advice,
65 Be not found here; hence, with your little ones.
To fright you thus, methinks I am too savage;
To do worse to you were fell cruelty,
Which is too nigh your person. Heaven preserve you!
I dare abide no longer.   [*Exit.*
Lady Macduff.   Whither should I fly?
70 I have done no harm. But I remember now
I am in this earthly world; where to do harm
Is often laudable, to do good sometime
Accounted dangerous folly: why then, alas,
Do I put up that womanly defence,
75 To say I have done no harm?

Enter Murderers.

                                    What are these faces?
1 Murderer. Where is your husband?
Lady Macduff. I hope, in no place so unsanctified
Where such as thou mayst find him.
1 Murderer.   He's a traitor.
Son. Thou liest, thou shag-ear'd villain!
1 Murderer.   [*Stabbing him.*] What, you egg!
80 Young fry of treachery!
Son.   He has kill'd me, mother:
Run away, I pray you!   [*Dies.*
                [*Exit* LADY MACDUFF, *crying "Murder!"*
                [*Exeunt* Murderers, *following her.*

62. IN YOUR STATE OF HONOUR I AM PERFECT—Perfectly acquainted with
your rank.
63. DOUBT—Fear.
67. FELL CRUELTY—Direct cruelty.
79. SHAG-EAR'D—Shaggy eared or shaggy haired.
80. YOUNG FRY OF TREACHERY!—Son of a traitor.

SCENE 3. *England. Before the King's palace.*

Enter MALCOLM *and* MACDUFF.

Malcolm.   Let us seek out some desolate shade, and there
Weep our sad bosoms empty.

Macduff.   Let us rather
Hold fast the mortal sword, and, like good men,
Bestride our down-fall'n birthdom. Each new morn
5 New widows howl, new orphans cry, new sorrows
Strike heaven on the face, that it resounds
As if it felt with Scotland, and yell'd out
Like syllable of dolour.

Malcolm.   What I believe, I'll wail;
What know, believe; and what I can redress,
10 As I shall find the time to friend, I will.
What you have spoke, it may be so perchance.
This tyrant, whose sole name blisters our tongues,
Was once thought honest: you have lov'd him well;
He hath not touch'd you yet. I am young; but something
15 You may deserve of him through me, and wisdom
To offer up a weak, poor, innocent lamb
T' appease an angry god.

Macduff.   I am not treacherous.

Malcolm.   But Macbeth is.
A good and virtuous nature may recoil

1. LET US SEEK OUT SOME DESOLATE SHADE—What Malcolm proposes is,
in effect, that instead of trying to redress their wrongs, they lose themselves
in some wild distant land and try to forget them. This makes Malcolm
seem to be a kind of spiritless fellow. It should be remembered that he
does not trust Macduff at first, and that throughout most of the scene he
puts himself in an unfavorable light in order to try Macduff's sincerity.

3. MORTAL—Deadly.

4. BESTRIDE OUR DOWN-FALL'N BIRTHDOM—Stand astride our fallen native
land as a knight does the body of a comrade who has fallen in battle.

6. IT—Heaven.

8. LIKE SYLLABLE OF DOLOUR—A similar cry of pain or grief.

10. TIME TO FRIEND—A friendly or favorable time.

10. I WILL—Note the reserved nature of Malcolm's entire speech. He
implies that as bad as things are, Macduff's account is overdrawn. "I will
bewail," he says, "what I believe, and I'll believe only what I know." He
professes to be unimpressed by Macduff.

14–17. BUT SOMETHING . . . AN ANGRY GOD—Malcolm suggests that it might
be worth Macduff's while to betray him (Malcolm) to Macbeth.

19–20. A GOOD AND VIRTUOUS NATURE MAY RECOIL IN AN IMPERIAL CHARGE—
Macduff's reply to Malcolm's suggestion is to assert that he is not treacherous.
To this Malcolm retorts, "No, but Macbeth is. And although you may not

20 In an imperial charge. But I shall crave your pardon;
That which you are, my thoughts cannot transpose
Angels are bright still, though the brightest fell:
Though all things foul would wear the brows of grace,
Yet grace must still look so.
　Macduff.　　　　　　I have lost my hopes.
25 　*Malcolm.* Perchance even there where I did find my doubts.
Why in that rawness left you wife and child,
Those precious motives, those strong knots of love,
Without leave-taking? I pray you,
Let not my jealousies be your dishonours,
30 But mine own safeties: you may be rightly just,
Whatever I shall think.
　Macduff.　　　　　Bleed, bleed, poor country!
Great tyranny, lay thou thy basis sure,
For goodness dare not check thee; wear thou thy wrongs;
The title is affeer'd! Fare thee well, lord:
35 I would not be the villain that thou think'st
For the whole space that's in the tyrant's grasp,
And the rich East to boot.
　Malcolm.　　　　　Be not offended:

be, yet a good and virtuous man acts contrary (recoil) to his nature when the king lays him under command (imperial charge)."

20–21. BUT I SHALL CRAVE YOUR PARDON . . . CANNOT TRANSPOSE—Malcolm's apology is none at all. What he says is, "I beg your pardon for insinuating that you are treacherous, but whatever the truth is, whether you are treacherous or not my thinking you one thing or the other will not make you what I think you to be." Malcolm, in assuming this attitude, is perhaps more irritating to Macduff than he would be if he accused Macduff outright of treachery, for he seems to be quite disinterested in Macduff's and his country's cause.

22–24. ANGELS ARE BRIGHT STILL . . . YET GRACE MUST STILL LOOK SO—Malcolm says in effect, "I really have no right to accuse you (although I have my own opinion), for some angels are still bright even though the brightest (Lucifer) did fall, and virtue must continue to wear its own looks although vice frequently assumes the outward appearance of virtue."

24. I HAVE LOST MY HOPES—Macduff is discouraged and disappointed. How different have been both Malcolm and his reception from what he must have expected!

25. PERCHANCE EVEN THERE WHERE I DID FIND MY DOUBTS—Malcolm interprets "hopes" in a different sense from that in which Macduff uses it. He says in effect, "Your leaving your wife and child behind is the circumstance which has caused me to doubt your sincerity and to suspect that you came with 'hopes' of enticing me back to Scotland to betray me."

26. RAWNESS—Hastiness, without making adequate provision for their care.

29. JEALOUSIES—Suspicions. The sense is: "Do not interpret my suspicions as insults to you but rather as precautions for myself."

34. AFFEER'D—Confirmed, i.e., "great tyranny's" title.

I speak not as in absolute fear of you.
I think our country sinks beneath the yoke;
40 It weeps, it bleeds; and each new day a gash
Is added to her wounds: I think withal
There would be hands uplifted in my right;
And here from gracious England have I offer
Of goodly thousands: but, for all this,
45 When I shall tread upon the tyrant's head,
Or wear it on my sword, yet my poor country
Shall have more vices than it had before;
More suffer, and more sundry ways than ever,
By him that shall succeed.
    Macduff.   What should he be?
50   *Malcolm.*   It is myself I mean; in whom I know
All the particulars of vice so grafted,
That, when they shall be open'd, black Macbeth
Will seem as pure as snow; and the poor state
Esteem him as a lamb, being compar'd
55 With my confineless harms.
    Macduff.   Not in the legions
Of horrid hell can come a devil more damn'd
In evils to top Macbeth.
    Malcolm.   I grant him bloody,
Luxurious, avaricious, false, deceitful,
Sudden, malicious, smacking of every sin
60 That has a name: but there's no bottom, none,
In my voluptuousness; your wives, your daughters,
Your matrons, and your maids, could not fill up
The cistern of my lust, and my desire
All continent impediments would o'erbear,
65 That did oppose my will. Better Macbeth
Than such an one to reign.
    Macduff.   Boundless intemperance
In nature is a tyranny; it hath been

---

43. ENGLAND—The king of England.
48. AND MORE SUNDRY WAYS—And in more sundry ways.
52. OPEN'D—Disclosed.
55. CONFINELESS HARMS—Unlimited vices.
58. LUXURIOUS—Licentious.
59. SUDDEN—Violent, quick to anger.
64. CONTINENT IMPEDIMENTS—Restraining motives.

Th' untimely emptying of the happy throne,
And fall of many kings. But fear not yet
70 To take upon you what is yours: you may
Convey your pleasures in a spacious plenty,
And yet seem cold, the time you may so hoodwink.
We have willing dames enough; there cannot be
That vulture in you, to devour so many
75 As will to greatness dedicate themselves,
Finding it so inclined.

    Malcolm.   With this there grows,
In my most ill-compos'd affection such
A stanchless avarice that, were I king,
I should cut off the nobles for their lands,
80 Desire his jewels and this other's house:
And my more-having would be as a sauce
To make me hunger more, that I should forge
Quarrels unjust against the good and loyal,
Destroying them for wealth.

    Macduff.   This avarice
85 Sticks deeper, grows with more pernicious root
Than summer-seeming lust, and it hath been
The sword of our slain kings: yet do not fear;
Scotland hath foisons to fill up your will
Of your mere own: all these are portable,
90 With other graces weigh'd.

    Malcolm.   But I have none: the king-becoming graces,
As justice, verity, temperance, stableness,
Bounty, perseverance, mercy, lowliness,
Devotion, patience, courage, fortitude,
95 I have no relish of them; but abound

---

71. CONVEY—Pursue in secret.
72. THE TIME YOU MAY SO HOODWINK—You may so deceive the world.
76. WITH THIS—In addition to this.
77. ILL-COMPOS'D AFFECTION—Nature made up of vices.
78. STANCHLESS—Insatiable.
80. HIS—This one's.
86. SUMMER-SEEMING—Like the summer, quickly passing, youthful.
87. THE SWORD OF OUR SLAIN KINGS—That which has slain our kings.
88. FOISONS—Abundance.
89. YOUR MERE OWN—That which is absolutely your own.
89. PORTABLE—Endurable. The sense is that all these vices are endurable if counterbalanced by other virtues.
95. RELISH—Savor, smack.

In the division of each several crime,
Acting it many ways. Nay, had I power, I should
Pour the sweet milk of concord into hell,
Uproar the universal peace, confound
100 All unity on earth.
  Macduff.   O Scotland, Scotland!
  Malcolm. If such a one be fit to govern, speak:
I am as I have spoken.
  Macduff.   Fit to govern!
No, not to live. O nation miserable,
With an untitled tyrant bloody-scepter'd,
105 When shalt thou see thy wholesome days again,
Since that the truest issue of thy throne
By his own interdiction stands accurs'd,
And does blaspheme his breed? Thy royal father
Was a most sainted king: the queen that bore thee,
110 Oftener upon her knees than on her feet,
Died every day she liv'd. Fare thee well!
These evils thou repeat'st upon thyself
Hath banish'd me from Scotland. O my breast,
Thy hope ends here!
  Malcolm.   Macduff, this noble passion,
115 Child of integrity, hath from my soul
Wip'd the black scruples, reconcil'd my thoughts
To thy good truth and honour. Devilish Macbeth
By many of these trains hath sought to win me
Into his power; and modest wisdom plucks me
120 From over-credulous haste; but God above
Deal between thee and me! for even now
I put myself to thy direction, and
Unspeak mine own detraction; here abjure
The taints and blames I laid upon myself,
125 For strangers to my nature. I am yet
Unknown to woman, never was forsworn,
Scarcely have coveted what was mine own,

96. IN THE DIVISION—Variation.
107. INTERDICTION—Pronouncement.
108. BLASPHEME HIS BREED—Slander his parentage.
111. DIED EVERY DAY SHE LIV'D—Each day of her life was a preparation
for death.
118. TRAINS—Lures, devices.
123. HERE ABJURE—I here disavow.

At no time broke my faith, would not betray
The devil to his fellow, and delight
130 No less in truth than life: my first false speaking
Was this upon myself. What I am truly,
Is thine and my poor country's to command;
Whither, indeed, before thy here-approach,
Old Siward, with ten thousand warlike men,
135 Already at a point, was setting forth:
Now we'll together; and the chance of goodness
Be like our warranted quarrel! Why are you silent?
    Macduff. Such welcome and unwelcome things at once
'Tis hard to reconcile.

Enter a Doctor.

140   *Malcolm.* Well; more anon.—Comes the king forth, I pray
      you?
    Doctor. Ay, sir; there are a crew of wretched souls
That stay his cure: their malady convinces
The great assay of art; but at his touch,
Such sanctity hath heaven given his hand,
145 They presently amend.
    Malcolm.   I thank you, doctor.   [*Exit* Doctor.
    Macduff. What's the disease he means?
    Malcolm.   'Tis call'd the evil:
A most miraculous work in this good king;
Which often, since my here-remain in England,
I have seen him do. How he solicits heaven,
150 Himself best knows: but strangely-visited people,
All swoln and ulcerous, pitiful to the eye,

135. AT A POINT—Prepared, armed at point.
136–137. THE CHANCE OF GOODNESS BE LIKE OUR WARRANTED QUARREL—May
the chances of success be as good as the outcome of our quarrel.
142. STAY HIS CURE—Wait his healing touch. Edward the Confessor was
said to have had the gift of healing scrofula, a blood and skin disease, by
"touching," and to have passed this gift to his successors. All the kings of
England from Edward down are said to have "touched" to cure this disease.
This episode has nothing to do with the play, but is generally believed to
have been introduced as a compliment to King James who witnessed the
play, and who himself "touched" many.
142–143. THEIR MALADY CONVINCES THE GREAT ASSAY OF ART—Their disease
overcomes the best effort of professional skill.
149. SOLICITS—Invokes and obtains the aid of.
150. STRANGELY-VISITED—Strangely-afflicted.

The mere despair of surgery, he cures,
Hanging a golden stamp about their necks,
Put on with holy prayers: and 'tis spoken,
155 To the succeeding royalty he leaves
The healing benediction. With this strange virtue,
He hath a heavenly gift of prophecy,
And sundry blessings hang about his throne,
That speak him full of grace.

Enter Ross.

Macduff.   See, who comes here?
160 *Malcolm.* My countryman; but yet I know him not.
Macduff. My ever-gentle cousin, welcome hither.
Malcolm. I know him now. Good God, betimes remove
The means that makes us strangers!
Ross.   Sir, amen.
Macduff. Stands Scotland where it did?
Ross.   Alas, poor country,
165 Almost afraid to know itself! It cannot
Be call'd our mother, but our grave: where nothing,
But who knows nothing, is once seen to smile;
Where sighs and groans and shrieks that rend the air,
Are made, not mark'd; where violent sorrow seems
170 A modern ecstasy: the dead man's knell
Is there scarce ask'd for who; and good men's lives
Expire before the flowers in their caps,
Dying or ere they sicken.
Macduff.   O, relation
Too nice, and yet too true!
Malcolm.   What's the newest grief?

152. MERE—Utter, complete.
153. GOLDEN STAMP—A coin of gold.
160. BUT YET I KNOW HIM NOT—Malcolm recognizes him as a countryman
by his dress, but is suspicious of him.
162. BETIMES—Forthwith, soon.
163. MEANS—Cause.
167. WHO KNOWS NOTHING—Such as the idiot and the fool.
169. NOT MARK'D—They are so common as no longer to excite notice.
170. A MODERN ECSTASY—A state of feeling which has become commonplace.
173–174. RELATION TOO NICE—Account or story too accurate.

427

175 *Ross.* That of an hour's age doth hiss the speaker,
Each minute teems a new one.
    Macduff. How does my wife?
    Ross. Why, well.
    Macduff. And all my children?
    Ross. Well too.
    Macduff. The tyrant has not batter'd at their peace?
    Ross. No; they were well at peace when I did leave 'em.
180   *Macduff.* Be not a niggard of your speech: how goes 't?
    Ross. When I came hither to transport the tidings
Which I have heavily borne, there ran a rumour
Of many worthy fellows that were out;
Which was to my belief witness'd the rather,
185 For that I saw the tyrant's power a-foot:
Now is the time of help; your eye in Scotland
Would create soldiers, make our women fight,
To doff their dire distresses.
    Malcolm. Be 't their comfort
We are coming thither: gracious England hath
190 Lent us good Siward and ten thousand men;
An older and a better soldier none
That Christendom gives out.
    Ross. Would I could answer
This comfort with the like! But I have words
That would be howl'd out in the desert air,
195 Where hearing should not latch them.
    Macduff. What concern they?
The general cause? or is it a fee-grief
Due to some single breast?
    Ross. No mind that's honest
But in it shares some woe; though the main part
Pertains to you alone.
    Macduff. If it be mine,

175. DOTH HISS THE SPEAKER—Whoever tells of an atrocity which is only an hour old is regarded much as the player who is hissed for presenting "old stuff."
176. TEEMS—Brings forth.
179. WELL AT PEACE—These are grisly puns.
183. OUT—Up in arms, in rebellion.   188. DOFF—Put off, get rid of.
194. WOULD BE—Ought to be, should only be.
195. LATCH—Catch.
196–197. FEE-GRIEF DUE TO SOME SINGLE BREAST—Private grief which concerns one man only.

200 Keep it not from me, quickly let me have it.
    Ross. Let not your ears despise my tongue for ever,
Which shall possess them with the heaviest sound
That ever yet they heard.
    Macduff.   Hum! I guess at it.
    Ross. Your castle is surpris'd; your wife and babes
205 Savagely slaughter'd: to relate the manner,
Were, on the quarry of these murder'd deer,
To add the death of you.
    Malcolm.   Merciful heaven!
What, man! ne'er pull your hat upon your brows;
Give sorrow words: the grief that does not speak
210 Whispers the o'er-fraught heart and bids it break.
    Macduff. My children too?
    Ross.   Wife, children, servants, all
That could be found.
    Macduff.   And I must be from thence!
My wife kill'd too?
    Ross.   I have said.
    Malcolm.   Be comforted:
Let's make us medicines of our great revenge,
215 To cure this deadly grief.
    Macduff. He has no children.—All my pretty ones?
Did you say all? O hell-kite! All?
What, all my pretty chickens and their dam
At one fell swoop?
220   *Malcolm.* Dispute it like a man.
    Macduff.   I shall do so;
But I must also feel it as a man:
I cannot but remember such things were,
That were most precious to me. Did heaven look on,
And would not take their part? Sinful Macduff,
225 They were all struck for thee! naught that I am,

---

206. QUARRY—Heap, used to designate the game killed.
207. TO ADD THE DEATH OF YOU—Would be to cause your death.
210. WHISPERS—As we say "bespeaks." 210. O'ER-FRAUGHT—Over-laden.
216. HE—Malcolm. Macduff means that it is easy to see that Malcolm
has no children. He talks of revenge. Revenge will not bring back those
whom Macbeth has slain. Macduff is overcome by his grief; he thinks rather
of those whom he will see no more than of revenge. This comes later.
220. DISPUTE IT—Resist it.
225. NAUGHT—Worthless.

Not for their own demerits, but for mine,
Fell slaughter on their souls. Heaven rest them now!
   Malcolm. Be this the whetstone of your sword: let grief
Convert to anger; blunt not the heart, enrage it.
230   *Macduff.* O, I could play the woman with mine eyes,
And braggart with my tongue! But, gentle heavens,
Cut short all intermission; front to front
Bring thou this fiend of Scotland and myself;
Within my sword's length set him; if he scape,
235 Heaven forgive him too!
   Malcolm.   This tune goes manly.
Come, go we to the king; our power is ready;
Our lack is nothing but our leave. Macbeth
Is ripe for shaking, and the powers above
Put on their instruments. Receive what cheer you may:
240 The night is long that never finds the day.   [*Exeunt.*

235. FORGIVE HIM TOO—If for any reason I let him escape, why, then let
Heaven let him escape too.
237. OUR LACK IS NOTHING BUT OUR LEAVE—We lack nothing but taking
leave of the king.
239. PUT ON THEIR INSTRUMENTS—Set their agents at work to shake Macbeth.

ACT V

SCENE 1. *Dunsinane. Ante-room in the Castle.*

Enter a Doctor *of Physic and a* Waiting-Gentlewoman.

Doctor. I have two nights watch'd with you, but can perceive
no truth in your report. When was it she last walk'd?
   Gentlewoman. Since his majesty went into the field, I have
seen her rise from her bed, throw her night-gown upon her,
5 unlock her closet, take forth paper, fold it, write upon 't, read
it, afterwards seal it, and again return to bed; yet all this while
in a most fast sleep.
   Doctor. A great perturbation in nature, to receive at once
the benefit of sleep, and do the effects of watching! In this

3. WENT INTO THE FIELD—To put down the "many worthy fellows that
were out." See Act IV, Scene 3.
4. NIGHT-GOWN—Dressing robe.
8. PERTURBATION—Disturbance.
9. DO THE EFFECTS OF WATCHING—Do things as if she were awake.

10 slumbery agitation, besides her walking and other actual performances, what, at any time, have you heard her say?

Gentlewoman. That, sir, which I will not report after her.

Doctor. You may to me; and 'tis most meet you should.

Gentlewoman. Neither to you nor any one; having no witness
15 to confirm my speech.

Enter LADY MACBETH, *with a taper.*

Lo, you, here she comes! This is her very
guise; and, upon my life, fast asleep. Observe her; stand close.

Doctor. How came she by that light?
20 *Gentlewoman.* Why, it stood by her:
she has light by her continually; 'tis her
command.

Doctor. You see, her eyes are open.

Gentlewoman. Ay, but their sense are
25 shut.

Doctor. What is it she does now?
Look, how she rubs her hands.

Gentlewoman. It is an accustom'd ac-
tion with her, to seem thus washing her hands; I have known
30 her continue in this a quarter of an hour.

Lady Macbeth. Yet here's a spot.

Doctor. Hark! she speaks: I will set down what comes from
her, to satisfy my remembrance the more strongly.

Lady Macbeth. Out, damned spot! out, I say!—One, two;
35 why, then 'tis time to do 't.—Hell is murky!—Fie, my lord,
fie! a soldier, and afeard? What need we fear who knows it,
when none can call our power to account?—Yet who would

12. WILL NOT REPORT—Will not repeat. What she has heard is of such
a damaging nature that she fears getting herself into trouble if she repeats
it; she implies in her next speech that what she has heard is something
which she dare not report without a confirming witness. What did she hear
Lady Macbeth say?

18. STAND CLOSE—Keep out of sight.

34. ONE, TWO—Lady Macbeth seems to hear the bell which she struck
to signal Macbeth that his drink was ready and that it was "time to do 't."
The student should note that Lady Macbeth's disordered mind recalls dis-
connected scraps of what had passed between her and her husband, mixed
with horrid reminiscences of the crime itself.

have thought the old man to have had so much blood in him?
Doctor. Do you mark that?

40 *Lady Macbeth.* The thane of Fife had a wife; where is she now?—What, will these hands ne'er be clean?—No more o' that, my lord, no more o' that: you mar all with this starting.
Doctor. Go to, go to; you have known what you should not.
Gentlewoman. She has spoke what she should not, I am
45 sure of that: heaven knows what she has known.
Lady Macbeth. Here's the smell of the blood still: all the perfumes of Arabia will not sweeten this little hand. Oh, oh, oh!
Doctor. What a sigh is there! The heart is sorely charg'd.
Gentlewoman. I would not have such a heart in my bosom
50 for the dignity of the whole body.
Doctor. Well, well, well,—
Gentlewoman. Pray God it be, sir.
Doctor. This disease is beyond my practice: yet I have known those which have walk'd in their sleep who have died
55 holily in their beds.
Lady Macbeth. Wash your hands; put on your night-gown; look not so pale. I tell you yet again, Banquo's buried; he cannot come out on 's grave.
Doctor. Even so?
60 *Lady Macbeth.* To bed, to bed; there's knocking at the gate: come, come, come, come, give me your hand: what's done cannot be undone: to bed, to bed, to bed. [*Exit.*
Doctor. Will she go now to bed?
Gentlewoman. Directly.
65 *Doctor.* Foul whisperings are abroad: unnatural deeds.
Do breed unnatural troubles: infected minds
To their deaf pillows will discharge their secrets:
More needs she the divine than the physician.
God, God forgive us all! Look after her;
70 Remove from her the means of all annoyance,
And still keep eyes upon her. So, good night:
My mind she has mated, and amaz'd my sight:
I think, but dare not speak.
Gentlewoman. Good night, good doctor. [*Exeunt.*

48. SORELY CHARG'D—Heavy, heavily laden.   68. DIVINE—Priest.
70. MEANS OF ALL ANNOYANCE—Things with which she might harm herself.
71. STILL—Always.   71. KEEP EYES UPON HER—Why?
72. MATED—Confounded, bewildered.

SCENE 2. *The country near Dunsinane.*

Drum and colours. Enter MENTEITH, CAITHNESS, ANGUS,
LENNOX, *and* Soldiers.

Menteith. The English power is near, led on by Malcolm,
His uncle Siward, and the good Macduff:
Revenges burn in them; for their dear causes
Would to the bleeding and the grim alarm
5 Excite the mortified man.
    Angus.   Near Birnam wood
Shall we well meet them; that way are they coming.
    Caithness. Who knows if Donalbain be with his brother?
    Lennox. For certain, sir, he is not: I have a file
Of all the gentry: there is Siward's son,
10 And many unrough youths, that even now
Protest their first of manhood.
    Menteith.   What does the tyrant?
    Caithness. Great Dunsinane he strongly fortifies:
Some say he's mad; others, that lesser hate him,
Do call it valiant fury: but, for certain,
15 He cannot buckle his distemper'd cause
Within the belt of rule.
    Angus.   Now does he feel
His secret murders sticking on his hands;
Now minutely revolts upbraid his faith-breach;
Those he commands move only in command,
20 Nothing in love: now does he feel his title
Hang loose about him, like a giant's robe
Upon a dwarfish thief.
    Menteith.   Who then shall blame

3. DEAR CAUSES—Grievous complaints.
4. BLEEDING—Bloody deeds.
4. ALARM—Call to arms.
5. EXCITE THE MORTIFIED MAN—Rouse the holy or religious man.
8. FILE—List.
10. UNROUGH—Smooth-faced, beardless.
11. PROTEST THEIR FIRST OF MANHOOD—Declare themselves no longer mere
boys but men, making this the first act of their manhood.
15. DISTEMPER'D CAUSE—Diseased cause. Macbeth's cause is compared to a
body swollen with dropsy which cannot be buckled in. The sense of the lines
is: He cannot control his rebellious subjects nor make his plans go right.
18. MINUTELY REVOLTS—Revolts breaking out every minute.
18. UPBRAID HIS FAITH-BREACH—Rebuke his breach of allegiance to Duncan.

433

His pester'd senses to recoil and start,
When all that is within him does condemn
25 Itself for being there?
   Caithness.   Well, march we on,
To give obedience where 'tis truly ow'd:
Meet we the medicine of the sickly weal;
And with him pour we in our country's purge
Each drop of us.
   Lennox.   Or so much as it needs
30 To dew the sovereign flower and drown the weeds.
Make we our march towards Birnam.   [*Exeunt, marching.*

23. PESTER'D—Perplexed, irritated.
23. TO RECOIL AND START—For recoiling and starting, that is, for acting, as we say, by fits and starts. We have here a good description of Macbeth alternating between fits of dark depression and starts of "valiant fury."
24–25. WHEN ALL THAT IS WITHIN HIM DOES CONDEMN ITSELF FOR BEING THERE—When Macbeth turns his thoughts inward, he finds nothing but what should be condemned. It is then he "recoils" to feverish activity.
27. MEDICINE OF THE SICKLY WEAL—*i.e.* Malcolm who can restore the commonwealth to health.
28. PURGE—The figure of "medicine" for a "sickly weal" is continued. The sense is: Each of us devote ourselves to restoring our country to health—to purging it.
30. DEW THE SOVEREIGN FLOWER—Revive or nourish the true king (Malcolm.)

SCENE 3. *Dunsinane. A room in the castle.*

Enter MACBETH, *the* Doctor, *and* Attendants.

Macbeth. Bring me no more reports; let them fly all:
Till Birnam wood remove to Dunsinane
I cannot taint with fear. What's the boy Malcolm?
Was he not born of woman? The spirits that know
5 All mortal consequences have pronounc'd me thus:
"Fear not, Macbeth; no man that's born of woman
Shall e'er have power upon thee." Then fly, false thanes,
And mingle with the English epicures:
The mind I sway by and the heart I bear
10 Shall never sag with doubt nor shake with fear.

1. THEM—His thanes and their soldiers. He has been receiving reports of their desertions.
3. TAINT—Become infected.
8. ENGLISH EPICURES—Holinshed records that the Scotch (whose barren country had accustomed them to plain living and few comforts) looked upon the English not without contempt as gormandizers.
9. SWAY BY—By which I am ruled.

Enter a Servant.

The devil damn thee black, thou cream-fac'd loon!
Where got'st thou that goose look?
Servant.   There is ten thousand—
Macbeth.   Geese, villain?
Servant.   Soldiers, sir.
Macbeth.   Go prick thy face, and over-red thy fear,
15 Thou lily-liver'd boy. What soldiers, patch?
Death of thy soul! those linen cheeks of thine
Are counsellors to fear. What soldiers, whey-face?
Servant.   The English force, so please you.
Macbeth.   Take thy face hence.   [*Exit* Servant.
                                        ·Seyton! I am sick at heart,
20 When I behold—Seyton, I say!—This push
Will chair me ever, or disseat me now.
I have liv'd long enough: my way of life
Is fall'n into the sear, the yellow leaf;
And that which should accompany old age,
25 As honour, love, obedience, troops of friends,
I must not look to have; but, in their stead,
Curses, not loud but deep, mouth-honour, breath,
Which the poor heart would fain deny, and dare not.
Seyton!

Enter SEYTON.

30 *Seyton.*   What's your gracious pleasure?
Macbeth.   What news more?
Seyton.   All is confirm'd, my lord, which was reported.

11. LOON—Stupid fellow. Despite his boast, Macbeth starts at the pallid face of the servant, and tried to bolster his own confidence by his own "valiant fury."
14. OVER-RED—Smear your blood over your pallid face; that is, take courage.
15. LILY-LIVER'D—Cowardly. The liver was believed to be the seat of courage, much as the heart is still spoken of as the seat of pity.
15. PATCH—Fool.
16. LINEN CHEEKS—Colorless cheeks.
17. ARE COUNSELLORS TO FEAR—Cause all who see them to fear.
17. WHEY-FACE—What is the color of whey?
19. SEYTON!—Macbeth calls the officer who attends him. Between calls, he gives way to one of his black fits which alternate with moods of fury.
20. PUSH—Attack.
21. CHAIR ME EVER, OR DISSEAT ME NOW—Will make my seat secure if I win, or disseat me if I lose in the coming attack.

Macbeth.   I'll fight, till from my bones my flesh be hack'd.
Give me my armour.
   Seyton.   'Tis not needed yet.
   Macbeth.   I'll put it on.
35 Send out moe horses, skirr the country round;
Hang those that talk of fear.   Give me mine armour.
How does your patient, doctor?
   Doctor.   Not so sick, my lord,
As she is troubled with thick-coming fancies,
That keep her from her rest.
   Macbeth.   Cure her of that.
40 Canst thou not minister to a mind diseas'd,
Pluck from the memory a rooted sorrow,
Raze out the written troubles of the brain,
And with some sweet oblivious antidote
Cleanse the stuff'd bosom of that perilous stuff
45 Which weighs upon the heart?
   Doctor.   Therein the patient
Must minister to himself.
   Macbeth.   Throw physic to the dogs, I'll none of it.
Come, put mine armour on; give me my staff.
Seyton, send out.   Doctor, the thanes fly from me.
50 Come, sir, dispatch.   If thou couldst, doctor, cast
The water of my land, find her disease,
And purge it to a sound and pristine health,
I would applaud thee to the very echo,
That should applaud again.   Pull 't off, I say.
55 What rhubarb, senna, or what purgative drug,

35. MOE—More.
35. SKIRR—Scour.
42. RAZE OUT—Erase, blot out.
43. OBLIVIOUS—Causing forgetfulness.
47. PHYSIC—The whole practice of medicine.
48. COME, PUT MINE ARMOUR ON; GIVE ME MY STAFF—Note the signs of Macbeth's great perturbation.   He orders his armor put on, then pulled off, and finally brought after him.   He must talk and he must be doing something. "Come, put mine armour on; give me my staff" is addressed to one (the armorer) whose duty it was to put the armor on.
49. SEYTON, SEND OUT—To Seyton he turns with the direction to send out for further news; next he addresses the Doctor, and in the same breath orders the armorer to be quick about his business.
50. CAST—Inspect, examine.
52. PURGE IT—Restore my land.
52. PRISTINE—Original, former.
54. PULL 'T OFF—Macbeth here directs his armorer to pull his armor off.

Would scour these English hence?   Hear'st thou of them?
Doctor.   Ay, my good lord; your royal preparation
Makes us hear something.
   Macbeth.   Bring it after me.
I will not be afraid of death and bane,
60 Till Birnam forest come to Dunsinane.
   Doctor. [*Aside.*] Were I from Dunsinane away and clear,
Profit again should hardly draw me here.   [*Exeunt.*

58. BRING IT AFTER ME—This probably refers to the armor which had been pulled off.
59. BANE—Ruin, destruction.

SCENE 4.   *Country near Birnam wood.*

Drum and colours.   Enter MALCOLM, *old* SIWARD *and his* Son,
MACDUFF, MENTEITH, CAITHNESS, ANGUS, LENNOX, ROSS,
and Soldiers, *marching.*

Malcolm.   Cousins, I hope the days are near at hand
That chambers will be safe.
   Menteith.   We doubt it nothing.
Siward.   What wood is this before us?
   Menteith.   The wood of Birnam.
Malcolm.   Let every soldier hew him down a bough,
5 And bear 't before him: thereby shall we shadow
The numbers of our host, and make discovery
Err in report of us.
   Soldiers.   It shall be done.
Siward.   We learn no other but the confident tyrant
Keeps still in Dunsinane, and will endure
10 Our sitting down before 't.
   Malcolm.   'Tis his main hope:
For, where there is advantage to be given,
Both more and less have given him the revolt,

2. CHAMBERS WILL BE SAFE—The allusion is probably to the chamber in which Duncan was murdered.
5. SHADOW—Conceal.
6–7. MAKE DISCOVERY ERR IN REPORT OF US—Make watchers or scouts (discovery) unable to report accurately of our number.
10. SITTING DOWN BEFORE 'T—Besieging it.
11. ADVANTAGE TO BE GIVEN—The sense is: Whenever there has been favorable opportunity.
12. MORE AND LESS—Great and small.

437

And none serve with him but constrained things,
Whose hearts are absent too.

Macduff.   Let our just censures
15 Attend the true event, and put we on
Industrious soldiership.

Siward.   The time approaches
That will with due decision make us know
What we shall say we have and what we owe.
Thoughts speculative their unsure hopes relate,
20 But certain issue strokes must arbitrate;
Towards which, advance the war.   [*Exeunt, marching.*

13. CONSTRAINED THINGS—Creatures who are forced to.
14–15. LET OUR JUST CENSURES ATTEND THE TRUE EVENT—Let our final judgment await the actual outcome.
18. WHAT WE SHALL SAY WE HAVE AND WHAT WE OWE—Time will show us how our account stands.
19–20. THOUGHTS SPECULATIVE . . . MUST ARBITRATE—Speculating about the outcome of an issue is only to give expression to hopes—which are not decisive. Fighting alone will yield a decisive result.

SCENE 5. *Dunsinane. Within the castle.*

Enter MACBETH, SEYTON, *and* Soldiers, *with drum and colours.*

Macbeth. Hang out our banners on the outward walls;
The cry is still, "They come." Our castle's strength
Will laugh a siege to scorn; here let them lie
Till famine and the ague eat them up.
5 Were they not forc'd with those that should be ours,
We might have met them dareful, beard to beard,
And beat them backward home.   [*A cry of women within.*
                              What is that noise?

Seyton. It is the cry of women, my good lord.   [*Exit.*

Macbeth. I have almost forgot the taste of fears:
10 The time has been, my senses would have cool'd
To hear a night-shriek, and my fell of hair
Would at a dismal treatise rouse and stir
As life were in 't: I have supp'd full with horrors;
Direness, familiar to my slaughterous thoughts,
15 Cannot once start me.

5. FORC'D—Reënforced.
11. FELL OF HAIR—"Fell" means skin of an animal. Hence, "fell of hair" here means scalp.
12. TREATISE—Story.

Re-enter SEYTON.

Wherefore was that cry?
Seyton. The queen, my lord, is dead.
Macbeth. She should have died hereafter;
There would have been a time for such a word.
To-morrow, and to-morrow, and to-morrow,
20 Creeps in this petty pace from day to day,
To the last syllable of recorded time;
And all our yesterdays have lighted fools
The way to dusty death. Out, out, brief candle!
Life's but a walking shadow; a poor player
25 That struts and frets his hour upon the stage
And then is heard no more. It is a tale
Told by an idiot, full of sound and fury,
Signifying nothing.

Enter a Messenger.

Thou com'st to use thy tongue; thy story quickly.
30 *Messenger.* Gracious my lord,
I should report that which I say I saw,
But know not how to do 't.
Macbeth.   Well, say, sir.
Messenger. As I did stand my watch upon the hill,
I look'd toward Birnam, and anon, methought,
35 The wood began to move.
Macbeth.   Liar and slave!
Messenger. Let me endure your wrath, if 't be not so:
Within this three mile may you see it coming;
I say, a moving grove.
Macbeth.   If thou speak'st false,
Upon the next tree shalt thou hang alive,
40 Till famine cling thee: if thy speech be sooth,
I care not if thou dost for me as much.

---

17. SHE SHOULD HAVE DIED HEREAFTER—Had she not died now, she would
have died hereafter.
18. THERE WOULD HAVE BEEN A TIME FOR SUCH A WORD—And there would
have come a time when I should have had to hear of it. Why not now?
40. CLING—Wither. 40. BE SOOTH—Be the truth.

I pull in resolution, and begin
To doubt th' equivocation of the fiend
That lies like truth: "Fear not, till Birnam wood
45 Do come to Dunsinane"; and now a wood
Comes toward Dunsinane. Arm, arm, and out!
If this which he avouches does appear,
There is nor flying hence nor tarrying here.
I 'gin to be a-weary of the sun,
50 And wish th' estate o' the world were now undone.
Ring the alarum-bell! Blow, wind! come, wrack!
At least we'll die with harness on our back.   [*Exeunt.*

42. I PULL IN RESOLUTION—I am no longer so certain of the outcome.
43. EQUIVOCATION—Deceit through double meaning.
47. HE AVOUCHES—The messenger assures me of.
50. TH' ESTATE O' THE WORLD WERE NOW UNDONE—The whole world might
fall into destruction.
51. WRACK—Ruin.
52. HARNESS—Armor.

SCENE 6. *Dunsinane. Before the castle.*

Drum and colours. Enter MALCOLM, *old* SIWARD, MACDUFF, *and
their* Army, *with boughs.*

Malcolm. Now near enough; your leavy screens throw down,
And show like those you are. You, worthy uncle,
Shall, with my cousin, your right noble son,
Lead our first battle: worthy Macduff and we
5 Shall take upon 's what else remains to do,
According to our order.
Siward.   Fare you well.
Do we but find the tyrant's power to-night,
Let us be beaten, if we cannot fight.
Macduff. Make all our trumpets speak; give them all breath,
10 Those clamorous harbingers of blood and death.   [*Exeunt.*
                              [*Alarums continued.*

2. SHOW LIKE THOSE YOU ARE—Appear in your own likenesses without
your camouflage.
4. FIRST BATTLE—Vanguard, division of an army.
6. OUR ORDER—The order of battle decided upon beforehand.
10. HARBINGERS—Forerunners, because blown to give the signal to begin the
battle.

SCENE 7. *Another part of the field.*

Enter MACBETH.

Macbeth. They have tied me to a stake; I cannot fly,
But, bear-like, I must fight the course. What's he
That was not born of woman? Such a one
Am I to fear, or none.

Enter young SIWARD.

5   *Young Siward.* What is thy name?
Macbeth.   Thou 'lt be afraid to hear it.
Young Siward. No; though thou call'st thyself a hotter name
Than any is in hell.
Macbeth.   My name's Macbeth.
Young Siward. The devil himself could not pronounce a title
More hateful to mine ear.
Macbeth.   No, nor more fearful.
10   *Young Siward.* Thou liest, abhorred tyrant; with my
    sword
I'll prove the lie thou speak'st.
                 [*They fight, and young* SIWARD *is slain.*
Macbeth.   Thou wast born of woman.
But swords I smile at, weapons laugh to scorn,
Brandish'd by man that's of a woman born.   [*Exit.*

Alarums. Enter MACDUFF.

Macduff. That way the noise is. Tyrant, show thy face!
15 If thou be'st slain, and with no stroke of mine,
My wife and children's ghosts will haunt me still.
I cannot strike at wretched kerns, whose arms
Are hir'd to bear their staves: either thou, Macbeth,
Or else my sword, with an unbatter'd edge,
20 I sheathe again undeeded. There thou shouldst be;

    1. TIED ME TO A STAKE—Macbeth compares himself to the bear in the
popular Elizabethan sport of bear-baiting. The bear was tethered to a stake
at the end of a rope about fifteen feet long. Relays of dogs were set on him.
The "sport" consisted in watching the ensuing battle.
    9. FEARFUL—To be feared.
    17. KERNS—Light-armed foot soldiers.
    20. UNDEEDED—Unused.
    20. THERE—Where the noise is—the noise Macduff notes in the first line of
his speech.

441

By this great clatter, one of greatest note
Seems bruited. Let me find him, fortune!
And more I beg not.   [*Exit. Alarums.*

Enter MALCOLM *and old* SIWARD.

Siward. This way, my lord. The castle's gently render'd.
25 The tyrant's people on both sides do fight;
The noble thanes do bravely in the war;
The day almost itself professes yours,
And little is to do.
Malcolm.   We have met with foes
That strike beside us.
Siward.   Enter, sir, the castle. [*Exeunt. Alarums.*

22. SEEMS BRUITED—Seems to be indicated.
24. GENTLY RENDER'D—Surrendered without much resistance.
25. ON BOTH SIDES—Many have come over to Malcolm.
29. STRIKE BESIDE—Strike aside, that is, do not try to hit us. The sense is:
They do not oppose us.

SCENE 8. *Another part of the field.*

Enter MACBETH.

Macbeth. Why should I play the Roman fool, and die
On mine own sword? whiles I see lives, the gashes
Do better upon them.

Enter MACDUFF.

Macduff.   Turn, hell-hound, turn!
Macbeth. Of all men else I have avoided thee:
5 But get thee back; my soul is too much charg'd
With blood of thine already.
Macduff.   I have no words,
My voice is in my sword; thou bloodier villain
Than terms can give thee out!   [*They fight.*
Macbeth.   Thou losest labour:
As easy mayst thou the intrenchant air

1. PLAY THE ROMAN FOOL—Kill myself, as Brutus and Cassius do in
Shakespeare's *Julius Cæsar.*
2. LIVES—Living foes.
8. THAN TERMS CAN GIVE THEE OUT—Than can be described in words.
8. THOU LOSEST LABOUR—Your efforts to kill me will be useless.
9. INTRENCHANT—The "un-cuttable," that is, in the sense that it cannot
be cut apart as a material thing can.

10 With thy keen sword impress as make me bleed:
Let fall thy blade on vulnerable crests;
I bear a charmed life, which must not yield
To one of woman born.
    Macduff.   Despair thy charm;
And let the angel whom thou still hast serv'd
15 Tell thee, Macduff was from his mother's womb
Untimely ripp'd.
    Macbeth. Accursed be that tongue that tells me so,
For it hath cow'd my better part of man!
And be these juggling fiends no more believ'd,
20 That palter with us in a double sense;
That keep the word of promise to our ear,
And break it to our hope. I'll not fight with thee.
    Macduff. Then yield thee, coward,
And live to be the show and gaze o' the time:
25 We'll have thee, as our rarer monsters are,
Painted upon a pole, and underwrit,
"Here may you see the tyrant."
    Macbeth.   I will not yield,
To kiss the ground before young Malcolm's feet,
And to be baited with the rabble's curse.
30 Though Birnam wood be come to Dunsinane,
And thou oppos'd, being of no woman born,
Yet I will try the last: before my body
I throw my warlike shield: lay on, Macduff;
And damn'd be him that first cries, "Hold, enough!"
                    [*Exeunt fighting. Alarums.*

12. MUST NOT YIELD—Does not have to yield.
13. DESPAIR—Put no trust or hope of safety in.
14. ANGEL—Demon, spirit.
15–16. MACDUFF . . . RIPP'D—That is, Macduff was not "born" in the ordinary sense of a natural birth. Such an exception had never occurred to Macbeth who had interpreted the witches' prophecy to mean that he need fear no man whatever.
18. COW'D MY BETTER PART OF MAN—Filled my whole being with fear.
19. JUGGLING—Deceiving.
20. PALTER—Equivocate.
21–22. THAT KEEP . . . OUR HOPE—That tell us what sounds all right but does not turn out as they lead us to hope.
26. PAINTED UPON A POLE—Macduff says: "Yield and be put on exhibition in a cage over which suspended from a pole will be a painted cloth bearing 'Here you may see the tyrant.' "
32. TRY THE LAST—Try the last resort.

Retreat.   Flourish.   Enter with drum and colours, MALCOLM,
   old SIWARD, ROSS, *the other* Thanes, *and* Soldiers.

35   *Malcolm.*   I would the friends we miss were safe arriv'd.
   Siward.   Some must go off; and yet, by these I see,
So great a day as this is cheaply bought.
   Malcolm.   Macduff is missing, and your noble son.
   Ross.   Your son, my lord, has paid a soldier's debt:
40 He only liv'd but till he was a man;
The which no sooner had his prowess confirm'd
In the unshrinking station where he fought,
But like a man he died.
   Siward.   Then he is dead?
   Ross.   Ay, and brought off the field: your cause of sorrow
45 Must not be measur'd by his worth, for then
It hath no end.
   Siward.   Had he his hurts before?
   Ross.   Ay, on the front.
   Siward.   Why then, God's soldier be he!
Had I as many sons as I have hairs,
I would not wish them to a fairer death:
50 And so his knell is knoll'd.
   Malcolm.   He's worth more sorrow,
And that I'll spend for him.
   Siward.   He's worth no more:
They say he parted well, and paid his score;
And so God be with him!   Here comes newer comfort.

Re-enter MACDUFF, *with* MACBETH's *head.*

Macduff.   Hail, king! for so thou art: behold, where
      stands

36. GO OFF—Die.
36. BY THESE I SEE—Those killed, who were evidently few.
41. HIS PROWESS CONFIRM'D—His prowess confirmed the fact that he had reached manhood.
42. IN THE UNSHRINKING STATION—Without shrinking from the place where he fought.
46. BEFORE—On the front.
52. PARTED—Departed.
With MACBETH's *head*—According to Holinshed, Macduff after "cutting his head from his shoulders, he set it upon a pole."
54. STANDS—The head is on the end of a pike or shaft.

55 Th' usurper's cursed head. The time is free.
   I see thee compass'd with thy kingdom's pearl,
   That speaks my salutation in their minds;
   Whose voices I desire aloud with mine:
   Hail, King of Scotland!
       All.   Hail, King of Scotland! [*Flourish.*
60   *Malcolm.* We shall not spend a large expense of time
   Before we reckon with your several loves,
   And make us even with you. My thanes and kinsmen,
   Henceforth be earls, the first that ever Scotland
   In such an honour nam'd. What's more to do,
65 Which would be planted newly with the time,
   As calling home our exil'd friends abroad
   That fled the snares of watchful tyranny;
   Producing forth the cruel ministers
   Of this dead butcher and his fiend-like queen,
70 Who, as 'tis thought, by self and violent hands
   Took off her life; this, and what needful else
   That calls upon us, by the grace of Grace,
   We will perform in measure, time, and place:
   So, thanks to all at once and to each one,
75 Whom we invite to see us crown'd at Scone.

                              [*Flourish. Exeunt.*

   55. TIME—Age, the world.
   56. COMPASS'D WITH THY KINGDOM'S PEARL—Surrounded by thy kingdom's
   pearls, that is, the thanes, who encircle him as the pearls in a crown encircle
   the head of a king.
   57. THAT SPEAK MY SALUTATION IN THEIR MINDS—Who already regard you,
   as I shall salute you, that is, as king of Scotland.
   61. RECKON WITH YOUR SEVERAL LOVES—Cast up the account of each of you
   who has been a friend (in order to see what will make us even with you).
   64-65. WHAT'S MORE TO DO, WHICH WOULD BE PLANTED NEWLY WITH THE
   TIME—The other things that remain to be done under the new order.
   68. PRODUCING FORTH THE CRUEL MINISTERS—Bringing to justice the agents
   employed by Macbeth to do his murders.

                         FOR INTERPRETATION

                                ACT I

SCENE I:
   If you were producing this scene, how would you set the stage to create
a "desert place"? Should the stage be well lighted? Should the witches
be distinctly seen by the audience? How would you have them attired?

How should they speak? What action would you suggest to accompany their dialogue? What would be the most important line? Why?

SCENE 2:

The Gentleman's Magazine for March, 1889, gives the following description of the stage setting for Scene 2 used by Charles J. Kean at the Princess Theater, London: "The scene was discovered in night and silence; a couple of semi-savage armed kerns were on guard, prowling to and fro with stealthy steps. A distant trumpet call was heard, another in reply, another, and yet another; a roll of the drum—an alarum. In an instant the whole camp was alive with kerns and gallowglasses, who circled around the old king and the princes. . . . The Bleeding Sergeant was carried in upon a litter, and the scene was illuminated with the ruddy glare of burning pine knots." Do you call this a good setting? Discuss. Enumerate the important items of information gathered from Scene 2. What do you learn from it as to Malcolm's ability as a soldier? What does Duncan's closing speech tell you? What inferences as to the character of Macbeth can you draw from this scene? Is Macbeth a better soldier than Malcolm? How can you tell? Is there any evidence that Macbeth is a more able man than Duncan?

SCENE 3:

What stage setting would you suggest for this scene? What do the stage directions call for? To what does Macbeth refer in his opening remark: "So foul . . . a day I have not seen"? What action on the part of the witches is called for before the entrance of Macbeth? Find lines which tell. What does the scene tell you of the appearance of the witches? How would you have Macbeth differ from Banquo in manner and bearing? Find lines which indicate how the part of Macbeth should be acted, especially after meeting with the witches. What information does the scene give? Enumerate important items. What do the witches promise Macbeth? Banquo? Are you more interested in the events or in the characters? Does one character seem more important than the other? Discuss.

What is the effect of the prophecy upon Macbeth? Is he afraid of the witches? What is his manner toward them? In what tone does he speak to them? Whose questions, those of Banquo or Macbeth, seem the more like disinterested inquiries prompted by natural curiosity? Which seems the more interested in the prophecies? What is the effect upon Macbeth of the announcement that he has been made thane of Cawdor? Banquo states wisely one of the ill effects of fortune-telling. Quote his lines on the subject. Does Macbeth feel, as Banquo does, that the witches are evil? Does he feel that they are good? Find lines which tell. Which man seems to have the stronger moral character? What evidence is there that Macbeth has an active imagination? What is the "horrid image" that "doth unfix my hair"? What is the effect of this "horrid image"

upon him? Why doesn't the same "horrid image" trouble Banquo? Can
Macbeth put evil aside? What does he mean by saying, "Come what
come may, time and the hour runs through the longest day"? Does Macbeth practice any deception in this scene? Do you think Macbeth has
been turning over in his mind possible means whereby he might attain
the throne before the meeting with the witches? Do you think the witches
originate evil ambition in Macbeth or is it there when he meets them?
Discuss.

What characteristics does Banquo have in common with Macbeth?
How does he differ from Macbeth? Which do you like the better, Macbeth or Banquo? Can you tell why? Which seems to have the warmer
human sympathy?

SCENE 4:

Suggest a setting for this scene. What persons other than those mentioned would be on the stage? What "stage business" would you suggest
for the scene? Is Duncan seated or standing? What action accompanies
Duncan's speech to Banquo? Compare Macbeth's bearing and manner
with Banquo's. What distinction would you make between them? Which
is the more natural? Which is the more reserved and formal? How
would you have Macbeth act at hearing Duncan announce that he intended Malcolm to succeed him?

Of the three, Macbeth, Duncan, and Banquo, which seems the most
able man and the one best fitted to be king? Why? What are the differences between Duncan's estimate of Macbeth and your own? Is Duncan a good judge of men? Which man, Banquo or Macbeth, seems to
possess the more likable personality? Why doesn't Duncan embrace
Macbeth as he does Banquo? Read the speeches of Macbeth to Duncan.
Do they seem sincere? Are they over-drawn? How do you explain
Macbeth's eagerness to bear word of Duncan's coming to Lady Macbeth?
Does Macbeth wish the death of Duncan? Has he fully resolved to kill
him? If not, what holds him back—is it conscience or "horrible imaginings"? or lack of favorable opportunity? Do you think Macbeth will go
through with it if any one discourages him?

SCENE 5:

The scene is laid in Macbeth's castle—possibly in the great hall whose
walls of heavy masonry are hung with thick tapestries or adorned with
trophies of the hunt and of battle. It is a somewhat somber and rather
cheerless place. In the foreground there is perhaps a massive table to
which Lady Macbeth comes as she reads the letter. But our interest is
not so much in the setting as in the characters. This is a famous scene.
It has called forth the best efforts of some of the greatest Shakespearean
actresses. The part of Lady Macbeth is difficult to do, and easy to overdo.
To get the most from the scene one must try to see the characters and
hear them as they speak.

Lady Macbeth enters reading the letter. Her face, her manner, and her voice betray her excitement. Her words are charged with emotion. What is her facial expression? the expression in her eyes? What emotions play over her face? In what tone of voice does she speak? How does her voice change as she goes on in her speech? Note particularly her reply to the messenger: "Thou art mad to say it." Is this a usual reply? How is the line spoken? What is Lady Macbeth's manner in her next speech? What state of mind does it indicate? Contrast the manner of Macbeth with that of Lady Macbeth. Which is the more intense? What is Macbeth's manner and tone in the speech: "Tomorrow, as he purposes"? What is his manner when he speaks: "We will speak further"? Does he act eager? in full accord with his wife?

Do you infer from this scene that Macbeth and Lady Macbeth have talked of Macbeth's ambition to be king? Do you think that they have ever spoken of the murder of Duncan?

Read carefully Lady Macbeth's characterization of her husband. Does she thoroughly understand him? Is it the "milk of human kindness" which holds him back from catching "the nearest way"? Is he without the "illness," or unscrupulousness, which should attend ambition? Is it true that he "wouldst wrongly win"? Does her characterization of him seem true or only partly accurate? How do you account for Macbeth's reserve in this scene? Has he fully resolved to murder Duncan? If not, what holds him back? What is your opinion of Lady Macbeth? Is she a "fiend-like" woman? Do you think she has a conscience? Has she more or less conscience than Macbeth? Read the following comment on Lady Macbeth by Stopford Brooke (*On Ten Plays of Shakespeare*). She "was not by nature a bad woman, but a woman who became bad by long cherishing an ambition for the crown. This desire was made much stronger by that which was good in her—by her love for her husband. From the time she receives Macbeth's letter, she is the victim of one of those unbridled impulses whose outburst is the result of inward thoughts and passions directed to one end, increasing during years of silence, and at last reaching the highest point of expression. . . . Such an impulse arises quickly into action, and is quickly exhausted. It came on Lady Macbeth in a moment—on the reception of Macbeth's letter. That voiced the possibility of the hopes being realized over which she had brooded so long, and the wild image of the reality seized on her brain. Then comes the news that Duncan is coming to spend the night, and the fury of her impulse falls upon her. She sees, hears, feels nothing but the death of the king. When Macbeth enters, the impulse is doubled by her love for him, by her consciousness that in his thought he is at one with her."

What is your opinion of this estimate of Lady Macbeth? Does it seem to you consistent with the facts of the scene? Would this "impulse" be strong enough to overcome conscience? Is it true that where a person has for a long time cherished the desire for something that a

sudden and unexpected opportunity to obtain the thing may lead to immediate action and cause other considerations to be forgotten for the
time? Is such action in accord with the "laws of human nature"? Is
Lady Macbeth acting contrary to what you would expect in a woman?
Why and how? What characteristics do Macbeth and Lady Macbeth have
in common? How do they differ?

SCENE 6:

Where does this scene take place? What time of day is it? What do
the stage directions call for? What "stage business" would you suggest
for the scene? How does the manner of Lady Macbeth here differ from
her manner in the last scene? What action does Duncan's closing speech
call for?

How does Lady Macbeth act her part? Do you think Macbeth would
have acted the part as well? Why or why not? What words of Duncan
and Banquo indicate that each has an eye for beauty? Has Macbeth
disclosed any such characteristic? What seem to be his special interests?

SCENE 7:

This is another great scene. Macbeth has left the banquet table. Now
that the meek and gentle Duncan sits at his board, he is unsettled by the
prospect of the assassination. He leaves his guests; he must be alone to
think, to turn the matter over in his mind. He cannot let the idea of
killing Duncan alone, yet he cannot bring himself to it. He has almost decided against it when Lady Macbeth enters. What does Macbeth do while
he is thinking aloud in the opening soliloquy? What is Lady Macbeth's
manner when she enters? How does Macbeth voice his objections? Is his
manner firm and determined? Which shows the greater intensity, Macbeth or Lady Macbeth? How does Lady Macbeth speak the words, "We
fail"? How does Macbeth's manner change during the closing speeches?

Read the speeches of Macbeth carefully. What reasons does he find
against the killing of Duncan? Does he anywhere say that it is morally
wrong to do so? What does he seem to fear most? Does he speak like
a man who has a strong moral sense, or strong conscience? Do you get
the impression that at the bottom it is the moral aspect of the assassination which troubles him? What inference as to Macbeth's character do
you draw from his ready acquiescence after Lady Macbeth points out that
the guilt may be put upon Duncan's chamberlains? Is Lady Macbeth
her natural self in this scene? Does it prove her a cold-blooded fiend?
Is she without conscience? How do you account for her actions? In
what state of mind is she? What is the effect of Macbeth's lukewarmness
on her?

Read again Lady Macbeth's characterization of Macbeth at the opening
of Scene 5. To what extent does Macbeth's manner here bear out her
estimate of him? What evidences does the scene give of Lady Macbeth's force of will? Is there any evidence that Macbeth has a high

admiration of Lady Macbeth's spirit? What difference in attitude toward the murder of Duncan do you note in Macbeth and Lady Macbeth?

ACT II

SCENE I:

Capell's idea of the setting intended is as follows: "A large court, surrounded all or in part by an open gallery; chambers opening into that gallery; the gallery ascended into by stairs, open likewise; with addition of a college-like gateway, into which opens a porter's lodge." What lighting effects are called for? What part in this scene calls for great acting?

What effect is created by the moonless, starless night? by Banquo's uneasiness? by the reference to Duncan's measureless content? by the mention of the weird sisters? by the reference to the signal bell? by the airdrawn dagger smeared with "gouts of blood"? by Macbeth's description of the night? by the ringing of the bell? by the closing lines of Macbeth's speech?

What contrast between Banquo and Macbeth does the scene present? Do you think that the prophecy of the witches has begun to "work" on Banquo? What instance is there in this scene of Macbeth's imagination? Do you get the impression that Macbeth is forcing himself to do the murder? Or is he eager to get Duncan out of the way? Why does Macbeth's imagination trouble him?

SCENE 2:

Where is Lady Macbeth? In what attitude is she? Where is Macbeth? Can any noise be heard from the chambers? What lighting effect is called for? Where is Macbeth when he calls "Who's there? What, ho!" In what tone of voice does he call? Why does Lady Macbeth exclaim, "My husband!"? In what tones do they speak?

What contrasts do Macbeth and Lady Macbeth present in this scene? Which has the firmer self-control? the more active imagination? Is there any evidence that it is the moral hideousness of the deed which troubles Macbeth? What is Lady Macbeth's attitude toward the murder? Is Lady Macbeth without conscience, or has she suppressed her scruples by sheer force of will? Why cannot Macbeth take the same attitude toward the crime that Lady Macbeth does? What evidence is there in this scene that Lady Macbeth's love for her husband and her desire to see him have his ambition are at the bottom of her action? Is there anything in the scene to indicate that Lady Macbeth is not without tenderness in her nature? Is Macbeth a coward? Is he "infirm of purpose"?

SCENE 3:

This scene presents a sudden and somewhat startling contrast. While the agonized cry of Macbeth, "Wake Duncan with thy knocking! I wouldst thou couldst!" yet lingers in our ears, the drunken porter stum-

451

bles from his lodge and goes with wavering gait to answer the knocking. As he fumbles at the chains and bolts, he pretends in his befuddled fancy to be porter at the gate of hell!

How do Macbeth and Lady Macbeth carry off their parts in this situation? What is the effect of Macbeth's announcement that he has killed the grooms? Does it surprise you? Why or why not? What is the effect of Macbeth's extravagant language? Does he talk too much?

Speaking of Lady Macbeth and Macbeth after the murder, Stopford Brooke says, "The next day their ideas are entirely changed. Macbeth, having exhausted all his objections, all his fears, and having irreparably committed his murder is absolutely changed from the trembling, reasoning, white-hearted personage of the murder scene. He is cool, determined, quick in action, ruthless. He sticks at nothing—the murder of the grooms. . . . As great a change comes upon Lady Macbeth. The storm of impulse is over. She has slept it away, or it has died in the silent sleeplessness of that dreadful dawn which brought her down to face the terror-stricken crowd and to faint away. She has awakened to the horror of what she has done; and she returns to her natural self—as she was, before the temptation she had cherished rose into fierce action, and transported her beyond herself." Do you agree with this comment? Does it seem to be borne out by the facts of the scene? Is Lady Macbeth's swoon real or pretended? If it is real, how do you account for it? How does Macbeth's manner here compare with his manner in the preceding scene? What term does Macduff apply to Lady Macbeth in this scene? Read carefully the speech of Macbeth beginning, "Had I but died an hour before this chance." Is this speech such a one as you would expect from Macbeth? Does it excite your sympathy for him? Is it sincere? Why might Macbeth feel thus?

SCENE 4:

Just where outside the castle is this scene laid? What sort of setting would you suggest? Enumerate the pieces of definite information given in the scene. Attention is focused on which character? Do you think any one as yet suspects Macbeth? How do you think Macduff should read his lines here? Discuss.

ACT III

SCENE 1:

Suggest a setting and "stage business" for this scene. What tells us that Banquo has begun to suspect Macbeth? What contrast is there between the action of Macbeth before the murder of Duncan and his action here as he questions Banquo to find out the latter's plans? Does Macbeth see any "air-drawn" dagger here? What conclusion do you draw from his matter-of-factness?. What troubles Macbeth now that he is king? Find lines which tell.

What characteristics of Banquo does Macbeth enumerate? Do you think Macbeth has any special reason to fear Banquo? What other motive than fear prompts his next murder? Do you think his arguments with the murderers were needed to persuade them to kill Banquo? Why does he talk so long to them? Is Macbeth the same man he was at the beginning of the play?

SCENE 2:

Where is this scene laid? Why do you think Lady Macbeth inquires about Banquo? Why does she wish to speak with Macbeth? Is there any evidence that she dislikes being alone? What does the scene tell you of the relationship between the two? Does Macbeth now need her to spur him on? Does she seem to possess the energy and vigor which she did in Act I? Does she seem remorseful? repentant? What does Macbeth mean by saying, "Full of scorpions is my mind"? What troubles Macbeth's peace? Does Macbeth show any sign of repentance? regret? Is he hesitating and indecisive now? What shows that Lady Macbeth is still ready to plot murder? Do you think she knows of Macbeth's plans for Banquo? Why does he not tell her? Are Macbeth and Lady Macbeth really fond of each other?

SCENE 3:

Where is the scene laid? What lighting effect does it call for? What effect should the setting aim to produce? Where is Banquo when he first speaks? How has Macbeth's plan failed? It has been suggested that Macbeth is the Third Murderer. What arguments can you find for and against this contention?

SCENE 4:

Describe a setting for the scene. What in the scene would make it spectacular? Where is Lady Macbeth seated? Why does Macbeth "mingle with society"? What is his manner? Does he speak as though he had something on his mind? Describe his movements. What action accompanies Macbeth's words, "See, they encounter thee with their hearts' thanks"? Can the audience see the murderer? Does the audience see any ghost in this scene? What information with respect to Macduff does the scene give?

Does the sight of Banquo's blood affect Macbeth as did the sight of Duncan's? Why or why not? Do you feel any pity for Macbeth here? What causes Macbeth's "fit" to come on him again? What does he mean by "my fit"? How does his language to the murderer beginning "Then comes my fit again" differ from his previous speeches? Do you think things would have been "perfect" for him if Fleance had been killed? Why or why not? What change evidently comes over Macbeth's mood? Compare actions of Macbeth and Lady Macbeth. Does Lady Macbeth remain mistress of the situation? Of what other occasions does this remind you? Is Macbeth a coward? How does he describe his predicament? Quote the lines. What does he plan to do next?

SCENE 5:

How has the preceding scene prepared us for Scene 5? What information important to the plot does the scene provide? With what words is the downfall of Macbeth predicted? By what means will it come about?

SCENE 6:

What is the tone of the speech with which Lennox opens the scene? What important pieces of information does the scene give? It centers interest on what character? How does it affect your attitude toward Macbeth? What hint does it give as to the outcome of the play?

ACT IV

SCENE 1:

Macready, a famous actor, suggested the following opening: "Let the witches be placed in different parts of the cavern. Suppose one at the mouth, intently on the watch; another near the cauldron, cowering over the livid flame . . . the third witch on the side opposite the entrance, seated perhaps on a fragment of stone, her arms folded, and rocking to and fro upon the rock, as it were, in impatience. Let not a word be spoken, till the audience have time to study the picture. 'Tis to the point, and they are sure to feel it, if you will allow them. The familiars—the brinded cat, the hedge-pig, and the Harpier—are supposed to be stationed outside the cavern to give notice of the approach of Hecate. The First Witch hears her familiar, 'Thrice the brinded cat hath mew'd.' The eyes of the other witches are instantly turned towards her; a pause ensues during which they all remain motionless. The witch near the cauldron hears her familiar; she starts from her cowering attitude, 'Thrice, and once the hedge-pig whined.' Another pause here. Now at length the Third Witch springs upon her feet, 'Harpier cries'; and then addressing her sisters, ' 'Tis time, 'tis time.' "

What action on the part of the witches follows this opening? What is Macbeth's manner as he enters the cavern? Is he timid or imperious in bearing and speech? With what facial expression do you imagine the witches watched Macbeth? From what spot did the apparitions rise? What new information does the scene present? What fresh interest does it arouse in the fortunes of Macbeth? What is the effect of the announcement that Macduff has fled to England? What does Macbeth decide to do?

Compare Macbeth's attitude toward murder now with his attitude before the murder of Duncan. Why is the killing of Macduff's wife and children worse than the killing of Duncan? What new trait is coming to the front in Macbeth under the assurance of the witches? Is his "security" breeding over-confidence and recklessness?

SCENE 2:

Describe a setting and "stage business" for this scene. What direct

454

characterization of Macduff occurs in the scene? Do you think he was wise to leave his wife and children? What kind of child is Macduff's son? Does the audience like him? What kind of woman was Lady Macduff?

SCENE 3:

What is the significance of the setting of this scene? When did Malcolm last appear in the play? What kind of person does he seem to be? How does he compare in force of character, soldierly ability, general competence to govern, with Macbeth? with Macduff? Does he impress you as a forceful character? Do you think he would be a match for Macbeth in battle? in personal combat? With what suspicions does he regard Macduff at first? Why? What causes him to drop his suspicions? What direct characterization of Macbeth is given in this scene? Do any of the new sins of which he is said to be guilty surprise you? What has been the effect of Macbeth's crimes upon his character? upon his reign? How does Ross break the news to Macduff? What impression of Macduff does the scene give you? Do you believe that fear for his own life led him to flee from Scotland, leaving his wife and children? Why does Malcolm talk of revenge when he hears of the murder of Macduff's wife and children? Why doesn't Macduff talk as Malcolm does? Are Macduff's actions true to life?

ACT V

SCENE 1:

What is the manner of the Doctor and the Gentlewoman? In what tones do they talk? What is Lady Macbeth's manner? What actions accompany her various speeches? What change has taken place in her face? Does Lady Macbeth speak in the same confident, forceful manner which characterized her speeches in Acts I and II? Stopford Brooke says, "She [Lady Macbeth] has awakened to the horror of what she has done . . . Her conscience awakes—'What's done cannot be undone.' It is only the awakened conscience which dwells in the irreparable past. Macbeth does not. He seeks only to secure the future. She lives in the ghastliness of the past." Does this strike you as an accurate explanation of what has gone on in Lady Macbeth?

This is the last scene in which Lady Macbeth appears. What is the final impression it leaves with the audience? Is one inclined to pity the Queen? to gloat over her unhappiness? to loathe her? Do you think the scene would have any deeper significance if Lady Macbeth were awake instead of asleep?

SCENE 2:

Describe a setting and "stage business" for this scene. What important information do you learn from the scene? How? What does it tell you of Macbeth's actions? of his fortunes? Who has remained loyal to him? How large a force is opposed against him?

SCENE 3:

Is Macbeth's manner agitated or calm and self-possessed? How does the pale face of the servant affect him? When did you last see Macbeth and Lady Macbeth together? What is his attitude toward her present state? What feelings now animate Macbeth? In what famous words does Macbeth express the thought that "crime does not pay"? Quote the lines. Why do you think he continues to fight? Has he lost any of his physical courage? of his vigor and energy? Why must he keep doing something? Have you any pity for him? Has your attitude toward either Macbeth or Lady Macbeth changed since the first act? What are the "thick-coming fancies" which trouble Lady Macbeth? What confidence does Macbeth have in the prophecies?

SCENE 4:

What setting and "stage business" would you suggest for this scene? Would you have the soldiers hew down the boughs on the stage or not? How would you handle this incident? What kind of man does Malcolm seem to be? Discuss.

SCENE 5:

Where is this scene laid? What activity is suggested? What is Macbeth's manner? What cry is heard? What is the manner of Macbeth as he comments on the death of Lady Macbeth? Why is it that the cry of the women does not cool Macbeth's senses? When was the time that his "senses would have cool'd to hear a night-shriek"? What effect has his course had on his feelings? What is his attitude toward the death of Lady Macbeth? Is his description of life true of life in general or only of his life? What is the manner of the messenger who interrupts his thoughts? Why does Macbeth call the messenger "liar and slave"? What is the effect of the announcement on him? Does his mind tell him that his cause is lost? Why does he not commit suicide? or attempt to make his escape? How does he endeavor to keep his spirits up? Does his physical courage remain with him? How can you tell?

SCENE 6:

Why is this scene so short? What are Malcolm and Macduff taking upon themselves to do? Do you want to see a general battle or do you wish to see Macduff meet Macbeth? Why?

SCENE 7:

From Macbeth's speech what do you learn about how the battle is going? How does Macbeth's victory over young Siward heighten your interest in the approaching scene? What climax do you look forward to?

SCENE 8:

Why does Macbeth say to Macduff, "My soul is too much charg'd with blood of thine already"? When he says again, "I will not fight with thee" does he really wish to spare Macduff? Has his bravery left him at the last? Or is there another explanation? Why does he renew the fight? How is the outcome of the fight made known? Why? What further information is given about the queen? What impression does Malcolm make in this last scene? Does the reader feel satisfied with the outcome?

GENERAL QUESTIONS IN INTERPRETATION:

1. The purpose of the play is undoubtedly to present a study of character changes developing in Macbeth and Lady Macbeth under the lash of ambition. Formulate a sentence stating in general terms (that is, not using the name *Macbeth*) just what kind of change has occurred and how it has come about. Could this sentence be considered the statement of the theme of the play? Why or why not?

2. Which character do you think has changed more—that of Macbeth or that of his wife? Discuss.

3. Do you think Macbeth and Lady Macbeth truly loved each other? How do you judge?

4. What elements of good were there in the characters of each? Explain why the presence of both good and bad, weak and strong characteristics increases the power and appeal of the play.

5. Do you think the witches were introduced into the play (*a*) merely for dramatic effect, (*b*) because Elizabethans believed such supernatural powers would lead men to do wrong, (*c*) as symbols of man's own evil nature, or (*d*) for some other reason?

6. Show how the character of Banquo serves to demonstrate the fact that similar circumstances and similar influences will have different effects upon different kinds of people. Was Macbeth's downfall inevitable because of the circumstances that surrounded him? Or was it inevitable because, being the kind of man he was, he reacted to them in a given way? Could Banquo have shared in Macbeth's guilt? Why didn't he? At what point or points could Macbeth have warded off his career of crime?

7. What do you consider the most interesting character portrayed in the play? Why?

8. Make a list of from five to ten memorable passages from the play. Memorize from 25 to 50 lines of your own choosing.

EXTENDED ACTIVITIES

THE CROWNING ACHIEVEMENT OF ELIZABETHAN
LITERATURE WAS THE DRAMA

FOR ACQUAINTANCE WITH AUTHORS

CHRISTOPHER MARLOWE (1564–1593)—"DOCTOR FAUSTUS"

Kit Marlowe, of all the Elizabethans who flung cape over shoulder, was perhaps the most dashing, the most tempestuous, and the most appealing. Born the same year as Shakespeare, he had much of Shakespeare's power, many of his poetic gifts, but none of his stability. Marlowe's early work shows as much promise as Shakespeare's, but Marlowe was dead at twenty-nine, his only bequest to the world four tragedies, full of greatness and littleness. Shakespeare lived to be fifty-two, acclaimed by the king, the author of more than fifty-seven plays, owner of a comfortable house in his old home town—a ripe harvest of early promise.

Marlowe, who was the son of a poor shoemaker, managed to spend some years at Cambridge, absorbing some knowledge and a lot of life. He attached himself to the tawdry fringe of society connected with the theater. He probably began by acting, but later turned to writing for the Earl of Nottingham's companies. His first play, *Tamburlaine,* with an ambition-maddened hero, took the theaters by storm. His second play, *Dr. Faustus,* was equally popular. Its theme of a man sel'ing his soul for the price of *all knowledge* held a strange fascination for grasping, superstitious Elizabethans. His two other plays were *The Jew of Malta,* a drama centered about thirst for wealth, and *Edward II,* an early historical play. Both repeated his earlier successes.

Little is known about Marlowe's life aside from his playwrighting. He may have been a government spy; he probably incurred the disapproval of the Church. He knew Sir Walter Raleigh and probably all of the theatrical crowd. He was stabbed in a poor tavern in a dispute over the bill. His assailant was released from charges of murder on a plea of self defense.

Marlowe's characters lived lives as tempestuous and tragic as their author's. The poet gave the English stage its first genuine tragedy and its first dramatic blank verse. He made his "mighty line" not an exercise in iambics but an instrument of power and drama.

WILLIAM SHAKESPEARE (1564–1616)—"MACBETH"

William Shakespeare, greatest of all the Elizabethans and greatest of all dramatists, grew up in Stratford-on-Avon, a busy little village of fifteen hundred inhabitants. He was born of excellent parentage. His mother was Mary Arden, daughter of a wealthy landowner of Wilmecote, a neighboring village. His father, John Shakespeare, was an honored citizen and officer of the village. Will was a typical Elizabethan boy. He punted on the river, played the sixteenth-century version of cop and robber in the meadows across the Avon, and growled about his lessons. As a youngster he must have stood more than once, mouth gaping, to see the traveling theatrical companies parade over Clopton bridge and up to the marketplace—banners flying, drums beating, costumes gaudy in the breeze, the trumpeters' blasts calling the villagers to the afternoon performance. Perhaps when he was twelve, he saw Queen Elizabeth herself passing through Stratford with her splendid retinue on her "progress" to a nearby nobleman's castle. Until he was eighteen, Shakespeare knew only the little town of Stratford; but it was full of the bustle and color of Elizabethan days.

For its bearing on Shakespeare's education, too much has probably been made of the remark by Ben Jonson that he had "small Latine and less Greek." It is a relative statement, and must be considered in light of the wide acquaintance with the ancient classics which passed for learning in those days. Shakespeare was no university man, it is true; but he certainly had far more schooling than Abraham Lincoln. He must have attended the King's New Grammar School at Stratford, which was a good school, until he was fourteen or fifteen. The course of study was in those days, even in what we call the grades, well ballasted with Latin authors, such as Virgil, Ovid, and Cicero; and the "making of latines" was begun early. For all Jonson's remark, Shakespeare had a better acquaintance with Latin than the average high-school or college graduate of our day, and there is evidence that he read many Latin authors, especially Ovid, with enjoyment.

Moreover, school in those days was heroic business. It usually opened at six o'clock in the morning and held until five in the afternoon. It was believed too "that the best Scholemaster . . . was the greatest beater." It is small wonder that Shakespeare's references to schools are generally uncomplimentary, and that he describes "the whining schoolboy, with his satchel and shining morning face" as "creeping like a snail unwillingly to school." But it was not book learning which made Shakespeare great; it was rather his ability to portray men from first-hand acquaintance with them.

In 1582 Shakespeare married Anne Hathaway, and three children were born to them, Susannah, Hamnet, and Judith. From boyhood Shakespeare had been interested in amateur dramatics and in working with traveling troupes of players that came to Stratford. About 1588 or 1589 he went to London to try his luck at playing. Meager records indicate that he acted in various capacities from stagehand to callboy and eventually as an actor "and did acte exceeding well." Plays which would fill the house were in great demand by the ever-increasing companies of professional actors, just as scenarios which will draw the crowd are in demand in our day. Here again Shakespeare was evidently quick to sense opportunity, and he set himself to supplying the need. The first company of players with whom he became associated was the Earl of Pembroke's Men, and for this company he wrote his earlier plays, most of which are revisions or adaptions of older plays which had long been favorites with the public.

In 1592 and 1593 outbreaks of the plague caused the closing of the theaters in London. Pembroke's Men went on a tour in the country, but meeting with no success, they returned to the city, sold their stock of plays and disbanded. From the time the company went on tour until 1594, Shakespeare was apparently connected with no theater or troupe. During this period he turned to writing poetry with the purpose possibly of establishing a reputation as a literary man. It should be remembered that in his time plays were not published for the reading public, nor were they regarded as worthy the name of literature. He now wrote the poems *Venus and Adonis*, and *Lucrece*, and began the *Sonnets*. These poems were well received and raised their author to a place of eminence in the literary world.

In 1594, the famous company of players, The Lord Chamberlain's Men, later known as The King's Men, was organized. It numbered among its members the most able and popular actors of the day, and it is significant of Shakespeare's reputation that he was taken in as full sharer apparently from the outset. With this company Shakespeare was actively associated as actor and as playwright for nearly twenty years. For it he wrote thirty-two of the thirty-seven plays which have come down to us in the *Folio of 1623,* and he had without doubt a hand in the writing and revision of many more.

Of Shakespeare's career as an actor next to nothing is known. Possibly his fame as a playwright quite eclipsed his reputation as an actor, and for that reason, we hear little of his appearance on the boards.

Of Shakespeare's engaging personality and of his uprightness of character there is the testimony of many who knew him. Jonson said, "I lov'd the man and doe honour his memory, on this side Idolatry, as much as any. He was, indeed, honest, and of an open and free nature." He was evidently a most companionable man, open and gracious, without any touch of affectation. Men spoke of him as "good Will." Aubrey wrote, "He was a handsome, well shap't man: very good company, and a very ready and pleasant smooth wit."

Shakespeare's death occurred in April, 1616. He was buried simply in

the church at Stratford. Although he deserved a place in Westminster
Abbey with England's great, his body was never removed there. Tradition has it that local superstition accounts for this, for the inscription
on his tombstone, said to have been written "by himselfe a little before
his death," reads as follows:

GOOD FREND FOR IESVS SAKE FORBEARE,
TO DIGG THE DVST ENCLOASED HEARE:
BLESE BE Y ͤ MAN Y ͭ SPARES HES STONES,
AND CVRST BE HE Y ͭ MOVES MY BONES·

BEN JONSON (1573–1637)

"Literary dictator" of the brilliant circle of dramatists at the court
of James I was the versatile Ben Jonson—poet, actor, dramatist, critic,
and song writer. As prolific a writer as Shakespeare, Jonson wrote more
exclusively for his own time; his elabor-
ate masques, comedies of manners, and
classical tragedies have gone out of
fashion, but in his own lifetime he was
respected as a master. Like Shakespeare
and Marlowe, Jonson early attached himself to the theater. Although born the
son of an educated clergyman, he was
raised by his stepfather, a bricklayer, and
for a time followed that trade. Through
diligent reading and the influence of good
teachers he acquired a much more thorough classical education than Shakespeare
or Marlowe. After a brief period of
military service he began writing for the
theater: comedy, tragedy, history, and
some thirty-seven masques—the pageant
entertainment so popular at court.

Unlike Shakespeare and Marlowe, Jon-
son was convinced that truly great drama must be ordered and stately,
following the rules set down by Greek and Roman critics. He was not
afraid to criticize the extravagance and lack of unity in the English drama
and by the use of satire and ridicule, he set out to improve the manners
and morals of his countrymen. On the accession of James I in 1603 he
was named the first poet laureate. Ben Jonson was highly regarded as a
poet and scholar and exerted a profound influence on the classical writers
of the eighteenth century. In his lyrics he is more the Elizabethan and
less the classical scholar; it is for these that he is still read today.

OF LITERARY FORM AND STYLE

CONCERNING ELIZABETHAN DRAMA

Macbeth is a Tragedy

A tragedy, in the Shakespearean sense at least, is a play in which the chief character, or hero, is defeated in the thing which he wishes to accomplish or gain. There is nothing in this definition to distinguish the true tragedy from the *tragedy of blood,* or from the *melodrama;* yet there is a sure distinction between them. In the tragedy of blood or in the melodrama, the interest of the audience is held by events, sensational in themselves, which thrill, startle, or excite. In the tragedy proper our interest is not so much in the happenings, however startling they may be, as in the significance of the events in the lives of the persons concerned. We find ourselves absorbed in the persons of the drama—watching the effects of their deeds upon their fortunes and upon their souls. Events are not made to happen just for their own sake; they are inextricably bound up with character. The thing which any given person does is inevitable. We are interested not so much in deeds as in the reasons and consequences.

Macbeth is a true tragedy. There are in it, however, incidents of the thriller type. The murder of Banquo and of Macduff's son, and the killing of young Siward take place on the stage. The murder of Duncan, although not done before the audience has its element of horror. Macbeth himself is killed off the stage, but his bleeding head is borne in on a pole by Macduff. There are, moreover, a number of scenes of sound and fury, not to overlook the appearance of the witches and the apparitions—sights which must have been powerfully moving to the superstitious audience. Yet these melodramatic features—however much they pleased the groundlings—are not the things which make the play live. For instance, it is not the killing of Duncan which interests us; it is the behavior of Macbeth and Lady Macbeth—the effect of murder upon two human souls laid bare before us. Pity and terror hold us spellbound while we reflect upon the irrevocable nature of the deed.

Macbeth and Lady Macbeth rise above the action. All of Shakespeare's great characters are persons of unusual qualities. Macbeth and Lady Macbeth are no exceptions. They are not the "deep-dyed" villains of a blood-and-thunder melodrama; nor are they petty cutthroats. There is nothing vulgar or ordinary about either of them; and whatever the emotions with which we witness their crimes, we are not disgusted with them, nor can we view them with contempt. There are blendings of good and bad in both. Part of the conflict of the play concerns which elements will win.

The student should remember, moreover, that *Macbeth* was written to be acted. Drama is more than dialogue. It includes the acting, the stage setting and scenery, lighting effects, and everything that is implied under the head of *stage business*—the roll of thunder, alarums, the tramp of approaching soldiers, the commotion of battle scenes, and the like. All of these elements are synthesized, or united, to produce a single dramatic effect. To get the most from a play, the reader must see and "hear" its performance in his imagination.

Elements of Play Construction

There are certain traditional features of play construction which it is helpful to understand. The most important element is the *plot*, or the planned development of the action. The stages of the plot may be indicated thus:

The *Introduction*—The part which gives the situation out of which the conflict rises, and furnishes the reader or beholder with whatever information he needs in order to understand the play.

The *Rising Action*—The part in which the conflict is developed and increases in intensity and interest with the fortunes of the chief character in ascendance.

The *Turning Point*—The moment when through some fatal error the fortunes of the hero cease to rise.

The *Falling Action*—The part in which the tide of circumstance is flowing against the chief character, and it is apparent that his fortunes are on the decline.

The *Catastrophe*—The definite defeat of the chief character.

The *Conclusion*—The brief conclusion, after the catastrophe, which brings the play to a satisfactory close.

In the organization and management of the incidents of the play, the dramatist endeavors to keep the interest of his audience by so placing incidents that he creates *suspense* and *climax*. A good illustration of suspense is to be seen in the assassination scene (Act II, Scene 2) where the audience is suddenly aroused by Macbeth's "Who's there? What, ho!" to the possibility that "they have awak'd" (Duncan and the grooms). This is followed very quickly by a climax—the appearance of Macbeth, his hands covered with blood whose shaken voice announces, "I have done the deed"; and then the scene goes on to another point of suspense created by the knocking at the gate. The climax in any situation, scene, or act is the point of greatest intensity. It will be noted that within a scene as in this one, there may seem to be a series of climaxes. The so-called climax of the play itself is similarly the point of greatest intensity. It may, but it does not always, coincide with the crisis, or with the turning point. In a five-act drama the turning point and the climax usually appear in the third act.

The *conflict* in a drama, to which allusion has been made, is the struggle between the chief character and the forces opposing him in the achievement of his desires. It is sometimes called the soul of the drama, for it is on this contention that interest centers. There is always an outward, visible conflict between characters or groups of characters; and there is in great drama, as in *Macbeth,* an inward struggle between contending forces in the chief character himself.

In the representation of the conflict, Shakespeare employs a number of methods to produce and to heighten the emotional effect of incidents and scenes. He makes frequent use of *contrast,* alternating exciting incidents and scenes with those which are mild and unexciting. The effect of a mild scene following a tense one is to furnish *relief,* or to let down the tension, and by contrast to make the tense scene more effective. The student will find a number of instances of this device in *Macbeth.* Occasionally relief is accompanied by a humorous touch, as in the incident of the drunken porter, who imagines himself devil-porter at the gate of hell; and no sooner do we set ourselves to laugh than the grim truth of the situation strikes us, making the relief itself reinforce the effect of the preceding scene.

After the crisis and, more especially after the turning point, when interest is likely to lag, there will be found scenes and incidents which stir emotions not touched in the first part of the play, as the scene between Lady Macduff and her son, or again there may be, as in Act V, a succession of battle scenes, with their alarms and commotion—scenes which, to judge from their frequency in Shakespeare's plays, must have had a strong appeal for his audience.

Whatever the effects produced by the management of scenes and incidents, or by acting and stage business, it should be remembered that *Macbeth* is a great piece of literature. This is the reason why a mere reading of the play can move one so powerfully. Although seeing the play or reading it with a knowledge of the theater, increases one's appreciation of it, it is nevertheless true that the great appeal of *Macbeth* is in a large measure independent of these things. The intensity of Lady Macbeth's passion, her fierce energy, and her all-compelling will; or Macbeth quite unmanned by terrors of the mind, these scenes *compel* the imagination of the reader so that he enters spiritually into the situation. Moreover, the lines of the play, instead of being mere instruments to develop the action, do themselves express broad human truths. Passage after passage startles our attention with compelling power or beauty. It is here that the creative genius of Shakespeare is manifest.

ON THE DIFFERENCES BETWEEN SHAKESPEAREAN AND MODERN DRAMA

Although what we may call the fundamental qualities of great drama remain today what they were in Shakespeare's time, the drama, nevertheless, has in the three centuries since his death undergone many changes. The more conspicuous of these changes may be roughly classified into two groups: (1) changes in the subject matter or material of the drama, and (2) changes in the technique or handling of it.

The first set of changes may be said to include those which have resulted from changes in the social order and in life generally during the last three hundred years. If the student will but casually review the plays of Shakespeare which he has read in high school, he will note that they reflect a society very different from ours. He will find, for example, that the chief characters in Shakespeare are persons of high station in life. In no case will he find plays built about what we are accustomed to call ordinary men and women. Modern and contemporary drama deals for the most part with persons from the ordinary walks of life. Probably the chief reason for this difference is to be found in the changes in ideas as to the worth and consequence of the individual, or the common man, which have attended the development of democracy throughout the world in the past three centuries.

With these changes in ideas as to the worth and significance of the individual has come a corresponding increase in interest in his affairs. As a consequence we find the situations or stories used by modern playwrights very different from those used by Shakespeare. The stories which Shakespeare worked into his plays were for the most part stories involving unusual circumstances, if not artificial situations, or they were stories of great actions. Among modern dramatists there is a strong tendency toward what is sometimes called "naturalism." They show a preference for natural situations taken from life itself as we actually live it.

There is also to be observed in modern and contemporary drama a tendency to deal with various social problems, such as divorce and prison reform, and to make the drama in such cases a vehicle for conveying to the audience the ideas or point of view of the author on such matters. Such plays sometimes are interesting because they deal with timely subjects, but they often lack the enduring qualities which make a play live. After interest in the particular problem dealt with has died out, all too frequently is it found that the play has died with it. In the case of Shakespeare, however, it may be said that his plays have lived in spite of the fact that many of the things which interested his audience have no attraction for us. They live for one reason, because human nature can be as truly portrayed in a king as in a commoner; and although modern drama may seem more significant to us because it deals with modern conditions of life, yet no dramatist of our day equals Shakespeare as interpreter of character and of life.

The second set of changes reflected by the modern drama—changes in technique—may be said to be in the main directly or indirectly the result of the development of the theater itself. It will be observed that there was a much closer or a more intimate relationship between player and audience in the Elizabethan theater than there is in the modern playhouse, where the separation of audience from player is complete. The stage which once projected out into the yard, or as we should call it the auditorium, has receded until all that is left is a narrow strip, called the *proscenium,* between footlights and curtain, while the orchestra pit is all that remains of the *yard* or *pit* where once the groundlings stood. In the modern theater, the action all takes place on what corresponds to the *inner stage* of the Elizabethan playhouse.

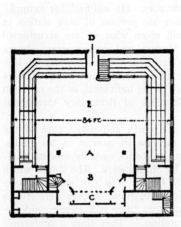

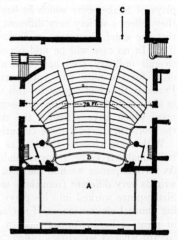

THE FORTUNE THEATER
(London, 1599)

A The Front Stage. *B* The Middle Stage. *C* The Back Stage. *E* The Pit, or Yard. The dotted line shows the curtains which might be drawn to cut off the back stage.

THE EMPIRE THEATER
(New York, 1930)

A The Stage, showing how it has receded. *B* The Proscenium. This is all that is left of what in the *Fortune Theater* is designed by *A* and *B*.

The physical separation of audience from player in our theaters has given rise to a feeling that the *soliloquy* and the *aside,* which are found so frequently in Shakespeare, are "unnatural"—that people do not speak thus in real life and that the dramatist ought not to have his characters address the audience directly. This unnaturalness seems never to have troubled either Shakespeare or his audience. Modern dramatists, as a rule, avoid both *soliloquy* and *aside.* They try in some other way to get to their audiences the necessary information; and they put upon their audiences the responsibility of drawing a good many inferences as to character and motives.

The fact that plays could be given only in the light of day and that the Elizabethan theater was lacking in scenery put upon Shakespeare the necessity for constantly reminding his audience of the setting. As M. Jusserand has put it, it was this lack of scenery which forced Shakespeare "to make up for the deficiency . . . by his wonderful descriptions of landscapes, castles, and wild moors. All that poetry would have been lost had he had painted scenery at his disposal." Modern scene design and the use of electrical appliances have revolutionized the technique of the playwright.

466

The fact that there was no curtain as we understand it in the Elizabethan playhouse also had its effect upon the technique of the drama—an effect observable in *Macbeth*. One of the problems caused by the absence of a curtain was how to get characters on and off the stage without making their entrances and exits mechanical and awkward. An examination of modern plays will show that the curtain frequently rises and invariably falls with characters upon the stage. An examination of the scenes in *Macbeth* will reveal the fact that all characters enter at the beginning of a scene or during it, and that all have made their exits at the end. The stage had to be cleared at the end of each scene.

It is probable, too, that change of scene was understood to indicate change of place, and in this connection it should be remembered that Elizabethan audiences were without the information which is given in printed programs in our theaters; and while there is evidence to indicate that on occasion there was displayed a painted cloth bearing the location of the scene, this does not seem to have been the general practice.

There remains to say something of one of the most conspicuous differences between the Shakespearean and the modern drama—the difference in language or dialogue. Shakespeare's plays are written in verse, specifically in the unrhymed iambic pentameter line. Some of the world's greatest poetry is to be found in the mouths of his characters. An examination of modern plays will show that the speech of the characters has been devised to square with what the dramatist regards as the way in which such persons would naturally speak. It is invariably prose, it is "conversational," and it is in the peculiar idiom of the character. The modern drama seems to us more natural, more life-like, more realistic.

QUESTIONS IN APPRECIATION:

ACT I

1. Scene 1: What do you think is the purpose of this brief scene? What mood does it set? What sort of play does it lead one to expect?

2. Scene 2: How does this scene furnish important information about the opening situation? about important characters? Which of the major characters appear in it? Which character has been mentioned in both opening scenes? What effect is produced by delaying his appearance upon the stage?

3. Scene 3: What is the purpose of the conversation among the weird sisters before the arrival of Macbeth and Banquo? How are the predictions of the witches made to appear significant? What hints does the scene give that Macbeth is already inclined to help fulfill them? By what devices are we inclined to trust Banquo and to suspect the purposes of his companion? Would a modern playwright use these same devices? Why or why not?

4. Scene 4: Do you think Scene 4 belongs to the *introduction* of the play? Or has the *rising action* begun? Give the reasons for your answer. What further glimpses does it give of the working of Macbeth's mind?

467

How? What element of suspense is created? Lines 7–11 and 12–13 are often quoted. Why? What is the general tone of the conversation in this scene?

5. Scene 5: What is the obvious purpose of scene 5? Why would it be more effective on the stage than in print? Why would Lady Macbeth's part in the scene be difficult to act? What elements in the scene—not true to ordinary conduct—would a modern playwright try to avoid? What devices would he use instead? Discuss.

6. Scene 6: What is the atmosphere or mood of this scene? Why is it well that the tension is lessened? What sort of feelings does it arouse toward Duncan? toward Lady Macbeth? Why does Macbeth not appear?

7. Scene 7: Show how Macbeth's soliloquy at the beginning of the scene foreshadows events to come. What creates the dramatic tension in the scene? What sort of conflict is being presented—mental or physical? Which character appears the stronger? By what means? What do you consider the finest lines spoken in the scene? Why?

ACT II

1. Scene 1: How do we learn that it is midnight? that there are neither stars nor moon? Why do you think the scene opens with Banquo and Fleance? Why would this scene of Macbeth's be difficult for an actor to portray? What traits of his character are uppermost in the scene?

2. Scene 2: Why was it advisable in the Shakespearean theater for the murders to be done off-stage? Do you think the murder of Duncan would be any more effective if done in sight of the audience? Discuss. What devices create an atmosphere of suspense and horror? How does the reader feel toward Macbeth at the close of the scene? What dramatic purpose is accomplished by having Lady Macbeth smear the grooms with blood? What effective bit of business closes the scene?

3. Scene 3: What is the dramatic effect of opening this scene with the porter's bit of clowning? Is the situation true to life—that is, are situations of tragedy often interrupted with pieces of unconscious humor or trifling incidents? Discuss. What special irony is there in this situation? What other dramatic purpose does the incident serve besides that of relieving tension? How is an ominous atmosphere restored before the discovery of the murder? How is it contrived to let the audience know the plans of Malcolm and Donalbain? What is the effect of Lady Macbeth's swoon?

4. Scene 4: What purpose is this short scene intended to serve? Could the information in it as well be included at the end of the third scene? Is this an appropriate scene with which to end Act II? Discuss. Is the play still in the course of its rising action? How can you tell?

ACT III

1. Scene 1: Why is Banquo's opening speech important? What purpose is served by the dialogue between Macbeth and Banquo? How does

this scene affect the reader's attitude toward Macbeth? What emotions would an audience feel during the course of this scene?

2. Scene 2: If *Macbeth* were a "blood and thunder" drama would Scene 2 be needed? Why, or why not? What does the scene add to the play?

3. Scene 3: How does the author indicate the kind of lighting required for Scene 3? Why would this scene be a difficult one to manage on the Elizabethan stage? Why do you think the murder of Banquo was enacted before the audience, and not merely reported in a later scene? Dramatically what is the most important feature of the scene? Why?

4. Scene 4: Why would Scene 4 be difficult to stage? Do you think the ghost should be visible to the audience? Why or why not? Do you think Shakespeare meant the ghost to be seen? Why would Macbeth's part in the scene be difficult to play? What will be the effect of Macbeth's conduct upon the banquet guests? Do you think that this scene or the preceding one contains the *turning point* of the play? Give the reasons for your choice.

5. Scene 5: Do you think Scene 5 is necessary in the development of the play? If so, why? If not, why was it included? Discuss.

6. Scene 6: Why do you think that Act III closes with these two short scenes—5 and 6? Is it apparent that the *falling action* has set in? If so, how? Which scene in Act III represents a climax of interest? Give the reasons for your choice.

ACT IV

1. Scene 1: In what respects is the witches' cavern an effective opening for Act IV? What mood does the scene establish? What evidence is there in the dialogue with the witches that Macbeth's fortunes are falling? Is he aware of it? Discuss. How does the conversation with Lennox advance the plot? Does it disclose fresh developments in the character of Macbeth? If so, what?

2. Scene 2: Is this scene necessary in the unfolding of the plot, or could the murder of Macduff's family have just as well been reported directly? Why do you think it was included? Discuss. What is the purpose of the conversation between Lady Macduff and her son? What is the tone of the conversation? What dramatic effect is produced by the two warnings? Why do you think only the one child is murdered before the audience? What effect does the scene have on the reader's attitude toward Macbeth? With what feelings would an audience watch the scene?

3. Scene 3: Enumerate the important steps in the advancement of the plot which Scene 3 presents. What is the effect of such a long scene? With what feeling and atmosphere does the scene open? How does it close? Does it in any way create a feeling of suspense? Discuss. How does the author make Macduff's grief seem real? Why do you think Shakespeare usually closes his scenes with a rhymed couplet? What is

the effect of the closing lines in this passage? Why is this a good closing scene for the fourth act?

ACT V

1. Scene 1:. What emotional effect should the first scene produce? What details of setting will help secure such an effect? What is the most dramatic moment in the scene? Why? Does the audience share the feelings of the Doctor and the Gentlewoman? Discuss. Why do you think this scene is written in prose?

2. Scene 2: This and the following scenes are all short. Why? Do you think in general the scenes of the *falling action* should be shorter than those of the rising action? Discuss. What hint is there in the last line of Scene 2 that catastrophe is approaching for Macbeth?

3. Scene 3: How does this scene indicate Macbeth's agitation of mind? Mention definite details. What feelings would the scene excite in the audience? What is the dramatic effect of Macbeth's reference to the words of the witches?

4. Scene 4: What is the purpose of this very short scene? Is it good stage business to let the audience know how the first part of the witches' prophecy is to be fulfilled? Discuss.

5. Scene 5: Show how Scene 5 helps hasten the falling action of the play. What catastrophe has already occurred? What else is foreshadowed? How does Macbeth win some shreds of admiration?

6. Scenes 6 and 7: What dramatic purpose do Scenes 6 and 7 serve? How could such short scenes be managed in the Elizabethan theater? How do modern theaters provide for many short, changing scenes? What important steps in the falling action are accomplished in these two short scenes?

7. Scene 8: How has the author achieved a sense of climax in the final scene of the play? Why is the last scene necessary in rounding out the portrait of Macbeth? Is it good stage business to have Macbeth killed off-stage? Discuss. What is the effect of the closing speeches of Malcolm, Ross, and Siward? Does the reader have a feeling that the play has progressed to an *inevitable* conclusion? Discuss.

FOR FURTHER READING

ADAMS, JOSEPH QUINCY, *Life of Shakespeare; Shakespearean Playhouses*
ANDERSON, MAXWELL, *Elizabeth, the Queen* (Drama)
BENNETT, JOHN, *Master Skylark*
ROLFE, W. J., *Shakespeare, The Boy*
SHAKESPEARE, WILLIAM, *Hamlet*
THORNDIKE, A. H., *Shakespeare's Theater*

470

THE SEVENTEENTH AND EIGHTEENTH CENTURIES
1620-1780

THE COFFEEHOUSE AND THE LITERARY CLUB

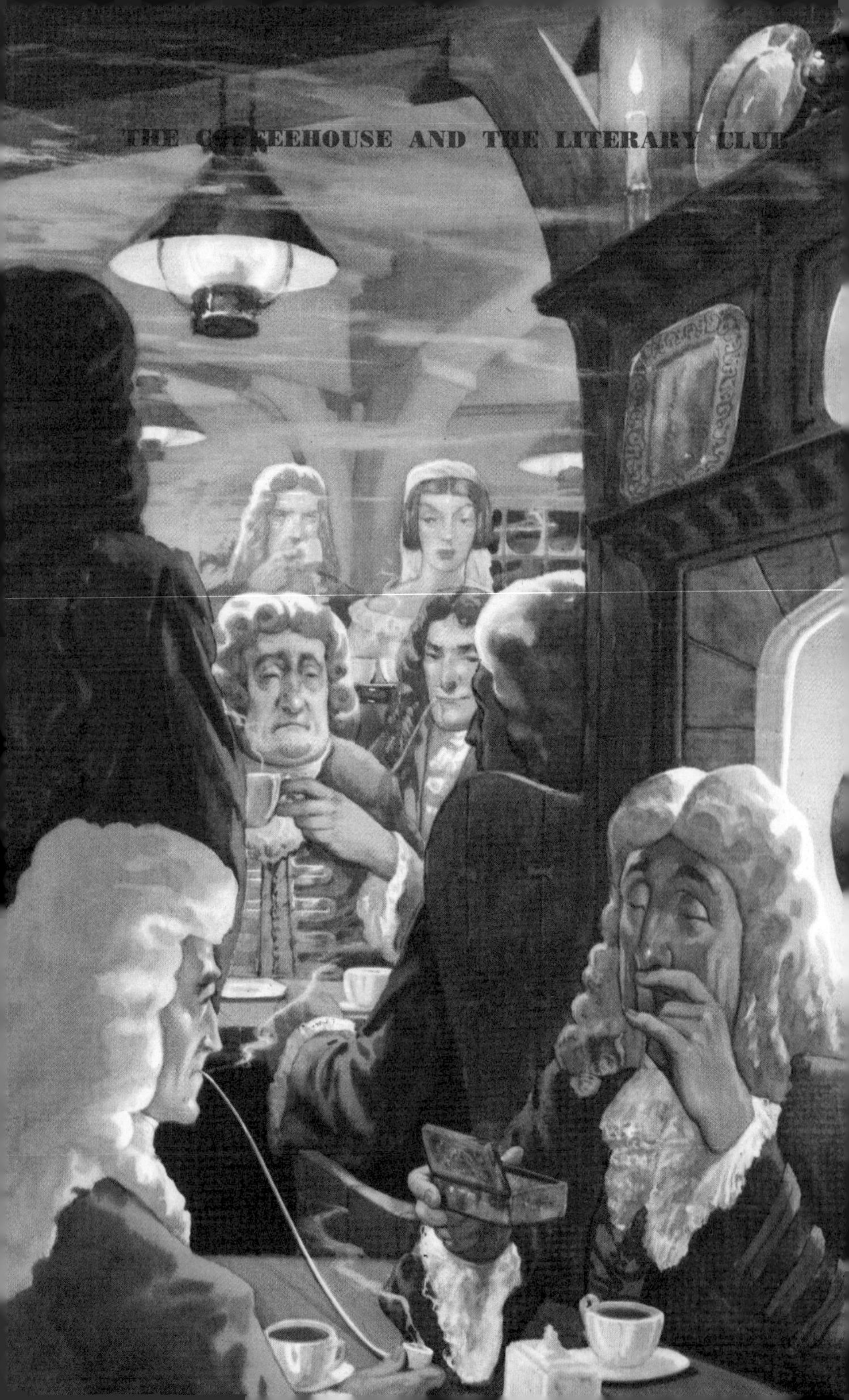

ENGLAND'S TURBULENT SEVENTEENTH CENTURY

(1620–1700)

Never before or since has there been such a breath-takingly dramatic hundred years in English history as the one that was ushered in in 1600. On that New Year's day Elizabeth was still queen. Before the bells were to ring out the end of the century in 1699, there had been eight different "administrations" and four major revolutions of government. England had rebelled against a king, indicted and beheaded him; tried out a republican commonwealth; restored her monarchy; rebelled again —unsuccessfully, with fearful toll in executions; and finally, without bloodshed won a "glorious revolution" and a Bill of Rights.

At first, after the death of Elizabeth in 1603, all seemed well. The son of her cousin Mary Stuart, Queen of Scots, had been called to the throne. As James I of England, he opened the dynasty of Stuart kings and in-augurated the policies that were responsible for most of the troubles of the century. But throughout his own reign of twenty-two years, England was still enjoying the surge of power and well-being fostered by Elizabeth. Shakespeare lived into the thirteenth year of James's reign; Francis Bacon and Ben Jonson maintained Elizabethan traditions of brilliance in literature; and James himself sponsored the translation of the Bible which brought a fitting conclusion to the poetic achievements inspired by the Queen.

But the spirit was changing. Even before the death of Shakespeare, the delight in life and the vigor born of the Renaissance was fading. The younger playwrights—men like Beaumont and Fletcher—were running off cheaper, frothier comedies. A hushed-up scandal tarnished the name of Bacon and toppled him from office. Rumors of discontent riffled the air. Behind the changing spirit loomed a divided England. Men were sifting into two parties—Puritan and Cavalier. With the ascension of Charles I in 1625, the cleavage was sharply defined.

The roots of the trouble went back to days before Elizabeth. In the reign of her father, Henry VIII, the Reformation which converted England from Catholicism to Protestantism had been regarded by some as only a partial reform. The pattern of church government and worship

471

remained much the same. The bishops still had centralized authority, and surviving medieval customs tended to stifle the spirit of devotion. A group of extreme Protestants arose who wished to "purify" the Church of its worldly formality. They were therefore known as *Puritans*. Those Puritans who wished to withdraw from the State Church were called *Separatists*. When the government later refused to allow them to set up a church of their own, the Separatists were the group that migrated to America.

The divisions begun under Henry VIII lost their edge during Elizabeth's almost tolerant reign. But with the coming of the Stuarts, religious difficulties flared afresh. At heart the Stuarts were Catholic; but realizing that the country would not change from Protestantism, they gave tacit support to the Church of England, as the State Church was called. And they encouraged rather than discouraged those tendencies in it which the Puritans disapproved. It was during the reign of James I that the *Mayflower* sailed for America.

James had not been a wise ruler. He had announced his faith in the doctrine that kings rule by Divine Right and that they are therefore independent of the will of the people or their parliaments. His son Charles I was also arrogant, self centered—and ill advised. He made extravagant demands for money and treated Parliament as if it existed only to vote him revenues. When it balked, Charles tried to dismiss it. Then came trouble. The Puritan party, established to uphold the principles of freedom in religion, now became equally concerned about civil freedom. As abuses grew, it took its stand with Parliament against the King. In 1642 Civil War broke out, and the Puritans under the leadership of Oliver Cromwell put an army in the field.

There were men who came to the defense of Charles—some because the habit of loyalty is strong; some out of real devotion to their monarch. The King had a winning personality; when he chose, he could be gracious and generous. His followers—chiefly young men who enjoyed the easy pleasures of the Court—were called *Cavaliers*. The term originally meant "horsemen" or "knights"; but through the seventeenth century, it indicated the party loyal to the king. After the fall of the Stuarts, it was replaced by the term *Tory*.

After three years of struggle, Charles and his Cavaliers were defeated at Naseby. Charles was imprisoned in the Tower of London, accused of high treason against his country, and sentenced to death. On a scaffold in 1649, with surprising dignity, he paid for his follies with his life. Europe was aghast and many of the English were horrified. It was then that the Puritan poet, John Milton, wrote his masterly prose documents explaining and defending the actions of Parliament.

A republican commonwealth was organized with Oliver Cromwell at its head. In 1653 the Puritan leader was given the title of "Lord Protector of England." He was a sincere and high-minded person with a genuine gift for government, but he lived only five years longer. His son, Richard

Cromwell, proved completely inadequate as a successor, and the Puritan power evaporated.

In the eleven years between the death of Charles I and the abdication of Richard Cromwell, the Puritans tried to establish a republican type of government with Parliament acting as a truly representative body. Their honest purpose was to secure civil freedom to the English people. But many of the leaders were themselves intolerant. In their attempt to curb vice and immorality, they passed too-stringent laws, prohibiting all manner of innocent amusements. Nor did they grant to members of other religious sects that same freedom of worship which they desired themselves. Instead they imposed their own brand of Protestantism as the uniform religion of England, Scotland, and Ireland.

And so unrest stirred again. Men sighed for "the good old days" and dreamed romantically of "bonnie Prince Charlie," escaped to France. The son of the dead monarch was living pleasantly in Paris, surrounded by the Cavaliers who had risked wealth, position, even their lives for him and his father. In 1660, two years after the death of Cromwell, the time seemed ripe for his return to England. The people welcomed him with extravagant joy and crowned him Charles II. He would bring them relief from the tiresome restrictions of Puritanism, and surely he would have learned the need of ruling wisely. These were the hopes of England in 1660. But Charles was a disappointing sovereign. Witty, handsome, easy-going, a prey to flattering favor-seekers, shamelessly immoral—he surrounded himself with men and women like him. And for twenty-five years he ruled with little thought for anything but the pleasures of the moment.

The early years of his reign were shaken by two great public disasters —the Plague of 1665 which raged up and down the narrow streets of London, killing people by the thousands; and the Fire of 1666 which destroyed all the center section of the capital—that part formerly known as the "City." When the section was rebuilt, stone foundations replaced old rat-ridden structures; and London never again was swept by plague. The famous architect, Sir Christopher Wren, helped design the rebuilding of the city. Such magnificent structures as St. Paul's Cathedral are the work of his genius. Wren was one of a number of able, honest men who lived in vivid contrast to the dissoluteness of the Court. Science flourished, and many arts. The Royal Society had been founded to honor distinguished men of learning, especially in the field of science. One of its early presidents was Sir Isaac Newton—the man who first formulated the law of gravitation.

It is not to be supposed that Puritanism had vanished with the breakdown of its political power. It is true that Charles had broken his promise of forgiveness and had punished some of those responsible for his father's death; but there were still thousands of Dissenters in England who chafed under the restoration of the English Church. And there were Catholics who hoped through the King's secret sympathies to win England back to the Church of Rome. When Charles died in 1685, these hopes intensified with the encouragement of the new monarch.

Charles's successor was his brother, James II. But there was another aspirant to the throne, the Duke of Monmouth, who claimed to be a son of Charles II. He and his army were defeated in the Battle of Sedgemoor. The Duke was executed, and the countryside was scoured for his followers. Jeffreys of Wem, Lord High Chancellor of England, sitting as judge ordered three hundred and twenty executions for treason. All the roads to London were lined with gibbets and dangling corpses. Hundreds of other participants in the rebellion were sold into bond slavery in the colonies. So James held the throne, but not for long. He was openly a Catholic and his attempts to establish Romanism as the State religion ran counter to deep-seated English prejudice. He eventually found himself without a friend.

Now James had a daughter Mary who had married William of Orange, of the Netherlands—a prince who was himself the grandson of Charles I. In 1688 a group of Englishmen invited Mary and her husband to come to England and take the throne. This time, there were no Cavaliers to come to the rescue. James with his family fled to France, and William and Mary—without the cost of a single life—became joint sovereigns of England. This was the "Bloodless" or "Glorious" Revolution of 1688. With James, his iniquitous judge, Lord Jeffreys, also escaped; but the judge later was captured and imprisoned in the Tower of London.

One of the grievances against James had been a family failing—a tendency to try to rule without deference to Parliament. That body now set forth a Declaration of Rights which William was required to accept before he could be proclaimed king. The declaration was incorporated in a Bill of Rights passed by Parliament in 1689. Provisions of the Bill forbade the levying of taxes without the consent of Parliament, the keeping of a standing army in times of peace, and interference with the administration of justice. Most important of all, it established the supremacy of acts of Parliament over the king's proclamations. This meant that the ministers who constituted the Cabinet would henceforth be responsible, not to the king but to Parliament. Henceforth no minister and no cabinet could hold office if Parliament refused its support. It was the document which transformed England into a *democratic* monarchy.

Cabinet government hastened the development of two political parties —the Whigs, or the Liberals; and the Tories, or the Conservatives, the traditional supporters of the king. Men who had earlier sided with Parliament and the Dissenters were the fathers of the Whigs; the Cavalier families produced the Tories. The Revolution and the Bill of Rights were tremendous victories for Whig principles.

In spite of its turbulent history, the seventeenth century saw great advances in commerce and industry. The East India Company and the Hudson Bay Company were thriving concerns. England tried to monopolize trade at sea. Rivalry over the wool trade provoked war with Holland

and won for England the Dutch colonies of New York and New Jersey. Streams of emigrants poured into the New World—Puritans going to New England, and Cavaliers to Virginia and Maryland. With these colonies the mother country had already established a profitable trade. The peace which followed the Revolution promised an era of real prosperity.

And in spite of swiftly changing fortunes men found time to write. Literature represented three main groups—the Puritans, the Cavaliers, and the Restoration enthusiasts. There was a good deal of religious prose: Browne's *Religion of a Physician,* Taylor's *Holy Living and Holy Dying,* Baxter's *Saints' Everlasting Rest,* Bunyan's *The Pilgrim's Progress* and *Grace Abounding.* Puritan thought had worked deep into the consciousness of the century. It touched the poetry, dominating the works of John Milton and giving a religious complexion to lyric verse. Many of the minor poets were clergymen. Even the Cavalier poets showed a leaning toward serious thought. Their verses have a matter-of-factness, a tendency to see life as it is, quite different from Elizabethan romancing. Only after the Restoration, was literature to lose its serious tone. Then came the cheerful daily jottings of Samuel Pepys in his *Diary,* Walton's placid little book on the joys of fishing, and Dryden's sophisticated comedies.

If these works did not flame with Elizabethan genius, they glowed with a warmth of their own. Bunyan's and Milton's interpretations of Christian thought were to influence mightily the whole western world. Together with Baxter, Taylor, Foxe (*Book of Martyrs*), and the Bible, they would comprise the whole library of many a New World home.

It was unfortunate that the century closed with a Drydenesque period of smart—sometimes tawdry—comedy, of pointed satire, and glittering jibe. The theater, closed during the Puritan regime, in restoration lost its glory, catering to a depraved and flippant audience.

All in all, midnight must have rung out the old year of 1699 on a people who felt that the Stuarts had brought England to a sorry state, but who cherished the hope that in the new regime established by the Glorious Revolution, the land would come again to her sober senses.

Puritan poetry and prose were soberly religious.

VIRTUE

GEORGE HERBERT

Living and writing before the differences between Puritan and Royalist had become open warfare, George Herbert shows a placidity in his verse like the calm before a storm. The thought with which "Virtue" opens is familiar enough—that the loveliest things in the world must pass away—but he carries the theme to a consoling conclusion. There is something that does not die.

SWEET day, so cool, so calm, so bright,
    The bridal of the earth and sky!
The dew shall weep thy fall tonight;
    For thou must die.

5   Sweet rose, whose hue, angry and brave,
    Bids the rash gazer wipe his eye,
Thy root is ever in its grave,
    And thou must die.

Sweet spring, full of sweet days and roses,
10   A box where sweets compacted lie,

My music shows ye have your closes,
And all must die.

Only a sweet and virtuous soul,
Like seasoned timber, never gives;
15 But though the whole world turn to coal,
Then chiefly lives.

11. MY MUSIC—The refrain of my verses.
15. THOUGH THE WHOLE WORLD TURN TO COAL—No matter what transformation takes place in the material world, nothing can destroy a virtuous soul.

FOR INTERPRETATION

1. Show how stanza 3 summarizes the thought of the first two stanzas. What is the meaning of *compacted* as it is used in line 10? What modern word from the same source shows a similar meaning? What is the *box* referred to in line 10? Express in your own words the meaning of line 12.

2. What is the one thing not subject to change and decay? Why do you think Herbert chose to liken it to "seasoned timber"? Discuss.

EASTER

GEORGE HERBERT

There is an appealingly simple spirituality about most of Herbert's verse. In the short lyric "Easter" he bridges the centuries between the first Resurrection Day and an Easter in his own life.

I GOT me flowers to straw Thy way,
I got me boughs off many a tree;
But Thou wast up by break of day,
And brought Thy sweets along with Thee.

5 Yet though my flowers be lost, they say
A heart can never come too late:
Teach it to sing Thy praise this day,
And then this day my life shall date.

1. STRAW—Strew.
4. THY SWEETS—The flowers of spring, symbolic of the renewed life springing from the Resurrection.

FOR INTERPRETATION

1. The first stanza of "Easter" takes the poet in his imagination to the first Easter day. What event in the life of Christ is suggested by the first two lines of the poem? What event is referred to in the third line? What part does the poet imagine for himself in these events?

2. Why should the poet's "flowers be lost"? What does the word *lost* mean here? How will the poet celebrate his Easter?

3. What spirit or feeling does this poem suggest? Discuss.

DEATH

JOHN DONNE

Though Donne was not a Puritan, there is a puritanic solemnity about much of his verse. His sonnet on Death reflects the religious mood of the times.

DEATH, be not proud, though some have called thee
Mighty and dreadful, for thou art not so:
For those whom thou think'st thou dost overthrow
Die not, poor Death: nor yet can'st thou kill me.
5 From Rest and Sleep, which but thy picture be,
Much pleasure, then from thee much more must flow;
And soonest our best men with thee do go—
Rest of their bones and souls' delivery!
Thou'rt slave to fate, chance, kings, and desperate men,
10 And dost with poison, war, and sickness dwell;
And poppy or charms can make us sleep as well
And better than thy stroke. Why swell'st thou then?
One short sleep past, we wake eternally,
And Death shall be no more: Death thou shalt die!

11. POPPY—Opium and other sleep-producing drugs are distilled from the poppy.
12. WHY SWELL'ST THOU?—Death is pictured as being swollen with pride.

FOR INTERPRETATION

1. In the first two lines what statement does the poet make to Death? What surprising statement does he make in the next two lines? What lines further on explain the meaning of lines 3 and 4?

2. What experiences does the poet say are "pictures of death"? Since these experiences are pleasant, what conclusion does Donne draw about the experience of Death?

3. In what sense is it true that Death is *slave* to "fate, chance, kings, desperate men"? Discuss.

4. According to the poet, what fact is it that causes Death to die?

5. Show how the poet has developed his theme by personifying Death throughout the poem.

ON HIS BLINDNESS

JOHN MILTON

From the days of his youth Milton had felt "called" to write a great religious poem. God had given him a talent which should be devoted to His service. In the mind of the poet there grew the plan of an epic retelling the story of the fall of man. It should explain the existence of sin in the world and "justify the ways of God to man." But at forty-three Milton found himself blind with his *Paradise Lost* unwritten—apparently never to be written. After a period of profound dejection, he composed a fourteen-line meditation "On His Blindness."

In the consoling closing lines of the sonnet he wrote more wisely than he knew. *Paradise Lost* did get written—great poetry, but of legendary rather than Scriptural theology, confusing rather than enlightening. Whereas the last line of this unpretentious sonnet has been a source of inspiration and comfort to helpless invalids ever since the day that Milton set it down.

WHEN I consider how my light is spent,
Ere half my days in this dark world and wide,
And that one talent which is death to hide
Lodged with me useless, though my soul more bent
5   To serve therewith my Maker, and present
My true account, lest He returning chide—
"Doth God exact day-labor, light denied?"
I fondly ask—But Patience, to prevent
That murmur, soon replies, "God doth not need
10   Either man's work, or His own gifts; who best

3. THAT ONE TALENT—Lines 3–7 are a reference to the parable of the talents told by Jesus and reported in the 25th chapter of the Gospel of St. Matthew, verses 14–30. If you are not familiar with the story, you will need to read it.
8. FONDLY—Foolishly.

479

Bear His mild yoke, they serve Him best. His state
Is kingly; thousands at His bidding speed,
And post o'er land and ocean without rest;
They also serve who only stand and wait."

FOR INTERPRETATION

1. Substitute two literal words for the figurative words *light* and *spent*
in the first line of the sonnet. How long does Milton expect to live,
according to line 2? What years do we generally call the middle age of
a man's life? How many years did Milton live in darkness? (Refer to
the biographical sketch in the EXTENDED ACTIVITIES section.)

2. In the years before Milton's blindness had the poet been using his
talent or hiding it? Discuss.

3. What is the meaning of the question asked in the seventh line?

4. Which of the two following statements do you think gives the correct interpretation for lines 9 and 10?

  a. Man does not need to serve God in the world, nor to devote his
    talents to God's use; *or*

  b. It is presumptuous for any *one* man to suppose that God cannot
    get along without his services, or without some specially man-
    conceived use of his services.

Who is the planner, God or man? Discuss.

5. Show how the last three lines of the poem help to determine the
meaning of lines 9 and 10. Why do you think the last line of the poem
would be of comfort to a hopeless cripple or to a bed-ridden invalid?
Discuss.

6. Summarize in your own words the thought of the sonnet. Be prepared to show how that thought was exemplified in the life of Milton,
or in the life of any other character in history or literature.

APOSTROPHE TO LIGHT

JOHN MILTON

In the twelve books of *Paradise Lost* Milton tells the old story of the
Garden of Eden and the fall of man. The central character of the epic is
Satan; for Milton makes the struggle in his plot a continuation of the
quarrel between Lucifer (later known as Satan) and God. The story of
the fallen angels is not told in the Bible, but it had been for centuries
popular tradition in church literature.

480

The scene of the first two books is laid in Hell, shortly after Lucifer had been hurled from Heaven. He and his companions at length arouse themselves from their confusion and begin to plot revenge. Satan has heard that a new world has been formed and suggests that they may anger God by leading Man astray. He himself undertakes the mission of discovering earth and spying out the prospects for revenge.

Most of Book III has its setting in Heaven. And so in the opening lines the poet pictures himself as returning to the realms of light after his imaginary visit in Hell. It is to be borne in mind that Milton wrote *Paradise Lost* after he had lost his eyesight; and in these opening lines he makes reference to his blindness. The passage presented forms merely an introduction to the third book. It tells nothing of the story, but it does suggest the tone of the whole work and it is a fair sample of Milton's impressive poetic style.

> HAIL, holy Light, offspring of Heav'n first-born! . . .
>   Before the sun,
> Before the heavens thou wert, and at the voice
> Of God, as with a mantle, didst invest
> 5   The rising world of waters dark and deep,
> Won from the void and formless infinite.
> Thee I revisit now with bolder wing,
> Escap't the Stygian pool, though long detained
> In that obscure sojourn, while in my flight,
> 10   Through utter and through middle darkness borne,
> With other notes than to th' Orphean lyre,
> I sung of Chaos and eternal Night,
> Taught by the heav'nly Muse to venture down
> The dark descent and up to reascend,
> 15   Though hard and rare. Thee I revisit safe,
> And feel thy sovran vital lamp; but thou

1. OFFSPRING OF HEAV'N FIRST-BORN—Milton is referring to the order of creation as related in the first book of *Genesis*: first, chaos without form, then light, then the firmament separated from the waters, and then land.

8. STYGIAN POOL—In Greek mythology, the River Styx was believed to separate the abode of the dead from the land of the living. Anything pertaining to the under-world might be described as *Stygian,* hence dark and horrible. Throughout *Paradise Lost* Milton intermingles pagan mythology with Hebrew history and tradition. The names and places of Greek myths are like a poetic vocabulary to him, nothing more.

11. ORPHEAN LYRE—A reference to the story that Orpheus with his music almost gained the release of his wife Eurydice from Hades. Milton's meaning here is that in writing the first two books he descended in imagination into Hell but that since his purpose was worthy, a *heavenly* muse showed him the difficult way between Hell and Heaven.

Revisit'st not these eyes, that roll in vain
To find thy piercing ray and find no dawn,
So thick a drop serene hath quencht their orbs,
20 Or dim suffusion veiled. Yet not the more
Cease I to wander where the Muses haunt
Clear spring or shady grove or sunny hill,
Smit with the love of sacred song; but chief
Thee, Sion, and the flow'ry brooks beneath,
25 That wash thy hallowed feet and warbling flow,
Nightly I visit; nor sometimes forget
Those other two equalled with me in fate,
So were I equalled with them in renown,
Blind Thamyris and blind Maeonides,
30 And Tiresias and Phineus, prophets old;
Then feed on thoughts that voluntary move
Harmonious numbers, as the wakeful bird
Sings darkling, and in shadiest covert hid
Tunes her nocturnal note. Thus with the year
35 Seasons return: but not to me returns
Day, or the sweet approach of ev'n or morn,
Or sight of vernal bloom, or summer's rose,
Or flocks, or herds, or human face divine;
But cloud instead and ever-during dark
40 Surrounds me, from the cheerful ways of men
Cut off, and for the book of knowledge fair

17. THOU REVISIT'ST NOT THESE EYES—Milton is still addressing *Light*. Though his imagination enables him to picture Heaven, actual light does not touch his blinded eyes.

21. WHERE THE MUSES HAUNT—The Muses were the nine goddesses believed to inspire poets, writers, artists, scholars; therefore they represent artistic effort of every kind. Milton's loss of sight has not discouraged him from writing. He composed *Paradise Lost* in his mind and dictated the lines to his daughters.

24. THEE, SION—The hill of Sion, or Zion, in Jerusalem is often associated with the "New Jerusalem," or Heaven. Milton imagines throughout the poem that a special "heavenly Muse" is inspiring him. This Muse has its home or *haunts* about the hill of Zion.

29. THAMYRIS—A singer of Thrace who believed that he could out-sing the Muses. For his presumption he was punished by the loss of his sight and of his gift for singing.

29. MAEONIDES—A name for Homer—also a blind poet—a native or son of Maeonia.

30. TIRESIAS—A blind singer of Thebes, punished by Athene with the loss of his sight but later endowed by her with a gift for prophecy and for interpreting the speech of birds and animals.

30. PHINEUS—A Greek sage who advised Jason about his search for the Golden Fleece.

Presented with a universal blank
Of nature's works, to me expunged and razed,
And wisdom at one entrance quite shut out.
45 So much the rather thou, celestial Light,
Shine inward, and the mind through all her powers
Irradiate; there plant eyes; all mist from thence
Purge and disperse, that I may see and tell
Of things invisible to mortal sight.

FOR INTERPRETATION

1. What is the meaning of *Heav'n* in the first line? What is the meaning of *heavens* in the third line? How does Milton show the distinction between the two meanings? In line 6 what words give a poetic description of *chaos?*

2. In your own words explain the meaning of line 7. What detained the poet in the "Stygian pool"? What is the "eternal night" referred to in line 12?

3. With what words does the poet say that he can see no light, however hard he try? Quote the lines.

4. Tell in your own words what you think Milton means by lines 23–26, especially by "nightly I visit."

5. Name at least two things that Milton has in common with each of the persons named in lines 29 and 30.

6. One of the sweetest singers of all birds is the nightingale. Why does Milton liken himself to it? In what lines does he make the comparison? Quote them.

7. Lines 34–44 contain a touching description of the lost beauty suffered by the poet through his blindness. Explain the meaning of lines 43–44. What is the "one entrance"? Enumerate at least five of the things which the poet says he can see no more. Which one do you think you would miss most of all if you were blind? Discuss. Be prepared to read this passage aloud, intelligently and sympathetically.

8. The last five lines of the selection tell what is to bring compensation to the poet for the loss of physical light. Study the lines carefully; then express the thought of them in simple prose. In what respect do the last three lines serve as a preparation, or *invocation,* for his writing of Book III? Discuss.

9. What do you learn from these 48 lines about:
   a. Milton's education and training?
   b. His mind and general intelligence?
   c. Any special abilities he possessed?
   d. His character and attitude toward life?

10. *For Extra Credit*: Read and prepare a report on the first two books

of *Paradise Lost.* You will find a carefully edited presentation of the first book in PROSE AND POETRY OF THE WORLD.

EVENING IN PARADISE

JOHN MILTON

In the first three books of *Paradise Lost* Milton showed his ability to describe in majestic terms sights of unearthly woe or splendor. The following brief passage from Book IV shows his skill in suggesting a natural landscape. The scene is the Garden of Eden before man has sinned.

> Now came still Evening on, and Twilight gray
> Had in her sober livery all things clad;
> Silence accompanied; for beast and bird,
> They to their grassy couch, these to their nests
> 5 Were slunk, all but the wakeful nightingale.
> She all night long her amorous descant sung:
> Silence was pleased. Now glowed the firmament
> With living sapphires; Hesperus, that led
> The starry host, rode brightest, till the Moon,
> 10 Rising in clouded majesty, at length
> Apparent queen, unveiled her peerless light,
> And o'er the dark her silver mantle threw.

FOR INTERPRETATION

1. What is the "sober livery" of Twilight? What comes with twilight?

2. In line 4 to what does *They* refer? To what does *these* refer?

3. Explain the meaning of the words "amorous descant." In what unusual way does the poet say that the nightingale's song was lovely?

4. With what words does the poet say that the stars came out? Explain the reference to Hesperus in line 8. What other poem that you have read recently refers also to Hesperus?

5. Quote the lines with which the poet says that the moon rose and lighted the landscape.

6. Does this description of evening appeal to more than your sense of sight? Discuss. Do you think it would be possible for a painter in any way to suggest this scene? What sort of musical composition might it inspire?

IN THE VALLEY OF HUMILIATION

JOHN BUNYAN

"As I walked through the wilderness of this world, I lighted on certain place where there was a Den, and I laid me down in that place to sleep: and as I slept, I dreamed a dream."

The writer was John Bunyan; the den was Bedford jail; and the dream grew into *The Pilgrim's Progress,* his great religious allegory. The book represents the life of any Christian as a pilgrim's journey toward the Celestial City. "Christian" flees from his home, with a burden of sins upon his back. He tumbles into the Slough of Despond, but is helped out by Evangelist. He picks up fellow travelers who weaken and turn back. He is misled by Mr. Worldly Wiseman, but Evangelist sets him right. He passes the roaring lions and finally reaches the House Beautiful where he is refreshed and rested and where he enjoys the friendship of the Christian virtues. Pleasant as the House Beautiful is, it is not his destination and he must push on. His friends provide him with armor and weapons. Again he sets out. Since he had been on the crest of the hill, he must now descend into the Valley of Humiliation.

But let us go a little way with Christian and participate in one of his adventures.

THEN he began to go forward; but Discretion, Piety, Charity, and Prudence would accompany him down to the foot of the hill. So they went on together, reiterating their former discourses, till they came to go down the hill. Then said Christian, As it was difficult coming up, so (so far as I can see) it is dangerous going down. Yes, said Prudence, so it is, for it is a hard matter for a man to go down into the Valley of Humiliation, as thou art now, and to catch no slip by the way; therefore, said they, are we come out to accompany thee down the hill. So he began to go down, but very warily; yet he caught a slip or two.

Then I saw in my dream that these good companions, when Christian was gone to the bottom of the hill, gave him a loaf of bread, a bottle of wine, and a cluster of raisins; and then he went on his way.

But now, in this Valley of Humiliation, poor Christian was hard put to it; for he had gone but a little way, before he espied a foul fiend coming over the field to meet him; his name is Apollyon.[1] Then did Christian begin to be afraid, and to cast in his mind whether to go back or to stand his ground. But he considered again that he had no armor for his back; and therefore thought that to turn the back to him might give him the greater advantage with ease to pierce him with his darts. Therefore he resolved to venture and stand his ground; for, thought he, had I no more in mine eye [2] than the saving of my life, it would be the best way to stand.

So he went on, and Apollyon met him. Now the monster was hideous to behold; he was clothed with scales, like a fish (and they are his pride); he had wings like a dragon, feet like a bear, and out of his belly came fire and smoke, and his mouth was as the mouth of a lion. When he was come up to Christian, he beheld him with a disdainful countenance, and thus began to question with him.

Apollyon. Whence come you? and whither are you bound?

Christian. I am come from the City of Destruction,[3] which is the place of all evil, and am going to the City of Zion.[4]

Apollyon. By this I perceive thou art one of my subjects, for all that country is mine, and I am the prince and god of it. How is it, then, that thou hast run away from thy king? Were it not that I hope thou mayest do me more service, I would strike thee now, at one blow, to the ground.

Christian. I was born, indeed, in your dominions, but your service was hard, and your wages such as a man could not live

[1] APOLLYON—A spirit of evil, the Destroyer. See *Revelation* 9:11.
[2] HAD I NO MORE IN MINE EYE—Were I considering nothing more.
[3] CITY OF DESTRUCTION—Worldly living.
[4] CITY OF ZION—The Celestial City, Heaven.

on, "for the wages of sin *is* death"; [5] therefore, when I was come to years, I did as other considerate persons do, look out, if, perhaps, I might mend myself.[6]

Apollyon. There is no prince that will thus lightly lose his subjects, neither will I as yet lose thee; but since thou complainest of thy service and wages, be content to go back: what our country will afford, I do here promise to give thee.

Christian. But I have let myself to another, even to the King of princes, and how can I, with fairness, go back with thee?

Then Apollyon broke out into a grievous rage, saying, I am an enemy to this Prince; I hate his person, his laws, and people; I am come out on purpose to withstand thee.

Christian. Apollyon, beware what you do; for I am in the king's highway, the way of holiness; therefore take heed to yourself.

Then Apollyon straddled quite over the whole breadth of the way, and said, I am void of fear in this matter: prepare thyself to die; for I swear by my infernal den, that thou shalt go no farther; here will I spill thy soul.

And with that he threw a flaming dart at his breast; but Christian had a shield in his hand,[7] with which he caught it, and so prevented the danger of that.

Then did Christian draw, for he saw it was time to bestir him: and Apollyon as fast made at him, throwing darts as thick as hail; by the which, notwithstanding all that Christian could do to avoid it, Apollyon wounded him in his head, his hand, and foot. This made Christian give a little back; Apollyon therefore followed his work amain, and Christian again took courage, and resisted as manfully as he could. This sore combat lasted for above half a day, even till Christian was almost quite spent; for you must know that Christian, by reason of his wounds, must needs grow weaker and weaker.

Then Apollyon, espying his opportunity, began to gather up close to Christian, and wrestling with him, gave him a dreadful fall; and with that Christian's sword flew out of his hand. Then

---

[5] FOR THE WAGES OF SIN IS DEATH—See *Romans* 6:23.

[6] MEND MYSELF—Improve my condition.

[7] A SHIELD IN HIS HAND—Christian had been armed in the House Beautiful with the "breast plate of righteousness," the "shield of faith," the "helmet of salvation," and the "sword of the Spirit, which is the Word of God." See *Ephesians* 6:12–18.

said Apollyon, I am sure of thee now. And with that he had almost pressed him to death, so that Christian began to despair of life: but as God would have it, while Apollyon was fetching of his last blow, thereby to make a full end of this good man, Christian nimbly stretched out his hand for his sword, and caught it, saying, "Rejoice not against me, O mine enemy: when I fall I shall arise"; [8] and with that gave him a deadly thrust, which made him give back, as one that had received his mortal wound. Christian perceiving that, made at him again, saying, "Nay, in all these things we are more than conquerors through him that loved us." [9] And with that Apollyon spread forth his dragon's wings, and sped him away, that Christian for a season saw him no more.

[8] REJOICE NOT AGAINST ME . . . I SHALL ARISE—See *Micah* 7:8.

[9] NAY, IN ALL THESE THINGS . . . THAT LOVED US—See *Romans* 8:37, 39 and *James* 4:7.

DID YOU READ WITH UNDERSTANDING?

1. Reread the selection with the thought of explaining the allegorical meaning of each character, place, object, and event. For instance, if the House Beautiful represents the Christian Church, what does the Valley of Humiliation mean? What would the "wine, bread, and cluster of raisins" signify? And so on.

2. Point out the places in the selection where Christian has used the Word of God as his "sword." What is the "thrust" that finally routs Apollyon?

3. Keeping the general outline of this incident in mind, give a parallel incident that might occur in the everyday life of any Christian, representing his descent into "the Valley of Humiliation." Make your incident realistic, not allegorical. Be prepared to present it orally or to write it out.

Cavalier and Restoration literature was witty and worldly.

SONG FROM *AGLAURA*

SIR JOHN SUCKLING

Typical of the getting-back-to-earth attitude of most Cavalier poets are the following lines of advice to an unhappy lover. This is good common sense, we admit, but the question, is, will it really help the poor fellow?

MB1   WHY so pale and wan, fond lover?
          Prithee, why so pale?
        Will, when looking well can't move her,
          Looking ill prevail?
B   5   Prithee, why so pale?

DB1   Why so dull and mute, young sinner?
          Prithee, why so mute?
        Will, when speaking well can't win her,
          Saying nothing do't?
B   10   Prithee, why so mute?

U   Quit, quit for shame! This will not move;
          This cannot take her.
        If of herself she will not love,
          Nothing can make her:
MB1   15 The devil take her!

FOR INTERPRETATION

1. Do you think there is good advice in the first stanza? Would the modern girl be more likely to favor a bright, healthy-looking suitor or one romantically "pale and wan"? Do you think seventeenth-century girls were any different from ours in their tastes?

2. Is silent brooding likely to be a symptom of an unfortunate love affair? Does it help the cause?

3. Do you agree with the sentiments expressed in the first four lines of the last stanza? Why or why not?

4. Why do you think the poet added the last line? Explain briefly how it typifies what we sometimes call a "Cavalier" attitude toward life?

GO, LOVELY ROSE!

EDMUND WALLER

Here is a poem in which the rejected lover speaks for himself—though with the help of a flower. Selecting a rose to be his "object lesson," he sends it to his adored one, with the following lines attached—

Go, LOVELY Rose!
Tell her that wastes her time and me,
That now she knows,
When I resemble her to thee,
5 How sweet and fair she seems to be.

Tell her that's young,
And shuns to have her graces spied,
That hadst thou sprung
In deserts, where no men abide,
10 Thou must have uncommended died.

Small is the worth
Of beauty from the light retired;
Bid her come forth,
Suffer herself to be desired,
15 And not blush so to be admired

Then die! that she
The common fate of all things rare
May read in thee;
How small a part of time they share
20 That are so wondrous sweet and fair.

FOR INTERPRETATION

1. What other seventeenth-century poem uses a similar theme—"the common fate of all things rare"—but with an entirely different application? How do you account for the difference in attitude in the two lyrics?

2. Compare the thought of "Go, Lovely Rose" with the thought expressed in the second stanza of Ben Jonson's song "To Celia"; and show how each poem is representative of the period that produced it.

3. Does Waller's poem end with an unhappy or with a pleasing note? Discuss.

TO THE VIRGINS, TO MAKE MUCH OF TIME

ROBERT HERRICK

The Cavalier poets seemed to be fond of giving advice to girls. Here is another word of warning—this one not addressed to any girl in particular but rather to all those who would escape the fate of spinsterhood.

GATHER ye rosebuds while ye may,
 Old time is still a-flying;
And this same flower that smiles today,
 Tomorrow will be dying.

5 The glorious lamp of heaven, the sun,
 The higher he's a-getting,
The sooner will his race be run,
 And nearer he's to setting.

That age is best which is the first,
10 When youth and blood are warmer;
But being spent, the worse and worst
 Times still succeed the former.

Then be not coy, but use your time,
And while ye may, go marry;
15 For, having lost but once your prime,
You may forever tarry.

FOR INTERPRETATION

1. The first stanza repeats the thought of what other poem that you
have read recently? Do you think the poet means this stanza to be considered *literally* or *figuratively?* Discuss.
2. What time of life does Herrick think is best? What time does he
think is the worst? Do you think people in general agree with him? Do
you agree? For another poem dealing with the ages of man's life, turn to
Browning's stanzas from "Rabbi Ben Ezra" in a later section of this book.

TO DIANEME

ROBERT HERRICK

Do you remember how Spenser praised the loveliness of his Elizabeth?
Herrick finds "Dianeme" beautiful, too, but what a difference there is in
his way of telling her so!

SWEET, be not proud of those two eyes
Which starlike sparkle in their skies;
Nor be you proud that you can see
All hearts your captives, yours yet free;
5 Be you not proud of that rich hair
Which wantons with the love-sick air;
Whenas that ruby which you wear,
Sunk from the tip of your soft ear,
Will last to be a precious stone
10 When all your world of Beauty's gone.

FOR INTERPRETATION

1. What is the "object lesson" used by this poet?
2. Is the statement of the last four lines *literally* true? A later poet,
John Keats, said "A thing of beauty is a joy forever." May he be
telling the truth also? Discuss.

THE UNFADING BEAUTY

THOMAS CAREW

Fading roses, transient loveliness—how many Cavalier poets made these their themes! But Thomas Carew suggests that there is another kind of beauty that never dies.

HE THAT loves a rosy cheek,
    Or a coral lip admires,
Or from starlike eyes doth seek
    Fuel to maintain his fires:
5 As old time makes these decay,
    So his flames must waste away.

But a smooth and steadfast mind,
    Gentle thoughts and calm desires,
Hearts with equal love combined,
10   Kindle never-dying fires.
Where these are not, I despise
    Lovely cheeks or lips or eyes.

FOR INTERPRETATION

1. In the first stanza, what metaphor is used for *love?* Point out three words in the last three lines which suggest that metaphor.
2. Is the metaphor of the first stanza continued in the second?
3. Do you agree in general with the thought of this poem? Discuss.
4. Of all the other lyrics you have read so far, which has a theme most nearly like the theme of "The Unfading Beauty"? Discuss.

TO LUCASTA, ON GOING TO THE WARS

RICHARD LOVELACE

Ladies of every generation have shrunk from seeing their men go off to war. When "Lucasta" tried to persuade her poet not to desert her for the hazardous lot of a soldier for King Charles, he left her with an unanswerable argument. And ever since, men who have chosen Duty before Love have liked to quote his lines.

493

TELL me not, sweet, I am unkind
　　That from the nunnery
Of thy chaste breast and quiet mind
　　To war and arms I fly.

5　True, a new mistress now I chase,
　　The first foe in the field;
And with a stronger faith embrace
　　A sword, a horse, a shield.

Yet this inconstancy is such
10　As you, too, shall adore;
I could not love thee, dear, so much,
　　Loved I not honor more.

FOR INTERPRETATION

1. Lucasta has apparently reproached her poet as being unfaithful to her. How does he turn her argument in his favor?

2. The last two lines of the poem have a clever turn. Are they also *true?* Discuss. Can you think of other circumstances in which they might apply? If so, give some examples.

TO ALTHEA, FROM PRISON

RICHARD LOVELACE

Richard Lovelace suffered imprisonment and loss of fortune for his loyalty to Charles I. But he wrote two stanzas that have made him famous—the closing lines of "To Lucasta" and the last stanza of "To Althea, from Prison."

WHEN Love with unconfinèd wings
　　Hovers within my gates,
And my divine Althea brings
　　To whisper at the grates;
5　When I lie tangled in her hair
　　And fettered to her eye,
The birds that wanton in the air
　　Know no such liberty.

494

When flowing cups run swiftly round
10   With no allaying Thames,
Our careless heads with roses bound,
Our hearts with loyal flames;
When thirsty grief in wine we steep,
When healths and draughts go free—
15   Fishes that tipple in the deep
Know no such liberty.

When, like committed linnets, I
With shriller throat shall sing
The sweetness, mercy, majesty,
20   And glories of my King;
When I shall voice aloud how good
He is, how great should be,
Enlargèd winds, that curl the flood,
Know no such liberty.

25   Stone walls do not a prison make,
Nor iron bars a cage;
Minds innocent and quiet take
That for an hermitage;
If I have freedom in my love
30   And in my soul am free,
Angels alone, that soar above,
Enjoy such liberty.

9. WHEN FLOWING CUPS—In English prisons, if a man or his friends had money, he could be supplied with wine and food beyond prison fare.
17. COMMITTED LINNETS—Caged songbirds.
19–20. THE SWEETNESS . . . OF MY KING—The followers of King Charles idealized him and gave him greater devotion than he deserved.

FOR INTERPRETATION

1. According to the first stanza, what kind of liberty may a man enjoy even in prison?
2. According to the second stanza, what kind of freedom could men enjoy in prison? Would this second stanza be generally true today?
3. According to the third stanza, what kind of liberty cannot be denied to prisoners? Is the thought of this stanza still true?
4. Do you believe that the thought of the fourth stanza is essentially true? Why do you think this stanza has been almost universally quoted?

From A DIARY

SAMUEL PEPYS

Have you ever wondered about ordinary folks in the days that now are history—about what they ate, how they dressed, what sorts of amusement they had? You need have no unsatisfied curiosities about such details in the days of Charles II. Thanks to the diaries of John Evelyn and Samuel Pepys we know as much about the folks in London then as we do about those in our own home town. Pepys's diary is especially revealing; for he wrote it in secret code, and then besides, he was a gossipy soul. He was as interested in clothes and food as any woman ever was, and he was always surrounded by people. He is frank in confessing his own misdemeanors—the crafty acceptance of a small bribe, or a little flirtation with the maid. He scolds his wife for being untidy, and then is sorry about it—all in all, a human sort of chap.

But here is the diary—a small portion of it—and you may see for yourself what manner of man was Samuel. The style has been imitated enough so that you should find it familiar.

Jan. 1st, 1660. (Lord's Day.) This morning (we living lately in the garret,[1]) I rose, put on my suit with great skirts,[2] having not lately worn any other clothes but them. Went to Mr. Gunning's chapel at Exeter House, where he made a very good sermon. Dined at home in the garret, where my wife dressed the remains of a turkey, and in the doing of it she burned her hand. I staid at home all the afternoon, looking over my accounts; then

---

[1] GARRET—In 1660, Pepys was just getting started financially. As he was a Royalist, he was eagerly hoping for a restoration of the monarchy.
[2] GREAT SKIRTS—A coat very full from waist to knees.

went with my wife to my father's, and in going observed the great posts which the City have set up at the Conduit in Fleet-street. *Mar. 5th, 1660.* To Westminster by water, only seeing Mr. Pinkney at his own house, where he showed me how he had alway kept the Lion and the Unicorn,[3] in the back of his chimney, bright, in expectation of the King's coming again. At home I found Mr. Hunt, who told me how the Parliament had voted that the Covenant be printed and hung in churches again. Great hopes of the King's coming again. To bed.

Mar. 6th, 1660. (Shrove Tuesday.) To the Bell, where were Mr. Eglin, Veezy, Vincent a butcher, one more, and Mr. Tanner, with whom I played upon a viall, and he a viallin, after dinner, and were very merry, with a special good dinner, a leg of veal and bacon, two capons and sausages and fritters, with abundance of wine. After that I went home, where I found Kate Sterpin who hath not been here a great while before. She gone I went to see Mrs. Jem, at whose chamber door I found a couple of ladies, but she not being there, we hunted her out, and found that she and another had hid themselves behind a door. Well, they all went down into the dining room, where it was full of tag, rag, and bobtail, dancing, singing, and drinking, of which I was ashamed, and after I had staid a dance or two I went away. This day I hear that the Lords do intend to sit, and great store of them are now in town, and I see in the Hall today. My Lord told me, that there was great endeavors to bring in the Protector [4] again; but he told me, too, that he did believe it would not last long if we were brought in; no, nor the King neither (though he seems to think that he will come in), unless he carry himself very soberly and well. Every body now drinks the King's health without any fear, whereas before it was very private that a man dare do it.

Oct 13th, 1660.[5] To my Lord's in the morning, where I met with Captain Cuttance, but my Lord not being up I went out to Charing Cross,[6] to see Major-General Harrison [7] hanged, drawn,

---

[3] LION AND UNICORN—The royal coat of arms.

[4] PROTECTOR—Richard Cromwell, the son of Oliver, who had succeeded his father but had resigned in May, 1659.

[5] *Oct. 13th, 1660*—In the meantime the King had returned. He made his royal entrance to London on May 29th.

[6] CHARING CROSS—A busy section of London.

[7] MAJOR-GENERAL HARRISON—One of the judges that had sentenced Charles I to be beheaded. Charles II had promised that there would be no reprisals for his father's death. Of course he did not keep the promise.

and quartered; which was done there, he looking as cheerful as any man could do in that condition. He was presently cut down, and his head and heart shown to the people, at which there was great shouts of joy. It is said that he said that he was sure to come shortly at the right hand of Christ to judge them that now had judged him; and that his wife do expect his coming again. Thus it was my chance to see the King beheaded at White Hall,[8] and to see the first blood shed in revenge for the blood of the King at Charing Cross. From thence to my Lord's, and took Captain Cuttance and Mr. Sheply to the Sun Tavern, and did give them some oysters. After that I went by water home, where I was angry with my wife for her things lying about, and in my passion kicked the little fine basket, which I bought her in Holland, and broke it, which troubled me after I had done it. Within all the afternoon setting up shelves in my study. At night to bed.

Nov. 22d, 1660. This morning came the carpenters to make me a door at the other side of my house, going into the entry, which I was much pleased with. At noon my wife and I walked to the Old Exchange, and there she bought her a white whisk and put it on, and I a pair of gloves, and so we took coach for Whitehall to Mr. Fox's, where we found Mrs. Fox within, and an alderman of London paying £1,000 or £1,400 in gold upon the table for the King, which was the most gold that ever I saw together in my life. Mr. Fox came in presently and did receive us with a great deal of respect; and then did take my wife and I to the Queen's presence-chamber, where he got my wife placed behind the Queen's chair, and I got into the crowd, and by and by the Queen and the two Princesses[9] came to dinner. The Queen a very little plain old woman, and nothing more in her presence in any respect nor garb than any ordinary woman. The Princess of Orange I had often seen before. The Princess Henrietta is very pretty, but much below my expectation; and her dressing of herself with her hair frizzed short up to her ears, did make her seem so much the less to me. But my wife standing near with two or three black patches[10] on, and well dressed, did seem to me much

---

[8] WHITE HALL—At that time the palace of the English kings.

[9] QUEEN AND THE TWO PRINCESSES—The mother of Charles, and his two sisters. The King was not married until 1662.

[10] BLACK PATCHES—Beauty-spots, much the fashion.

handsomer than she. Dinner being done, we went to Mr. Fox's again, where many gentlemen dined with us, and most princely dinner, all provided for me and my friends, but I bringing none but myself and wife, he did call the company to help to eat up so much good victuals. At the end of dinner, my Lord Sandwich's health was drunk in the gilt tankard that I did give to Mrs. Fox the other day. After dinner I took coach for my wife and me homewards, and I light at the Maypole in the Strand, and sent my wife home. I to the new playhouse and saw part of the "Traitor," a very good Tragedy; Mr. Moon did act the Traitor very well. I went home on foot, it being very late and dirty, and so weary to bed.

Feb. 27th, 1661. At the office all the morning, that done I walked in the garden with little Captain Murford, where he and I had some discourse concerning the Light-House again, and I think I shall appear in the business, he promising me that if I can bring it about, it will be worth £100 per annum. Then I called for a dish of fish, which we had for dinner, this being the first day of Lent; and I do intend to try whether I can keep it or no.

Feb. 28th, 1661. Early to wait on my Lord, and after a little talk with him I took boat at Whitehall for Redriffe, but in my way overtook Captain Cuttance and Teddiman in a boat and so ashore with them at Queenhithe, and so to a tavern with them to a barrel of oysters, and so away. Capt. Cuttance and I walked from Redriffe to Deptford, where I found both Sir William and Sir G. Carteret at Mr. Uthwayt's, and there we dined, and notwithstanding my resolution, yet for want of other victualls, I did eat flesh this Lent, but am resolved to eat as little as I can. This month ends with two great secrets under dispute but yet known to very few: first, Who the King will marry; and What the meaning of this fleet is which we are now sheathing to set out for the southward.

Apr. 4th, 1661. To my workmen, then to my Lord's, and there dined with Mr. Shepley. After dinner I went in to my Lord and there we had a great deal of musique, and then came my cozen Tom Pepys and there did accept of the security which we gave him for his £1,000 that we borrowed of him, and so the money to be paid next week. Then to the Privy Seal, and so with Mr. Moore to my father's, where some friends did sup there and we with them and late went home, leaving my wife still there. So to bed.

Apr. 4th, 1663. Up betimes and to my office. I returned home to dinner, whither by and by comes Roger Pepys, Mrs. Turner, her daughter, Joyce Norton, and a young lady, a daughter of Coll. Cockes, my uncle Wight, his wife and Mrs. Anne Wight. Very merry, at, before, and after dinner, and the more for that my dinner was great, and most neatly dressed by our only maid. We had a fricasee of rabbits and chickens, a leg of mutton boiled, three carps in a dish, a great dish of a side of lamb, a dish of roasted pigeons, a dish of four lobsters, three tarts, a lamprey pie (a most rare pie), a dish of anchovies, good wine of several sorts, and all things mighty noble and to my great content.

Apr. 5th, 1663. (Lord's day.) Up and spent the morning, till the Barber came, in reading in my chamber part of Osborne's Advice to his Son (which I shall not never enough admire for sense and language), and being by and by trimmed, to Church, myself, wife, Ashwell,[11] &c. Home to dinner, it raining, while that was prepared to my office to read over my vows with great affection and to very good purpose. So to dinner, and very well pleased with it. Then to church again, where a simple bawling young Scot preached. So home to my office alone till dark, reading some papers of my old navy precedents, and so home to supper, and, after some pleasant talk, my wife, Ashwell, and I to bed.

Apr. 19th, 1663. (Easter day.) Up and this day put on my close-kneed colored suit, which, with new stockings of the color, with belt, and new gilt-handled sword, is very handsome. To church alone, and so to dinner, where my father and brother Tom dined with us, and after dinner to church again, my father sitting below in the chancel. After church done, where the young Scotchman preaching I slept all the while, my father and I to see my uncle and aunt Wight, and after a stay of an hour there my father to my brother's and I home to supper, and after supper fell in discourse of dancing, and I find that Ashwell hath a very fine carriage,[12] which makes my wife almost ashamed of herself to see herself so outdone, but tomorrow she begins to learn to dance [13] for a month or two. So to prayers and to bed.

[11] ASHWELL—Mary Ashwell, maid to Mrs. Pepys, addressed without a title because she was a servant. Notice how the Pepyses have prospered.
[12] FINE CARRIAGE—That is, carries herself well.
[13] LEARN TO DANCE—To improve her carriage.

DID YOU READ WITH UNDERSTANDING?

1. In the entries for January and March, 1660, how many hints do you find that Pepys was in sympathy with Charles and was hoping for a restoration of the monarchy? Cite them.

2. From the *Diary*, what have you learned about fashions in clothes during the Restoration period? What have you learned about habits of eating? What, for instance, are the most striking differences between their dinner menus and ours? Should you like to have been a housemaid in a Restoration home? Why or why not?

3. What evidence do you find that Pepys was an educated man? What accomplishments did he have?

4. From these selections, what have you learned about kinds of entertainment popular in England in the 1660's? Name the forms of amusement that Pepys mentions in various entries. Are they very different from our own amusements? Discuss.

5. What details from these selections do you think Pepys would have omitted if he had not written his *Diary* in shorthand?

6. Cite at least one instance to prove that Pepys was not guilty of self-deception, that he did not "kid" himself.

7. What was the author's attitude toward religion? What faults of character do you find in him? What admirable traits does he have?

8. Be prepared to give a short description—either oral or written—of Samuel Pepys as you imagine him, covering his personal appearance, personality, and character.

A SONG FOR
ST. CECILIA'S DAY

JOHN DRYDEN

Most people are familiar with two lovely paintings of St. Cecilia, one by Raphael and one by Rubens, both representing her playing a musical instrument with angels sweeping down from the skies to listen. There is no doubt that the same pictures were in Dryden's mind when he composed his song for St. Cecilia's Day.

Cecilia was one of the early Christian martyrs, and Church tradition made her the patron saint of music. According to one story she invented an arrangement of musical pipes, a forerunner of the organ, which she used as an accompaniment for her hymns. During the seventeenth century it was the custom to hold festivals of music on St. Cecilia's Day. Composers and poets were invited to write special music and songs for these festivals. Dryden, as Poet Laureate, composed two such songs—

one in 1687 and a second, which he called "Alexander's Feast," in 1697. The poems are written in the irregular stanza form of the *ode,* and both have been greatly admired.

I

FROM harmony, from heavenly harmony
　　This universal frame began;
　　When Nature underneath a heap
　　　Of jarring atoms lay,
5　　And could not heave her head,
　The tuneful voice was heard from high,
　　　Arise, ye more than dead!

Then cold and hot and moist and dry
　　In order to their stations leap,
10　　And Music's power obey.
From harmony, from heavenly harmony
　　This universal frame began:
　　From harmony to harmony
　Through all the compass of the notes it ran,
15　The diapason closing full in Man.

II

What passion cannot Music raise and quell?
　　When Jubal struck the chorded shell,
　　His listening brethren stood around,
　　And, wondering, on their faces fell
20　　To worship that celestial sound:
Less than a god they thought there could not dwell
　　Within the hollow of that shell
　　That spoke so sweetly, and so well.
What passion cannot Music raise and quell?

III

25　　The trumpet's loud clangor
　　　Excites us to arms

15. DIAPASON—A chord including all notes or tones. Dryden is referring in these first two stanzas to the tradition that at the Creation, the heavenly bodies sang together.

17. JUBAL—According to the Hebrews, "the father of all such as play the lyre or pipes." He is named in *Genesis* 4:21. The King James Version translated *pipes* as *organ,* though of course the organ had not been imagined in Jubal's day.

With shrill notes of anger
And mortal alarms.
The double, double, double beat
30   Of the thundering drum
Cries, hark! the foes come;
Charge, charge, 'tis too late to retreat.

IV

The soft complaining flute
In dying notes discovers
35   The woes of hopeless lovers,
Whose dirge is whispered by the warbling lute.

V

Sharp violins proclaim
Their jealous pangs and desperation,
Fury, frantic indignation,
40   Depths of pains and height of passion
For the fair, disdainful dame.

VI

But oh! what art can teach,
What human voice can reach
The sacred organ's praise?
45   Notes inspiring holy love,
Notes that wing their heavenly ways
To mend the choirs above.

VII

Orpheus could lead the savage race,
And trees uprooted left their place,
50   Sequacious of the lyre;
But bright Cecilia raised the wonder higher:
When to her organ vocal breath was given,
An angel heard, and straight appeared—
Mistaking earth for heaven.

48. ORPHEUS—According to the Greeks, Orpheus, the son of Apollo, could play so beautifully upon his lyre that savage men and women were tamed and that rocks and trees would leave their places to follow him.

50. SEQUACIOUS OF—Following. This Latinism is a good example of the artificial, "elegant" diction that became the fashion in poetry during the Restoration period and that was to be in use for over a century.

GRAND CHORUS

55   *As from the power of sacred lays*
    The spheres began to move,
    And sung the great Creator's praise
    To all the blessed above;
    So when the last and dreadful hour
60   *This crumbling pagent shall devour,*
    The trumpet shall be heard on high,
    The dead shall live, the living die,
    And Music shall untune the sky.

FOR INTERPRETATION

1. Whose is the "tuneful voice" referred to in line 6? In line 10, do you think the word *Music* is to be taken literally? What other lines in the first two stanzas help you to the right answer? What was the last act of the Creation? What musical recognition was it given?

2. What figures of speech has Dryden used in the first two stanzas?

3. The earliest stringed instruments were made by stretching cords across empty tortoise shells. The Hebrews believed that Jubal made the first lyre; the Greeks believed that Hermes (Mercury) invented it and gave it to Apollo. Quote the lines with which Dryden describes Jubal's use of the lyre.

4. Line 16 expresses the theme for the stanzas that follow. According to the poet, what passions are aroused by musical instruments? Do you think Dryden's associations of emotions with the various instruments are appropriate? Discuss.

5. What special power did Orpheus' lyre possess? Cecilia's organ?

6. Why is the organ generally conceded to be the noblest of all musical instruments? Was the organ of Dryden's day like the organs of today? Look up the history of the organ before you answer.

7. Dryden opened his poem with reference to the Creation of the world. With what scene does he close the poem? What part shall Music play in this scene? What is the general effect created by the last stanza of the poem? Discuss.

8. If you were a great composer commissioned to write an orchestral score as an accompaniment to Dryden's ode, what kind of music would you use for the various parts of the poem? Write a musical outline, stanza by stanza, indicating the number and kind of instruments you would use, the kind of airs and harmony, and so on. How would you secure an effect of climax for the Grand Chorus?

EXTENDED ACTIVITIES

DIFFERENCES BETWEEN PURITAN AND CAVALIER
BROUGHT CIVIL WAR

HISTORY IN BRIEF

	The Stuarts	Events in America
1600-1699 (17th Century)	Charles I (1625-1649), executed 1649 Oliver Cromwell as Lord Protector, followed by his son, Richard (1649-1660) Charles II (1660-1685) (Plague of London, 1665) (Fire of London, 1666) James II (1685-1688) (The Bloodless Revolution) William and Mary (1688-1694) (The Bill of Rights) William III (1694-1702)	Settlement of colonies: Dover, N. H. 1623 Maine 1625 Delaware 1627 Maryland 1634 Connecticut 1635 North Carolina 1653 South Carolina 1659 New Netherlands 1664 New Netherlands changed to New York, 1664 King Philip's War, 1675-1678 King William's War, 1689-1697 Salem witchcraft persecutions

FOR ACQUAINTANCE WITH AUTHORS

THE "METAPHYSICAL" POETS

JOHN DONNE (1573–1631)—"DEATH"

Many of the truly great men of English letters have been preachers whose fame in their day rested upon their brilliant and moving sermons. Any writing they did was incidental to the tasks of their ministry. John Donne was one of the most famous of this distinguished group. His two and three hour sermons transported his listeners "to Heaven in holy raptures"; audiences at Whitehall, the King's Chapel, worried over the health of their beloved cleric. Tortuous and involved language damps our enthusiasm for his long sermons, but in his simple lyrics the goodness and genuineness of the man shines forth.

John Donne was the son of a Welsh ironmonger who died while John was a child. The boy's precocity was recognized and despite hardships he was educated at Cambridge. Soon after college, he renounced Catholicism and joined the Anglican faith. He accompanied Lord Essex, Elizabeth's ill-fated favorite, on his expeditions to the Azores and the continent. On his return to England Donne accepted a minor post in the house of the Lord Keeper of the Seal. There he met Ann More, niece of his master.

The two fell in love and were married; John was immediately dismissed by the Lord Keeper and imprisoned. Ann's devotion to her young husband won his release and he began practicing law to support Ann and his growing family. His faith and sincerity led friends to persuade him to enter the ministry where he was finally ordained in 1615. His success was rapid, but the death of his beloved wife left him with little pleasure in his appointment as royal chaplain and in his rising popularity as a poet.

GEORGE HERBERT (1593–1633)—"VIRTUE," "EASTER"

At a period when the excesses of Renaissance England were often too evident, the quiet, scholarly life of George Herbert is as welcome as were his graceful lyrics. Born in Wales, George Herbert early distinguished himself as a scholar and orator, and was appointed public orator there for eight years. Like Spenser he was hopeful of a position at court, but when none came he resigned himself to a quiet life in the Church. At thirty-seven he took clerical orders and was assigned to a tiny parish in New Bemerton.

His writing, like himself, was devoted to the service of the Church. His little church held services twice a day; many of the hymns he wrote himself. His poetry was filled with sincere religious feeling. As a model for other young clerics, he wrote *A Priest to the Temple,* a sort of handbook of useful rules for a country parson. He and his parish grew fond of each other, but after only three years at New Bemerton, Herbert died of tuberculosis.

PURITAN WRITERS

JOHN MILTON (1608–1674)—"ON HIS BLINDNESS," "APOSTROPHE TO LIGHT," "EVENING IN PARADISE"

It is easy to imagine young Will Shakespeare cutting classes, flunking a quiz now and then, playing a good game at shortstop. John Milton was of a different sort. He was a frail studious child, the son of a well-to-do banker and lawyer who had been disinherited for his Puritanism. Milton's father was passionately fond of music and had earned fame as a composer. The Milton household breathed an atmosphere of study, music, and piety. In this quiet, well-ordered, but sternly sober home, little John at eight years began under tutors a regime of studies which would have stifled a less greedy mind. At the age of twelve his school day began at six in the morning and lasted often until midnight.

After finishing the course at St. Paul's School, he entered Christ College, Cambridge. There, like Bacon, he found little that was challenging. Once, in utter disgust he described the curriculum as an "asinine feast of soused thistles and brambles." His quiet shyness, his long auburn hair and fair skin, and his Puritan ways earned for him the nickname of "Our

Lady of Christ's." His Puritan convictions deepened and after seven years at Cambridge he had about decided to enter the ministry. The intolerance of the Established Church led him, however, at the age of twenty-four to vow to give his life to writing poetry in the same way that a minister might give himself to religion.

For five years Milton retired to his father's country house at Horton; reading in English, Latin, Greek, French, Italian, and Hebrew; writing some and meditating. A period of travel in  Italy followed. He returned to set up a small school for boys where his strictness and impatience with failure must have made him respected but unloved. He had married a pretty young girl of eighteen, Mary Powell, daughter of a Cavalier squire. It was an unfortunate selection for the gay, fun-loving Mary was vastly unhappy in the sober Puritan household. At one time Mary left her staid husband to return to her home, but at last she was persuaded to come back.

Milton continued his teaching and writing until the Puritan-Cavalier disputes flamed into Civil War. For the next twenty years he gave his time to politics. Because of his ability as a writer and scholar, he entered the disputes as a pamphleteer, his violence enraging the Royalists and delighting the Puritans. With Cromwell's rise as "Protector" Milton became his secretary under the title of Latin Secretary to the Council of State. Part of his task was to carry on all the correspondence with foreign countries—in Latin. Warned by his physician that continued writing meant blindness, Milton remained at his post: handling the records, writing state documents, and defending the new government by pamphlets. His pamphlets covered all the political problems of his own day. Most are of little interest to us; his pamphlets on education and divorce were noteworthy for their advanced views; in *Areopagitica* he plead for freedom of the press.

The last years of Milton's life have been called his period of "defeat," but a glorious defeat it was. At forty-four he was totally blind; the tasks he had set for himself as a young man were scarcely begun. The Royalists had returned; no one man had exasperated them more than he. Puritans lost belongings, homes, and lives. Milton was forced to go into hiding but escaped the scaffold. He retired from active life and set himself to his great work, *Paradise Lost,* dictating the chapters to his three daughters who chafed at his severity and at having to read long hours to him in languages of which they understood not a word. In 1667 the poem was published; Milton received about twenty pounds for his years of labor. Its popularity, however, resulted in the sale of 1,200 copies within three months of publication. *Paradise Regained* and *Samson Agonistes* followed. Milton's success as a writer was assured. Although he lost much in the Great Fire of 1666 his last years were spent quietly and prosperously. Writers and readers of all lands recognized and paid tribute to his genius.

Had Milton died at thirty-four he would have been famous as one of the great lyricists. Had he died at forty-four he would have been revered as a great statesman and pamphleteer. Living to be sixty-six he added to both of these his best claim to fame, that of the greatest epic poet in English literature.

JOHN BUNYAN (1628–1688)—"IN THE VALLEY OF HUMILIATION"

In another age John Bunyan with his white-hot religious zeal and his great courage would probably have been one of the first martyrs thrown to the lions for the emperor's pleasure. As it was, he suffered a martyrdom equally real if not as spectacular—the martyrdom of his own mind and that of filthy English prisons.

As the son of a poor tinsmith, young John learned little more than to read and write. Even as a child he was considered eminently pious but

his sleep was broken by hideous dreams of punishment for his four great sins: dancing, ringing the church bells, playing tipcat (a sort of seventeenth century baseball), and swearing.

At twenty Bunyan married and under the influence of his pious wife and the religious books she brought with her he began to feel the call to preach. His simple faith and evident sincerity impressed the minds of the poor people who gathered to listen to him. With the re-establishment of the State Church and the Restoration in 1600, laws were passed prohibiting unlicensed preachers from holding public services. Bunyan nevertheless continued his services openly and was arrested while preaching one night in a

farmhouse. For nearly twelve years he was a prisoner in the village jail although his sentence would have been commuted had he promised never to preach again. Laboriously he began to put on paper the religious fervor that burned within him—a fervor that overflowed, despite his meager learning into nearly sixty works. But if he had written nothing besides *The Pilgrim's Progress*, he would forever be counted great.

The Pilgrim's Progress was immediately popular. After his release from prison, Bunyan continued writing and preaching, gathering more and more followers. His simple language and his sincerity won over even educated scholars. Before his death, this simple tinsmith's son whose life had shown him willing to suffer martyrdom for his faith, was known throughout England as "Bishop Bunyan."

THE CAVALIER POETS

ROBERT HERRICK (1591–1674)—"TO THE VIRGINS, TO MAKE MUCH OF TIME," "TO DIANEME"

Robert Herrick was branded as a Cavalier and Royalist because he was a vicar in the Established Church and not a Puritan, and perhaps, because he sometimes saw the beauty and brightness of life rather than its sinfulness. His elaborate, but sometimes witty, sermons were popular with the neighborhood gentry. His light tuneful poetry, devoted more to the charms of nature than the charms of religion, delighted the literary circles. In 1647 the Puritans ejected him from his parish, along with many others of Royalist leanings. At the return of Charles II he again took up his duties at the same vicarage where he served until his death.

THOMAS CAREW (1595–1645)—"THE UNFADING BEAUTY"

Thomas Carew, one of the earliest of the Cavalier song writers, was also the only one fortunate enough to live out his life before Charles I's execution and the resultant debacle of noblemen's hopes. Life was kind to Carew. Born of wealthy parents, Thomas went to Oxford at thirteen. His court career began as secretary to an ambassador whom he accompanied on missions to France and The Hague. Rising rapidly through services to the Crown, he became, in 1630, taster-in-ordinary to Charles I and one of the King's close confidants. Although his busy court life left him little leisure, Carew often wrote verses modeled after those of John Donne whom he admired tremendously. He knew Suckling and Jonson and was a respected member of both literary and court circles.

EDMUND WALLER (1606–1687)—"GO, LOVELY ROSE!"

It was the mark of a Cavalier gentleman to be able to turn an easy rhyme and Waller felt himself a true Cavalier gentleman. He lacked the personal charm of Herrick, but in his own age he was respected as a politician and a poet. He first sat in Parliament at the age of fifteen, continuing as a member now and again for the next sixty years. His part in a plot in the King's behalf resulted in his expulsion from the House by the Puritans, but Cromwell finally allowed him to return. At the Restoration he quickly presented his poem, "Upon His Majesty's Return," and kept his seat in Parliament and his reputation at court. He steadfastly refused to endorse the policies of the religious bigots, defending Nonconformists and Catholics alike. In his own day his lyrics were immensely popular; but only a few of the simplest are favorites today.

SIR JOHN SUCKLING (1609–1642)—"SONG FROM 'AGLAURA'"

John Suckling was the gayest of the whole gay crowd who danced and sang and bowled at the court of Charles I. At eighteen he inherited the huge estates left by his father who had been a Secretary of State under James I. Young John's talents ran to versifying rather than to statesmanship. He was handsome and witty, well-educated and well-traveled, the best card player and the best bowler at court. His clever verses, light and often cynical, made him a tremendous favorite with lords and ladies alike. Many a young writer must have looked at him and sighed with envy at his success.

Charles I's excessive demands and the rise of the Puritan party changed the picture overnight. As a trusted friend of the King, Suckling had to flee the country to save his life. Disconsolate and afraid to face poverty and banishment, he took poison shortly after reaching France.

RICHARD LOVELACE (1618–1658)—"TO LUCASTA, ON GOING TO THE WARS," "TO ALTHEA, FROM PRISON"

Richard Lovelace, devoted to the Royalist cause, lost his fortune, his fiancee, his health, and his freedom to the Parliamentarians—but not without a valiant struggle. Wealthy, handsome, and clever, Lovelace was popular among the circle of Charles I's court. After the break between the King and Parliament, Lovelace sponsored and presented to Parliament a petition defending the King. He was promptly thrown in prison. It was during this two years' imprisonment that he wrote his lyric, "To Althea." On his release he joined Charles I in France, sacrificing his estate to raise a regiment to support the French king in his attempt to put Charles again on the English throne. When the young Royalist was wounded in the King's service, his fiancee thought him dead and married another. Later he was captured and held as a prisoner on parole throughout the Civil War. Generous as long as he had money, to musicians and scholars, he died in near poverty the year that Richard Cromwell succeeded his father and there was once more hope for the Royalist cause.

RESTORATION WRITERS

JOHN DRYDEN (1631–1700)—"A SONG FOR ST. CECILIA'S DAY"

Born during the reign of Charles I, John Dryden lived through the Cromwell interlude, through the restoration of the last two Stuarts, and on into the period of William and Mary. He was a Puritan under Cromwell, and Episcopalian under Charles II, a Catholic under James II. But he refused to return to Protestantism under William and Mary, even though it meant the loss of royal favor.

In a century when politics dominated every phase of life, including writing, Dryden had been willing to seek advancement by writing flattering and timely verses. He had, for instance, written a poem in honor of Cromwell; but he also wrote one to welcome Charles II. And he devoted the best years of his life to writing cheap plays to please the court—plays that featured spirits fluttering through the air and stabbed heroines who came to life to deliver appropriate epilogues. The plays brought

Dryden financial independence. Later he turned to political satires. Many a man lost his reputation and his job through the poison of Dryden's pen.

He had been appointed Poet Laureate in 1668, but lost the office some twenty years later under William and Mary. During the last years of his life he turned public attention once more to the masterpieces of Greek and Roman literature by translating Homer and Virgil into rhymed couplets. Comfortably stretched out in the arm chair reserved for him each night at Will's Coffee House, he held forth on the rules of good writing. He was a real power; and many a young writer must have moved hesitantly into the circle near the firelight, his delight in meeting the great man tempered by fear of his still malevolent tongue.

SAMUEL PEPYS (1633–1703)—"DIARY"

How fortunate it is that an obscure clerk in the Admiralty enjoyed putting on paper the menu served at the coronation banquet of Charles II, the price of his wife's new petticoat, and the style of a waistcoat he envied! Through the dandified little clerk with the pretty wife we have a detailed record of nine of the most interesting years in England's history. Samuel Pepys was the fifth son of a family that had risen by sheer industry from yeoman farmers to the gentry. The young Samuel, inquisitive and ambitious, worked his way through Cambridge as a waiter. At twenty-two he married a clever, half-French girl, the Elizabeth of his diary, whose taste for pretty clothes worked such havoc with the Pepys's family budget.

Because of his energy and honesty, Pepys's career prospered. He became clerk of the king's ships, surveyor-general of the victualling office, and finally, Secretary to the Admiralty. In all his positions he was thoroughly competent, although when he entered as a clerk he was so ignorant of business that he scarcely knew the multiplication tables. When the plague ravaged London he remained at his desk when others fled to the country. Even after his public career was finished, his reputation led to his being consulted about navy affairs.

In 1669 his failing eyesight forced him to give up his diary which he had written in code that he might be completely frank. The diary was not deciphered until 1825, but since then the diligent little man's story has charmed all who read it.

OF LITERARY FORM AND STYLE

PURITAN INFLUENCE ON VERSE AND PROSE
Puritan Verse

The rise of the Puritan had been swift and his day was short, but in that brief reign he wrought an influence which the world still feels. English Puritans were often wealthy, influential persons. As a class they were intelligent and well educated. They appreciated music and art; but they viewed life soberly. Very shortly after the death of Elizabeth, that sober shading crept over the face of English verse. It was apparent even in lyric poetry. Many of the new writers were men of the Church. Even if they had not yet joined ranks with the Puritans, they nevertheless introduced into their own lives a kind of Puritanic austerity and spirituality.

Typical of such poets were John Donne and George Herbert. Critics later called these men, and other poets who followed their lead, the "metaphysical" poets, because their themes went beyond the physical aspects of life. Their work was likely to be deeply religious, but sometimes it took on a strain of the fantastic, mysterious, and obscure. And almost always it was tinged with melancholy.

If the foreshadowing of a great movement may be seen in the works of these minor poets, its enduring monument appears in the works of one master-writer—John Milton. In himself he personified the moral righteousness of the age. It burns in his precocious earnestness, in his devoutness, in his consecration to duty and to God. At the age of twenty-three we find him writing a sonnet of reproach because his life has shown "no bud or blossom." And yet he had already composed an impressive sheaf of English and Latin verse. There was no need for him to work for his living, but no man ever drove himself harder. There was no question in his mind as to what end he was born. It was to do the will of God in the world, and so he labored "as ever in my great Task-master's eye."

The volume of his collected poems shows the result of most of that work. More than half of the volume—and it is a large one—holds *Paradise Lost* and its sequel, *Paradise Regained*. There is also a long dramatic poem based on the Old Testament story of Samson, and a shorter, idyllic "Masque of Comus." The other hundred-odd pages contain the Latin poems written between his sixteenth and twenty-first years, his sonnets, his paraphrases of the Psalms, and various occasional poems.

Besides the sonnets, the twin poems "L'Allegro" and "Il Penseroso" are the best known of the shorter works. The first of the two is a picture of twenty-four hours as a man in a happy mood might want to spend them; the second is a picture of a night and day as a man in melancholy mood would like to spend them. Both poems are filled with references to Greek and Roman mythology, to books and music and study. Only an intellectual superman could conceive of hours so filled with knowledge, study, and meditation and call it pleasure. But Milton had a super-mind. An intellectual bent is evident in everything he wrote. Master of half a dozen languages, he seems familiar with all the works by all the writers in each of them. He knows by heart the Bible and its hard Old-Testament names. Glance through his roll-call of the evil spirits in the first book of *Paradise Lost* and remember that the poet was blind when he composed that stupendous catalogue of names! The very extent of his learning has been a stumbling block to readers.

There are pages of Milton that cannot be assimilated without the help of an encyclopedia. But in spite of difficult allusions, long sentences, hard words, and extended metaphors, there is that in Milton's verse which repays the study spent in reading it. His rhythms are magnificent and his conceptions lofty. And among his lines are many that are the essence of vast rich poetry. Like Shakespeare he has built word-combinations of universal and immortal appeal.

In *Paradise Lost* we are amazed at the dignity and power vested in Satan. He is an opponent worthy a Celestial foe, accepting his changed fortunes with defiance—

> "Hail horrors! hail
> Receive thy new possessor! one who brings
> A mind not to be changed by place or time:
> The mind is its own place, and in itself
> Can make a Heaven of Hell, a Hell of Heaven
> What matter where, if I be still the same!"

In fact one of the criticisms of the work is that it has made Satan rather than God its most heroic figure. Nevertheless the poem remains the one *artistic epic* in English literature. It is legendary in subject, heroic in dimensions, majestic in form, and truly representative in spirit and philosophy of the Puritan Age which produced it. However far short Milton may have come of his presumptive purpose of justifying God, he did produce a mighty work of art.

Puritan Prose

It is not surprising that the seventeenth century produced a great deal of good prose literature. Simple, straightforward English suited the serious purpose of the Puritan. Even Milton wrote prose during the years that he sacrificed to service in the affairs of state.

Mention has already been made of several volumes of religious prose which found a wide and appreciative reading circle in the New World as well as in the old—Browne's *Religion of a Physician,* Taylor's *Holy Living and Holy Dying,* Baxter's *Saints' Everlasting Rest.* These books were not controversial in nature, but were marked by reverence, tolerance, and sweetness of spirit. The writers were clergymen and doctors—professional men with a taste for study, deeply touched by the religious bent of the times.

But the most astonishingly successful book of the period was the work of a very different sort of man—a fervent evangelist of humble background and scant learning—John Bunyan. The name of his masterpiece is known to all who read the English tongue, for no other book except the Bible has been mentioned so often by other writers. Those who read it today are likely to be disappointed in the rather simple story of a Christian's journey through an unfriendly world. To appreciate its tremendous appeal in the days of our forefathers, we need to remember, first, that it appeared in a day when there were few *stories* in literature, and second, that our grandparents made its acquaintance at an early age when the fairy-tale element of the allegory kindled childish imaginations. Puritan children who played the game of make-believe with the scenes of *The Pilgrim's Progress* remembered the incidents as they grew older and interpreted them in the terms of their growing experience. Similarly people differing so greatly in times and personality as Cotton Mather, the Alcott sisters, and Theodore Roosevelt II are alike in naming it the most vividly remembered and most deeply influential reading of their youth. Bunyan's style is unassuming. But it has dignity and force. There is a distinctly Biblical flavor to his vocabulary and turn of sentences. Indeed, the book is the not unnatural product of a man of sensitive nature and vivid imagination whose chief schooling was a reading and rereading of the King James Version of the Holy Bible.

One other prose writer of the period deserves special mention—Izaak Walton, whose ninety years almost spanned the arc of the century. The book that has kept his name alive is his little treatise on fishermen and fishing—*The Compleat Angler*. Twentieth-century fishers still turn its pages with an appreciative smile. It tells no "fish stories." The reader rambles along an English country road, meets a shepherd, hears a milkmaid singing, casts a fly, catches a trout or two, and speculates upon the world and all the pleasant things in it. To day-dreaming anglers, especially to older men, the book seems to have captured the charm of the sport that gives man a chance to "loaf and invite his soul." Walton was not a Puritan. He took no militant part in the struggles of his day. But his books have the serenity and sweetness that marked the best prose of his puritanic age.

QUESTIONS IN APPRECIATION:

1. How does the lyric poetry of Puritan England differ in *subject matter* from the lyrics of Elizabethan England? Illustrate your answer by quoting typical titles of lyrics from both periods.

2. Are there any respects in which "Virtue" is like an Elizabethan lyric? Discuss.

3. Which poem do you think is easier to understand, "Virtue" or "Easter"? Does either poem have a touch of the mysticism which characterized the work of the metaphysical poets? Discuss.

4. Does Donne's sonnet on "Death" appeal primarily to the heart or to the intelligence of the reader? Give the reasons for your answer. In what respects is "Death" characteristic of Puritan lyric verse?

5. Compare the forms of the two sonnets "Death" and "On His Blindness." In what respects are they different? Which is harder to read aloud? Why?

6. Does Milton's sonnet appeal especially to the mind or to the heart? Or to both? Be prepared to defend your answer.

7. What references in Milton's poems show his familiarity with the Bible? What references show his familiarity with Greek literature?

8. What is an *apostrophe* (see *Appendix*)? Why have the opening lines to Book III of *Paradise Lost* been called an "apostrophe to Light"?

9. Which selection from Milton do you think has the most poetic appeal—the sonnet, the "Apostrophe to Light," or "Evening in Paradise"?

10. Select three adjectives which you think definitely describe the style of Milton's verse.

11. What is an allegory? Prove that the selection from *The Pilgrim's Progress* is allegorical.

12. How old a reader do you think would enjoy the story of Pilgrim's adventure with Apollyon? Why? How old a reader would find the most *meaning* in the selection? Why?

13. Summarize briefly the influence of Puritan thought on seventeenth-century poetry and prose.

CAVALIER LYRICS

To draw exact lines between the types of poetry produced during a given century is, of course, impossible. Writers reflect in various ways the influence of their times, and no one writer can be guaranteed always to write in the same fashion. However, any one who reads through the large amount of lyric verse written in the years following Elizabeth discovers that it is of two distinctly different sorts. There was a group of serious writers whose work was mainly religious. These we have considered with the Puritan poets because they reflect the sobering influence of Puritan ideals. And there is a second group, composed chiefly of young men who, for want of a better term, are usually called "Cavalier" or "Caroline" poets. Most of them were followers of King Charles. They wrote co-temporaneously with the Religious Poets and were not untouched by that influence. And yet their verse is in a class by itself.

It is marked first of all by a practical, down-to-earth attitude toward "life and love and all things else." Although modern slang was yet to coin the phrase, they seemed to be waging a "de-bunking" campaign in the field of poetry, especially love poetry. No Cavalier poet believed for one moment that his lady did "in herself contain all this world's riches that may far be found." Beautiful she might be—but, so what? Flowers fade and women grow old. One of two conclusions usually followed. The first was altogether worldly—"Gather ye rosebuds while ye may!" Make the most of today, you can't escape wrinkles tomorrow! The second was more in accord with George Herbert's philosophy—seek then that loveliness which does not die, *beauty of mind and spirit*. Thus even the gayest Cavalier shows sometimes a serious nature. In fact, so mixed up were the times that the author of some of the most worldly lyrics was himself a clergyman—Robert Herrick.

There are other characteristics of Cavalier verse. It is keen, clever, sometimes flippant, but always sensible. Each poem has a theme and is carefully constructed around it. Sometimes the theme is idealistic, sometimes cynical. But it is there, and well inscribed in an attractive setting. They were good craftsmen, these poets. Their work is never slipshod nor inconsequential. It makes sense; it challenges our thought. It is in direct contrast with Elizabethan lyrics which stir our hearts rather than our minds. It is thus much easier to analyze. A Shakespearean song delights our soul—who cares to know why? A seventeenth-century lyric excites our admiration, and we can trace step by step just how the poet did it. Suckling, Herrick, Lovelace, Carew—they were a brilliant set of writers, and their verse has the polish—and often the hardness—of a well-cut gem.

QUESTIONS IN APPRECIATION:

1. Be prepared to show how in any lyric of the Cavalier group each stanza contributes toward the development of the theme.

2. Make one list of titles of lyrics that develop a cynical or worldly theme. Make another list that express a worthy or idealistic theme. Which list is longer?

3. Review the lyrics in the Elizabethan section and also those in the Puritan group. Be prepared to show in class that there is a closer resemblance between the two groups of seventeenth-century poets than there is between either of those groups and the Elizabethans. Be very definite in your points of comparison.

4. True or false?—*Cavalier poets used figures of speech sparingly but skillfully.* Discuss.

5. Which single poem in the Cavalier group seems to you most artistic? Why? Which one do you think contains lines most worth remembering? Why?

LITERATURE OF THE RESTORATION

English literature for the last forty years of the seventeenth century mirrors the swing back from Puritan extremism as well as the gradual adoption of an elaborate, formal style based somewhat upon French models. But again we are reminded that there is no clean-cut cleavage between the old and the new. We know, for example, that Milton and Bunyan wrote their greatest works after the Restoration—and that both were well received. Nevertheless, tastes were changing; and the rising writers aimed at pleasing a different class of readers.

Charles II had been welcomed to the throne with extravagant hopes for a return of "good times." The first reaction against the Puritans affected the way of living. Theaters were reopened, music and dancing revived, and "pleasures of the world" were flaunted openly. The times are best reflected in two incidental pieces of literature, both diaries, and one at least making no pretense of being literature. That one is the detailed and frank, personal record kept by Samuel Pepys for the years between 1660 and 1669. It was written to please no one but the author. Yet the man who deciphered it more than a hundred years later discovered that here—

in spite of its apparently careless diary style—was real literature. The explanation is simple. All unconsciously Pepys had captured the everliving features of men and women. Fads and fashions change from year to year. Human nature never changes. That is the prime lesson we learn from writers like Chaucer, Shakespeare, and even Samuel Pepys. Under their touch a long-dead age revives in terms that we can believe and understand. We know Pepys himself, his pride in his pretty wife, his business associates, the rather frumpy queen and ordinary princesses. All are very real—the good mixed with the bad, and even the badness sometimes engaging.

The *Diary* of John Evelyn was much more carefully written and covers a much longer period of time—from 1640 to 1706. Although it lacks the human appeal of Pepys's work, it is extremely interesting reading. Evelyn tried to set down fairly and accurately the important events of his times. He was a Royalist; but he did not close his eyes to the faults of the King. In his account of the death of Charles II (February 4, 1685) he carefully weighs the graces of the King with his faults and finds him wanting—a wasted life and opportunity. Both diaries carry interesting accounts of the Coronation, the Plague, the Fire. And there are enlightening comments on popular amusements. Together the two diaries provide a panoramic picture of the Restoration years.

The conscious literary figure of the age was John Dryden—a man whose work shows the same shifting pattern as his life. Dryden was an opportunist. He rode before the gale and changed his ports to fit the wind. His writing reflects his changing loyalties in politics and religion. During the twenty-five years when Dryden was in his prime, Charles II was king. He had spent eleven years in a life of "refined" pleasure in Paris. Now he wanted for the English stage, plays in the French fashion —bright, witty, and not too nice. Dryden undertook to write them— three plays a year for twenty years—and not one of them worth saving. They were written in the rhymed couplet which Waller had made popular; and though there were occasional brilliant passages, most of them jingle emptily away. To prove that he could be a good poet if he chose, Dryden wrote one superior play, *All for Love,* in excellent blank verse. It is the only one still read.

Besides his plays he wrote a number of satires in verse. One was a bitter piece ridiculing a rival poet. One was an elaborate political satire upholding the policies of the king at the time of Monmouth's Rebellion. One was in defense of the Catholic Church, which he had joined after James II came to the throne. These satires are interesting now chiefly because he used the heroic couplet so expertly that it became the literary weapon of Alexander Pope and his followers in the next century. Of real merit poetically are his shorter poems, particularly the two odes written for St. Cecilia's Day.

Modern critics rate Dryden's prose more important than his verse— especially the critical essays which appeared as prefaces in his edited collections of earlier poets. In such criticisms he discards the over-elegance affected in his verse and talks in strong, simple terms. In fact one discriminating modern writer, Clifford Box, goes so far as to say that Dryden is the "supreme stylist in English prose," possessing "strength, speed, music, continuity, and range." And yet, unfortunately, with all his literary skill, Dryden misses the mark of greatness. We are not carried away by anything he wrote. His judgment strikes us as biased; and we look in vain for tenderness or warmth—for, indeed, a more humble but essential quality—sincerity.

QUESTIONS IN APPRECIATION:

1. Point out several ways in which the selections from Samuel Pepys's *Diary* disclose an attitude toward life quite different from that of the Puritan writers. Do you find in these selections any signs that some Puritan influence was still being felt? Discuss.

2. Bearing in mind the fact that Pepys was keeping a personal diary with no idea that anyone else would ever read it, how would you describe his style of writing? For example, does he use hard words or easy words? Is his thought, on the whole, clearly expressed? Does it sound more "modern" than the English of Shakespeare or Bacon? What words or expressions give the *Diary* a seventeenth-century flavor?

3. Why was John Dryden the most important literary figure of the Restoration period? Do you think modern readers would find the subject matter of his plays and satires interesting? Why or why not?

4. Is Dryden's "A Song for St. Cecilia's Day" as easy to read as the Cavalier lyrics? Give the reasons for your answer.

5. Does the poem show an evidence of an artificial or "refined" vocabulary and style? Discuss.

6. Look up the definition of an *ode* in the *Appendix*. Does Dryden's "Song" fit the definition in all respects? Discuss.

7. What do modern critics consider Dryden's greatest contribution to literature? What kept him from being a really great writer? Discuss.

FOR FURTHER READING

BELLOC, HILAIRE, *Cromwell*
BRYANT, ARTHUR, *Charles II*
DOYLE, SIR ARTHUR CONAN, *Micah Clarke*
DUMAS, ALEXANDRE, *The Black Tulip*
FAGAN, JAMES B., *And So to Bed* (Pepys)
MASEFIELD, JOHN, *Martin Hyde, the Duke's Messenger*
MILTON, "L'Allegro"; "Il Penseroso"; "Comus"
MORLEY, JOHN, *Oliver Cromwell*
PALGRAVE, FRANCIS TURNER (ed.) *The Golden Treasury*
QUILLER-COUCH, SIR ARTHUR, *The Splendid Spur*
SCOTT, SIR WALTER, *The Bride of Lammermoor; Rob Roy*

IV·II

With peace came a classic period of polish and restraint.

THE COMPLAISANT EIGHTEENTH
CENTURY

(1700–1780)

The hopes of the expiring seventeenth century seemed, in the eyes of the eighteenth to have been fulfilled. Since the effect of the Revolution of 1688 had been to settle comfortably the supremacy of Parliament over the throne, politics for the next two or three generations were just important enough to make life interesting.

Before the reign of William and Mary, Parliament had used its power in the negative fashion of a father who keeps his son short of money. By gradual and well-manipulated transition, Parliament now became the government. The monarch was left with little more than the power of personality and the weight of regality. William and Mary were agreeable to the new order—docile because of the way they had come to the throne and because they had competent Whig advisers. At the death of William, the crown passed quietly to the round and stolid head of Anne, sister of Mary, who became as thoroughly pious and respectable a queen as England ever had. In spite of her uninspiring personality, her reign proved an active period in literature and was further marked with brilliant military successes.

In 1714 at the death of the good Queen, the ascendancy of Parliament was assured. Anne's successor was George I, the Elector of Hanover, and great-grandson of James I. England waited complacently for the new ruler to make the journey from Germany to England. Affairs of state went on as usual. George, it developed, could speak no English, nor did he care to learn. Perhaps his most significant achievement was his selection of a Whig cabinet. Parliament went on its happy, argumentative way, pausing now and then to hear the reports of Cabinet ministers who had consulted—in very bad Latin—with the King. George would stop his card-playing long enough to sign the necessary bills, but it was a negligible interruption for he rarely bothered about hearing the text.

George II knew more of English and of England than his father, but he too allowed the Whigs to have their way. Fortunately for these Hanover monarchs and for England, there was Sir Robert Walpole to act as Prime Minister for twenty-one years. Walpole maintained his majority in Parliament by methods which would not be countenanced today; yet he secured during his administration tremendous commercial expansion and material prosperity for England. This growth in trade seemed unaffected by a series of wars with France. Louis XIV, King of France, had been friendly to the deposed Stuarts and bitterly opposed to William. England had feared that the French, like the Spaniards a hundred years earlier, would attempt an invasion of England. By 1690 the English and French were at war; and by the middle of the eighteenth century, there had been three separate contests between them. In America, these were known as King William's, Queen Anne's, and the French-and-Indian Wars. There were a number of famous battles on the continent of Europe, but none of them seemed to settle anything.

Wars, even then, cost money; and there was a consequent increase of taxes, especially on commodities. Smuggling of tea, tobacco, and silk became a profitable trade. Buccaneering flourished about the West Indies, and Captain Kidd badgered the Spanish Main. Inside England, communications were difficult and dangerous. Agriculture made no advance. Science and education seemed at a standstill. There was little interest in religion. And though the times were called prosperous, there was great inequality in the distribution of wealth and sharp distinctions in social classes. Over all lay a thick, unhealthy fog of complacency.

Only the wealthy found much enjoyment in life. The city had become the important center of living. Society flourished. There grew up an elaborate code of gallantry. Refinement and sophistication counted rather than virtue. Coffee was the favorite drink, and the coffeehouses became lounging rooms for writers, politicians, and dandies. Here men could learn the news, transact business, talk politics or art, or gossip. The coffeehouse was a modern newspaper, club, and business office rolled into one. Different groups had their favorite coffeehouses; and men who dined together more or less regularly became "clubs." The literary men gathered at Will's where, a generation earlier, John Dryden had held forth.

Men and women affected an elaborate dress to match their manners. Women wore extravagant headdresses and richly embroidered gowns. Hats were sometimes so large that the tops had to be removed from the sedan chairs. Men wore powdered wigs, cocked hats, and satin waistcoats. Talk was mincing and "elegant." With complete absorption in their own little world of fashion and politics, belles and beaux alike were carried unseeingly past the tenements and workshops of the poor. Behind this show of wealth was a heart-sickening backdrop of squalor and human misery. And this, in brief, was England through the reign of Queen Anne and the first two Georges.

Then in 1760, George III, twenty-five years old, handsome and well educated, came to the throne. There was great rejoicing. He seemed well mannered; and best of all he had shaken off the Hanover ties. He felt himself English and was resolved to be a real English ruler. In three years' time the Treaty of Paris was signed to end the wars with France; and the English found themselves in command of the sea, with acknowledged control over India, the Mediterranean, and America.

But the rejoicing was short-lived. Though George III had the manners of a country squire, he had the vices of a despot. Through a succession of prime ministers willing to be his obedient servants, he set out on a colonial policy which was to cost England her American colonies and to weaken her prestige throughout the world. An obstinate thickhead, he failed completely to understand the temper and character of the English in either the Old World or the New; but Parliament was in Tory control. Under the blundering leadership of Lord North, the bills were passed which provoked the American colonies into declaring and winning their independence; and few there were in England to realize the tremendous import of that loss.

In the meantime life at home was changing. Englishmen were shaking off some of their torpor to become aware of existing evils. In literature came the first demands for attention. A spirit of reform whispered through Parliament. The great William Pitt, and then his son, became leaders in government, with a genuine interest in human welfare. In religion, too, there was a revival, due chiefly to the zeal of John Wesley. From one end of the island to another he preached that religious faith is not a matter of organization of churches and acceptance of creeds, but a living reality in men's hearts—a power to change the world. Wesley and his followers were laughed at as "Method-ists." The name stuck, though it was not until the end of the century that the Methodists separated from the Established Church and became an independent religious organization. The new movement gave spiritual life to thousands who had had no former connection with the church.

Literature for the century again reflects the pattern of history. It falls into two clearly marked groupings, one contemporaneous with Queen Anne and the first Hanovers, and the other stretching from the ascension of George III to the end of the century.

Writers of the first period shared the complacency of the times. They called their period the "Augustan" or Golden Age of English literature, because they were sure that their works outshone anything that had been produced by Chaucer, Shakespeare, or Milton. Their interest in Greek and Roman models and their belief that regularity and finish made art truly great led them to apply the term "classic" to their works. Partly because of their interpretation of the term, *classicism* in literature has taken on a specialized meaning, indicating work in which *the emphasis is placed upon form rather than feeling* and in which *the interest centers in man in his social relations rather than in man as an individual.* Classicism is artificial in its demand for finish and perfection. And in its classic tendencies this early eighteenth century literature was in perfect accord with the elaborate fashions of the day.

Classic poetry shows its weakness and its strength in the works of Alexander Pope. He has been one of the most quoted writers in the English tongue, but is today one of the most seldom read. His work is marred by the artificiality of the age and by his own prejudice and occasional insincerity. The most original of his works was his mock epic, "The Rape of the Lock," still interesting because it gives a good, though humorously distorted, picture of social life in the days of Queen Anne and because it tells a good story cleverly. It is a perfect example of classic verse.

Classic art is well expressed in prose; and there were more prose writers than poets in the early part of the century. Jonathan Swift was a satirist of clever craftsmanship, whose caustic wit appeared in book-length prose. The essay also became popular, especially essays on manners and fashions. The prose of the period appears at its best in the society essays of Addison and Steele, two gentlemen who worked together on the *Tatler* and *Spectator* papers—publications which proved the forerunners of the literary magazine.

By 1745 the leaders of the classic movement had passed away and a new literary dictator was in the making. Dr. Samuel Johnson was a great uncouth fellow, crude in manners but sound of heart and possessed of an extraordinary personality. About him as a center there gathered a famous group of literary men. Johnson fancied himself a Tory and a classicist; but there were in his circle men who had become sensible of the errors of society and of the blind spots in conservative government. One of the group was Edmund Burke—an out-and-out Whig, unalterably opposed to the short-sighted policies of George III and his advisers. It was Burke who made the most valiant attempts to persuade Parliament to compromise with the American colonies. Other members of the Johnson circle, notably Oliver Goldsmith and Richard Sheridan, were interested in the theater and helped to accomplish its revival. They swung away from the stilted lines of classic drama to produce two or three excellent realistic comedies.

One other important feature of the age should be mentioned in passing —the appearance of the first English novels. The new form merits a study by itself, but we pause here to note that through the hands of Defoe, Richardson, Fielding, and Goldsmith it was well initiated before the century expired.

Such a sweeping century of achievement proves in review to have left surprisingly little that is of intrinsic interest. The "Augustan" writers overestimated the value of their work. Much of it is of historic significance; little is still read. The student will remember it best for the vogue of classicism in literature, for the wit of Alexander Pope preserved in certain quotations, for the satire of Swift, for the literary elegance and healthful influence of Addison and Steele, for the strange power wielded by Dr. Johnson, for a revival of the drama, for the emergence of three new literary forms—the newspaper, the magazine, and the novel—and for the awakening interest in humanity that paved the way for the Romantic Revival of the approaching nineteenth century.

Satire ridiculed men's faults and follies.

THE RAPE OF THE LOCK

ALEXANDER POPE

Every age has its belles and beaux, its glamor-girls and its "zoot-suit" wearers. None, however, could outdo the days of Queen Anne in extravagant vanity. It was a period of satins, laces, frills, and ribboned wigs for men; of "puffs, powders, patches" for women. Coiffures were tremendous—eighteen and twenty inches high and elaborated with birds, feathers, fruits, ships' models, and the like. The frivolities of court life were immortalized in Pope's mock "epic," "The Rape of the Lock," a condensation of which appears below.

The poem grew out of a real incident that had been reported to Pope by his friend, Mr. Caryll. It seems that a social feud was raging because Lord Petre had cut a curl from the head of Miss Arabella Fermor and was threatening to wear the lock, set under crystal, in a finger ring. The appearance of Mr. Pope's poem flattered Arabella's family; and peace was restored. Fictitious names, of course, were used; but London society easily recognized Arabella in the person of Belinda.

CANTO I

WHAT dire offense from amorous causes springs,   The Invoca-
What mighty contests rise from trivial things,   tion, addressed
I sing.—This verse to Caryll, Muse! is due;   to a new Muse,
This, e'en Belinda may vouchsafe to view.
5 Slight is the subject, but not so the praise,
  If she inspire, and he approve my lays.
    Say what strange motive, Goddess! could compel
A well-bred lord t' assault a gentle belle?   announces
Oh, say what stranger cause, yet unexplored,   the subject
10 Could make a gentle belle reject a lord?   in epic
In tasks so bold, can little men engage,   style.
And in soft bosoms dwells such mighty rage?   Scene 1—
    Sol through white curtains shot a timorous ray,   Belinda's
And oped those eyes that must eclipse the day.   room.
Time—almost noon.

3. TO CARYLL, MUSE—It was classic fashion for any long poem to begin with an invitation to one of the Muses to inspire the writer. Pope acknowledges the source of his inspiration by naming a new Muse for Mr. Caryll. The invocation to the Muse also announced the subject or the theme of the poem. Typical invocations are to be found in the opening lines of Homer's *Iliad* or Milton's *Paradise Lost*.

13. SOL—The sun.

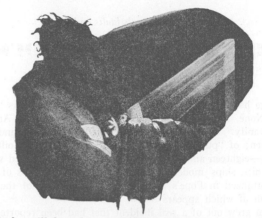

15 Belinda still her downy pillow pressed,
Her guardian sylph prolonged the balmy rest;
'Twas he had summoned to her silent bed
The morning dream that hovered o'er her head;
A youth more glittering than a birth-night beau,   Belinda
20 (That e'en in slumber caused her cheek to glow)   dreams.
Seemed to her ear his winning lips to lay,
And thus in whispers said, or seemed to say:
   "Fairest of mortals, thou distinguished care
Of thousand bright inhabitants of air!
25 Know, then, unnumbered spirits round thee fly,
The light militia of the lower sky.
These, though unseen, are ever on the wing,
Hang o'er the box, and hover round the Ring.
As now your own, our beings were of old,
30 And once enclosed in woman's beauteous mold;
Thence, by a soft transition, we repair
From earthly vehicles to these of air.
Think not, when woman's transient breath is fled,
That all her vanities at once are dead;
35 Succeeding vanities she still regards,
And though she plays no more, o'erlooks the cards.
Her joy in gilded chariots, when alive,

19. A YOUTH—To warn Belinda, her guardian sylph appeared, in her dreams, in the form of a handsome young man. Pope's first version of the poem had simply told the story of the theft of the curl and of the scandal it had aroused. Later he expanded the poem, adding the sylphs and sprites to furnish the supernatural element characteristic of epic verse.

And love of ombre, after death survive.
The light coquettes in sylphs aloft repair,
40 And sport and flutter in the fields of air.
'Tis these that early taint the female soul,
Instruct the eyes of young coquettes to roll,
Teach infant cheeks a bidden blush to know,
And little hearts to flutter at a beau.
45 "Of these am I, who thy protection claim,
A watchful sprite, and Ariel is my name. *Her guardian sprite intro-*
Late, as I ranged the crystal wilds of air, *duces himself,*
In the clear mirror of thy ruling star
I saw, alas! some dread event impend,
50 Ere to the main this morning sun descend,
But Heaven reveals not what, or how, or where. *and warns of impending*
Warned by the sylph, O pious maid, beware! *disaster.*
This to disclose is all thy guardian can:
Beware of all, but most beware of man!"
55 He said; when Shock, who thought she slept too long,
Leaped up, and waked his mistress with his tongue.
'Twas then, Belinda, if report say true, *Belinda*
Thy eyes first opened on a billet-doux; *awakes,*
Wounds, charms, and ardors were no sooner read,
60 But all the vision vanished from thy head.
And now, unveiled, the toilet stands displayed,
Each silver vase in mystic order laid. *dresses for*
First, robed in white, the nymph intent adores, *a party*
With head uncovered, the cosmetic powers.
65 A heavenly image in the glass appears,
To that she bends, to that her eyes she rears;
Th' inferior priestess, at her altar's side, *assisted by her maid*
Trembling begins the sacred rites of pride. *Betty and by the sylphs.*
Unnumbered treasures ope at once, and here
70 The various offerings of the world appear;
From each she nicely culls with curious toil,
And decks the goddess with the glittering spoil.

38. LOVE OF OMBRE—Ombre was the popular card game of the day, as much
a favorite as bridge is today.
55. SHOCK—Belinda's pet dog.
69. In lines 69–96, Belinda's dressing table is presented as an altar sacred to
Beauty; Belinda herself as a "nymph" or "goddess"; the appointments of the
table as "offerings"; the maid as a "priestess"; and so on.

This casket India's glowing gems unlocks,
And all Arabia breathes from yonder box.
75 The tortoise here and elephant unite,
Transformed to combs, the speckled, and the white.
Here files of pins extend their shining rows,
Puffs, powders, patches, bibles, billets-doux.

Now awful beauty puts on all its arms;
80 The fair each moment rises in her charms,
Repairs her smiles, awakens every grace,
And calls forth all the wonders of her face;
Sees by degrees a purer blush arise,
And keener lightnings quicken in her eyes.
85 The busy sylphs surround their darling care,
These set the head, and those divide the hair,
Some fold the sleeve, whilst others plait the gown;
And Betty's praised for labors not her own.

CANTO II

Not with more glories, in th' ethereal plain,   Belinda joins
The sun first rises o'er the purpled main,   a barge-party
on the
Thames.

83. A PURER BLUSH ARISE—The *blush* was rouge.
84. KEENER LIGHTNINGS—Girls sometimes put drops in their eyes to make
them appear more brilliant. It was a dangerous practice.

Than, issuing forth, the rival of his beams
Launched on the bosom of the silver Thames.
5 Fair nymphs, and well-dressed youths around her shone,
But every eye was fixed on her alone.
On her white breast a sparkling cross she wore,
Which Jews might kiss, and infidels adore.
Her lively looks a sprightly mind disclose,
10 Quick as her eyes, and as unfixed as those;
Favors to none, to all she smiles extends;
Oft she rejects, but never once offends.
Bright as the sun, her eyes the gazers strike,
And, like the sun, they shine on all alike.
15 Yet graceful ease, and sweetness void of pride,
Might hide her faults, if belles had faults to hide;
If to her share some female errors fall,
Look at her face, and you'll forget 'em all.
     This nymph, to the destruction of mankind,
20 Nourished two locks, which graceful hung behind

In equal curls, and well conspired to deck
With shining ringlets the smooth ivory neck.

Her ravishing
ringlets

Th' adventurous baron the bright locks admired;
He saw, he wished, and to the prize aspired.
25 Resolved to win, he meditates the way, are coveted by the Baron.
By force to ravish, or by fraud betray;
For when success a lover's toil attends,
Few ask, if fraud or force attained his ends.

[The Baron had erected an altar to Love on which he had sacrificed the souvenirs of all his former love affairs, praying the gods for success in his attempt to steal the curl. He asked "soon to obtain, and long possess the prize." Pope says that "the powers gave ear and granted *half* his prayer."]

But now secure the painted vessel glides,
30 The sunbeams trembling on the floating tides;
While melting music steals upon the sky,
And softened sounds along the waters die; ·
Smooth flow the waves, the zephyrs gently play,
Belinda smiled, and all the world was gay.
35 All but the sylph—with careful thoughts oppressed,
Th' impending woe sat heavy on his breast. Ariel senses danger
He summons straight his denizens. of air;
The lucid squadrons round the sails repair.
"Ye sylphs and sylphids, to your chief give ear!
40 Fays, fairies, genii, elves, and demons, hear!
"This day, black omens threat the brightest fair
That e'er deserved a watchful spirit's care; and tries to prevent it.
Some dire disaster, or by force, or sleight;
But what, or where, the fates have wrapped in night.
45 Whether the nymph shall break Diana's law,
Or some frail china jar receive a flaw;
Or stain her honor, or her new brocade;
Forget her prayers, or miss a masquerade;
Or lose her heart, or necklace, at a ball;
50 Or whether Heaven has doomed that Shock must fall.
Haste, then, ye spirits! to your charge repair;
The fluttering fan be Zephyretta's care;
The drops to thee, Brillante, we consign;
And, Momentilla, let the watch be thine;
55 Do thou, Crispissa, tend her favorite lock;
Ariel himself shall be the guard of Shock."

53. THE DROPS—Belinda's ear rings.

He spoke; the spirits from the sails descend;
Some, orb in orb, around the nymph extend;
Some thrid the mazy ringlets of her hair;
60 Some hang upon the pendants of her ear;

With beating hearts the dire event they wait,
Anxious and trembling for the birth of fate.

CANTO III

Close by those meads, forever crowned with flowers,
Where Thames with pride surveys his rising towers,
There stands a structure of majestic frame,
Which from the neighboring Hampton takes its name.
5 Here Britain's statesmen oft the fall foredoom
Of foreign tyrants and of nymphs at home;
Here thou, great Anna! whom three realms obey,
Dost sometimes counsel take—and sometimes tea.
Hither the heroes and the nymphs resort,
10 To taste awhile the pleasures of a court;
In various talk th' instructive hours they passed,
Who gave the ball, or paid the visit last;
One speaks the glory of the British Queen,
And one describes a charming Indian screen;
15 A third interprets motions, looks, and eyes;
At every word a reputation dies.

The party disembarks at Hampton Court—

as the guests of Queen Anne.

7. THREE REALMS—England, Ireland, and America. Notice the irony and mockery throughout this passage—lines 1–22.

Snuff, or the fan, supply each pause of chat,
With singing, laughing, ogling, and all that.
Meanwhile, declining from the noon of day,
20 The sun obliquely shoots his burning ray;
The hungry judges soon the sentence sign,
And wretches hang that jurymen may dine;
Belinda now, whom thirst of fame invites,
Burns to encounter two adventurous knights,
25 At ombre singly to decide their doom;
And swells her breast with conquests yet to come.
The skillful nymph reviews her force with care:

> Belinda and the Baron play at cards.

Let spades be trumps! she said, and trumps they were.

[Pope describes the game at length, as if it were a battle with the different cards for troops. The card table is presented as the battlefield. The present account has been condensed.]

The baron now his diamonds pours apace;
30 Th' embroidered king who shows but half his face,
And his refulgent queen, with powers combined,
Of broken troops an easy conquest find.
Clubs, diamonds, hearts, in wild disorder seen,
With throngs promiscuous strew the level green.

35 The knave of diamonds tries his wily arts,
And wins (oh shameful chance!) the queen of hearts.
At this the blood the virgin's cheek forsook,

A livid paleness spreads o'er all her look;
She sees, and trembles at th' approaching ill,
40 Just in the jaws of ruin, and codille.
And now (as oft in some distempered state)
On one nice trick depends the general fate.
An ace of hearts steps forth; the king unseen
Lurked in her hand, and mourned his captive queen:
45 He springs to vengeance with an eager pace,
And falls like thunder on the prostrate ace.
The nymph exulting fills with shouts the sky;   Belinda
                                                 wins.
The walls, the woods, and long canals reply.
    Oh thoughtless mortals! ever blind to fate,
50 Too soon dejected, and too soon elate.
Sudden, these honors shall be snatched away,
And cursed forever this victorious day.

    For lo! the board with cups and spoons is crowned,
The berries crackle, and the mill turns round;   Coffee is
                                                  served.
55 On shining altars of Japan they raise
The silver lamp; the fiery spirits blaze;
From silver spouts the grateful liquors glide,
While China's earth receives the smoking tide:
At once they gratify their scent and taste,
60 And frequent cups prolong the rich repast.
Straight hover round the fair her airy band;
Some, as she sipped, the fuming liquor fanned,
Some o'er her lap their careful plumes displayed,
Trembling, and conscious of the rich brocade.
65 Coffee (which makes the politician wise,
And see through all things with his half-shut eyes)
Sent up in vapors to the baron's brain
New stratagems the radiant lock to gain.
Ah, cease, rash youth! desist ere 'tis too late,
70 Fear the just gods, and think of Scylla's fate!
    But when to mischief mortals bend their will,   Clarissa lends
                                                     the Baron
How soon they find fit instruments of ill!   her scissors.

40. CODILLE—A term signifying defeat.
   54. THE BERRIES CRACKLE—The coffee was ground and brewed at the table.
Coffee mills and spirit lamps were part of the tea table equipment.
   58. CHINA'S EARTH—Porcelain cups.
   70. SCYLLA'S FATE—Scylla, who betrayed her father by sending one of his
hairs to an enemy, was changed by the gods into a bird.

531

Just then Clarissa drew with tempting grace
A two-edged weapon from her shining case:
75 He takes the gift with reverence, and extends
The little engine on his fingers' ends;
This just behind Belinda's neck he spread,
As o'er the fragrant steams she bends her head.
Swift to the lock a thousand sprites repair,
80 A thousand wings, by turns, blow back the hair;
And thrice they twitched the diamond in her ear;
Thrice she looked back, and thrice the foe drew near.

[At this critical moment Ariel discovered an earthly lover lurking in Belinda's heart and his power to protect her was cancelled.]

The peer now spreads the glittering forfex wide,
T' inclose the lock; now joins it, to divide.   The Baron
85 E'en then, before the fatal engine closed,   snips the
A wretched sylph too fondly interposed;   curls.

Fate urged the shears, and cut the sylph in twain,
(But airy substance soon unites again).
The meeting points the sacred hair dissever
90 From the fair head, forever, and forever!
Then flashed the living lightning from her eyes,
And screams of horror rend th' affrighted skies.   Belinda
Not louder shrieks to pitying Heaven are cast,   bewails
When husbands, or when lap-dogs breathe their last; her loss.

95 Or when rich China vessels, fallen from high,
 In glittering dust and painted fragments lie!
 "Let wreaths of triumph now my temples twine,"
 The victor cried; "the glorious prize is mine! The Baron gloats.
 What Time would spare, from steel receives its date,
100 And monuments, like men, submit to fate!
 What wonder then, fair nymph! thy hairs should feel,
 The conquering force of unresisted steel?"

CANTO IV

Not tyrants fierce that unrepenting die, Belinda rages,
Not Cynthia when her manteau's pinned awry,
E'er felt such rage, resentment, and despair,
As thou, sad virgin, for thy ravished hair.
5 Belinda burns with more than mortal ire,
 And fierce Thalestris fans the rising fire.
 "O wretched maid!" she spread her hands and cried,
 (While Hampton's echoes, "Wretched maid!" replied)
 "Was it for this you took such constant care and friend Thalestris
10 The bodkin, comb, and essence to prepare? "comforts" her.
 For this your locks in paper durance bound,
 For this with torturing irons wreathed around?
 For this with fillets strained your tender head,
 And bravely bore the double loads of lead?
15 Gods! shall the ravisher display your hair,
 While the fops envy, and the ladies stare!
 Honor forbid! at whose unrivalled shrine
 Ease, pleasure, virtue, all our sex resign.
 Methinks already I your tears survey,
20 Already hear the horrid things they say,
 Already see you a degraded toast,
 And all your honor in a whisper lost!
 How shall I, then, your helpless fame defend!
 'Twill then be infamy to seem your friend!
25 And shall this prize, th' inestimable prize,
 Exposed through crystal to the gazing eyes,

9. Lines 9–14 refer to the elaborate measures used in preparing a coiffure. At least six different ways of curling the hair are named. The "essence" of line 10 was probably steeped from flaxseed, much like the "wave-set" in use today.
 26. EXPOSED THROUGH CRYSTAL—Curls or braids of hair were often used in jewelry, sometimes with a protecting glass over them.

And heightened by the diamond's circling rays,
On that rapacious hand forever blaze?
Sooner let earth, air, sea, to chaos fall,
30 Men, monkeys, lap-dogs, parrots, perish all!"
     She said; then raging to Sir Plume repairs,
And bids her beau demand the precious hairs
(Sir Plume, of amber snuff-box justly vain,   *Sir Plume to the rescue!*
And the nice conduct of a clouded cane.)
35 With earnest eyes, and round unthinking face,
He first the snuff-box opened, then the case,
And thus broke out—"My lord, why, what the devil?
Zounds! damn the lock! 'fore Gad, you must be civil!
Plague on't! 'tis past a jest—nay prithee, pox!
40 Give her the hair," he spoke, and rapped his box.

"It grieves me much," replied the peer again,   *The Baron is unyielding.*
"Who speaks so well should ever speak in vain.
But by this lock, this sacred lock, I swear,
(Which never more shall join its parted hair;
45 Which never more its honors shall renew,
Clipped from the lovely head where late it grew)
That while my nostrils draw the vital air,

31. SIR PLUME—Thalestris' "boy-friend," Sir Plume, represents the ineffectual
dandy whose chief accomplishments were dressing fashionably, flourishing a
cane with an amber or meerschaum top, and using his snuffbox with elegant
grace. The snuff, by the way, was placed in the nostril to induce sneezing.

This hand, which won it, shall forever wear."
He spoke, and speaking, in proud triumph spread
50 The long-contended honors of her head.
Then see! the nymph in beauteous grief appears,
Her eyes half languishing, half drowned in tears;
On her heaved bosom hung her drooping head,
Which, with a sigh, she raised; and thus she said:
55 "Forever curs'd be this detested day,
Which snatched my best, my favorite curl away!
Happy! ah, ten times happy had I been,
If Hampton Court these eyes had never seen!
What moved my mind with youthful lords to roam?
60 Oh, had I stayed, and said my prayers at home!
'Twas this, the morning omens seemed to tell:
Thrice from my trembling hand the patch-box fell;
A sylph, too, warned me of the threats of fate,
In mystic visions, now believed too late!
65 Oh, hadst thou, cruel! been content to seize
Hairs less in sight, or any hairs but these!"

CANTO V

She said: the pitying audience melt in tears.
But Fate and Jove had stopped the baron's ears.
Then grave Clarissa graceful waved her fan;   Clarissa tries
Silence ensued, and thus the nymph began: to restore peace.
5   "Say, why are beauties praised and honored most,
The wise man's passion, and the vain man's toast?
What then remains but well our power to use,
And keep good humor still whate'er we lose?
And trust me, dear! good humor can prevail,
10 When airs, and flights, and screams, and scolding fail.
Beauties in vain their pretty eyes may roll;
Charms strike the sight, but merit wins the soul."
So spoke the dame, but no applause ensued;
Belinda frowned, Thalestris called her prude.   Thalestris
15 "To arms, to arms!" the fierce virago cries,   rouses the
And swift as lightning to the combat flies   forces to battle.
All sides in parties, and begin th' attack;
Fans clap, silks rustle, and tough whalebones crack;
Heroes' and heroines' shouts confus'dly rise,

20 And bass and treble voices strike the skies.
    No common weapons in the hands are found,
    Like gods they fight, nor dread a mortal wound.
        While through the press enraged Thalestris flies,
    And scatters death around from both her eyes,   *Contenders wield looks and words for weapons.*
25 A beau and witling perished in the throng,
    One died in metaphor, and one in song.
    "O cruel nymph! a living death I bear,"
    Cried Dapperwit, and sunk besides his chair.
    A mournful glance Sir Fopling upwards cast,
30 "Those eyes are made so killing"—was his last.
        When bold Sir Plume had drawn Clarissa down,
    Chloë stepped in and killed him with a frown;
    She smiled to see the doughty hero slain,
    But, at her smile, the beau revived again.
35   Now Jove suspends his golden scales in air,   *Jupiter's scales decide the outcome.*
    Weighs the men's wits against the lady's hair;
    The doubtful beam long nods from side to side;
    At length the wits mount up, the hairs subside.
        See, fierce Belinda on the Baron flies,
40 With more than usual lightning in her eyes;
    Just where the breath of life his nostrils drew,
    A charge of snuff the wily virgin threw;

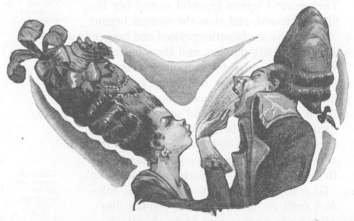

35. JOVE SUSPENDS HIS GOLDEN SCALES—In classic mythology Jupiter settled the outcome of men's contests by weighing with the scales of the Fates. The loser in the contest of Hector and Achilles, for instance, was determined when the side holding Hector's name sank down.

Sudden, with starting tears each eye o'erflows,
And the high dome reechoes to his nose.
45 "Restore the lock!" she cries; and all around
"Restore the lock!" the vaulted roofs rebound.
Not fierce Othello in so loud a strain
Roared for the handkerchief that caused his pain.
But see how oft ambitious aims are crossed,
50 And chiefs contend till all the prize is lost!
The lock, obtained with guilt, and kept with pain,
In every place is sought, but sought in vain:
With such a prize no mortal must be blessed,
So Heaven decrees! with Heaven who can contest?
55 Some thought it mounted to the lunar sphere,
Since all things lost on earth are treasured there.
There heroes' wits are kept in ponderous vases,   *The ringlets disappear from earth*
And beaux' in snuff-boxes and tweezer cases;
There broken vows and death-bed alms are found,
60 And lovers' hearts with ends of riband bound,
    But trust the Muse—she saw it upward rise,
Though marked by none but quick, poetic eyes:
A sudden star, it shot through liquid air,   *to become a new constellation in the heavens*
And drew behind a radiant trail of hair.
65 The sylphs behold it kindling as it flies,
And pleased pursue its progress through the skies.
    Then cease, bright nymph! to mourn thy ravished hair,
Which adds new glory to the shining sphere!   *and bring Belinda everlasting fame.*
Not all the tresses that fair head can boast,
70 Shall draw such envy as the lock you lost.
For, after all the murders of your eye,
When, after millions slain, yourself shall die;
When those fair suns shall set, as set they must,
And all those tresses shall be laid in dust:
75 This lock, the Muse shall consecrate to fame,
And 'midst the stars inscribe Belinda's name.

FOR INTERPRETATION

CANTO I:

1. What does Pope say is to be the theme of his poem? The Muse is to help him find the answer to what puzzling questions?

2. Who is Ariel? Who or what had he once been? What are the duties of the sylphs?

3. Point out the passages between lines 28 and 44 where Pope hints that he does not regard women very highly. In one of his *Epistles* he wrote,

> "Nothing so true as what you once let fall—
> *Most women have no characters at all."*

Be on the look-out all through this poem for lines in which he says or implies the same thing.

4. What made Belinda forget the warning of her sylph?

5. Explain the meaning of the phrase, "the trembling rites of pride," line 76. Who is trembling? Why?

6. Was there anything on Belinda's table not likely to be found on the dressing table of a modern girl? Are any of the usual present-day accessories missing? If so, what?

CANTO II:

1. In the opening lines of Canto II to whom does Pope compare Belinda in her beauty? What extravagant tribute does he pay to the grace with which she wore her jewels?

2. Lines 9–18 explain the secrets of Belinda's popularity. What are those secrets? Do they lie in her manner? in her looks? in both? Discuss. Do the same secrets work with the modern girl? Discuss.

3. Pope seldom describes nature in his verse, but Canto II contains an excellent six-line description of late afternoon on the river. Point out the lines. Have you ever heard any part of them quoted?

4. What are some of the "disasters" that Ariel fears may overtake Belinda? Name at least six.

5. Show how in lines 52–55 the poet has matched the name of the sprite to the duty assigned to each.

6. How does Pope, near the end of this canto, give a mock seriousness to the subject of the poem? Discuss.

CANTO III:

1. What effect does Pope secure when he links something serious with something trivial, as in lines 7 and 8—"Here thou, great Anna . . . does sometimes *counsel* take and sometimes *tea*." Point out several other examples of the same device in this canto; in other cantos.

2. On the whole is Pope complimentary or uncomplimentary to the Queen? Discuss. Is he complimentary or uncomplimentary to her court? Quote the lines in which he implies the most severe criticisms.

3. What extended metaphor does Pope use in the description of the card game, lines 24–48? Point out the words which suggest the metaphor.

4. What effect did the coffee fumes have on the Baron? Who helped the Baron in his enterprise? How?

5. Why couldn't the sprites save the lock?

6. Quote the lines that describe Belinda's dismay. Quote the lines that express the triumph of the Baron.

CANTO IV:

1. How does Thalestris commiserate with Belinda? Will her words make Belinda feel better or worse? Why? Is Thalestris going to stand by Belinda in her "disgrace"? How do you judge?

2. What sort of man is Sir Plume? With what kind of voice do you think he makes his speech? What is the tone of the Baron's reply?

3. Why is Belinda so grief-stricken at her loss?

CANTO V:

1. What advice does Clarissa give? Is it good advice? How is it received?

2. When the battle lines are drawn with Belinda's friends on one side and the Baron's on the other, what kinds of weapons are used? Mention at least four named by the poet. Whom or what do you think the poet is ridiculing in this passage? Discuss.

3. What outcome of the battle is indicated by the fact that the part of the scales containing the men's wits mounted up? What other meaning did Pope also imply?

4. What really effective weapon did Belinda use to end the battle? In the meantime, what happened to the lock of hair? Why does this ending prove to be a particularly suitable one for the poem? Discuss.

5. Prove that Pope wrote the truth in lines 69 and 70. How does the poet prove it? In what lines? Explain the meaning of lines 71–72. What are the "fair suns" of line 73? Why is it the *Muse* that is inscribing Belinda's name among the stars?

OVERVIEW:

1. Write a sentence summary for each canto of the poem.

2. A *burlesque* treatment may treat a serious subject flippantly, or treat a trivial subject with mock seriousness. Which device did Pope use predominantly in "The Rape of the Lock"? Do you find any examples of the opposite device? Discuss.

3. Is Pope more uncomplimentary to the belles than to the beaux? Discuss. Quote lines to prove your points.

4. If you were Arabella Fermor or a member of her family, would you be flattered by the poem? Why or why not?

5. Would the poem lend itself particularly well to outdoor staging? to pageantry?

LIFE WITH THE GIANTS

JONATHAN SWIFT

Sometimes books written for children prove interesting to grown-ups, but the reverse is seldom true; children rarely enjoy a grown man's reading, particularly if it expresses views on politics, finance, customs or morals. There is one famous exception. *Gulliver's Travels* was written to show the politicians and statesmen of England how much the writer despised them and their country. It amused or enraged a current generation and then, according to precedent, it should have found a place with other satires in the musty chambers of forgotten books. It should have, but it didn't. The children discovered it. The satire, you see, is masqueraded under the guise of fairy-tale adventures in four amazing countries.

Best known is the land of Lilliput where the tallest men are six inches high and everything else is in diminutive proportion. Equally interesting, though not so familiar, is the land of giants, Brobdingnag.[1] There a man may be sixty feet tall and a palace seven miles in circumference. The following selection contains enough of the fairy tale to recommend it to little brother or sister; it also has enough mockery to show the curious student how an embittered man took vengeance on his countrymen.

[1] BROBDINGNAG—The general name of the country. Swift locates the land on an undiscovered continent between California and Japan. Its capital was called "Lorbrulgrud" which Gulliver translates as "Pride of the Universe."

THE King, who delighted in music, had frequent concerts at court, to which I was sometimes carried, and set in my box [2] on a table to hear them; but the noise was so great, that I could hardly distinguish the tunes. I am confident that all the drums and trumpets of a royal army, beating and sounding together just at your ears, could not equal it. My practice was to have my box removed from the places where the performers sat, as far as I could, then to shut the doors and windows of it, and draw the window curtains; after which I found their music not disagreeable.

I had learned in my youth to play a little upon the spinet. Glumdalclitch [3] kept one in her chamber, and a master attended twice a week to teach her: I call it a spinet, because it somewhat resembled that instrument, and was played upon in the same manner. A fancy came into my head that I would entertain the King and Queen with an English tune upon this instrument. But this appeared extremely difficult; for the spinet was near sixty foot long, each key being almost a foot wide, so that, with my arms extended, I could not reach to above five keys, and to press them down required a good smart stroke with my fist, which would be too great a labor, and to no purpose. The method I contrived was this. I prepared two round sticks about the bigness of common cudgels; they were thicker at one end than the other, and I covered the thicker ends with a piece of a mouse's skin,[4] that by rapping on them I might neither damage the tops of the keys, nor interrupt the sound. Before the spinet a bench was placed, about four foot below the keys, and I was put upon the bench. I ran sideling upon it that way and this, as fast as I could, banging the proper keys with my two sticks, and made a shift to play a jig, to the great satisfaction of both their Majesties: but it was the most violent exercise I ever underwent, and yet I could not strike above sixteen keys, nor, consequently, play the bass and treble together, as other artists do; which was a great disadvantage to my performance.

[2] BOX—Gulliver was kept in a box about twelve feet square and ten feet deep. It was lined with cloth and furnished with doll bed, etc. When Gulliver accompanied the king and queen on a progress through the realm, the box was strapped about the waist of "some grave or trusty servant."

[3] GLUMDALCLITCH—"Little Nurse," the name which Gulliver gave to the nine-year-old girl who became his care-taker. He describes her as "very good-natured, and not above forty feet high, being little for her age."

[4] MOUSE'S SKIN—The mice were the size of large English dogs.

The King, who, as I before observed, was a prince of excellent understanding, would frequently order that I should be brought in my box, and set upon the table in his closet. He would then command me to bring one of my chairs out of the box, and sit down within three yards' distance upon the top of the cabinet, which brought me almost to a level with his face. In this manner I had several conversations with him. I one day took the freedom to tell his Majesty, that the contempt he discovered towards Europe, and the rest of the world, did not seem answerable to those excellent qualities of mind he was master of. That, as inconsiderable as he took me to be, I hoped I might live to do his Majesty some signal service. The King heard me with attention, and began to conceive a much better opinion of me than he had ever before. He desired I would give him as exact an account of the government of England as I possibly could; because, as fond as princes commonly are of their own customs, he should be glad to hear of any thing that might deserve imitation.

Imagine with thyself, courteous reader, how often I then wished for the tongue of Demosthenes [5] or Cicero,[6] that might have enabled me to celebrate the praise of my own dear native country in a style equal to its merits and felicity.

I began my discourse by informing his Majesty that our dominions consisted of two islands, which composed three mighty kingdoms under one sovereign, besides our plantations in America. I dwelt long upon the fertility of our soil, and the temperature of our climate. I then spoke at large upon the constitution of an English Parliament, partly made up of an illustrious body called the House of Peers, persons of the noblest blood, and of the most ancient and ample patrimonies. I described that extraordinary care always taken of their education in arts and arms, to qualify them for being counselors born to the king and kingdom, to have a share in the legislature, to be members of the highest Court of Judicature, from whence there could be no appeal, and to be champions always ready for the defense of their prince and country, by their valor, conduct, and fidelity. That these were the ornament and bulwark of the kingdom, worthy followers of their most renowned ancestors, whose honor had been the reward of their virtue, from which their

---

[5] DEMOSTHENES—An Athenian orator and patriot (384–322 B.C.)
[6] CICERO—A Roman orator and patriot (106–43 B.C.)

posterity were never once known to degenerate. To these were joined several holy persons, as part of that assembly, under the title of Bishops, whose peculiar business it is to take care of religion, and of those who instruct the people therein. These were searched and sought out through the whole nation, by the prince and his wisest counselors, among such of the priesthood as were most deservedly distinguished by the sanctity of their lives, and the depth of their erudition; who were indeed the spiritual fathers of the clergy and the people.

That the other part of the Parliament consisted of an assembly called the House of Commons, who were all principal gentlemen, freely picked and culled out by the people themselves, for their great abilities and love of their country, to represent the wisdom of the whole nation. And these two bodies make up the most august assembly in Europe, to whom, in conjunction with the prince, the whole legislature [7] is committed.

I then descended to the Courts of Justice, over which the Judges, those venerable sages and interpreters of the law, presided, for determining the disputed rights and properties of men, as well as for the punishment of vice, and protection of innocence. I mentioned the prudent management of our treasury; the valor and achievements of our forces by sea and land. I computed the number of our people, by reckoning how many millions there might be of each religious sect, or political party among us. I did not omit even our sports and pastimes, or any other particular which I thought might redound to the honor of my country. And I finished all with a brief historical account of affairs and events in England for about an hundred years past.

This conversation was not ended under five audiences, each of several hours, and the King heard the whole with great attention, frequently taking notes of what I spoke, as well as memorandums of several questions he intended to ask me.

When I had put an end to these long discourses, his Majesty, in a sixth audience, consulting his notes, proposed many doubts, queries, and objections, upon every article. He asked what methods were used to cultivate the minds and bodies of our young nobility, and in what kind of business they commonly spent the first and teachable part of their lives. What course was taken to supply that assembly when any noble family became extinct.

[7] THE WHOLE LEGISLATURE—All legislation.

What qualifications were necessary in those who were to be created new lords. Whether the humor of the prince, a sum of money to a court lady, or a prime minister, or a design of strengthening a party opposite to the public interest, ever happened to be motives in those advancements. What share of knowledge these lords had in the laws of their country, and how they came by it, so as to enable them to decide the properties of their fellow-subjects in the last resort. Whether they were always so free from avarice, partialities, or want, that a bribe, or some other sinister view, could have no place among them. Whether those holy lords I spoke of were always promoted to that rank upon account of their knowledge in religious matters, and the sanctity of their lives, had never been compliers with the times while they were common priests, or slavish prostitute chaplains to some nobleman, whose opinions they continued servilely to follow after they were admitted into that assembly.

He then desired to know what arts were practiced in electing those whom I called commoners: whether a stranger with a strong purse might not influence the vulgar voters to choose him before their own landlord, or the most considerable gentleman in the neighborhood. How it came to pass, that people were so violently bent upon getting into this assembly, which I allowed to be a great trouble and expense, often to the ruin of their families, without any salary or pension: because this appeared such an exalted strain of virtue and public spirit, that his Majesty seemed to doubt it might possibly not be always sincere: and he desired to know whether such zealous gentlemen could have any views of refunding themselves for the charges and trouble they were at, by sacrificing the public good to the designs of a weak and vicious prince in conjunction with a corrupted ministry. He multiplied his questions, and sifted me thoroughly upon every part of this head, proposing numberless inquiries and objections, which I think it not prudent or convenient to repeat.

Upon what I said in relation to our Courts of Justice, his Majesty desired to be satisfied in several points: and this I was the better able to do, having been formerly almost ruined by a long suit in chancery, which was decreed for me with costs. He asked, what time was usually spent in determining between right and wrong, and what degree of expense. Whether advocates and orators had liberty to plead in causes manifestly known to be unjust, vexatious, or oppressive. Whether party in religion or politics were observed to be of any weight in the scale of justice. Whether those pleading orators [8] were persons educated in the general knowledge of equity, or only in provincial, national, and other local customs. Whether they or their judges had any part in penning those laws which they assumed the liberty of interpreting and glossing upon at their pleasure. Whether they had ever at different times pleaded for and against the same cause, and cited precedents to prove contrary opinions. Whether they were a rich or a poor corporation. Whether they receive any pecuniary reward for pleading, whether they were ever admitted as members in the lower senate.

He fell next upon the management of our treasury; and said he thought my memory had failed me, because I computed our taxes at above five or six millions a year, and when I came to mention the issues,[9] he found they sometimes amounted to more than double; for the notes he had taken were very particular in this point, because he hoped, as he told me, that the knowledge of our conduct might be useful to him, and he could not be deceived in his calculations. But, if what I told him were true, he was still at a loss how a kingdom could run out of its estate [10] like a private person. He asked me, who were our creditors; and where we should find money to pay them. He wondered to hear me talk of such chargeable and extensive wars; that certainly we must be a quarrelsome people, or live among very bad neighbors, and that our generals must needs be richer than our kings. He asked what business we had out of our own islands, unless upon the score of trade or treaty, or to defend the coasts with our fleet. Above all, he was amazed to hear me talk of a mercenary standing army in the midst of peace, and among a free people. He said, if we were governed by our own consent in the persons of our representatives, he could not imagine of whom we were afraid, or against whom we were to fight; and would hear my opinion, whether a private man's house might not better be defended by himself, his children, and family, than by half a dozen rascals picked up at a venture in the streets, for small wages, who might get an hundred times more by cutting their throats.

[8] THOSE PLEADING ORATORS—Lawyers.
[9] ISSUES—Bonds of indebtedness for expenditures.
[10] RUN OUT OF ITS ESTATE—Live beyond its income.

He was perfectly astonished with the historical account I gave him of our affairs during the last century, protesting it was only an heap of conspiracies, rebellions, murders, massacres, revolutions, banishments, the very worst effects that avarice, faction, hypocrisy, perfidiousness, cruelty, rage, madness, hatred, envy, lust, malice, or ambition could produce.

His Majesty in another audience was at the pains to recapitulate the sum of all I had spoken, compared the questions he made with the answers I had given, then taking me into his hands, and stroking me gently, delivered himself in these words, which I shall never forget nor the manner he spoke them in: My little friend Grildrig,[11] you have made a most admirable panegyric upon your country; you have clearly proved that ignorance, idleness, and vice, may be sometimes the only ingredients for qualifying a legislator; that laws are best explained, interpreted, and applied by those whose interest and abilities lie in perverting, confounding, and eluding them. I observe among you some lines of an institution, which in its original might have been tolerable, but these half erased, and the rest wholly blurred and blotted by corruptions. It doth not appear from all you have said, how any one virtue is required towards the procurement of any one station among you; much less that men are ennobled on account of their virtue, that priests are advanced for their piety or learning, soldiers for their conduct or valor, judges for their integrity, senators for the love of their country, or counselors for their wisdom. As for yourself (continued the King) who have spent the greatest part of your life in travelling, I am well disposed to hope you may hitherto have escaped many vices of your country. But by what I have gathered from your own relation, and the answers I have with much pains wringed and extorted from you, I cannot but conclude the bulk of your natives to be the most pernicious race of little odious vermin that nature ever suffered to crawl upon the surface of the earth.

[11] GRILDRIG—The Brobdingnagians' name for Gulliver, signifying "mannikin," or "little man."

DID YOU READ WITH UNDERSTANDING?

1. What evidence do you find in the first three paragraphs of Swift's carefulness about keeping all details in scale with the size of the people of Brobdingnag? Does he make any mistakes? Discuss.

2. To appreciate Gulliver's achievement in playing the spinet, try to imagine yourself playing a piano whose keys are a foot wide and whose keyboard is sixty feet long. Can you think of any better way of playing it than Gulliver devised? Do you think his scheme would work? Could he really play a jig tune on such a huge instrument? Discuss.

3. How does Swift prepare the reader to respect the judgment of the King? In describing the customs and government of England, does Gulliver seem to be praising his country or finding fault with it? Prove your point by referring to the text. Do you discover any traces of irony in Gulliver's words? If so, point them out.

4. What effect is gained by having the condemnation of England come from the King of Brobdingnag? What were some of the events that happened to England "during the last century"—that is, during the seventeenth century? Do you think that the King was justified in describing that period of English history as a "heap of conspiracies, rebellions, murders, massacres, revolutions," and so on? Discuss. Is there justice in any of the other condemnations of the King? If so, point out examples.

5. What do you discover in the life of Swift to account for his bitterness toward the Church and toward the Government? Discuss.

6. Does his condemnation of his country go beyond the limits of reason? Discuss.

FROZEN WORDS

JOSEPH ADDISON, WITH RICHARD STEELE

Our grandfathers called it spinning yarns. We call it telling tall stories. But no matter what the name, the fun of extravagant tale-telling remains. Often the teller refuses responsibility for his story and gives the credit to some earlier yarn-spinner like Sir John Mandeville. And indeed that famous traveler hardly surpassed the heights of imagination reached by Addison and Steele in working up the idea of weather so cold it could freeze a man's words.

THERE are no books which I more delight in than in travels, especially those that describe remote countries, and give the writer an opportunity of showing his parts without incurring any danger of being examined or contradicted. Among all the authors of this kind, our renowned countryman Sir John Mandeville has distinguished himself, by the copiousness of his invention,[1] and the greatness of his genius. The second to Sir John

[1] INVENTION—Imagination.

I take to have been, Ferdinand Mendez Pinto,[2] a person of infinite adventure, and unbounded imagination. One reads the voyages of these two great wits, with as much astonishment as the travels of Ulysses in Homer, or of the Red Cross Knight in Spenser. All is enchanted ground, and fairyland.

I have got into my hands, by great chance, several manuscripts of these two eminent authors, which are filled with greater wonders than any of those they have communicated to the public; and indeed, were they not so well attested, they would appear altogether improbable. I am apt to think the ingenious authors did not publish them with the rest of their works, lest they should pass for fictions and fables: a caution not unnecessary, when the reputation of their veracity was not yet established in the world. But as this reason has now no farther weight, I shall make the public a present of these curious pieces, at such times as I shall find myself unprovided with other subjects.

The present paper I intend to fill with an extract from St. John's Journal, in which that learned and worthy knight gives an account of the freezing and thawing of several short speeches, which he made in the territories of Nova Zembla.[3] I need not inform my reader, that the author of *Hudibras* [4] alludes to this strange quality in that cold climate, when, speaking of abstracted notions [5] clothed in a visible shape, he adds that apt simile,

<blockquote>Like words congealed in northern air.</blockquote>

Not to keep my reader any longer in suspense, the relation [6] put into modern language, is as follows:

"We were separated by a storm in the latitude of seventy-three, insomuch, that only the ship which I was in, with a Dutch and French vessel, got safe into a creek of Nova Zembla. We landed, in order to refit our vessels, and store ourselves with provisions. The crew of each vessel made themselves a cabin of turf and wood, at some distance from each other, to fence themselves against the inclemencies of the weather, which was severe beyond imagination. We soon observed, that in talking to one another we lost several of our words, and could not hear

---

[2] FERDINAND MENDEZ PINTO—Portuguese adventurer and traveler (1509–1583) in China and Japan. *Peregrinaçao* is a record of his adventures.

[3] NOVA ZEMBLA—Russian islands in the Arctic Ocean.

[4] *Hudibras*—A poem by Samuel Butler (1612–1680), a satire on the Puritans.

[5] ABSTRACTED NOTIONS—Abstract, or intangible, ideas.

[6] RELATION—Narrative.

one another at above two yards distance, and that too when we sat very near the fire. After much perplexity, I found that our words froze in the air, before they could reach the ears of the persons to whom they were spoken. I was soon confirmed in this conjecture, when, upon the increase of the cold, the whole company grew dumb, or rather deaf; for every man was sensible, as we afterwards found, that he spoke as well as ever; but the sounds no sooner took air than they were condensed and lost. It was now a miserable spectacle to see us nodding and gaping at one another, every man talking, and no man heard. One might observe a seaman that could hail a ship at a league's distance, beckoning with his hand, straining his lungs, and tearing his throat; but all in vain:

Nec vox nec verba sequuntur.[7]

"We continued here three weeks in this dismal plight. At length, upon a turn of wind, the air about us began to thaw. Our cabin was immediately filled with a dry clattering sound, which I afterwards found to be the crackling of consonants that broke above our heads, and were often mixed with a gentle

[7] *Nec vox nec verba sequuntur*—Neither voice nor words followed.

hissing, which I imputed to the letter *s*, that occurs so frequently in the English tongue. I soon after felt a breeze of whispers rushing by my ear; for those, being of soft and gentle substance, immediately liquefied in the warm wind that blew across our cabin. These were soon followed by syllables and short words, and at length by entire sentences, that melted sooner or later, as they were more or less congealed; so that we now heard everything that had been *spoken* during the whole three weeks that we had been *silent,* if I may use that expression. It was now very early in the morning, and yet, to my surprise, I heard somebody say, 'Sir John, it is midnight, and time for the ship's crew to go to bed.' This I knew to be the pilot's voice; and, upon recollecting myself, I concluded that he had spoken these words to me some days before, though I could not hear them until the present thaw. My reader will easily imagine how the whole crew was amazed to hear every man talking, and see no man opening his mouth. In the midst of this great surprise we were all in, we heard a volley of oaths and curses, lasting for a long while, and uttered in a very hoarse voice, which I knew belonged to the boatswain, who was a very choleric fellow, and had taken his opportunity of cursing and swearing at me, when he thought I could not hear him; for I had several times given him the strappado on that account, as I did not fail to repeat it for these his pious soliloquies, when I got him on shipboard.

"I must not omit the names of several beauties in Wapping,[8] which were heard every now and then, in the midst of a long sigh that accompanied them; as, 'Dear Kate!' 'Pretty Mrs. Peggy!' 'When shall I see my Sue again!' This betrayed several amours, which had been concealed until that time, and furnished us with a great deal of mirth in our return to England.

"When this confusion of voices was pretty well over, though I was afraid to offer at speaking, as fearing I should not be heard, I proposed a visit to the Dutch cabin, which lay about a mile farther up in the country. My crew were extremely rejoiced to find they had again recovered their hearing; though every man uttered his voice with the same apprehensions that I had done,

Et timide verba intermissa retentat.[9]

[8] WAPPING—A part of London, along the Thames.
[9] *Et timide . . . retentat*—And timidly held back the halting words.

"At about a half-a-mile's distance from our cabin we heard the groanings of a bear, which at first startled us; but, upon inquiry, we were informed by some of our company, that he was dead, and now lay in salt, having been killed upon that very spot about a fortnight before, in the time of the frost. Not far from the same place, we were likewise entertained with some posthumous snarls, and barkings of a fox.

"We at length arrived at the little Dutch settlement; and, upon entering the room, found it filled with sighs that smelt of brandy, and several other unsavory sounds, that were altogether inarticulate. My valet, who was an Irishman, fell into so great a rage at what he heard, that he drew his sword; but not knowing where to lay the blame, he put it up again. We were stunned with these confused noises, but did not hear a single word until about half-an-hour after; which I ascribed to the harsh and obdurate sounds of that language, which wanted more time than ours to melt, and become audible.

"After having here met with a very hearty welcome, we went to the cabin of the French, who, to make amends for their three weeks' silence, were talking and disputing with greater rapidity and confusion than I ever heard in an assembly, even of that nation. Their language, as I found, upon the first giving of the weather, fell asunder and dissolved. I was here convinced of an error, into which I had before fallen; for I fancied, that for the freezing of the sound, it was necessary for it to be wrapped up, and, as it were, preserved in breath: but I found my mistake when I heard the sound of a kit [10] playing a minuet over our heads. I asked the occasion of it; upon which one of the company told me that it would play there above a week longer; 'for,' says he, 'finding ourselves bereft of speech, we prevailed upon one of the company, who had his musical instrument about him, to play to us from morning to night; all which time was employed in dancing in order to dissipate our chagrin, and *tuer le temps*." [11]

Here Sir John gives very good philosophical reasons, why the kit could not be heard during the frost; but, as they are something prolix I pass them over in silence, and shall only observe, that the honorable author seems, by his quotations, to have been well versed in the ancient poets, which perhaps raised his

[10] KIT—A small violin with three strings.
[11] *Tuer le temps*—To kill time.

551

fancy above the ordinary pitch of historians, and very much contributed to the embellishment of his writings.

DID YOU READ WITH UNDERSTANDING?

1. Why do you think the authors pretended to be quoting an old manuscript in this essay? Why was Sir John Mandeville an appropriate "author" for it?

2. The third paragraph tells us what was the real source of inspiration for the essay. What single line suggested it?

3. How do the authors give an air of plausibility to their tale?

4. What are the two most humorous situations that develop when the sounds freeze?

5. Explain some of the phonetic differences between the English and the Dutch and the French languages. How did the authors allow for those differences in the thawing-out process?

6. What inconsistent statements do you find in the last two paragraphs?

7. Do you think the essay is intended to carry a hidden meaning, or was it written just for fun? Discuss.

SIR ROGER AT CHURCH

JOSEPH ADDISON, WITH RICHARD STEELE

One of the most lovable figures moving through the pages of English literature is the country gentleman. He is always delightful, and somehow very typically British. But at no time is he more lovable than in the person of Sir Roger de Coverley—an eccentric, good-hearted eighteenth-century landlord.

Steele introduced him in the second number of the *Spectator*, and he quickly became the feature of the paper. His ardent, if timorous, devotion to the widow was followed with as much eager suspense as are comic-strip love-adventures of modern heroes. When the co-author let him die, readers of the *Spectator* protested their loss and were not at all consoled by the magnificence of his funeral.

But here is the good squire alive, and very much himself!

SIR ROGER HIMSELF

The first of our society is a gentleman of Worcestershire, of ancient descent, a baronet, his name Sir Roger de Coverley. His great grandfather was inventor of that famous country-dance which is called after him. All who know that shire, are very well acquainted with the parts and merits of Sir Roger. He is a gentleman that is very singular in his behavior, but his singularities proceed from his good sense, and are contradictions to the manners of the world, only as he thinks the world is in the wrong. However, this humor creates him no enemies, for he does nothing with sourness or obstinacy; and his being unconfined to modes and forms, makes him but the readier and more capable to please and oblige all who know him. When he is in town, he lives in Soho-square.[1] It is said, he keeps himself a bachelor by reason he was crossed in love by a perverse beautiful widow of the next county to him. Before this disappointment, Sir Roger was what you call a fine gentleman, had often supped with Lord Rochester and Sir George Etherege, fought a duel upon his first coming to town, and kicked Bully Dawson[2] in a public coffeehouse for calling him youngster. But being ill used by the above mentioned widow, he was very serious for a year and a half; and though, his temper being naturally jovial, he at last got over it, he grew careless of himself, and never dressed[3] afterwards. He continues to wear a coat and doublet of the same cut that were in fashion at the time of his repulse, which, in his merry humors, he tells us, has been in and out[4] twelve times since he first wore it. He is now in his fifty-sixth year, cheerful, gay, and hearty; keeps a good house both in town and country; a great lover of mankind; but there is such a mirthful cast in his behavior, that he is rather beloved than esteemed; his tenants grow rich, his servants look satisfied; all the young women profess love to him, and the young men are glad of his company: when he comes into a house, he calls the servants by their names, and talks all the way upstairs to a visit. I must not omit, that Sir Roger is a justice of the quorum;[5] that he fills the chair at a quarter-session[6] with great abilities, and three months ago gained universal applause by explaining a passage in the game act.

[1] SOHO-SQUARE—A square in London.

[2] LORD ROCHESTER, SIR GEORGE ETHEREGE, BULLY DAWSON—The first, John Wilmot, an English poet and courtier of Charles II; the second, an English dramatist; the third, a notorious London sharper. These three are typical of the dissolute gentlemen prominent in London society in the closing years of the reign of Charles II.

[3] DRESSED—Dressed up.   [4] IN AND OUT—In and out of fashion.

[5] JUSTICE OF THE QUORUM—Justice of the peace.

[6] QUARTER-SESSION—A court held four times a year, trying many petty offences and exercising a minor civil jurisdiction.

SIR ROGER AT CHURCH

I am always very well pleased with a country Sunday, and think, if keeping holy the seventh day were only a human institution, it would be the best method that could have been thought of for the polishing and civilizing of mankind. It is certain the country people would soon degenerate into a kind of savages and barbarians, were there not such frequent returns of a stated time, in which the whole village meet together with their best faces, and in their cleanliest habits,[1] to converse with one another upon indifferent subjects, hear their duties explained to them, and join together in adoration of the Supreme Being. Sunday clears away the rust of the whole week, not only as it refreshes in their minds the notions of religion, but as it puts both the sexes upon appearing in their most agreeable forms, and exerting all such qualities as are apt to give them a figure in the eye of the village. A country fellow distinguishes himself as much in the churchyard, as a citizen does upon the 'Change, the whole parish-politics being generally discussed in that place either after sermon or before the bell rings.

My friend Sir Roger, being a good churchman, has beautified the inside of his church with several texts of his own choosing. He has likewise given a handsome pulpit-cloth, and railed in the communion-table at his own expense. He has often told me, that at his coming to his estate he found his parishioners very irregular; and that in order to make them kneel and join in the responses, he gave every one of them a hassock and a common prayer-book; and at the same time employed an itinerant singing-master, who goes about the country for that purpose, to instruct them rightly in the tunes of the psalms:[2] upon which they now very much value themselves, and indeed outdo most of the country churches that I have ever heard.

As Sir Roger is landlord to the whole congregation, he keeps them in very good order, and will suffer nobody to sleep in it besides himself; for if by chance he has been surprised into a short nap at sermon, upon recovering out of it he stands up and looks about him, and if he sees anybody else nodding, either wakes them himself, or sends his servant to them. Several other of the old knight's peculiarities break out upon these occasions.

[1] HABITS—Clothes.   [2] PSALMS—The earliest church hymns were paraphrases of the Psalms set to music.

Sometimes he will be lengthening out a verse in the singing psalms, half a minute after the rest of the congregation have done with it; sometimes when he is pleased with the matter of his devotion, he pronounces Amen three or four times to the same prayer: and sometimes stands up when everybody else is upon their knees, to count the congregation, or see if any of his tenants are missing.

I was yesterday very much surprised to hear my old friend in the midst of the service calling out to one John Matthews to mind what he was about, and not disturb the congregation. This John Matthews it seems is remarkable for being an idle fellow, and at that time was kicking his heels for his diversion. This authority of the knight, though exerted in that odd manner which accompanies him in all circumstances of life, has a very good effect upon the parish, who are not polite [3] enough to see anything ridiculous in his behavior; besides that the general good sense and worthiness of his character make his friends observe these little singularities as foils that rather set off than blemish his good qualities.

As soon as the sermon is finished, nobody presumes to stir till Sir Roger is gone out of the church. The knight walks down from his seat in the chancel between a double row of his tenants, that stand bowing to him on each side: and every now and then inquires how such an one's wife, or mother, or son, or father do, whom he does not see at church; which is understood as a secret reprimand to the person that is absent.

The chaplain [4] has often told me, that upon a catechising day,

[3] POLITE—Here, sophisticated.
[4] CHAPLAIN—Here, the resident clergyman, one of Sir Roger's household.

when Sir Roger has been pleased with a boy that answers well, he has ordered a Bible to be given him next day for his encouragement; and sometimes accompanies it with a flitch of bacon to his mother. Sir Roger has likewise added five pounds a year to the clerk's place; and, that he may encourage the young fellows to make themselves perfect in the church service, has promised upon the death of the present incumbent, who is very old, to bestow it according to merit.

The fair understanding between Sir Roger and his chaplain, and their mutual concurrence in doing good, is the more remarkable, because the very next village is famous for the differences and contentions that rise between the parson and the squire, who live in a perpetual state of war. The parson is always preaching at the squire; and the squire, to be revenged on the parson, never comes to church. The squire has made all his tenants atheists and tithe-stealers; while the parson instructs them every Sunday in the dignity of his order, and insinuates to them almost in every sermon that he is a better man than his patron. In short, matters are come to such an extremity, that the squire has not said his prayers either in public or private this half year; and that the parson threatens him, if he does not mend his manners, to pray for him in the face of the whole congregation.

Feuds of this nature, though too frequent in the country, are very fatal to the ordinary people; who are so used to be dazzled with riches, that they pay as much deference to the understanding of a man of an estate, as of a man of learning; and are very hardly brought to regard any truth, how important soever it may be that is preached to them, when they know there are several men of five hundred a year [5] who do not believe it.

[5] FIVE HUNDRED A YEAR—Five hundred pounds a year, about $2,500.

DID YOU READ WITH UNDERSTANDING?

1. What sorts of people are likely to be "rather beloved than esteemed"? What kind of people may be both beloved and esteemed? Discuss, with illustrations.

2. Explain the meaning of the last sentence in the first paragraph of "Sir Roger at Church." Is the statement still true, in a general way? Why or why not?

3. What do you think of the Squire's methods of encouraging devotion among his tenants? Discuss.

4. Which parts of the essay are a satire on Sir Roger himself? Which parts are a satire on English society or upon any special classes of people? Discuss.

5. In what respects is Sir Roger like other country gentlemen you have read about—such as Squire Cass in *Silas Marner?* Do you think there are still country gentlemen of his sort in England? Why or why not?

6. Does the reader feel scornful of Sir Roger in the end, or sympathetic toward him? Why?

Samuel Johnson's Club was a literary power.

From LIFE OF
SAMUEL JOHNSON

JAMES BOSWELL

A present-day newspaper man, sports enthusiast, and radio celebrity— John Kieran—has named as the book, barring the Bible or the complete works of Shakespeare, he would choose for a desert-island companion— Boswell's *Life of Samuel Johnson.* There is this to be said about his choice —the biography is an amazing and entertaining book. As Mr. Kieran points out, "The Great Bear of English Literature rambled all over the field of learning;" and James Boswell, hanging on in "open-eared admiration" took pains to jot down every word that the Doctor spoke. Johnson had his share of human vanity, but even he once cried out in protest to his companion, "Sir, you have but two topics, yourself and me. I am sick of both." Boswell meekly recorded the rebuke but altered not one degree in his dog-like devotion. The excerpts below will furnish some idea of "the astonishing couple and the imperishable book" that sprang from their association.

THE LITERARY CLUB

In February [1764] was founded that Club which existed long
without a name, but at Mr. Garrick's [1] funeral became dis-
tinguished by the title of "The Literary Club." Sir Joshua
Reynolds had the merit of being the first proposer of it, to which
Johnson acceded; and the original members were Sir Joshua
Reynolds, Dr. Johnson, Mr. Edmund Burke, Dr. Nugent, Mr.
Beauclerk, Mr. Langton, Dr. Goldsmith, Mr. Chamier, and Sir
John Hawkins.[2] They met at the Turk's Head, in Gerrard
Street, Soho,[3] one evening in every week, at seven, and generally
continued their conversation till a pretty late hour. This club
has been gradually increased to its present number, thirty-five.
After about ten years, instead of supping weekly, it was resolved
to dine together once a fortnight during the meeting of Parliament.

Not very long after the institution of [the] Club Sir Joshua
Reynolds was speaking of it to Garrick. "I like it much," said
he; "I think I shall be of you." When Sir Joshua mentioned
this to Dr. Johnson, he was much displeased. *"He'll be of us,"*
said Johnson; "how does he know we will *permit* him? The first
Duke in England has no right to hold such language." However,
when Garrick was regularly proposed some time afterwards,
Johnson warmly and kindly supported him, and he was accordingly elected, was a most agreeable member, and continued to
attend our meetings to the time of his death.

[1] MR. GARRICK—David Garrick, famous actor and theatrical manager. Although not one of the original members of the Club, he was made a member
shortly after its organization.

[2] SIR JOSHUA REYNOLDS . . . SIR JOHN HAWKINS—In addition to the name of
Dr. Johnson himself, the most familiar names are those of Sir Joshua Reynolds,
famous portrait painter; Mr. Edmund Burke, famous orator who is remembered
for his speech "On Conciliation with the American Colonies"; and Dr. Goldsmith, author of "The Deserted Village" and *The Vicar of Wakefield.*

[3] SOHO—A section of London.

JOHNSON'S REGARD FOR CONVERSATION

Another evening Dr. Goldsmith and I called on him [Johnson]
with the hope of prevailing on him to sup with us at the Mitre.[1]
We found him indisposed and resolved not to go abroad.
"Come, then," said Goldsmith, "we will not go to the Mitre to-

[1] THE MITRE—A popular tavern of the day.

night, since we cannot have the big man [2] with us." Johnson
then called for a bottle of port, of which Goldsmith and I par-
took, while our friend, now a water drinker, sat by us. GOLD-
SMITH. "I think, Mr. Johnson, you don't go near the theaters
now. You give yourself no more concern about a new play than
if you had never had anything to do with the stage." JOHNSON.
"Why, sir, our tastes greatly alter. The lad does not care for
the child's rattle. As we advance in the journey of life, we drop
some of the things which have pleased us; whether it be that we
are fatigued and don't choose to carry so many things any farther,
or that we find other things which we like better." BOSWELL.
"But, sir, why don't you give us something in some other way?"
GOLDSMITH. "Aye, sir, we have a claim upon you." JOHNSON.
"No, sir, I am not obliged to do any more. No man is obliged
to do as much as he can do. A man is to have part of his life
to himself. If a soldier has fought a good many campaigns, he
is not to be blamed if he retires to ease and tranquillity. A
physician who has practiced long in a great city may be excused
if he retires to a small town, and takes less practice. Now, sir,
the good I can do by my conversation bears the same proportion
to the good I can do by my writings that the practice of a physician, retired to a small town, does to his practice in a great city."
BOSWELL. "But I wonder, sir, you have not more pleasure in
writing than in not writing." JOHNSON. "Sir, you *may* wonder."

[2] BIG MAN—Johnson was an extremely large man.

JOHNSON CONVERSES WITH HIS FRIENDS

On Friday, May 7, I breakfasted with him [Johnson] at Mr.
Thrale's [1] in the Borough.[2] I dined with him this day at the
house of my friends, Messieurs Edward and Charles Dilly, book-
sellers in the Poultry.[3]

BOSWELL. "I am well assured that the people of Otaheite [4]
who have the bread tree, the fruit of which serves them for bread,
laughed heartily when they were informed of the tedious process
necessary with us to have bread—plowing, sowing, harrowing,

[1] MR. THRALE—Henry Thrale, at whose home Johnson spent much time.
[2] BOROUGH—A section of London.   [3] POULTRY—A section of London.
[4] OTAHEITE—Tahiti, an island in the southern Pacific. This passage is a good
illustration of the way in which Boswell would introduce any subject under the
sun, merely to draw out some kind of comment or reaction from Johnson.

reaping, threshing, grinding, baking." JOHNSON. "Why, sir, all ignorant savages will laugh when they are told of the advantages of civilized life. Were you to tell men who live without houses, how we pile brick upon brick, and rafter upon rafter, and that after a house is raised to a certain height, a man tumbles off a scaffold, and breaks his neck, he would laugh heartily at our folly in building; but it does not follow that men are better without houses. No, sir (holding up a slice of a good loaf), this is better than the bread tree."

He repeated an argument, which is to be found in his *Rambler*,[5] against the notion that the brute creation is endowed with the faculty of reason: "Birds build by instinct; they never improve; they build their first nest as well as any one they ever build." GOLDSMITH. "Yet we see if you take away a bird's nest with the eggs in it, she will make a slighter nest and lay again." JOHNSON. "Sir, that is because at first she has full time and makes her nest deliberately. In the case you mention she is pressed to lay, and must therefore make her nest quickly, and consequently it will be slight."

I introduced the subject of toleration. JOHNSON. "Every society has a right to preserve public peace and order, and therefore has a good right to prohibit the propagation of opinions which have a dangerous tendency." MAYO.[6] "I am of opinion, sir, that every man is entitled to liberty of conscience in religion; and that the magistrate cannot restrain that right." JOHNSON. "Sir, I agree with you. Every man has a right to liberty of conscience, and with that the magistrate cannot interfere. People confound liberty of thinking with liberty of talking; nay, with liberty of preaching. Every man has a physical right to think as he pleases; for it cannot be discovered how he thinks. He has not a moral right, for he ought to inform himself, and think justly. But, sir, no member of a society has a right to *teach* any doctrine contrary to what the society holds to be true. The magistrate may be wrong in what he thinks; but while he thinks himself right, he may and ought to enforce what he thinks." MAYO. "Then, sir, we are to remain always in error, and truth never can prevail; and the magistrate was right in persecuting the first Christians." JOHNSON. "I am afraid there is no other

---

[5] *Rambler*—A series of short essays on morals, manners, and literature.
[6] MAYO—The Reverend Doctor Mayo, a member of the Club.

way of ascertaining the truth but by persecution on the one hand and enduring it on the other." GOLDSMITH. "But how is a man to act, sir? Though firmly convinced of the truth of his doctrine, may he not think it wrong to expose himself to persecution? Has he a right to do so? Is it not, as it were, committing voluntary suicide?" JOHNSON. "Sir, as to voluntary suicide, as you call it, there are twenty thousand men in an army who will go without scruple to be shot at, and mount a breach for five pence a day."

[This conversation lasted a long time.]

During this argument, Goldsmith sat in restless agitation, from a wish to get in and *shine*. Finding himself excluded, he had taken his hat to go away, but remained for some time with it in his hand, like a gamester, who, at the close of a long night, lingers for a little while to see if he can have a favorable opening to finish with success. Once when he was beginning to speak, he found himself overpowered by the loud voice of Johnson, who was at the opposite end of the table and did not perceive Goldsmith's attempt. Thus disappointed of his wish to obtain the attention of the company, Goldsmith in a passion threw down his hat, looking angrily at Johnson, and exclaimed in a bitter tone, "*Take it*." When Toplady [7] was going to speak, Johnson uttered some sound which led Goldsmith to think that he was beginning again and taking the words from Toplady. Upon which, he seized this opportunity of venting his own envy and spleen, under the pretext of supporting another person: "Sir," said he to Johnson, "the gentleman has heard you patiently for an hour; pray allow us now to hear him." JOHNSON (sternly). "Sir, I was not interrupting the gentleman. I was only giving him a signal of my attention. Sir, you are impertinent." Goldsmith made no reply, but continued in the company for some time.

[7] TOPLADY—The Reverend Doctor Toplady, a member of the Club.

JOHNSON AND GOLDSMITH

He [Johnson] and Mr. Langton and I went together to the Club, where we found Mr. Burke, Mr. Garrick, and some other members, and amongst them our friend Goldsmith, who sat silently brooding over Johnson's reprimand to him after dinner. Johnson perceived this, and said aside to some of us, "I'll make Goldsmith forgive me"; and then called to him in a loud voice,

"Dr. Goldsmith—something passed today where you and I dined; I ask your pardon." Goldsmith answered placidly, "It must be much from you, sir, that I take ill." And so at once the difference was over, and they were on as easy terms as ever, and Goldsmith rattled away as usual.

Goldsmith's incessant desire of being conspicuous in company was the occasion of his sometimes appearing to such disadvantage as one should hardly have supposed possible in a man of his genius. One evening, in a circle of wits, he found fault with me for talking of Johnson as entitled to the honor of unquestionable superiority. "Sir," said he, "you are for making a monarchy of what should be a republic." He was still more mortified when, talking in a company with fluent vivacity, a German who sat next to him and perceived Johnson rolling himself as if about to speak, suddenly stopped him, saying, "Stay, stay—Toctor Shonson is going to say something." This was, no doubt, very provoking, especially to one so irritable as Goldsmith, who frequently mentioned it with strong expressions of indignation.

It may also be observed that Goldsmith was sometimes content to be treated with an easy familiarity, but, upon occasions, would be consequential and important. An instance of this occurred in a small particular. Johnson had a way of contracting the names of his friends; as Beauclerk, Beau; Boswell, Bozzy; Langton, Lanky; Murphy,[1] Mur; Sheridan,[2] Sherry. I remember one day, when Tom Davies[3] was telling what Dr. Johnson said, "We are all in labor for a name to Goldy's play," Goldsmith seemed displeased that such a liberty should be taken with his name, and said, "I have often desired him not to call me 'Goldy.'" Tom was remarkably attentive to the most minute circumstance about Johnson. I recollect his telling me once, on my arrival in London, "Sir, our great friend has made an improvement on his appellation of old Mr. Sheridan. He calls him now 'Sherry derry.'"

[1] MURPHY—An editor and critic.
[2] SHERIDAN—Richard Brinsley Sheridan, famous playwright of the day, remembered for *The Rivals* and *The School for Scandal*.
[3] TOM DAVIES—Thomas Davies, an actor and bookseller.

SELECTED QUOTATIONS FROM JOHNSON

"Before dinner men meet with great inequality of understanding; and those who are conscious of their inferiority, have the modesty not to talk. But when they have drunk wine, every man feels himself happy, and loses that modesty, and grows impudent and vociferous; but he is not improved; he is only not sensible of his defects."

"A man of sense and education should meet a suitable companion in a wife. It is a miserable thing when the conversation can only be such as, whether the mutton should be boiled or roasted, and probably a dispute about that."

"What we read with inclination makes a much stronger impression. If we read without inclination half the mind is employed in fixing the attention; so there is but one half to be employed on what we read."

"If a man does not make new acquaintance as he advances through life, he will soon find himself left alone. A man, Sir, should keep his friendship in constant repair."

"If a man begins to read in the middle of a book and feels an inclination to go on, let him not quit it to go to the beginning. He may perhaps not feel again the inclination."

DID YOU READ WITH UNDERSTANDING?

1. Check the date for the founding of the Literary Club with the dates of Johnson's life. How old was Johnson when the Club was founded? How many years was it in existence before Johnson died?

2. Prepare brief reports—oral or written—on the following members of the club: Sir Joshua Reynolds, David Garrick, Edmund Burke, Oliver Goldsmith. You will find information about Goldsmith in succeeding pages of this book.

3. So many of Boswell's comments about Goldsmith are unfavorable that it has been suggested that Boswell was jealous of the other writer. From the selections you have read, does the idea seem plausible? Discuss, proving your points by reference to the text.

4. What traits of Johnson's character are disclosed in these selections? For instance, does he show qualities of leadership? Was he kind? harsh? tolerant? generous? conceited? intelligent? and so on. Is your impression of the man favorable or unfavorable? Discuss.

5. In a similar manner discuss Boswell's personality and character as it is revealed in these selections. Do you think he would make a good friend and companion? Why or why not?

6. Be prepared to discuss in informal debate any of the selected quotations from Johnson. With each quotation, decide first whether you agree or disagree, and why.

From SHE STOOPS TO CONQUER

OLIVER GOLDSMITH

Oliver Goldsmith was forever finding himself in an embarrassing situation. On one occasion in his youth—a very unusual occasion because he happened to have money in his pockets—he inquired of a lad in a village for "the best house in town." The chap knew very well that the traveler was inquiring about an inn, but for a prank took his words literally and directed him to the home of a squire, the wealthiest man in the village. Goldsmith swaggered into the house, called the squire "my good man," and ordered the servants about in grand manner. The squire sensed the mistake, and led his "guest" on. When Goldsmith was ready to leave, he called for his bill, and only then discovered his mistake. His humiliation was overwhelming. But with uncommon sense, he later made good use of the experience. When he decided to write a comedy of manners, he built his plot around just such a mistake. The result was that he turned the most embarrassing moment of his young manhood into one of the real successes of his career—the still amusing farce, *She Stoops to Conquer*.

As a sample of eighteenth century comedy, a few scenes from the play are presented below.

DRAMATIS PERSONAE

YOUNG MARLOW, a bashful young man
HARDCASTLE, a country squire
KATE, his daughter
TONY LUMPKIN, his roguish stepson
JEREMY, a servant to MARLOW
MAID
HASTINGS, friend and traveling companion of Marlow
CONSTANCE NEVILLE, niece of Mrs. Hardcastle, in love
      with Hastings

All the scenes presented take place within the Hardcastle mansion—a comfortable, rambling structure not unlike a good wayside inn in style and appointments.

The opening scene of the play introduces the reader to the Hardcastle household. The Squire is expecting guests from the city—the son of his old friend, Sir Charles Marlow, and young Marlow's friend, a Mr. Hastings. Hardcastle and Sir Charles are trying to arrange a marriage between the daughter of the one and the son of the other, and the young man is coming to meet Kate for the first time. He has always been strangely shy with young ladies of his own station in life, but very free and easy with servant girls. Hastings is in love with Kate's cousin Constance Neville, and hopes on this visit to arrange an elopement, since Mrs. Hardcastle will not consent to Connie's marrying any one but her loutish son, Tony Lumpkin. Mr. Hardcastle is coaching his servants in the proper way to welcome their expected guests.

In the meantime Marlow and Hastings have lost their way and stopped at the local inn for directions. Tony is there with some of his cronies; and for a joke tells the travelers that they are a long way from their destination but that there is an excellent inn about a mile down the road. He then directs them to his stepfather's house.

When the young men arrive at the Hardcastle home, they mistake the friendliness of their host for boldness on the part of a landlord; and they in turn give the impression of being most unmannerly guests. Hastings shortly learns of their mistake; but in order to perfect the plans for his elopement, he decides not to enlighten Marlow just yet. When Kate Hardcastle returns from a walk, he tells Marlow that she has stopped in at the inn by chance and introduces the two. In an agony of shyness, Marlow keeps his eyes on the ground, makes a few stammering speeches, and excuses himself. And this is the young man who has been, unknowingly, trying to put the girl's father "in his place." No wonder Hardcastle and Kate have formed two very different opinions of the chap!

Act III opens with Hardcastle wondering about the strange manners of Sir Charles's son.

ACT III

Scene i.

Enter Hardcastle.

Hardcastle. What could my old friend Sir Charles mean by recommending his son as the modestest young man in town? To me he appears the most impudent piece of brass that ever spoke with a tongue. He has taken possession of the easy chair by the fire-side already. He took off his boots in the parlor, and desired me to see them taken care of. I'm desirous to know how his impudence affects my daughter. She will certainly be shocked at it.

Enter Miss Hardcastle, *plainly dressed*.

Hardcastle. Well, my Kate, I see you have changed your dress,[1] as I bid you; and yet, I believe, there was no great occasion.

---

[1] CHANGED YOUR DRESS—Kate's father disliked elaborate clothes. Early in the day Kate might dress up in fashion and call upon her friends, but in the evening she dressed simply to please her father.

Miss Hardcastle. I find such a pleasure, sir, in obeying your commands, that I take care to observe them without ever debating their propriety.

Hardcastle. And yet, Kate, I sometimes give you some cause, particularly when I recommended my *modest* gentleman to you as a lover today.

Miss Hardcastle. You taught me to expect something extraordinary, and I find the original exceeds the description.

Hardcastle. I was never so surprised in my life! He has quite confounded all my faculties.

Miss Hardcastle. I never saw anything like it; and a man of the world, too!

Hardcastle. Ay, he learned it all abroad; what a fool was I, to think a young man could learn modesty by traveling. He might as soon learn wit at a masquerade.

Miss Hardcastle. It seems all natural to him.

Hardcastle. A good deal assisted by bad company and a French dancing-master.

Miss Hardcastle. Sure, you mistake, papa. A French dancing-master could never have taught him that timid look—that awkward address—that bashful manner.

Hardcastle. Whose look, whose manner, child?

Miss Hardcastle. Mr. Marlow's: his *mauvaise honte* [2] his timidity, struck me at the first sight.

Hardcastle. Then your first sight deceived you; for I think him one of the most brazen first sights that ever astonished my senses.

Miss Hardcastle. Sure, sir, you rally.[3] I never saw any one so modest.

Hardcastle. And can you be serious! I never saw such a bouncing, swaggering puppy since I was born. Bully Dawson [4] was but a fool to him.

Miss Hardcastle. Surprising! He met me with a respectful bow, a stammering voice, and a look fixed on the ground.

Hardcastle. He met me with a loud voice, a lordly air, and a familiarity that made my blood freeze again.

Miss Hardcastle. He treated me with diffidence and respect; censured the manners of the age; admired the prudence of girls

---

[2] *Mauvaise honte*—Shyness, bashfulness.   [3] RALLY—Joke.
[4] BULLY DAWSON—A notorious braggart or swashbuckler of the time.

that never laughed; tired me with apologies for being tiresome; then left the room with a bow, and "Madam, I would not for the world detain you."

Hardcastle. He spoke to me as if he knew me all his life before; asked twenty questions, and never waited for an answer; interrupted my best remarks with some silly pun; and when I was in my best story of the Duke of Marlborough and Prince Eugene, he asked if I had not a good hand at making punch. Yes, Kate, he asked your father if he was a maker of punch!

Miss Hardcastle. One of us must certainly be mistaken.

Hardcastle. If he be what he has shown himself, I'm determined he shall never have my consent.

Miss Hardcastle. And if he be the sullen thing I take him, he shall never have mine.

Hardcastle. In one thing then we are agreed—to reject him.

Miss Hardcastle. Yes—but upon conditions. For if you should find him less impudent, and I more presuming; if you find him more respectful, and I more importunate—I don't know —the fellow is well enough for a man—Certainly we don't meet many such at a horse-race in the country.

Hardcastle. If we should find him so—But that's impossible. The first appearance has done my business. I'm seldom deceived in that.

Miss Hardcastle. And yet there may be many good qualities under that first appearance.

Hardcastle. Ay, when a girl finds a fellow's outside to her taste, she then sets about guessing the rest of his furniture. With her a smooth face stands for good sense, and a genteel figure for every virtue.

Miss Hardcastle. I hope, sir, a conversation begun with a compliment to my good sense, won't end with a sneer at my understanding!

Hardcastle. Pardon me, Kate. But if young Mr. Brazen can find the art of reconciling contradictions, he may please us both, perhaps.

Miss Hardcastle. And as one of us must be mistaken, what if we go to make farther discoveries?

Hardcastle. Agreed. But depend on 't, I'm in the right.

Miss Hardcastle. And, depend on 't, I'm not much in the wrong. [*Exeunt.*

[While Constance and Hastings are arranging their elopement, Kate has learned from one of the maids about Marlow's blunder.]

SCENE 2.

Enter MISS HARDCASTLE *and* Maid.

Miss Hardcastle. What an unaccountable creature is that brother of mine, to send them to the house as an inn; ha! ha! I don't wonder at his impudence.

Maid. But what is more, madam, the young gentleman, as you passed by in your present dress, asked me if you were the barmaid. He mistook you for the barmaid, madam!

Miss Hardcastle. Did he? Then, as I live, I'm resolved to keep up the delusion. Tell me, Pimple, how do you like my present dress? Don't you think I look something like Cherry in the *Beaux' Stratagem?* [1]

Maid. It's the dress, madam, that every lady wears in the country, but when she visits or receives company.

Miss Hardcastle. And are you sure he does not remember my face or person?

Maid. Certain of it.

Miss Hardcastle. I vow I thought so; for though we spoke for some time together, yet his fears were such that he never once looked up during the interview. Indeed, if he had, my bonnet would have kept him from seeing me.

Maid. But what do you hope from keeping him in his mistake?

Miss Hardcastle. In the first place, I shall be *seen,* and that is no small advantage to a girl who brings her face to market. Then I shall perhaps make an acquaintance, and that's no small victory gained over one who never addresses any but the wildest of her sex. But my chief aim is to take my gentleman off his guard, and, like an invisible champion of romance, examine the giant's force before I offer to combat.

Maid. But are you sure you can act your part, and disguise your voice so that he may mistake that, as he has already mistaken your person?

Miss Hardcastle. Never fear me. I think I have got the true bar cant [2]—Did your honor call?—Attend the Lion there.—Pipes

---

[1] CHERRY IN THE *Beaux' Stratagem*—Cherry was the daughter of the innkeeper in the comedy, the *Beaux' Stratagem.*

[2] CANT—Mode of speaking.

and tobacco for the Angel.—The Lamb has been outrageous this half hour!

Maid. It will do, madam. But he's here. [*Exit* Maid.

Enter MARLOW.

Marlow. What a bawling in every part of the house; I have scarce a moment's repose. If I go to the best room, there I find my host and his story; if I fly to the gallery,³ there we have my hostess with her curtsey down to the ground. I have at last got a moment to myself, and now for recollection. [*Walks and muses.*]

Miss Hardcastle. Did you call sir? Did your honor call?

Marlow. [*Musing.*] As for Miss Hardcastle, she's too grave and sentimental for me.

Miss Hardcastle. Did your honor call? [*She still places herself before him, he turning away.*]

Marlow. No, child. [*Musing.*] Besides, from the glimpse I had of her, I think she squints.

Miss Hardcastle. I'm sure, sir, I heard the bell ring.

Marlow. No, no. [*Musing.*] I have pleased my father, however, by coming down, and I'll tomorrow please myself by returning. [*Taking out his tablets and perusing.*]

Miss Hardcastle. Perhaps the other gentleman called, sir?

Marlow. I tell you no.

Miss Hardcastle. I should be glad to know, sir. We have such a parcel of servants.

Marlow. No, no, I tell you. [*Looks full in her face.*] Yes, child, I think I did call. I wanted—I wanted—I vow, child, you are vastly handsome.

Miss Hardcastle. Oh, la, sir, you'll make one ashamed.

Marlow. Never saw a more sprightly, malicious eye. Yes, yes, my dear, I did call. Have you got any of your—a—what d' ye call it, in the house?

Miss Hardcastle. No, sir, we have been out of that these ten days.

Marlow. One may call in this house, I find, to very little purpose. Suppose I should call for a taste, just by way of trial, of the nectar of your lips; perhaps I might be disappointed in that too.

Miss Hardcastle. Nectar? nectar? That's a liquor there's no

³ GALLERY—Hallway, passageway.

call for in these parts. French, I suppose. We keep no French wines here, sir.

Marlow. Of true English growth, I assure you.

Miss Hardcastle. Then it's odd I should not know it. We brew all sorts of wines in this house, and I have lived here these eighteen years.

Marlow. Eighteen years! Why, one would think, child, you kept the bar before you were born. How old are you?

Miss Hardcastle. Oh, sir, I must not tell my age. They say women and music should never be dated.

Marlow. To guess at this distance, you can't be much above forty. [*Approaching.*] Yet nearer, I don't think so much. [*Approaching.*] By coming close to some women, they look younger still; but when we come very close indeed— [*Attempting to kiss her.*]

Miss Hardcastle. Pray, sir, keep your distance. One would think you wanted to know one's age as they do horses, by mark of mouth.

Marlow. I protest, child, you use me extremely ill. If you keep me at this distance, how is it possible you and I can be ever acquainted?

Miss Hardcastle. And who wants to be acquainted with you? I want no such acquaintance, not I. I'm sure you did not treat

Miss Hardcastle, that was here a while ago, in this obstropalous [4] manner. I'll warrant me, before her you looked dashed, and kept bowing to the ground, and talked, for all the world, as if you was before a justice of peace.

Marlow. [*Aside.*] Egad, she has hit it, sure enough! [*To her.*] In awe of her, child? Ha! ha! ha! A mere awkward, squinting thing! No, no. I find you don't know me. I laughed and rallied her a little; but I was unwilling to be too severe. No, I could not be too severe, curse me!

Miss Hardcastle. Oh, then, sir, you are a favorite, I find, among the ladies!

Marlow. Yes, my dear, a great favorite. And yet, hang me, I don't see what they find in me to follow. At the Ladies' Club in town I'm called their agreeable Rattle. Rattle, child, is not my real name, but one I'm known by. My name is Solomons; Mr. Solomons, my dear, at your service. [*Offering to salute her.*]

Miss Hardcastle. Hold, sir, you are introducing me to your club, not to yourself. And you're so great a favorite there, you say?

Marlow. Yes, my dear. There's Mrs. Mantrap, Lady Betty Blackleg, the Countess of Sligo, Mrs. Langhorns, old Miss Biddy Buckskin, and your humble servant, keep up the spirit of the place.

Miss Hardcastle. Then it's a very merry place, I suppose?

Marlow. Yes, as merry as cards, suppers, wine, and old women can make us.

Miss Hardcastle. And their agreeable Rattle, ha! ha! ha!

Marlow. [*Aside.*] Egad! I don't quite like this chit. She looks knowing, methinks. You laugh, child?

Miss Hardcastle. I can't but laugh to think what time they all have for minding their work, or their family.

Marlow. [*Aside.*] All's well; she don't laugh at me. [*To her.*] Do *you* ever work, child?

Miss Hardcastle. Ay, sure. There's not a screen or a quilt in the whole house but what can bear witness to that.

Marlow. Odso! then you must show me your embroidery. I embroider and draw patterns myself a little. If you want a judge of your work, you must apply to me. [*Seizing her hand.*]

    Enter HARDCASTLE, *who stands in surprise.*

[4] OBSTROPALOUS—Obstreperous.

Miss Hardcastle. Ay, but the colors don't look well by candle-light. You shall see it all in the morning. [*Struggling.*]

Marlow. And why not now, my angel? Such beauty fires beyond the power of resistance. Pshaw! the father here! My old luck; I never nicked seven that I did not throw ames ace [5] three times following. [*Exit* MARLOW.

Hardcastle. So, madam! So I find *this* is your *modest* lover. This is your humble admirer, that kept his eyes fixed on the ground, and only adored at humble distance. Kate, Kate, art thou not ashamed to deceive your father so?

Miss Hardcastle. Never trust me, dear papa, but he's still the modest man I first took him for; you'll be convinced of it as well as I.

Hardcastle. By the hand of my body, I believe his impudence is infectious! Didn't I see him seize your hand? Didn't I see him haul you about like a milkmaid? And now you talk of his respect and his modesty, forsooth!

Miss Hardcastle. But if I shortly convince you of his modesty, that he has only the faults that will pass off with time, and the virtues that will improve with age, I hope you'll forgive him.

Hardcastle. The girl would actually make one run mad! I tell you I'll not be convinced. I am convinced. He has scarcely been three hours in the house, and he has already encroached on all my prerogatives. You may like his impudence, and call it modesty; but my son-in-law, madam, must have very different qualifications.

Miss Hardcastle. Sir, I ask but this night to convince you.

Hardcastle. You shall not have half the time, for I have thoughts of turning him out this very hour.

Miss Hardcastle. Give me that hour, then, and I hope to satisfy you.

Hardcastle. Well, an hour let it be then. But I'll have no trifling with your father. All fair and open; do you mind me?

Miss Hardcastle. I hope, sir, you have ever found that I considered your commands as my pride; for your kindness is such that my duty as yet has been inclination.[6] [*Exeunt.*

---

[5] NICKED SEVEN . . . THROW AMES ACE—Expressions in dice throwing. The meaning is "I never made a lucky throw that I didn't follow it with three unlucky ones."

[6] MY DUTY AS YET HAS BEEN INCLINATION—The things I have so far been required to do have been the things I wanted to do.

ACT IV

SCENE 3.

MARLOW *on stage. Enter* HARDCASTLE.

Hardcastle. I no longer know my own house. It's turned all topsy-turvy. His servants have got drunk already. I'll bear it no longer; and yet, from my respect for his father, I'll be calm. [*To him.*] Mr. Marlow, your servant. I'm your very humble servant. [*Bowing low.*]

Marlow. Sir, your humble servant. [*Aside.*] What's to be the wonder now?

Hardcastle. I believe, sir, you must be sensible, sir, that no man alive ought to be more welcome than your father's son, sir. I hope you think so?

Marlow. I do from my soul, sir. I don't want much entreaty. I generally make my father's son welcome wherever he goes.

Hardcastle. I believe you do, from my soul, sir. But though I say nothing to your own conduct, that of your servants is insufferable. Their manner of drinking is setting a very bad example in this house, I assure you.

Marlow. I protest, my very good sir, that is no fault of mine. If they don't drink as they ought, *they* are to blame. I ordered them not to spare the cellar; [1] I did, I assure you. [*To the side-scene.*] Here, let one of my servants come up. [*To him.*] My positive directions were, that as I did not drink myself, they should make up for my deficiencies below.

Hardcastle. Then they had your orders for what they do? I'm satisfied!

Marlow. They had, I assure you. You shall hear from one of themselves.

Enter Servant, *drunk.*

Marlow. You, Jeremy! Come forward, sirrah! What were my orders? Were you not told to drink freely, and call for what you thought fit, for the good of the house?

Hardcastle. [*Aside.*] I begin to lose my patience.

Jeremy. Please your honor, liberty and Fleet-street forever!

---

[1] I ORDERED THEM NOT TO SPARE THE CELLAR—Since Marlow believed that a certain charge for wine would be included in his bill even though he was not drinking it, he told his servants to order as much as they wanted.

Though I'm but a servant, I'm as good as another man. I'll drink for no man before supper, sir! Good liquor will sit upon a good supper, but a good supper will not sit upon—hiccup— upon my conscience, sir.   [*Exit.*

Marlow. You see, my old friend, the fellow is as drunk as he can possibly be. I don't know what you'd have more, unless you'd have the poor devil soused in a beer barrel.

Hardcastle. Zounds! he'll drive me distracted, if I contain myself any longer. Mr. Marlow, sir! I have submitted to your insolence for more than four hours, and I see no likelihood of its coming to an end. I'm now resolved to be master here, sir, and I desire that you and your drunken pack may leave my house directly.

Marlow. Leave your house!—Sure, you jest, my good friend? What? when I am doing what I can to please you!

Hardcastle. I tell you, sir, you don't please me; so I desire you'll leave my house.

Marlow. Sure you cannot be serious? at this time of night, and such a night? You only mean to banter me.

Hardcastle. I tell you, sir, I'm serious! and now that my passions are roused, I say this house is mine, sir; this house is mine, and I command you to leave it directly.

Marlow. Ha! ha! ha! A puddle in a storm. I shan't stir a step, I assure you. [*In a serious tone.*] This your house, fellow! It's my house. This is my house. Mine, while I choose to stay. What right have you to bid me leave this house, sir? I never met with such impudence, curse me; never in my whole life before.

Hardcastle. Nor I, confound me if ever I did! To come to my house, to call for what he likes, to turn me out of my own chair, to insult the family, to order his servants to get drunk, and then to tell me, "This house is mine, sir!" By all that's impudent, it makes me laugh. Ha! ha! ha! Pray, sir, [*Bantering.*] as you take the house, what think you of taking the rest of the furniture? There's a pair of silver candlesticks, and there's a fire-screen, and here's a pair of brazen-nosed bellows; perhaps you may take a fancy to them?

Marlow. Bring me your bill, sir; bring me your bill, and let's make no more words about it.

Hardcastle. There are a set of prints, too. What think you of the *Rake's Progress* ² for your own apartment?

Marlow. Bring me your bill, I say, and I'll leave you and your infernal house directly.

Hardcastle. Then there's a mahogany table that you may see your face in.

Marlow. My bill, I say.

Hardcastle. I had forgot the great chair for your own particular slumbers, after a hearty meal.

Marlow. Zounds! bring me my bill, I say, and let's hear no more on 't.

Hardcastle. Young man, young man, from your father's letter to me, I was taught to expect a well-bred, modest man as a visitor here, but now I find him no better than a coxcomb and a bully; but he will be down here presently, and shall hear more of it.

[*Exit.*

Marlow. How's this! Sure I have not mistaken the house? Everything looks like an inn; the servants cry "Coming"; the attendance ³ is awkward; the barmaid, too, to attend us. But she's here, and will further inform me. Whither so fast, child? A word with you.

Enter MISS HARDCASTLE.

Miss Hardcastle. Let it be short, then. I'm in a hurry. [*Aside.*] I believe he begins to find out his mistake. But it's too soon quite to undeceive him.

Marlow. Pray, child, answer me one question. What are you, and what may your business in this house be?

Miss Hardcastle. A relation of the family, sir.

Marlow. What! a poor relation?

Miss Hardcastle. Yes, sir, a poor relation, appointed to keep the keys, and to see that the guests want nothing in my power to give them.

Marlow. That is, you act as the barmaid of this inn.

Miss Hardcastle. Inn! O law—what brought that into your head? One of the best families in the country keep an inn!— Ha! ha! ha! old Mr. Hardcastle's house an inn!

² *Rake's Progress*—A famous set of prints or drawings by a celebrated English artist.

³ ATTENDANCE—Service.

Marlow. Mr. Hardcastle's house! Is this house Mr. Hardcastle's house, child?

Miss Hardcastle. Ay, sure. Whose else should it be?

Marlow. So, then, all's out, and I have been infernally imposed on. Oh, confound my stupid head, I shall be laughed at over the whole town! I shall be stuck up in caricatura [4] in all the print-shops. The *Dullissimo-Macaroni.*[5] To mistake this house of all others for an inn, and my father's old friend for an innkeeper! What a swaggering puppy must he take me for! What a silly puppy do I find myself! There, again, may I be hanged, my dear, but I mistook you for the barmaid.

Miss Hardcastle. Dear me! dear me! I'm sure there's nothing in my *behavior* to put me upon a level with one of that stamp.

Marlow. Nothing, my dear, nothing. But I was in for a list of blunders, and could not help making you a subscriber. My stupidity saw everything the wrong way. I mistook your assiduity for assurance, and your simplicity for allurement. But it's over—this house I no more show *my* face in.

Miss Hardcastle. I hope, sir, I have done nothing to disoblige you. I'm sure I should be sorry to affront any gentleman who has been so polite, and said so many civil things to me. I'm sure I should be sorry [*Pretending to cry.*] if he left the family upon my account. I'm sure I should be sorry people said anything amiss, since I have no fortune but my character.

Marlow. [*Aside.*] By Heaven! she weeps! This is the first mark of tenderness I ever had from a modest woman, and it touches me. [*To her.*] Excuse me, my lovely girl; you are the only part of the family I leave with reluctance. But, to be plain with you, the difference of our birth, fortune, and education, make an honorable connection impossible; and I can never harbor a thought of seducing simplicity that trusted in my honor, or bringing ruin upon one whose only fault was being too lovely.

Miss Hardcastle. [*Aside.*] Generous man! I now begin to admire him. [*To him.*] But I am sure my family is as good as Miss Hardcastle's; and though I'm poor, that's no great mis-

[4] CARICATURA—Caricatures.
[5] *Dullissimo-Macaroni*—During this period the term "macaroni" meant a fop or a dandy. *Dullissimo-Macaroni* would therefore mean "the very dullest or most stupid of all dandies."

fortune to a contented mind; and, until this moment, I never thought that it was bad to want [6] fortune.

Marlow. And why now, my pretty simplicity?

Miss Hardcastle. Because it puts me at a distance from one, that, if I had a thousand pound I would give it all to.

Marlow. [*Aside.*] This simplicity bewitches me so, that if I stay I'm undone. I must make one bold effort and leave her. [*To her.*] Your partiality in my favor, my dear, touches me most sensibly; and were I to live for myself alone, I could easily fix my choice. But I owe too much to the opinion of the world, too much to the authority of a father; so that—I can scarcely speak it—it affects me! Farewell.   [*Exit.*

Miss Hardcastle. I never knew half his merit till now. He shall not go if I have power or art to detain him. I'll still preserve the character in which I *stooped to conquer,* but will undeceive my papa, who, perhaps, may laugh him out of his resolution.   [*Exit.*

[Needless to say, in Act V, Kate makes her CONQUEST; all mistakes are cleared up, and both pairs of lovers are happily engaged.]

[6] WANT—Lack.

DID YOU READ WITH UNDERSTANDING?

SCENE 1:

1. What impression has Mr. Hardcastle formed of young Marlow? Why?

2. What sort of impression has Marlow made upon Kate? In this first scene of the third act is either Kate or her father hopeful about the proposed match between Kate and Marlow? Which one thinks that the young man is not so impossible as he seems? Discuss.

3. Why does Hardcastle call his guest "Mr. Brazen"?

SCENE 2:

1. What important information about Marlow does Kate learn from the maid?

2. Why does Kate decide to let Marlow continue in his delusion that the house is an inn and that she is a barmaid or waitress in it? Why will Marlow not recognize her as the young lady to whom he had been formally presented an hour or so earlier?

3. How does Kate finally engage Marlow's attention? What is the effect upon him? Marlow describes himself as what kind of fellow among the ladies? Is he telling the truth, do you think, or exaggerating?

4. Why is Kate's father surprised when he finds Kate and Marlow together?

5. How much time does Kate ask in which to prove to her father that Marlow is not an improper young man?

SCENE 3:

1. What is the source of misunderstanding between Marlow and his host in the third scene of our selection? Does the testimony of the servant make matters better or worse? Explain.

2. Point out several instances in the scene in which Marlow and Hardcastle completely miss the point of each other's words—as when Marlow uses the term "house" in the sense of *hotel* and his host in the sense of *home*.

3. What sarcastic suggestions does Hardcastle make near the close of the scene?

4. What finally suggests the idea to Marlow that he may have made a mistake?

5. Why doesn't Kate tell him at once that she is Hardcastle's daughter?

6. How does Marlow feel about his blunder? What does he propose to do? How does Kate hope to keep him in the house? Why does she now consider Marlow a desirable young man?

7. Explain the significance of the title of the play—*She Stoops to Conquer*.

OVERVIEW:

1. In what general respects did Marlow's idea of *good manners* differ from ours?

2. What evidence is there that there were sharp class distinctions in eighteenth-century England?

3. Would an American girl like young Marlow? Why or why not? Why did Kate not resent his conduct?

EXTENDED ACTIVITIES

WITH PEACE CAME A CLASSIC PERIOD OF POLISH
AND RESTRAINT

HISTORY IN BRIEF

	The Stuarts	The House of Hanover	Events in America
1700-1780 (18th Century)	Anne (1702-1714) (England and Scotland united as Great Britain, 1707) (War with France)		Queen Anne's War, 1702-1713
		George I (1714-1727) (War with France) (Walpole Minister) George II (1727-1760) (War with Spain) (War with France) (Clive in India, 1750) George III (1760-1820) (Peace of Paris, 1763) (Lord North Minister, 1770-1782) (War with American colonies, 1775-1783) (War with Spain, 1779-1783) (War with Holland, 1780-1783)	French and Indian Wars, 1755-1763 Montreal and all Canada surrendered to England, 1760 The Stamp Act, 1765 The Boston Tea Party, 1773 Battles of Lexington and Concord, 1775 Declaration of Independence, July 4, 1776 Surrender of Cornwallis, 1781

FOR ACQUAINTANCE WITH AUTHORS

ALEXANDER POPE (1688–1744)—"THE RAPE OF THE LOCK"

A strange misshapen little figure dominates the early eighteenth century. Hunchbacked, dwarfed, and a Catholic, Alexander Pope's chances of fame seemed small; for after the Bloodless Revolution of 1688 Catholics were held in nearly as much disfavor as were the Puritans during the Restoration. But Pope's intellect, his ability to say "what oft was thought but ne'er so well expresst," and his clever spitefulness brought him fame and fortune. At seventeen he was hailed as a prodigy by the London "wits." His first published work was the "Essay on Criticism," a résumé of the rules for writing poetry copied after the French. In the next year appeared "The Rape of the Lock," and the young ladies dangled a curl in front of their gallants in the hope that Mr. Pope might celebrate them as he had Arabella. When Pope was only twenty-five, he published his translation of Homer which brought him nation-wide acclaim, eight thousand pounds, and a beautiful country estate near London—the Twickenham so often mentioned in letters of the writers of the Queen Anne period.

Pope, like Dryden, became embroiled in politics. The Age of Queen Anne was an age of political intrigue. The government tottered, as Whigs and Tories fought for power. As never before or since, men of letters were admitted to the inner political circles and won political appointments through their well-aimed attacks. Pope's sharp tongue and sharper pen were much sought after.

Nearly always ill, often petulant and spiteful, Pope nevertheless was loved and respected by his own circle. Swift was his friend, as was Addison. His witty, compact verses were believed the ultimate achievement in English poetry.

JONATHAN SWIFT (1667–1745)—"LIFE WITH THE GIANTS"

The tragedy in the life of Jonathan Swift is reflected in his characterization of his countrymen as "the most pernicious race of little odious vermin that nature ever suffered to crawl upon the surface of the earth." Behind the bitterness of that sentence lies a lifetime of disappointment and disillusionment.

Swift came from a good Irish family and was educated at Trinity in Dublin and later at Oxford. But he was poor. It was a time of general snobbishness and bitter prejudices. Intelligence and learning were respected, but poverty was a personal disgrace. Swift was impelled to take a position as secretary to Sir William Temple, a wealthy relative who treated him with condescending contempt. In an attempt to become independent he took orders in the Church and was assigned to a parish in Ireland. Like Spenser, he thoroughly detested the country; but unlike the poet, he worked conscientiously for the welfare of the Irish people. After a short stay in his first parish he returned to the services of Sir William at Moor Park, preferring to be in England even in an unpleasantly inferior position. At Moor Park, Swift met Esther Johnson, a beautiful girl whom he grew to love. The affection seemed a lasting one; and the happiest of Swift's works are the letters he wrote to her as his "Stella." Yet Swift never married, returning Esther's devotion to him with cruel extremes of affection and neglect.

When Temple died, Swift returned to the Church, again in Ireland. He hoped through his very real ability to secure advancement, but one of his earliest satires had offended the Queen and the appointments he hoped for never came. However, in the years between 1700 and 1713 he divided his time between London and Ireland. In London he became the most powerful writer of political pamphlets. For three years he enjoyed prosperity and fame. When Queen Anne died, he hoped to be made bishop of an English diocese. His appointment was to the deanship of St. Patrick's Cathedral in Dublin. Thoroughly embittered, Dean Swift went to Ireland to stay, returning to London only for brief visits concerned with the publications of his works. He did his work well in Ireland and eventually won the respect of his people. From time to time he was distressed by illness, and a brain affliction finally destroyed his reason. He died hopelessly insane.

JOSEPH ADDISON (1672–1719)— "FROZEN WORDS," "SIR ROGER AT CHURCH"

Joseph Addison epitomizes the eighteenth century. Meticulously bewigged and beruffled, he was a thoroughly respectable and respected gentleman. He was a competent scholar, a politician and a statesman, a conversationalist and a coffee drinker. His sense of humor, satiric in the

eighteenth-century manner, was tempered with much good nature and some kindliness; here he parts company with many of the other leading writers of his day.

From his early school days Addison was marked for fame. At fifteen he went to Oxford where his skill in Latin versifying brought him favor after favor. He won a pension, traveled abroad for three years, came forth with polished little verses at the proper times and began his political rise. Ultimately he became Secretary of Ireland, then Secretary of State. In his leisure he wrote pamphlets, verses, opera, formal tragedy and—what is most important—copy for the *Tatler* and *Spectator*.

At Oxford he had known slightly a good natured and rather lazy young Irishman, Dick Steele. When in 1709 an amusing little sheet of news and gossip entitled the *Tatler* appeared, Addison recognized it as the work of his school fellow, Steele. He noticed that the articles of literary criticism were weak; now and again he sent in reviews, criticisms, and ideas. Soon the two men were working together; they published a new paper, the *Spectator*, which was to be free of political argument and devote itself to education and to the reform of the foibles of mankind. The editors intended that young ladies find a copy of the *Spectator* on their breakfast trays instead of their hand mirrors. And the young ladies did! The paper flourished; Addison lost much of his formality to genial good humor and raillery at foolish customs. As his state career demanded more time, he was forced to give up his writing; too many people knew of his connection with the gossipy little sheet that now had a circulation of 10,000. The last eight years of his life were devoted entirely to politics; he died at forty-seven leaving behind him the correct but genial Mr. Spectator who in so many respects was Mr. Addison himself.

RICHARD STEELE (1672–1729)—"FROZEN WORDS," "SIR ROGER AT CHURCH"

Richard Steele was born the same year as Addison, went to the same college, and collaborated with him on the *Tatler* and *Spectator*. Here the similarities between the two men end. Steele was a rollicking Irishman

—sentimental, generous, often in debt. He was never a success although he tried politics and soldiering and writing.

In 1707 he somehow landed the job of "gazeteer," publishing news dispatches for the government. Often the news was late and trivial; Steele grew weary of his dull job. On borrowed money he decided to try a new sort of gazette in which the news would give place to comments on the events and to interesting articles that would appeal to the middle-class reader. Thus was born the *Tatler*. Steele's fortunes for a time looked brighter. His next magazine, the *Spectator*, published in collaboration with Addison, was immensely popular. In 1715 under George I he was knighted. After the *Spectator*, he tried six other magazines, all more or less successful. In debt as usual, he finally had to retire to his wife's estate in Wales where the living was cheaper, the temptations fewer. But the sentimental Irishman who wept as easily as he laughed had started the eighteenth century on a perusal of its faults and the discovery of its heart.

OLIVER GOLDSMITH (1729–1774)—"SHE STOOPS TO CONQUER"

The gaudy little figure of Noll Goldsmith bobbed in and out of eighteenth-century life—into the theaters, the print shops, the book stalls, Johnson's Literary Club, high society and low. Fame came to him after nearly a lifetime of blunders and disappointments. Born in Dublin, the pock-marked youngster with a taste for the flamboyant in clothes, worked his way as a sizar in Trinity College. He was early distinguished for his escapades rather than his scholarship and left without a degree.

At the wish of his relatives he applied for orders in the Church. His arrival in a scarlet suit to apply for ordination helped win him rejection. Relatives contributed a purse for him to start to America, but he got as far as Cork. The kind-hearted Goldsmith clan supplied another purse for him to study law in London; Oliver got as far as Dublin. Once more, this time with dire threats, the clan sent him on his way—to Leyden to study medicine. There Oliver spent two years acquiring a light smattering of medicine but winning more renown for his flute playing than for his knowledge. Determined to tour Europe, his finances exhausted as usual, he set out on foot with his flute, playing for bed and board throughout Flanders, Switzerland, and France.

By 1756 he had reappeared in England. Then began his attempts at money-making. His jobs were many, his earnings scant. He was an apothecary's assistant, a proof reader, tutor; and finally, after all else had failed, a hack writer. He had at last found his niche—or his publisher had! It was found that, coerced sufficiently, Goldsmith could write anything: children's books, articles, reviews, zoology, history, philosophy, and fiction. In addition, his output was readable and popular. About this time Samuel Johnson discovered the young, underrated journalist, rescued him from his demanding publisher, and brought him into the circle of the Literary Club. At last Goldsmith found a welcoming public; he began writing for the first time under his own name. Comedy, tragedy, letters, poetry, and a novel poured from his pen; and he easily earned the fame due his literary genius.

After "The Traveler" and "The Deserted Village" came the delightful comedy, *She Stoops to Conquer*, the first true comedy in a period when a play's success had depended upon the quantity of gentle weeping it provoked. It is said that Johnson rushed out to sell the manuscript of Goldsmith's famous novel, *The Vicar of Wakefield*, while the author himself argued with his threatening landlady. Goldsmith was completely successful, but with success came increased expenditures; he was never more than a step ahead of his creditors—and that a short one! The strain of always working under the pressure of debt finally contributed to breaking his health and spirit. In a space of sixteen years Goldsmith wrote a series of essays, a poem, a novel, and two dramas; any one of which would have been sufficient to entitle him to an enduring place in literature.

JAMES BOSWELL (1740–1795)—"LIFE OF SAMUEL JOHNSON"

The man who was to give the world a book possessing "more of life than any work ever yet appeared" began humbly enough as a Scotch lawyer who found clients hard to get. James Boswell was really much less interested in his legal cases than he was in his hobby of celebrity-hunting. The book that has made him famous was not at all an accident. He had evidently early made up his mind to search out the most likely man in London, study him closely, and write a book about him. Samuel Johnson was the subject that he selected; and when he finally achieved an introduction to the Doctor, he attached himself to the man like a shadow. Johnson was big and Boswell small, and the couple were often likened to a lumberly bear with a devoted little terrier frisking about him.

It took Boswell seven years after the death of Johnson to arrange and edit the mass of notes in which he had recorded the very words and gestures of his master. When the *Life of Samuel Johnson* finally appeared, it presented not only the portrait of one man but an encyclopediac fund of information about eighteenth-century life. The little Scotch lawyer had insured immortality not only for himself, but for the curious lion of classic letters—Samuel Johnson.

OF LITERARY FORM AND STYLE

CLASSICISM IN LITERATURE

In the study of literature, the term *classicism* has come to have a specialized meaning. It denotes a conventional way of writing. It implies following an accepted pattern, and it places great emphasis upon the *form* or *manner* of presentation. The usual characteristics of classic literature may be summarized as follows:

In *subject,* classicism is interested in art rather than in nature, and in man as a member of society rather than as an individual. It therefore deals with clubs and politics, with churches, schools, societies, and man's relations to them. It is concerned with rank and social position and behavior. It deals more with man's manners and accomplishments than with his heart. It counts a display of emotion or sentiment as ill-bred or weak. It shows more interest in art and artificial effects than in nature. A man of classic mind would take more pleasure in smooth lawns and clipped hedges than in the tumbled splendor of the Alps. Classic literature, then, deals chiefly with men and women, brilliantly clad, moving decorously in court or ballroom or formal garden. Their conversation may sparkle with wit, or be distinguished by reason and logic. It glitters, but it does not burn.

In *form,* classic art must be precise and polished. What one says is counted of less importance than how one says it. Writing may be done by rule. Poetry should be syllable-perfect in rhythm, flawless in expression. Words should be dignified and refined. A cottage is a "bower"; a peasant is a "rustic" or a "swain"; a crowd is a "train"; and so on. The poet forgets the language of life for formalized diction and elaborate elegance. Classic literature abounds in figures of speech, particularly in long, complicated metaphors and in similes drawn from ancient mythology. Clever imitation may be counted of more worth than originality, and ornateness preferable to simplicity and strength. Whether expressed in prose or verse, classic writing is smooth, regular, scholarly, *impressive* with long words and long sentences carefully contrived. Any *feeling* aroused by such art is, of course, cold and remote. Its appeal is to the mind rather than to the heart. At its best, it pleasantly skims the surface of life. It shows the dress and mannerisms of man, but not his emotions. The classic writer does not put himself into his work except as an observer or critic. Hence his literature is likely to be critical, satiric, supercilious. It may provoke smiles, but not heart-stirring laughter.

English literature during most of the eighteenth century was marked by just such characteristics, so that the period is often known as the Age of Classicism. The writings were predominantly prose; but there was one major poet and one extremely popular poetic form—the *heroic couplet.*

THE HEROIC COUPLET, AND EIGHTEENTH-CENTURY VERSE

Because classic art places so much emphasis on polish and regularity of form, its favorite verse pattern became the precisely balanced *closed,* or *heroic, couplet.* The ten-syllable iambic line of the couplet falls easily into English speech; and when rhymed in pairs it clicks off with clocklike precision, especially if the pauses are arranged to fall at the ends of the lines. In the closed or heroic couplet, there is usually a minor pause at the end of the first line and a major pause at the end of the second line—

> "Honor and shame from no condition rise:
> Act well your part, there all the honor lies."

Such a couplet is well suited to expressing truths or witticisms, neatly, compactly. It lends itself well to satire and to moralizing. Eighteenth-century writers gave it almost a monopoly in their verse.

Not that they had discovered it! It was the form used by Chaucer in his *Canterbury Tales*—

> "Tending to moral virtue was his speech,
> And gladly would he learn, and gladly teach."

Shakespeare—although he wisely kept his dramas unrhymed—liked to round out a scene with one closed couplet—

> "Away, and mock the time with fairest show;
> False face must hide what the false heart doth know."

John Dryden found it just the form he wanted for his wit-spangled comedies. He also proved its stinging aptness for satire.

But it remained for Alexander Pope to demonstrate the full range of its possibilities. In most of his work, Pope is the typical classicist. The artificiality of the period in which he lived is reflected by the fact that whatever he wrote he put into verse—criticism, debate, rebuke; essay, or letter—everything went into rhymed couplets. And his couplets varied to suit his needs. In poems like the "Essay on Criticism" and "Essay on Man," the form proved itself a neat container for odd lots of wisdom or opinion. In "The Rape of the Lock" and the "Dunciad" ("Poem of the Dunces") it became a two-edged dagger, but delicate! There was not the hacking bluntness of Dryden's satire; Pope's was finely drawn and tipped with wit. In his translations of Homer, which were admired out of all proportion to their merit, Pope demonstrated how not to use the couplet. For a long serious poem, the rhymed lines are monotonous and undignified. The form that was brilliant in his mock epic was weak and inappropriate as a medium for the real thing.

Two of Pope's poems not in the heroic couplet have become famous— an "Ode on St. Cecilia's Day," similar to those by Dryden, composed when Pope was only twenty; and a splendid hymn, "The Universal Prayer." The prayer is Christian in its philosophy but so broad in its terms that it speaks for every one who worships a spiritual God. Many critics consider it the finest of all Pope's works.

In the first half of the eighteenth century there was no other poet to come anywhere near Pope in ability or reputation. Men who did write in verse, followed his patterns. There were philosophical discussions, classic translations, political and literary satires, all written in rhymed couplets, but lacking the touch that gave Pope's distinction. Had life been kinder and had he lived in a less artificial age, this man whose bitter satire won him a fearful respect might have become one of the truly great in literature. As it is he has given the world a store of apt quotations and a few fine lines.

QUESTIONS IN APPRECIATION:

1. Summarize the important characteristics of *classic literature* in (*a*) subject matter, (*b*) form, and (*c*) mood or feeling.

2. Show how "The Rape of the Lock" qualifies in all three respects as an example of classic literature.

3. Point out at least four respects in which "The Rape of the Lock" imitates the form or style of the *epic*.

4. Describe the form of the heroic couplet, giving its rhythm, meter, rhyme scheme, and any other distinguishing characteristic.

5. For what kind of verse is the heroic couplet especially suitable? For what kind of poetry is it not suitable? What are its disadvantages?

6. From "The Rape of the Lock" select lines or pairs of lines which illustrate the following devices:

    a. The use of *irony* for satire effect, as in the line,

> "In various talk th' *instructive* hours they pass."

    b. The pairing of important with trifling things for satiric or humorous effect, as in the lines,

> "Not louder shrieks to pitying Heaven are cast,
> When *husbands,* or when *lap-dogs* breathe their last."

c. The use of extravagantly exaggerated expressions for burlesque effect, as in the lines,

"Sudden these honors shall be snatched away,
And *cursed forever* this *victorious day.*"

d. The use of subtly disparaging remarks about either men or women, as in the lines,

"There heroes' wits are kept in ponderous vases,
And *Beaux'* in *snuff-boxes* and *tweezer cases.*"

e. The especially effective use of metaphor or simile.

f. The especially successful use of the heroic couplet for descriptive effect.

7. What would you select as the most clever, or the most significant lines in the whole poem? Why?

8. What did you learn about eighteenth-century life from reading "The Rape of the Lock"? What did you learn about the author himself—about his ability as a poet? about his attitude toward life?

9. Do you consider "The Rape of the Lock" a good poem? Why or why not?

CLASSIC PROSE

At its best classic prose is clear, forceful, and direct—lighted sometimes by wit but only occasionally mellow with humor. At its worst it is heavy, cumbersome, overloaded with long hard words and round-about expressions. It served as a vehicle for almost every possible kind of writing—satire, fantasy, argument, biography, letters, memoirs, essays, oratory, history, and fiction. Adequate mention cannot be made of all the kinds of writing turned out by the tireless scholars of the eighteenth century. And a disproportionately small number of works proved great enough to live. These we shall discuss briefly.

The Satires

Dryden and Pope had set a fashion for satire in verse which spilled over into prose. Individuals and institutions alike were victims. Education, history, government, religion—nothing was safe from the barbed words with double meaning.

Jonathan Swift was the most powerful of the prose satirists. In his hands satire became a political weapon. Pamphlets ridiculing leaders and policies were distributed like handbills about the streets of the city. Since Swift had a brilliant imagination and a kind of perverted genius, he was employed by the party in power, first by the Whigs and then by the Tories, to demolish their rivals. Two of his longer satires were allegories—*The Battle of the Books,* on the advantages of classic learning over "modern" learning; and *The Tale of a Tub,* intended to support the Church of England as opposed to the Dissenters and the Catholics.

Swift overshot his mark and succeeded only in antagonizing all three churches.

The most surprising of all Swift's works was *Gulliver's Travels,* written to vent his spite against all men everywhere. It tells of Gulliver's adventures in four imaginary countries: Lilliput, or the land of tiny folk; Brobdingnag, or the land of the giants; Laputa, or the floating island of the scientists; and the land of the Houyhnhnms, where degraded human beings called Yahoos were the servants of fine, intelligent horses. Swift's venom grows devastating as the book progresses, so that the last two voyages prove unpleasant reading. But the direct, realistic style in which the first two voyages have been related has made them popular with young readers, who care nothing at all about the ironic purpose underlying them. They have become Swift's most enduring work.

Two other prose writers, Joseph Addison and Sir Richard Steele, used satire skillfully. Such essays as "The Coquette's Heart," "Fan Drill," and the "Sir Roger de Coverley" papers show English classic prose at its best. They deal with polite society; they reflect the polish and sophistication of the age; they are lightly satiric and delicately impersonal; they are gracefully written and smooth. There is an important difference between their kind of satire and that of Swift or Pope. The essays are pleasant reading because their fun is never aimed at individuals. They ridicule types and fashions but not some certain man or woman. When Pope's "The Rape of the Lock" came out, everyone knew the name of the girl and the incident that inspired it. Society tittered at the real Sir Plume of the "round, unthinking face." There was spite behind the work. But the Beau and Coquette of whom Steele and Addison wrote are no more nor less real than Harold Teen and Lilloms. The mark of a gentleman is kindness; and being gentlemen, Steele and Addison never stepped beyond the bounds of courtesy. One other point should be made about their work. It was their admitted intention, through satire, to make vice unattractive and virtue popular. Thus it is only the silly, trashy weaknesses of men that are held up to ridicule. And even in such an eccentric character as Sir Roger, there are fundamental human virtues of kindness and honor that endear him to the reader.

The Light Essay and the Literary Magazine

Not all the essays of the classic period were satires. To appreciate the eighteenth-century development of the essay one must become acquainted with a newcomer in the field of English letters—the *literary magazine.*

Periodicals had increased enormously during the century. Back in 1622 the first weekly newspaper had appeared, but it was not until 1702 than there was a regular daily paper. Daniel Defoe was one of the earliest journalists, and one of the best. To him is given the credit for writing the first "interview" and of featuring the "leading editorial." Moreover, he contributed literally thousands of essays to his paper *The*

Review over a nine-year period. Here was the germ of an idea upon which Richard Steele capitalized. Borrowing Swift's pen-name of "Isaac Bickerstaff" and Defoe's idea of dressing up a paper with literary contributions, Steele issued his *Tatler*. It was a pleasantly gossipy little paper, coming out three times a week. Each issue featured a neatly turned-out essay. The paper was not a news-spreading agency; it was merely entertaining. A new type of periodical had been discovered. From it in direct descent has come the modern magazine. The *Tatler* ran for two years, Joseph Addison serving as co-author in the later issues. When it was discontinued the two friends introduced a similar publication called the *Spectator,* which proved even more popular. Thereafter the light periodical featuring an entertaining or uplifting essay became a fixture in English life. Nearly every author of the century tried his hand at editing one.

The essays featured in the periodicals were quite different from those which Bacon had introduced. Instead of being instructive they were amusing. They presented serio-comic character studies, or they told a little story. They commented on fashions—fans, snuff-boxes, hair-do's, wigs. Some were allegories, or semi-serious bits of philosophy or moralizing. Any diverting subject might furnish the editor with his essay for the day. But however light the subject, the authors kept the aloof, impersonal manner of classic prose. In the *Tatler* and *Spectator* essays, for instance, the person who does the talking is the imaginary Mr. Bickerstaff. It is ostensibly his opinions—not Addison's or Steele's that are being expressed.

The essays that proved most popular were collected and bound in book form. Those that have enjoyed the widest reading were the *Spectator* essays, and the *Sir Roger de Coverley Papers.*

QUESTIONS IN APPRECIATION:

1. In this selection from Gulliver's adventures in Brobdingnag, how does Swift manage to keep the interest of the reader? Does the selection make one curious to read more of *Gulliver's Travels?* Why or why not?

2. Compare this selection with the Addison-Steele essays and with other classic prose as to general *readability.* Is it easier to read or harder to read? Why?

3. Look up, if necessary, the definitions for *irony* and *satire.* What is the difference in meaning between the two terms?

4. What evidences do you find that the story of Gulliver's adventures was intended as a satire on English manners, customs, and institutions? Point out any passages that are ironic.

5. Which of the Addison-Steele essays is not a satire? Does it contain any ironic sentences? If so, point them out. How can you tell that the essay is not a satire?

6. Has virtue or kindliness been made attractive in either of these essays? Discuss.

7. Do you find these essays easy or hard reading? Why? Which did you find most entertaining?

8. In his *Autobiography*, Benjamin Franklin tells how he used essays from the *Spectator* papers as self-devised exercises to develop a good style of writing. Do you think that the essays could be used as models of style today? Why or why not?

Miscellaneous Prose Works

Most of the writers that have been discussed became well known because of one thing each could do exceptionally well. But they were versatile men, often producing works of various types. Addison, for example, won great acclaim in his day for a long poem written in heroic couplets to glorify the Duke of Marlborough and his victory at Blenheim. And Swift produced one work that was not ironic—his *Journal to Stella*, a collection of letters written to Esther Johnson during the period of his success in London. Defoe was a prolific writer, producing works of almost every type and winning real distinction for his fiction.

The second forty years of the eighteenth century is often called the "Age of Johnson," after Samuel Johnson, of whom Boswell has written. It seems strange today that books of English literature usually contain more literature about the big man than by him. But most of Johnson's works are too ponderous for profitable reading. A sentence of 180 words is not unusual. Some run even longer. He loved hard words. In his dictionary, he actually did define *network* as "anything reticulated or decussated at equal distances with interstices between the intersections." It was jokingly said that he made the words and sentences of his essays hard so that readers would have to buy his dictionary. As Johnson grew older, he spent more time in conversation than in writing. It is his personality as revealed through these conversations that Boswell has preserved for us in his biography. Hence Boswell's work has become more important than anything written by the master that he worshipped.

The *Life of Samuel Johnson* is a tremendous work. Its fame is not dependent upon any excellence of style on the part of the author, but upon the minute and lifelike portraits it presents. Boswell was a good reporter. The *Life* is an almost literal transcription from his notebooks. Between the eccentricity of his subject and his own curious industry, the little lawyer managed to produce a unique work.

Another writer of the Johnsonian school was Edmund Burke. Though Americans know Burke chiefly through his speech *On Conciliation with the American Colonies,* his collected works fill fourteen volumes. He is typical of the scholarly bent of the age. He was well trained in the classics and filled his speeches with references to the ancients. His style is "rhetorical"—filled with adjectives and dressed-up, round-about expressions. Yet he used words precisely. His organization was always excellent. He had an orderly mind and an enthusiasm for justice. He was a distinguished member of the House of Commons.

In the hands of Johnson and his contemporaries, English prose grew more and more heavy. Mention should be made, however, of one other writer, Edward Gibbon, who wrote a history combining careful fact with conscious literary style. His subject was *The Decline and Fall of the Roman Empire*. In six volumes, it covers the fortunes of Rome from the reign of Trajan in 98 A.D. to the fall of the Byzantine Empire in 1453. It is a masterly piece of work—though heavy—and its almost flawless expression makes it a fitting finale to the list of classic prose of the eighteenth century.

QUESTIONS IN APPRECIATION:

1. Review briefly the method used by Boswell in writing his *Life of Johnson*. In the present selection, point out some peculiarities of form which are a result of Boswell's method.

2. Do you think that Boswell's method would be good for biographers in general to use? Why or why not?

3. If a writer expresses his own opinions about the persons or subjects in his writings, he is said to be using a *subjective* treatment. If he merely presents his characters as any onlooker might see them, leaving the reader to form his own opinions, he is using an *objective* treatment. Is Boswell's method, on the whole, subjective or objective? What are the advantages of that sort of treatment? Are there any disadvantages?

THE DRAMA FROM SHAKESPEARE TO GOLDSMITH AND SHERIDAN

As we have already noted, there was a sharp decline in English drama after the death of Shakespeare. The reason lay partly in the inferiority of the later plays and partly in the active opposition of the Puritans. Except for Ben Jonson, there were no strong dramatists in the early seventeenth century. Plays often made sport of immorality and vice, and thus gave the rising Puritans cause for objections. Sentiment became so strong that in 1642, all theaters were closed. There was rigid enforcement of the edict, the penalties for violation including public whippings and confiscation of property.

With the accession of Charles II in 1660, the theaters were reopened, but again—as we have seen—the plays were bad. Even Dryden in his twenty years of playwriting did nothing to elevate the character of the stage. However, two significant changes in theatrical techniques did develop: women were allowed upon the stage so that feminine roles need no longer be acted by boys, and movable scenery came into general use. Quite elaborate stage effects were used in presenting some of Dryden's plays. But the moral tone of the theater was low. After 1688, plays were frequently suppressed and playhouses closed.

Gradually a reaction set in. Fearing that all plays might again be banned, a group of dramatists appeared who were determined to "purify" the stage. They began to produce plays overloaded with sentiment and given to moralizing. The "sentimental" comedy became especially popular. Tragedy and comedy alike were devoted to presenting codes of conduct and to proving that virtue is always rewarded and evil is punished. The result was a highly artificial type of play. There was a tendency to follow the classic models of Greek and Roman drama. Tragedies were often written in rhymed couplets, and the dialogue sounded stilted. Farces were presented, depending for their humor on puns, mechanical devices, and mimicry.

Samuel Johnson, the literary leader of the later eighteenth century wrote a tragedy *Irene* which was not successful on the stage. His more important contribution to English drama was indirect—his influence on the group of writers surrounding him and his encouragement of actors and playwrights of ability. The best known of his protégés were David Garrick, the actor; Richard Brinsley Sheridan, author of *The Rivals* and *The School for Scandal;* and Oliver Goldsmith. Already successful as a poet and novelist, Goldsmith's great contribution to the drama was his comedy of manners, *She Stoops to Conquer.* In the words of Dr. Johnson, it attained "the great end of comedy, making an audience merry." It and Sheridan's two plays have been making audiences merry ever since. Both *The Rivals* and *She Stoops to Conquer* have been popular in amateur theatricals, and are often used by high schools and colleges for class plays.

She Stoops to Conquer deserves its popularity. It has a clever, well-constructed plot; for besides the main interest in Kate and Marlow, there are complications in the side issue of Connie's and Hastings' love affair. Mrs. Hardcastle is set on having Connie marry her son Tony; but Tony having no liking for the match, is glad to help Connie and Hastings upset his mother's schemes. There is the matter of Connie's jewels, which also gives rise to some suspense and some hilarity. Tony Lumpkin is the high-comedy character of the play. Besides the trick he plays on the heroes, his loutish behavior is good for a laugh whenever he treads upon the boards.

Historically speaking, the importance of Goldsmith's and Sheridan's comedies lies in the fact that they marked a return to a natural, realistic type of play—a play that drew its situations and characters from life and that was wholesome and entertaining. Goldsmith had his characters talk like the people of his day. He discarded artificial verse and high-flown speeches. And from his time, English drama took a turn for the better. The theater once more became respectable, with no sacrifice of its entertaining values.

QUESTIONS IN APPRECIATION:

1. Where did Goldsmith get the idea for the plot of *She Stoops to Conquer?* Explain.

2. Do the scenes which you have read sound *plausible?* Are the mistakes and misunderstandings such as could actually happen? Discuss.

3. What evidence do you find that Goldsmith was using natural, everyday language in his dialogue? Remember that allowances must be made for the greater formality in eighteenth century family life. Husband and wife, for instance, usually addressed each other as "Mrs. Hardcastle" or "Mr. Hardcastle," and so on.

4. What is there about the play that would make it *act well?* Why do you think it remains popular? Discuss.

THE ENGLISH NOVEL TAKES FORM

It is readily agreed that the first long stories which may be called *novels* appeared in England in the eighteenth century. It is not so easy to say just which book was the *first* English novel. In the new literary form, which presented a study of life in the guise of a story, two elements combine—the *romantic,* or imaginative, and the *realistic.* Those novels in which the romantic element prevails are sometimes called "romances" to distinguish them from the realistic representations of life and its problems.

In the year 1719 there appeared in England an unusual book. It told the story of a shipwrecked sailor who had spent nearly thirty years on a small tropic island, alone except for an escaped cannibal slave who became his servant. It was an imaginary story, although probably suggested by the experience of a real sailor, Alexander Selkirk, who had lived on a deserted island for three years before being picked up by a passing ship. The thing that commended the story to readers then and which still keeps it in active circulation is its convincingly vivid detail. The reader is easily fooled into believing that here is an account of actual shipwreck and escape. The subject is romantic, but the treatment is realistic. In other words, *Robinson Crusoe* by Daniel Defoe is a long prose story combining both the romantic and realistic elements of the novel. Yet for some strange reason most literary critics dismiss it as a romantic adventure tale, and award the title of "the first English novel" to Samuel Richardson's *Pamela,* which appeared some twenty years later. The decision is not a vital one, to be sure; but it is significant to note that *Robinson Crusoe* is one of the two pieces of eighteenth-century fiction still enjoyed by a wide circle of readers, whereas *Pamela* goes unread, except by the curious scholar.

Richardson's book was a literary accident. The author was a printer who decided to publish a model letter-writer for the use of trades-people of little learning. He hit upon the idea of having the letters tell a story, and then became so much interested in his heroine—a poor but virtuous serving girl—that he continued the project into several volumes. Unconcerned about the letter-forms, the reading public gobbled up the sentimental story. Richardson followed his success with two more long stories told by letters—*Clarissa Harlowe* and the *History of Sir Charles Grandison.* Because these books are concerned with human emotions growing out of real life situations, they are certainly novels; and their author, Samuel Richardson, is usually called the first English novelist.

Other writers were quick to adopt the new form. Henry Fielding set out to ridicule the sentimentality of *Pamela* by doing a parody of it in *Joseph Andrews*. But Fielding, too, became interested in his character and turned out a vigorous, humorous, realistic story. He wrote three other novels, *Tom Jones* proving to be the best of them and the only one still read—and even it, not widely. Tobias Smollett and Laurence Sterne wrote long novels, once gladly read; and Horace Walpole, the statesman, produced a romantic medieval tale, *The Castle of Otranto*. With the exception of the Walpole romance, the novels were long, running into several volumes and marred by the coarseness of their realism.

The one book to keep *Robinson Crusoe* company on the shelves known to the general reader is Oliver Goldsmith's slim little volume, *The Vicar of Wakefield*. Drawing heavily upon scenes from his own household and modeling his vicar after preachers in his family, Goldsmith has told a lifelike story of eighteenth century home life. True, the trials of the vicar are almost melodramatic in their rapid succession; true, too, all misfortunes are overcome in an almost fairy-tale conclusion; yet the book is good reading and smacks of reality. It was a favorite with our grandparents and still proves a pleasant friend to those who like to make acquaintances among the folks of other centuries.

FOR FURTHER READING

BANGS, JOHN KENDRICK, *A Houseboat on the Styx*
BUCHAN, JOHN, *Midwinter* (Dr. Samuel Johnson)
DEEPING, WARWICK, *Apples of Gold*
DEFOE, DANIEL, *Robinson Crusoe*
DICKENS, CHARLES, *A Tale of Two Cities*
ELIOT, GEORGE, *Adam Bede*
GOLDSMITH, OLIVER, *The Vicar of Wakefield*
MORLEY, FRANK V. (ed.), *Everybody's Boswell*
MORROW, HONORE WILLSIE, *Let the King Beware!*
NEWTON, A. EDWARD, *Doctor Johnson* (Drama)
ORCZY, BARONESS, *The Scarlet Pimpernel*
SABATINI, RAPHAEL, *Captain Blood*
THACKERAY, WILLIAM MAKEPEACE, *Henry Esmond, Esq.; The Virginians*
TINKER, CHAUNCEY BREWSTER, *Young Boswell*

THE AGE OF ROMANTICISM
1780-1840

"SWEET IS THE LORE THAT NATURE BRINGS"

Transition poets broke away from classicism.

ENGLAND IN A CHANGING WORLD

(1780-1840)

The overlapping of period into period is especially marked at the opening of the nineteenth century. The thoughts that shaped most events from 1800 to 1850 had their roots in the last thirty years of the period just past. England had learned something from the American Revolution. In 1783, Sir William Pitt, a liberal, had become Prime Minister. Wisely he adopted a generous policy toward the remaining colonies of the Crown. And as English trade expanded wealth increased and the country prospered.

But across the channel there was trouble. When the French Revolution broke open, Englishmen in general were in sympathy with the desperate peasant classes. Young idealists hurried abroad to do what they could to help. But as the Revolution became more and more violent and the guillotine became the instrument of the Reign of Terror, English sympathy cooled. The extreme measures of inexperienced republican leaders alarmed the rest of Europe; and by 1793 all but the most radical youngsters were opposed to the new Republic. Every one watched with concern the rise of young Bonaparte. And suddenly England found herself again at war. There was no peace in Europe until the Battle of Waterloo, fought in 1815 upon the fields of Belgium, disposed of Napoleon and his dreams of world conquest. Then the great powers met in Vienna to settle the peace of Europe. England came out of the wars more powerful than before. She had gained new territory and new respect. The victory of Lord Nelson at Trafalgar in 1805 had reaffirmed her supremacy on the sea; and she was generally conceded the most powerful of the existing empires.

In the meantime, she had been going through a revolution of her own—though of an entirely different sort. Nations, like people, change gradually yet show the effects suddenly. Only with nations, the times of change are marked in centuries, not years. After the breakdown of feudalism, English life had settled into a quiet pattern. The cities, except London, were not large. Most of the population was rural and agricultural. Industry had been carried on within the home. In the cloth-making centers, for example, the looms were in the homes; and the life of the whole fam-

595

ily revolved about the weaving. In the pottery districts each family had its potter's wheel, and the whole household worked at the trade. Families had been grouped together in hamlets, each house having a small vegetable garden. Perhaps there would be a cow, a pig or two, and some geese. Wares were sold from the homes or bartered at market. Through the fifteenth, sixteenth, seventeenth, and early eighteenth centuries, life in rural Britain presented much the same sort of picture.

And then suddenly within a period of about sixty years everything was changed. Industry moved from the home to the factory; and hamlets, sometimes in the space of a single generation, grew into cities. The immediate causes for the change were a series of inventions which made possible and profitable large scale production. The most important single factor was the development of the steam engine; but there were many revolutionizing devices—among them the fly shuttle, the spinning jenny, the spinning mule, and the power loom. At the same time, new methods in smelting accelerated the output of iron and steel.

A change-over from a system of handwork in the home to a system of factory production could not take place without much individual hardship and opposition. Here was worked out an early chapter in the now too-familiar story of the struggle between man and machines. England was suffering its Industrial Revolution. For two or more generations there was fretted out a period of turmoil and tragedy for Britain's laboring millions. It had been natural at first that children should go into the mills. At home they had helped with the weaving. But the conditions of factory work were utterly different, and no account seems to have been taken of a child's slender strength and endurance. The unhappiness that followed the change from a semi-rural life to existence in tenement rooms in a smoky city; the employment of women at heavy tasks for fourteen and sixteen hour stretches; the poorly paid hazardous work in mines—all these elements were at first considered the necessary accompaniments of a machine age.

Then a few souls began to ask questions and to remonstrate. Even before the death of Dr. Johnson, there developed a tendency to protest existing conditions. Poets in a reactionary mood, described the simple joys that had been a part of country living even when farms were poor and the tenants humble. Gray's "Elegy Written in a Country Churchyard," Goldsmith's "The Deserted Village," Burns's "The Cotter's Saturday Night" are nostalgic pictures of a disappearing way of living.

As the nineteenth century opened, men adopted a more realistic attitude. The changes had come to stay. The time when "every rood of ground maintained its man" would never return. It couldn't return; there was no longer land enough to go around. But the fact that men had moved into cities did not need to mean that they must live in filthy tenements. The fact that mills were given over to huge production programs did not have to mean that children should become their slaves, or that limits could not be set to working hours. Standards to govern working conditions could be adopted. They must be. And so the sentimentality of the late eighteenth century gave way to practical efforts for reform in the nineteenth. Finally in 1832 the great Reform Bill was passed. From that time to the present, England has pushed ahead slowly in the task of safeguarding the welfare of her industrial workers. Most of her prime ministers in the intervening years were liberal minded. William IV, who came to the throne in 1830, was in sympathy with the people; and he was succeeded seven years later by the humanitarian Victoria. At her accession the ground work in adjusting to an industrialized empire had been accomplished. She guaranteed the right sort of building up.

History records changes. Literature makes them real to us. Books like *Silas Marner* and *The Little Minister,* though written in a later day, bring us into the homes of weaving communities in the days of hand looms. The reader shares the poverty and toil of the workers,—sometimes their terror and rebellion at the threat of change. Scores of excellent British novels have had their settings in the period of this industrial upheaval.

At the time that the changes were in progress, the most apparent reaction in literature was a movement toward liberalism of spirit and toward a sympathetic interpretation of men. *Romanticism*—which represents the opposite swing of the pendulum from *classicism*—became the literary mode. The great romanticists in English poetry were contemporaneous with the years of the Industrial Revolution—from 1770 to 1835, approximately. Those were the years that brought forth the poems of Burns and Blake, of Wordsworth, Coleridge, Byron, Shelley, Keats—great liberalists, all of them, and concerned with fundamental human experiences as the subject for literature. Some of the writers took part in activities that helped hasten measures of reform. But all encouraged the movement, because all believed in the significance of individual human beings. Their enthusiasm and freshness of spirit was an inspiration to the age. Even the prose of the period was freed from the formality of classic tradition. It had become warm and lively. As the century approached its middle years, it was apparent that mentally and spiritually, England was keeping pace with a changing world.

ELEGY WRITTEN IN A COUNTRY CHURCHYARD

THOMAS GRAY

A country burying-ground—especially an old one—has a curious fascination for anyone of imaginative mind. In England the churchyard cemeteries are very old. One knows that the people buried in them were humble; for according to European custom, persons of rank were buried within the churches, in vaults or crypts beneath the floors.

At Stoke Poges in Buckinghamshire lies an old churchyard, once the haunt of a dreamy poet, Thomas Gray. Gray liked to wander among the graves, looking at the simple monuments and deciphering the inscriptions. Poorly worded, almost ludicrous in their awkwardness, the epitaphs told of the poverty of the neighborhood. As Gray tried to repicture the simple lives remembered there, he wondered what difference it might have made had these folks had the privileges of education and contact with public affairs. Did this spot hold the remains of some possible genius, forever hidden from the world? Fired by such fancies, Gray wrote an elegy to celebrate the "unhonored dead." His tribute has become one of the best known poems in the English language. To it, in conclusion, he added the lines that he chose for his own epitaph when he should be laid to rest in some such quiet spot.

THE curfew tolls the knell of parting day;
The lowing herd winds slowly o'er the lea;
The plowman homeward plods his weary way,
And leaves the world to darkness and to me.

5 Now fades the glimmering landscape on the sight,
And all the air a solemn stillness holds,
Save where the beetle wheels his droning flight,
And drowsy tinklings lull the distant folds;

Save that from yonder ivy-mantled tow'r
10 The moping owl does to the moon complain
Of such as, wandering near her secret bow'r,
Molest her ancient solitary reign.

Beneath those rugged elms, that yew-tree's shade,
Where heaves the turf in many a mold'ring heap,
15 Each in his narrow cell forever laid,
The rude forefathers of the hamlet sleep.

The breezy call of incense-breathing Morn,
The swallow twitt'ring from the straw-built shed,
The cock's shrill clarion, or the echoing horn,
20 No more shall rouse them from their lowly bed.

For them no more the blazing hearth shall burn,
Or busy housewife ply her evening care;
No children run to lisp their sire's return,
Or climb his knees the envied kiss to share.

25 Oft did the harvest to their sickle yield,
Their furrow oft the stubborn glebe has broke;
How jocund did they drive their team a-field!
How bowed the woods beneath their sturdy stroke!

Let not Ambition mock their useful toil,
30 Their homely joys and destiny obscure;

26. GLEBE—Turf, sward.
29. AMBITION—Those who have made it their purpose to achieve power,
fame, wealth, and the like. Similarly, *Grandeur*, in line 31, refers to those who
have such wealth and power.

Nor Grandeur hear with a disdainful smile
The short and simple annals of the poor.

The boast of heraldry, the pomp of pow'r,
And all that beauty, all that wealth e'er gave,
35 Awaits alike the inevitable hour:
The paths of glory lead but to the grave.

Nor you, ye proud, impute to these the fault,
If Memory o'er their tomb no trophies raise,
Where, through the long-drawn aisle and fretted vault,
40 The pealing anthem swells the note of praise.

Can storied urn or animated bust
Back to its mansion call the fleeting breath?
Can Honor's voice provoke the silent dust,
Or Flatt'ry soothe the dull, cold ear of Death?

45 Perhaps in this neglected spot is laid
Some heart once pregnant with celestial fire;
Hands that the rod of empire might have swayed,
Or waked to ecstasy the living lyre.

But Knowledge to their eyes her ample page,
50 Rich with the spoils of time, did ne'er unroll;
Chill Penury repressed their noble rage,
And froze the genial current of their soul.

Full many a gem of purest ray serene
The dark unfathomed caves of ocean bear;
55 Full many a flower is born to blush unseen,
And waste its sweetness on the desert air.

33. BOAST OF HERALDRY—Family pride; *inherited rank,* indicated by family coats-of-arms.
41. STORIED URN—Burial urns inscribed with records of achievements and honors.
41. ANIMATED—Lifelike.
43. PROVOKE—Arouse, awaken.
46. PREGNANT WITH CELESTIAL FIRE—Filled with heaven-sent genius.
51. PENURY REPRESSED THEIR NOBLE RAGE—Poverty stifled or smothered their talents.
52. FROZE THE GENIAL CURRENT OF THEIR SOUL—Prevented them from following their natural bents.

600

Some village-Hampden that with dauntless breast
The little tyrant of his fields withstood,
Some mute inglorious Milton, here may rest,
60   Some Cromwell guiltless of his country's blood.

Th' applause of list'ning senates to command,
The threats of pain and ruin to despise,
To scatter plenty o'er a smiling land,
And read their hist'ry in a nation's eyes,

65   Their lot forbade: nor circumscribed alone,
Their growing virtues, but their crimes confined;
Forbade to wade through slaughter to a throne,
And shut the gates of mercy on mankind;

The struggling pangs of conscious truth to hide,
70   To quench the blushes of ingenuous shame,
Or heap the shrine of Luxury and Pride
With incense kindled at the Muse's flame.

Far from the madding crowd's ignoble strife,
Their sober wishes never learned to stray;
75   Along the cool sequestered vale of life
They kept the noiseless tenor of their way.

Yet e'en these bones from insult to protect,
Some frail memorial still erected nigh,
With uncouth rhymes and shapeless sculpture decked,
80   Implores the passing tribute of a sigh.

57. HAMPDEN—An English squire who refused to pay the "tax of ship money," thus starting the argument which led to the Puritan Revolution.
58. LITTLE TYRANT OF HIS FIELDS—His landlord.
61–64. Notice the punctuation in this stanza, which must be read together with the following stanza. *Lot* (l. 65) is the subject of the main clause; *forbade* is the verb; and the infinitives *to command, to despise, to scatter* and *read* are the objects.
65. CIRCUMSCRIBED—Set limits to. The thought is that if their lot prevented them from being benefactors of mankind, it may also have prevented them from causing widespread pain and suffering. It thus "confined their crimes."
69–72. This stanza must be read in connection with the preceding one. The infinitives *to hide, to quench,* and *heap* are the objects of *forbade* in line 67. Gray is here referring to the practice of patronage under which an author would dedicate his work to a wealthy or influential person expecting to receive money or favors in return.

601

Their name, their years, spelt by th' unlettered Muse,
The place of fame and elegy supply;
And many a holy text around she strews,
That teach the rustic moralist to die:

85   For who, to dumb Forgetfulness a prey,
This pleasing, anxious being e'er resigned,
Left the warm precincts of the cheerful day,
Nor cast one longing, ling'ring look behind?

On some fond breast the parting soul relies,
90   Some pious drops the closing eye requires;
E'en from the tomb the voice of nature cries,
E'en in our ashes live their wonted fires.

For thee who, mindful of th' unhonored dead,
Dost in these lines their artless tale relate,
95   If chance, by lonely Contemplation led,
Some kindred spirit shall inquire thy fate,

Haply some hoary-headed swain may say,
"Oft have we seen him at the peep of dawn,
Brushing with hasty steps the dews away,
100   To meet the sun upon the upland lawn.

"There, at the foot of yonder nodding beech
That wreathes its old fantastic roots so high,
His listless length at noontide would he stretch,
And pore upon the brook that babbles by.

105   "Hard by yon wood, now smiling as in scorn,
Mutt'ring his wayward fancies, he would rove;

81. UNLETTERED MUSE—Uneducated poet or rhymster.
84. TEACH THE RUSTIC MORALIST TO DIE—Texts intended to give comfort in the face of death.
93. THEE—Gray himself. In this and the six following stanzas, Gray does what probably every human being does at one time or another—he pictures his own death and funeral. He imagines some stranger noticing the inscription on his tombstone and inquiring about him from some old farmer ("hoary-headed swain"). Lines 98–120 describe Gray as the peasants might have understood him, and then go on to tell of his death and burial. The last three stanzas form the modest epitaph which Gray wrote for himself.

Now drooping, woeful—wan, like one forlorn
Or crazed with care or crossed in hopeless love.

"One morn I missed him from the customed hill,
110   Along the heath, and near his fav'rite tree.
Another came, nor yet beside the rill,
  Nor up the lawn, nor at the wood was he;

"The next, with dirges due, in sad array,
  Slow through the churchway path we saw him borne:
115 Approach and read (for thou canst read) the lay
  Graved on the stone beneath yon aged thorn."

THE EPITAPH

Here rests his head upon the lap of Earth,
  A youth to Fortune and to Fame unknown:
Fair Science frowned not on his humble birth,
120   *And Melancholy marked him for her own.*

Large was his bounty, and his soul sincere;
  Heaven did a recompense as largely send:
He gave to Mis'ry (all he had) a tear,
  He gained from Heav'n ('twas all he wished) a friend.

125 *No farther seek his merits to disclose,*
  Or draw his frailties from their dread abode,
(There they alike in trembling hope repose),
  The bosom of his Father and his God.

FOR INTERPRETATION

Although Gray has chosen a simple subject for his "Elegy," he has kept the long words of classic poetry. Yet so popular was the poem with our parents and grandparents that many of its lines have passed into common speech *in quotation.*

1. The first three stanzas are introductory, planned to set the mood for the poem. What things does the reader see? What does he hear? What does he feel? Choose three adjectives of your own to describe the kind of mood or feeling set by the first twelve lines.

2. Which stanza describes the cemetery? What kinds of trees grew there? What was the "narrow cell"?

3. Which three stanzas present imaginary scenes from the daily lives of those now lying in the churchyard? Are the pictures happy or sad?

4. What is the general thought of lines 29–36? What is the connection —expressed or implied—between the humble villagers of the churchyard and the "paths of glory"?

5. Quote the lines in the succeeding stanzas which express the following thoughts:

   a. The absence of suitable markers or memorials does not mean necessarily that the men were unworthy.

   b. Splendid monuments cannot alter the fact of death.

Quote the lines which indicate that England's "honored dead" are buried within the churches. Which English church holds the tombs of her greatest men?

6. Restate in simple prose the meaning of lines 45 and 46. Quote a later stanza which says that the same sort of thing happens often in the realm of nature.

7. In lines 45–60 what undeveloped talents does Gray suggest may have been buried in that "neglected spot"? Do you think that Gray approved or disapproved of the Puritan Revolution of the seventeenth century? How can you tell?

8. In which stanzas does Gray say that lack of opportunity may have prevented great misfortunes or unhappiness at the same time that it robbed men of fame and success? Do you think that Gray is right? In your discussion follow some of these thoughts to a conclusion:

   a. Name some men in history who "waded through a slaughter to a throne." Were they all men from privileged circumstances? Do you think they would have become famous no matter what their original circumstances were?

   b. Can you name some men or women of humble origin who have been the cause of great human suffering? How were they able to win or wield power?

9. Do you think Gray's ideas as presented in the first 72 lines are an argument for or against the principle that there should be equal opportunities for all persons? Discuss.

10. Which lines say that even these simple graves bear markers of some sort? Which lines say that it is a common trait of human nature to want to be missed and mourned?

11. How can the reader tell that Gray is writing of himself in lines 93–96? What do we learn about Gray's habits, in the stanzas that follow? What was he doing when he acted like one "crazed with care or crossed in hopeless love"?

12. What does the parenthetical expression, "for thou canst read" imply about the educational status of the community?

13. It is customary in an epitaph to mention the virtues of the one remembered. What virtues does Gray claim in his epitaph?

14. How does the "Elegy" prove that Gray was interested in ordinary

men and women? Which passages in it show the most effective use of poetic imagination?

15. Why do you think this poem became a favorite in Gray's time and for many succeeding generations? Make a list of lines or expressions from it which you have heard quoted. Which passages from it do you consider most worthy of memorization? Why?

THE CLOD AND THE PEBBLE

WILLIAM BLAKE

In every generation men and women have asked, "What is love?" William Blake seems to think that the answer will vary according to the one who gives it. The clod of clay, yielding and gentle, emblem of self-giving, makes one reply. The pebble, hard and self-protective, finds an exactly opposite answer.

L   "Love seeketh not itself to please,
                 Nor for itself hath any care,
             But for another gives its ease,
                 And builds a Heaven in Hell's despair."

M   5   So sung a little Clod of Clay,
                 Trodden with the cattle's feet,
             But a Pebble of the brook
                 Warbled out these meters meet:

D   "Love seeketh only Self to please,
         10   To bind another to Its delight,
             Joys in another's loss of ease,
                 And builds a Hell in Heaven's despite."

FOR INTERPRETATION

1. Think of some characters from life or from books who would say with the clay, "Love seeketh not itself to please . . . but for another gives its ease." List the names of at least five persons who have shown this kind of love in their lives; and indicate what sacrifice each made for love. Did any of them find a *heaven* in their despair?

2. Would you say that this first kind of love is found only in certain

relationships; such as in the love of parents for their children, or may it be found in any kind of human relationships? Discuss.

3. Robert Browning wrote a poem called "My Last Duchess" which illustrates perfectly the pebble's kind of "love." You will find the poem in a later section of the book. An old Italian duke is supposed to be talking. You will find him a hard, stony little soul. List two or three other characters from history or literature—people who have thought of love merely as something to please themselves, who have tried to "bind others to their delight." Have these persons found happiness? Or have they turned possible happiness into misery? for others? for themselves also?

4. Would you say that the pebble's kind of love is found only in certain kinds of human relationships (in the case of the duchess, it was between husband and wife), or may it be found in any relationship?

5. Which kind of emotion do you think most people have in mind when they speak of *love*—the clod's or the pebble's? Discuss.

THE TIGER

WILLIAM BLAKE

Man stands in bewilderment before the contrasts of nature. On the one hand we see the uplifting freshness of trees and flowers; on the other hand the destructive fury of the hurricane. There are volcanos; and there are snowflakes. And behind these paradoxes—what? What creative mind and force? "The Tiger" expresses man's bafflement, in simple but compelling imagery.

TIGER, Tiger, burning bright
In the forests of the night,

606

What immortal hand or eye
Could frame thy fearful symmetry?

5   In what distant deeps or skies
Burnt the fire of thine eyes?
On what wings dare he aspire?
What the hand dare seize the fire?

And what shoulder, and what art,
10   Could twist the sinews of thy heart?
When thy heart began to beat,
What dread hand forged thy dread feet?

What the hammer? What the chain?
In what furnace was thy brain?
15   What the anvil? What dread grasp
Dared its deadly terrors clasp?

When the stars threw down their spears,
And watered heaven with their tears,
Did He smile His work to see?
20   Did He who made the Lamb make thee?

Tiger, Tiger, burning bright
In the forests of the night,
What immortal hand or eye
Dare frame thy fearful symmetry?

FOR INTERPRETATION

1. Why do you think Blake chose the Tiger as especially symbolic of the mysteries of creation? Discuss. If you are not sure of the answer now, come back to it after you have considered the following questions.

2. Is there foundation in fact for Blake's poetic fancy which sees the tiger *"burning bright* in the forests of the *night"*? Explain.

3. What does *symmetry* mean? Is there symmetry in all living creatures? Why is the tiger's well described as a "fearful symmetry"?

4. What characteristics peculiar to the tiger are implied in the following expressions: (*a*) the fire of thine eyes? (*b*) the sinews of thy heart? (*c*) thy dread feet? (*d*) the deadly terrors of thy brain?

5. With what matching expressions does Blake suggest the Power that could create a tiger? List at least four.

6. What do you think was Blake's intention in writing the first two lines of the fifth stanza? What deeper question lies behind line 19? What deeper question lies behind line 20?

7. Does Blake answer his questions in the last stanza?

8. What kind of thoughts or feelings does this poem excite in the reader? Can you see any reasons why some critics have considered this short lyric to be the most truly poetic verse written in the eighteenth century? Would you agree? Why or why not?

From AUGURIES OF INNOCENCE

WILLIAM BLAKE

Can you do the things suggested in the four lines below? If so, you may count yourself wise. But Blake says that they are "signs of innocence." Of course philosophers and poets have long said that the innocent are the truly wise, and that if we would understand the Kingdom of Heaven we must become as little children. Perhaps Blake had some such thought in mind when he said that these are the "Auguries of Innocence."

> To SEE a world in a grain of sand,
> And a heaven in a wild flower;
> Hold infinity in the palm of your hand,
> And eternity in an hour.

FOR INTERPRETATION

1. Is there the same mystery involved in accounting for the existence of a single grain of sand that there is in accounting for the existence of a world? Discuss.

2. What element not present in sand or earth characterizes a *plant* or *flower?* What does a flower bear or produce? Why have flowers been used so often as the symbol of immortality? How can one "see a heaven in a wild flower"? Explain.

3. Is the bit of space that may be measured by the palm of one's hand *really* separated from the infinity of space that surrounds us? Discuss.

4. Are the limits that men set upon time *real?* Does time actually have a beginning and ending? In what respect is an "hour" a part of the eternity of time?

5. For the poet (a) a grain of sand is a symbol of what? (b) a flower is a symbol of what? (c) a bit of space is a symbol of what? (d) an hour is a symbol of what?

6. What are *auguries*? Why do you think the poet called these four things auguries of *innocence*? Explain.

JOHN ANDERSON, MY JO

ROBERT BURNS

Most of Robert Burns's poetry is written in Scotch brogue. The poet used dialect deliberately. It was not that he knew no better. You will notice that when it pleased him, he could turn out stanzas in pure English, polished and smooth as those of any classic poet. You will note, too, that his verses are marked with quotations from other writers—from his contemporaries, Gray and Goldsmith, and from the earlier poets—Pope and Dryden and Milton. No, his use of dialect was not due to ignorance.

Burns used dialect because—however well educated a Scotchman may be—when he is with those he loves and trusts, he drops naturally into brogue. It is the cozy, familiar speech of the home. John Muir, the Scotch-born American naturalist, has said that no matter how hot a Scotch argument waxed, so long as the men used dialect, you could know that all was friendly beneath; but if one man "put his English on"—then look out! Burns, writing for his neighbors and cronies, uses the daily speech, homelike and comfortable as their old clothes. He "puts his English on" only when he wants dignity for a dedication, as in the first stanza of "The Cotter's Saturday Night," or when he turns aside to moralize a bit.

Familiar songs like "Auld Lang Syne" and "Comin' Through the Rye" have given us some practice with Burns's speech. Try reading some of the following newer lines aloud until you can get them smoothly.

> JOHN ANDERSON, my jo, John,
> When we were first acquent,
> Your locks were like the raven,
> Your bonie brow was brent;
> 5 But now your brow is beld, John,
> Your locks are like the snaw;

1. JO—Sweetheart.
4. BRENT—Smooth, unwrinkled.
5. BELD—Bald.

> But blessings on your frosty pow,
> John Anderson, my jo.

> John Anderson, my jo, John,
> 10   We clamb the hill thegither;
> And mony a canty day, John
> We've had wi' ane anither;
> Now we maun totter down, John,
> And hand in hand we'll go,
> 15   And sleep thegither at the foot,
> John Anderson, my jo.

11. CANTY—Happy.
13. MAUN—Must.

FOR INTERPRETATION

1. Who is speaking in "John Anderson, My Jo"? How old would you guess John Anderson to be? What kind of wife do you think he had? How can you tell?

2. Name at least two familiar English or American songs which express the same sentiment that is expressed in "John Anderson, My Jo." Do you think that some long-married couples really experience this sort of companionship?

WHISTLE O'ER THE LAVE O'T

ROBERT BURNS

One of the important ends served by imagination is that it gives one insight into how other people live. Poets make frequent use of this sort of imagination. Burns did not live long enough for an experience like that of John Anderson; and certainly his Jean was not like Maggie in the following poem, "Whistle O'er the Lave O't." But it is more than likely that the poet knew families of both sorts. Most of us do.

> FIRST when Maggie was my care,
> Heav'n, I thought, was in her air,
> Now we're married—speir nae mair,
> But whistle o'er the lave o't!

3. SPEIR NAE MAIR—Ask no more.
4. THE LAVE O'T—The rest of it.

5 Meg was meek, and Meg was mild,
Sweet and harmless as a child—
Wiser men than me's beguil'd;
Whistle o'er the lave o't!

How we live, my Meg and me,
10 How we love, and how we gree,
I care na by how few may see—
Whistle o'er the lave o't!
Wha I wish were maggot's meat,
Dish'd up in her winding-sheet,
15 I could write—but Meg maun see 't
Whistle o'er the lave o't!

15. MAUN—Might.

FOR INTERPRETATION

1. Who is speaking in "Whistle O'er the Lave O't"? How did Maggie and her husband get along together?

2. What American slang expression might be substituted for "Whistle o'er the lave o't"?

3. What is the poetic effect of "John Anderson, My Jo"? Of "Whistle O'er the Lave O't"? Does either poem tell us anything about Burns's life? about Burns's personality? Discuss.

AFTON WATER

ROBERT BURNS

As a young man Burns was often in love. So it is that in certain lyrics we see the rivers, the birds, the flowers of Scotland through the eyes of a lover. Many of the poems were written to his "Highland Mary"; but whether or not "Mary" was always the same girl we cannot tell. At any rate one of the Highland's loveliest little rivers—the Afton—has been endeared to the world through such a love song.

B   Flow gently, sweet Afton! among thy green braes,
     Flow gently, I'll sing thee a song in thy praise;
B1   My Mary's asleep by thy murmuring stream,
B   Flow gently, sweet Afton, disturb not her dream.

LG*1*   5   Thou stock dove whose echo resounds thro' the glen,
          Ye wild whistling blackbirds, in yon thorny den,
          Thou green crested lapwing thy screaming forbear,
B*1*   I charge you, disturb not my slumbering Fair.

MG   How lofty, sweet Afton, thy neighboring hills,
     10 Far mark'd with the courses of clear, winding rills;
B*1*   There daily I wander as noon rises high,
          My flocks and my Mary's sweet cot in my eye.

LG   How pleasant thy banks and green valleys below,
          Where, wild in the woodlands, the primroses blow;
     15 There oft, as mild Ev'ning weeps over the lea,
B*1*   The sweet-scented birk shades my Mary and me.

LG*1*   Thy crystal stream, Afton, how lovely it glides,
B*1*   And winds by the cot where my Mary resides;
LG   How wanton thy waters her snowy feet lave,
     20 As, gathering sweet flowerets, she stems thy clear
            wave.

U   Flow gently, sweet Afton, among thy green braes,
          Flow gently, sweet river, the theme of my lays;
B*1*   My Mary's asleep by thy murmuring stream,
LG   Flow gently, sweet Afton, disturb not her dream.

  1. BRAES—Small hills.
  5. STOCK DOVE—European wild pigeon.
  7. LAPWING—Plover; noted for its shrill, wailing cry.
 12. COT—Cottage; humble home.
 15. LEA—Grass or pasture land; untilled land.   16. BIRK—Birch.
 19. LAVE—Wash; flow against.   22. LAYS—Songs.

FOR INTERPRETATION

1. In the first stanza Burns tells us that "Mary's asleep." What lines later on in the poem indicate that it is a natural sleep, and not the sleep of death?

2. Do we share with the poet any other sensations than those of sight and sound? If so, what?

3. The musical setting for the song is probably as well known as the words. Do you think the music increases our enjoyment of the poem? Discuss.

OF A' THE AIRTS

ROBERT BURNS

One of the loveliest of all Burns's love songs is known by its first line,
"Of A' the Airts the Wind Can Blaw." Fittingly enough it was written
for Jean Armour, the girl that he married.

Of a' the airts the wind can blaw,
  I dearly like the west,
For there the bonie lassie lives,
  The lassie I lo'e best:
5 There wild woods grow, and rivers row,
  And monie a hill between;
But day and night my fancy's flight
  Is ever wi' my Jean.

I see her in the dewy flowers,
10 I see her sweet and fair;
I hear her in the tunefu' birds,
  I hear her charm the air:
There's not a bonie flower that springs
  By fountain, shaw, or green,
15 There's not a bonie bird that sings,
  But minds me o' my Jean.

1. AIRTS—Directions.   5. ROW—Roll.
14. SHAW—Wood.   16. MINDS—Reminds.

FOR INTERPRETATION

1. What picture of Jean does the poem suggest? List several specific
details, and quote the lines from the poem which give us each impression.
2. If you were going to compose a musical setting for "Of A' the Airts,"
what tempo would you use? what key? what voice?

A MAN'S A MAN FOR A' THAT

ROBERT BURNS

In the late years of the eighteenth century the British Isles hummed
with democratic doctrines. Revolutions, first in America and then in

France, had started Britishers thinking about "the rights of man." Ardent in his sympathies for poor men everywhere, Burns poured his articles of faith into what might be called the *theme-poem* of Democracy—"A Man's a Man for A' That." The "a' that" of the poem stands for all the external differences between men—dress, rank, manners, and the like. But for all that, says Burns, it's the Man himself that counts.

Is THERE for honest poverty
 That hings his head, an' a' that;
The coward slave—we pass him by,
 We dare be poor for a' that!
5 For a' that, an' a' that,
  Our toils obscure an' a' that,
The rank is but the guinea's stamp,
 The Man's the gowd for a' that.

What though on hamely fare we dine,
10 Wear hoddin gray, an' a' that;
Gie fools their silks, and knaves their wine,
 A Man's a Man for a' that:
For a' that, and a' that,
 Their tinsel show, an' a' that;
15 The honest man, tho' e'er sae poor,
 Is king o' men for a' that.

Ye see yon birkie ca'd a lord,
 Wha struts, an' stares, an' a' that;
Tho' hundreds worship at his word,
20 He's but a coof for a' that:
For a' that, an' a' that,
 His ribband, star, an' a' that:
The man o' independent mind
 He looks an' laughs at a' that.

2. HINGS—Hangs.
7. GUINEA—An English gold coin worth about $5.11.
8. GOWD—Gold. Burns meant that it is the gold, not the mark, or stamp, which makes the coin valuable.
9. HAMELY—Common; coarse.
10. HODDIN GRAY—Coarse gray woolen.
17. BIRKIE—Conceited fellow.
20. COOF—Fool.
22. RIBBAND, STAR—Symbols of orders of nobility, and of such orders as the Order of the Star and Garter.

25   A prince can mak a belted knight,
     A marquis, duke, an' a' that;
     But an honest man's aboon his might,
     Gude faith, he maunna fa' that!
     For a' that, an' a' that,
30   Their dignities an' a' that;
     The pith o' sense, an' pride o' worth,
     Are higher rank than a' that.

     Then let us pray that come it may,
     (As come it will for a' that),
35   That Sense and Worth, o'er a' the earth,
     Shall bear the gree, an' a' that.
     For a' that, an' a' that,
     It's coming yet for a' that,
     That Man to Man, the world o'er,
40   Shall brothers be for a' that.

27. ABOON—Above.   28. MAUNNA FA'—Can not manage that.
36. BEAR THE GREE—Have the first place.

FOR INTERPRETATION

1. Does Burns mean in the first three lines that all poor men are "coward slaves"? Under what conditions dare a man be poor and proud?

2. Explain the meaning of the figure of speech which Burns uses in lines 7 and 8.

3. What kind of differences between men is the poet referring to in the second stanza? What are some of the things in life that might be classed as "tinsel show"?

4. What other poet, or poets, have expressed thoughts similar to the one in lines 15 and 16?

5. What kind of differences between men is the poet referring to in the third stanza? Do such distinctions exist even in America? Discuss.

6. Quote lines written by one of Burns's contemporaries which express a thought the same as that in lines 25–29. What does the poet say is the real indication of rank?

7. Do you think that the world is any closer today to the ideal expressed in the last stanza than it was in Burns's day? Which nation do you think has come the closest to realizing those ideals? Do you believe that real brotherhood among men will ever prevail? Discuss.

8. "The best aristocracy is the aristocracy of character." Point out lines in this poem which say the same thing. Do you believe that aristocracy of character and democracy of conduct can live side by side?

THE COTTER'S SATURDAY NIGHT

ROBERT BURNS

The Scotchman as we see him represented in his own literature is very different from the Scotchman known to the joke-smith. In native prose as well as in poems like those by Burns, the typical Scotchman is a sober, industrious, affectionate man. Frugal he must be, because his life is so cruelly poor—but stingy, never. His great interests are his family and his religion.

He is a stern father, not easily expressing his emotion; but beneath the surface is an uncommonly tender heart. The Scotch virtues seem hard, like granite, but Scotch men and women know the meaning of "love that seeketh not itself to please."

A picture of the homelife that breeds such virtues is presented in "The Cotter's Saturday Night." The scene is a farm home in the fall of the year. The family is large and the soil poor, and so the older children have all left home to work for more prosperous families nearby. These "older" children may be anywhere from eight or nine years to the late teen ages. But at twilight on Saturday, they all come home to spend the evening.

The poem opens with a dedication to Robert Aiken, a gentleman who had befriended Burns. The cotter—or *cottager*—appears first in the second stanza, after Burns has shed his English and dropped into "guid braid Scots."

INSCRIBED TO ROBERT AIKEN, ESQ.

Let not Ambition mock their useful toil,
Their homely joys, and destiny obscure;
Nor Grandeur hear, with a disdainful smile,
The short and simple annals of the poor.

MY LOVED, my honored, much respected friend!
No mercenary bard his homage pays;
With honest pride, I scorn each selfish end,
My dearest meed a friend's esteem and praise:
5   To you I sing, in simple Scottish lays,
The lowly train in life's sequester'd scene;
The native feelings strong, the guileless ways,
What Aiken in a cottage would have been;
Ah, tho' his worth unknown, far happier there, I ween!

10   November chill blaws loud wi' angry sugh;
The short'ning winter-day is near a close;
The miry beasts retreating frae the pleugh;
The black'ning trains o' craws to their repose.
The toil-worn cotter frae his labor goes—
15   This night his weekly moil is at an end,—
Collects his spades, his mattocks, and his hoes,
Hoping the morn in ease and rest to spend,
And weary, o'er the moor, his course does hameward bend.

At length his lonely cot appears in view,
20   Beneath the shelter of an aged tree;
Th' expectant wee-things, toddlin, stacher through
To meet their dad, wi' flichterin' noise and glee.
His wee bit ingle, blinkin bonilie,

10. SUGH—Sough, or rushing sound.
12. FRAE THE PLEUGH—From the plough.
13. CRAWS—Crows.   15. MOIL—Toil or labor.
16. MATTOCKS—Implements for digging.
21. STACHER—Toddle or stagger.
22. FLICHTERIN'—Fluttering.   23. INGLE—Fireplace or fire.

His clean hearth-stane, his thrifty wifie's smile,
25   The lisping infant, prattling on his knee,
Does a' his weary kiaugh and care beguile,
   And makes him quite forget his labor and his toil.

Belyve the elder bairns come drapping in,
   At service out, amang the farmers roun';
30 Some ca' the pleugh, some herd, some tentie rin
   A cannie errand to a neebor town.
Their eldest hope, their Jenny, woman-grown,
   In youthfu' bloom, love sparkling in her e'e,
Comes hame, perhaps to shew a braw new gown,
35 Or deposite her sair-won penny-fee,
   To help her parents dear if they in hardship be.

With joy unfeigned, brothers and sisters meet,
   And each for other's weelfare kindly spiers;
The social hours, swift-winged, unnoticed fleet;
40   Each tells the uncos that he sees or hears.
The parents, partial, eye their hopeful years;
   Anticipation forward points the view.
The mother, wi' her needle and her sheers,
   Gars auld claes look amaist as weel's the new;
45 The father mixes a' wi' admonition due:

Their master's and their mistress's command
   The yonkers a' are warnèd to obey,
And mind their labors wi' an eydent hand,
   And ne'er, tho' out o' sight, to jauk or play:
50 "And O be sure to fear the Lord alway,

26. KIAUGH—Trouble, anxiety.
28. BELYVE—By and by.
28. ELDER BAIRNS—Older children.
30. CA'—Drive.
30. TENTIE RIN—Heedfully run.
31. CANNIE—Carefully.
34. BRAW—Handsome.
35. SAIR-WON—Hard earned.
38. SPIERS—Inquires.
40. UNCOS—Strange happenings.
44. GARS AULD CLAES—Makes old clothes.
48. EYDENT—Ardent, diligent.
49. JAUK—Trifle.

And mind your duty duly, morn and night;
 Lest in temptation's path ye gang astray,
Implore His counsel and assisting might:
They never sought in vain that sought the Lord aright."

55 But hark! a rap comes gently to the door.
 Jenny, wha kens the meaning o' the same,
Tells how a neebor lad came o'er the moor,
 To do some errands and convoy her hame.
 The wily mother sees the conscious flame
60 Sparkle in Jenny's e'e, and flush her cheek;
 With heart-struck anxious care enquires his name,
While Jenny hafflins is afraid to speak;
Weel-pleased the mother hears it's nae wild, worthless rake.

With kindly welcome Jenny brings him ben:
65 A strappin' youth, he takes the mother's eye;
Blythe Jenny sees the visit's no ill-taen;
 The father cracks of horses, pleughs, and kye.
 The youngster's artless heart o'erflows wi' joy,
But blate and laithfu', scarce can weel behave;
70 The mother, wi' a woman's wiles, can spy
What makes the youth sae bashfu' and sae grave,
Weel-pleased to think her bairn's respected like the lave.

Oh happy love, where love like this is found!
 Oh heart-felt raptures! bliss beyond compare!
75 I've pacèd much this weary, mortal round,
 And sage experience bids me this declare:
 "If Heaven a draught of heavenly pleasure spare,
One cordial in this melancholy vale,
 'T is when a youthful, loving, modest pair
80 In other's arms breathe out the tender tale,
Beneath the milk-white thorn that scents the evening gale."

62. HAFFLINS—Halfway, partly.
64. BEN—Into the parlor.
67. CRACKS—Talks.
67. KYE—Cattle.
69. BLATE AND LAITHFU'—Shy and bashful.
72. LAVE—Others, the rest.

Is there, in human form, that bears a heart,
A wretch! a villain! lost to love and truth!
That can, with studied, sly, ensnaring art,
85   Betray sweet Jenny's unsuspecting youth?
Curse on his perjured arts! dissembling, smooth!
Are honor, virtue, conscience, all exiled?
Is there no pity, no relenting ruth,
Points to the parents fondling o'er their child?
90   Then paints the ruined maid, and their distraction wild?

But now the supper crowns their simple board:
The halesome parritch, chief o' Scotia's food:
The sowpe their only hawkie does afford,
That 'yont the hallan snugly chows her cood.
95   The dame brings forth, in complimental mood,
To grace the lad, her weel-hained kebbuck, fell,
And aft he's prest and aft he ca's it guid;
The frugal wifie, garrulous, will tell
How 't was a towmond auld sin' lint was i' the bell.

100   The cheerfu' supper done, wi' serious face
They round the ingle form a circle wide;
The sire turns o'er, wi' patriarchal grace,
The big ha'-Bible, ance his father's pride;
His bonnet rev'rently is laid aside,
105   His lyart haffets wearing thin and bare;
Those strains that once did sweet in Zion glide,
He wales a portion with judicious care,
And "Let us worship God!" he says, with solemn air.

They chant their artless notes in simple guise;
110   They tune their hearts, by far the noblest aim:

92. HALESOME PARRITCH—Wholesome porridge—oatmeal, of course.
93. SOWPE—Sup of milk.
93. HAWKIE—Cow.
94. 'YONT THE HALLAN—Beyond the partition.
96. WEEL-HAINED KEBBUCK, FELL—Well-kept strong cheese.
99. TOWMOND AULD, etc.—Twelve-month old since flax was in the flower.
103. HA'-BIBLE—Hall Bible, that is the Bible belonging in the hall, or living room.
105. LYART HAFFETS—Grey locks.
107. WALES—Chooses.

Perhaps "Dundee's" wild-warbling measures rise,
Or plaintive "Martyrs," worthy of the name;
Or noble "Elgin" beets the heavenward flame,
The sweetest far of Scotia's holy lays.
115   Compared with these, Italian trills are tame;
The tickled ears no heart-felt raptures raise;
Nae unison hae they with our Creator's praise.

The priest-like father reads the sacred page:
How Abram was the friend of God on high;
120   Or Moses bade eternal warfare wage
With Amalek's ungracious progeny;
Or how the royal bard did groaning lie
Beneath the stroke of Heaven's avenging ire;
Or Job's pathetic plaint and wailing cry;
125   Or rapt Isaiah's wild, seraphic fire;
Or other holy seers that tune the sacred lyre.

Perhaps the Christian volume is the theme:
How guiltless blood for guilty man was shed;
How He Who bore in Heaven the second name
130   Had not on earth whereon to lay His head;
How His first followers and servants sped;
The precepts sage they wrote to many a land;
How he, who lone in Patmos banishèd,
Saw in the sun a mighty angel stand,
135   And heard great Bab'lon's doom pronounced by Heaven's
command.

Then kneeling down to heaven's Eternal King,
The saint, the father, and the husband prays;

111. DUNDEE'S, MARTYRS, ELGIN—Names of hymns.
113. BEETS—Fans.
119. ABRAM—See *Genesis* xv.
120. MOSES—See *Exodus* xvii.
121. AMALEK'S UNGRACIOUS PROGENY—The descendants of Amalek, a heathen tribe that attacked the Israelites in the desert.
122. ROYAL BARD—King David.
127. CHRISTIAN VOLUME—The New Testament.
133. HE—Saint John, who was imprisoned on the island of Patmos in the Ægean Sea. He wrote the Book of Revelation referred to in the next lines.

Hope "springs exulting on triumphant wing,"
And thus they all shall meet in future days,
140   There ever bask in uncreated rays,
No more to sigh or shed the bitter tear,
    Together hymning their Creator's praise,
In such society, yet still more dear,
While circling Time moves round in an eternal sphere.

145 Compared with this, how poor Religion's pride,
    In all the pomp of method and of art,
When men display to congregations wide
    Devotion's ev'ry grace except the heart!
The Power, incensed, the pageant will desert,
150 The pompous strain, the sacerdotal stole;
    But haply, in some cottage far apart,
May hear, well pleased, the language of the soul,
And in His Book of Life the inmates poor enroll.

Then homeward all take off their sev'ral way;
155   The youngling cottagers retire to rest;
The parent-pair their secret homage pay,
    And proffer up to Heaven the warm request
That He Who stills the raven's clam'rous nest,
And decks the lily fair in flow'ry pride,
160   Would, in the way His wisdom sees the best,
For them and for their little ones provide,
But chiefly in their hearts with grace divine preside.

From scenes like these old Scotia's grandeur springs,
That makes her loved at home, revered abroad:
165 Princes and lords are but the breath of kings,
    "An honest man's the noblest work of God."
And certes in fair virtue's heavenly road,
The cottage leaves the palace far behind:
    What is a lordling's pomp? a cumbrous load,
170 Disguising oft the wretch of human kind,
Studied in arts of hell, in wickedness refined!

150. SACERDOTAL STOLE—Priestly garment.
166. A quotation from Alexander Pope.
167. CERTES—Certainly.

O Scotia! my dear, my native soil!
For whom my warmest wish to Heaven is sent!
Long may thy hardy sons of rustic toil
175   Be blest with health and peace and sweet content!
And O may Heaven their simple lives prevent
From luxury's contagion, weak and vile!
Then, howe'er crowns and coronets be rent,
A virtuous populace may rise the while,
180   And stand a wall of fire around their much-loved isle.

O Thou, Who poured the patriotic tide
That streamed thro' Wallace's undaunted heart,
Who dared to nobly stem tyrannic pride,
Or nobly die, the second glorious part!
185   (The patriot's God peculiarly Thou art,
His friend, inspirer, guardian, and reward!)
Oh never, never Scotia's realm desert,
But still the patriot and the patriot-bard
In bright succession raise, her ornament and guard!

182. WALLACE—A Scottish leader of the thirteenth century.

FOR INTERPRETATION

Gilbert Burns, Robert's brother, has said of this poem, "Robert had frequently remarked to me that he thought there was something peculiarly venerable in the phrase, 'Let us worship God,' as used by a decent, sober head of a family, introducing family worship. To this sentiment of the author, the world is indebted for 'The Cotter's Saturday Night.' " The description of the cotter is an almost exact likeness of Burns's father.

1. Where did Burns find the quotation with which he introduces his poem? What words or expressions from the first stanza sound like quotations from the same source? What does the first stanza do besides make acknowledgment to Mr. Aiken?

2. What change in atmosphere or feeling accompanies the change from pure English to dialect?

3. What similarities in setting do you find in the second stanza of "The Cotter's Saturday Night" and in the opening stanzas of Gray's "Elegy"? What are the important differences? Point out the details in this second stanza that help to establish the mood for the poem.

4. What details in the third stanza stand out in bright contrast to those in the preceding description? Has the mood changed again? Discuss.

5. Quote one or two expressions from the fourth stanza that indicate the extreme poverty of the home.

6. What is the attitude of the brothers and sisters toward each other?

7. Repeat in your own words the advice that the father gives his children.

8. How do the father and the mother treat Jenny's "boy-friend"? Why is the mother pleased to see that the lad acts shy and awkward?

9. How do stanzas nine and ten (lines 73–90) differ from those that preceded and follow? Do you think that they make an important contribution to the poem? Discuss.

10. What would an average American family think of the supper described in the eleventh stanza? What adjective does Burns use in the next stanza to describe the supper?

11. How does the whole family participate in the service of worship? Which stanza of the poem refers to the Old Testament? Which stanza refers to the New Testament? Would you say that Burns had learned something from the family worship in his home? Why or why not? How did the service of worship close? How does the poet feel about the significance of such worship? Which stanza expresses his feeling about it?

12. What do the parents do after the children have left or gone to bed?

13. Why do you think that Burns wrote the last five stanzas in pure English? What other poets does he quote in the closing stanzas? What special prayer does Burns offer for Scotland?

14. "The Cotter's Saturday Night" has been called a "perfect picture of noble poverty." Do you agree with that description? Discuss. Burns said in his opening stanza that Mr. Aiken might have found a happier life if he too had lived in such a cottage. Could there be some truth in the statement? What was it that secured happiness to the Cotter's family? Would the same prescription for happiness work in a mansion as well as in a cottage?

EXTENDED ACTIVITIES

TRANSITION POETS BROKE AWAY FROM CLASSICISM

HISTORY IN BRIEF

	The House of Hanover	Events in America
1780-1799 (18th Century)	George III (1760-1820) (Fall of the Bastille, 1789) (Reign of Terror in France, 1793) (Irish Rebellion, 1798)	Constitutional Convention, 1787 Constitution signed, 1788-1790 Washington president, 1789 Washington's farewell, 1796 Death of Washington, 1799
1800-1840 (19th Century)	(Union of Great Britain and Ireland, 1801) (War with France, 1803-1815) (War with the United States, 1812-1814) (Battle of Waterloo, 1815) George IV (1820-1830) William IV (1830-1837) (Great Reform Bill, 1832) (Slavery abolished in Empire, 1833)	Louisiana Purchase, 1803 War with Great Britain, 1812-1814 Missouri Compromise, 1820 Monroe Doctrine, 1823 American writers appear: Washington Irving (1783-1859) Nathaniel Hawthorne (1804-1864) Edgar Allan Poe (1809-1849)

FOR ACQUAINTANCE WITH AUTHORS

THOMAS GRAY (1716-1771)—"ELEGY WRITTEN IN A COUNTRY CHURCH-
YARD"

The life of Thomas Gray reflects somewhat the changes taking place in the late
eighteenth century. The story of his early
life reads like an early romantic novel. His
father, although well-to-do, refused to do
anything for his son; his devoted mother,
through millinery, supported herself and
Thomas and managed to send him to Eton
and Cambridge. At college the intelligent
but shy student made few friends; throughout his life he was not a "clubbable" man as
were his earlier contemporaries—Johnson,
Pope, and Dryden. He became in maturity
not a politician or a statesman but a college
professor.

Most of Gray's life was spent at Cambridge, first as a student and later as professor of history and modern languages. He

wrote little but wrote carefully and thoughtfully with much revision. The "Elegy Written in a Country Churchyard" was published after seven years of revision, when Gray was thirty-five. His poetry was much what the man was—quiet, somewhat somber, neat, and intellectual rather than impassioned. In his maturity he cared little for fame; the laureateship was offered him after Southey's death but he refused it. For him "to be employed was to be happy"—and his preferred employment was with his books in the little room at Cambridge.

WILLIAM BLAKE (1757–1827)—"THE CLOD AND THE PEBBLE," "THE TIGER," "AUGURIES OF INNOCENCE"

There seems little in the dull facts of the life of William Blake—second son of a London hosier, apprentice at fifteen to an engraver, underpaid magazine illustrator—that would explain the excellence of his work. Even in his lifetime he was almost a legend. Charles Lamb once said of him, "Blake is a real name, I assure you, and a most extraordinary man if he be still living. He paints in watercolors marvelous strange pictures, visions of his brain. . . . His poems have been sold hitherto only in manuscript. I never read them . . . but there is one to a tiger which I have heard recited which is glorious. But alas! I have not the book; for the man is flown, whither I know not—to Hades or a Mad House." But Blake had gone to neither place. He was quietly laboring at his second-rate engraving job to earn enough to support himself and his family. At night he and his wife would work on his own engravings that he loved to do and that no one wanted to buy. During his sleep he would be wakened by strange visions and he would get up to write long mystical poems that no one bought and few read. He and his wife invented a new method of engraving called "illuminated printing," but the exquisite volumes went unsold. Most people thought Blake quite mad; only a few realized his genius and encouraged him. Not until the early nineteenth century was it agreed that the strange William Blake, between his twelfth and twentieth years, had written some of the most beautiful lyrics in the English language, and that his engravings and watercolors entitled him to first rank among all artists.

ROBERT BURNS (1759–1796)—"JOHN ANDERSON, MY JO," "WHISTLE O'ER THE LAVE O'T," "AFTON WATER," "OF A' THE AIRTS," "A MAN'S A MAN FOR A' THAT," "THE COTTER'S SATURDAY NIGHT"

The simple, tender lyrics that poured their good Scotch burr from the tongue of Robert Burns are far removed from the tinkling elegance of the eighteenth century. As a person he was equally distant from his contemporaries. Robert Burns was a Scotch peasant to whom song came as naturally as thought; the only things he knew well were Scotland and his own heart and of them he wrote, sometimes with tenderness, often with humor, but always with truthfulness. He might have belonged to any century but he belongs to all centuries and to all men.

As a child Burns knew the simple peasant life, long hours of work brightened with a few simple pleasures. His father, from whom Burns modeled the father in "The Cotter's Saturday Night," wanted an education for his children, but there was always too little money and too much work. At fifteen Burns was the principal laborer on the farm, his only reading snatched over the plow or at his lunch. He left the farm to study surveying, but his father's death left him to manage the rented fields that seemed to become stonier and less fertile at each move. He had already begun writing, giving more time to it than to the stubborn soil. Restless as always and embittered at a girl's refusal to marry him, he decided to emigrate to Jamaica. To earn passage money he sold his first book of poetry; it was immediately popular. Edinburgh society demanded acquaintance with the "rustic prodigy"; Burns was feted and toasted, but more as a strange exhibit than as a brilliant writer. Bewildered and disillusioned, he began to drink and to cultivate companions who seemed to him more sincere than the socialites he had met.

Early in 1788 he returned to his boyhood home where he married Jean Armour, the sweetheart he had left when he planned on Jamaica. "To give the rest of my story in brief," he wrote, "I have married 'my Jean' and taken a farm." The poet was accustomed to say that the most happy period of his life was the first winter he spent on this farm. But his happiness was short-lived. Although he wrote furiously and passionately for the next seven years, poverty and unrest remained his lot. He died at forty-seven, old and broken before his time, not suspecting the lasting fame that would be his.

OF LITERARY FORM AND STYLE

ROMANTICISM IN LITERATURE

One cannot improve upon Victor Hugo's brief definition of *romanticism* as the spirit of "liberalism in literature." As you may guess, romantic literature differs from classic literature in every main point of criticism. It transfers the emphasis from the form of expression to *meaning* and *feeling;* and it enlarges its range to accept any aspect of life as a possible subject for art. The general characteristics of *romantic literature* may be summarized thus.

In *subject*, romanticism is interested in nature rather than art, and in man as a human being rather than as a member of society. It encourages the imagination, and looks for freshness of ideas and sincerity of thought.

The romanticist writes of other men with sympathetic understanding. He also writes of himself—of his ideals, his disappointments, his ordinary experiences. He likes children and tries to understand them. He is concerned about the unfortunate and wants to help them. His sympathies overflow into the field of nature; any living creature may become the subject of his thought and therefore of his pen. Burns wrote a poem to a mouse; Blake makes a plea for gentleness in our dealings with bird and dog and horse. The true romanticist agrees with Coleridge that "He prayeth best who loveth best *all things,* both great and small." He enjoys nature as it really is, writing of daisies, buttercups, and noisy swallows. He sees nature as one with man, and both a manifestation of God. The romanticist is usually an idealist, hopeful for the upward strivings of man.

The *form* of romantic art is ever subordinate to the thought. Inspiration is more important than rules or models. The message one has to give should determine the way it is presented. And so there is much variety in romantic expression. Each writer is free to develop his own style, to say what he needs to say in the fashion best suited to him. The romanticist uses simple language; short, direct sentences; even a conversational style, or a homely dialect. He likes natural rhythms in his verse and easy rhymes. He turns away from classic figures of speech in favor of illustrations drawn from nature. The classicist writes—

> "Hesperus entreats thy light,
> Goddess, excellently bright!"

The romanticist says—

> "Fair as a star when only one
> Is shining in the sky."

The romanticist thinks of words, not as ornaments, but as the means of expressing his thoughts and feelings—thus as most successfully used when we are least conscious of them. There is little regularity or uniformity in romantic art. It is, instead, fresh and original and inspiring.

In *spirit* or *mood,* romantic literature is warm and friendly. The romantic writer is not ashamed to show his own feelings. He shares with us his joys, his enthusiasms, his fears, and his sorrows. And he sees with understanding eyes into the hearts of others. He sometimes is stirred to revolt. He points out the injustices in life and tries to arouse men to action against them. He is likely to be hopeful, optimistic. He is a dreamer, sometimes sentimentalizing over the past, but more often looking ahead, planning and building. Because he gives rein to his imagination, his moods are many, ranging from the quiet melancholy of Thomas Gray to the mercurial temperament of Robert Burns who is tender or reverent or hilarious as the moment finds him.

The romantic spirit finds its best expression in lyric poetry; but prose also quickens to its influence.

THE LATE EIGHTEENTH-CENTURY SHIFT TO ROMANTICISM

As has been mentioned before, there are no hard, fast lines setting off literary periods and movements. Even while the influence of classicism was at its height in eighteenth-century England, there were a few writers who turned away from the heroic couplet to other more natural forms. There was, for example, James Thomson, who published in 1730 his poem, "The Seasons," written in unrhymed verse and filled with delightful glimpses of nature. William Collins and William Cowper were two other poets who early turned away from satire and criticism to write of natural scenes and simple, homelike incidents. Collins wrote a number of interesting odes and "Eclogues," or pastoral poems. Cowper gained recognition for a long poem dealing with everyday life to which he gave the curious name "The Sofa." Today he is best remembered for such hymns as "God Moves in a Mysterious Way" and for his humorous tale in verse, "John Gilpin's Ride."

As the eighteenth century passed into its last decades, the reaction against classicism became stronger. Samuel Johnson was a defender of Pope and his followers; but some of the members of the Literary Club were experimenting with romantic subjects. Foremost in the group was Oliver Goldsmith, whose own humble origin gave him a real sympathy with poor men everywhere. In his essays, *A Citizen of the World,* he followed the classic fashion, writing as an amused and condescending observer of London society; but in *The Vicar of Wakefield* he tells a romantic story of the ups and downs in the life of a country clergyman. We have seen that the comedy *She Stoops to Conquer* features such natural yet amusing situations as may arise in daily life. His poem "The Deserted Village" lies halfway between the precincts of classic and romantic literature.

There were other transition poets showing similar tendencies—an interest in man and nature, an inclination to give free expression to their feelings, though still bound by the conventions of classic form. Gray's "Elegy" is a transition poem parallel in most respects to "The Deserted Village." As you check the poem, point by point, you will notice that in form it is certainly classic. The wording is formal and dignified; there are bits of satire; there is the "elegance" of manner aspired to by most eighteenth-century poets. But the subject of the poem—the idealized longing for good old days, the pictures of village life, the sympathy for the working man—this is certainly romantic. So too is the feeling of general melancholy. Because the poem combines so clearly characteristics of both classic and romantic literature, it is called a "transition" poem. Its author stands at the half-way mark in the swing to romanticism which was overtaking English literature.

Two eighteenth-century poets—Robert Burns and William Blake—went farther along the romantic way. In fact, Blake shows no slightest trace of classic influence. Burns was, in the beginning, much influenced by earlier poets. There are occasional stanzas all through his works in which he shows a classic precision of phrase; but for the most, his Scotch dialect proves a good homespun cloak for homelike themes. Burns knew every rhythm and stanza form, from simple doggerel to the Spenserian stanza. Many of his songs were composed to fit old Scotch airs; others just seemed to sing themselves. Those that have become most dearly loved are in common speech and easy form, but overflowing with human affection. Romanticist at heart, Burns proved an inspiration to the poets who followed him.

Blake was one of those strange geniuses who follow no one's lead. He did what he must do in art and in literature. His inspiration, he said, came from God. His poems seemed almost to write themselves. His introduction to "Songs of Innocence" tells how a child called to him, laughing, from a cloud—

> " 'Piper, sit thee down and write
> In a book, that all may read.'
> So he vanished from my sight;
> And I plucked a hollow reed,
>
> "And I made a rural pen
> And I stained the water clear,
> And I wrote my happy songs
> Every child may joy to hear."

We can almost believe that he wrote his poems just that way. They are about trees and clouds and butterflies, tigers, sunflowers, lambs, children; about love and hate and misery. They deal with dreams and philosophies, science, wisdom, nonsense. And they are so childishly simple in form that the bigness of ideas is astonishing. He is like no English poet who came before him; and of those that follow, the American Emily Dickinson comes the closest to his mystic combination of sense and fancy dressed in little words that are crystal clear.

With the lyrics of Burns and Blake, the eighteenth century had said farewell to classicism. English literature was poised for a romantic outpouring in the dawning nineteenth century.

QUESTIONS IN APPRECIATION:

"Elegy Written in a Country Churchyard"

1. Which stanzas in the "Elegy" present pleasing descriptions of nature? Be prepared to read aloud those you like best. What kind of words has Gray used in these stanzas?

2. Which stanzas give descriptions of village life? What kinds of words has Gray used here?

3. In which stanzas has Gray used hard words or especially dignified or complicated sentences? Point out at least five such stanzas. Why do you think his style is more formal in these passages?

4. What evidence is there that Gray used his imagination freely in

writing the poem? Do you think his fancies are too far fetched or are they reasonable? Discuss.

5. In mood and feeling is the poem romantic or classic? in subject? in form? Discuss.

Blake's Lyrics

1. Upon what figures of speech has Blake based his poem "The Clod and the Pebble"? Explain them.

2. Is the rhythmic pattern of the poem elaborate or simple? What interesting design may be seen in the *thought pattern* of the poem?

3. Why do you think Blake gives two definitions of love? Does he indicate any personal choice between them? That is, does he indicate that he agrees with one and disagrees with the other?

4. How do the figures of speech in "The Tiger" affect the reader's mental picture of the tiger? For instance, is your own conception of the tiger changed after reading Blake's poem?

5. Does the poem carry the mind of the reader beyond the tiger itself? Is the appeal in this poem primarily to the mind? to the heart? to the imagination? Or is it to all three? What is the appeal of "The Clod and the Pebble"?

6. What do you think was Blake's philosophy of life? That is, what was his attitude toward men? toward children? toward animals? toward nature? toward God? Does he present his philosophy directly or indirectly?

7. What qualities of romantic literature do Blake's poems embody?

Burns's Lyrics

1. Why did Robert Burns write most of his poems in Scotch dialect? How can the reader tell that lack of education was not the reason?

2. How many different stanza forms are represented in the present group by Burns? Why do you think Burns chose the particular form he did for "Afton Water"?

3. Explain why, in literary criticism, a *romantic* subject does not mean necessarily a subject concerning love. May it concern love? Why or why not? Which subjects in this group of poems by Burns do you consider particularly *romantic*—that is, typical of romantic literature?

4. From at least four poems select at least six stanzas which are examples of good descriptive writing. Practice reading them aloud until you can present them smoothly. Be prepared to read any of these stanzas before the class.

5. Does Burns use many figures of speech in his poetry? From what sources does he draw his figures?

6. Does Burns's work show any of the characteristics of *classicism?* Which single poem by Burns do you consider the best example of romanticism in literature? Why?

7. Why do you think Burns has been called "the working man's poet"?

Burns's poems proved an inspiration to many later poets, among them the American farm poet, John Greenleaf Whittier. Review in your mind some of Whittier's poems such as "Snowbound," "In School Days," "The Eternal Goodness," "Telling the Bees," "The Poor Voter on Election Day," and the like. What points of similarity do you find in the works of the two poets?

8. What songs or poems by Burns not represented here do you know? Which of all the poems by Burns do you like the best? Why?

Overview

1. Summarize the important characteristics of romantic literature in (*a*) subject matter, (*b*) form, and (*c*) feeling.

2. From the poems in this section, point out illustrations of these various characteristics. For example, name at least one poem that shows an interest in children; one that illustrates the use of simple words, and so on.

3. Explain what is meant by the *transition poets*. Show, point by point, why Gray's "Elegy" is a good example of a transition poem.

4. As you glance over the poems in this section, do you notice a similarity in poetic form, or do you find many different forms?

5. Which two poems (not including those written in dialect) have used the most hard words? Which poet has used the greatest proportion of short easy words? Which type of poem do you enjoy most? Which do you think is the better kind of poetry? Discuss.

FOR FURTHER READING

BARRIE, JAMES, *A Window in Thrums; The Little Minister*
CARLYLE, THOMAS, *Essay on Burns*
DICK, I. C., *Burns's Songs, Now First Printed with the Melodies for which They Were Written*
ELIOT, GEORGE, *Silas Marner*
FITCH, CLYDE, *Beau Brummel* (drama)
IRVING, WASHINGTON, *Life of Goldsmith*
LANE, ELINOR, *Nancy Stair* (Burns)
MOORE, FRANK F., *The Jessamy Bride*
MULOCK, DINAH CRAIK, *John Halifax, Gentleman*
SHERIDAN, RICHARD BRINSLEY, *The School for Scandal; The Rivals* (drama)
SMITH, D. N., *The Oxford Book of Eighteenth Century Verse*
SNYDER, FRANKLIN BLISS, *Robert Burns*
TARKINGTON, BOOTH, *Monsieur Beaucaire* (drama)
THOMAS, AUGUSTUS, *Oliver Goldsmith* (drama)

V·II

Romanticism flowered in the nineteenth century.

POEMS FOR LUCY

WILLIAM WORDSWORTH

When Wordsworth was twenty-nine, he wrote a group of five unusually appealing poems, sometimes known as the "Lucy lyrics." Part of their charm lies in the fact that although they seem to tell a story, there is no clue to the truth behind the story. Who was Lucy? Did she really live? Did Wordsworth know her in his Cambridge days when he spent his holidays among the hills? Did she live in a country cottage and die in early girlhood? Was that why Wordsworth hurried abroad after taking his degree? And was that why he went back to live "beside the springs of Dove"?

Or was Lucy only a dream maiden, born of his lonely reveries? There is no way of knowing. Wordsworth gave the lines no titles, left no notes about them. He wrote the poems, that is all. But they breathe a sense of reality. In each there is a poignancy of grief more convincing than ever Poe expressed for a lost Lenore or an Annabel Lee.

> "But she is in her grave, and oh
> The difference to me!"

The poet who wrote these lines must have met the mystery of death. But who? or when? or how? Only the poems can answer. Three of the five "Lucy lyrics" follow.

THREE YEARS SHE GREW

The careless reader often misses the point of this first poem. In all but the last stanza, Nature is speaking. She has found a lovely child and has decided to take charge of her growing-up. Like a fairy godmother, she promises to give the girl various natural beauties and graces. Nature keeps her promises, but no more.

> THREE years she grew in sun and shower,
> Then Nature said, "A lovelier flower
> On earth was never sown;
> This Child I to myself will take;

5 She shall be mine, and I will make
   A Lady of my own.

   "Myself will to my darling be
   Both law and impulse: and with me
   The Girl, in rock and plain,
10 In earth and heaven, in glade and bower,
   Shall feel an overseeing power
   To kindle or restrain.

   "She shall be sportive as the fawn
   That wild with glee across the lawn,
15 Or up the mountain springs;
   And hers shall be the breathing balm,
   And hers the silence and the calm
   Of mute insensate things.

   "The floating clouds their state shall lend
20 To her; for her the willow bend;
   Nor shall she fail to see
   Even in the motions of the Storm
   Grace that shall mold the Maiden's form
   By silent sympathy.

25 "The stars of midnight shall be dear
   To her; and she shall lean her ear

In many a secret place
Where rivulets dance their wayward round,
And beauty born of murmuring sound
30 Shall pass into her face.

"And vital feelings of delight
Shall rear her form to stately height,
Her virgin bosom swell;
Such thoughts to Lucy I will give
35 While she and I together live
Here in this happy dell."

Thus Nature spake.—The work was done—
How soon my Lucy's race was run!
She died, and left to me
40 This heath, this calm, and quiet scene;
The memory of what has been,
And never more will be.

FOR INTERPRETATION

1. How old was Lucy when Nature took charge of her? What indication is there in the first stanza that Nature intends to have Lucy grow up to full maturity?

2. How do we know that Nature kept her promises?

3. Describe Lucy as you think she must have been when Nature's work was finished. How old do you think she was? Why?

4. What indication is there in this poem that the poet knew Lucy? that he felt a sense of loss at her death?

5. For comparison with an American poem on a similar theme, look up William Cullen Bryant's "O Fairest of the Rural Maids."

SHE DWELT AMONG THE
UNTRODDEN WAYS

Here is a poem that tells its story so simply and clearly that it needs no introduction.

G   SHE dwelt among the untrodden ways
     Beside the springs of Dove;

A maid whom there were none to praise,
And very few to love:

LG1   5   A violet by a mossy stone
Half hidden from the eye;
MG1   Fair as a star, when only one
Is shining in the sky.

DG1   She lived unknown, and few could know
     10   When Lucy ceased to be;
DB1   But she is in her grave, and oh
The difference to me!

FOR INTERPRETATION

1. Why were there none to praise Lucy and few to love her? Point out all the different ways in which the poet suggests that Lucy lived in a remote, lonely place.

2. What do we learn about Lucy herself from figures of speech used in the second stanza? Was she the kind of girl who would have attracted attention in a city? in any large gathering? How do you know?

3. What kind of person appreciates a single star? or prefers one wood violet to a large bouquet?

4. How does the third stanza convey the impression of sincere emotion? Would the feeling of grief be stronger if the poet said more about it? Why or why not?

5. What points of similarity do you find between the story suggested in this lyric and the one suggested in "Three Years She Grew"? Do you think the poems are about the same Lucy? Why or why not?

6. Do you think that the Lucy mentioned in these poems was imaginary or real? Why?

A SLUMBER DID MY
SPIRIT SEAL

Most persons feel a misleading sense of security until death strikes within the family or within the circle of close, close friends. We hear of tragedies about us with a feeling of—"but that sort of thing doesn't happen to *me.*" Then when it does come, there is a space of numbed bewilderment. And the world never seems quite the same place again. This is how a poet tells of such an experience——

A SLUMBER did my spirit seal;
I had no human fears:
She seemed a thing that could not feel
The touch of earthly years.

5 No motion has she now, no force;
She neither hears nor sees;
Rolled round in earth's diurnal course,
With rocks, and stones, and trees.

FOR INTERPRETATION

1. How does this poem suggest that death came suddenly, without warning? Why is there an element of bewilderment to those left when death comes suddenly?

2. What picture does the first stanza suggest—what kind of person? What realization is the poet forcing upon himself in the second stanza?

3. This lyric is the only one of the five "Lucy lyrics" in which the name "Lucy" does not appear. Why do we feel sure that it belongs in the group?

4. Do you think a poet would be likely to write such lines about an imaginary experience? Why or why not? Compare this poem in point of feeling with such a poem as Poe's "To One in Paradise" (see PROSE AND POETRY OF AMERICA), which was written from fancy, not from life. What gives Poe's lyric a sense of unreality?

SHE WAS A PHANTOM OF DELIGHT

WILLIAM WORDSWORTH

Wordsworth was no different from other men when he fell in love. He first saw the girl he was to marry as something lovely to look at, "a moment's ornament." Longer acquaintance with Mary showed him more and more to admire in her, and to wonder at. The lyric which he wrote to his wife two or three years after their marriage is all the finer compliment because it is expressed in terms of everyday living. It is doubtful that any woman ever received a more sincere and thoughtfully beautiful tribute.

SHE was a phantom of delight
When first she gleamed upon my sight;

  A lovely apparition, sent
  To be a moment's ornament:
5 Her eyes as stars of twilight fair;
  Like twilight's, too, her dusky hair;
  But all things else about her drawn
  From Maytime and the cheerful dawn;
  A dancing shape, an image gay,
10 To haunt, to startle, and way-lay.

  I saw her upon nearer view,
  A Spirit, yet a Woman too!
  Her household motions light and free,
  And steps of virgin-liberty;
15 A countenance in which did meet
  Sweet records, promises as sweet;
  A Creature not too bright or good
  For human nature's daily food;
  For transient sorrows, simple wiles,
20 Praise, blame, love, kisses, tears, and smiles.

  And now I see with eye serene
  The very pulse of the machine;
  A Being breathing thoughtful breath,
  A Traveler between life and death;
25 The reason firm, the temperate will,
  Endurance, foresight, strength, and skill;
  A perfect Woman, nobly planned,
  To warn, to comfort, and command;
  And yet a Spirit still, and bright
30 With something of angelic light.

FOR INTERPRETATION

 1. Show how the three stanzas of "She Was a Phantom of Delight" give a *progressive* picture of Mary Wordsworth. What does each succeeding stanza add to the portrait?

 2. Mention several details of her appearance and personality as presented in the first stanza.

 3. Two lines in the second stanza also deal with her appearance—but especially with her character as revealed by her appearance. Quote the lines, and explain them. What, besides her beauty, has the poet learned

to admire? Which lines in the second stanza make Mrs. Wordsworth seem like a very real person? Do you think that the second stanza was written of Mary before or after her marriage? Discuss.

4. Has close association lessened or deepened the poet's appreciation of Mary? How can we tell? The third stanza furnishes what further insight into her personality? Has daily contact caused her charm to "fade into the common light of day"? Quote lines that give the answer.

5. Does this poem tell why Wordsworth's marriage was a happy one? Discuss.

6. Notice the date for Wordsworth's marriage (see his biography). Do you think that the fact that the poet found real happiness with Mary means that the Lucy of the first group of lyrics was an imaginary girl?

TO A SKYLARK

WILLIAM WORDSWORTH

The two song birds that have given the greatest inspiration to poets of the Old World—the nightingale and the skylark—represent two different kinds of music. The nightingale sings in the dusk of evening from the cover of woods or thickets. The melody is wonderfully sweet, but melancholy. The skylark sings high on the wing, in bright sunlight. Its song is one of clear, pure joy. In fact, some poets have asked the question—how can any living creature overflow with so much happiness? In the following lyric—the second one written by Wordsworth to the skylark—he suggests an answer to the question.

ETHEREAL minstrel! pilgrim of the sky!
Dost thou despise the earth where cares abound?
Or, while the wings aspire, are heart and eye
Both with thy nest upon the dewy ground?
5   Thy nest which thou canst drop into at will,
Those quivering wings composed, that music still!

Leave to the nightingale her shady wood;
A privacy of glorious light is thine,
Whence thou dost pour upon the world a flood
10   Of harmony, with instinct more divine:
Type of the wise, who soar but never roam,
True to the kindred points of heaven and home.

FOR INTERPRETATION

1. Why is the expression "pilgrim of the sky" especially suitable?

2. What two different centers of interest are suggested in the first stanza? How?

3. What two lines suggest the great contrast between the nightingale and the skylark?

4. What does the word "soar" mean, literally? What kind of thoughts or actions does it suggest poetically? What does the word "roam" mean, literally? What meaning does it suggest poetically? What kind of person do you think is meant by the words—"the wise, who soar but never roam"?

5. From what two sources does the skylark draw his happiness? May men find happiness from the same two sources? Discuss.

LINES WRITTEN IN EARLY SPRING

WILLIAM WORDSWORTH

The workings of a man's mind are curious. Sometimes the enjoyment of a certain place or situation may make him think of something else just because it is different. So Wordsworth sitting at ease under a tree on a perfect spring day is carried in his thought to the city with its noise, confusion and worry. He ponders the difference between the life of nature and the life that man has built up for himself. And he does not find the balance in man's favor. To what extent do you think he is right?

I HEARD a thousand blended notes,
While in a grove I sate reclined,
In that sweet mood when pleasant thoughts
Bring sad thoughts to the mind.

5 To her fair works did Nature link
The human soul that through me ran;
And much it grieved my heart to think
What man has made of man.

Through primrose tufts, in that green bower,
10 The periwinkle trailed its wreaths;

And 't is my faith that every flower
Enjoys the air it breathes.

The birds around me hopped and played;
Their thoughts I cannot measure,
15 But the least motion which they made
It seemed a thrill of pleasure.

The budding twigs spread out their fan,
To catch the breezy air;
And I must think, do all I can,
20 That there was pleasure there.

If this belief from heaven be sent,
If such be Nature's holy plan,
Have I not reason to lament
What man has made of man?

FOR INTERPRETATION

1. The following are thoughts for general discussion, before considering the poem in detail:
   a. Is nature more often happy than depressed or depressing?
   b. Does nature more often bring man happiness or distress?
   c. Is nature, in any mood, at any time of year, usually more pleasing to look at than man-made habitations, especially cities? Does man *usually* add ugliness or beauty to the natural scene?
   d. Is much of man's suffering man-made? Most of it?
Before answering these questions take a good look around the neighborhood in which you live, and ask yourself whether the relation between man and nature in your locality is typical or exceptional. Try to make allowance for exceptional conditions as you give your answers.

2. How would the reader know, even without the title to tell him, that the lines of this poem were written in early spring?

3. What seems to be the spirit of nature on this spring day? What did the poet believe was *Nature's holy plan* for man? How can you tell?

4. List at least a half dozen things that may have been in the poet's mind when he grieved about "what man has made of man."

5. Do you find in this poem any evidence that Wordsworth considered Nature as an aspect of God? Discuss.

6. Try to express the theme, or central thought, of this poem in a single sentence.

THE WORLD IS TOO MUCH WITH US

WILLIAM WORDSWORTH

One advantage of the old Greek religion—thinks the poet—was that believing there was a deity in every tree or stream or flower or star made men aware of the natural beauty around them. In fact, the pagan myths gave romance to every object in nature and so increased man's enjoyment in it. In outgrowing ancient superstitions, man has lost too often the power to see anything of the Divine in nature. And that, to Wordsworth, seemed a tragic loss.

THE world is too much with us; late and soon,
Getting and spending, we lay waste our powers;
Little we see in Nature that is ours;
We have given our hearts away, a sordid boon!
5 The sea that bares her bosom to the moon;
The winds that will be howling at all hours,
And are upgathered now like sleeping flowers;
For this, for everything, we are out of tune;
It moves us not.—Great God! I'd rather be
10 A Pagan suckled in a creed outworn;
So might I, standing on this pleasant lea,
Have glimpses that would make me less forlorn;
Have sight of Proteus rising from the sea;
Or hear old Triton blow his wreathèd horn.

11. SO MIGHT I—If then I might.
13. PROTEUS—"The Old Man of the Sea," a lesser deity under Poseidon (Neptune), who could transform himself into any shape that pleased him.
14. TRITON—A sea-god, son of Poseidon, who blew upon a sea-shell trumpet to raise or calm the waves.

FOR INTERPRETATION

1. In what sense is the word *world* used in the first line? What two words in the next line help the reader to understand the right meaning?
2. Give some definite examples of what you think the poet means when he says that men have given their hearts away in return for some *sordid* boon. (What does the word *boon* really mean?)
3. Do you think Wordsworth enjoyed the winds even when they were *howling?* Give the reasons for your answer.

4. Do you think Wordsworth means literally that he would like to return to heathen beliefs? If so, why? If not, what do the last six lines of the sonnet mean? Discuss.

5. Point out the respects in which the thought of this sonnet is similar to the theme of "Lines Written in Early Spring."

MY HEART LEAPS UP

WILLIAM WORDSWORTH

From childhood to manhood Nature seemed to be the strongest influence in Wordsworth's life. He drew more inspiration from it than from books or people. It is bewildering to try to think what kind of man the poet would have been, had he grown up in the center of the city of London. Possibly then he would not have become a poet at all.

LG1	My HEART leaps up when I behold
	A rainbow in the sky:
B1	So was it when my life began;
MB1	So is it now I am a man;
DB1 5	So be it when I shall be old,
B	Or let me die!
L	The Child is father of the Man;
U	And I could wish my days to be
	Bound each to each by natural piety.

9. NATURAL PIETY—A feeling of religion, or devotion, drawn from nature.

FOR INTERPRETATION

1. Do most children feel a thrill at the sight of a rainbow? Are there other things in nature which appeal to children—sunsets? northern lights? stars? and the like? Base your answers on what you remember from your own childhood and also on what you have observed in other children.

2. Do most people as they grow older seem to lose a sense of wonder in the beauties of nature? Do you think most grown people enjoy a rainbow *more* or *less* than children do? Or do you think that finding pleasure in nature is a matter of temperament rather than age? Discuss.

3. Line 7 sounds like a contradiction, but in a sense it is really true. How can a *child* be *father* of a man? *What* man?

4. What is the source of Wordsworth's religious faith? What elements in nature most often speak of God to men? Why? Do you think most people have something of what Wordsworth calls "natural piety"?

From ODE ON INTIMATIONS OF IMMORTALITY

WILLIAM WORDSWORTH

If you were asked to prepare a discussion on the subject of man's immortality—that is, on whether or not you believe that a man's spiritual life continues after his body dies—where would you go for material? Would you turn to books—to the Bible? to the sacred writings of other religions? to the works of philosophers and psychologists? Would you ask other people for their views—teachers? ministers? older persons with a reputation for wisdom? Possibly you would look for evidence from all such sources.

One of Wordsworth's longer lyrics presents the reasons for his belief in the immortality of the human soul. Strangely he has not drawn his conclusions from any of the usual sources, but rather from *things that he remembers from his own childhood*—from almost indefinable recollections of feelings and impressions.

To understand the "Ode," one must bear in mind the close relationship that Wordsworth felt to nature, the deep impressions made on him as a child by the beauty of the countryside, and also the sensitive nature of childhood itself. Even the most matter-of-fact person will admit that children have a greater emotional intensity than grown people. Childhood griefs are sharp out of all proportion to their causes. And childhood joys have a keenness that almost approaches ecstasy. Just remember how you used to look forward to Christmas! or to the circus! Wasn't there something almost unearthly about the season and your enjoyment of it? Because Wordsworth found his greatest delight in sunsets and rainbows, in lights on the water or frost patterns on the pond, his childhood ecstasies were associated with the outdoor world. From his remembrance of them he draws a unique argument for belief in an ever-living human soul. See if you can follow the thread of his thought through these selected stanzas from his "Ode."

THERE was a time when meadow, grove, and stream,
    The earth, and every common sight,
        , To me did seem
     Appareled in celestial light,
5 The glory and the freshness of a dream.
It is not now as it hath been of yore;
      Turn whereso'er I may,
        By night or day,
The things which I have seen I now can see no more.

10   The rainbow comes and goes,
      And lovely is the rose;
      The Moon doth with delight
Look round her when the heavens are bare;
      Waters on a starry night
15   Are beautiful and fair;
     The sunshine is a glorious birth;
     But yet I know, where'er I go,
That there hath passed away a glory from the earth.

Our birth is but a sleep and a forgetting;
20 The soul that rises with us, our life's star,
     Hath had elsewhere its setting,
      And cometh from afar;
     Not in entire forgetfulness,
     And not in utter nakedness,
25 But trailing clouds of glory, do we come
     From God, Who is our home.
Heaven lies about us in our infancy!
    Shades of the prison-house begin to close
     Upon the growing boy,

30 But he beholds the light, and whence it flows.
    He sees it in his joy;
  The youth, who daily farther from the east
   Must travel, still is Nature's priest,
   And by the vision splendid
35   Is on his way attended;
  At length the man perceives it die away,
  And fade into the light of common day.

  Earth fills her lap with pleasures of her own;
  Yearnings she hath in her own natural kind,
40 And, even with something of a mother's mind,
   And no unworthy aim,
   The homely nurse doth all she can
  To make her foster child, her inmate man,
   Forget the glories he hath known,
45 And that imperial palace whence he came.

    · · · · ·

   O joy! that in our embers
   Is something that doth live;
   That nature yet remembers
   What was so fugitive!
50 The thought of our past years in me doth breed
  Perpetual benediction—not indeed
  For that which is most worthy to be blest,
  Delight and liberty, the simple creed
  Of childhood, whether busy or at rest,
55 With new-fledged hope still fluttering in his breast;——
   Not for these I raise
   The song of thanks and praise;
   But for those obstinate questionings
   Of sense and outward things;
60   Fallings from us, vanishings;
   Blank misgivings of a creature
  Moving about in worlds not realized;
  High instincts before which our mortal nature
  Did tremble like a guilty thing surprised;
65   But for those first affections,
   Those shadowy recollections,

Which, be they what they may,
Are yet the fountain-light of all our day,
Are yet a master-light of all our seeing;
70   Uphold us, cherish, and have power to make
Our noisy years seem moments in the being
Of the eternal silence; truths that wake,
      To perish never;
Which neither listlessness, nor mad endeavor,
75   Nor man nor boy,
Nor all that is at enmity with joy,
Can utterly abolish or destroy!
Hence, in a season of calm weather
      Though inland far we be,
80   Our souls have sight of that immortal sea
      Which brought us hither;
    Can in a moment travel thither,
And see the children sport upon the shore,
And hear the mighty waters rolling evermore.

85 What though the radiance which was once so bright
Be now forever taken from my sight,
    Though nothing can bring back the hour
Of splendor in the grass, of glory in the flower?
    We will grieve not, rather find
90   Strength in what remains behind;
    In the primal sympathy
    Which having been must ever be;
    In the soothing thoughts that spring
    Out of human suffering;
95   In the faith that looks through death,
In years that bring the philosophic mind.

And O ye fountains, meadows, hills, and groves,
Forebode not any severing of our loves!
Yet in my heart of hearts I feel your might;
100 I only have relinquished one delight
To live beneath your more habitual sway.
I love the brooks which down their channels fret,
Even more than when I tripped lightly as they;

The innocent brightness of a new-born day
105   Is lovely yet;
The clouds that gather round the setting sun
Do take a sober coloring from an eye
That hath kept watch o'er man's mortality;
Another race hath been, and other palms are won.
110 Thanks to the human heart by which we live,
Thanks to its tenderness, its joys, and fears,
To me the meanest flower that blows can give
Thoughts that do often lie too deep for tears.

108. MORTALITY—Death, dying. Wordsworth here is apparently thinking of some time when he has watched a sunset after the death of some one dear to him.

109. PALMS—In ancient athletic contests laurel crowns or palm branches were awarded as symbols of victory. The line is apparently a reference to St. Paul's comparison of life to an athletic contest, as in *II Timothy* 4:7— "I have fought the good fight, I have finished my course." When a good life ends, the poet thinks of a race as having been won and of the runner as receiving palms of victory when he enters eternity.

FOR INTERPRETATION

Wordsworth's "Ode on Intimations of Immortality" is not an easy poem to understand at first reading; but it is one that becomes more and more filled with meaning as it grows familiar. It has become one of the best loved of all English poems. Among the notes left by the author is this explanation of the thought that underlies the first two stanzas: "To that dream-like vividness and splendor which invests objects of sight in childhood, every one, I believe, if he would look back, could bear testimony." The rest of the poem is Wordsworth's interpretation of the experience described in stanzas one and two.

1. What is the meaning of the word "celestial" (l. 4)? What does the poet mean when he says that every common sight was once "appareled in celestial light"? Do you recall any feeling or experience from your own childhood that corresponds with that of Wordsworth? Discuss.

2. Reread the poem, "My Heart Leaps Up," comparing its thought with that of the second stanza of the "Ode." Do the two seem to agree, or to contradict each other? What do you think is the full meaning of the second stanza? When do we most appreciate *sunshine* as a "glorious birth"?

3. *Death* is often spoken of as a "sleep and a forgetting." In what sense could *birth* be considered a going-to-sleep process? What would be "forgotten" at birth?

4. When we speak of the moon or of a star as "rising" for us, what

is it doing for some other part of the world? Explain the figure of speech presented in lines 20–22.

5. Show how lines 23–26 explain the "celestial light" of the first stanza.

6. According to Wordsworth, we are closest to heaven at what period in our lives? What do you think is meant by the "prison-house" of line 28? What does the term "east" represent in line 32? What general characteristics of young people account for the poet's saying that youth ". . . by the vision splendid is on his way attended"?

7. What common experience in life is summarized in lines 36 and 37? Discuss. Do you think that Wordsworth, like other men, has seen the vision die away "and fade into the common light of day"? Support your answer by quotations from other lines in this poem or from other of his poems.

8. Lines 38–45 present a figurative struggle between what two forces for the soul of man? "Earth" in line 38 is in contrast with what opposite idea? What other poem or poems by Wordsworth express a similar thought?

9. Lines 46–84 are the hardest to understand because they are the most abstract. Read the stanza through carefully to see if you can find the answers to these questions:

  a. Out of all the experiences of his childhood why is the poet most grateful for "those first affections, those shadowy recollections" of the glory that seemed to clothe every common sight when he was young? What have they led him to believe about man's soul?

  b. Are the poet's ideas about immortality the outgrowth of reasoning and logic, or of instinctive feeling? Discuss.

  c. Trace the relationship in thought between lines 19–26 in the third stanza and the general thought of the fifth stanza. Show how Wordsworth has carried his belief in immortality a step beyond the usual thought on the subject.

10. What is meant by the "eternal silence" in line 72? By that "immortal sea" in line 80? How can one "in a moment travel thither"?

11. What loss is the poet discussing in lines 85–95? What does he mention as some of the gains that come with years to older people (lines 90–96)? What is *philosophy?* What is a "philosophic mind"? Do you believe that older people take a more philosophic attitude toward life than young people? Discuss.

12. What is the central thought of the closing stanza of the "Ode"? What do you think is the *one delight* of line 100? Explain the thought of lines 106–107. How is line 108 related to them? What kind of thoughts can even the humblest flower give to Wordsworth? Why? What other romantic poet could see deep significance in a wild flower? Does this closing stanza agree with or contradict the thought expressed in "My Heart Leaps Up"?

13. How does the "Ode" give evidence of the fact that Wordsworth's religion was a kind of "natural piety"? Discuss.

14. What American poet and philosopher also drew much of his religious faith from nature?

15. Which stanza in the "Ode" seems the easiest to understand? Which stanza seems to have the most depth of meaning? Which one do you think is most beautiful, both in thought and expression? Which lines from the "Ode" have you heard quoted?

16. Do you think the "Ode" would be hard to memorize? Why or why not? Select from ten to twenty lines that you think especially worth knowing, and commit them to memory.

KUBLA KHAN

SAMUEL TAYLOR COLERIDGE

In the summer of 1797 Coleridge, who was in ill health, went to a farm house near Porlock, England, hoping the rest would cure him. One morning as he sat reading *Purchas's Pilgrimage* he fell asleep in his chair. The last words he read were: "In Xanadu did Cublai Can build a stately Palace, encompassing sixteene miles of plaine ground with a wall, wherein are fertile Medowes, pleasant Springs, delightfull Streames, and all sorts of beasts of chase and game, and in the middest thereof a sumptuous house of pleasure." He said upon awakening that he had composed during his sleep about three hundred lines telling of magnificent scenes of oriental splendor. He immediately began writing them down and had completed fifty-four lines when he was interrupted by a visitor who stayed an hour. Coleridge was never able to remember any more of the dream.

In Xanadu did Kubla Khan
A stately pleasure-dome decree,
Where Alph, the sacred river, ran
Through caverns measureless to man
5 Down to a sunless sea.
So twice five miles of fertile ground
With walls and towers were girdled round;
And here were gardens bright with sinuous rills,
Where blossomed many an incense-bearing tree;
10 And here were forests ancient as the hills,
Enfolding sunny spots of greenery.

But O that deep romantic chasm which slanted
Down the green hill athwart a cedarn cover!
A savage place! as holy and enchanted
15 As e'er beneath a waning moon was haunted
By woman wailing for her demon-lover!
And from this chasm, with ceaseless turmoil seething,
As if this earth in fast thick pants were breathing,
A mighty fountain momently was forced;
20 Amid whose swift half-intermitted burst,
Huge fragments vaulted like rebounding hail,
Or chaffy grain beneath the thresher's flail;
And 'mid these dancing rocks at once and ever
It flung up momently the sacred river.
25 Five miles meandering with a mazy motion,
Through wood and dale the sacred river ran,
Then reached the caverns measureless to man,
And sank in tumult to a lifeless ocean;
And 'mid this tumult Kubla heard from far
30 Ancestral voices prophesying war!

The shadow of the dome of pleasure
Floated midway on the waves;

TITLE—*Khan*, which has various spellings, means king or emperor. Kubla (or Kublai) Khan was the rich and powerful founder of the Mongol dynasty of China. He lived from 1216(?) to 1294. Medieval travelers have written of the splendors of his court.
1. XANADU—A region of Tartary.
3. ALPH—Probably an imaginary name suggested by the Alpheus, a river of southern Greece which plunges underground and flows under the sea, emerging in Sicily.

Where was heard the mingled measure
From the fountain and the caves.
35   It was a miracle of rare device,
A sunny pleasure-dome with caves of ice!
A damsel with a dulcimer
In a vision once I saw;
It was an Abyssinian maid,
40   And on her dulcimer she played,
Singing of Mount Abora.
Could I revive within me
Her symphony and song,
To such a deep delight 't would win me,
45   That with music loud and long
I would build that dome in air,
That sunny dome! those caves of ice!
And all who heard should see them there,
And all should cry, "Beware! beware!
50   His flashing eyes, his floating hair!
Weave a circle round him thrice,
And close your eyes with holy dread,
For he on honey-dew hath fed,
And drunk the milk of Paradise."

41. MOUNT ABORA—There is Mount Amara of fabled beauty in Abyssinia.

FOR INTERPRETATION

1. Try to picture the geography of the scene: Where did the "sacred river" have its source (lines 12–24)? How long did it run above ground? And where did it end (lines 25–28 and 1–5)? Where, along the banks of the river, was the pleasure palace located (lines 31–36)? Do you think the "caves of ice" are the same as the "caverns measureless to man"?

2. Describe the grounds that surround the palace. How do you think the palace itself looked? of what style of architecture? built of what materials? Are these details described in the poem or merely suggested?

3. Does the "damsel with a dulcimer" (l. 37) have anything to do with the pleasure dome? How can you tell? What do lines 45–47 mean?

4. Who is being described in lines 50–55? What is suggested as the effect of feeding on *honey-dew* and drinking the *milk of Paradise?*

5. Which lines in the poem suggest what kind of story the poet intended to tell? What makes the reader feel that there would be supernatural elements in the story? Are any of the details in these 54 lines actually impossible or contrary to nature? Why does the reader find these opening lines interesting even though the whole story remains untold?

JOCK O' HAZELDEAN

SIR WALTER SCOTT

The happiest ballads are those that tell of an elopement where all goes well. Jock was just another Lochinvar, and true love won the day.

DB1		"WHY weep ye by the tide, ladie?
B		Why weep ye by the tide?
DB1		I'll wed ye to my youngest son,
		And ye sall be his bride;
B	5	And ye sall be his bride, ladie,
		Sae comely to be seen"—
M		But aye she loot the tears down fa'
U		For Jock o' Hazeldean.
DB1		"Now let this wilfu' grief be done,
	10	And dry that cheek so pale;
		Young Frank is chief of Errington,
		And lord of Langley-Dale;
		His step is first in peaceful ha',
		His sword in battle keen"—
M	15	But aye she loot the tears down fa'
U		For Jock o' Hazeldean.
DB1		"A chain of gold ye sall not lack,
		Nor braid to bind your hair;
		Nor mettled hound, nor managed hawk,
	20	Nor palfrey fresh and fair;
		And you, the foremost o' them a',
		Shall ride our forest queen"—
M		But aye she loot the tears down fa'
U		For Jock o' Hazeldean.
M	25	The kirk was decked at morning tide,
L		The tapers glimmered fair;
M		The priest and bridegroom wait the bride,
		And dame and knight are there.

1. LADIE—Lady. Do not confuse with "laddie."
7. LOOT—Let.   13. HA'—Hall.
19. METTLED HOUND NOR MANAGED HAWK—Spirited hunting dog nor trained hawk.   20. PALFREY—Riding horse.   25. KIRK—Church.

653

They sought her baith by bower and ha'
30   The ladie was not seen!
U   She's o'er the Border, and awa'
Wi' Jock o' Hazeldean.

FOR INTERPRETATION

1. Who speaks the lines in quotation marks? How can you tell?
2. What actual information are we given about the bridegroom? What else may the reader guess about the groom?
3. What does the poem tell us about Jock of Hazeldean? What do you think Jock was like?
4. Do we have any information about the lady, either direct or indirect? What do you think she was like?

SOLDIER, REST!

SIR WALTER SCOTT

Near the end of the first canto of *The Lady of the Lake*, Ellen, the heroine, has come upon an unfortunate hunter who has lost his party and his horse. The girl takes him in a skiff to her island home and makes him welcome with traditional Scotch hospitality. The stranger introduces himself as "The Knight of Snowdoun, James Fitz-James," adding that in company with Lord Moray he had that morning——

> ". . . chased a stalwart stag in vain,
> Outstripped his comrades, missed the deer,
> Lost his good steed, and wandered here."

But when he tries courteously to discover whose home he is visiting and who his hostess may be, Ellen parries the question and sings a song to divert his attention. She is accompanied in the singing by an unseen harp. The last stanza she invents, as she sings, to fit the circumstances of her guest.

SOLDIER, rest! thy warfare o'er,
    Sleep the sleep that knows not breaking;
Dream of battled fields no more,
    Days of danger, nights of waking.
5 In our isle's enchanted hall,
    Hands unseen thy couch are strewing,
Fairy strains of music fall,
    Every sense in slumber dewing,

654

Soldier, rest! thy warfare o'er,
10 Dream of fighting fields no more;
Sleep the sleep that knows not breaking,
Morn of toil, nor night of waking.

No rude sound shall reach thine ear,
Armor's clang or war-steed champing,
15 Trump nor pibroch summon here
Mustering clan or squadron tramping.
Yet the lark's shrill fife may come
At the daybreak from the fallow,
And the bittern sound his drum,
20 Booming from the sedgy shallow.
Ruder sounds shall none be near,
Guards nor warders challenge here,
Here's no war-steed's neigh and champing,
Shouting clans or squadrons stamping.

25 Huntsman, rest! thy chase is done;
While our slumbrous spells assail ye,
Dream not, with the rising sun,
Bugles here shall sound reveille.
Sleep! the deer is in his den;
30 Sleep! thy hounds are by thee lying;
Sleep! nor dream in yonder glen
How thy gallant steed lay dying.
Huntsman, rest! thy chase is done;
Think not of the rising sun,
35 For at dawning to assail ye
Here no bugles sound reveille.

15. PIBROCH—A set of variations for the Scotch bagpipes, either warlike or mournful.

19. BITTERN—A kind of heron that nests in marshy places and that makes a peculiar booming sound.

28. REVEILLE—The bugle call for rising in the morning is pronounced rĕv'ĕ-lē in the United States. The British pronunciation is rĕ-vāl'yă.

FOR INTERPRETATION

The popularity of *The Lady of the Lake* was largely due to the faithful descriptions of Scotch scenes and life in the beautiful wooded foothills lying between Stirling castle, the residence of James V, and Loch Lomond.

Ellen's Isle is in lovely Loch Katrine—"Loch" of course being dialect for "Lake." Even this short lyric has some touches of local color.

1. The first two stanzas are ostensibly from an old song. What two meanings might be intended by "the sleep that knows not breaking"? Do the first two stanzas indicate which meaning is preferred here?

2. From what you know of Scotch history, why is the warlike note of the second stanza appropriate? What natural sounds does the song say will replace the sounds of war?

3. How does Ellen change the beginning of the third stanza to fit her guest? Why does she not use the expression "sleep that knows not breaking" in this stanza?

4. What lines or expressions in the song are especially suggestive of Scotland?

THE DESTRUCTION OF SENNACHERIB

GEORGE GORDON, LORD BYRON

One of Byron's favorite books was the Old Testament of the Bible, from which he drew the inspiration for many of his poems. For instance,

his narrative lyric, "The Destruction of Sennacherib," retells one of the remarkable stories from the book of *Kings*.

From 705 B.C. to 681, Sennacherib was king of Assyria—then at the
height of its power. The northern kingdom of Israel had already fallen
to the Assyrians, and now the cities of Judea were being taken. Altogether two hundred thousand Hebrews had been carried off captive. With
a huge army Sennacherib then laid siege to Jerusalem. But he made the
mistake of boasting and ridiculing the Hebrews for their trust in Jehovah. The Jews had fallen into evil ways, but they had a good king,
Hezekiah, who now offered a solemn prayer entreating God not to let the
Assyrian make good his boasts. The Lord heard Hezekiah's prayer and
promised, "concerning the king of Assyria, he shall not come into this
city, nor shoot an arrow there, nor come before it with shield . . . by
the way that he came, by the same shall he return." It was further fore-
told that Sennacherib should die by the sword in his own land.

History bears record of the strange disaster that overtook the Assyrian
host. Over night a pestilence swept the army, killing one hundred and
eighty-five thousand men. Sennacherib fled to his own country, where
he was slain by two of his sons. Jerusalem, for the time, had been saved
from her enemies.

M		The Assyrian came down like a wolf on the fold,
D		And his cohorts were gleaming in purple and gold;
L		And the sheen of their spears was like stars on the sea,
D		When the blue wave rolls nightly on deep Galilee.

L	5	Like the leaves of the forest when Summer is green,
		That host with their banners at sunset were seen:
D		Like the leaves of the forest when Autumn hath blown,
		That host on the morrow lay withered and strewn.

Gı		For the Angel of Death spread his wings on the blast,
	10	And breathed in the face of the foe as he passed;
D		And the eyes of the sleepers waxed deadly and chill,
		And their hearts but once heaved, and forever grew still!

Bı		And there lay the steed with his nostril all wide,
		But through it there rolled not the breath of his pride;
	15	And the foam of his gasping lay white on the turf,
D		And cold as the spray of the rock-beating surf.

B   And there lay the rider distorted and pale,
          With the dew on his brow and the rust on his mail:
D   And the tents were all silent, the banners alone,
L 20 The lances unlifted, the trumpet unblown.

G   And the widows of Ashur are loud in their wail,
D   And the idols are broke in the temple of Baal;
U   And the might of the Gentile, unsmote by the sword,
          Hath melted like snow in the glance of the Lord!

    21. ASHUR—Assyria.
    22. BAAL—A general term for a god, especially a god of the fields, worshipped by the heathen neighbors of the ancient Hebrews.
    23. GENTILE—A term used by the Jews for any one not of their faith. Here it refers to the Assyrians.

FOR INTERPRETATION

    The full story of Hezekiah and Sennacherib is told in *II Kings*, the eighteenth and nineteenth chapters. It is interesting reading.
    1. Explain the figure with which Byron describes the attack of the Assyrians. How does the poet suggest the size of the attacking army?
    2. With what figure does he represent the contrast in the army before and after the pestilence had struck? Why is it a particularly good figure?
    3. Byron, like the writer of *Kings*, does not use the term "pestilence." With what words does he relate the fate of the army? What details does he add to make the picture more realistic?
    4. Why, in view of the whole story, are lines 21–24 especially effective?

SHE WALKS IN BEAUTY

GEORGE GORDON, LORD BYRON

    A friend of Byron, who had made a collection of Hebrew melodies, suggested that the poet write a group of lyrics to fit the songs. Most of the twenty-three poems that grew out of the suggestion were on Old Testament themes—some of them stories, like "The Destruction of Sennacherib."
    Another melody gave Byron the inspiration for what has proved to be one of the loveliest of all his lyrics—"She Walks in Beauty Like the Night." It presents the portrait of a dark-haired, dark-eyed maiden graced with those qualities of ideal womanhood which Jewish tradition has immortalized in stories like those of Ruth and Rachel and Esther.

SHE walks in beauty, like the night
Of cloudless climes and starry skies;
And all that's best of dark and bright
Meet in her aspect and her eyes:
5   Thus mellowed to that tender light
Which heaven to gaudy day denies.

One shade the more, one ray the less,
Had half impaired the nameless grace
Which waves in every raven tress,
10   Or softly lightens o'er her face;
Where thoughts serenely sweet express
How pure, how dear their dwelling place.

And on that cheek, and o'er that brow,
So soft, so calm, so eloquent,
15   The smiles that win, the tints that glow,
But tell of days in goodness spent,
A mind at peace with all below,
A heart whose love is innocent!

FOR INTERPRETATION

1. What countries does Byron suggest by the expression, "cloudless climes and starry skies"? Why, in those lands, is the night more pleasing than the day?

2. Why would the beauty of such a maiden appropriately be likened to the beauties of night? Mention several specific qualities of night which Byron ascribes to the girl, either directly or indirectly.

3. Why does this lyric have a universal appeal?

THE OCEAN

GEORGE GORDON, LORD BYRON

The finest lines and stanzas that Byron wrote are to be found in *Childe Harold's Pilgrimage*, which he described as the most thoughtful of his works and as the one in which he took the greatest pleasure. The poem records impressions—most of them written on the scene—of the "countries of chivalry, history, and fable—Spain, Greece, Asia Minor, and

Italy." Byron wanted his work to preserve something of his "respect for what is venerable and feeling for what is glorious."

The title he explained by saying that he had invented a character to serve as a thread to give "connection" to the work. He used an old-fashioned term for knight—"childe"—to be in keeping with the Spenserian stanza in which the work was written. He insisted that Childe Harold was fictitious; but all readers identified the young nobleman with Byron himself. And so in the last canto, from which the passage on the ocean was taken, he drops the disguise.

The stanzas on "The Ocean" make a fitting conclusion to the last canto, for Byron loved the sea. He makes no empty boast in the last stanza. He was an excellent swimmer; and once, to prove that it could be done, he swam the treacherous Hellespont. The passage was written in Italy, the Mediterranean being his immediate inspiration.

THERE is a pleasure in the pathless woods,
There is a rapture on the lonely shore,
There is society, where none intrudes,
By the deep Sea, and music in its roar:
5   I love not Man the less, but Nature more,
From these our interviews, in which I steal
From all I may be, or have been before,
To mingle with the Universe, and feel
    What I can ne'er express, yet cannot all conceal.

10   Roll on, thou deep and dark blue Ocean—roll!
Ten thousand fleets sweep over thee in vain;
Man marks the earth with ruin—his control
Stops with the shore; upon the watery plain
The wrecks are all thy deed, nor doth remain
15   A shadow of man's ravage, save his own,
When, for a moment, like a drop of rain,
He sinks into thy depths with bubbling groan,
    Without a grave, unknelled, uncoffined, and unknown.

His steps are not upon thy paths—thy fields
20   Are not a spoil for him,—thou dost arise
And shake him from thee; the vile strength he wields
For earth's destruction thou dost all despise,
Spurning him from thy bosom to the skies,
And send'st him, shivering in thy playful spray
25   And howling, to his gods, where haply lies

His petty hope in some near port or bay,
And dashest him again to earth:—there let him lay.

The armaments which thunderstrike the walls
Of rock-built cities, bidding nations quake,
30   And monarchs tremble in their capitals,
The oak leviathans, whose huge ribs make
Their clay creator the vain title take
Of lord of thee, and arbiter of war—
These are thy toys and, as the snowy flake,
35   They melt into thy yeast of waves, which mar
Alike the Armada's pride or spoils of Trafalgar.

27. THERE LET HIM LAY—This is a particularly unfortunate example of
Byron's carelessness and indifference. *Lay* is of course incorrectly used here
for *lie*, not through ignorance, but because it rhymed and it was too much
trouble to find a correct way of ending the stanza. The error is the more
surprising since it occurs in a favorite passage of the author's favorite poem.

36. ARMADA'S PRIDE—A reference to England's defeat of a huge Spanish fleet
during the reign of Elizabeth.

36. SPOILS OF TRAFALGAR—A reference to the naval battle in 1805 in which
England defeated a combined French and Spanish fleet and again proved her
supremacy on the sea.

Thy shores are empires, changed in all save thee—
Assyria, Greece, Rome, Carthage, what are they?
Thy waters washed them power while they were free,
40 And many a tyrant since; their shores obey
The stranger, slave, or savage; their decay
Has dried up realms to deserts: not so thou;—
Unchangeable, save to thy wild waves' play,
Time writes no wrinkle on thine azure brow:
45   Such as creation's dawn beheld, thou rollest now.

Thou glorious mirror, where the Almighty's form
Glasses itself in tempests; in all time,—
Calm or convulsed, in breeze, or gale, or storm,
Icing the pole, or in the torrid clime
50 Dark-heaving—boundless, endless, and sublime,
The image of eternity, the throne
Of the Invisible; even from out thy slime
The monsters of the deep are made; each zone
Obeys thee; thou goest forth, dread, fathomless, alone.

55 And I have loved thee, Ocean! and my joy
Of youthful sports was on thy breast to be
Borne, like thy bubbles, onward; from a boy
I wantoned with thy breakers—they to me
Were a delight; and if the freshening sea
60 Made them a terror—'twas a pleasing fear,
For I was as it were a child of thee,
And trusted to thy billows far and near,
And laid my hand upon thy mane—as I do here.

FOR INTERPRETATION

1. In the stanza of *Childe Harold's Pilgrimage* immediately preceding this passage on the ocean, Byron had expressed the wish to live in some lonely spot far from all human kind. In the first stanza of this selection, what reason does he give for such a wish? What line is in the nature of an apology for his desire to be away from men? In what sense is the word *society* used in line 3? In which lines of the first stanza does Byron confess certain noble aspirations? What inspires them?

2. In what sense may it be said that man's fleets sweep over the ocean *in vain?* With what kind of *ruin* does man mark the shore? To what extent is it true that "his control stops with the shore"?

3. In the third stanza what strength is it that "man wields for earth's destruction"? In what sense is it true that strength leaves no mark upon the ocean?

4. What were some of the *armaments* used in Byron's day? What others should be added today to make the list complete? Are these armaments still "toys" to "melt into the yeast of waves"? What are the "oak leviathans" of line 31? What changes in wording would be needed to bring this line up to date? Who is meant by the "clay creator"? Is he really "lord of the sea"? Discuss.

5. Explain the meaning of line 37. How did the waves of the ocean once "wash power" to Rome and Carthage? How could it bring them *tyrants?* What has been the fate of Assyria? Greece? Rome? Carthage? What part has the ocean played in their changing fortunes? With what striking figure of speech does the poet say that the ocean remains unchanged through all the passage of years?

6. Why is the ocean an appropriate symbol for, or mirror of, God? In what sense is it an "image of eternity"? a "throne of the invisible"? What is meant by "Each *zone* obeys thee"? by "Thou goest forth, dread, fathomless, alone"?

7. Show how the point of view of the seventh stanza is different from that of the preceding stanzas. Why do you think Byron found so much pleasure in swimming? With what effective figure of speech does he close the passage? Why is it appropriate? Do you think the passage on the ocean would have had a stronger conclusion if it had closed with the sixth stanza? Or are you glad that the seventh stanza was added?

THE CLOUD

PERCY BYSSHE SHELLEY

To the dreamer lying on his back under a summer sky a cloud is an invitation. And poor in spirit is the boy or girl who has not sometime gone sailing across that dome of sky. Shelley in such a day-dream fancied himself a spirit of the cloud. Then he pictured all the transformations through which, as a cloud being, he would pass. It is his idealized cloud that speaks in the following stanzas. As you read, notice the brilliance of the pictures suggested and the exquisite melody of the lines.

L1   I BRING fresh showers for the thirsting flowers,
     From the seas and the streams;
L2   I bear light shade for the leaves when laid
     In their noonday dreams.

L3   5   From my wings are shaken the dews that waken
             The sweet buds every one,
G1   When rocked to rest on their mother's breast,
             As she dances about the sun.
B1   I wield the flail of the lashing hail,
     10   And whiten the green plains under,
           And then again I dissolve it in rain,
             And laugh as I pass in thunder.

D1   I sift the snow on the mountains below,
             And their great pines groan aghast;
M1   15   And all the night 'tis my pillow white,
             While I sleep in the arms of the blast.
G1   Sublime on the towers of my skyey bowers,
             Lightning my pilot sits;
D   In a cavern under is fettered the thunder,
     20   It struggles and howls at fits;
L1   Over earth and ocean, with gentle motion,
             This pilot is guiding me,
G1   Lured by the love of the genii that move
             In the depths of the purple sea;
L   25   Over the rills, and the crags, and the hills,
             Over the lakes and the plains,
           Wherever he dream, under mountain or stream,
             The Spirit he loves remains;
           And I all the while bask in heaven's blue smile.
     30   Whilst he is dissolving in rains.

M   The sanguine Sunrise, with his meteor eyes,
             And his burning plumes outspread,
           Leaps on the back of my sailing rack,
             When the morning star shines dead,
     35   As on the jag of a mountain crag,
             Which an earthquake rocks and swings,
           An eagle alit one moment may sit
             In the light of its golden wings.
           And when sunset may breathe, from the lit sea
             beneath,
     40   Its ardors of rest and of love,

D   And the crimson pall of eve may fall
          From the depth of heaven above,
      With wings folded I rest, on mine airy nest,
          As still as a brooding dove.

G1 45 That orbèd maiden with white fire laden,
          Whom mortals call the Moon,
L   Glides glimmering o'er my fleece-like floor,
          By the midnight breezes strewn;
      And wherever the beat of her unseen feet,
    50   Which only the angels hear,
      May have broken the woof of my tent's thin roof,
          The stars peep behind her and peer;
      And I laugh to see them whirl and flee,
          Like a swarm of golden bees,
    55 When I widen the rent in my wind-built tent,
          Till the calm rivers, lakes, and seas,
      Like strips of the sky fallen through me on high,
          Are each paved with the moon and these.

M   I bind the Sun's throne with a burning zone,
    60   And the Moon's with a girdle of pearl;
      The volcanoes are dim, and the stars reel and swim,
          When the whirlwinds my banner unfurl.
      From cape to cape, with a bridge-like shape,
          Over a torrent sea,
    65 Sunbeam-proof, I hang like a roof—
          The mountains its columns be.
      The triumphal arch through which I march
          With hurricane, fire, and snow,
      When the Powers of the air are chained to my chair,
    70   Is the million-colored bow;
      The sphere-fire above its soft colors wove,
          While the moist earth was laughing below.

G   I am the daughter of Earth and Water,
          And the nursling of the Sky;
    75 I pass through the pores of the ocean and shores;
          I change, but I cannot die.

For after the rain when with never a stain
The pavilion of heaven is bare,
And the winds and sunbeams with their convex˙
gleams,
80   Build up the blue dome of air,
I silently laugh at my own cenotaph,
And out of the caverns of rain,
L   Like a child from the womb, like a ghost from
the tomb,
U   I arise and unbuild it again.

81. CENOTAPH—An empty tomb.

FOR INTERPRETATION

A thoughtful reading of this poem discloses the fact that in it Shelley
has his Cloud take on all the shapes and forms that may ever be seen in
the sky, at any time of day or night, in any season. He also suggests
what the scientist would call the "functions" of the Cloud—that is, all
the changes in weather and atmosphere that accompany various cloud
formations. And finally he touches upon the strange nature of the cloud
—that it is really the unending cycle through which moisture is gathered
up and redistributed over the earth.

1. What time of year does the first stanza suggest? What kind of
clouds? What kind of weather? Have you experienced such a rain as is
described in these first twelve lines? In what month is it most likely
to come? What is meant by "their mother's breast" (l. 7)? How and
when does she "dance about the sun"?

2. What time of year do lines 13-16 suggest? Does the rest of the
stanza keep the same picture? How can you tell? Who is the *pilot* of
the cloud? Through how many lines is this figure continued? Who do
you think is the "Spirit" of line 28? Can you read a meaning into lines
21-28? Who is "dissolving the rain" (l. 30)? What cloud shapes do you
see as you read this second stanza? Describe them.

3. Which lines in the third stanza describe the effect of the sunrise on
the cloud? Which lines describe the sunset? What are the different
meanings of the word *sanguine*? Which meaning or meanings do you
think are meant in line 31? What does the word *pall* mean? What are
the two sources of color for the cloud in lines 39-44? Describe the difference between the sunrise and the sunset clouds.

4. What time of year is suggested in the fourth stanza? Which words
give that impression? What new and different picture does Shelley use
for the moon? What does he call the cloud-form? Why?

5. Does the fifth stanza present one picture or a series of pictures?
Explain. What do you think is the "burning zone" of line 59? What is

the meaning of the expression, "When the Powers of the air *are chained to my chair*"? What is the "sphere-fire above"? Show how lines 71 and 72 describe the conditions that cause a rainbow. Do you need to revise your answer to the first question in this section?

6. How are clouds formed? In what sense is the cloud a "daughter of *earth* and *water*"? Why does the cloud appropriately call the clear sky its "cenotaph"? Why does Shelley use the word *unbuild* in the last line of the poem? To what does *it* refer? Does the last stanza suggest a definite picture or scene? If so, of what sort? Why does this stanza form a suitable conclusion for the poem? Discuss.

TO A SKYLARK

PERCY BYSSHE SHELLEY

It is said that the inspiration for Shelley's poem "To a Skylark" was a flood of melody that cascaded down upon the poet and his wife one morning when they were wandering along an English lane. It was a familiar song enough, but this time the mood was right and Shelley caught in his lines the soaring joy of the bird even while he questioned the secret of such joy.

HAIL to thee, blithe spirit!
Bird thou never wert,

667

That from heaven, or near it,
Pourest thy full heart
5   In profuse strains of unpremeditated art.

Higher still and higher
From the earth thou springest
Like a cloud of fire;
The blue deep thou wingest,
10   And singing still dost soar, and soaring ever
singest.

In the golden lightning
Of the sunken sun,
O'er which clouds are brightening,
Thou dost float and run,
15   Like an unbodied joy whose race is just begun.

The pale purple even
Melts around thy flight;
Like a star of heaven,
In the broad daylight
20   Thou art unseen, but yet I hear thy shrill delight,

Keen as are the arrows
Of that silver sphere,
Whose intense lamp narrows
In the white dawn clear,
25   Until we hardly see, we feel that it is there.

All the earth and air
With thy voice is loud,
As, when night is bare,
From one lonely cloud
30   The moon rains out her beams, and heaven is
overflowed.

What thou art we know not;
What is most like thee?

From rainbow clouds there flow not
Drops so bright to see
35 As from thy presence showers a rain of melody.

Like a poet hidden
In the light of thought,
Singing hymns unbidden,
Till the world is wrought
40 To sympathy with hopes and fears it heeded not;

Like a high-born maiden
In a palace tower,
Soothing her love-laden
Soul in secret hour
45 With music sweet as love, which overflows her
bower;

Like a glowworm golden
In a dell of dew,
Scattering unbeholden
Its aërial hue
50 Among the flowers and grass, which screen it
from the view;

Like a rose embowered
In its own green leaves,
By warm winds deflowered,
Till the scent it gives
55 Makes faint with too much sweet those heavy-
wingèd thieves.

Sound of vernal showers
On the twinkling grass,
Rain-awakened flowers,
All that ever was
60 Joyous, and clear, and fresh, thy music doth surpass.

Teach us, sprite or bird,
What sweet thoughts are thine;

I have never heard
Praise of love or wine
65 That panted forth a flood of rapture so divine.

Chorus Hymeneal
Or triumphal chaunt
Matched with thine, would be all
But an empty vaunt—
70 A thing wherein we feel there is some hidden want.

What objects are the fountains
Of thy happy strain?
What fields, or waves, or mountains?
What shapes of sky or plain?
75 What love of thine own kind? what ignorance
of pain?

With thy clear keen joyance
Languor cannot be;
Shadow of annoyance
Never came near thee;
80 Thou lovest—but ne'er knew love's sad satiety.

Waking or asleep
Thou of death must deem
Things more true and deep
Than we mortals dream,
85 Or how could thy notes flow in such a crystal
stream?

We look before and after,
And pine for what is not;
Our sincerest laughter
With some pain is fraught;
90 Our sweetest songs are those that tell of saddest
thought.

66. CHORUS HYMENEAL—Wedding music; from Hymen, the god of marriage.

Yet if we could scorn
Hate, and pride, and fear;
If we were things born
Not to shed a tear,
95 I know not how thy joy we ever should come
near.

Better than all measures
Of delightful sound,
Better than all treasures
That in books are found,
100 Thy skill to poet were, thou scorner of the ground!

Teach me half the gladness
That thy brain must know,
Such harmonious madness
From my lips would flow,
105 The world should listen then, as I am listening now.

FOR INTERPRETATION

1. What is the general subject of the first twelve stanzas of the poem?
What is the important question asked by the poet in the last nine stanzas?
2. What are the two distinguishing qualities of the song of the skylark? (Turn to Wordsworth's poem on the same subject if you have
forgotten.) Notice how in the first part of the poem the poet emphasizes
these two qualities. What unusual simile has the poet used in the second
stanza? What qualities does it imply?
3. Why does the poet compare the lark to a "star of heaven *in the
broad daylight*"? Quote the lines that give the answer.
4. What kind of moon is the poet describing in the fifth stanza? What
kind of sky and moon in the sixth stanza? Why are these two pictures
suggestive of the lark's song? What different kind of comparison does
the poet make in the seventh stanza?
5. The seventh stanza asks a question, to which the next four stanzas
give special answers. You will note that each stanza describes something lovely that is *unseen* but that gives evidence of its presence in
some other way: the unknown poet by what? the tower-locked maiden by
what? the glow-worm by what? (Note that this is a glow-worm, not a fire-
fly.) the leaf-hidden rose by what? Why does the poet consider these
suitable similes for the skylark?
6. Why does the poet find it hard to account for the happiness of the

671

lark? Is it because all human life is sad? Or because *he* had not been
able to find happiness? Discuss.

7. Explain the phrase, "love's sad satiety." When had Shelley known
such satiety? What do lines 81–85 imply about the poet's attitude toward death and immortality? Is the thought of lines 86–90 generally
true for human beings? Do you agree with the last line—do most people like the story of Elaine better than the story of Gareth and Lynette?
or *Romeo and Juliet* better than *A Comedy of Errors?* Do you think
lines 91–96 are essentially true, or are they poetic *hyperbole?*

8. You have read two other poems about the skylark—Shakespeare's
"Hark, Hark! the Lark," and Wordsworth's "To a Skylark." If you
review them you will discover that the Shakespeare lyric overflows with
the same kind of joy as the lark. Why? What feelings or circumstances
inspired that lyric? And you will note that Wordsworth gives an explanation of what he believes the secret of the happiness of the lark. What
difference in the lives and characters of Shelley and Wordsworth would
account for the difference in their interpretation of the bird's song? Discuss. Could you choose one of the three as the *best* lyric about a skylark?
Or would you say that each has its own excellence and that there can be
no choice among them? Do you have a personal favorite, or do you
like all three? Discuss.

ODE TO THE WEST WIND

PERCY BYSSHE SHELLEY

Shelley has told us that his "Ode to the West Wind" was "conceived
and chiefly written in a wood that skirts the Arno, near Florence, Italy."
It was a day when the wind was gathering clouds for the beginning of
the autumn rains. By sunset the rains came with a tempest of hail and
with "that magnificent thunder and lightning peculiar to the . . . regions."

To appreciate the beauty of the poem, the reader should be aware of
its design, which is based upon various sets of *threes*. The wind acts
upon three things—the dead leaves of earth (Stanza I), the clouds of
heaven (Stanza II), and the waves of the sea (Stanza III). The fourth
stanza gathers together the three pictures; and in it and the last stanza
the poet presents this "wild west wind" as a symbol of himself—"tameless and swift and proud." The stanzas, like sonnets, have fourteen lines,
except that they are broken into sets of threes and a couplet, and that
the interlocking rhyming words (all but the first group) appear in sets of
threes. As you read, notice the exquisite blending of thought and design.

I

L O wild West Wind, thou breath of Autumn's being,
 Thou, from whose unseen presence the leaves dead
 Are driven, like ghosts from an enchanter fleeing,

M Yellow, and black, and pale, and hectic red,
5 Pestilence-stricken multitudes; O thou,
 Who chariotest to their dark wintry bed

D The wingèd seeds, where they lie cold and low,
 Each like a corpse within its grave, until
L Thine azure sister of the spring shall blow

10 Her clarion o'er the dreaming earth, and fill
 (Driving sweet buds like flocks to feed in air)
 With living hues and odors plain and hill;

 Wild Spirit, which art moving everywhere;
U Destroyer and preserver; hear, O hear!

II

M 15 Thou on whose stream, 'mid the steep sky's commotion,
 Loose clouds like earth's decaying leaves are shed,
 Shook from the tangled boughs of heaven and ocean,

 Angels of rain and lightning; there are spread
 On the blue surface of thine airy surge,
20 Like the bright hair uplifted from the head

 Of some fierce Mænad, even from the dim verge
 Of the horizon to the zenith's height,
 The locks of the approaching storm. Thou dirge

D Of the dying year, to which the closing night
25 Will be the dome of a vast sepulcher,
 Vaulted with all thy congregated might

 Of vapors, from whose solid atmosphere
U Black rain, and fire, and hail will burst; O hear!

III

L   Thou who didst waken from his summer dreams
30   The blue Mediterranean, where he lay,
        Lulled by the coil of his crystalline streams,

        Beside a pumice isle in Baiae's bay,
        And saw in sleep old palaces and towers
        Quivering within the wave's intenser day,

35   All overgrown with azure moss and flowers
        So sweet, the sense faints picturing them! thou
M   For whose path the Atlantic's level powers

        Cleave themselves into chasms, while far below
        The sea-blooms and the oozy woods which wear
40   The sapless foliage of the ocean, know

        Thy voice, and suddenly grow gray with fear,
        And tremble and despoil themselves; O hear!

IV

Lı   If I were a dead leaf thou mightest bear;
Gı   If I were a swift cloud to fly with thee;
Bı 45   A wave to pant beneath thy power, and share

        The impulse of thy strength, only less free
        Than thou, O uncontrollable! If even
        I were as in my boyhood, and could be

        The comrade of thy wanderings over heaven,
50   As then, when to outstrip thy skyey speed
        Scarce seemed a vision, I would ne'er have striven

21. MÆNAD—A frenzied priestess of Bacchus, the god of wine.
32. BAIAE—A site of many ruins of ancient luxury near Naples. The region is volcanic, hence "pumice" or volcanic isle.
39–42. The explanation of these lines is to be found in Shelley's notes as follows: "The phenomenon alluded to at the conclusion of the third stanza is well known to naturalists. The vegetation at the bottom of the sea, of rivers, and of lakes, sympathizes with that of the land in the change of seasons, and is consequently influenced by the winds which announce it."

As thus with thee in prayer in my sore need.
O lift me as a wave, a leaf, a cloud!
I fall upon the thorns of life! I bleed!

D 55 A heavy weight of hours has chained and bowed
One too like thee—tameless, and swift, and proud.

V

M Make me thy lyre, even as the forest is;
What if my leaves are falling like its own!
D The tumult of thy mighty harmonies

60 Will take from both a deep, autumnal tone,
Sweet though in sadness. Be thou, spirit fierce,
U My spirit! Be thou me, impetuous one!

Bɪ Drive my dead thoughts over the universe
Like withered leaves to quicken a new birth!
U 65 And, by the incantation of this verse,

Scatter, as from an unextinguished hearth
Ashes and sparks, my words among mankind!
Be through my lips to unawakened earth

The trumpet of a prophecy! O Wind,
L 70 If winter comes, can spring be far behind?

FOR INTERPRETATION

1. Why does the west wind seem symbolic of autumn? With what phrase does Shelley suggest this fact? What other things of earth besides the leaves is the wind blowing? Where? Who do you think is the west wind's "azure sister of the spring"?

2. Again Shelley shows his fondness for figures of speech. In Stanza II he uses at least four figurative representations of the clouds. Point out each of these four similes or metaphors. Which one links this stanza with the preceding one? Show how the last line of the second stanza describes part of the experience which inspired the poem.

3. Is it generally true that under-water life—both in fresh and salt water—undergoes seasonal changes? What effect does the west wind of fall have on the Mediterranean? What is the meaning of lines 33–34?

4. Show how the opening lines of the fourth stanza tie together the imagery of the first three stanzas. What other line in the stanza refers to the same three ideas? In what respects does Shelley see himself like the west wind? What prayer does he make to the wind? Why?

5. How old was Shelley when he died? How old does he sound in the first three lines of the fifth stanza? What does this last stanza tell us about the hopes and aspirations of the poet? Did his poetry have a share in bringing about social reforms? Why or why not?

6. This poem ends with one of the few hopeful notes to be found in Shelley's verse. Quote the line that promises something of joy to come. How does the first stanza of the ode prepare for this hint of hopefulness?

A LAMENT

PERCY BYSSHE SHELLEY

One July day in 1822 Shelley said, "If I die tomorrow, I have lived to be older than my father. I am ninety years of age." The next day his sailing boat capsized, and he and two companions were drowned. The two following lyrics, among the last that he wrote, echo the thought just quoted. They sound like the words of an old, old man.

O WORLD! O Life! O Time!
On whose last steps I climb,
    Trembling at that where I had stood before;
When will return the glory of your prime?
5   No more—oh, never more!

Out of the day and night
A joy has taken flight;
    Fresh spring, and summer, and winter hoar,
Move my faint heart with grief, but with delight
10   No more—oh, never more!

A DIRGE

PERCY BYSSHE SHELLEY

D*i*		ROUGH wind, that moanest loud
G*i*		Grief too sad for song;
L		Wild wind, when sullen cloud
D		Knells all the night long;
D	5	Sad storm, whose tears are vain,
M		Bare woods, whose branches strain,
D		Deep caves and dreary main,
U		Wail, for the world's wrong!

FOR INTERPRETATION

1. What words in "A Lament" sound as if Shelley had had a forewarning of his death? What words in the first stanza sound as if they had been written by an old man instead of by one of thirty years or less?

2. Do young people or old people take more delight in changing seasons? Why? What makes the second stanza of "A Lament" sound particularly tragic?

3. What is usually wrong when any one person says, "The world's wrong"? Discuss. Were the actual circumstances of Shelley's life tragic? Or were his misfortunes largely of his own making?

From ENDYMION

JOHN KEATS

It seems appropriate to preface any selections from the poetry of John Keats with the first five lines of his poem "Endymion." They are the summary of his poetic creed—in fact, of the creed of his life.

A THING of beauty is a joy forever:
    Its loveliness increases; it will never
Pass into nothingness; but still will keep
A bower quiet for us, and a sleep
5   Full of sweet dreams, and health, and quiet breathing.

FOR INTERPRETATION

The poem "Endymion" takes its name from the Greek legend of the beautiful youth beloved by Diana and therefore doomed by Jupiter to an everlasting sleep. In sleep his beauty was preserved, though Diana's love could never be fulfilled. Keats used the story as a symbol of man's unsatisfied searchings for ideal beauty.

1. Name a half dozen things generally conceded to be beautiful. Do any of these things last forever? How can their "loveliness increase"?

2. Writing about the imagination, Keats said, "What the Imagination seizes as Beauty must be Truth, whether it existed before or not. . . . The Imagination may be compared to Adam's dream; he awoke and found it truth." How does this thought help to explain the meaning of the first three lines of our selection?

3. Do psychologists believe that the restfulness of one's sleep depends upon the kind of thoughts that fill the mind before one goes to sleep? Discuss. What would be Keats's recipe for sweet and sound sleep?

ODE ON A GRECIAN URN

JOHN KEATS

Keats found his best inspiration not, as Wordsworth did in the beauty of nature, but in his own imagination and in any sort of lovely impression that touched it. From his boyhood, Greek legends and Greek literature had delighted him; and his pleasure in nature was complete when he peopled it with the dream creatures of old Greek lore. Just as enjoyment in American landscape takes on a romantic tone by our thinking of the canoes that once skimmed our lakes and the Indians that glided through our forests, so Keats liked to think of nymphs playing in mountain streams or of priests leading garlanded processions to the shrines of ancient gods.

The poet loved to study objects of ancient art, particularly classic vases with their sculptured ornaments. One marble vase had a decorative band which showed a group of men and women going to offer a sacrifice. They were playing various instruments and dancing as they went—a happy scene. And here was Keats in nineteenth-century England enjoying a holiday that had taken place two thousand years before. It was another illustration of his belief that "a thing of beauty is a joy forever." And the ode which he wrote about the vase proves that in the hands of an artist the beauty of temporal things increases. The beauty of one Greek vase in the British Museum has been made full of meaning to readers of poetry all through the world.

THOU still unravished bride of quietness,
Thou foster-child of silence and slow time,
Sylvan historian, who canst thus express
A flowery tale more sweetly than our rhyme:
5   What leaf-fringed legend haunts about thy shape
Of deities or mortals, or of both,
    In Tempe or the dales of Arcady?
What men or gods are these? What maidens loth?
What mad pursuit? What struggle to escape?
10   What pipes and timbrels? What wild ecstasy?

Heard melodies are sweet, but those unheard
Are sweeter; therefore, ye soft pipes, play on;
Not to the sensual ear, but, more endeared,
    Pipe to the spirit ditties of no tone.
15   Fair youth, beneath the trees, thou canst not leave
Thy song, nor ever can those trees be bare;
    Bold Lover, never, never canst thou kiss,
Though winning near the goal—yet, do not grieve;
She cannot fade, though thou hast not thy bliss,
20   Forever wilt thou love, and she be fair!

Ah, happy, happy boughs! that cannot shed
Your leaves, nor ever bid the Spring adieu;
And, happy melodist, unwearièd,
    Forever piping songs forever new;
25   More happy love! more happy, happy love!
Forever warm and still to be enjoyed,
    Forever panting, and forever young;
All breathing human passion far above,
That leaves a heart high-sorrowful and cloyed,
30   A burning forehead, and a parching tongue.

1. Because undisturbed and unmolested, the urn has retained its original beauty and purity.
2. So-called because it has been preserved by silence and time.
3. SYLVAN HISTORIAN—The vase. A *historian,* because it keeps a record of an ancient scene; and *sylvan* because there is a country background to the scene and because it is bordered with leaves and flowers.
7. TEMPE—A valley in Greece, famed for its beauty and sacred to Apollo, the sun god.
7. ARCADY—A district of Greece inhabited by simple, contented people. It has become a symbol of peace and happiness.

679

Who are these coming to the sacrifice?
To what green altar, O mysterious priest,
Lead'st thou that heifer lowing at the skies,
And all her silken flanks with garlands dressed?
35 What little town by river or sea shore,
Or mountain-built with peaceful citadel,
Is emptied of this folk, this pious morn?
And, little town, thy streets for evermore
Will silent be; and not a soul to tell
40 Why thou art desolate, can e'er return.

O Attic shape! Fair attitude! with brede
Of marble men and maidens overwrought,
With forest branches and the trodden weed;
Thou, silent form, dost tease us out of thought
45 As doth eternity. Cold Pastoral!
When old age shall this generation waste,
Thou shalt remain, in midst of other woe
Than ours, a friend to man, to whom thou say'st,
"Beauty is truth, truth beauty,"—that is all
50 Ye know on earth, and all ye need to know.

41. ATTIC SHAPE—The urn. "Attic" means "Athenian." Attic sculpture is marked by its simplicity and purity.
41. BREDE—Decoration.
45. PASTORAL—That which pictures rural life and scenes.

FOR INTERPRETATION

1. Read the poem through once, looking for the descriptions of the scenes carved on the vase. What are the different figures doing? Do you think the little town is represented? Why or why not? the streets? the altar? How much of what the poet describes appears on the vase? How much does his imagination supply?

2. Do you think the vase really expresses a "flowery tale more sweetly" than the poet's rhyme? That is, do you think you could read as much into the vase as he did? Discuss.

3. What are some of the instruments being played by the figures on the frieze? How can these "unheard melodies" be enjoyed? By whom? Do you think these "ditties of no tone" are sweeter than heard music? Discuss.

4. What happiness is denied to the lover on the vase? What compensating good fortune does he enjoy (lines 17-20 and 25-28)? What

words do lines 29 and 30 modify? Is there some literal truth in the thought expressed by the second and third stanzas? Discuss.

5. To what part of the scene does the fourth stanza refer? What do you think the last three lines of the stanza mean?

6. In what sense is the word *attitude* used in line 41? What likeness is there in the thoughts inspired by this centuries-old vase and by eternity (lines 44–45)? What *generation* does Keats mean in line 46? Explain the meaning of the next four lines. Have they proved to be true?

7. In the questions which follow the lines from "Endymion" there is a quotation by Keats. How does that quotation help explain the meaning of line 49? Would the so-called "realists" in art and literature agree with Keats? Do you agree with him? Discuss.

8. Express in a single sentence the theme of the ode.

ODE TO A NIGHTINGALE

JOHN KEATS

Keats is said to have sat down and written off his "Ode to a Nightingale" after returning from a walk with Fanny Brawne. It was in the late spring, not long after the death of the poet's brother. The ode compresses into its eight stanzas all the richness of a May evening. There is an undertone of sadness in keeping with the melancholy note of the nightingale. Already Keats must have known that he had not long to live. But he knew, too, how to use the "viewless wings of poesy" to carry him, for a time, away from "sorrow and leaden-eyed despair."

My heart aches, and a drowsy numbness pains
    My sense, as though of hemlock I had drunk,
Or emptied some dull opiate to the drains
    One minute past, and Lethe-wards had sunk:
5 'Tis not through envy of thy happy lot,
    But being too happy in thine happiness—
      That thou, light-wingèd Dryad of the trees,
        In some melodious plot
    Of beechen green, and shadows numberless,
10   Singest of summer in full-throated ease.

O, for a draught of vintage, that hath been
    Cooled a long age in the deep-delvèd earth,
Tasting of Flora and the country green,
    Dance, and Provençal song, and sun-burnt mirth!
15 O for a beaker full of the warm South,
    Full of the true, the blushful Hippocrene,
      With beaded bubbles winking at the brim,
        And purple-stainèd mouth;
    That I might drink, and leave the world unseen,
20   And with thee fade away into the forest dim:

Fade far away, dissolve, and quite forget
    What thou among the leaves hast never known,
The weariness, the fever, and the fret
    Here, where men sit and hear each other groan;
25 Where palsy shakes a few, sad, last gray hairs;
    Where youth grows pale, and specter-thin and dies;
      Where but to think is to be full of sorrow
        And leaden-eyed despairs;
    Where Beauty cannot keep her lustrous eyes
30   Or new Love pine at them beyond tomorrow.

    2. hemlock—A drug made from hemlock, a poisonous herb.
    4. lethe-wards—According to Greek mythology, Lethe was the river in Hades from which the blessed dead drank forgetfulness before going into the Elysian Fields. Its waters destroyed all memory of earth with its joys and sorrows and thus enabled the souls to be happy in Elysium.
    13. flora—Goddess of flowers and the spring.
    14. provençal song—Songs of the troubadours of Provençal in southern France.
    16. hippocrene—A spring sacred to the goddesses who presided over poetry, art and sciences (the Muses).

Away! away! for I will fly to thee,
　Not charioted by Bacchus and his pards,
　But on the viewless wings of Poesy,
　　Though the dull brain perplexes and retards:
35　Already with thee! tender is the night,
　And haply the Queen-Moon is on her throne,
　　Clustered around by all her starry Fays;
　　　But here there is no light,
　Save what from heaven is with the breezes blown
40　　Through verdurous glooms and winding mossy ways.

I cannot see what flowers are at my feet,
　Nor what soft incense hangs upon the boughs,
But, in embalmèd darkness, guess each sweet
　Wherewith the seasonable month endows
45　The grass, the thicket, and the fruit-tree wild;
　White hawthorne, and the pastoral eglantine;
　　Fast fading violets covered up in leaves;
　　　And mid-May's eldest child,
　The coming musk-rose, full of dewy wine,
50　　The murmurous haunt of flies on summer eves.

Darkling I listen; and, for many a time
　I have been half in love with easeful Death,
Called him soft names in many a musèd rhyme,
　To take into the air my quiet breath;
55　Now more than ever seems it rich to die,
　To cease upon the midnight with no pain,
　　While thou are pouring forth thy soul abroad
　　　In such an ecstasy!
　Still wouldst thou sing, and I have ears in vain—
60　　To thy high requiem become a sod.

Thou wast not born for death, immortal Bird!
　No hungry generations tread thee down;
The voice I hear this passing night was heard
　In ancient days by emperor and clown:

32. BACCHUS—God of wine. His chariot is often represented as being drawn
by two leopards (pards).
37. FAYS—Fairies.
60. REQUIEM—Hymn for the dead.

65   Perhaps the self-same song that found a path
      Through the sad heart of Ruth, when, sick for home,
      She stood in tears amid the alien corn;
      The same that oft-times hath
      Charmed magic casements, opening on the foam
70   Of perilous seas, in faëry lands forlorn.

      Forlorn! the very word is like a bell
      To toll me back from thee to my sole self!
      Adieu! the fancy cannot cheat so well
      As she is famed to do, deceiving elf.
75   Adieu! adieu! thy plaintive anthem fades
      Past the near meadows, over the still stream,
      Up the hill-side; and now 'tis buried deep
      In the next valley-glades.
      Was it a vision, or a waking dream?
80   Fled is that music:—Do I wake or sleep?

64. CLOWN—Peasant.
66. RUTH—In the Old Testament story, Ruth left her own land of the
Moabites to go with her mother-in-law back to Bethlehem. There in a strange
land she provided for Naomi and herself by gleaning the stalks of grain (*corn*
was the general term used for grain) left in the fields by the reapers.

FOR INTERPRETATION

1. What is the mood with which the poet begins the poem? Is it
caused by sadness or by happiness? Quote the lines that give the poet's
answer to the question. Is it possible sometimes for the heart to ache
with *too much happiness?* Who is the "light-winged Dryad of the trees"?
What words in the first stanza suggest the place and the time of year?
2. What kind of drink does the poet wish for in the second stanza?
Why? What effect does he want it to have?
3. The third stanza is a poetic summary of the woes of life. What is
the connection, if any, between the nightingale and these sorrows?
4. What common word would we use for the expression, "the viewless
wings of poesy"? The first two lines of the fourth stanza are a reference
to what wish expressed earlier in the poem? How has the poet changed
his mind? Beginning with line 35, where does the poet find himself?
What kind of night is it? Why does the poet say, "But *here* there is no
light, save _____"? Save *what?* How much light is there? Explain.
5. How can the poet tell what flowers there are? Which flowers does
he name and how does he recognize them?
6. Why does Keats call the nightingale "Darkling" (l. 51)? What is

684

the poet's attitude toward death on this May evening? How would he
like to die? Why would the nightingale's song be an appropriate *requiem?*

7. Again the poet has changed his fancy. Why does he say in lines
61–70 that we should not associate death with the nightingale? Explain
the thought of the stanza.

8. What happens to the poet in the last stanza? Explain the meaning
of lines 73–74. Why do the last lines form an appropriate conclusion to
the poem? Discuss.

9. What particular qualities of the nightingale and its song are suggested in this ode? Explain why a skylark could not have inspired this
sort of poem. Can you, nevertheless, find a line in Shelley's poem, "To
a Skylark" that might be used to describe Keats's poem? Try it.

IN A DREAR-NIGHTED
DECEMBER

JOHN KEATS

To meet death suddenly is not the hardest experience that human beings are called upon to face. It takes more courage to accept the reality
of a slowly approaching fate—a fading away from life that no human
hand can stop. It is not strange that Keats envied the winter-numbed
landscape which, too, had experienced a kind of death but without the pain
of knowing what it was losing.

D		In a drear-nighted December,
L		Too happy, happy tree,
D		Thy branches ne'er remember
		Their green felicity:
L	5	The north cannot undo them,
		With a sleety whistle through them;
		Nor frozen thawings glue them
		From budding at the prime.
D		In a drear-nighted December,
L	10	Too happy, happy brook,
M		Thy bubblings ne'er remember
		Apollo's summer look;
L		But with a sweet forgetting,
		They stay their crystal fretting,
	15	Never, never petting
		About the frozen time.

U	Ah! would 'twere so with many
	A gentle girl and boy!
G1	But were there ever any
20	Writhed not at passèd joy?
L	To know the change and feel it,
M	When there is none to heal it,
D	Nor numbèd sense to steel it,
M	Was never said in rhyme.

FOR INTERPRETATION

Before considering the following questions be sure that you know the meaning of these words: *felicity, fretting* (as it is used in line 14); *petting* (as it is used in line 15).

1. The first four lines of the poem express one advantage that Keats thinks a tree in winter has over human beings. Do you agree that the tree is happier because it cannot remember the summertime? Discuss. What do you think line 6 means? lines 7 and 8? What second advantage does the dead tree of winter have? Would every one agree that this advantage is denied to human beings? Or is there a sense in which people, too, may renew their lives? Discuss. What would Wordsworth say?

2. The second stanza repeats the thought of what part of the first stanza? What did Keats have in mind when he wrote "but with a *sweet forgetting*"?

3. Under what circumstances would Keats wish for a girl and boy the happy unconsciousness of tree and frozen brook? Does this poem of his suggest something of the feeling which he says cannot be expressed?

4. Review the facts of the lives of Byron, Shelley, and Keats. Was the tragedy in Keats's life of his own making or did it lie in circumstances which he could not control? Explain. What advantages did Byron and Shelley have which were denied to Keats? Is there bitterness in the poem "In a Drear-Nighted December" or merely tragedy? Discuss.

WHEN I HAVE FEARS THAT
I MAY CEASE TO BE

JOHN KEATS

Byron and Shelley in the last weeks before they died expressed the thought that life for them was lived out. Neither had anything left to hope for or enjoy. Keats regretted approaching death because of the things he would leave behind. In a sonnet—"When I Have Fears That I May Cease to Be"—he tells us what those two things were.

WHEN I have fears that I may cease to be
Before my pen has gleaned my teeming brain,
Before high-pilèd books, in charact'ry,
Hold like rich garners the full-ripened grain;
5   When I behold, upon the night's starred face,
Huge cloudy symbols of a high romance,
And think that I may never live to trace
Their shadows, with the magic hand of chance;
And when I feel, fair creature of an hour,
10   That I shall never look upon thee more,
Never have relish in the faery power
Of unreflecting love; then on the shore
Of the wide world I stand alone, and think
Till love and fame to nothingness do sink.

FOR INTERPRETATION

1. How much poetry did Keats believe he could produce if he could be given time in which to write it down (l. 1–4)? What two words tell us that his mind is filled with ideas for writing? What words tell us that he wanted to work over and perfect the things that he would write?

2. Which lines tell us that he had dreamed or planned the plot of some great story that he feared would never get written?

3. Which lines tell us that his second regret is in leaving the girl he loved? With what words does he refer to the girl? What do you think is the meaning of *"unreflecting* love"?

4. When Shelley thought of his own unhappiness, he wrote "Wail, for the world's wrong." When Keats thought of the things life could not give him, what did he say? Quote the lines that give the answer. What two words in the last line of the sonnet name the things Keats thought would be denied to him? Was he right about both? Discuss. Where do you think Keats was when he refers to standing "on the shore of the wide world"? What kind of thoughts could make his own misfortunes sink into "nothingness"? Discuss.

5. Is there strength or weakness in Keats's farewell to the world? courage or fear? Discuss.

EXTENDED ACTIVITIES

ROMANTICISM FLOWERED IN THE NINETEENTH CENTURY

FOR ACQUAINTANCE WITH AUTHORS

WILLIAM WORDSWORTH (1770–1850)—"THE LUCY LYRICS," "SHE WAS A PHANTOM OF DELIGHT," "LINES WRITTEN IN EARLY SPRING," "THE WORLD IS TOO MUCH WITH US," "MY HEART LEAPS UP," "TO A SKYLARK," "ODE ON IMITATIONS OF IMMORTALITY"

The quiet rhythmic movement of Wordsworth's nature lyrics hardly calls to mind the hot-headed rebel the poet was in his youth. But both the calmness and the rebellion were part of his nature and influenced his poetry. Wordsworth grew up in the Lake District—one of the loveliest stretches of country in all England. The spirit of those hills with their tarns and clear blue lakes became a part of his being, influencing him far more than anything in his formal schooling.

After the death of his parents, at the age of seventeen, he entered Cambridge where he was not too happy. Far more than his studies, he enjoyed the holidays which took him back to his solitary hills. But in spite of his protests against courses of study and the—to him—always-tedious classics, he did earn his degree. At the magic age of twenty-one, he went to France and was caught in the enthusiasm of the Revolution. For a space he was pure rebel. He fell in love with Annette Vallon, a lovely French girl, whom he wanted to marry. Both families objected, because Wordsworth had no money and no career. With youthful hot-headedness, he joined the Girondist party and seemed headed straight for the guillotine when his guardians ordered him home. He went, determined to return some day for Annette. The day never came.

The excesses of the French Revolution and the rise of Napoleon Bonaparte sobered him, as they did other English sympathizers. In 1795 a friend who had had faith in William's poetic inclinations left him a legacy of about five thousand dollars with the request that he should try to make his living at writing. He settled down with his sister Dorothy in Dove Cottage—so called because of the little Dove River near by—in his own Lake Country. When he was thirty-two, he married his cousin and childhood playmate, Mary Hutchinson. He brought his bride to Dove Cottage, where the three—William, Mary, and Dorothy—lived a completely tranquil and companionable life. The poet had the leisure he needed to roam the countryside, to think, and to write. All his finest poetry was written in Dove Cottage.

Shortly after his return from France he had met Coleridge who proved a kindred spirit. Wordsworth turned his own rebellious instincts from politics to literature, and the two friends started a revolution in poetry.

688

Their revolt was directed against the formalism of the eighteenth century and against the kind of writing sponsored by Alexander Pope and Samuel Johnson. Literature, they believed, should be a simple, sincere expression of the beauty and charm that invests everyday living. To prove the point, they published jointly a volume of poems called *Lyrical Ballads*. In the introduction they presented their theories of poetry—the theories which were to dominate the literature of England for fifty years and which would remain a kind of Bible for ro-

mantic poets always. At first the book was unnoticed except for some unfavorable criticism. It was most appreciated in America —perhaps because the American himself loved nature and so could understand the works of a man who wrote ". . . the common face of Nature spake to me rememberable things."

But slowly recognition came to Wordsworth in his own country. His beliefs were popularized by more exuberant poets like Scott and Byron. He had been given a small government post in his own county which insured him a living, and he was later able to move to a more impressive house, Rydal Mount, not far from Dove Cottage. When he was seventy-three, he was made Poet Laureate, enjoying the honor until his death at the age of eighty. His best work had been done in a score of years from 1797 on— work so impressive in its simplicity and beauty that it has affected poetic writing ever since.

SAMUEL TAYLOR COLERIDGE (1772–1834)—"KUBLA KHAN"

Literature reflects the upheavals in men's thinking. History shows that each period of complacency is followed by the appearance of small groups of men who question the state of things as they are. The few increase in strength, instituting reforms. Then again complacency rules until the cycle brings back the questioners. Coleridge as a young man belonged to the small group who questioned Alexander Pope and all the ideas in government, religion, and art which the eighteenth century had accepted. In our own day, Coleridge would have been a leader of some radical group on a school campus—youthful but much in earnest. Like Wordsworth, maturity calmed his revolt and confined his "reforms" to the field of poetry.

Coleridge had a brilliant mind. He read easily before he was four and entertained his father's friends with intelligent conversation when he was seven. The son of a vicar, he was to be educated for the ministry as were his three older brothers; but Samuel had other plans. In Cambridge at fifteen, he showed little interest in the church. He read incessantly and filled his room with earnest students who discussed Burke's latest pamphlet, argued about religion, and wrote snatches of verse.

Unconcerned about his studies, he left school and enlisted in the Dragoons but was rescued from a military career by his family. In the interlude, he met Robert Southey and the two dreamers, captivated by the French Revolution and its promises of democracy, decided that they, too, would found a new order—a "pantisocracy" on the banks of the Susque-

hanna in America. They married two sisters and planned their ideal community—only to realize that they had no money to take them to America. Southey settled down to make a business career of writing. He was so successful that much of the time thereafter he supported not only his own family but also that of his less practical brother-in-law.

Coleridge turned to writing, lecturing, journalism, and even to preaching in a Unitarian church. He always captivated his audience, but was careless about keeping appointments and collecting his fees. He had published a small volume of poems for which he was well paid, but which had little sale. Then he met Wordsworth, the stronger character who was to influence the rest of his life. The publication of *Lyrical Ballads* gave him the chance to express his revolutionary ideas about poetry and to exemplify them with some notable verse —especially with his fanciful tale, "The Rime of the Ancient Mariner."

The rest of his life was spent quietly in writing, dreaming, visiting his friends—especially the Wordsworths—and fighting ill health and drugs, which he had begun taking to relieve intense neuralgia. He grew torpid and fat, but remained an amazing conversationalist, exerting an influence equal perhaps to that of Samuel Johnson. Unfortunately there was no Boswell to write down his words. His poetry was fragmentary. Unconscious of fame, he dreamed away the last years of his life in the company and care of a friendly physician. Like his "Kubla Khan," his life seems an unfinished tale.

SIR WALTER SCOTT (1771–1832)—"JOCK O' HAZELDEAN," "SOLDIER, REST"

Not all the early Romantic writers were misunderstood and persecuted by the public they sought to please. Scott's earliest work found ready acceptance. More than that, his own charm and personality made himself and the Scottish highlands equally popular. The importance of temperament and heredity in a writer's life is illustrated in the lives of Lord Byron and Sir Walter Scott, writing contemporaries. Both were noticeably lame from childhood. Byron remained morbidly conscious of his crooked foot; Scott early adapted himself to his defect. The one disgusted all England with his sardonic temper; the other as laird of his castle on the Tweed kept open house for writers and statesmen alike. Byron died miserably in Greece while His Majesty's government placed a vessel at Scott's disposal when his physician recommended a sea voyage. Scott wrote too much and too hurriedly for his work to achieve the excellence or permanence of Byron's, but he left with his voluminous heritage of books the memory of a sweet and sympathetic character.

Born of an old Scottish Border family, Scott grew up amid the ballads and legends of the Highland clans. His lameness forced him to rely on books and stories for amusement rather than sports. At ten he had already collected a large store of ballads and tales. During his vacations from school he would ramble over the country, collecting the folklore and landscape he later popularized. Parental influence led him to the study of law at the University of Edinburgh, but he practiced only desultorily, closing up shop in good weather to set out on his beloved rambles. Appointed to the post of sheriff of Selkirkshire where the light duties and good salary pleased him, he began writing poetry in earnest. The long romantic poems were welcomed by a public  grown suddenly landscape conscious. With his marriage to the daughter of a French refugee, a promotion in office, and two successful poems, Scott's future seemed assured.

Unfortunately, the forty-year-old Scott was a far better poet than business man. Entangled with a publishing firm, he lost his entire fortune by its failure and incurred debts to over five hundred thousand dollars. The last years of his life were spent in a desperate attempt to pay back every penny. With great difficulty he kept the splendid castle he had built in the Highland country. The death of his wife and his own weakened health only added to his determination. Anonymously, to earn money speedily, he published his novel, *Waverley*, the first of a series of twenty-nine historical novels all written after he was forty-three. The novel was tremendously successful; more stories poured from the pen of "The Great Unknown." Readers snatched at each new volume offered for sale. At the time of his death he had almost completely cleared himself of his debts, but the strain had been too great on his never-robust health.

GEORGE GORDON, LORD BYRON (1788–1824)—"THE DESTRUCTION OF SEN-
NACHERIB," "SHE WALKS IN BEAUTY," "THE OCEAN"

"I have not loved the world nor the world me," despaired Byron when, as a young man he left England forever. The words were partly truth and partly pose. The world had showered favors at his feet; London society and London letters proclaimed him the greatest genius of the century. Europe agreed. But the handsome lord of the shrewish temper and maimed foot flouted fame and favor to become, by his own choice, "a wandering outlaw of his own dark mind."

Byron's character developed early a combination of passionate temper, pride, and sensitivity. His father was an unprincipled spendthrift who fled to France, leaving behind a tempestuous Scotch wife, a beautiful child with

a crippled foot, and a stack of unpaid bills. At ten the child inherited the title of "Lord Byron" and the estate of Newstead Abbey, to which he and his mother moved. The boy was badly spoiled and his mother was not a wise guardian. Most of the money coming to George was being held until he came of age, and the household was pinched for funds. Lady Byron tried one scheme after another to cure her son's limp, succeeding only in making him unhappily conscious of his defect. He determined to win attention in other ways.

In school at Harrow and then at Cambridge he excelled in boxing and swimming— and fits of temper. His title set him apart from the "commoners" and his lack of money from other young noblemen. He was shy and sensitive, but pride made him a show-off who delighted in shocking faculty and students. He was intelligent and loved to read—not a bad student when left to his own bent—but impatient of discipline, and "touchy." Nevertheless he won at college a few trusted friends who were faithful to him through the feverish years that followed.

He published "Hours of Idleness," a slight volume of verse, while he was still in college. A literary review pounced upon it and satirized the writer no less than the verses. Stung by the attack, Byron answered with "English Bards and Scotch Reviewers"—venomous satire in verses more clever than the review's. It helped along his reputation for a hot head and a heart "as hard as a Highlander's heel-piece."

Soon after his graduation, Byron received part of the money attached to his title, and he set out on a tour of Europe. Travel gave a touch of maturity to his poetry, and he really worked at the first two cantos of *Childe Harold's Pilgrimage*. Published upon his return it became immediately popular—tremendously so. Society seized upon the slim young lord with his mocking eyes who watched from the doorway while others waltzed. Ladies literally swooned at his entrance into a drawing room. Byron loved it. He entertained lavishly at Newstead Abbey, sat in the House of Lords, and conquered the hearts of scores of young women. He decided that he should marry to provide an heir to his estate. The bride should be nobly born and wealthy; and he selected quiet, intelligent, but thoroughly practical Annabella Milbanke. The two were completely incompatible. Annabella was horrified at the strange creature she had married; Byron was bored. A baby daughter was born, for whom Byron professed real affection; but his conduct grew more and more erratic. On the first anniversary of their marriage, Annabella with her daughter returned to her parents. It was a day when the appearance of married happiness must be preserved at all costs. Byron found himself ostracized from the homes that had received him like a son. With a grimace and a shrug he accepted the situation as part of his heritage from the "mad Gordons."

It was then that he left England never to return. In Switzerland he met Shelley, also an outcast, and the two rambled and talked for days. In Greece and Italy Byron was as happy as his own disposition could make him. He wrote two more cantos for *Childe Harold*. These and his other works continued to find enthusiastic sale in England, Europe, and America. His fortunes prospered, but his health was dissipated.

In Greece he became absorbed in the Greek dreams of independence. He organized a force to meet the Turks, furnishing it with his own funds. And he gave tirelessly of himself to the cause. Before he could see battle, he contracted rheumatic fever and died in camp at Missolonghi on April 19, 1824—an embittered man, "old" at thirty-six, but destined, strangely enough, to become a hero in a land not his own. Greece still honors him as a truly great man.

PERCY BYSSHE SHELLEY (1792–1822)—"THE CLOUD," "TO A SKYLARK," "ODE TO THE WEST WIND," "A LAMENT," "A DIRGE"

The parents of Percy Shelley must have been bewildered at the child they fostered. Timothy Shelley, the father—Member of Parliament; respected, thorough-going, eighteenth-century baronet—and Lady Shelley—how they both must have sighed over the auburn-haired, blue-eyed boy and wondered where ever he got his mad ideas. As for young Percy, he was quite indifferent to what they or any one else thought. The world, for him, was a place of his own making, centering about himself and his ideas. Unlike Byron, who pretended an indifference he did not feel, Shelley hardly realized that the world his family knew had cast him off.

Percy was a precocious youngster who, at the age of twelve, was doubting world systems of ethics and morality. At Eton his liberal beliefs and violent rages earned him the epithet of "Mad Shelley." The frail looking boy refused to condone the floggings of the masters and the brutal hazings of the older boys—practices then believed a necessary feature of a boy's education. Stubbornly, passionately he resisted all attempts to whip him into submission. At Oxford his shrill voice—arguing chemistry, metaphysics, German literature, theology—won him tongue-lashings from sleepy students. During his first term he had printed a pamphlet "On the Necessity of Atheism" and had had it scattered over the campus. The outraged authorities had him expelled. His father cut off the boy's allowance until he should "come to his senses." But Shelley never did.

Unconcerned, he went to London, living on donations from his sisters' pocket money sent him by a pretty classmate of theirs—Harriet Westbrook. Shelley found Harriet a good pupil for his radical ideas, until the girl discovered that she was about to be expelled from school. Then she

begged Shelley to elope with her to save her from "persecution." While both were in their teens, they were married. On a small allowance furnished by their two families, they wandered through Britain, Harriet playing at housekeeping and Shelley teaching and writing the thoughts with which he would re-make the world. Troubles brewed. Harriet was merely a pretty, not very intelligent, child. Separation was inevitable. When it came, Harriet was heartbroken and eventually died a suicide.

In the meantime Shelley had fallen in love with Mary Godwin, daughter of the radical writer, William Godwin, and of Mary Wollstonecraft, first champion of woman's rights. Shelley persuaded Mary to go with him to France; and after the death of Harriet they were married. Mary Godwin, herself a brilliant woman, made Shelley a loyal, loving wife enduring for his sake the lot of an outcast from society. She herself was a writer and later wrote the romance of *Frankenstein*.

The Shelley household, always cluttered with extra people whom the poet was befriending, had moved to Italy. There Shelley did his best work. His desk was a pine stump in the middle of a grove of trees. At meal time, some one had to hunt him out, tracking him by wads of crumpled paper that littered the forest floor. His work received little public encouragement. The poet's revolutionary ideas about religion, states' rights, morality led men to close their eyes to the beauty of his verse.

At thirty Shelley died, drowned in a storm that overturned his sailboat, the *Ariel*. Like Byron, Shelley had felt himself lived out and old. Lack of recognition had not troubled him; but he had found the earth an alien place—he was like a spirit from another world.

JOHN KEATS (1795–1821)—"ENDYMION," "ODE ON A GRECIAN URN," "ODE TO A NIGHTINGALE," "IN A DREAR-NIGHTED DECEMBER," "WHEN I HAVE FEARS"

"Beauty is truth, truth beauty—that is all ye know on earth and all ye need to know." That a consumptive young man who had grown up around a livery stable, who had lost his two favorite brothers and his mother through tuberculosis, and who had renounced the girl he loved because of his own ill health could write those shining lines is a tribute to the young romanticists at their best. It would seem to take diligent searching to find beauty in the drabness of Keats's life, but the young poet found it and preserved it in some of the most richly beautiful lines in English poetry.

John Keats was born in London, where his father kept a large stable. As a boy, John helped out about the stable and attended school at Enfield. He was an eager student; but the great schools of Eton, Harrow, Oxford, or Cambridge were not for boys like him. He was orphaned at fifteen and apprenticed to a surgeon. For nearly seven years he tried to like his profession, but books and writing were much more real to him. In 1817 he gave up medicine and surgery with the resolve to make writing his profession. His first two volumes of verse were bitterly attacked; but Keats acknowledged the faults and set about to correct them. Leigh Hunt, an older poet and editor, befriended Keats and published some of his verses in a new magazine, *The Examiner.* Lamb and Shelley, too, encouraged the promising young writer.

When Keats was twenty-three he fell in love with Fanny Brawne, a girl of eighteen. For a time the poet was overwhelmingly happy; and in the next year and a half produced his greatest poems. But in the meantime his brother Tom had died; and the dread consumptive disease had fastened itself upon John. Knowing his heritage and his poverty, he refused to consider marriage. In September, 1820, he went to Italy in an attempt to save his life; but there in February he died, four months after his twenty-fifth birthday. He was the third and youngest of a tragic group of young romanticists; but among his poems, written in less than four years' time, are some that take their place with the masterpieces of our literature. The world has wondered since what riches it lost through the fulfillment of the fate that Keats foresaw—

> "When I have fears that I may cease to be
> Before my pen has gleaned my teeming brain—"

MINOR POETS OF THE ROMANTIC PERIOD

There were other poets writing in the early nineteenth century—some of them influential in their own day, but now remembered chiefly for one or two single works or for their association with other men.

Foremost among them was Robert Southey, the friend of Wordsworth and Coleridge. He was an industrious writer, working at literature as at a trade for over fifty years and producing over one hundred volumes. His best work was done in prose; but his early ballads show promise. His several long poems are forgotten, and he is best remembered today for one brief lyric, "The Battle of Blenheim." It is a clever satire on the futility of war and would rate as a good poem in any age.

Thomas Moore, the Irishman, is remembered for three songs and for his enduring friendship with Byron. The two men became acquainted in London where Moore had gone to study law. Their love of poetry and music made a bond between them. Byron inscribed some of his poems to Moore; and Moore wrote Byron's biography. On his own account, Moore wrote songs dealing especially with sentiment and with Irish themes. The world still sings his "Minstrel Boy," "The Harp That Once Through Tara's Halls," and "Oft in the Stilly Night."

Leigh Hunt was one of the literary critics and editors who made it a policy to encourage promising new writers. He will always be remembered with gratitude for the hand he held out to John Keats. He was friendly also to the early efforts of Byron and Shelley. Hunt himself wrote steadily for thirty years, much of his work being in prose, especially in the field of literary criticism. And a few of his poems have become famous. He was the author of "Abou Ben Adhem" and "King Francis and the Lions."

Thomas Hood was a master of melody and champion of the unfortunate. His verses all have a pleasing rhythm, easy to read and easy to remember. He was particularly interested in the poor workers of Industrial England, and some of his best known poems were written in the interests of reform. There was, for example, his "Song of the Shirt" with its dull refrain of "Work—work—work!"

To name all the poets of the age would produce a long list. It was a period that had become interested in verse. Men who could turn off appropriate lyrics in an easy manner found a good market for their work. But as in other ages, the financial fortunes of the living poet proved no indication of his fame after death. Men who made good livings from their verse are now, for the most part, classed among the minor poets, if they are not completely forgotten. Men whose first works were ridiculed or ignored—Wordsworth, Coleridge, Keats among them—have positions of first rank among the English poets.

OF LITERARY FORM AND STYLE

THE ROMANTIC POETS OF THE NINETEENTH CENTURY

We have seen how the swing to romanticism began in the later eighteenth century. But it was not until the beginning of the nineteenth century that the new movement really gained headway. Blake's lyrics went almost unnoticed by his generation. Burns's poems had found enthusiastic readers in Scotland, England, and America; yet they had no apparent influence in changing the poetic fashions of the period. But in 1797, with the publication of *Lyrical Ballads* by Wordsworth and Coleridge, thought was consciously directed toward the *romantic movement*. The two writers knew what they were doing. And they explained both purpose and methods in the preface to their book.

Critics at first laughed at them. Then other poets began showing the same tendencies. Scott told some stories in verse—historic tales with rousing action laid against settings of natural beauty. The poetry was easy, almost careless, but *The Lady of the Lake* and *The Lay of the Last Minstrel* were enthusiastically received. Then Byron published the first two cantos of *Childe Harold's Pilgrimage*—glorified travelogues in Spenserian stanzas, with delightful descriptions of European scenes. The work became a best-seller overnight, captivating Europe and America as well as England. The romantic movement was established.

From 1800 to 1850 some of England's greatest poets appeared, each emphasizing some aspect of liberalism in verse. Though they were all romanticists, the work of each was marked by individual distinctions of matter and style. These are easily discernible in a study of representative works of each writer.

THE POETRY OF WORDSWORTH

Wordsworth may be considered the pace-setter of nineteenth century romanticism. A study of the characteristics of romantic literature as presented in the preceding pages, checked against the selections from Wordsworth's poetry, discloses the fact that there is scarcely a point not exemplified in the poems. There is the emphasis upon thought, the evident sincerity of feeling, freshness of inspiration, and utter simplicity of form. There is an interest in all humble commonplace things, and an understanding of the beauty that lies in human relationships and in everyday surroundings. Everything that lives or supports life becomes meaningful. In his works nature has replaced art.

It is precisely in this last respect that one finds the distinguishing feature of Wordsworth's poetry—in the fact that his inspiration came from nature and that he cultivated a natural style of expression. He does not write much about men—never about men in crowds and crowded habitations. Only one of his well known poems has its setting in the city—his "Sonnet Composed upon Westminster Bridge," and it was written early in the morning when the life of the city was asleep. Nor was Wordsworth interested—after the flare-up of his youth—in politics or world events. The world he lived in was bounded by his Windermere lakes and hills; and the folks he wrote about were solitary creatures who moved among them. He found the things of nature lovely enough to be worth portraying for their own sakes. And so he wrote about daffodils and rainbows and skylarks. He sometimes read a meaning from them; but he never used them as object lessons to clothe some hobby of his own. To him the existence of such a world was proof of the Being of God. He saw the Spirit of God manifest in all natural life; and the great lessons of courage, endurance, faith, charity, hopefulness—these were taught from the book of nature.

To appreciate Wordsworth's naturalness of style one need only compare any of his lyrics—even a deeply philosophical one like his "Ode on Immortality" with lines from Gray's "Elegy" or from Goldsmith's "The Deserted Village." Gray wrote——

> "But knowledge to their eyes her ample page
> Rich from the spoils of time did ne'er unroll;
> Chill penury repressed their noble rage,
> And froze the genial current of the soul."

He meant only, "They had no chance to go to school or to develop their talents." Wordsworth wrote——

> "Our birth is but a sleep and a forgetting:
> The soul that rises with us, our life's Star,
> Hath had elsewhere its setting,
> And cometh from afar."

There are no big words here and no strange ones. Yet the idea is immense. Wordsworth believed that ideas and images are best passed on to others in easy natural words. And he proved that it can be done.

QUESTIONS IN APPRECIATION:

Poems for Lucy

1. Point out several characteristics of romantic literature apparent in the *form* of these lyrics.

2. Which of the poems give the strongest impression of grief and loss? How has the poet given a sense of reality to this feeling?

3. Has Wordsworth proved in these lyrics that simple words may present lovely pictures and express real feeling? Discuss.

"She Was a Phantom of Delight"

1. Readers who were used to the elegance of classic literature objected to some of Wordsworth's commonplace terms. What words in the second and third stanzas of this poem do you think might have been called not "poetic"? Name at least two. How do you feel about their use? Do they add to or detract from the effectiveness of the poem? Discuss.

2. Reread the two sonnets from Spenser's "Amoretti." What are the most striking points of difference between them and this poem written for Mrs. Wordsworth? Which single lyric do you think pays the highest compliment? Why?

Nature Lyrics

1. The *poetic* quality of certain words depends upon their power to suggest more than their literal meaning. Wordsworth had skill in selecting such words, as is apparent in a lyric like "To a Skylark." What does *ethereal* mean? What other qualities does it *suggest?* Name at least four other poetically suggestive words that the poet has used in the lyric.

2. How many words in "My Heart Leaps Up" are of more than one syllable? more than two syllables? How does the size of the words compare with the size of the thought? What is a *paradox* (see the *Appendix*)? What paradox do you find in the poem? Explain it.

3. In "Lines Written in Early Spring" is the reader more interested in what Wordsworth says, or in how he says it? Reread the discussion of Wordsworth's poetry. Show why this lyric might be described as a "typical" Wordsworth poem.

4. Is "The World Is Too Much With Us" an Italian sonnet or an Elizabethan sonnet? How can you tell? In what respect do the figures of speech and the general manner of expression in this sonnet differ from those of most Wordsworth poems?

5. Do the last three poems in this group show more similarity in *thought* or in *form?* Discuss. Which one do you think presents its message most effectively? Why?

"Ode on Intimations of Immortality"

1. What is an ode (see the *Appendix*)? Does "Intimations of Immortality" meet all the qualifications of an ode? Discuss, point by point.

2. Figures of speech are used in literature (*a*) to add to the beauty of a selection, or (*b*) to present an idea more clearly. Point out three or four figures in the ode that seem to have been used merely for ornament. Point out at least four figures that help make the meaning clear.

3. For purposes of comparison, review briefly "The Rape of the Lock." Is the poetic form of Wordsworth's ode more simple or more difficult than that of "The Rape of the Lock"? Discuss. What general differences do you note in vocabulary? in sentence form? in the type of figures used? What are the most important differences in the subject matter of the two poems? What feelings are aroused by Pope's poem? What feelings are awakened by Wordsworth's? What differences do you note in the total effectiveness of the two poems? Can the same reader enjoy both poems in different ways and for different reasons? Discuss.

4. Would you consider the "Ode" the most truly representative poem, in the present group of selections, of the Wordsworth ideal of poetry? Why or why not?

Overview

1. Make a list of the subjects Wordsworth has written about in these poems. What generalization can you make about his favorite subjects?

2. How many different stanza forms has he used? Which one shows

the most finish? Which one seems most musical? Which ones seem especially well suited to the subjects and purposes of their poems?

3. How many footnotes were used in this group of poems? Compare with the number of notes in Gray's "Elegy in a Country Churchyard." How do you explain the difference?

4. Make a list of from five to ten lines, not consecutive, selected from the various poems, which for poetic effectiveness are worthy of being remembered.

5. Which poem do you like best of all? Prepare to tell why in a brief oral or written theme.

THE POETRY OF COLERIDGE

The particular romantic genius of Coleridge was an ability to clothe natural scenes with a dreamlike quality of unreality and to write of apparitions and phantom landscapes as naturally as if they were real. In imaginative inventiveness he holds first place among poets. It is unfortunate that so much of his work was left unfinished, that so many of his dreams never did get written down. "Kubla Khan" is a tantalizing fragment. "Christabel" leaves off at a point where a serial-writing novelist says "To be continued"—where suspense makes the next chapter a *must*. But the next chapter—or canto—didn't get written. We shall never know what tragedy the proposed three cantos were to unfold. We do know from "The Rime of the Ancient Mariner" that the poet could plan a complete narrative and that he could bring it to a perfect conclusion. To appreciate Coleridge at his best, one should read and reread the tale of the Mariner.

It is interesting to note that Coleridge could get all manner of weird effects by apparently artless arrangements of common words. His description of the phantom "Life-in-Death" who played at dice for the soul of the Ancient Mariner is described in the most ordinary words, but note the extraordinary effect—

"Her lips were red, her looks were free,
Her locks were yellow as gold:
Her skin was white as leprosy,
The nightmare Life-in-Death was she,
Who thicks man's blood with cold."

He has the same uncanny touch in "Christabel" and "Kubla Khan."

Coleridge's verse has more melody than Wordsworth's; but he uses the same easy rhymes and meters—usually iambic lines, rhymed in twos or threes, alternately or in succession. His short lyrics are graceful, even when touched with melancholy. His most famous poems were written in the year or two of his first association with Wordsworth; but at intervals in his later years a set of exquisite verses would appear to show that the skill was there when he had the will to use it.

QUESTIONS IN APPRECIATION:

1. Choose a single word to name or describe the mood suggested by "Kubla Khan." What is the general musical effect of the poem?

2. Most of Wordsworth's figures of speech were drawn from nature. Do Coleridge's come from the same source? Discuss.

3. Do you discern any apparent plan for the telling of the story? What kind of story do you think it would have been? Why?

4. Make a list of the most important differences between Wordsworth's poetry and Coleridge's. What points of similarity do you find?

THE WORKS OF SIR WALTER SCOTT

Sir Walter Scott holds somewhat the same place in English literature that Washington Irving holds in American letters. And we should note in passing that the two men knew and admired each other. Both, because of their genial personalities, helped to make literature popular. Both were spokesmen for a particular locality—Irving for the Dutch communities of old New York, and Scott for the Border country of his native land. And both men found the richest source of literary material to be the store of impressions gathered in their boyhood rambles over the countryside. Scott's happiest days were spent with a grandmother in the hills near the English Border. He loved to talk with the Scotch folk, drawing them out for legends and bits of local history. Many of their songs he learned. In early manhood he had hunted over every part of the scene which he used in *The Lady of the Lake*. He was devoted to his country; proud of her history and her traditions. And he made use of his accumulated lore in three important fields: in the collection and preservation of Scotch ballads; in the writing of three long narrative poems; and in the invention of the popular historical novel.

In 1765 an Irish bishop had published a remarkable work—the first collection of British folk ballads—Thomas Percy's *Reliques of Ancient English Poetry*. It made people aware of the value of this primitive oral literature. A copy of the book came into Scott's hands and was read and reread with delight. He had himself been storing up Border ballads; and in the years 1802 and 1803 he published his three-volume *Minstrelsy of the Scottish Border*. It proved an important addition to the store of folk literature. Off and on, Scott wrote original ballads in the modern manner. An enlightening comparison of the differences between the folk ballad and the literary ballad may be made by checking "Jock o' Hazeldean" against "Lochinvar." In the one we have the dialect story, whose events are suggested rather than described, leaving much for the reader to guess behind the lines. In the other we have the complete story smoothly told in easy galloping stanzas. Scott's best work in shorter poems is in the field of the ballad.

When he was in his early thirties—about seven years after Wordsworth and Coleridge had published their *Lyrical Ballads*—Scott tried an experiment. He produced *The Lay of the Last Minstrel,* a long narrative poem in Scotch setting. Its success was instantaneous. Critics were dubious about whether it was good poetry, but the people loved it. *Marmion,* three years later was equally successful; and when in 1810 his publishers put out a third poem, *The Lady of the Lake,* in a *de luxe* edition selling at about ten dollars a copy, twenty thousand books were sold. This third narrative is the best of the three poems. It tells a good story, and it presents a series of lovely pictures of the Loch Katrine country and the Trosach foothills.

And now realizing that his best gift was his ability to tell a tale, Scott turned to prose. His novels—particularly those that deal with Scotch and English history—were as sensational in their success as his poems had been. From his hands the historical novel flared into the literary scene with an appeal that it has never lost. Scott not only showed how to make men and women of history seem real; he showed also how important the background may become in a story. If *Ivanhoe, The Talisman,* and *Kenilworth* are the best of his historical novels, *The Heart of Midlothian* gives the most unforgettable picture of Scotch peasantry and Scotch womanhood. Because his novels are acknowledged his greatest contribution to literature, and because they obviously cannot be represented in an anthology of this type, Scott is here represented by a typical dialect ballad and by a song from *The Lady of the Lake.*

QUESTIONS IN APPRECIATION:

1. Review the definition of the folk ballad. (See the *Appendix.*) In what respects is "Jock o' Hazeldean" a typical folk ballad?

2. Does it seem likely, in view of the rank and wealth suggested for the family of Frank of Errington, that the person who is quoted in the first three stanzas actually spoke in dialect? Why, then, do you think the dialect is used?

3. Though the poem is short, it shows some of the elements of good story-telling. What are they?

4. For the narrative portions of *The Lady of the Lake* Scott used *iambic tetrameter.* (See the section on versification in the *Appendix.*) Why do you think he chose a different form for the various songs that appear in it? Copy "Soldier, Rest!" and mark the accented and unaccented syllables and indicate the rhyming scheme. Describe the stanza pattern of the song.

5. Do you think it a good plan to break a long narrative poem with lyrics like this one? Why or why not?

6. What touches in the song might make it a favorite with Scotch readers? Does it also appeal to the general reader? Discuss.

7. Scott realized that he was a better story teller than he was a poet. Compare these two selections by Scott with lyrics by Wordsworth, Coleridge, or Byron. Do you discover any essential poetic element lacking in Scott's work? If so, what is it?

THE POETRY OF BYRON

The poetry of Byron shows extremes to match the ups and downs of his life. There is much that is careless, cheap, or showy; much that is good; and some that is great enough to justify the praise given it in nineteenth-century Europe where Byron was hailed as the brightest star of the romantic revival.

Byron wrote easily. He was at home in every meter. His "English Bards and Scotch Reviewers," written when he was twenty, is in heroic couplets, pointed and clever as any from the pen of Dryden or Pope. And the comments, though unkind, are often all too true. He found the weak spot of each contemporary, criticizing Southey for writing too much; Wordsworth for being too, too simple; Coleridge for taking a "pixie for a muse"; Scott for writing for money. Most of his days Byron aimed shafts at the first three, partly because he did not agree with their theories of poetry, partly because he believed their shifts from the liberal politics of their youth to the conservatism of middle age was a "selling out" process. Byron was enough younger to remain a hot-headed radical, contemptuously intolerant of changing viewpoints. To Scott Byron later apologized.

And yet Byron—though he would have admitted no influence from the Wordsworth-Coleridge type of poetry—almost at once slipped away from the Dryden-Pope style which he had admired as a school boy. Like Wordsworth, he found his greatest inspiration in nature; like Southey he had a facility for writing on any subject for any occasion. He had a natural sense of rhythm which guided him to the right forms for the right subjects. He had the ear and eye and spirit of a poet—and sometimes the heart of one. When his feelings were aroused he could write glowingly. His "The Prisoner of Chillon" with its preceding sonnet tells its story simply and touchingly. It will always be a favorite. *Childe Harold* has passages of unusual beauty and has contributed a surprising number of expressions into the currency of daily speech—"merry as a marriage bell"; "on with the dance, let joy be unconfined"; "and he, their sire, butchered to make a *Roman holiday*"—these and many, many more are evidence of his skill with words. And there is a pleasing color and vitality about all his best work.

Common criticisms are that he liked to see himself as the hero of his poems; that he was often careless; that he let politics and prejudice override poetic taste; and that he is often stagey and affected rather than sincere. There was a time when few people could judge Byron impartially; some praised him—and his works—extravagantly, and sympathized with his unfortunate fate; others condemned him utterly and discounted his works because of his life. The present sees him as a man of great talent who sometimes used it well; as a man of personal charm, sometimes sinned against, but more often sinning; as one who tossed aside the greatest opportunities that came to him and fed his soul on husks of bitterness. Something of all this is in his poetry. The best of his work is very good indeed; the rest can be forgotten.

QUESTIONS IN APPRECIATION:

"The Destruction of Sennacherib"

1. There are six striking similes in "The Destruction of Sennacherib." Point out each one. Do you think the use of these similes adds to the effectiveness of the poem? Discuss. (See the humorous verses by Ogden Nash, "Very Like a Whale," in PROSE AND POETRY OF AMERICA. Do you think Nash is justified in his references to this poem? Why or why not?)

2. There are also a number of striking metaphors. How many do you find? List them.

3. What is the general rhythmic effect of the poem? How has Byron gained this particular effect?

4. Why do you think the poem is unusually easy to memorize? Why do you think the adjectives "colorful" and "picturesque" are used to describe such a poem?

"She Walks in Beauty"

1. There is unusual poetic appeal in the two opening lines of "She Walks in Beauty." What creates this poetic effect? Why, for instance, are they more effective than the simple statement, "She is as beautiful as night"? Discuss.

2. What keeps the description from being somber? Is there anything "bright" about night? What are the points of brightness in the portrait?

3. What mood does the poem create? Point out several words or phrases which help to suggest that mood.

4. Do you think that Byron was wise not to make this lyric a description of any one heroine? not to mention directly his source of inspiration? Discuss.

"The Ocean"

1. Byron said that he chose the Spenserian stanza for *Childe Harold's Pilgrimage* because it was a verse form suited to any mood and any subject. Do you think that it was an effective form to use for this passage about the ocean? Would a simple stanza like that in Wordsworth's "Lines Written in Early Spring" have done as well? Would heroic couplets have been better? or blank verse? Discuss.

2. Do all seven stanzas present the same mood? If not, indicate the ones that are different and name the moods for each.

3. Byron again has shown his ability to use figurative language with powerful effect. Choose what you think are the four finest figures in the passage, and be prepared to explain them.

4. What characteristics of romantic literature do you find in the stanzas on "The Ocean"? Are there any passages in which Byron has expressed

views similar to those of other romantic poets like Wordsworth and
Coleridge and Scott? Discuss.

5. What evidence do you find that Byron wrote *Childe Harold's Pilgrimage* thoughtfully and seriously? What blemish mars this particular
passage from it? Which lines from this selection have you heard quoted?

6. Select at least one stanza for memorization.

Overview

1. Compare the forms in which the various poems by Byron are written. Does he show a fondness for any particular style? Or does he
vary the form to suit the subject?

2. In which of these poems does the poet appear to speak for himself?
Which poem is most personal? Does Byron seem to present himself
fairly, or is the picture overdrawn? Discuss.

3. Though Byron professed to scorn the works of the romantic "Lake
Poets"—Wordsworth, Coleridge and Southey—he is always classed with
them as a romantic poet. What are the most important romantic qualities to be found in his work? What are the important differences between his work and the works of Wordsworth and Coleridge?

4. It was Byron's rising fame as a poet that decided Scott to turn
from poetry to prose. Judging by the selections you have read from the
works of both, would you say that Byron was the better poet? Discuss.

THE POETRY OF SHELLEY

The poetry of Shelley is distinguished, first of all, by its exquisite
music. Everything he wrote sings with melody. He was a natural poet,
possessing the instinctive lyric power of the lark he envied. But he was
also an artist, knowing his poetic forms and using them expertly. There
is rich variety in his works. He loved to try new combinations of rhyme
and rhythms. He was master of the old forms too—blank verse, the
sonnet (though he felt it stiff), and the Spenserian stanza which he used
with surpassing beauty for "Adonais," the elegy written for Keats. Nor
can it be said that Shelley sacrificed meaning for form. There is superb
blending of sense, mood, and melody in all his verse.

The limitations of his poetry are found in the limitations of his philosophy. He never did find the answers he sought to the riddles of the
universe. And so he made his exit from life weeping. There is an under-
current of sadness in even his loveliest lyrics. He could not quite fulfill
the aspirations expressed in his "Ode to the West Wind"—"scatter my
words among mankind . . . to quicken a new birth." He had discovered
no secret meaning. There was nothing for him to pass on except his own
intense appreciation of everything that was lovely to eye or ear or heart;
but that one thing he could do with a skill no writer has surpassed. To
interpret the loveliness was beyond his power. He had no key. As one
critic has put it, Shelley merely *"lost himself"* in nature."

QUESTIONS IN APPRECIATION:

"The Cloud"

1. It is worth while to note the special devices which Shelley has used to secure the effect of dancing melody in "The Cloud." If you mark the accented and unaccented syllables, you will see that he has combined feet of two and three syllables—usually *iambics* with *anapests*. It is the extra unaccented syllables that give the lilt to the lines. And if you study the rhyming scheme you will note that each long line has a rhyming word within it. With these suggestions in mind, work out the pattern for the first stanza. Indicate the number of feet to a line, and the rhyming scheme. How has Shelley varied this pattern in the following stanzas? In general is the pattern the same throughout?

2. There are so many metaphors and similes in Shelley's verse that it is impractical to try to discuss them all. One should merely observe the effect of the figures as a whole and note the most striking ones. "The Cloud" is, of course, an example of extended *personification*. In addition to this main figure, what similes and metaphors are used of the cloud itself? Point out several of each. Shelley also liked to make use of the devices of *alliteration* and *onomatopoeia*. Do you think that the use of so many different figures is poetically effective? Or is it confusing?

3. Be prepared to discuss orally or in writing the poetic effect of Shelley's figurative language.

4. The fourth stanza of this poem is considered one of the most musical combinations of words in the English language. Since its general pattern is about the same as that of the other stanzas, how do you account for the especially melodious quality of these lines? Is the imagery of the stanza in keeping with its delightful sound effects? Discuss.

5. Will familiarity with this poem increase your enjoyment of cloud "sky-scapes"? Does an understanding of the poem give one anything besides the *pleasure* of its pictures and sound effects? Discuss.

"To a Skylark"

1. Shelley invented an unusual stanza for his "To a Skylark"—a stanza that seems to imitate, or at least suggest, the spiral flight of the bird. If you scan the lines, you will discover that four short lines of each stanza are *trochaic trimeter* and that the long line is *iambic hexameter*. Trochaic and iambic feet are seldom combined into a rhythmic pattern; yet notice how effective the form is for this particular poem. Pick out the single stanza which seems to you best to represent the *soaring flight* of the bird. Which one stanza sounds most *joyous*? Which one sounds most *richly melodious*? Which one sounds *saddest*? How has the poet secured these different effects with the same stanza pattern? Discuss.

2. Probably no other poet has used so many different similes so well in so few lines as did Shelley for his skylark. Count the number of similes that appear in the first twelve stanzas. Why is the effect not confusing?

Why did the poet not continue the use of similes in the last nine stanzas? What are the most poetic metaphors in the lyric? (Point out at least six.) Are these metaphors used of the lark itself, or of surrounding details or circumstances? Cite some examples to prove your answer. What other figures of speech do you find in the poem? (Check with the list in the *Appendix*.)

"Ode to the West Wind"

1. Study carefully the form of the "Ode to the West Wind." How does the stanza differ from a sonnet? How does it resemble a sonnet? What special name is given to the three-line interlocking rhyming pattern—aba bcb cdc, and so on? (See *Appendix*.)

2. Point out the ways in which Shelley has shaped his thoughts in accordance with a definite design. In what respects does the ode come closer to perfection of form than either of the two preceding poems? In what respects is the ode similar to the two preceding poems?

3. Even though there is evidence of great care in the construction of this ode and a kind of perfection in its form, it is a *romantic* poem. Why? With what other romantic writers may Shelley be compared—in subject, style, mood? Discuss.

"A Lament" and "A Dirge"

What well-known American poet somewhat resembles Shelley in the form and tone of his verse? Do you think he may have drawn part of his inspiration from Shelley? Why or why not?

Overview

1. Which of Shelley's poems has the happiest tone? Which has the saddest? Which shows the most careful design? Which seems to have the most natural rhythm and form? Which shows the most effective use of figures of speech? Which seems the most sincere expression of the poet's thought and feeling? Which poems indicate his failure to find a satisfactory answer to the questions of life? Which best exemplify his skill in reproducing the beauties of nature? Which poem do you like the best? Why?

2. Which other poet that you have studied shows the same sense of dissatisfaction and despair? Is there any other poet who approaches Shelley in the musical quality of his verse? Discuss. What are the most apparent differences between Wordsworth's poetry and Shelley's? How do you account for these differences?

THE POETRY OF KEATS

The poetry of John Keats is remarkable for the richness of its poetic effects. Keats had the temperament of a poet. His was the gift of finding beauty and meaning in every circumstance of life. He had besides a natural gift for poetic expression. And finally, he was possessed of a devotion to poetry that made him take infinite pains with everything he wrote. The result is that his works give an impression of concentrated poetry—like a thick, heavy syrup or a rich, exotic preserve. One does not sit down to read pages of Keats at a time, as one may read Scott or Byron. Rather one reads in small portions, tasting slowly to get the full flavor of every line and phrase.

The perfection of Keats's expression is matched by a fine idealism of thought. There is the same singleness of direction in his thinking that there is in Wordsworth. Where the older poet may be said to have worshiped at the shrine of Nature, Keats worshiped Beauty. He believed that man's highest mission was to find the beauty that does exist in the world, to give expression to it, to preserve it, and whenever possible to create new beauty. Any hardship or sorrow or suffering could be borne if one could find in it some deep, true meaning, or could clothe it with loveliness. From the earliest of his poems, such as the sonnet "On the Grasshopper and Cricket," to his last published volume with its odes on the nightingale and a Grecian urn, this one theme shines clear like a thread of gold.

Like the other romanticists, Keats appreciated nature. His descriptions of the natural scene are passages of exquisite loveliness. But he also found stimulation in the works of other writers. Spenser, Shakespeare—especially the sonnets—English translations of the Greek poets, medieval legends—these were enchanted reading to him. His narrative and dramatic poems reflect both medieval and classic themes. "The Eve of St. Agnes"—a luxurious telling of an old legend in Spenserian stanzas—and "Hyperion"—an unfinished Grecian drama in blank verse—these are evidence of his ability to clothe old themes in enchanting new dress. One wonders what tale it was he saw traced in the heavens—his "huge, cloudy symbols of a high romance." Another medieval legend? Perhaps. But our regrets that Keats could not live out his poetic destiny is matched with grateful wonder that in four years of serious writing, he could give to the world so much pure poetry. Be sure that if you have any poetic sense, the beauty of Keats's works will grow upon you through the years.

QUESTIONS IN APPRECIATION:

From "Endymion"

1. How can you tell that "Endymion" is not written in blank verse? How can you tell that it is not written in heroic couplets? The first four lines give you the clue to its form. How would you describe it?

2. Why do you think the first line of the poem has become such a familiar quotation? Discuss.

"Ode on a Grecian Urn"

1. What is the general poetic effect of the poem? Does it use as many

figures of speech as Shelley's poems do? Does it appeal especially (a) to the senses, (b) to the mind, (c) to the emotions, (d) to the imagination? Or does it appeal to a combination of two or more? Discuss.

2. Which lines in the poem do you think especially true? Which lines are especially lovely? Which lines should you remember always? Why?

"Ode to a Nightingale"

1. The beauty of some poetry is apparent at first reading. There is other poetry that seems to increase in beauty as one becomes more and more familiar with it. In which group would you place the poetry of Keats? Why? Is Keats's "Ode to a Nightingale" easy to understand? Does it repay study? Discuss. Do you think it would have greater appeal to old people or to young folks? Why?

2. You have undoubtedly noticed that Keats was not as fond of similes as were Byron and Shelley. He did, however, use many metaphors. And he specialized in a figure called the *transferred epithet*—that is, the use of an adjective or modifying phrase, not before the word it logically modifies, but before a word associated with it in meaning. For example in the seventh stanza of the ode, Keats speaks of the *"alien corn."* But it was Ruth who was the alien; the grain was native to the fields of Bethlehem. This is a *transferred epithet*. Point out at least four other examples of this figure from the poem.

3. Does a poem like the "Ode to a Nightingale" make the reader *think* as well as *feel?* There is sadness in the ode. Is there also *despair*—as in Shelley's last lyrics?

4. What evidence is there in the ode that Keats considered the *form* of poetry important? Judging by the ode, would you say that Keats is a *pure* romanticist? Or does his work show a blending of classic and romantic qualities? Discuss.

"In a Drear-Nighted December"

1. Keats has used an ingenious stanza form for this lyric. Indicate the pattern of rhythm and rhyme. The last word of the last line of each stanza rhymes with what other word? What is the poetic effect of this form?

2. What feeling does the poem leave with the reader? Why?

"When I Have Fears That I May Cease to Be"

1. Does Keats's sonnet fulfill all the requirements of the ideal sonnet?

2. Point out the most expressive figures of speech in the sonnet and explain them. What is there that lifts this sonnet above mere "prettiness" of expression and makes it worthy of the name *poetry* rather than *verse?*

Overview

1. How does the poetic form of Keats's works compare in general with the poetic form of the other romanticists? In answering the question,

keep in mind these points—the kind of words he uses; the kind of stanza forms he favors; the choice of poetic ornaments, figures of speech, and the like. Compare, for example, the stanza form of Keats's two odes with the form of Wordsworth's ode on immortality. Compare his vocabulary with that of Wordsworth or Coleridge; and his rhythms with those of Scott or Byron.

2. One commentator has said that Keats "has enriched the poetic vocabulary more than any other writer since Milton," mentioning such expressions as the "deep-damasked wings" of the moth and the "calm-throated thrush." Make a list of ten expressions of similar poetic quality and appeal.

3. In how many of the poems you have read by Keats does his theme deal directly with *beauty*? Name the poems. In how many of Keats's poems has the author contrived to give beauty to thoughts that concern suffering or pain? What is the usual tone of Keats's poetry? Discuss.

4. In how many of the poems that you know has Keats referred to Grecian ideals or subjects? In what respects does he show himself familiar with the works of other poets? Discuss.

5. *For Extra Credit*: Read and prepare an oral report on Keats's narrative, "The Eve of St. Agnes." Bring a copy of the poem to class with you and be prepared to read two or three stanzas from it by way of illustration when you make your report.

6. What do you think you will remember about the poetry of Keats? Do you think that in general older people enjoy Keats more than pupils of high school age? Why or why not?

FOR FURTHER READING

BARRINGTON, E., *Glorious Apollo* (Byron)
COLVIN, SIDNEY, *John Keats, His Life and Poetry*
DE SELICOURT, ERNEST, *Dorothy Wordsworth*
DRINKWATER, JOHN, *The Pilgrim of Eternity* (Byron)
HALL, HOWARD JUDSON, ed., *Selected Poems of William Wordsworth*
KNIGHT, W. A., *Through the Wordsworth Country*
LOWELL, AMY, *John Keats*
MAUROIS, ANDRE, *Ariel* (Shelley); *Byron*
RANNIE, D. W., *Wordsworth and His Circle*
RIVES, AMALIE, *The Castaway* (Byron)
SCOTT, SIR WALTER, *The Lady of the Lake*
TRELAWNEY, E. J., *Records of Byron, Shelley, and the Author*
WINCHESTER, C. T., *Wordsworth, How to Know Him*
WYLIE, ELINOR, *Orphan Angel* (Shelley)

VIII

Prose writers developed the familiar essay and the novel.

A DISSERTATION UPON ROAST PIG

CHARLES LAMB

Before the American Indian introduced wild turkey to the white man, the Englishman's favorite holiday dish was roast pig. Not roast pork, mind you, but young pig—from three to six weeks old—roasted whole with appropriate stuffing and served with a festive apple in his mouth! One who has enjoyed the tender sweetness of a crisply browned loin of pork can easily imagine the delicacy of its baby brother. 'Tis small wonder that Lamb was inspired to rhapsodize in its praise.

In the opening paragraphs, Lamb qualifies as a member of the "tall-story club." We can see the twinkle in his eye as he gravely recounts the wasteful method by which man learned to cook his food. There's an idea to speculate upon! How *did* man first get the idea of cooking his meat? There may be logical flaws in Lamb's explanation, but it makes a right good tale.

MANKIND, says a Chinese manuscript, which my friend M—[1] was obliging enough to read and explain to me, for the first seventy thousand ages ate their meat raw, clawing or biting it from the living animal, just as they do in Abyssinia to this day. This period is not obscurely hinted at by their great Confucius [2] in the second chapter of his *Mundane Mutations,* where he designates a kind of golden age by the term *Cho-fang,* literally the Cook's holiday. The manuscript goes on to say that the art of roasting, or rather broiling (which I take to be the elder brother), was accidentally discovered in the manner following. The swineherd, Ho-ti, having gone out into the woods one morning, as his manner was, to collect mast for his hogs, left his cottage in the care of his eldest son, Bo-bo, a great lubberly

---

[1] M—Thomas Manning. The Chinese manuscript is, of course, purely imaginative.

[2] CONFUCIUS—Famous Chinese philosopher and teacher (551–478 B.C.). The allusion is used to give an air of authenticity to the tale.

boy, who being fond of playing with fire, as younkers of his age commonly are, let some sparks escape into a bundle of straw which, kindling quickly, spread the conflagration over every part of their poor mansion, till it was reduced to ashes. Together with the cottage (a sorry antediluvian makeshift of a building, you may think it), what was of much more importance a fine litter of new-farrowed pigs, no less than nine in number, perished. China pigs have been esteemed a luxury all over the East from the remotest periods that we read of. Bo-bo was in utmost consternation, as you may think, not so much for the sake of the tenement,[3] which his father and he could easily build up again with a few dry branches, and the labor of an hour or two, at any time, as for the loss of the pigs. While he was thinking what he should say to his father, and wringing his hands over the smoking remnants of one of these untimely sufferers, an odor assailed his nostrils, unlike any scent which he had before experienced. What could it proceed from?—not from the burnt cottage—he had smelt that smell before—indeed this was by no means the first accident of the kind which had occurred through the negligence of this unlucky young firebrand. Much less did it resemble that of any known herb, weed, or flower. A premonitory moistening at the same time overflowed his nether lip. He knew not what to think. He next stooped down to feel the pig, if there were any signs of life in it. He burnt his fingers, and to cool them he applied them in his booby fashion to his mouth. Some of the crumbs of the scorched skin had come away with his fingers, and for the first time in his life (in the world's life indeed, for before him no man had known it) he tasted—*crackling!* Again he felt and fumbled at the pig. It did not burn him so much now, still he licked his fingers from a sort of habit. The truth at length broke into his slow understanding, that it was the pig that smelt so, and the pig that tasted so delicious; and, surrendering himself up to the newborn pleasure, he fell to tearing up whole handfuls of the scorched skin with the flesh next to it, and was cramming it down his throat in his beastly fashion, when his sire entered amid the smoking rafters, armed with retributory cudgel, and finding how affairs stood, began to rain blows upon the young rogue's shoulders, as thick as hailstones, which Bo-bo heeded

[3] TENEMENT—Here, merely "dwelling."

not any more than if they had been flies. The tickling pleasure, which he experienced in his lower regions, had rendered him quite callous to any inconveniences he might feel in those remote quarters. His father might lay on, but he could not beat him from his pig, till he had fairly made an end of it, when, becoming a little more sensible of his situation, something like the following dialogue ensued.

"You graceless whelp, what have you got there devouring? Is it not enough that you have burnt me down three houses with your dog's tricks, and be hanged to you, but you must be eating fire, and I know not what—what have you got there, I say?"

"O, father, the pig, the pig, do come and taste how nice the burnt pig eats."

The ears of Ho-ti tingled with horror. He cursed his son, and he cursed himself that ever he should beget a son that should eat burnt pig.

Bo-bo, whose scent was wonderfully sharpened since morning, soon raked out another pig, and fairly rending it asunder, thrust the lesser half by main force into the fists of Ho-ti, still shouting out, "Eat, eat, eat the burnt pig, father, only taste—O Lord,"— with such-like barbarous ejaculations, cramming all the while as if he would choke.

Ho-ti trembled in every joint while he grasped the abominable thing, wavering whether he should not put his son to death for an unnatural young monster, when the crackling scorching his fingers, as it had done his son's, and applying the same remedy to them, he in his turn tasted some of its flavor, which, make what sour mouths he would for a pretense, proved not altogether displeasing to him. In conclusion (for the manuscript here is a little tedious) both father and son fairly sat down to the mess, and never left till they had dispatched all that remained of the litter.

Bo-bo was strictly enjoined not to let the secret escape, for the neighbors would certainly have stoned them for a couple of abominable wretches, who could think of improving upon the good meat which God had sent them. It was observed that Ho-ti's cottage was burnt down now more frequently than ever. Nothing but fires from this time forward. Some would break out in broad day, others in the nighttime. As often as the sow farrowed, so sure was the house of Ho-ti to be in a blaze; and Ho-ti himself, which was the more remarkable, instead of chastising his son, seemed to grow more indulgent to him than ever. At length they were watched, the terrible mystery discovered, and father and son summoned to take their trial at Pekin,[4] then an inconsiderable assize town. Evidence was given, the obnoxious food itself produced in court, and verdict about to be pronounced, when the foreman of the jury begged that some of the burnt pig, of which the culprits stood accused, might be handed into the box. He handled it, and they all handled it, and burning their fingers, as Bo-bo and his father had done before them, and Nature prompting to each of them the same remedy, against the face of all the facts, and the clearest charge which judge had ever given,—to the surprise of the whole court, townsfolk, strangers, reporters, and all present—without leaving the box, or any manner of consultation, whatever, they brought in a simultaneous verdict of Not Guilty.

The judge, who was a shrewd fellow, winked at the manifest iniquity of the decision; and, when the court was dismissed, went privily, and bought up all the pigs that could be had for love or money. In a few days his Lordship's town house was observed to be on fire. The thing took wing, and now there was nothing to be seen but fires in every direction. Fuel and pigs grew enormously dear all over the district. The insurance offices one and all shut up shop. People built slighter and slighter every day, until it was

[4] PEKIN—Now Peiping, a principal city of northern China.

feared that the very science of architecture would in no long time be lost to the world. Thus this custom of firing houses continued, till in process of time, says my manuscript, a sage arose, like our Locke,[5] who made a discovery, that the flesh of swine, or indeed of any other animal, might be cooked (*burnt*, as they called it) without the necessity of consuming a whole house to dress it. Then first began the rude form of a gridiron. Roasting by the string, or spit, came in a century or two later, I forget in whose dynasty. By such slow degrees, concludes the manuscript, do the most useful, and seemingly the most obvious arts, make their way among mankind.

Without placing too implicit faith in the account above given, it must be agreed that if a worthy pretext for so dangerous an experiment as setting houses on fire (especially in these days) could be assigned in favor of any culinary object, that pretext and excuse might be found in Roast Pig.

Of all the delicacies in the whole *mundus edibilis*,[6] I will maintain it to be the most delicate—*princeps obsoniorum*.[7]

I speak not of your grown porkers—things between pig and pork—those hobbydehoys—but a young and tender suckling—under a moon old—guiltless as yet of the sty—with no original speck of the *amor immunditiæ* [8] the hereditary failing of the first parent, yet manifest—his voice as yet not broken, but something between a childish treble, and a grumble—the mild forerunner or *præludium,* of a grunt.

He must be roasted. I am not ignorant that our ancestors ate them seethed, or boiled but what a sacrifice of the exterior tegument!

There is no flavor comparable, I will contend, to that of the crisp, tawny, well-watched, not over-roasted, *crackling,* as it is well called—the very teeth are invited to their share of the pleasure at this banquet in overcoming the coy, brittle resistance—with the adhesive oleaginous—O call it not fat—but an indefinable sweetness growing up to it—the tender blossoming of fat—fat cropped in the bud—taken in the shoot—in the first innocence—the cream and quintessence of the child-pig's yet pure food—the lean, no lean, but a kind of animal manna—or, rather, fat and lean (if it

[5] LOCKE—John Locke (1632–1704), an English philosopher.
[6] *Mundus edibilis*—World of food, eatables.
[7] *Princeps obsoniorum*—Chief of dainties.
[8] *Amor immunditiæ*—Love of dirt.

must be so), so blended and running into each other, that both together make but one ambrosian result, or common substance.

Behold him, while he is doing—it seemed rather a refreshing warmth, than a scorching heat, that he is so passive to. How equably he twirleth round the string!—Now he is just done. To see the extreme sensibility of that tender age, he hath wept out his pretty eyes—radiant jellies—shooting stars——

See him in the dish, his second cradle, how meek he lieth!—wouldst thou have had this innocent grow up to the grossness and indocility which too often accompany maturer swinehood? Ten to one he would have proved a glutton, a sloven, an obstinate, disagreeable animal—wallowing in all manner of filthy conversation—from these sins he is happily snatched away—

> Ere sin could blight, or sorrow fade,
> Death came with timely care—[9]

his memory is odoriferous—no clown curseth, while his stomach half rejecteth, the rank bacon—no coal-heaver bolteth him in reeking sausages—he hath a fair sepulchre in the grateful stomach of the judicious epicure—and for such a tomb might be content to die.

He is the best of sapors. Pineapple [10] is great. She is indeed almost too transcendent—a delight, if not sinful, yet so like to sinning, that really a tender-conscienced person would do well to pause—too ravishing for mortal taste, she woundeth and excoriateth the lips that approach her—like lovers' kisses, she biteth—she is a pleasure bordering on pain from the fierceness and insanity of her relish—but she stoppeth at the palate [11]—she meddleth not with the appetite—and the coarsest hunger might barter her consistently for a mutton chop.

Pig—let me speak his praise—is no less provocative of the appetite, than he is satisfactory to the criticalness of the censorious palate. The strong man may batten on him, and the weakling refuseth not his mild juices.

Unlike to mankind's mixed characters, a bundle of virtues and vices, inexplicably intertwisted, and not to be unraveled without hazard, he is good throughout. No part of him is better

---

[9] These lines are from Coleridge's "Epitaph on an Infant."
[10] PINEAPPLE—A rare delicacy in eighteenth-century England.
[11] SHE STOPPETH AT THE PALATE—Pleases the taste without satisfying one's hunger.

or worse than another. He helpeth, as far as his little means extend, all around. He is the least envious of banquets. He is all neighbors' fare.

I am one of those who freely and ungrudgingly impart a share of the good things of this life which fall to their lot (few as mine are in this kind) to a friend. I protest I take as great an interest in my friend's pleasures, his relishes, and proper satisfactions, as in mine own. "Presents," I often say, "endear Absents." Hares, pheasants, partridges, snipes, barndoor chickens (those "tame villatic fowl" [12]), capons, plovers, brawn, barrels of oysters, I dispense as freely as I receive them. I love to taste them, as it were, upon the tongue of my friend. But a stop must be put somewhere. One would not, like Lear,[13] "give everything." I make stand upon pig. Methinks it is an ingratitude to the Giver of all good flavors, to extra-domiciliate,[14] or send out of the house, slightly (under pretext of friendship, or I know not what), a blessing so particularly adapted, predestined, I may say, to my individual palate—it argues an insensibility.

I remember a touch of conscience in this kind at school. My good old aunt, who never parted from me at the end of a holiday without stuffing a sweetmeat, or some nice thing, into my pocket, had dismissed me one evening with a smoking plum-cake, fresh from the oven. On my way to school (it was over London Bridge) a gray-headed old beggar saluted me (I have no doubt at this time of day that he was a counterfeit). I had no pence to console him with, and in the vanity of self-denial, and the very coxcombry of charity, schoolboy like, I made him a present of—the whole cake. I walked on a little, buoyed up, as one is on such occasions, with a sweet soothing of self-satisfaction; but before I had got to the end of the bridge, my better feelings returned, and I burst into tears, thinking how ungrateful I had been to my good aunt, to go and give her good gift away to a stranger, that I had never seen before, and who might be a bad man for aught I knew; and then I thought of the pleasure my aunt would be taking in thinking that I—I myself, and not another—would eat her nice cake—and what should I say to her

[12] "TAME VILLATIC FOWL"—From John Milton's *Samson Agonistes.*
[13] LEAR—The tragic hero of Shakespeare's *King Lear,* who gave up his kingdom to his children before his death.
[14] EXTRA-DOMICILIATE—Lamb uses an Anglicized expression in its literal Latin meaning, translating it for the reader in the following words.

the next time I saw her—how naughty I was to part with her pretty present—and the pleasure and the curiosity I had taken in seeing her make it, and her joy when she sent it to the oven, and how disappointed she would feel that I had never had a bit of it in my mouth at last—and I blamed my impertinent spirit of alms-giving, and out-of-place hypocrisy of goodness, and above all I wished never to see the face again of that insidious good-for-nothing, old gray imposter.

Our ancestors were nice in their method of sacrificing these tender victims. We read of pigs whipped to death with something of a shock, as we hear of any other obsolete custom. The age of discipline is gone by, or it would be curious to inquire (in a philosophical light merely) what effect this process might have towards intenerating and dulcifying a substance, naturally so mild and dulcet as the flesh of young pigs. It looks like refining a violet. Yet we should be cautious, while we condemn the inhumanity, how we censure the wisdom of the practice. It might impart a gusto——

I remember an hypothesis, argued upon by the young students, when I was at St. Omer's,[15] and maintained with much learning and pleasantry on both sides, "Whether, supposing that the flavor of a pig who obtained his death by whipping (*per flagellationem extremam*) superadded a pleasure upon the palate of a man more intense than any possible suffering we can conceive in the animal, is man justified in using that method of putting the animal to death?" I forget the decision.

His sauce[16] should be considered. Decidedly, a few bread crumbs, done up with his liver and brains, and a dash of mild sage. But banish, dear Mrs. Cook, I beseech you, the whole onion tribe. Barbecue your whole hogs to your palate, steep them in shalots, stuff them out with plantations of the rank and guilty garlic; you cannot poison them, or make them stronger than they are—but consider, he is a weakling—a flower.

[15] ST. OMER'S—An imaginative touch. Lamb attended a charity school not, by the way, "over London Bridge."
[16] HIS SAUCE—Dressing.

DID YOU READ WITH UNDERSTANDING?

1. The subject matter of Lamb's discussion on roast pig is clearly divided into two parts. What is the general subject of the first part of the essay? Are both parts of the essay humorous? Discuss.

2. Tell briefly the story of Bo-bo and the "burnt pigs." Aside from the intentional absurdities of the story, there is one point that makes it seem very unlikely that man learned to cook his meat by accidentally tasting *burnt* pig. What is the flaw? Discuss.

3. How was meat roasted in Lamb's day? Why must the pig be well watched while it was cooking?

4. Explain the difference between *roast pig* and *roast pork*. Why is roast pig much more expensive and therefore much rarer today than it was in Lamb's day? Why is pineapple no longer a luxury?

5. Explain the meaning of Lamb's pun, "Presents endear Absents." Explain his sentence, "I love to taste them [delicacies] upon the tongue of my friend."

6. What do you think was the real cause of the schoolboy's tears after his generosity to the beggar? What does the story of the plum cake have to do with the discussion on roast pig?

7. Has Lamb convinced you that roast pig is a real delicacy? that it was his favorite dish? If so, how did he do it? Discuss.

DREAMS

THOMAS DE QUINCEY

People are always interested in dreams. If the conversation lags at any gathering, let some one mention an unusual dream and instantly the ball of talk starts rolling again. No doubt this common interest is one reason for the continued popularity of Thomas de Quincey's *Confessions of an English Opium Eater,* for much of that work is given over to a discussion of his opium dreams. Strange as are the dreams of health, they are pallid in comparison with the dreams that accompany fever, sleep induced by anesthetics or drugs, or, in fact, any abnormal physical condition.

Contrary to general belief, the dreams that follow drugs are not pleasant, but horrifying and depressing. In his *Confessions,* de Quincey makes reference to the "pains" of opium. In this selection, note that almost immediately he speaks of his "acutest suffering." He shares with Poe and Coleridge the faculty of describing such weird, unreal experiences with convincingly vivid detail.

I now pass to what is the main subject of these latter confessions, to the history and journal of what took place in my dreams; for these were the immediate and proximate cause of my acutest suffering.

The first notice I had of any important change going on in this part of my physical economy was from the re-awakening of a state of eye generally incident to childhood, or exalted states of irritability. I know not whether my reader is aware that many children, perhaps most, have a power of painting, as it were, upon the darkness, all sorts of phantoms; in some, that power is simply a mechanic affection of the eye; others have a voluntary, or a semi-voluntary power to dismiss or to summon them; or, as a child once said to me when I questioned him on this matter, "I can tell them to go, and they go; but sometimes they come, when I don't tell them to come." Whereupon I told him that he had almost as unlimited a command over apparitions as a Roman centurion over his soldiers.—In the middle of 1817, I think it was, that this faculty became positively distressing to me: at night, when I lay awake in bed, vast processions passed along in mournful pomp; friezes of never-ending stories, that to my feelings were as sad and solemn as if they were stories drawn from times before Œdipus [1] or Priam [2]—before Tyre [3]—before Memphis.[4] And, at the same time a corresponding change took place in my dreams; a theater seemed suddenly opened and lighted up within my brain, which presented nightly spectacles of more than earthly splendor. And the four following facts may be mentioned, as noticeable at this time:

1. That, as the creative state of the eye increased, a sympathy seemed to arise between the waking and the dreaming states of the brain in one point—that whatsoever I happened to call up and to trace by a voluntary act upon the darkness was very apt to transfer itself to my dreams; so that I feared to exercise this faculty; for, as Midas [5] turned all things to gold, that yet baffled his hopes and defrauded his human desires, so whatsoever things capable of being visually represented I did but think of in the darkness, immediately shaped themselves into phantoms of the eye; and, by a process apparently no less inevitable, when thus once traced in faint and visionary colors, like writings in sympathetic ink, they were drawn out by the fierce chemistry of my dreams, into insufferable splendor that fretted my heart.

[1] ŒDIPUS—King of Thebes, whose story is told in Greek mythology.
[2] PRIAM—King of ancient Troy, father of Hector and Paris.
[3] TYRE—An ancient city in Phoenicia.
[4] MEMPHIS—An ancient city in Egypt.
[5] MIDAS—King of Phrygia, who was granted the power of turning everything he touched into gold.

2. For this, and all other changes in my dreams, were accompanied by deep-seated anxiety and gloomy melancholy, such as are wholly incommunicable by words. I seemed every night to descend, not metaphorically, but literally to descend, into chasms and sunless abysses, depths below depths, from which it seemed hopeless that I could ever re-ascend. Nor did I, by waking, feel that I *had* re-ascended. This I do not dwell upon; because the state of gloom which attended these gorgeous spectacles, amounting at last to utter darkness, as of some suicidal despondency, cannot be approached by words.

3. The sense of space, and in the end, the sense of time, were both powerfully affected. Buildings, landscapes, &c. were exhibited in proportions so vast as the bodily eye is not fitted to receive. Space swelled, and was amplified to an extent of unutterable infinity. This, however, did not disturb me so much as the vast expansion of time; I sometimes seemed to have lived 70 or 100 years in one night; nay, sometimes had feelings representative of a millennium passed in that time, or, however, of a duration far beyond the limits of any human experience.

4. The minutest incidents of childhood, or forgotten scenes of later years, were often revived: I could not be said to recollect them; for if I had been told of them when waking, I should not have been able to acknowledge them as parts of my past experience. But placed as they were before me, in dreams like intuitions, and clothed in all their evanescent circumstances and accompanying feelings, I *recognized* them instantaneously. I was once told by a near relative of mine, that having in her childhood fallen into a river, and being on the very verge of death but for the critical assistance which reached her, she saw in a moment her whole life, in its minutest incidents, arrayed before her simultaneously as in a mirror; and she had a faculty developed as suddenly for comprehending the whole and every part. This, from some opium experiences of mine, I can believe; I have, indeed, seen the same thing asserted twice in modern books, and accompanied by a remark which I am convinced is true; viz. that the dread book of account, which the Scriptures speak of is, in fact, the mind itself of each individual. Of this at least, I feel assured, that there is no such thing as *forgetting* possible to the mind; a thousand accidents may, and will interpose a veil between our present consciousness and the secret in-

scriptions on the mind; accidents of the same sort will also rend away this veil; but alike, whether veiled or unveiled, the inscription remains for ever; just as the stars seem to withdraw before the common light of day, whereas, in fact, we all know that it is the light which is drawn over them as a veil—and that they are waiting to be revealed when the obscuring daylight shall have withdrawn.

Having noticed these four facts as memorably distinguishing my dreams from those of health, I shall now cite a case illustrative of the first fact; and shall then cite any others that I remember, either in their chronological order, or any other that may give them more effect as pictures to the reader.

I had been in youth, and even since, for occasional amusement, a great reader of Livy,[6] whom, I confess, that I prefer, both for style and matter, to any other of the Roman historians: and I had often felt as most solemn and appalling sounds, and most emphatically representative of the majesty of the Roman people, the two words so often occurring in Livy—*Consul Romanus;* [7] especially when the consul is introduced in his military character. I mean to say that the words king—sultan—regent, &c. or any other titles of those who embody in their own persons the collective majesty of a great people, had less power over my reverential feelings. I had also, though no great reader of history, made myself minutely and critically familiar with one period of English history, viz. the period of the Parliamentary War,[8] having been attracted by the moral grandeur of some who figured in that day, and by the many interesting memoirs which survive those unquiet times. Both these parts of my lighter reading,[9] having furnished me often with matter of reflection, now furnished me with matter for my dreams. Often I used to see, after painting upon the blank darkness a sort of rehearsal whilst waking, a crowd of ladies, and perhaps a festival, and dances. And I heard it said, or I said to myself, "These are English ladies from the unhappy times of Charles I. These are the wives and the daughters of those who met in peace, and sate at the same table, and were allied by

---

[6] LIVY—A Roman historian (59 B.C.–17 A.D.).

[7] *Consul Romanus*—The title given to the chief magistrate of ancient Rome.

[8] PARLIAMENTARY WAR—The civil war which deposed Charles I and made Cromwell Protector of England. It began in August, 1642.

[9] LIGHTER READING—An interesting sidelight on the author's wide reading. Livy is considered heavy reading in college today.

marriage or by blood; and yet, after a certain day in August 1642, never smiled upon each other again, nor met but in the field of battle; and at Marston Moor, at Newbury, or at Naseby [10] cut asunder all ties of love by the cruel saber, and washed away in blood the memory of ancient friendship."—The ladies danced, and looked as lovely as the court of George IV. Yet I knew, even in my dream, that they had been in the grave for nearly two centuries.—This pageant would suddenly dissolve: and, at a clapping of hands would be heard the heartquaking sound of *Consul Romanus*: and immediately came "sweeping by," in gorgeous paludaments,[11] Paulus or Marius,[12] girt round by a company of centurions, with the crimson tunic hoisted on a spear, and followed by the *alalagmos* [13] of the Roman legions.

Many years ago, when I was looking over Piranesi's Antiquities of Rome, Mr. Coleridge, who was standing by, described to me a set of plates by that artist, called his *Dreams,* and which record the scenery of his own visions during the delirium of a fever: Some of them (I describe only from memory of Mr. Coleridge's account) represented vast Gothic halls: on the floor of which stood all sorts of engines and machinery, wheels, cables, pulleys, levers, catapults, &c. &c. expressive of enormous power put forth, and resistance overcome. Creeping along the sides of the walls, you perceive a staircase; and upon it, groping his way upwards, was Piranesi himself: follow the stairs a little further, and you perceive it come to a sudden and abrupt termination, without any balustrade, and allowing no step onwards to him who had reached the extremity, except into the depths below. Whatever is to become of poor Piranesi, you suppose, at least, that his labors must in some way terminate here. But raise your eyes, and behold a second flight of stairs still higher: on which again Piranesi is perceived, but this time standing on the very brink of the abyss. Again elevate your eye, and a still more aerial flight of stairs is beheld: and again is poor Piranesi busy on his aspiring labors: and so on, until the unfinished stairs and Piranesi both are lost in the upper gloom of the hall.—With the same power of endless growth and self reproduction did my architecture proceed in

---

[10] MARSTON MOOR, NEWBURY, NASEBY—Battles in the Parliamentary War.
[11] PALUDAMENTS—Military cloaks.
[12] PAULUS, MARIUS—The former a Roman consul (died 216 B.C.); the latter a Roman consul and general (155–86 B.C.).
[13] *Alalagmos*—A word coined from the war cry of the Romans.

dreams. In the early stage of my malady, the splendors of my dreams were indeed chiefly architectural: and I beheld such pomp of cities and palaces as was never yet beheld by the waking eye, unless in the clouds.

And now came a tremendous change, which, unfolding itself slowly like a scroll, through many months, promised an abiding torment; and, in fact, it never left me until the winding up of my case.[14] Hitherto the human face had mixed often in my dreams, but not despotically nor with any special power of tormenting. But now that which I have called the tyranny of the human face began to unfold itself. Perhaps some part of my London life might be answerable for this. Be that as it may, now it was that upon the rocking waters of the ocean the human face began to appear; the sea appeared paved with innumerable faces, upturned to the heavens: faces, imploring, wrathful, despairing, surged upward by thousands, by myriads, by generations, by centuries:— my agitation was infinite,—my mind tossed—and surged with the ocean.

[14] WINDING UP OF MY CASE—By phenomenal willpower, de Quincey broke himself of the habit of taking drugs.

DID YOU READ WITH UNDERSTANDING?

1. Coleridge began one of his poems, "My eyes make pictures when they are shut." If you share with him and de Quincey this power to paint pictures in the dark, how do your experiences correspond with those described in the first part of the second paragraph of this essay?

2. Explain the allusion to Midas in the first numbered paragraph. Do you think that it is a common experience to have one's dreams grow out of one's last waking thoughts? Can you furnish any illustrations?

3. Jot down at least three ways in which de Quincey's dream experiences differed from the dreams of a person in normal health.

4. What is de Quincey's theory about *forgetting?* Do you agree with him?

5. What two periods of history often furnished him with material for his dreams?

6. Which of all the dream experiences described do you think would be the most disturbing? Why?

EXTENDED ACTIVITIES

≈ V-III ≈

FOR ACQUAINTANCE WITH AUTHORS

CHARLES LAMB (1775–1834)—"A DISSERTATION UPON ROAST PIG"

It does not take a large man to make a hero; it does take courage. Charles Lamb was a small man, shabby and insignificant looking. He did nothing sensational, but he was heroic just the same. He had the courage to accept the support of himself, his sister, his father, and—at times— other dependents. Though he loved deeply, he was strong enough not to consider a marriage that would have been selfish and perhaps unwise. And he was brave enough to care for his insane sister Mary in the periods of temporary relief and to walk with her to the asylum when a fit of violence was coming on. Here was the most cruel tragedy of his life. One day in his early twenties he had come home to learn that Mary had killed their mother. The girl was put into an institution, her brother paying the fees out of his slender earnings. When her mind cleared, Lamb took her home to keep her busy and amused until the next spell should come on. For the rest of his life the care of Mary was his chief concern.

There was heroism, too, in Lamb's smiling acceptance of everyday hardships. The family had always been poor. For seven years Charles was a charity student in the Bluecoat School of Christ's Hospital. Most English boys found little but suffering in the charity schools. Lamb absorbed an excellent education and made one good friend, Samuel Coleridge. Because of a slight stammer Lamb was unfitted for a career in the church—the only way charity-school students might then obtain a free college education. At fourteen, his school days came to an end and he went out to earn his living. For thirty-three years he was a clerk in the India House. Some would have found the long hours over a clerk's desk tiring and monotonous; but Lamb liked people and he enjoyed the bustle and stir of business. In his last years of leisure, retired on a pension by the company he had faithfully served, he was almost homesick for the office.

725

Lamb showed an early interest in writing, but his first works were poems and plays, now little remembered. He had always been interested in Elizabethan drama, and his first successful works grew out of this field. In 1807 he and Mary published their *Tales from Shakespeare*—short, easily read synopses of the important plays of the poet. Lamb was almost forty-five when he began contributing to the *London Magazine* little sketches which he signed "Elia." Thus began the famous *Essays of Elia*. Addison and Steele a century before had made the essay entertaining; Lamb made it personal. The *Essays of Elia* and its successors are as self-revealing as an autobiography. And in between the lines shines the writer's happy, courageous spirit. There is no sham about it; Lamb did really find happiness in what seem to us unhappy circumstances. He had a sense of fun, an appreciation of books and people, and a brave heart. Out of these he fashioned a pleasant and noble life.

THOMAS DE QUINCEY (1785–1859)—"DREAMS"

Picture for a moment a tiny man with gentle manners, a man with a delicate womanly face illumined by brilliant eyes, a man somehow marked with mystery—and you have a notion of Thomas de Quincey. Carlyle once said that he looked like a beautiful little child but that there was an expression in his face that said, "Behold, this child has been in Hell." De Quincey himself has explained the look in his *Confessions of an English Opium Eater,* his most famous book. At different periods in his life he was a slave of the drug, at one time using enormous quantities of it. Before he died he had broken the habit, but the marks of his suffering were never erased.

His father, who was wealthy, died when Thomas was seven, leaving the lad to the guardianship of relatives. They were conscientious but not understanding. De Quincey particularly hated the first school in which he was placed. He was a brilliant boy, a great reader, and proficient beyond his years—and his teachers—in Latin and Greek. At fourteen he ran away. For weeks he tramped through Wales and then nearly starved in London. He was finally found and persuaded to enter Oxford. He remained for the four years; but terrified at the thought of the examinations he again fled, never to return to school.

A great admirer of Wordsworth and Coleridge, he moved as a young man to the Lake District, into the very Dove Cottage where Wordsworth had lived. He dabbled a bit in literature because it pleased him but did no regular writing until an unwise investment cost him his fortune. Then he began to contribute steadily to various literary magazines. There was a constant market for his articles which were unusual in learning and in style. The "Confessions" appeared serially in the *London Magazine*. Their popularity was sensational.

His later years were restless ones, spent chiefly in Edinburgh. He would rent a room, live in it alone for weeks (letting no one know where he was), fill it with books and papers until he could no longer work in the litter, then lock the door and go off to find another room. At his death, it is said, six such rooms were discovered.

All sorts of subjects he treated with distinction: history, recent and ancient; literature; manners; customs; morals; personalities. His vocabulary was prodigious; he was never at a loss for words. The reader brings these judgments against him: his sentences are often too elaborate to be easily understood; he often is led away from his subject; and he is not averse to gossiping about his neighbors. Contemporaries judged him a scholar, a wit, a man of the world, a philosopher, and a genius. Time has taken little from that reputation.

OF LITERARY FORM AND STYLE

ROMANTIC PROSE

The romantic spirit found its finest expression in lyric poetry, but prose, too, was affected by the new influence. The familiar essay shows most clearly the change in mood and subject. The essayist is no longer afraid to talk about himself. He confesses his likes and dislikes, his little whims and fancies. He talks freely about his mistakes and failings, about his plans for the future. He takes us into his home and shows us his books and his china. He discusses the food he likes and the clothes he wears. He talks about the friends he knows and the interesting things they do. Lamb and de Quincey were masters of the familiar essay. In their literary criticism, the men used a familiar style and presented their opinions from a personal point of view.

But even these writers had not freed themselves entirely from classic traditions. Their educations had been classic, and their vocabularies were stocked with resounding Latinisms. De Quincey, particularly, used the sonorous balanced sentence of the eighteenth century. In Lamb, however, in spite of the learned diction, there is a distinctly conversational tone.

MAGAZINES OF LITERARY CRITICISM

The years from 1800 to 1820 saw the establishment of the famous magazines of literary criticism: *The Edinburgh Review, The Quarterly Review, Blackwoods, The Examiner,* and *The London Magazine.* With the exception of the last two, these were very conservative periodicals and were distinctly unfriendly to romantic writers. The first works of Wordsworth, Coleridge, Keats, and Byron were all ridiculed by *The Edinburgh Review* and *The Quarterly;* and it was the adverse criticism of the two magazines that called forth Byron's satiric retaliation, "English Bards and Scotch Reviewers."

It was Leigh Hunt, himself a poet, who began *The Examiner,* and he proved a loyal friend to the younger poets. Time has revealed that he was the best critic of them all. The writers to whom he opened his pages are the ones that the world calls great.

Two other poets should be mentioned for their work in literary criticism —Samuel Coleridge and Robert Southey. Coleridge was an inspired lecturer, but he was unable to hold himself to a task long enough adequately to release his brilliant mind. Two prose works deserve mention— his *Sketches of My Literary Life and Opinions* and the collected *Essays on Shakespeare.* Robert Southey was Coleridge's friend. He too wrote critical essays, but his best prose is in his biographies, *The Life of Nelson* and *Lives of the British Admirals.*

A prose writer of the period who reached some prominence was Walter Savage Landor. He was a stormy fellow, but his prose is surprisingly placid. He is best known for his *Imaginary Conversations,* a work that is classic both in subject and in manner. It is based upon his great reading in history and literature, and is of value chiefly because of the way in which it has caught the spirit of ages long ago.

William Hazlitt was a literary scholar—a friend of Lamb, Coleridge, Wordsworth, and de Quincey. He was an authority on Shakespeare and the Elizabethan age. His work was critical rather than imaginative. Among his works may be mentioned *Lectures on English Poets, A Life of Napoleon,* and a series of essays, *Table Talk.*

QUESTIONS IN APPRECIATION:

"A Dissertation upon Roast Pig"

1. *Burlesque,* you may remember, may treat a serious subject flippantly, or a slight subject with mock seriousness. Did Lamb make use of either type of burlesque in his "A Dissertation upon Roast Pig"? Discuss.

2. An *anachronism* is an error, sometimes intentional, in which an article or custom is ascribed to a period before the time when it first existed or came into use. If a boy were describing Caesar's campaign in Britain and had the Roman legions using machine guns or talking over short-wave radios, that would be an anachronism. For comic effect Lamb uses several anachronisms in the story of Bo-Bo. Point out as many anachronisms as you can discover.

3. What other humorous devices, besides those already discussed, has Lamb used in the essay? Discuss.

4. Do writers still make use of burlesque treatment for humorous effect? of anachronisms? of the other devices used by Lamb? Why or why not?

5. In what respects does the style of Lamb differ from the style of Francis Bacon? In what respects does the style of Lamb differ from the style of Addison and Steele? In what respects, if any, are the essays by these different authors alike? Does Lamb more closely resemble Bacon or Addison and Steele? Discuss.

6. Describe and illustrate the following types of essays—(*a*) the formal essay, (*b*) the familiar essay, (*c*) the personal essay. Which type of essay do you like best? Why?

"Dreams"

1. How could you tell, merely from reading this selection, that de Quincey was an unusually well-educated man? that he had an unusual degree of intelligence?

2. What is there about de Quincey's way of writing that makes his work on "Dreams" understandable to the ordinary reader?

3. Select for class discussion one example of de Quincey's ability to describe a weird experience so that any one can share it with him. In discussion, point out the ways that he secures his effects.

4. A successful modern novelist and essayist advised high school students of news and journalism to read de Quincey to improve their own style. Do you think it was good advice? Why or why not?

5. What characteristics of romantic literature do you notice in de Quincey's works?

THE GROWTH OF THE ENGLISH NOVEL

After its christening in the eighteenth century, the novel settled down to lusty growth in the nineteenth century. In the first fifty years it responded to the romantic influences around it. Several women writers appeared, the first of them delighting in the sentimental and mysterious possibilities of the new form. Frances Burney, afterward Madame d'Arblay, continued Richardson's stories of the human heart—considerably modernized—in her romances *Evelina* and *Cecilia.* Then Mrs. Ann Radcliffe wrote a thriller, *The Mysteries of Udolpho,* which set a fashion for tales of mystery and terror. The most famous of the terror tales proved to be Mary Godwin Shelley's *Frankenstein,* as well known in the twentieth century as in its own day.

But the most important contributions to the novel came from Walter Scott and Jane Austen, two gifted writers of totally different talents.

When Scott was just a young man he started an adventurous novel, but laid it aside while he did his narrative poems. Nine years later he came upon the manuscript in a cabinet with some fishing tackle. He read it eagerly, enjoying it as if some one else had written it. Then he sat down to finish it. In three weeks' time the job was done. He called it *Waverley* and sent it off to the publishers with the request that it be published anonymously. It was an instant success. In the next four years six more books appeared with the by-line, "By the author of *Waverley.*" Every one wondered who the new author could be, but it was many years before Scott disclosed his secret. For seventeen years, Scott wrote about two books a year—at first only about Scotland and the Scotch. But he had discovered the historical novel; and he branched out to include England in *Kenilworth* and *Ivanhoe,* France in *Quentin Durward,* and Palestine in *The Talisman.* The magic touch with which he made people of the past live again won for him the title of "The Wizard of the North."

Entirely different in subject and manner were the books of Jane Austen, who wrote of uneventful English village life. Her romantic heroes, sometimes seem to be in the picture only because of a handsome profile and well-setting coat. But Jane's novels are the stories of her own life, with imaginary trimmings. And the heroes? Well, there just weren't any; hence the air of unreality about her handsome men. However, she and her sisters were well supplied with patronizing relatives and eccentric family characters—the types that sparkle through her pages.

Jane's father was an Episcopalian minister, and she was the youngest of his seven children. Her early life held much of the trivial comedy of *Pride and Prejudice.* Something of a flirt in her youth, she was pretty and one of the town's belles—"as impatient of poor dancing as of poor sense." But neither she nor her sister married, and after her father's death the girls and their mother became dependent upon wealthier members of the family.

Jane had begun writing at fourteen, but it was not considered genteel for a "maiden lady" to write novels. One by one, her six books appeared anonymously. They were entirely different from the horror stories then the vogue and from Scott's dashing romances. It was slowly that they took hold upon the reading public. But a few critics recognized her charm and defended the simple stories. Scott, Lamb, and Tennyson became her champions. Scott once wrote of her work, "The big bow-wow I can do myself like anyone going; but the exquisite touch which renders commonplace things interesting from the truth of description and sentiment is denied to me." Today his judgment is that of the reading world. Prim little Miss Austen wrote with genius and truth, and with her pen set the novel well on the road to realism. Her best works are the well-known *Pride and Prejudice, Emma,* and *Sense and Sensibility.*

FOR FURTHER READING

AUSTEN, JANE, *Northanger Abbey; Pride and Prejudice; Sense and Sensibility*

BRIGHOUSE, HAROLD, "The Night of 'Mr. H.' " (Lamb) (drama)

DE QUINCEY, THOMAS, *Joan of Arc*

GRAY, ELIZABETH J., *Young Walter Scott*

LAMB, CHARLES (A. C. Ward, ed.), *Everybody's Lamb;* (Russell D. Gilman, ed.) *Letters*

LAMB, CHARLES and MARY, *Tales from Shakespeare*

NORDHOFF, CHARLES, and HALL, JAMES NORMAN, *Mutiny on the Bounty; Men Against the Sea; Pitcairn's Island*

SCOTT, SIR WALTER, *The Heart of Midlothian; Kenilworth; Quentin Durward; The Talisman*

SOUTHEY, ROBERT, *The Life of Nelson*

THE VICTORIAN ERA
1840-1900

VII

The Victorian Era was essentially an age of prose.

VICTORIAN ENGLAND

(1840–1900)

In the year 1837 an eighteen-year-old girl became Queen of England. And for the next sixty-four years the country was whole-heartedly *Victorian*. Because for many people that term is associated curiously with too-ornate gilt frames, plush furniture, and a stuffy moralizing attitude toward life, it is well to consider just what Victorian England was like.

In the first place, it was intensely loyal to the Queen. The people were proud of the dignity and graciousness with which Victoria had accepted her crown. Her gravity—in spite of her youth—was reassuring. She set at once about learning the details of government, becoming eventually one of the wisest and best informed rulers of any realm. She conscientiously refrained from playing politics, but there was never a time that she was ignorant of what went on in the various parts of her empire. For the second time in British history she proved the extraordinary ability with which a queen may rule a realm, and for a third time she gave a queen's name to an era of culture and artistic achievement.

We are close enough to the period of her reign to be fairly familiar with its history. Her uncle, William IV, you may remember, had been a Liberal and had sponsored the passing of the Reform Bill. England was already headed in the right direction. Victoria conscientiously lent support to every feasible step forward. For twenty-one years she had the fine assistance of her husband, Prince Albert, an intelligent and tactful man. He had married into a difficult situation, but in time he had won the respect of the empire. Fortunately he had a sense of humor, which his queen had not, and he eased what might have been more than one embarrassing situation for both. After his death in 1861 Victoria worked alone with her ministers and their cabinets. She numbered among her ministers some of the greatest names in English statesmanship—Lord Palmerston, Benjamin Disraeli, and William Gladstone.

Through the various ministeries England made a way of progress: she fought and won the Crimean War; suppressed the Indian Mutiny; established better government in Ireland; acquired stock in the Suez Canal; increased her holdings in Africa, China, and India; strengthened her position in Egypt; fought and won another African war; and celebrated two jubilees for her queen—one on the fiftieth and one on the sixtieth anniversary of her accession.

731

The story of Victoria's long reign is faithfully but charmingly told in the modern play, *Victoria Regina,* by Laurence Housman. Victoria was a real personality, distinguished by her unswerving integrity of character and purpose. She was honest, thorough, truly religious, devoted to her family and her kingdom. Her lack of humor was compensated for in part by an innate kindness. She imposed upon her court extremely conservative standards of conduct; but her own high ideals and adherence to them freed her from the suspicion of priggishness and hypocrisy. The people she honored were men and women of actual worth. Though they may at times have wished for royalty not quite so unbending, they respected her always. As a nation her subjects gave her fiercely proud affection.

In England, as in America, the last half of the nineteenth century was marked with rapid progress in science, education, literature, and art. The inventions which had already upset and reorganized England's industries were improved and multiplied. The use of the cotton gin in America meant vastly increased raw materials for the looms of England. The gradual substitution of steamships for sailing vessels meant amazing shortening of the time used in transportation between supply centers all over the world and British factories. The passing of the sailing vessels marked the end of the chapter for one of England's most picturesque, though hazardous, professions—sailor-seamanship. British men continue to man the ships of the world, but the ships are a different kind. Whatever such changes cost in picturesqueness was gained a hundred-fold in general wealth. These were boom times for industry and transportation.

And doggedly England kept at the job of social progress—cutting down factory hours, providing free schools for working men's children, improving living conditions, making books and music available. Many of the best writers and speakers of the period worked tirelessly at the job of making life more worth living for the laboring masses. England tried to take stock of her systems of education, to bring them up to date and make them practical. Matthew Arnold, John Ruskin, and Thomas Huxley were among the scholarly leaders who were interested in more liberal and effective education for England's commoners.

The years about the middle of the century were a period of spiritual unrest. Experimental methods in science overwhelmed men with discoveries in chemistry, physics, and biology. There were those who believed that the universe could not be explained in terms of chemistry and mechanics, and that there was no longer need to reckon with a spiritual force, or God. Such views were upsetting to men who had been brought up in strictly orthodox homes. The publication of *The Origin of Species* by Charles Darwin in 1859 was of profound importance because it gave a reasonable theory to account for the belief in organic evolution, a doctrine which had already engaged the attention of the scientists. The result was a sharp questioning of religious faith and a temporary wave of atheistic philosophy. The doubts of the period may be found in some of

Tennyson's poems written in the middle period of his life, and in the works of Matthew Arnold who never did regain his lost assurance. It took more than a half century for philosophers in general to discover that there is no quarrel between science and God; that science may point at error in man's *assumptions* of belief; but that mechanics alone can never explain a universe. There are indeed those who believe that the troubles of the twentieth century are an outgrowth of the materialistic philosophy which —in spite of the Queen, for she was never swayed by it,—dominated the later Victorian years.

The writing of the period was prolific. There were scores of books expounding the theories of the age. Men were interested in history, economics, social problems, art, politics, science—in fact in every field of human learning. Many of the specialists in these varied fields were also good writers, and so some of the works produced in the interests of religion or science and the like have taken their places on the shelves of good literature.

While non-fiction prose thus reached a new "high" in expression, fiction itself assumed a powerful influence. England's great novelists—Charles Dickens, George Eliot, William Thackeray—and a host of others were producing significant novels that touched all sorts of lives and dealt with all manner of themes. Some were out-and-out propaganda of one sort or another—usually in a good cause. In their pages are reflected the spiritual uncertainty, the economic problems, the ethical and moral questions of the times. The men and women who filled their pages—Mr. Micawber, Becky Sharpe, Hetty Sorrel, Jane Eyre—these have become as well known to the world as the great folks of history. It was flood tide for the English novel. The last years of the century also saw the short story make a beginning in Britain. However, it is the present century that has seen the real flowering of the British short story.

There were poets also. There were Tennyson and Browning who represented well the underlying strength and soundness of the times. There were poets only less great who reflected varying movements and interests or who expressed their own personal genius in verse. And there were many minor poets. Browning and Tennyson were poets of good cheer. Nothing ever seemed to cloud Browning's happy outlook on life or to disturb his faith in the ultimate goodness of the world and its Maker. He was not a poser. He was sincere, matter of fact, healthily happy. Tennyson had his periods of distress and doubt, but he worked through them to a triumphant assurance. He gave voice in his poetry to his own philosophy; but he also expressed the highest ideals and aspirations of his times. He was sensitive to changing conditions about him; thus his thoughtful work over a long lifetime reflects unusually well all that was most significant in the days of Queen Victoria. The contributions of the lesser poets will be discussed with their works in the closing pages of the unit. It is really Tennyson and Browning and the prose writers—both scholars and novelists—that give the picture of Victorian England.

733

Prose touched the fields of history, science, criticism, and philosophy.

THE STORMING OF THE
BASTILLE

THOMAS CARLYLE

It has remained for a twentieth-century invention to furnish a satisfactory simile for Carlyle pouring forth his almost incoherent account of the French Revolution. He was a glorified radio announcer, standing, as it were, at the ringside of the battle of the century—the seething eighteenth century in France. Though the battle was fought and won six years before Carlyle was born, it comes to us hot from his pages as if, instead, he were being borne by the crowd through the streets of Paris, microphone to his lips, shouting to the world the moment-by-moment blows that are felling the Bastille.

"And now, friends, we switch you over to our announcer, Mr. Thomas Carlyle, who will pick up the story. Here we are—"

THE Bastille [1] is besieged!

On, then, all Frenchmen that have hearts in your bodies! Roar with all your throats of cartilage and metal, ye sons of

---

[1] BASTILLE—The former state-prison of France, begun in 1370, one of the strongest fortresses and most dreaded prisons of Europe. On July 14, 1789, the mobs of Paris stormed the fortress and demanded its surrender. The governor of the prison pretended to comply, then had his soldiers fire into the mob and the fight was on.

liberty; stir spasmodically whatsoever of utmost faculty is in you, soul, body, or spirit, for it is the hour! Smite thou, Louis Tournay, cartwright of the Marais, old soldier of the Regiment Dauphine;[2] smite at that outer drawbridge chain, though the fiery hail whistles around thee! Never, over nave or felloe, did thy axe strike such a stroke. Down with it, man; down with it to Orcus;[3] let the whole accursed edifice sink thither, and tyranny be swallowed up forever! Mounted, some say, on the roof of the guard-room, some "on bayonets stuck into joints of the wall," Louis Tournay smites, brave Aubin Bonnemère (also an old soldier) seconding him. The chain yields, breaks; the huge drawbridge slams down, thundering. Glorious! and yet, alas! it is still but the outworks. The eight grim towers with their invalide musketry,[4] their paving-stone and cannon-mouths still soar aloft intact; ditch yawning impassable, stone-faced; the inner drawbridge with its back toward us; the Bastille is still to take!

To describe the siege of the Bastille (thought to be one of the most important in history) perhaps transcends the talent of mortals. . . . Paris, wholly,[5] has got to the acme of its frenzy, whirled all ways by panic madness. At every street-barricade there whirls, simmering, a minor whirlpool, strengthening the barricade, since God knows what is coming; and all minor whirlpools play distractedly into that grand fire-maelstrom which is lashing round the Bastille.

And so it lashes and roars. Cholat, the wine-merchant, has become an impromptu cannoneer. See Georget, of the marine service, fresh from Brest,[6] play the King of Siam's cannon. Singular (if we were not used to the like). Georget lay last night taking his ease at his inn; the King of Siam's cannon also lay, knowing nothing of *him* for a hundred years; yet now, at the right instant, they have got together, and discourse eloquent music; for, hearing what was toward, Georget sprang from the Brest diligence, and ran. Gardes Francaises,[7] also, will be here

---

[2] REGIMENT DAUPHINE—Regiment of the prince.

[3] ORCUS—In Roman mythology, the underworld, the abode of the dead.

[4] INVALIDE MUSKETRY—The handful of soldiers defending the Bastille; *invalide* meaning originally a wounded soldier, later, any veteran.

[5] PARIS, WHOLLY—A mob of about 12,000 citizens, armed with whatever they could lay hands on.

[6] BREST—The seaport nearest Paris.

[7] GARDES FRANCAISES—French guards.

with real artillery. Were not the walls so thick! Upward from the esplanade, horizontally from all neighboring roofs and windows, flashes one irregular deluge of musketry, without effect. The invalides lie flat, firing comparatively at their ease from behind stone; hardly through port-holes show the tip of a nose. We fall, shot, and make no impression!

Let conflagration rage of whatsoever is combustible! Guard rooms are burnt, invalides mess-rooms. A distracted "peruke-maker with two fiery torches" is for burning "the saltpeters of the arsenal," had not a woman run screaming, had not a patriot, with some tincture of natural philosophy, instantly struck the wind out of him (butt of musket on pit of stomach), overturned barrels, and stayed the devouring element. A young, beautiful lady seized, escaping, in these outer courts, and thought, falsely, to be de Launay's [8] daughter, shall be burnt in de Launay's sight; she lies, swooned, on a paillasse; [9] but, again, a patriot—it is brave Aubin Bonnemère, the old soldier—dashes in, and rescues her. Straw is burnt; three cartloads of it, hauled hither, go up in white smoke, almost to the choking of patriotism itself; so that Elie had, with singed brows, to drag back one cart, and Réole, the "gigantic haberdasher," another. Smoke as of Tophet,[10] confusion as of Babel,[11] noise as of the crack of doom!

Blood flows, the aliment of new madness. The wounded are carried into houses of the Rue Cerisaie,[12] the dying leave their last mandate not to yield till the accursed stronghold fall. And yet, alas! how fall? The walls are so thick! Deputations, three in number, arrive from the Hôtel-de-Ville.[13] . . . These wave their town flag in the arched gateway, and stand, rolling their drum, but to no purpose. In such crack of doom de Launay cannot hear them, dare not believe them; they return, with justified rage, the whew of lead still singing in their ears. What to do? The firemen are here, squirting with their firepumps on the invalides cannon to wet the touch-holes; they unfortunately cannot squirt so high, but produce only clouds of spray. Individuals

---

[8] DE LAUNAY—The governor of the prison. He was killed by the mob.

[9] PAILLASSE—Bed of straw.

[10] TOPHET—Part of a valley near Jerusalem, used for burning refuse; hence, hell.

[11] BABEL—The tower described in *Genesis* xi:9; hence, confusion of sound, tumult.

[12] RUE CERISAIE—A neighboring street.

[13] HÔTEL-DE-VILLE—Town-house, guild-hall.

of classical knowledge propose *catapults.* Santerre, the sonorous brewer of the suburb Saint-Antoine, advises rather that the place be fired by "a mixture of phosphorous and oil of turpentine spouted up through forcing-pumps." O Spinola-Santerre,[14] hast thou the mixture *ready?* Every man his own engineer! And still the fire-deluge abates not; even women are firing, and Turks—at least one woman (with her sweetheart) and one Turk. Gardes Francaises have come; real cannon, real cannoneers. Usher Maillard is busy; half-pay Elie, half-pay Hulin, rage in the midst of thousands.

How the great Bastille clock ticks (inaudible) to its inner court, there, at its ease, hour after hour; as if nothing special, for it or the world, were passing! It tolled one when the firing began, and is now pointing toward five, and still the firing slakes not. Far down in their vaults, the seven prisoners hear muffled din as of earthquakes; their turnkeys answer vaguely.

Woe to thee, de Launay, with thy poor hundred invalides! . . . What shall de Launay do? One thing only de Launay could have done—what he said he would do. Fancy him sitting, from the first, with lighted taper, within arm's-length of the powder-magazine; motionless, like an old Roman senator, or bronze lamp-holder; coldly apprising Thuriot,[15] and all men, by a slight motion of his eye, what his resolution was. Harmless he sat there, while unharmed; but the king's fortress, meanwhile, could, might, would, or should in nowise be surrendered, save to the king's messenger; one old man's life is worthless, so it be lost with honor; but think, ye brawling *canaille,* how will it be when a whole Bastille springs skyward? In such statuesque, taper-holding attitude, one fancies de Launay might have left Thuriot, the red clerks of the Basoche,[16] curé of St. Stephen, and all the tagrag and bobtail of the world, to work their will.

And yet, withal, he could not do it. Hast thou considered how each man's heart is so tremulously responsive to the hearts of all men? Hast thou noted how omnipotent is the very sound of many men? How their shriek of indignation palsies the strong soul? Their howl of contumely withers with unfelt pangs? . . .

[14] SPINOLA-SANTERRE—Santerre was a leader of the mob; Spinola was an Italian general who fought valiantly with the Spanish against the Netherlands in the early seventeenth century.

[15] THURIOT—A revolutionary leader.

[16] RED CLERKS OF BASOCHE, etc.—The revolutionists.

Great is the combined voice of men, the utterance of their *instincts,* which are truer than their *thoughts;* it is the greatest a man encounters, among the sounds and shadows which make up this world of time. He who can resist that, has his footing somewhere *beyond* time. Distracted he hovers between two—hopes in the middle of despair; surrenders not his fortress; declares that he will blow it up, seizes torches to blow it up, and does not blow it. Unhappy old de Launay, it is the death agony of the Bastille and thee! Jail, jailoring, and jailor, all three, such as they may have been, must finish.

For four hours now has the world-bedlam roared; call it the world-chimera, blowing fire! The poor invalides have sunk under their battlements, or rise only with reversed muskets; they have made a white flag of napkins, go beating the chamade, or seeming to beat, for one can hear nothing. The very Swiss [17] at the portcullis look weary of firing, disheartened in the fire-deluge; a port-hole at the drawbridge is opened, as by one that would speak. See Huissier Maillard, the shifty man! On his plank, swinging over the abyss of that stoned ditch, plank resting on parapet, balanced by weight of patriots, he hovers perilous— such a dove toward such an ark! Deftly, thou shifty ushers; one man already fell and lies smashed, far down there against the masonry! Usher Maillard falls not; deftly, unerringly, he walks, with outspread palm. The Swiss holds a paper through the port-hole; the shifty usher snatches it and returns. Terms of surrender: Pardon, immunity to all! Are they accepted? *"Foi d'officer* (on the word of an officer)," answers half-pay Hulin, or half-pay Elie—for men do not agree on it—"they are!" Sinks the drawbridge, Usher Maillard bolting it when down; rushes in the living deluge; the Bastille is fallen!

Victorie! La Bastille est prise! [18]

[17] swiss—Swiss mercenaries.

[18] *Victorie! La Bastille est prise*—Victory! The Bastille is taken.

DID YOU READ WITH UNDERSTANDING?

If there are pupils in the class who have studied French, it would be helpful for them to list on the blackboard all French names and words occurring in the essay, indicating the correct pronunciation for each and, if translatable, the meaning.

  1. If you are not familiar with the main events of the French Revolu-

tion, review them briefly. Why was the fall of the Bastille important?

2. What kind of people made up the mob that stormed the prison? Were there any former soldiers or government employees? How many different kinds of trades or occupations were represented? Count the ones mentioned by Carlyle.

3. Did any forces try to come to the rescue of the prison and its defenders? How can you tell on which side the different groups were fighting?

4. Who was de Launay? Why did he threaten to blow up the Bastille? Why didn't he do it? Do you think he should have? Discuss.

5. Why was the Bastille with its thick walls surrendered so quickly? What is meant by "the living deluge" in the last sentence?

6. Relate briefly the main order of events in the fall of the prison.

7. What does the author mean when he says in the next-to-the-last paragraph that "the utterance of men's *instincts* is truer than their *thoughts*"? Do you agree with him? Discuss.

LONDON IN 1685

THOMAS BABINGTON MACAULAY

Concerning *history*, Macaulay once wrote, "It should invest with the reality of human flesh and blood, beings whom we are all too much inclined to consider as personified qualities in an allegory; call up our ancestors before us with all their peculiarities of language, manners, garb; show us over their houses, seat us at their tables, rummage their old fashioned wardrobes, explain the uses of their ponderous furniture."

In a conscientious effort to meet that definition he wrote five full-size volumes on sixteen years of English history. And he did it so well that the volumes became best-sellers in their day. When the books first issued from the press, while the author was still in doubt about the success of his work, he wrote in his diary, "At all events, I have aimed high; I have tried to do something to be remembered; I have had the year 2000, or even 3000, often in my mind; I have sacrificed nothing to temporary fashions of thought and style; and if I fail, my failure will be honorable."

But he did not fail. Nearly a hundred years have passed since the words were written; and the *History of England* had an assured place among the world's great books. It is enlightening and entertaining reading.

The position of London, relatively to the other towns of the empire, was, in the time of Charles the Second far higher than at present. For at present the population of London is little more than six times the population of Manchester or of Liverpool. In the days of Charles the Second the population of London was more than seventeen times the population of Bristol or of Norwich. It may be doubted whether any other instance can be mentioned of a great kingdom in which the first city was more than seventeen times as large as the second. There is reason to believe that, in 1685, London had been, during about half a century, the most populous capital in Europe. The inhabitants, who are now[1] at least nineteen hundred thousand, were then probably a little more than half a million. London had in the world only one commercial rival, now long outstripped, the mighty and opulent Amsterdam.

Of the metropolis, the City, properly so called, was the most important division. At the time of the Restoration it had been built, for the most part, of wood and plaster;[2] the few bricks that were used were ill baked; the booths where goods were exposed to sale projected far into the streets, and were overhung by the upper stories. A few specimens of this architecture may still be seen in those districts which were not reached by the great fire.[3] That fire had, in a few days, covered a space of little less than a square mile with the ruins of eighty-nine churches and of thirteen thousand houses. But the city had risen again with a celerity which had excited the admiration of neighboring countries. Unfortunately, the old lines of the streets had been to a great extent preserved; and those lines, originally traced in an age when even princesses performed their journeys on horseback, were often too narrow to allow wheeled carriages to pass each other with ease, and were therefore ill adapted for the residence of wealthy persons in an age when a coach and six was a fashionable luxury. The style of building was, however, far superior to that of the city which had perished. The ordinary material was brick, of much better quality than had formerly been used.

We should greatly err if we were to suppose that any of the streets and squares then bore the same aspect as at present. The

---

[1] NOW—The first volume of the *History,* from which this selection is taken, was published in 1848. The estimated population in 1933 was 4,396,421 for London proper and 8,202,818 for London and its suburbs.

[2] BUILT OF WOOD AND PLASTER—For this reason the houses and buildings were infested with rats, spreaders of disease. It is interesting to note that after the great fire the city was never again the victim of a great plague such as that which raged in 1665.

[3] GREAT FIRE—The great fire of London in 1666.

great majority of the houses, indeed, have, since that time, been wholly or in great part rebuilt. If the most fashionable parts of the capital could be placed before us, such as they then were, we should be disgusted by their squalid appearance and poisoned by their noisome atmosphere. In Covent Garden a filthy and noisy market was held close to the dwellings of the great. Fruit women screamed, carters fought, cabbage stalks and rotten apples accumulated in heaps at the thresholds of the Countess of Berkshire and of the Bishop of Durham. The center of Lincoln's Inn Fields [4] was an open space where the rabble congregated every evening, within a few yards of Cardigan House and Winchester [5] House, to hear mountebanks harangue, to see bears dance, and to set dogs at oxen.

The houses were not numbered. There would indeed have been little advantage in numbering them; for of the coachmen, chairmen, porters, and errand boys of London, a very small portion could read. It was necessary to use marks which the most ignorant could understand. The shops were therefore distinguished by painted signs, which gave a gay and grotesque aspect

---

[4] LINCOLN'S INN FIELDS—The largest square in London, named from its proximity to Lincoln's Inn.

[5] CARDIGAN . . . WINCHESTER—Great residences.

to the streets. The walk from Charing Cross to Whitechapel [6] lay through an endless succession of Saracen's Heads, Royal Oaks, Blue Bears, and Golden Lambs, which disappeared when they were no longer required for the direction of the common people.

When the evening closed in, the difficulty and danger of walking about London became serious indeed. The garret windows were opened, and pails were emptied, with little regard to those who were passing below. Falls, bruises, and broken bones were of constant occurrence. For, till the last year of the reign of Charles the Second, most of the streets were left in profound darkness. Thieves and robbers plied their trade with impunity; yet they were hardly so terrible to peaceable citizens as another class of ruffians. It was a favorite amusement of dissolute young gentlemen to swagger by night about the town, breaking windows, upsetting sedans, beating quiet men, and offering rude caresses to pretty women. The machinery for keeping the peace was utterly contemptible. There was an act of Common Council which provided that more than a thousand watchmen should be constantly on the alert in the city, from sunset to sunrise, and that every inhabitant should take his turn of duty. But the act was negligently executed. Few of those who were summoned left their homes; and those few generally found it more agreeable to tipple in alehouses than to pace the streets.

It ought to be noticed that, in the last year of the reign of Charles the Second, began a great change in the police of London,—a change which has perhaps added as much to the happiness of the great body of the people as revolutions of much greater fame. An ingenious projector, named Edward Heming, obtained letters patent conveying to him, for a term of years, the exclusive right of lighting up London. He undertook, for a moderate consideration, to place a light before every tenth door, on moonless nights, from Michaelmas to Lady Day, [7] and from six to twelve of the clock. Those who now see the capital all the year round, from dusk to dawn, blazing with a splendor compared with which the illuminations for La Hogue [8] and Blenheim [9] would have looked

---

[6] CHARING CROSS TO WHITECHAPEL—Across London.

[7] MICHAELMAS TO LADY DAY—September 29 to March 25.

[8] LA HOGUE—The English victory of La Hogue. This naval battle was fought between the English and the French in the war which Louis XIV brought against England in an attempt to put King James II back on the throne after the English had expelled him.

[9] BLENHEIM—The battle in which Marlborough defeated the French in 1704.

pale, may perhaps smile to think of Heming's lanterns, which glimmered feebly before one house in ten during a small part of one night in three. But such was not the feeling of his contemporaries. His scheme was enthusiastically applauded and furiously attacked. The friends of improvement extolled him as the greatest of all the benefactors of his city. What, they asked, were the boasted inventions of Archimedes [10] when compared with the achievement of the man who had turned the nocturnal shades into noonday? In spite of these eloquent eulogies, the cause of darkness was not left undefended. There were fools in that age who opposed the introduction of what was called the new light as strenuously as fools in our age have opposed the introduction of vaccination and railroads, as strenuously as the fools of an age anterior to the dawn of history doubtless opposed the introduction of the plough and of alphabetical writing. Many years after the date of Heming's patent, there were extensive districts in which no lamp was seen.

[10] ARCHIMEDES—An ancient Greek scientist.

DID YOU READ WITH UNDERSTANDING?

Find, if possible, a map of London. Locate upon it the limits of the city proper. Locate also the parts of the city which you have read about in this and other selections—such places as Westminster, Covent Garden, Fleet Street, Lincoln's Inn Fields, and the like.

1. Why are the streets of old London narrow and crooked? Why were shops, inns, and places of business not designated by street number in 1685? How were they designated? In an essay "On the Naming of Streets" written before the present war, a modern English essayist, Max Beerbohm protested against the rebuilding of some sections of London, with streets being widened, straightened, and renamed. Do you think in such a case that progress should be sacrificed to sentiment? or sentiment to progress? Do you think a new plan should be laid out for post-war rebuilding? Or should England try to reproduce all the old landmarks?

2. Which period (so far as you can judge) has produced the greater changes—the years between the death of Charles II and Macaulay's *History,* or the years between 1850 and today? Illustrate by specific examples.

3. Do we in modern America still face some of the problems that bothered city dwellers in the seventeenth century? Discuss. What was America like in 1685? Which one American was responsible for the introduction of most of our improvements of city life—such improvements as street lighting, fire protection, public libraries, and the like? When did he live?

4. What other writers have given us descriptions of London life during the period Macaulay wrote about? Were they historians? Is there any advantage in our reading about customs, manners, and events of other days? Discuss.

OF BOOKS, OF READING, OF NATIONS

JOHN RUSKIN

Sesame [1] *and Lilies* is the title given to two lectures which Ruskin delivered in 1864 before a group of working men at Manchester. The first lecture, which is about books, has the special title "Of Kings' Treasuries." The address closed with a plea to have more good books made easily available to the people of England, for these books would be the "Sesame which opens doors—doors not of robbers', but of kings' treasuries." The second lecture, "Of Queens' Gardens," presents Ruskin's view on education for women and on woman's place in the world. The three selections which follow are from the first lecture. The "King's Treasuries," as you have guessed, are the riches to be found in books.

OF BOOKS

ALL books are divisible into two classes,—the books of the hour, and the books of all time. Mark this distinction; it is not one of quality only. It is not merely the bad book that does not last, and the good one that does; it is a distinction of species. There are good books for the hour, and good ones for all time; bad books for the hour, and bad ones for all time. I must define the two kinds before I go farther.

The good book of the hour, then,—I do not speak of the bad ones,—is simply the useful or pleasant talk of some person whom you cannot otherwise converse with, printed for you. Very useful often, telling you what you need to know; very pleasant often, as a sensible friend's present talk would be. These bright accounts of travel; good-humored and witty discussions of question; lively or pathetic story-telling in the form of novel; firm

---

[1] *Sesame*—In the story of *Ali Baba and the Forty Thieves* from *The Arabian Nights*, "Open Sesame (Sĕs'à-mē)" was the magic phrase which would open the entrance to the robbers' cave.

fact-telling, by the real agents concerned in the events of passing history,—all these books of the hour, multiplying among us as education becomes more general, are a peculiar possession of the present age. We ought to be entirely thankful for them, and entirely ashamed of ourselves if we make no good use of them. But we make the worst possible use if we allow them to usurp the place of true books; for strictly speaking, they are not books at all, but merely letters or newspapers in good print. Our friend's letter may be delightful or necessary today,—whether worth keeping or not, is to be considered. The newspaper may be entirely proper at breakfast-time, but assuredly it is not reading for all day; so, though bound up in a volume, the long letter which gives you so pleasant an account of the inns and roads and weather last year at such a place, or which tells you that amusing story, or gives you the real circumstances of such and such events, however valuable for occasional reference, may not be in the real sense of the word, a "book" at all, nor, in the real sense, to be "read." A book is essentially not a talked thing, but a written thing, and written not with a view of mere communication, but of permanence. The book of talk is printed only because its author cannot speak to thousands of people at once; if he could he would, —the volume is mere *multiplication* of his voice. You cannot talk to your friend in India; if you could, you would. You write instead; that is mere *conveyance* of voice. But a book is written, not to multiply the voice merely, not to carry it merely, but to perpetuate it. The author has something to say which he perceives to be true and useful, or helpfully beautiful. So far as he knows, no one has yet said it; so far as he knows, no one else can say it. He is bound to say it clearly and melodiously if he may; clearly, at all events. In the sum of his life he finds this to be the thing or group of things manifest to him,—this, the piece of true knowledge or sight which his share of sunshine and earth has permitted him to seize. He would fain set it down forever, engrave it on rock if he could, saying, "This is the best of me; for the rest, I ate and drank and slept, loved and hated, like another. My life was as the vapor, and is not; but this I saw and knew,— this, if anything of mine, is worth your memory." This is his "writing"; it is in his small human way, and with whatever degree of true inspiration is in him, his inscription or scripture. That is a "Book."

OF READING

VERY ready we are to say of a book, "How good this is,—
that's exactly what I think!" But the right feeling is, "How
strange that is! I never thought of that before, and yet I see it is
true; or if I do not now, I hope I shall some day." But whether
thus submissively or not, at least be sure that you go to the author
to get at *his* meaning, not to find yours. Judge it afterward if you
think yourself qualified to do so; but ascertain it first. And be
sure also, if the author is worth anything, that you will not get at
his meaning all at once—nay, that at his whole meaning you will
not for a long time arrive in any wise. Not that he does not say
what he means, and in strong words too; but he cannot say it all,
and what is more strange, *will* not, but in a hidden way and in
parable, in order that he may be sure you want it. I cannot quite
see the reason of this, nor analyze that cruel reticence in the
breasts of wise men which makes them always hide their deeper
thought. They do not give it you by way of help, but of reward,
and will make themselves sure that you deserve it before they allow you to reach it. But it is the same with the physical type of
wisdom, gold. There seems, to you and me, no reason why the
electric forces of the earth should not carry whatever there is of
gold within it at once to the mountain-tops; so that kings and
people might know that all the gold they could get was there, and
without any trouble of digging, or anxiety, or chance, or waste of
time, cut it away, and coin as much as they needed. But Nature
does not manage it so. She puts it in little fissures in the earth,
nobody knows where; you may dig long and find none; you must
dig painfully to find any.

And it is just the same with men's best wisdom. When you
come to a good book, you must ask yourself, "Am I inclined to
work as an Australian miner would? Are my pickaxes and shovels
in good order, and am I in good trim, myself, my sleeves well
up to the elbow, and my breath good, and my temper?" And
keeping the figure a little longer, even at a cost of tiresomeness,
for it is a thoroughly useful one, the metal you are in search of
being the author's mind or meaning, his words are as the rock
which you have to crush and smelt in order to get at it. And
your pickaxes are your own care, wit, and learning; your smelting
furnace is your own thoughtful soul. Do not hope to get any good

746

author's meaning without those tools and that fire; often you will need sharpest, finest chiseling and patientest fusing, before you can gather one grain of the metal.

And, therefore, first of all, I tell you earnestly and authoritatively (I *know* I am right in this), you must get into the habit of looking intensely at words, and assuring yourself of their meaning, syllable by syllable—nay, letter by letter. For though it is only by reason of the opposition of letters in the function of signs, to sounds in the function of signs, that the study of books is called "literature," and that a man versed in it is called, by the consent of nations, a man of letters instead of a man of books or of words, you may yet connect with that accidental nomenclature this real fact,—that you might read all the books in the British Museum (if you could live long enough) and remain an utterly "illiterate," uneducated person; but that if you read ten pages of a good book, letter by letter,—that is to say, with real accuracy,—you are forevermore in some measure an educated person. The entire difference between education and non-education (as regards the merely intellectual part of it) consists in this accuracy. A well-educated gentleman may not know many languages, may not be able to speak any but his own, may have read very few books. But whatever language he knows, he knows precisely; whatever word he pronounces, he pronounces rightly. Above all, he is learned in the *peerage* of words, knows the words of true descent and ancient blood, at a glance, from the words of modern *canaille,* remembers all their ancestry, their intermarriages, distant relationships, and the extent to which they were admitted, and offices they held, among the national *noblesse* of words at any time and in any country. But an uneducated person may know, by memory, many languages, and talk them all, and yet truly know not a word of any,—not a word even of his own.

OF NATIONS

As IN nothing is a gentleman better to be discerned from a vulgar person, so in nothing is a gentle nation (such nations have been) better to be discerned from a mob, than in this,— that their feelings are constant and just, results of due contemplation, and of equal thought. You can talk a mob into anything; its feelings may be—usually are—on the whole, generous and right; but it has no foundation for them, no hold of them; you may tease or tickle it into any, at your pleasure; it thinks by infection, for the most part, catching an opinion like a cold, and there is nothing so little that it will not roar itself wild about, when the fit is on;—nothing so great but it will forget in an hour, when the fit is past. But a gentleman's, or a gentle nation's, passions are just, measured, and continuous. A great nation, for instance, does not spend its entire national wits [1] for a couple of months in weighing evidence of a single ruffian's having done a single murder; and for a couple of years see its own children murder each other by their thousands or tens of thousands a day, considering only what the effect is likely to be on the price of cotton,[2] and caring nowise to determine which side of battle is in the wrong. Neither does a great nation send its poor little boys to jail for stealing six walnuts; and allow its bankrupts to steal their hundreds of thousands with a bow, and its bankers, rich with poor men's savings, to close their doors "under circumstances over which they have no control," with a "by your leave"; and large landed estates to be bought by men who have made their money by going with armed steamers up and down the China Seas, selling opium at the cannon's mouth,[3] and altering, for the benefit of the foreign nation, the common highwayman's demand of "your money *or* your life," into that of "your money *and* your life." Neither does a great nation allow the lives of its innocent poor to be parched out of them by fog fever, and rotted out of them by dunghill plague, for the sake of sixpence a life extra per week to its landlords; and then debate, with driveling tears, and diabolical sympathies, whether it ought not piously to save, and nursingly cherish, the lives of its murderers. Also, a great nation having made up its mind that hanging is quite the wholesomest process for its homicides in general, can yet with mercy distinguish between the degrees of guilt in homicides, and does not yelp like a pack of frost-pinched wolf-cubs on the blood track of an unhappy

---

[1] DOES NOT SPEND ITS ENTIRE NATIONAL WITS, etc.—This and the following illustrations Ruskin took from abuses current in England in 1864.

[2] EFFECT . . . ON THE PRICE OF COTTON—In spite of recent reform legislation, shocking conditions still existed in factories which continued to employ child labor.

[3] SELLING OPIUM AT THE CANNON'S MOUTH—One of Great Britain's blackest sins was her enforcing trade in opium when the Chinese government wished to prohibit traffic in the drug.

crazed boy, or gray-haired clodpate Othello,[4] "perplexed i' the extreme," at the very moment that it is sending Minister of the Crown to make polite speeches to a man who is bayoneting young girls in their fathers' sight, and killing noble youths in cool blood, faster than a country butcher kills lambs in spring. And, lastly, a great nation does not mock Heaven and its Powers, by pretending belief in a revelation which asserts the love of money to be the root of *all* evil, and declaring, at the same time, that it is actuated, and intends to be actuated, in all chief national deeds and measures, by no other love.

No nation can last, which has made a mob of itself, however generous at heart. It must discipline its passions, and direct them, or they will discipline *it*, one day, with scorpion-whips. Above all, a nation cannot last as a money-making job: it cannot with impunity,—it cannot with existence,—go on despising literature, despising science, despising art, despising nature, despising compassion, and concentrating its soul on Pence.

---

[4] CRAZED BOY, OR . . . CLODPATE OTHELLO—A reference to two sensational murders of the time, the "Othello" being a man who had killed his wife in a frenzy of jealousy. "Perplexed i' the extreme" is a quotation from Shakespeare's *Othello*.

DID YOU READ WITH UNDERSTANDING?

OF BOOKS:

1. Explain why Ruskin's classification of books is not one of *quality*, but one of *species*. Why does he not discuss *bad books*? Why would there not be any *bad books for all time*?

2. Explain why Ruskin calls books of travel or books that discuss current affairs not really books, but "letters" or "newspapers." Do you think Ruskin would classify the books that are coming out now about the war and post-war problems—even the good ones—as real *books*? Discuss.

3. Explain in your own words what Ruskin means by a *book*. How long do you think it takes a man or woman to write such a book? Discuss.

4. Which prose selections in this volume of English literature are from what Ruskin would classify as "good books for all time"? Discuss.

5. What kinds of printed matter today serve as mere *multiplication* or *conveyance* of voice? Find the list of current "best-sellers" from the book section of your Sunday newspaper. How many of the books listed there do you think will become *books for all time*? What are some of the bases of your judgment?

OF READING:

1. Do you think Ruskin would advise the student of English to study Latin? French? German? other languages? Why or why not?

2. What is meant by the *peerage* of words? by their *ancestry?* by their *intermarriages?* What would be Ruskin's attitude toward such expressions as "enthuse," "contact" (as a verb), "yeah"? Why?

3. Explain how Ruskin's figure for "digging out the meaning" of an author might be applied to the right kind of study habits. What additional "tools" does the student have at his disposal? Discuss *pro* and *con:* *The first and most important step in an effective study program is for the pupil to convince himself that study is work.*

OF NATIONS:

1. Do you think Ruskin had his own country, England, in mind when he mentions the things a "gentle nation" should not have done? How can you tell? List at least five specific national wrongs or abuses of the nineteenth century to which Ruskin refers indirectly.

2. Which, if any, of the abuses he describes may be found in twentieth-century America? Can you name similar national sins of which we should be aware, but which are peculiar to America? The mayors, representatives, governors of today were in high school a generation ago. A score of years from now the control of our government will be in *your* hands. What can you do to prepare yourselves for the responsibility?

A LIBERAL EDUCATION

THOMAS HENRY HUXLEY

The pupil who has read thoughtfully the prose selections up to this point must have observed certain great differences between the older systems of education and modern American systems. He must have noticed the classical complexion of English learning. Children barely able to talk were set at work upon the Greek alphabet and the rules of Latin grammar. A good scholar, ten or twelve years old, could turn out original verses in Latin—in fact, was expected to. De Quincey tells us that one of his diversions in his early teens was to translate the daily newspapers into Greek. All of which brings us to a second observation, that the older English system was very rigid and very thorough. There was little variation in the subjects taught or the classics read in the different schools; and the amount of reading—in English, Latin, and Greek literature and philosophy—expected of the young scholar seems to us staggering. For five hundred years the same traditions governed the classrooms of England. It was education for culture rather than for use. With these facts in mind, you will appreciate the revolutionary nature of Huxley's address on the subject "A Liberal Education" from which the following essay has been taken.

SUPPOSE it were perfectly certain that the life and fortune of every one of us would, one day or other, depend upon his winning or losing a game of chess. Don't you think that we should all consider it to be a primary duty to learn at least the names and the moves of the pieces; to have a notion of gambit, and a keen eye for all the means of giving and getting out of check? Do you not think that we should look with a disapprobation amounting to scorn, upon the father who allowed his son, or the state which allowed its members, to grow up without knowing a pawn from a knight?

Yet it is a very plain and elementary truth, that the life, the fortune, and the happiness of every one of us, and, more or less, of those who are connected with us, do depend upon our knowing something of the rules of a game infinitely more difficult and complicated than chess. It is a game which has been played for untold ages, every man and woman of us being one of the two players in a game of his or her own. The chessboard is the world, the pieces are the phenomena of the universe, the rules of the game are what we call the laws of Nature. The player on the other side is hidden from us. We know that his play is always fair, just, and patient. But also we know, to our cost, that he never overlooks a mistake, or makes the smallest allowance for ignorance. To the man who plays well, the highest stakes are paid, with that sort of overflowing generosity with which the strong shows delight in strength. And one who plays ill is check-mated—without haste, but without remorse.

My metaphor will remind some of you of the famous picture in which Retzsch [1] has depicted Satan playing at chess with man for his soul. Substitute for the mocking fiend in that picture, a calm, strong angel who is playing for love, as we say, and would rather lose than win—and I should accept it as an image of human life.

Well, what I mean by Education is learning the rules of this

[1] RETZSCH—Moritz Retzsch (1779–1857), a German painter and etcher.

mighty game. In other words, education is the instruction of the intellect in the laws of Nature, under which name I include not merely things and their forces but men and their ways; and the fashioning of the affections and of the will into an earnest and loving desire to move in harmony with those laws. For me education means neither more nor less than this. Anything which professes to call itself education must be tried by this standard, and if it fails to stand the test, I will not call it education, whatever may be the force of authority, or of numbers, upon the other side.

It is important to remember that, in strictness, there is no such thing as an uneducated man. Take an extreme case. Suppose that an adult man, in the full vigor of his faculties, could be suddenly placed in the world, as Adam is said to have been, and then left to do as he best might. How long would he be left uneducated? Not five minutes. Nature would begin to teach him, through the eye, the ear, the touch, the properties of objects. Pain and pleasure would be at his elbow telling him to do this and avoid that; and by slow degrees the man would receive an education, which, if narrow, would be thorough, real, and adequate to his circumstances, though there would be no extras and very few accomplishments.

And if to this solitary man entered a second Adam, or better still, an Eve, a new and greater world, that of social and moral phenomena, would be revealed. Joys and woes, compared with which all others might seem but faint shadows, would spring from the new relations. Happiness and sorrow would take the place of the coarser monitors, pleasure and pain; but conduct would still be shaped by the observation of the natural consequences of action; or, in other words, by the laws of the nature of man.

To every one of us the world was once as fresh and new as to Adam. And then, long before we were susceptible of any other mode of instruction, Nature took us in hand, and every minute of waking life brought its educational influence, shaping our actions into rough accordance with Nature's laws, so that we might not be ended untimely by too gross disobedience. Nor should I speak of this process of education as past for any one, be he as old as he may. For every man the world is as fresh as it was at the first day, and as full of untold novelties for him who has the eyes to see them. And Nature is still continuing her patient education of us in that great university, the universe, of which we are all members—Nature having no Test-Acts.[2]

Those who take honors in Nature's university, who learn the laws which govern men and things and obey them, are the really great and successful men in this world. The great mass of mankind are the "Poll," [3] who pick up just enough to get through without much discredit. Those who won't learn at all are plucked; [4] and then you can't come up again. Nature's pluck means extermination.

Thus the question of compulsory education is settled so far as Nature is concerned. Her bill on that question was framed and passed long ago. But, like all compulsory legislation, that of Nature is harsh and wasteful in its operation. Ignorance is visited as sharply as willful disobedience—incapacity meets with the same punishment as crime. Nature's discipline is not even a word and a blow, and the blow first; but the blow without the word. It is left to you to find out why your ears are boxed.

The object of what we commonly call education—that education in which man intervenes and which I shall distinguish as artificial education—is to make good these defects in Nature's methods; to prepare the child to receive Nature's education, neither incapably nor ignorantly, nor with willful disobedience; and to understand the preliminary symptoms of her displeasure, without waiting for the box on the ear. In short, all artificial education ought to be an anticipation of natural education. And a liberal education is an artificial education, which has not only prepared a man to escape the great evils of disobedience to natural laws, but has trained him to appreciate and to seize upon the rewards, which Nature scatters with as free a hand as her penalties.

That man, I think, has had a liberal education, who has been so trained in youth that his body is the ready servant of his will, and does with ease and pleasure all the work that, as a mechanism, it is capable of; whose intellect is a clear, cold, logic engine, with all its parts of equal strength, and in smooth working

[2] TEST-ACTS—Until 1871 there was enforced in all English universities a Test-Act, requiring every student to subscribe to the articles of belief of the Church of England before he could come up for a degree.
[3] POLL—An English college term for one who receives an ordinary degree without honors or distinction.
[4] PLUCKED—English slang for failed; like "flunked."

order; ready, like a steam engine, to be turned to any kind of work, and spin the gossamers as well as forge the anchors of the mind; whose mind is stored with a knowledge of the great and fundamental truths of Nature and of the laws of her operations; one who, no stunted ascetic, is full of life and fire, but whose passions are trained to come to heel by a vigorous will, the servant of a tender conscience; who has learned to love all beauty, whether of Nature or of art, to hate all vileness, and to respect others as himself.

Such an one and no other, I conceive, has had a liberal education; for he is, as completely as a man can be, in harmony with Nature. He will make the best of her, and she of him. They will get on together rarely; she as his ever beneficent mother; he as her mouthpiece, her conscious self, her minister and interpreter.

DID YOU READ WITH UNDERSTANDING?

1. In a dictionary or encyclopedia find an explanation of the game of *chess* and the terms used in it—such terms as *gambit, check, checkmate, pawn,* and *knight;* or have some class member who plays the game make the explanations.

2. Put Huxley's definition of education into your own words. Distinguish between *pleasure* and *happiness,* and between *pain* and *sorrow.*

3. Explain the sentence, "Nature's pluck means extermination." Can you name any persons who may be said to have "taken honors in Nature's university"? Give an illustration of Nature's method of teaching, "the blow without the word."

4. Would you be satisfied with this statement of the objective of education—"to learn to love all beauty, whether of nature or of art, to hate all vileness, and to respect others as oneself"? If not, how would you change it?

5. Was Huxley an atheist? Prove the correctness of your answer by reference to the essay. How do you think Huxley would judge the education offered by the usual American high school?

6. Make an outline of what seems to you to be an ideal program of studies for a senior high school. How many electives would you allow? What courses should be required? Discuss.

Short story and the novel flourished.

MARKHEIM

ROBERT LOUIS STEVENSON

"YES," said the dealer, "our windfalls are of various kinds. Some customers are ignorant, and then I touch a dividend on my superior knowledge. Some are dishonest," and here he held up the candle, so that the light fell strongly on his visitor, "and in that case," he continued, "I profit by my virtue."

Markheim had but just entered from the daylight streets, and his eyes had not yet grown familiar with the mingled shine and darkness in the shop. At these pointed words, and before the near presence of the flame, he blinked painfully and looked aside.

The dealer chuckled. "You come to me on Christmas Day," he resumed, "when you know that I am alone in my house, put up my shutters, and make a point of refusing business. Well, you will have to pay for that; you will have to pay for my loss of time, when I should be balancing my books; you will have to pay, besides, for a kind of manner that I remark in you today, very strongly. I am the essence of discretion, and ask no awkward question; but when a customer cannot look me in the eye, he has to pay for it." The dealer once more chuckled; and then, changing to his usual business voice, though still with a note of irony, "You can give, as usual, a clear account of how you came into the possession of the object?" he continued. "Still your uncle's cabinet? A remarkable collector, sir!"

And the little pale, round-shouldered dealer stood almost on tiptoe, looking over the top of his gold spectacles, and nodding his head with every mark of disbelief. Markheim returned his gaze with one of infinite pity, and a touch of terror.

"This time," said he, "you are in error. I have not come to sell, but to buy. I have no curios to dispose of; my uncle's cabinet is bare to the wainscot; even were it still intact, I have done well on the Stock Exchange, and should more likely add to it than otherwise, and my errand today is simplicity itself. I seek a Christmas present for a lady," he continued, waxing more fluent as he struck into the speech he had prepared; "and certainly I owe you every excuse for thus disturbing you upon so small a matter. But the thing was neglected yesterday; I must produce my little compliment at dinner; and, as you very well know, a rich marriage is not a thing to be neglected."

There followed a pause, during which the dealer seemed to weigh this statement incredulously. The ticking of many clocks among the curious lumber of the shop, and the faint rushing of the cabs in a near thoroughfare, filled up the interval of silence.

"Well, sir," said the dealer, "be it so. You are an old customer after all; and if, as you say, you have the chance of a good marriage, far be it from me to be an obstacle. Here is a nice thing for a lady now," he went on, "this hand glass—fifteenth century, warranted; comes from a good collection, too; but I reserve the name, in the interests of my customer, who was just like yourself, my dear sir, the nephew and sole heir of a remarkable collector."

The dealer, while he thus ran on in his dry and biting voice, had stooped to take the object from its place; and, as he had done so, a shock had passed through Markheim, a start both of hand and foot, a sudden leap of many tumultuous passions to the face. It passed as swiftly as it came, and left no trace beyond a certain trembling of the hand that now received the glass.

"A glass," he said hoarsely, and then paused, and repeated it more clearly. "A glass? For Christmas? Surely not!"

"And why not?" cried the dealer. "Why not a glass?"

Markheim was looking upon him with an indefinable expression. "You ask me why not?" he said. "Why, look here—look in it—look at yourself! Do you like to see it? No! nor I—nor any man."

The little man had jumped back when Markheim had so suddenly confronted him with the mirror; but now, perceiving there was nothing worse on hand, he chuckled. "Your future lady, sir, must be pretty hard favored," said he.

"I ask you," said Markheim, "for a Christmas present, and you give me this—this reminder of years, and sins and follies—this hand-conscience! Did you mean it? Had you a thought in your mind? Tell me. It will be better for you if you do. Come, tell me about yourself. I hazard a guess now, that you are in secret a very charitable man?"

The dealer looked closely at his companion. It was very odd, Markheim did not appear to be laughing; there was something in his face like an eager sparkle of hope, but nothing of mirth.

"What are you driving at?" the dealer asked.

"Not charitable?" returned the other, gloomily. "Not charitable; not pious; not scrupulous; unloving, unbeloved; a hand to get money, a safe to keep it. Is that all? Is that all, man, is that all?"

"I will tell you what it is," began the dealer, with some sharpness, and then broke off again into a chuckle. "But I see this is a love match of yours, and you have been drinking the lady's health."

"Ah!" cried Markheim, with a strange curiosity. "Ah, have you been in love? Tell me about that."

"I!" cried the dealer. "I in love! I never had the time, nor have I the time today for all this nonsense. Will you take the glass?"

"Where is the hurry?" returned Markheim. "It is very pleasant to stand here talking; and life is so short and insecure that I would not hurry away from any pleasure—no, not even from so mild a one as this. We should rather cling, cling to what little we can get, like a man at a cliff's edge. Every second is a cliff, if you think upon it—a cliff a mile high—high enough, if we fall, to dash us out of every feature of humanity. Hence it is best to talk pleasantly. Let us talk of each other; why should we wear this mask? Let us be confidential. Who knows, we might become friends."

"I have just one word to say to you," said the dealer. "Either make your purchase, or walk out of my shop."

"True, true," said Markheim. "Enough fooling. To business. Show me something else."

The dealer stooped once more, this time to replace the glass upon the shelf, his thin blond hair falling over his eyes as he did so. Markheim moved a little nearer, with one hand in the pocket of his greatcoat; he drew himself up and filled his lungs; at the same time many different emotions were depicted together on his face—terror, horror, and resolve, fascination and a physical repulsion; and through a haggard lift of his upper lip, his teeth looked out.

"This, perhaps, may suit," observed the dealer; and then, as he began to re-arise, Markheim bounded from behind upon his victim. The long, skewerlike dagger flashed and fell. The dealer struggled like a hen, striking his temple on the shelf, and then tumbled on the floor in a heap.

Time had some score of small voices in that shop, some stately and slow as was becoming to their great age; others garrulous and hurried. All these told out the seconds in an intricate chorus of tickings. Then the passage of a lad's feet, heavily running on the pavement, broke in upon these smaller voices and startled Markheim into the consciousness of his surroundings. He looked about him awfully. The candle stood on the counter, its flame solemnly wagging in a draught; and by that inconsiderable movement, the whole room was filled with noiseless bustle and kept heaving like a sea. The tall shadows nodding, the gross blots of darkness swelling and dwindling as with respiration, the faces of the portraits and the china gods changing and wavering like images in water. The inner door stood ajar, and peered into that leaguer of shadows with a long slit of daylight like a pointing finger.

From these fear-stricken rovings, Markheim's eyes returned to the body of his victim, where it lay both humped and sprawling, incredibly small and strangely meaner than in life. In these poor, miserly clothes, in that ungainly attitude, the dealer lay like so much sawdust. Markheim had feared to see it, and, lo! it was nothing. And yet, as he gazed, this bundle of old clothes and pool of blood began to find eloquent voices. There it must lie; there was none to work the cunning hinges or direct the miracle of loco-motion—there it must lie till it was found. Found! ay, and then? Then would this dead flesh lift up a cry that would ring over England, and fill the world with the echoes of pursuit. Ay, dead or not, this was still the enemy. "Time was that when the brains were out," [1] he thought; and the first word struck into his mind. Time, now that the deed was accomplished—time, which had closed for the victim, had become instant and momentous for the slayer.

The thought was yet in his mind, when, first one and then an-other, with every variety of pace and voice—one deep as the bell from the cathedral turret, another ringing on its treble notes the prelude of a waltz—the clocks began to strike the hour of three in the afternoon.

The sudden outbreak of so many tongues in that dumb chamber staggered him. He began to bestir himself, going to and fro with the candle, beleaguered by moving shadows, and startled to the soul by chance reflections. In many rich mirrors, some of home designs, some from Venice or Amsterdam, he saw his face re-peated and repeated, as it were an army of spies; his own eyes met and detected him; and the sound of his own steps, lightly as they fell, vexed the surrounding quiet. And still as he continued to fill his pockets, his mind accused him, with a sickening itera-tion, of the thousand faults of his design. He should have chosen a more quiet hour; he should have prepared an alibi; he should not have used a knife; he should have been more cautious, and only bound and gagged the dealer and not killed him; he should have been more bold, and killed the servant also; he should have done all things otherwise; poignant regrets, weary, incessant toil-ing of the mind to change what was unchangeable, to plan what was now useless, to be the architect of the irrevocable past. Meanwhile, and behind all this activity, brute terrors, like the scurrying of rats in a deserted attic, filled the more remote cham-bers of his brain with riot; the hand of the constable would fall heavy on his shoulder, and his nerves would jerk like a hooked fish; or he beheld, in galloping defile, the dock, the prison, the gallows, and the black coffin.

Terror of the people in the street sat down before his mind

---

[1] TIME WAS THAT WHEN THE BRAINS WERE OUT—A reference to *Macbeth*, Act III, Scene 4.

like a besieging army. It was impossible, he thought, but that
some rumor of the struggle must have reached their ears and set
on edge their curiosity; and now, in all the neighboring houses,
he divined them sitting motionless and with uplifted ear—prying
and hearkening and weaving the rope that was to hang him.
Sometimes it seemed to him he could not move too softly; the
clink of the tall Bohemian goblets rang out loudly like a bell;
and alarmed by the bigness of the ticking, he was tempted to stop
the clocks. And then, again, with a swift transition of his terrors,
the very silence of the place appeared a source of peril, and a
thing to strike and freeze the passer-by; and he would step more
boldly, and bustle aloud among the contents of the shop, and
imitate, with elaborate bravado, the movements of a busy man
at ease in his own house.

But he was now so pulled about by the different alarms that,
while one portion of his mind was still alert and cunning, another
trembled on the brink of lunacy. One hallucination in particular
took a strong hold on his credulity. The neighbor hearkening
with white face beside his window, the passer-by arrested by a
horrible surmise on the pavement—these could at worst suspect,
they could not know; through the brick walls and shuttered windows only sounds could penetrate. But here within the house,
was he alone? He knew he was; he had watched the servant set
forth sweethearting, in her poor best, "out for the day" written in
every ribbon and smile. Yes, he was alone, of course; and yet, in
the bulk of empty house above him, he could surely hear a stir
of delicate footing—he was surely conscious, inexplicably conscious of some presence. Ay, surely; to every room and corner of
the house his imagination followed it; and now it was a faceless
thing, and yet had eyes to see with; and again it was a shadow of
himself; and yet again behold the image of the dead dealer, re-
inspired with cunning and hatred.

At times, with a strong effort, he would glance at the open door
which still seemed to repel his eyes. The house was tall, the sky-
light small and dirty, the day blind with fog; and the light that
filtered down to the ground story was exceedingly faint, and
showed dimly on the threshold of the shop. And yet, in that strip
of doubtful brightness, did there not hang wavering a shadow?

Suddenly, from the street outside, a very jovial gentleman began to beat with a staff on the shop-door, accompanying his blows

with shouts and railleries in which the dealer was continually called upon by name. Markheim, smitten into ice glanced at the dead man. But no! he lay quite still; he was fled away far beyond earshot of these blows and shoutings; he was sunk beneath seas of silence; and his name, which would once have caught his notice above the howling of a storm, had become an empty sound. And presently the jovial gentleman desisted from his knocking and departed.

Here was a broad hint to hurry what remained to be done, to get forth from this accusing neighborhood, to plunge into a bath of London multitudes, and to reach, in the other side of day, that haven of safety and apparent innocence—his bed. One visitor had come; at any moment another might follow and be more obstinate. To have done the deed, and yet not to reap the profit, would be too abhorrent a failure. The money, that was now Markheim's concern; and as a means to that, the keys.

He glanced over his shoulder at the open door, where the shadow was still lingering and shivering; and with no conscious repugnance of the mind, yet with a tremor of the belly, he drew near the body of his victim. The human character had quite departed. Like a suit half-stuffed with bran, the limbs lay scattered, the trunk doubled, on the floor; and yet the thing repelled him. Although so dingy and inconsiderable to the eye, he feared it might have more significance to the touch. He took the body by the shoulders, and turned it on its back. It was strangely light and supple, and the limbs, as if they had been broken, fell into the oddest postures. The face was robbed of all expression; but it was as pale as wax, and shockingly smeared with blood about one temple. That was, for Markheim, the one displeasing circumstance. It carried him back, upon the instant, to a certain fair day in a fishers' village: a gray day, a piping wind, a crowd upon the street, the blare of brasses, the booming of drums, the nasal voice of a ballad singer; and a boy going to and fro, buried over head in the crowd and divided between interest and fear, until, coming out upon the chief place of concourse, he beheld a booth and a great screen with pictures, dismally designed, garishly colored: Brownrigg with her apprentice; the Mannings with their murdered guest; Weare in the death grip of Thurtell; [2] and a score besides

---

[2] BROWNRIGG, THE MANNINGS, THURTELL—Notorious murderers, popular subjects for waxwork displays.

of famous crimes. The thing was as clear as an illusion; he was once again that little boy; he was looking once again, and with the same sense of physical revolt, at these vile pictures; he was still stunned by the thumping of the drums. A bar of that day's music returned upon his memory; and at that, for the first time, a qualm came over him, a breath of nausea, a sudden weakness of the joints, which he must instantly resist and conquer.

He judged it more prudent to confront than to flee from these considerations; looking the more hardily in the dead face, bending his mind to realize the nature and greatness of his crime. So little a while ago that face had moved with every change of sentiment, that pale mouth had spoken, that body had been all on fire with governable energies; and now, and by his act, that piece of life had been arrested, as the horologist, with interjected finger, arrests the beating of the clock. So he reasoned in vain; he could rise to no more remorseful consciousness. At best, he felt a gleam of pity for one who had been endowed in vain with all those faculties that can make the world a garden of enchantment, one who had never lived and who was now dead. But of penitence, no, not a tremor.

With that, shaking himself clear of these considerations, he found the keys and advanced towards the open door of the shop. Outside, it had begun to rain smartly; and the sound of the shower upon the roof had banished silence. Like some dripping cavern, the chambers of the house were haunted by an incessant echoing, which filled the ear and mingled with the ticking of the clocks. And, as Markheim approached the door, he seemed to hear, in answer to his own cautious tread, the steps of another foot withdrawing up the stair. The shadow still palpitated loosely on the threshold. He threw a ton's weight of resolve upon his muscles, and drew back the door.

The faint, foggy daylight glimmered dimly on the bare floor and stairs; on the bright suit of armor posted, halbert in hand, upon the landing; and on the dark wood-carvings, and framed pictures that hung against the yellow panels of the wainscot. So loud was the beating of the rain through all the house that, in Markheim's ears, it began to be distinguished into many different sounds. Footsteps and sighs, the tread of regiments marching in the distance, the chink of money in the counting, and the creaking of doors held stealthily ajar, appeared to mingle with the patter of the drops upon the cupola and the gushing of the water in the pipes. The sense that he was not alone grew upon him to the verge of madness. On every side he was haunted and begirt by presences. He heard them moving in the upper chambers; from the shop, he heard the dead man getting to his legs; and as he began with a great effort to mount the stairs, feet fled quietly before him and followed stealthily behind. If he were but deaf, he thought, how tranquily he would possess his soul! And then again, and hearkening with ever fresh attention, he blessed himself for that unresting sense which held the outposts and stood a trusty sentinel upon his life. His head turned continually on his neck; his eyes which seemed starting from their orbits, scouted on every side, and on every side were half-rewarded as with the tail of something nameless vanishing. The four-and-twenty steps to the first floor were four-and-twenty agonies.

On that first story, the doors stood apart, three of them like three ambushes, shaking his nerves like the throats of cannon. He could never again, he felt, be sufficiently immured and fortified from men's observing eyes; he longed to be home, girt in by walls, buried among bedclothes, and invisible to all but God. And at that thought he wondered a little, recollecting tales of other murderers and the fear they were said to entertain of heavenly avengers. It was not so, at least, with him. He feared the laws of nature, lest, in their callous and immutable procedure, they should preserve some damning evidence of his crime. He feared tenfold more, with a slavish, superstitious terror, some scission in the continuity of man's experience, some willful illegality of nature. He played a game of skill, depending on the rules, calculating consequence from cause; and what if nature, as the defeated tyrant overthrew the chessboard, should break the mold of their succession? The like had befallen Napoleon (so writers said) when the winter changed the time of its appearance. The like might befall Markheim: the solid walls might become transparent and reveal his doings like those of bees in a glass hive; the stout planks might yield under his foot like quicksands and detain him in their clutch; ay, and there were soberer accidents that might destroy him: if, for instance, the house should fall and imprison him beside the body of his victim; or the house next door should fly on fire, and the firemen invade him from all sides. These things he feared; and, in a sense, these things might be called the hands of God reached forth against sin. But about God himself he was at ease; his act was doubtless exceptional, but so were his excuses, which God knew; it was there, and not among men, that he felt sure of justice.

When he had got safe into the drawing room, and shut the door behind him, he was aware of a respite from alarms. The room was quite dismantled, uncarpeted besides, and strewn with packing cases and incongruous furniture; several great pier-glasses, in which he beheld himself at various angles, like an actor on a stage; many pictures, framed and unframed, standing, with their faces to the wall; a fine Sheraton sideboard, a cabinet of marquetry, and a great old bed, with tapestry hangings. The windows opened to the floor; but by great good fortune the lower part of the shutters had been closed, and this concealed him from the neighbors. Here, then, Markheim drew in a packing case before the cabinet, and began to search among the keys. It was a long business, for there were many; and it was irksome, besides; for, after all, there might be nothing in the cabinet, and time was on the wing. But the closeness of the occupation sobered him. With the tail of his eye he saw the door—even glanced at it from time to time directly, like a besieged commander pleased to verify the good estate of his defences. But in truth he was at peace. The rain falling in the street sounded natural and pleasant. Presently, on the other side, the notes of a piano were wakened to the music of a hymn, and the voices of many children took up the air and words. How stately, how comfortable was the melody! How fresh the youthful voices! Markheim gave ear to it smilingly, as he sorted out the keys; and his mind was thronged with answerable ideas and images; church-going children and the pealing of the high organ; children afield, bathers by the brookside, ramblers on the brambly common, kite-flyers in the windy and cloud-navigated sky; and then, at another cadence of the hymn, back again to church, and the somnolence of summer Sundays, and the high, genteel voice of the parson.

And as he sat thus, at once busy and absent, he was startled to his feet. A flash of ice, a flash of fire, a bursting gush of blood, went over him, and then he stood transfixed and thrilling. A step mounted the stair slowly and steadily, and presently a hand was laid upon the knob, and the lock clicked, and the door opened.

Fear held Markheim in a vice. What to expect he knew not, whether the dead man walking, or the official ministers of human justice, or some chance witness blindly stumbling in to consign him to the gallows. But when a face was thrust into the aperture, glanced round the room, looked at him, nodded and smiled as if in friendly recognition, and then withdrew again, and the door closed behind it, his fear broke loose from his control in a hoarse cry. At the sound of this the visitant returned.

"Did you call me?" he asked, pleasantly, and with that he entered the room and closed the door behind him.

Markheim stood and gazed at him with all his eyes. Perhaps there was a film upon his sight, but the outlines of the newcomer seemed to change and waver like those of the idols in the wavering candlelight of the shop; and at times he thought he knew him; and at times he thought he bore a likeness to himself; and always, like a lump of living terror, there lay in his bosom the conviction that this thing was not of the earth and not of God.

And yet the creature had a strange air of the commonplace, as he stood looking on Markheim with a smile; and when he added: "You are looking for the money, I believe?" it was in the tones of everyday politeness.

Markheim made no answer.

"I should warn you," resumed the other, "that the maid has left her sweetheart earlier than usual and will soon be here. If Mr. Markheim be found in this house, I need not describe to him the consequences."

"You know me?" cried the murderer.

The visitor smiled. "You have long been a favorite of mine," he said; "and I have long observed and often sought to help you."

"What are you?" cried Markheim: "the devil?"

"What I may be," returned the other, "cannot affect the service I propose to render you."

"It can," cried Markheim, "it does! Be helped by you? No, never; not by you! You do not know me yet; thank God, you do not know me!"

"I know you," replied the visitant, with a sort of kind severity or rather firmness. "I know you to the soul."

"Know me!" cried Markheim. "Who can do so? My life is but a travesty and slander on myself. I have lived to belie my nature. All men do; all men are better than this disguise that grows about and stifles them. You see each dragged away by life, like one whom bravos have seized and muffled in a cloak. If they had their own control—if you could see their faces, they would be altogether different, they would shine out for heroes and saints! I am worse than most; my self is more overlaid; my excuse is known to me and God. But, had I the time, I could disclose myself."

"To me?" inquired the visitant.

"To you before all," returned the murderer. "I supposed you were intelligent. I thought—since you exist—you would prove a reader of the heart. And yet you would propose to judge me by my acts! Think of it; my acts! I was born and I have lived in a land of giants; giants have dragged me by the wrists since I was born out of my mother—the giants of circumstance. And you would judge me by my acts! But can you not look within? Can you not understand that evil is hateful to me? Can you not see within me the clear writing of conscience, never blurred by any willful sophistry, although too often disregarded? Can you not read me for a thing that surely must be common as humanity —the unwilling sinner?"

"All this is very feelingly expressed," was the reply, "but it regards me not. These points of consistency are beyond my province, and I care not in the least by what compulsion you may have been dragged away, so as you are but carried in the right direction. But time flies; the servant delays, looking in the faces of the crowd and at the pictures on the boardings, but still she keeps moving nearer; and remember, it is as if the gallows itself were striding towards you through the Christmas streets! Shall I help you; I, who know all? Shall I tell you where to find the money?"

"For what price?" asked Markheim.

"I offer you the service for a Christmas gift," returned the other.

Markheim could not refrain from smiling with a kind of bitter triumph. "No," said he, "I will take nothing at your hands; if I were dying of thirst, and it was your hand that put the pitcher to my lips, I should find the courage to refuse. I may be credulous, but I will do nothing to commit myself to evil."

"I have no objection to a death-bed repentance," observed the visitant.

"Because you disbelieve their efficacy!" Markheim cried.

"I do not say so," returned the other; "but I look on these things from a different side, and when the life is done my interest falls. The man has lived to serve me, to spread black looks under color of religion, or to sow tares in the wheat field, as you do, in a course of weak compliance with desire. Now that he draws so near to his deliverance, he can add but one act of service—to repent, to die smiling, and thus to build up in confidence and hope the more timorous of my surviving followers. I am not so hard a master. Try me. Accept my help. Please yourself in life as you have done hitherto; please yourself more amply, spread our elbows at the board; and when the night begins to fall and the curtains to be drawn, I tell you, for your greater comfort, that you will find it even easy to compound your quarrel with your conscience, and to make a truckling peace with God."

"And do you, then, suppose me such a creature?" asked Markheim. "Do you think I have no more generous aspirations than to sin, and sin, and sin, and, at last, sneak into heaven? My heart rises at the thought. Is this, then, your experience of mankind? or is it because you find me with red hands that you presume such baseness? and is this crime of murder indeed so impious as to dry up the very springs of good?"

"Murder has to me no special category," replied the other. "All sins are murder, even as all life is war. I behold your race, like starving mariners on a raft, plucking crusts out of the hands of famine and feeding on each other's lives. I follow sins beyond the moment of their acting; I find in all that the last consequence is death; and to my eyes, the pretty maid who thwarts her mother with such taking graces on a question of a ball, drips no less visibly with human gore than such a murderer as yourself. Do

I say that I follow sins? I follow virtues also; they differ not by
the thickness of a nail, they are both scythes for the reaping angel
of Death. Evil, for which I live, consists not in action but in
character. The bad man is dear to me; not the bad act, whose
fruits, if we could follow them far enough down the hurtling
cataract of the ages, might yet be found more blessed than those
of the rarest virtues. And it is not because you have killed a
dealer, but because you are Markheim, that I offered to forward
your escape."

"I will lay my heart open to you," answered Markheim. "This
crime on which you find me is my last. On my way to it I have
learned many lessons; itself is a lesson, a momentous lesson.
Hitherto I have been driven with revolt to what I would not; I
was a bond-slave to poverty, driven and scourged. There are
robust virtues that can stand in these temptations; mine was not
so: I had a thirst for pleasure. But today, and out of this deed,
I pluck both warning and riches—both the power and a fresh
resolve to be myself. I become in all things a free actor in the ·
world; I begin to see myself all changed, these hands the agents
of good, this heart at peace. Something comes over me out of
the past; something of what I have dreamed on Sabbath evenings
to the sound of the church organ, of what I forecast when I shed
tears over noble books, or talked, an innocent child, with my
mother. There lies my life; I have wandered a few years, but
now I see once more my city of destination."

"You are to use this money on the Stock Exchange, I think?"
remarked the visitor; "and there, if I mistake not, you have already lost some thousands?"

"Ah," said Markheim, "but this time I have a sure thing."

"This time, again, you will lose," replied the visitor quietly.

"Ah, but I keep back the half!" cried Markheim.

"That also you will lose," said the other.

The sweat started upon Markheim's brow. "Well, then, what
matter?" he exclaimed. "Say it be lost, say I am plunged again
in poverty, shall one part of me, and that the worse, continue until
the end to override the better? Evil and good run strong in me,
hailing me both ways. I do not love the one thing, I love all. I
can conceive great deeds, renunciations, martyrdoms; and though
I be fallen to such a crime as murder, pity is no stranger to my
thoughts. I pity the poor; who knows their trials better than

myself? I pity and help them; I prize love, I love honest laughter; there is no good thing nor true thing on earth but I love it from my heart. And are my vices only to direct my life, and my virtues to lie without effect, like some passive lumber of the mind? Not so; good, also, is the spring of acts."

But the visitant raised his finger. "For six-and-thirty years that you have been in this world," said he, "through many changes of fortune and varieties of humor, I have watched you steadily fall. Fifteen years ago you would have started at a theft. Three years back you would have blanched at the name of murder. Is there any crime, is there any cruelty or meanness, from which you still recoil?—five years from now I shall detect you in the act! Downward, downward, lies your way; nor can anything but death avail to stop you."

"It is true," Markheim said huskily, "I have in some degree complied with evil. But it is so with all: the very saints, in the mere exercise of living, grow less dainty, and take on the tone of their surroundings."

"I will propound to you one simple question," said the other; "and as you answer, I shall read to you your moral horoscope. You have grown in many things more lax; possibly you do right to be so; and at any account, it is the same with all men. But granting that, are you in any one particular, however trifling, more difficult to please with your own conduct, or do you go in all things with a looser rein?"

"In any one?" repeated Markheim, with an anguish of consideration. "No," he added, with despair, "in none! I have gone down in all."

"Then," said the visitor, "content yourself with what you are, for you will never change; and the words of your part on this stage are irrevocably written down."

Markheim stood for a long while silent, and indeed it was the visitor who first broke the silence. "That being so," he said, "shall I show you the money?"

"And grace?" cried Markheim.

"Have you not tried it?" returned the other.. "Two or three years ago, did I not see you on the platform of revival meetings, and was not your voice the loudest in the hymn?"

"It is true," said Markheim; "and I see clearly what remains for me by way of duty. I thank you for these lessons from my soul; my eyes are opened, and I behold myself at last for what I am."

At this moment, the sharp note of the doorbell rang through the house; and the visitant, as though this were some concerted signal for which he had been waiting changed at once in his demeanor.

"The maid!" he cried. "She has returned, as I forewarned you, and there is now before you one more difficult passage. Her master, you must say, is ill; you must let her in, with an assured but rather serious countenance—no smiles, no over-acting, and I promise you success! Once the girl within, and the door closed, the same dexterity that has already rid you of the dealer will relieve you of this last danger in your path. Thenceforward you have the whole evening—the whole night, if needful—to ransack the treasures of the house and to make good your safety. This is help that comes to you with the mask of danger. Up!" he cried, "up, friend; your life hangs trembling in the scales; up, and act!"

Markheim steadily regarded his counselor. "If I be condemned to evil acts," he said, "there is still one door of freedom open— I can cease from action. If my life be an ill thing, I can lay it down. Though I be, as you say truly, at the beck of every small temptation, I can yet, by one decisive gesture, place myself beyond the reach of all. My love of good is damned to barrenness; it may, and let it be! But I have still my hatred of evil; and from that, to your galling disappointment, you shall see that I can draw both energy and courage."

The features of the visitor began to undergo a wonderful and lovely change: they brightened and softened with a tender triumph; and, even as they brightened, faded and dislimned. Markheim did not pause to watch or understand the transformation. He opened the door and went downstairs very slowly, thinking to himself. His past went soberly before him; he beheld it as it was, ugly and strenuous like a dream, random as chance-medley— a scene of defeat. Life, as he thus reviewed it, tempted him no longer; but on the further side he perceived a quiet haven for his bark. He paused in the passage, and looked into the shop, where the candle still burned by the dead body. It was strangely silent. Thoughts of the dealer swarmed into his mind, as he stood gazing. And then the bell once more broke out into impatient clamor.

He confronted the maid upon the threshold with something like a smile.

"You had better go for the police," said he: "I have killed your master."

DID YOU READ WITH UNDERSTANDING?

1. What kind of man is the dealer? What indications are there as to whether or not he is an honest dealer? Is the reader inclined at any time to sympathize with him? Why or why not?

2. In what indirect ways does the reader learn that Markheim is a thief? What is the first hint? When do you begin to realize that Markheim is not an ordinary kind of thief? What is there unusual in his manner? in his speech?

3. Why did the hand-mirror upset him so? Did it trouble the dealer in the same way? Do you think Markheim had come to the shop with the intention of murdering the dealer? Discuss.

4. Why was Markheim eager to discover some redeeming trait in the dealer? What difference would it make whether the dealer was secretly charitable or pious or had been in love?

5. What were Markheim's first reactions after the murder? Were they such as most men would feel under the circumstances? List the varying emotions which Markheim experienced between the time of the murder and the moment when, looking for the keys to the cabinet, he heard the step on the stairs. Are any of these emotions preparatory to the experience which follows? Discuss.

6. Who do you think Markheim's visitor was? Do you think he was a real person? the creature of Markheim's imagination? a spirit of evil? a good spirit? Markheim's own conscience? Discuss.

7. In the conversation between Markheim and his visitor, what further traits of Markheim's character are disclosed? Was Markheim able to read his own character right? from the beginning? Is he essentially honest in appraising himself? How do you judge?

8. Why did Markheim seem so certain that God would understand and condone his acts? In what respect was he disappointed in his visitor? Why did he refuse to accept help in finding the money? or to escape before the servant returned? or to murder the servant in order to save himself? Was the visitor disappointed in Markheim's decision? How can you tell? How does this consideration help determine your answer to question 6 above?

9. Were you disappointed in the ending of the story? Why or why not? Do you think such a man as Markheim was and had been could really give himself up? Do you think he would later regret his decision? Discuss.

EXTENDED ACTIVITIES

THE VICTORIAN ERA WAS ESSENTIALLY AN AGE OF PROSE

VII

HISTORY IN BRIEF

	The House of Hanover	Events in America
1840-1899 (19th Century)	Victoria (1837-1901) (Marriage to Albert, 1840) (Crimean War, 1853-1856) (Indian Mutiny, 1857-1858) (Proclaimed sovereign of India, 1858) (Death of Albert, 1861) (Second Reform Bill, 1867) (Boers' Revolt, 1880-1881) (Fiftieth Anniversary, 1887) (Diamond Jubilee, 1897)	Mexican War, 1846-1848 Poets reflect the spirit of America: William Cullen Bryant (1794-1878) Ralph Waldo Emerson (1803-1882) Henry Wadsworth Longfellow (1807-1882) John Greenleaf Whittier (1807-1892) Oliver Wendell Holmes (1809-1894) James Russell Lowell (1819-1891) Walt Whitman (1819-1892) Fugitive Slave Law, 1850 Dred Scott Case, 1857 John Brown's Raid, 1859 Abraham Lincoln, president, 1860 War between the States, 1861-1865 Lincoln assassinated, 1865 Purchase of Alaska, 1867 Westward expansion, 1870-1900 War with Spain, 1898

FOR ACQUAINTANCE WITH AUTHORS

THOMAS CARLYLE (1795-1881)—"THE STORMING OF THE BASTILLE"

Not unlike the dour, rugged country from which he came was Thomas Carlyle. He had the rather common Scotch combination of a crusty exterior and a sweet, sound core.

There are four important settings in the drama of Carlyle's life. The first is a farmer's cottage at Ecclefechan, near Dumfries in Scotland. Thomas himself is a peasant lad—sturdy, ruddy-cheeked, accustomed to hard work. He is the oldest child and his parents have decided that he is to be a Presbyterian minister. At fourteen, therefore, he sets off on foot for the University of Edinburgh, eighty miles away.

The second scene is a poor student's lodgings at college. Carlyle is friendless and miserable. The indigestion which tormented him the rest of his days has begun—undoubtedly the result of privation. But he has found an enthusiasm in German literature and philosophy—an enthusiasm which inspired his own first writings and which was the one happy association of his college years.

The third scene is not a parsonage but a farmhouse. Carlyle was convinced that he was not to be a minister. After some luckless experimenting with jobs, he settled down to write. In 1826 he had married Jane

Welsh, a beautiful girl who had also some genius as a writer. Though her father was a physician, Jane owned a farm at Craigenputtock; here the couple decided to live while Thomas was getting established. It was a lonely place, and life was hard—especially for Jane, who baked bread, scrubbed floors, washed clothes, and wheedled her husband. Carlyle responded by writing *The Life of Burns* and *Sartor Resartus* (reflective of his interest in German philosophy). It was at Craigenputtock that Carlyle first entertained Emerson and made a life-long friend. At the end of seven years he was finding a regular market for his writings and decided to leave the farm.

For the next forty-seven years a house in Cheyne Row, Chelsea, in London is the setting. It was here that fame came to Thomas; it was here that he and Jane entertained the wise and great of England. Carlyle's books had always commanded readers, but it took *The French Revolution* with its unusual style and vigor to make him famous. The book was published in 1837. When the last line was written, Carlyle gave his wife the manuscript, with the words, "This I could tell the world, 'You have not had for a hundred years any book that comes more directly and flamingly from the heart of a living man.'" And Mrs. Carlyle after reading it through, replied, "A work of genius, dear!"

From the appearance of *The French Revolution* until the death of Mrs. Carlyle in 1865, the author was busy lecturing and writing. His house became a Mecca for everyone interested in books and philosophy. But when Jane Carlyle died, Thomas was a broken man. His last fifteen years were sadly lonely.

Many anecdotes are told of the Scotchman's flaming temper and general ill humor and of his amazing meekness in moments of great stress. He confessed that during the years he was working on *Frederick the Great* he "devastated homelife and happiness,"—but then, he was ever given to exaggeration. And when the manuscript for the first volume of *The French Revolution,* which he had lent to John Stuart Mill, was destroyed through the carelessness of a servant, Carlyle's only concern was to keep Mill from knowing how disastrous the loss was! The whole thing had to be rewritten, and not a note had been saved.

Carlyle lived to be eighty-five, crotchety and beloved to the last. At his death he was taken for burial back to the little Scotch town where he was born.

THOMAS B. MACAULAY (1800–1859)—"LONDON IN 1685"

"If I had to choose a lot from all that there are in human life, I am not sure that I should prefer any to that which has fallen to me. I am sincerely and thoroughly contented."

This remarkable statement comes from a letter written by Thomas Macaulay when he was at the height of his career. He would probably have counted it the final blessing that he died very suddenly at the comparatively early age of fifty-nine, while he was still happily active.

Macaulay had a rare combination of natural gifts. His mind was phenomenally quick and retentive. He could read at three, was studying serious books at five, talked like an encyclopedia at six, had written a *Compendium of Universal History* at ten; and instead of being a self-conscious little prig, was a pretty child whom everyone adored. In maturity he could read like lightning and he seemed to remember, literally, everything that he had ever read. He could recite at will from *Paradise Lost,* from novels or histories or newspapers.

He had, besides, a tall, fine figure, excellent health, and a happy disposition. Everyone liked him. More, everyone respected him. He was thoroughly honest and conscientious in his business and political life. In Parliament, besides being its most eloquent speaker, he was a trustworthy leader. He accepted some high offices—such as a cabinet position—and refused others. At no time did he sacrifice his honor to success. Once he was not reelected to Parliament because of his loyalty to an unpopular cause. A later election, however, returned him to his seat. Two years before his death he was made Baron Macaulay of Rothley.

With money he was also fortunate. His father had been wealthy but lost his money when Macaulay was a young man. Thomas then set vigorously to work to make a living for himself and his brothers and sisters. He eventually built up a fortune of his own. He never married but made his home with a sister and her sons.

The success that he enjoyed in other things came to him also as a writer. In fact the sale of his works contributed largely to his fortune. When he was twenty-five, his *Essay on Milton* appeared in the *Edinburgh Review.* It was a sensational success. For the next twenty years he contributed to magazines, essays on literary and historical themes—essays like those on Bunyan, Addison, and Goldsmith; on Lord Clive, Warren Hastings, and William Pitt. Then he began the *History of England* on which he worked until his death. The five volumes that he finished covered only sixteen years of history. Scholars have estimated that the work completed on the scale that he had started would have filled fifty volumes.

Macaulay made history and literature popular. He wrote, not for scholars, but for everyone. His style was direct, easy to read. He chose details with an eye to human interest and did not hesitate to overdraw the curious or appealing. Unfortunately, most historians do not endorse his tendency to exaggerate; and his work is recommended more as introduction to the subject than for intensive study. Macaulay fol-

lowed the same principles in writing literary criticisms, with a similar result. His books are always read with pleasure. No student finds them
dull; but they must be read with the proverbial grain of salt. The heroes
were probably not quite so good nor the villains quite so bad as he drew
them. Historical facts, though, are easy to find; it is not so easy to make
them come alive, and a certain liveliness of subject was Macaulay's
greatest contribution to the art of writing.

JOHN RUSKIN (1819-1900)—"OF BOOKS, OF READING, OF NATIONS"

It is refreshing to read of a reformer sincere enough to try putting his
theories into practice and sensible enough to have practical ideas. That
is the kind of man Ruskin was. Of course, he was sometimes prejudiced
and unreasonable; but many of his undertakings were successful and his
influence was wholly good. His own wealth had not blinded him to the
injustices of the day, and he worked and put his money to work to correct
them. He became interested in social conditions in a roundabout way,
the chain beginning in his childhood.

Ruskin's father was a wine-merchant,
wealthy and interested in art; his mother
was very religious. The household discipline
was strict and the young child had few toys
and many whippings. Like Macaulay, he
showed great intelligence as a youngster.
Fortunately, his parents encouraged his literary enthusiasms. From childhood he drew,
and wrote verses and stories. At Oxford he
left a distinguished record and after graduation went to Italy to fit himself for the art
career he had chosen. When only twenty-
four, he published the introductory volume
of *Modern Painters* (anonymously because
of his youth), in which he warmly defended
nineteenth-century art, especially the work
of the landscape painter, Joseph William

Turner. The book created something like a revolution in taste, and within
the next ten years Ruskin became the art dictator of England. His views
raised or lowered prices in a sales room; his proteges found themselves
spectacularly successful. Besides *Modern Painters,* he had written *The
Seven Lamps of Architecture; Pre-Raphaelism* (a defense of one of the
newer movements in art and poetry); and *The Stones of Venice*—all
before he was forty-one.

It was at this time that his love for art led him to realize the need for
changes in living-and-working conditions in England. He did not think
of art as a pleasure to be reserved for a wealthy few. He thought of it
as something to enrich and beautify the lives of everyone. What use was

there in writing about the glories of Gothic architecture in Venice when a million Londoners were living in tenement slums? Ruskin set to work to get rid of the slums. He did not, to be sure, wipe them out, but he did much to improve the conditions of the working-man and to put within his reach things that were inspiring. Ruskin's father had left him about three-quarters of a million dollars, and most of this fortune Ruskin used in works of public welfare.

His writings from 1860 on, all reveal this new interest. Many of them were delivered as lectures to schools or clubs for working-men. From 1870 to 1879 Ruskin was also connected with Oxford as professor of fine arts. The students found his lectures profoundly moving—as one of them said, "far above the religious height of the most solemn service I have ever heard."

THOMAS HENRY HUXLEY (1825–1895)—"A LIBERAL EDUCATION"

Huxley in the nineteenth century was a popularizer of science as Macaulay was a popularizer of history; Ruskin of art; and—in a way— Newman of religion. Huxley, like his distinguished contemporaries, was a precocious youngster who educated himself through reading. At sixteen he was apprenticed to a medical man whose work in the London slums aroused Huxley's interest and sympathy in the frightful working conditions then prevalent. When he received his degree of Bachelor of Medicine at twenty he was too young to enter the College of Surgeons. As an alternative, Huxley spent the next years as assistant surgeon on the *S. S. Rattlesnake* where he gathered information on navy conditions and flora and fauna off the coast of Australia—as well as paid court to his future wife, a pretty Australian girl.

His scientific monographs had already brought him some repute. His fame increased rapidly; and in 1852, at the time when Ruskin was virtually an art dictator, Huxley became as nearly a science dictator. Although he now ranked as one of the foremost anatomists of his time, he gave up his work to popularize Darwin and his revolutionary theories. In addition, he worked tirelessly lecturing to workingmen's groups, and trying to improve their conditions. Nearly always ill, Huxley rarely showed his depression; he was clever and witty, keen for a fight and quick to forget it. His technical writings are many and authoritative. In literature he is remembered chiefly for these works: *Lay Sermons,* containing the famous essay "On a Piece of Chalk"; *Science and Culture;* and his *Autobiography,* which reveals a gracious personality.

ROBERT LOUIS STEVENSON (1850–1894)—"MARKHEIM"

Robert Louis Stevenson wrote brave books, but braver than all his books was his life. And brave, you remember means *gay* as well as *courageous.* He did not let ill health keep him from living fully and richly. His father and grandfather were famous lighthouse engineers, but Louis had no inclination to follow their profession. He and his father compromised by Louis' agreeing to study law. At the University of Edinburgh he studied with little enthusiasm, preferring the friendship and easy chat of school-mates to the dull routine of classes. Although he passed the bar examina-tions, Stevenson never practiced law. Still in search of robust health, he spent some happy months in France, living near Fontainebleau in the artists' colony at Barbizon. Essays sent back to England were printed in English magazines and immediately won a reading public. His account of a canoe trip through Belgium and France, *An Inland Voyage*, gained for him fame as well as a fiancee. During the trip he had met an American woman, Mrs. Osbourne, older than he but sympathetic to the young man and his writing aspirations.

After the success of *Travels with a Don-key*, the account of his wanderings through France, Stevenson's career was settled. Most of the fourteen years remaining to him were filled with his writing and with his pilgrimages in search of a healthful climate. In California he married Mrs. Osbourne and settled there to write. Their dream was realized when in 1888 they hired a yacht at San Francisco and sailed for the South Seas. In Samoa near Apia, Stevenson seemed to have found the ideal climate for his tubercular condition. There he spent six of his happiest years with his wife and stepchildren. The natives called him *Tusitala*, Teller of Tales, and built the "Road of the Loving Heart" up to the door of Valima, the Stevenson villa. At his own request he was buried on the mountaintop behind his home, his epitaph his lovely stanza "Requiem."

OF LITERARY FORM AND STYLE

VICTORIAN PROSE—NON-FICTION

The Age of Romanticism had been a revolutionary time; it was fol-lowed by a period of conservatism. The literature of the later nine-teenth century was a combination of romanticism and classicism, with classicism—in form, at least—predominating. Prose shows both influ-ences. The novel reached its stage of highest development; and for the first time the short story appears in English literature. But a great deal of the writing was not fiction. Its general tone was sober, and it dis-plays an interest in many new subjects. Discoveries in science, the de-velopment of new theories, general industrial expansion—these brought a wealth of new ideas to be discussed. A glance at the fields of activity represented by the essayists of the age will indicate a great diversity of subject. Carlyle was a philosopher; Macaulay, a member of Parliament; Ruskin a critic of art, and a social reformer; Huxley a scientist. It is interesting to note that their works were serious. There is nothing that approaches the light essay in their prose.

The French Revolution was Carlyle's masterpiece. It remains his most readable work, perhaps chiefly because here was a subject admirably suited to the Scotchman's explosive style. This style is undoubtedly a handicap to the general reader. In his more deeply philosophical works, besides the sometimes chaotic sentences, there is a complicated allegory to perplex the reader. As a result, Carlyle, a leading figure in literary London fifty years ago, has today fewer readers than his more smooth-spoken contemporaries—Ruskin or Newman or Macaulay.

Thomas Macaulay's essays, though well written, are now seldom read. His fame rests upon one stirring narrative poem, "Horatius at the Bridge," and upon his *History of England*. With all its shortcomings, the latter work is outstanding. It was written with an honest purpose. Years of labor were spent in gathering the material. It sparkles with the brilliance of an extraordinary genius. It carries its message in an easy, direct style. For these reasons, it is not only history but art, and therefore enduring.

John Ruskin was a precise scholar. In his autobiography, he gives us an account of early years that helps explain this precision:

"I had Walter Scott's novels and the *Iliad* (Pope's translation) for my only reading when I was a child, on week days; on Sunday their effect was tempered by *Robinson Crusoe* and *The Pilgrim's Progress,* my mother having it deeply in her heart to make an evangelical clergyman of me.

"I had, however, still better teaching, and that compulsorily and every day of the week. My mother forced me, by steady daily toil, to learn long chapters of the Bible by heart, as well as to read it every syllable through, aloud, hard names and all, from *Genesis* to the *Apocalypse* [*Revelation*] about once a year; and to that discipline—patient, accurate, and resolute —I owe not only a knowledge of the book which I find occasionally serviceable, but much of my general power of taking pains, and the best part of my taste in literature. Once knowing the 32d of *Deuteronomy,* or the 119th *Psalm,* the 15th of 1st *Corinthians,* The Sermon on the Mount, and most of the *Apocalypse,* every syllable by heart, and having always a way of thinking with myself what words meant, it was not possible for me, even in the foolishest times of my youth to write entirely superficial or formal English."

It is not strange that from such a childhood grew a man sober, sincere, painstaking. Books were to him something almost sacred, but only when they too were sincere and painstaking. With this honesty in reading and study, it is not surprising that Ruskin was distressed by insincerity and greed in life. He saw things straight. Why should it not be possible to conceive a nation which would think straight and act soberly? The idea seemed not impossible of achievement. Ruskin was an idealist, but he also had a good measure of common sense. He believed that the means to national reform lay in national education and he devoted himself and his writings to the promotion of it.

Thomas Henry Huxley is remembered as one of the most important scientists of Victorian England. Actively interested in the rapid developments being made in physics, chemistry, and biology, he was influential in making science generally popular. His educational background was the traditional classic one. Nor did he despise it. He was conservative in his literary tastes and recommended to every English child a careful study of the Bible, Chaucer, and Shakespeare as a means to literary culture of the highest kind. He did believe that practical and cultural education should unite in showing men how to live wisely and happily. He was liberal and tolerant. Living in a controversial age, he himself avoided controversies. He wanted learning to be accurate and useful; and he proved that, granted these two qualities, it may also be beautiful.

Three other prose writers merit special mention—Robert Louis Stevenson, who did distinguished work in every type of literature; Matthew Arnold, who was both scholar and poet; and John Henry Newman, who was a churchman and theologian.

Stevenson's first literary ventures were his *Travels with a Donkey* and *An Inland Voyage*—pleasant narratives of two European trips told with the engaging charm of the light essay. His *Virginibus Puerisque* is a collection of later and more serious essays.

Himself a teacher, Matthew Arnold believed in education for culture rather than for use, and his essays make their greatest appeal to the man of learning. He has even a delicate satire with which to jibe the unbeliever—of his doctrine. His best essays are in four main groups: *Essays in Criticism, Culture and Anarchy, Friendship's Garland,* and *Discourses in America.* "Sweetness and Light" from *Culture and Anarchy* is an excellent illustration of Arnold's favorite subject and his style.

Cardinal Newman's writings have a personal significance. We feel that what he wrote he believed and practiced. He was a teacher and preacher of singular sweetness of character. The greatest part of his thirty-six volumes are of first interest to the theologian, but during a voyage through the Mediterranean he composed the famous hymn "Lead Kindly Light." To his credit also belong two novels; a remarkable series of essays, *The Idea of a University;* and a goodly quantity of poetry. His writings disclose his wide learning, his clear expression, and his gentle nature.

When we add to this list of writers of non-fiction, the roll of Victorians who carried the English novel to its crest, we realize how much excellent prose was produced in the last fifty years of the nineteenth century. With its reaching out into new fields and its broad interests in humanity, it has retained the spirit of the romanticists; but in its emphasis on culture and its interest in form the new prose makes acknowledgment to certain classic virtues. The best of it strikes a good balance between two extremes.

QUESTIONS IN APPRECIATION:

"The Storming of the Bastille"

1. Why do you think Carlyle used the present tense to write of an event that had happened a half century earlier? Why are there few adjectives and adverbs in the account? Do you find Carlyle's writing easy or hard to understand? Why?

2. What do you think was Carlyle's purpose in naming the occupations of the different leaders in the fight—such as "Louis Tournay, cartwright," "Georget of the marine service," and so on?

3. Does Carlyle sympathize with the mob? or with the defenders of the prison? How does he let us know? Does he enlist the sympathies of the readers for his side? If so, how? If not, why not?

"London in 1685"

1. How does Macaulay's style compare with that of other prose writers you have studied this term? Is it harder or easier to read? Why? Do you think that the fact that Macaulay had in mind readers of the year 2000 and later, may have had some effect on his style? Discuss.

2. The selection you have just read is but a small part of the chapter from which it was taken. What evidence do you find even in these paragraphs that Macaulay was living up to his definition of the purpose of *history?* In your answer give examples of ways the author made the people of 1685 seem real; or of details he gives us of the way they lived.

3. Do you think Macaulay's *History of England* will still have readers in the year 2000? Why or why not?

"Of Books, Of Reading, Of Nations"

1. Have you had to "dig" for the meaning in these selections from Ruskin? Or has the main thought in each been clearly presented? Discuss. Ruskin uses words with careful regard to their meaning; but would you say he shows a preference for long, hard words? Prove your answer by specific examples from your reading.

2. Do you see any evidence of Biblical influence in Ruskin's writings? If so, point out some examples.

3. What are the important points of difference between the kind of writing Ruskin is doing in *Sesame and Lilies* and the kind of writing Lamb did in his essays, like "A Dissertation upon Roast Pig"? Which has the more logical organization? Why?

4. Would the selection "Of Nations" be more effective if the author had specifically named the countries and the evils instead of referring to them indirectly? Discuss. Do you think the fact that the selections were first delivered as lectures might have affected the author's policy here?

5. What have you learned from reading these three selections?

"A Liberal Education"

1. Do Thomas Huxley's ideas on education sound revolutionary to us? Discuss. How does he make his points convincing?

2. Figures of speech may serve for clearness as well as for ornament. Point out at least two instances where Huxley has made his ideas clear through the use of similes. What other figures of speech has he used with good effect? Point them out and explain them.

3. What evidence do you find in the essay that Huxley was a scientist? That he also had a good general and cultural education?

Overview

1. In what respects does the writing of these four Victorians sound more *modern* than that of the other prose writers whose works you have read? Which one sounds most like a twentieth-century selection? Can you explain why?

2. Which of the four shows the strongest romantic tendencies? Which one has used the most classic type of expression? Which one did you find the most interesting reading? Why? Was it because of the subject matter or because of the way it was written? Discuss.

3. Do you think that if you were given five paragraphs from other works typical of these same writers you could tell which was the work of Macaulay? which was the work of Carlyle? of Ruskin? of Huxley? If you could, you have learned something about the meaning of *style* in writing.

4. Write three or four sentences in which you summarize your impressions of Victorian non-fiction prose.

THE SHORT STORY APPEARS IN ENGLAND

It is strange that the most popular form in modern literature—the short story—should be the latest type to be developed. Story-telling is a natural means of entertainment, and prose narratives are found in the oldest writings. But these narratives are usually long and rambling, with no apparent attempt having been made to shape them into brief, artistic units. The art of compressing a story into one short telling had developed first in poetry. Ballads and somewhat longer narrative poems had been popular for centuries before it was discovered that the same sort of thing could be done in prose.

And then the discovery was made in America,—probably accidentally. At any rate, Washington Irving—in his playing around with Dutch legends—perfected a few excellent short stories, such as "Rip Van Winkle" and "The Legend of Sleepy Hollow." Then Hawthorne and Poe adopted the new form and made of it a distinct art.

Even with this lead, English writers were slow in taking up the innovation. The English short story may be said to have begun with Robert Louis Stevenson, when in 1877 he published "A Lodging for the

Night." Stevenson was a born story teller, and to give his talent proper expression he developed a polished style. He has described his method. He studied other great writers, and in self-imposed exercises he painstakingly imitated them. He was a close student of Hawthorne particularly, and most of his stories—like the American's—inquire into the moral nature of man. He was of course also familiar with Poe's technique and theories, with his emphasis upon tone and mood. But Stevenson had his own genius, too—a knack of telling an absorbing story, and a liking for adventure tempered by a knowledge of life and an understanding of people. This combination gives a sense of reality even to a story like "Markheim," removing it from the whimsical fantasy that Hawthorne delighted in and also from the exaggerated distortions of Poe. Stevenson, moreover, had a wide range of interests and a mastery of many styles so that he appeals to readers of various tastes. "Markheim" represents the peak of his work in the short story.

Almost at the same time that Stevenson's stories were winning readers, three other Englishmen began experimenting in the field—Kipling, Barrie, and Hardy; but because all three lived on well into the next century, it is customary to group them with the modern writers. Kipling did the most work in his early years; and his Victorian period introduced a new scene to English letters—the scene of the British colonial empire, especially India. He sounded a vigorous new note; and his productivity, together with the promise of Hardy and Barrie meant that the short story was at home in England by the end of the century.

QUESTIONS IN APPRECIATION:

1. The title of "Markheim" indicates that the chief interest in the story centers upon *character* rather than upon *setting* or *plot*. Would you say that it is a story of character portrayal or of character development?

2. To what extent does the setting influence the development of the story? Does it react upon or influence the character? Discuss, referring to specific instances.

3. What elements of suspense carry along the interest of the reader? What are the things we wonder about in the development of the story? What point represents the climax of interest? Has the reader been prepared for it, or does it come as a surprise?

4. Are there evidences in the story that it was carefully planned—that the ending was in the writer's mind from the beginning? Discuss. What is the *theme* around which the story is built? Express it in a single sentence.

5. Recall some of the stories by the American writer Hawthorne—"Feather-Top," "The Minister's Black Veil," "The Great Stone Face," "Ethan Brand," and the like. What points of similarity do you discover between "Markheim" and a typical Hawthorne tale? Discuss. In what respects does Stevenson's story resemble a typical tale by Edgar Allan

Poe? What elements in the story show Stevenson's own craftsmanship?

6. Stevenson had a masterly touch with figures of speech. Notice, for example, the two sentences following the account of the murder: *"Time had some score of small voices in that shop, some stately and slow* as was becoming to their great age; other *garrulous and hurried. All those told out the seconds in an intricate chorus of tickings."* Select for class citation at least five other examples of effective imagery. Select for reading aloud at least three paragraphs which you consider examples of exceptionally good writing.

7. What combination of qualities makes "Markheim" one of the world's great stories? Discuss.

THE GOLDEN AGE OF THE NOVEL

The sixty years bounded approximately by the dates 1830 to 1890 saw the novel develop as a form of literary art to its present important position as the world's favorite kind of reading. The period, which saw novelists of distinction appearing in every country, was one of particular power in England. There were novels written purely for entertainment; there were novels designed to propound broad problems of ethics and morals, or to awaken public concern for social abuses, or to popularize a particular philosophy. Like the non-fiction prose, the Victorian novel was a serious piece of work. Our best picture of it is to be obtained through glimpses of the men and women who worked with it.

Charles Dickens (1812–1870), the second in a family of eight children, was born in humble circumstances and brought up in slums and shabby streets. His father was a clerk in a navy pay-office and for some time the family lived in comfortable circumstances. The father was irresponsible and care-free, however, and finally, when Charles was about ten years old, was arrested and put into a debtors' prison. The lad's dreams of school and college were shattered and "he found himself in a row of ragged boys in a great dreary factory, putting the same kinds of labels on the same kinds of blacking bottles from morning till night." The degradation and misery of these days sank deep into the sensitive boy's soul, and of this particular dark spot in his life he could never speak.

After about two years Charles' father was released from prison and upon the unexpected receipt of a legacy, the financial condition of the family began to improve. Charles was sent to a private school where he remained for three or four years. At the age of seventeen he secured a position as a newspaper reporter, and this work gave him an intimate knowledge of London people in every walk of life. It was while connected with the paper that Dickens began to think of using his leisure hours for writing about the scenes and characters which he daily saw. His first articles, *Sketches by Boz,* appeared in the paper on which he worked, and because of their popularity, he was encouraged to write other character sketches which appeared first in monthly installments and

later in book form. These were the *Pickwick Papers,* and within a year
40,000 copies were sold. Dickens' popularity was now assured and the
rest of his life was success after success.

The events of his childhood and his youth had impressed his imagination and influenced the whole of his literary career so profoundly that to
the very end of his life there was not a single work in which some of the
characters, some of the places, were not derived from his early recollections. His own childhood may be read in *David Copperfield.* His father,
his mother, his old landlady, his companions in the blacking factory, and
the quaint, grotesque figures of the alleys live in the characters of his
books. The prison, the lawyer's office, the tavern, warehouses, and shabby
streets furnished him with scenes and settings. All that he had learned in
his rough initiation into life was poured out into his stories. The bitter
memories of his own childhood sufferings gave him great sympathy for
children and for the middle and lower classes. He detested cruelty and
indifference and oppression and in his stories he attacked many public
abuses and aided in many reforms. In *Oliver Twist* he attacked the
work-house and in *Little Dorrit,* the debtors' prison. In *Nicholas
Nickleby* and *Dombey & Son* he exposed the cruelty practiced in English
schools and helped put a stop to the shameful exploitation of children for
commercial purposes. He knew well how to produce laughter and horror
and tears, and "it is for his deeply human heart that the world will continue to love the memory of Charles Dickens."

William Makepeace Thackeray (1811–1863) was a man of altogether
different temperament from Dickens. He was not concerned with social
problems, but endeavored to see life whole and see it steadily. He possessed a penetrating insight into human nature, seeing through sham and
pretense and viewing life without illusion. His method is that of the
realist who endeavors to picture things faithfully and accurately as they
are. The characters in his books come from the higher social levels. His
novel, *Henry Esmond,* laid in the days of Queen Anne, is regarded as one
of the greatest of English novels. A close second to it is *Vanity Fair,*
with its shrewd, cold glamour-girl of the Napoleonic wars, Becky Sharpe.
The Newcomes and *Pendennis* deal with Victorian life; the latter dealing
at length with the problems of the English college boy. In addition to
these Thackeray wrote a sequel to *Henry Esmond,* entitled *The Virginians.*
In all his works, Thackeray maintains the attitude of an observer of life,
pausing sometimes for a long parenthetical aside to his reader, often in
ironic mood.

The important woman novelist of the Victorian era was Mary Ann
Evans (1819–1880), better known by her pen-name, George Eliot. "You
may try, but you can never imagine what it is to have a man's force of
genius in you, and yet to suffer the slavery of being a girl," she once wrote.
From her earliest childhood, Mary Ann Evans was torn between a desire
to follow her own intellectual bent and her conviction that a woman's
place was in the home doing the duties which naturally fall to the daughter

or wife of the house. She was thirty-seven years old before she definitely launched herself on a literary career and then she chose a *nom de plume* because she felt that as a woman she would not gain any recognition in the literary field.

Although she lived during the years of scientific discovery and progress of the last quarter of the nineteenth century, it is events of her girlhood before railroads, telegraphs or factories, which appear in most of her writings. Her first novel was *Adam Bede,* followed the next year by *The Mill on the Floss.* The latter is largely a story of her own childhood and of her brother Isaac to whom she was deeply devoted. Other well-known novels from her pen are *Silas Marner, Romola,* and *Felix Holt.* As a novelist, she ranks with Dickens and Thackeray. Her works are serious—sometimes gripping—stories concerned with problems of personal conduct as interpreted by society. *Adam Bede* tells the most powerful story; *The Mill on the Floss* is the warmest and most realistic; *Silas Marner,* the shortest, is most expertly told.

Robert Louis Stevenson looked upon fiction as a means of escape. He contended that it should be to the grown man what play is to the child. *Treasure Island* is one of the greatest adventure stories in our literature; and he wrote romances with many of the same characteristics: *Kidnapped, The Master of Ballantrae, David Balfour,* and the unfinished romances, *St. Ives* and *West of Hermiston.* Shorter than these romances, and unique in its symbolic representation of a psychological theme is his *Dr. Jekyll and Mr. Hyde,* a book that is "creepy" out of all proportion to the incidents it relates. It is a curious fact that the gentle Stevenson put so much blood and fire into his narratives that their appeal is limited almost entirely to masculine readers. Girls seldom care for his novels.

George Meredith (1828–1909) is entitled to a place among the great English novelists. His recognition by the public was belated and may be said to have been delayed until after his death. Meredith began as a poet. His attitude toward life, or his philosophy, is best illustrated by his masterpiece, *The Egoist.* According to him, it is out of egoism that come all the ills that flesh is heir to. The antidote to this is what he calls the Comic Spirit or the "genius of thoughtful laughter" which, by making folly, vanity, and ambition appear ridiculous, destroys them. Meredith's chief novels are *Evan Harrington, The Egoist, The Ordeal of Richard Feverel,* and *Diana of the Crossways.*

With the listings of these five writers and their works, the roll call of the Victorian novel is by no means complete. There were scores of writers, each with at least one good book to his credit. Among them one might mention the following: Edward Bulwer-Lytton, who did a thrilling historical novel inspired by nineteenth century archeological explorations —*The Last Days of Pompeii;* Benjamin Disraeli, Prime Minister of England, who as Lord Beaconsfield, wrote four romances; Charlotte Brontë, author of *Jane Eyre,* a perennial favorite; her sister Emily Brontë, author of *Wuthering Heights;* Elizabeth Gaskell, who produced in *Cran-*

ford, a slight little novel in the Jane Austen style, full of gossipy village life; Richard Blackmore, who tells a rousing seventeenth-century romance in *Lorna Doone;* Charles Reade, who has written one of the fine historical novels of all time in *The Cloister and the Hearth;* Dinah Craik Mulock, whose *John Halifax, Gentleman* is one of the best of all English stories; Samuel Butler, author of *The Way of All Flesh;* Wilkie Collins, who wrote an all-time mystery thriller in *The Moonstone;* and George Gissing who centered his attention upon poverty and hardship and who did a notable piece of work in *New Grub Street.*

There are other names that might be added; but the list is imposing enough to prove the remarkable range and variety of the Victorian novel. The period was indeed a golden age for this, the highest artistic type of prose literature.

FOR FURTHER READING

BLACKMORE, RICHARD D., *Lorna Doone*
BRONTË, CHARLOTTE, *Jane Eyre*
BRONTË, EMILY, *Wuthering Heights*
BULWER-LYTTON, EDWARD, *The Last Days of Pompeii*
CARLYLE, J. B. W., *Jane Welsh Carlyle: Letters to Her Family*
CARROLL, LEWIS, *Alice's Adventures in Wonderland*
COLLINS, WILKIE, *The Moonstone*
COLLINGWOOD, STUART DODGSON (ed.), *Life and Letters of Lewis Carroll*
DICKENS, CHARLES, *Oliver Twist; David Copperfield; A Tale of Two Cities*
ELIOT, GEORGE, *Adam Bede; The Mill on the Floss*
GASKELL, ELIZABETH C., *The Life of Charlotte Brontë; Cranford*
GOODRICH, ARTHUR FREDERICK AND PALMER, ROSE A., *Caponsacchi* (drama)
GUEDALLA, PHILIP, *The Hundred Years* (1837–1937)
HARDY, THOMAS, *Under the Greenwood Tree*
KIPLING, RUDYARD, *Plain Tales from the Hills; The Light That Failed*
LEACOCK, STEPHEN, *Charles Dickens, His Life and Work*
MACAULAY, THOMAS B., *Lays of Ancient Rome*
MACFARLANE, KATHRYN JEAN, *Divide the Desolation* (Emily Brontë)
MAUROIS, ANDRE, *Disraeli; The Miracle of England*
MEREDITH, GEORGE, *The Egoist*
MULOCK, DINAH CRAIK, *John Halifax, Gentleman*
ROMIEU, EMILIE AND GEORGES, *Three Virgins of Haworth* (Brontë sisters)
SITWELL, EDITH, *Victoria of England*
STEVENSON, ROBERT LOUIS, *The Merry Men and Other Tales and Fables; Dr. Jekyll and Mr. Hyde; The Black Arrow*
STRACHEY, LYTTON, *Eminent Victorians; Queen Victoria*
THACKERAY, WILLIAM MAKEPEACE, *The Newcomes; Vanity Fair; Henry Esmond*
WILLIAMS, BLANCHE COLTON, *George Eliot*

VI·II

Victorian poetry was thoughtful and idealistic.
Tennyson and Browning were the great spokesmen of the era.

THE LADY OF SHALOTT

ALFRED TENNYSON

In "The Lady of Shalott" Tennyson is giving symbolic expression to the story which he later told more realistically in the idyll of "Lancelot and Elaine." "The Lady of Shalott" was written during an early period of the poet's career when he was especially concerned with musical effects. It ranks with Shelley's lyrics among the most pleasingly melodious poems in all the world.

I

L   On either side the river lie
    Long fields of barley and of rye,
    That clothe the wold and meet the sky;
    And thro' the field the road runs by
U 5   To many-tower'd Camelot;
M   And up and down the people go,
    Gazing where the lilies blow
    Round an island there below,
U   The island of Shalott.

L 10 Willows whiten, aspens quiver,
    Little breezes dusk and shiver
    Thro' the wave that runs forever
    By the island in the river
U   Flowing down to Camelot.
M 15 Four gray walls, and four gray towers,
    Overlook a space of flowers,
    And the silent isle embowers
U   The Lady of Shalott.

5. CAMELOT—The place of King Arthur's court.

787

M		By the margin, willow-veil'd
	20	Slide the heavy barges trail'd
		By slow horses; and unhail'd
		The shallop flitteth silken-sail'd
U		Skimming down to Camelot:
G1		But who hath seen her wave her hand?
	25	Or at the casement seen her stand?
		Or is she known in all the land,
U		The Lady of Shalott?

B1		Only reapers, reaping early
		In among the bearded barley,
	30	Hear a song that echoes cheerly
		From the river winding clearly,
U		Down to tower'd Camelot:
B1		And by the moon the reaper weary,
		Piling sheaves in uplands airy,
	35	Listening, whispers, " 'Tis the fairy
U		Lady of Shalott."

II

M		There she weaves by night and day
		A magic web with colors gay.
		She has heard a whisper say,
	40	A curse is on her if she stay
U		To look down to Camelot.
G1		She knows not what the curse may be,
		And so she weaveth steadily,
		And little other care hath she,
U	45	The Lady of Shalott.

M		And moving thro' a mirror clear
		That hangs before her all the year,
		Shadows of the world appear.
		There she sees the highway near
U	50	Winding down to Camelot:
L1		There the river eddy whirls,
B1		And there the surly village churls,

46. MIRROR—The Lady of Shalott is weaving into a web of tapestry the sights reflected in her mirror, so placed that it catches the life passing by the castle on the road below.

G1
U

And the red cloaks of market girls,
    Pass onward from Shalott.

G
DB1
MB1

U
B

G1
U

55 Sometimes a troop of damsels glad,
An abbot on an ambling pad,
Sometimes a curly shepherd-lad,
Or long-hair'd page in crimson clad,
    Goes by to tower'd Camelot:
60 And sometimes thro' the mirror blue
The knights come riding two and two:
She hath no loyal knight and true,
    The Lady of Shalott.

M

D

U
G1

U

But in her web she still delights
65 To weave the mirror's magic sights,
For often thro' the silent nights
A funeral, with plumes and lights
    And music, went to Camelot:
Or when the moon was overhead,
70 Came two young lovers lately wed;
"I am half sick of shadows," said
    The Lady of Shalott.

III

M

U
G1

U

A bowshot from her bower eaves
He rode between the barley sheaves,
75 The sun came dazzling thro' the leaves,
And flamed upon the brazen greaves
    Of bold Sir Lancelot.
A red-cross knight forever kneel'd
To a lady in his shield,
80 That sparkled on the yellow field,
    Beside remote Shalott.

L

U

The gemmy bridle glitter'd free,
Like to some branch of stars we see
Hung in the golden Galaxy.
85 The bridle bells rang merrily
    As he rode down to Camelot:

82. GEMMY—Set with gems.
84. GALAXY—The Milky Way.

M And from his blazon'd baldric slung
A mighty silver bugle hung,
And as he rode his armor rung,
U 90 Beside remote Shalott.

L All in the blue unclouded weather
Thick-jewel'd shone the saddle leather,
The helmet and the helmet feather
Burn'd like one burning flame together,
U 95 As he rode down to Camelot.
M As often thro' the purple night,
Below the starry clusters bright,
Some bearded meteor, trailing light,
U Moves over still Shalott.

B 100 His broad clear brow in sunlight glow'd;
On burnish'd hooves his war horse trode;
From underneath his helmet flow'd
His coal-black curls as on he rode,
U As he rode down to Camelot.
B 105 From the bank and from the river
He flashed into the crystal mirror,

| | | "Tirra lirra," by the river |
| U | | Sang Sir Lancelot. |

G1		She left the web, she left the loom,
	110	She made three paces thro' the room,
		She saw the water lily bloom,
		She saw the helmet and the plume,
U		She look'd down to Camelot.
G1		Out flew the web and floated wide;
	115	The mirror crack'd from side to side;
		"The curse is come upon me," cried
U		The Lady of Shalott.

IV

D		In the stormy east wind straining,
		The pale yellow woods were waning,
	120	The broad stream in his banks complaining,
		Heavily the low sky raining
U		Over tower'd Camelot:
D		Down she came and found a boat
		Beneath a willow left afloat,
	125	And round about the prow she wrote
U		*The Lady of Shalott.*

M		And down the river's dim expanse
		Like some bold seer in a trance.
		Seeing all his own mischance—
	130	With a glassy countenance
U		Did she look to Camelot.
M		And at the closing of the day
		She loosed the chain, and down she lay;
		The broad stream bore her far away,
U	135	The Lady of Shalott.

G		Lying, robed in snowy white
		That loosely flew to left and right—
		The leaves upon her falling light—
		Thro' the noises of the night
U	140	She floated down to Camelot:

L   And as the boat head wound along
     The willowy hills and fields among,
     They heard her singing her last song,
U   The Lady of Shalott.

D 145 Heard a carol, mournful, holy,
     Chanted loudly, chanted lowly,
     Till her blood was frozen slowly,
     And her eyes were darken'd wholly,
U   Turn'd to tower'd Camelot,
G1 150 For ere she reach'd upon the tide
     The first house by the waterside,
     Singing in her song she died,
U   The Lady of Shalott.

M   Under tower and balcony,
  155 By garden wall and gallery,
     A gleaming shape she floated by,
     Dead pale between the houses high,
U   Silent into Camelot.
M   Out upon the wharfs they came,
  160 Knight and burgher, lord and dame,
     And round the prow they read her name,
U   *The Lady of Shalott.*

L   Who is this? and what is here?
     And in the lighted palace near
  165 Died the sound of royal cheer;
D   And they cross'd themselves for fear,
U   All the knights at Camelot:
B1   But Lancelot mused a little space;
     He said, "She has a lovely face;
  170 God in His mercy lend her grace,
U   The Lady of Shalott!"

FOR INTERPRETATION

PART I:

1. What do you think is the purpose of the first four stanzas of the poem? Discuss.

2. What information is given about the Lady of Shalott? What suggestion is there in Part I that there is a touch of fantasy about the poem?

PART II:

1. Does the poem say that the Lady of Shalott is in a tower room? Do you think she is? Why or why not? What are the conditions of the curse that has been placed upon her?

2. What is the first suggestion that her life is lonely? What is the mirror's reflection that makes the lady herself realize it?

3. If you have read the idyll of "Lancelot and Elaine," point out the respects in which Elaine's life at Astolot was like that of the Lady of Shalott.

PART III:

1. Describe Sir Lancelot as the Lady of Shalott saw him in her mirror. Is this a realistic description or an idealized one? (Compare with the description of Lancelot as Elaine first looked upon his face, as told in the idyll.)

2. What did the Lady of Shalott do that brought the curse upon her?

3. Reading behind the symbolism, explain the meaning of the following: What do you think the *web* represents? What is signified by her leaving the mirror for the window? (Do you think the window was open? Why or why not?) What further meaning may be implied in the fact that she *looked down to Camelot?*

PART IV:

1. What time of year is suggested by the first three parts of the poem? What time of year is suggested by Part IV? Do you think the poet intended to indicate the passage of time? or merely to adapt the setting to the mood of this part of the story? Discuss.

2. What is the most important point of difference between Elaine's journey on the barge to Camelot and the voyage of the Lady of Shalott? In what respects are the stories alike?

3. In the present poem, what was the cause of the Lady's death? In what way may that be considered symbolic of the fate of Elaine?

4. Who greeted the arrival of the barge in Camelot? What is the significance of Lancelot's words with which the poem closes? What do they show about the nature of the knight? (Compare with the speech of Lancelot over the bier of Elaine.)

OVERVIEW:

1. *For Extra Credit:* Read Tennyson's "Lancelot and Elaine." Point out some of the differences in the details between "Lancelot and Elaine" and "The Lady of Shalott." What are some of the parallels in the general theme?

2. Do you think that any one who did not know the story of Lancelot and Elaine would enjoy the story of the Lady of Shalott? Why or why not? Why do you think children are fond of this poem?

ULYSSES

ALFRED TENNYSON

The average reader lays aside the *Odyssey* of Homer with some misgivings at its conclusion. Could Ulysses after twenty years of warfare and of wandering settle down to peaceful domesticity? Would the faithful Penelope remain so charming after all those years of waiting? Somehow the usually accepted "happily-ever-after" ending is threatened in this instance with a number of possible snags. Tennyson, with poetic insight, saw the greatest hazard to retirement in the restless nature of Ulysses. And so this more realistic poet has written a new ending to an old story— or rather he carries on where the older poet stopped. Ulysses is speaking as the poem opens.

> It LITTLE profits that an idle king,
> By this still hearth, among these barren crags,
> Matched with an aged wife, I mete and dole
> Unequal laws into a savage race,
> 5   That hoard, and sleep, and feed, and know not me.
> I cannot rest from travel; I will drink
> Life to the lees. All times I have enjoyed
> Greatly, have suffered greatly, both with those

That loved me, and alone; on shore, and when
10 Through scudding drifts the rainy Hyades
Vext the dim sea. I am become a name;
For always roaming with a hungry heart,
Much have I seen and known; cities of men
And manners, climates, councils, governments,
15 Myself not least, but honored of them all;
And drunk delight of battle with my peers,
Far on the ringing plains of windy Troy.
I am a part of all that I have met;
Yet all experience is an arch wherethrough
20 Gleams that untraveled world whose margin fades
Forever and forever when I move.
How dull it is to pause, to make an end,
To rust unburnished, not to shine in use!
As though to breathe were life! Life piled on life
25 Were all too little, and of one to me
Little remains; but every hour is saved
From that eternal silence, something more,
A bringer of new things; and vile it were
For some three suns to store and hoard myself,
30 And this gray spirit yearning in desire
To follow knowledge like a sinking star,
Beyond the utmost bound of human thought.

This is my son, my own Telemachus,
To whom I leave the scepter and the isle—
35 Well-loved of me, discerning to fulfill
This labor, by slow prudence to make mild
A rugged people, and through soft degrees
Subdue them to the useful and the good.
Most blameless is he, centered in the sphere
40 Of common duties, decent not to fail
In offices of tenderness, and pay
Meet adoration to my household gods,
When I am gone. He works his work, I mine.

There lies the port; the vessel puffs her sail;
45 There gloom the dark, broad seas. My mariners,

10. HYADES—Rain nymphs, placed in the sky by Jupiter.

Souls that have toiled, and wrought, and thought with
   me—
That ever with a frolic welcome took
The thunder and the sunshine, and opposed
Free hearts, free foreheads—you and I are old;
50 Old age hath yet his honor and his toil.
Death closes all; but something ere the end,
Some work of noble note, may yet be done,
Not unbecoming men that strove with Gods.
The lights begin to twinkle from the rocks;
55 The long day wanes; the slow moon climbs; the deep
Moans round with many voices. Come, my friends,
'Tis not too late to seek a newer world.
Push off, and sitting well in order smite
The sounding furrows; for my purpose holds
60 To sail beyond the sunset, and the baths
Of all the western stars, until I die.
It may be that the gulfs will wash us down;
It may be we shall touch the Happy Isles,
And see the great Achilles, whom we knew.
65 Though much is taken, much abides; and though
We are not now that strength which in old days
Moved earth and heaven, that which we are, we are—
One equal temper of heroic hearts,
Made weak by time and fate, but strong in will
70 To strive, to seek, to find, and not to yield.

63. HAPPY ISLES—The Islands of the Blest, sometimes confused with the
Elysian Fields, the home of heroes after death.

FOR INTERPRETATION

Before discussing the poem, review the story of Ulysses (Odysseus),
and be prepared to tell it *briefly* to the class. Notice particularly the
details of the hero's homecoming.

1. According to Tennyson, what has Ulysses been doing since his
return? Does he feel himself fitted for this kind of work? Why or why
not? With what feelings does he look back on his years of wandering
and war? Read aloud the lines that give the answer.

2. Was he satisfied with the achievements of the past? How does he
think old age should be spent? What lines tell what he hoped to do?

3. Who is Telemachus? How does he differ in nature from Ulysses? What qualities of the ideal ruler does he possess? Discuss.

4. To whom is Ulysses speaking from line 45 on to the end of the poem? What picture of declining years does he present? Quote the lines with which Ulysses expresses his *purpose*. Does he have some definite goal in mind? Discuss. With what lines does the poet sum up the spirit of Ulysses?

5. What do you think is the theme of the poem? Can you find a line or lines from the poem that state it?

From LOCKSLEY HALL

ALFRED TENNYSON

In the year 1842 there were no electric lights, no automobiles, no radios, no telephones, and of course no airplanes. But the streets of London were by this time gaslighted. The steam engine had been invented and put to use propelling boats and locomotives at a speed—for the latter—of some fifteen miles an hour. Men had become aware of the possibilities of applied science. Those with vision foresaw some of the inventions which have become commonplaces with us.

A remarkably accurate prediction of this sort was made, not by a scientist, but by the poet, Alfred Tennyson. In the volume of poems published in 1842 was "Locksley Hall"—an imaginative story of a young man disappointed in love who turns for consolation to the world of work. As a whole the poem is no masterpiece, but it contains some splendid lines; such as, "Yet I doubt not through the ages one increasing purpose runs," and the even more famous, "In the spring a young man's fancy lightly turns to thoughts of love." Of greatest interest today is the passage in which the disappointed young man looks forward to taking his place among "the throngs of men." As you read, remember that these lines were written more than a hundred years ago.

B1   Men, my brothers, men the workers, ever
           reaping something new;
    That which they have done but earnest of the
           things that they shall do!

    For I dipt into the future, far as human eye
           could see,

2. EARNEST—"Earnest" money. That is, the uses to which man has already put science are like a "down payment" or a proof of the things that he will be able to do.

797

Saw the vision of the world, and all the wonder that would be;

MB 5 Saw the heavens fill with commerce, argosies
of magic sails,

DB Pilots of the purple twilight, dropping down
with costly bales;

G Heard the heavens fill with shouting, and
there rain'd a ghastly dew
From the nations' airy navies grappling in
the central blue;

L Far along the world-wide whisper of the
southwind rushing warm,

M 10 With the standards of the peoples plunging
thro' the thunder-storm;

D Till the war-drum throbb'd no longer, and
the battle-flags were furl'd

U In the Parliament of Man, the Federation of
the World.

There the common sense of most shall hold a
fretful realm in awe,
And the kindly earth shall slumber, lapped in
universal law.

FOR INTERPRETATION

1. Do we still say, as we look into the future, that considering advances
made in the last century, no prediction seems too rash for the future?
Cite some illustrations.

2. How long a time does the poet seem to allow for the fulfilment of
his predictions? Did he underestimate or overestimate the time?

3. What do lines 4–5 predict? For how long a time has that prediction
been realized? What do lines 7–8 predict? When did that prophecy first
come true? How long after Tennyson wrote the poem was the prophecy
being fulfilled in the skies over London?

4. What do lines 9–12 foretell? Has there been any attempt at fulfilling this prediction? Discuss. Are we any nearer fulfilling it today
than in Tennyson's time? Do lines 13–14 express an ideal possible of

achievement? Discuss. If we consider the accuracy of Tennyson's first predictions as "earnest" of his wisdom, what encouragement does it offer for the fulfilment of his last predictions? Discuss.

BREAK, BREAK, BREAK

ALFRED TENNYSON

The shock of grief has a transforming effect on one's own life, but the rest of the world goes on as before. It is hard, always, to reconcile the two facts. Tennyson knew this feeling on a day when he sat overlooking the sea, longing for the companion who had recently been taken from him.

D   BREAK, break, break,
             On thy cold gray stones, O Sea!
B1   And I would that my tongue could utter
             The thoughts that arise in me.

MB1   5   O, well for the fisherman's boy,
             That he shouts with his sister at play!
DB1   O, well for the sailor lad,
             That he sings in his boat on the bay!

M   And the stately ships go on
      10   To their haven under the hill;
D   But O for the touch of a vanish'd hand,
             And the sound of a voice that is still!

D   Break, break, break,
             At the foot of thy crags, O Sea!
L   15   But the tender grace of a day that is dead
D   Will never come back to me.

FOR INTERPRETATION

1. Does the landscape seem in sympathy with the poet's grief?
2. Just what does Tennyson see as he looks out and down from his hilltop? Name at least three things,—and as many more as you can.
3. Does he resent the unconcern of the rest of the world? How can you tell? What lines best express the sense of his personal loss?

From IN MEMORIAM

ALFRED TENNYSON

Arthur Hallam, the friend and confidant of Tennyson's young manhood, died in 1833. The event made an unusual impression on the poet because, added to the sense of personal grief, came perplexing questions concerning what had been his fundamental faiths. Why, if there was Divine justice, should a gifted and good young man die? Were the new philosophers right who denied a God with any personal interest in human beings? Was there indeed a human immortality? For years Tennyson wrestled with these and similar questions. And through that time he wrote down his thoughts in lyrics—some very short, others of many stanzas. Those that were in any way the outgrowth of his affection for Hallam, he kept together, using for them a special stanza form.

In 1850 there were one hundred and thirty lyrics which he published together under the title of *In Memoriam.* They show a growth in vision and understanding. The early poems reflect mostly the bewilderment of his grief—

> "O life as futile, then, as frail!
> O for thy voice to soothe and bless!
> What hope of answer, or redress?
> Behind the veil, behind the veil."

In the later ones, he sets his personal experience against the background of universal life and of eternity. And in the end there grows within him a faith larger and stronger than that of his youth, a belief in

> "That God, which ever lives and loves,
> One God, one law, one element,
> And one far-off divine event,
> To which the whole creation moves."

The separate lyrics are designated merely by number. They are of many moods, and concern many incidental themes. The following selections will introduce you to some of the finest thoughtful poetry of the last century.

XXVII

If you had to be a prisoner, would you wish that you had never known freedom? Is the animal better off than man because it has no sense of right or wrong? Is it better never to love than to have to suffer separation from a dear one? Tennyson gives his answers to these questions in the following stanzas.

I ENVY not in any moods
The captive void of noble rage,

The linnet born within the cage,
That never knew the summer woods;

5 I envy not the beast that takes
His license in the field of time,
Unfetter'd by the sense of crime,
To whom a conscience never wakes;

Nor, what may count itself as blest,
10   The heart that never plighted troth
But stagnates in the weeds of sloth;
Nor any want-begotten rest.

I hold it true, whate'er befall;
I feel it, when I sorrow most;
15   'T is better to have loved and lost
Than never to have loved at all.

3. LINNET—A singing bird, caged in England as we cage canaries.
12. NOR ANY WANT-BEGOTTEN REST—Rest or contentedness which is the result
of never having known a high desire.

LIV

Is there really a divine and growing purpose guiding the destiny of
the ages? Is there a meaning to the sin and the waste and the losses of
life? When the following lines were written, the poet *hoped*, but he was
not confident in his hope.

O, YET we trust that somehow good
Will be the final goal of ill,
To pangs of nature, sins of will,
Defects of doubt, and taints of blood;

5 That nothing walks with aimless feet;
That not one life shall be destroy'd,
Or cast as rubbish to the void,
When God hath made the pile complete;

That not a worm is cloven in vain;
10   That not a moth with vain desire
Is shrivell'd in a fruitless fire,
Or but subserves another's gain.

Behold, we know not anything;
   I can but trust that good shall fall
15   At last—far off—at last, to all,
   And every winter change to spring.

So runs my dream; but what am I?
   An infant crying in the night;
   An infant crying for the light,
20   And with no language but a cry.

CXXVI AND CXXVII

Again Tennyson shows himself to have a touch of prophetic insight. In lyrics CXXVI and CXXVII, which really belong together, it is almost as if he were seeing through a crystal ball the fury of two world wars and their accompanying changes. Some of the thrones did topple in World War I. But "social justice" was by no means established. Is ours the great æon that must "sink in blood"? Is World War II the predicted conflict? If so, there is comfort in the faith that believes the outcome will be a new order in which "All is well."

The first of these two lyrics serves merely as an introduction to the stanzas of the second. Tennyson pictures the spirit of his friend as now "living in God" and thus being able to see human affairs with the understanding of eternal values.

CXXVI

Love is and was my lord and king,
   And in his presence I attend
   To hear the tidings of my friend,
Which every hour his couriers bring.

5   Love is and was my king and lord,
   And will be, tho' as yet I keep
   Within the court on earth, and sleep
Encompass'd by his faithful guard,

And hear at times a sentinel
10   Who moves about from place to place,
   And whispers to the worlds of space,
In the deep night that all is well.

1. LOVE—Tennyson's faith is in a God of love. He made love a guiding principle of his life. This lyric expresses the poet's belief that his friend's spirit lives and forms a bond between this world and eternity.

CXXVII

And all is well, tho' faith and form
Be sunder'd in the night of fear;
15   Well roars the storm to those that hear
A deeper voice across the storm,

Proclaiming social truth shall spread,
And justice, even tho' thrice again
The red fool-fury of the Seine
20   Should pile her barricades with dead.

But ill for him that wears a crown,
And him, the lazar, in his rags!
They tremble, the sustaining crags;
The spires of ice are toppled down,

25   And molten up, and roar in flood;
The fortress crashes from on high,
The brute earth lightens to the sky,
And the great Æon sinks in blood

And compass'd by the fires of hell;
30   While thou, dear spirit, happy star,
·O'erlook'st the tumult from afar,
And smilest, knowing all is well.

16. STORM—The social disturbances of Tennyson's day.
22. LAZAR—Beggar. The two extremes of social injustice are represented by the crowned head on one hand and the beggar on the other.
24. SPIRES OF ICE—The artificial distinctions of society—of class, of caste, of race, etc.—which allow a small proportion of men to enrich themselves at the cost of the impoverished masses.

FOR INTERPRETATION

XXVII:

1. How would you answer the first question in the introduction to this lyric? Would the bird hatched in a cage be happier than the one caught and brought from the woods to captivity? Discuss.

2. Do you agree with the poet that it is better to be a man knowing what *good* is, though often falling short of it, than to be like a beast with no sense of right and wrong? Why or why not?

3. In what respect is the man who has seen and lost his eyesight *richer*

than the man who has never seen at all? What things can the person born deaf not even *imagine?* In what sense was Tennyson's life richer after Hallam's death than if he had never known the man? Do you agree with the poet in the thought of the closing lines of the lyric?

LIV:

1. Is it true that a long view of events *often* shows that what looked like misfortunes proved to be blessings? Cite at least one example from history. Cite one example, if possible, from your own life or from the life of some one you know. Is the reverse situation sometimes true?

2. Express in your own words the theme of the first three stanzas. Quote, if you can, a sentence from some other book or piece or literature which expresses the same thought.

3. Lines 14–16 echo a thought expressed by what other poet whose works you have recently studied? What feeling does the poet suggest in lines 13–20?

CXXVI AND CXXVII:

1. To understand the meaning of these three stanzas one must study the metaphor in which it is expressed. The key is contained in the first line. *Who* or *what* is the king? Who "waits in the presence" of the king? Why? What do you think could be meant by the *couriers* of the king? What is meant by keeping "within the court on earth"? Who is the *faithful guard?* Who do you think is the *sentinel?*

2. Explain the relationship in thought between the third stanza of CXXVI and the last stanza of CXXVII. Who is the "dear spirit" in line 30?

3. Mention briefly some of the political, economic, and social disturbances in England during the nineteenth century. Which lines seem to refer to them?

4. At what times before 1850 had heaps of dead reddened the waters of the Seine? To which occasion do you think Tennyson is referring in his "red fool-fury" (l. 19)? Why does he use those words? How many times since 1850 has the Seine been the scene of the destruction of war?

5. What reforms does the poet say need to be accomplished? Why does the beggar need to tremble? How does Tennyson think those reforms will come about? Quote the lines with which the poet says the reforms will come. Do you think he is right? Discuss.

6. To what extent has history in the last ninety years proved the poet correct in his prophecies? For example, what *crowns* have fallen since 1850? When did most of them go? Are we any closer to the achievement of *social justice* today? Discuss.

7. Why does the "spirit" over-looking the conflict *smile?* How does the underlying thought of this lyric differ in spirit from LIV, which was written several years earlier? Do you see any indication of growth or maturity in the poet? Discuss.

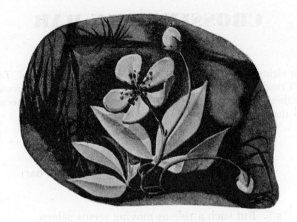

FLOWER IN THE CRANNIED WALL

ALFRED TENNYSON

Because a flower lives—though briefly—and holds within its seeds the promise of other flowers, it has always seemed to poets especially full of meaning. Blake saw "a heaven in a wild flower." Tennyson believed it to be the clue to the mysteries of life. If only he could read it!

L
B1

FLOWER in the crannied wall,
I pluck you out of the crannies,
I hold you here, root and all, in my hand,
Little flower—but *if* I could understand
5   What you are, root and all, and all in all,

U

I should know what God and man is.

FOR INTERPRETATION

1. Why should a flower growing out of a cranny in a rock seem especially significant?

2. What are some of the miracles involved in the life of a flower that even a botanist or biologist cannot completely comprehend? Luther Burbank called a green leaf the "most wonderful thing in the world." In what respects is a flower even more complex and mysterious? Discuss.

3. What do you think Tennyson meant when he said he would know about God and man *if* he could understand what a flower is? Discuss.

CROSSING THE BAR

ALFRED TENNYSON

In his eighty-first year, with all doubts and misgivings settled, Tennyson wrote "Crossing the Bar." Its quiet assurance has been a source of comfort to those who are facing death themselves or who have seen others dear to them go out across the bar.

L		SUNSET and evening star,
GI		And one clear call for me!
D		And may there be no moaning of the bar,
L		When I put out to sea,
M	5	But such a tide as moving seems asleep,
		Too full for sound and foam,
		When that which drew from out the bound-
		less deep
		Turns again home.
L		Twilight and evening bell,
D	10	And after that the dark!
GI		And may there be no sadness of farewell,
		When I embark;
M		For though from out our bourne of time
		and place
BI		The flood may bear me far,
U	15	I hope to see my Pilot face to face
		When I have crossed the bar.

FOR INTERPRETATION

To one who knows the sea and harbors, the imagery of the poem is beautifully clear. Birth is the tide that bears the soul into the world from the boundless deep of eternity. Death is the turning of the tide that carries one back across the harbor bar again into eternity and home.

1. Is it a deep, flooding tide, or a shallow sea that makes the crossing of a bar noisy? Explain. What kind of death does the poet wish for in the second stanza? Is he referring to the physical manner of dying, or to the attitude with which he and his family shall meet his death? Discuss. What meaning is suggested to you by the tide "too full for sound and foam"?

2. What accompanying sights and sounds are suggestive of peace and assurance? Name them, and explain the ideas associated with each.

3. What is the meaning of the word *bourne?* Explain its use in the fourth stanza. What is the relationship between the passenger and the pilot? Does the passenger see the pilot during the crossing? What does the pilot do? What must be the attitude of the passenger? Why might the passenger want to see his pilot after he had "crossed the bar"? What do you think is the poet's full meaning in the last stanza? Discuss.

4. Why do you think Tennyson asked his son to be sure that this poem was placed last in any collection of his works? With the musical setting that has been provided for it, "Crossing the Bar" has become a favorite song with those who have suffered bereavement. Can you tell why?

THE YEAR'S AT THE SPRING

ROBERT BROWNING

In his dramatic poem "Pippa Passes," Browning presents a little Italian girl from a silk factory, singing as she enjoys her one holiday of the year. Her path crosses those of four persons, each facing a great crisis; and each is helped by the unknowing singer. "The Year's at the Spring" is the song with which Pippa began her day.

LGI		The year's at the spring,
MGI		And day's at the morn;
LGI		Morning's at seven;
MGI		The hillside's dew-pearled;
MBI	5	The lark's on the wing;
DBI		The snail's on the thorn;
G		God's in His heaven—
U		All's right with the world.

FOR INTERPRETATION

Pippa's song really speaks for itself. Notice how it builds up to a crescendo of happiness. An interesting point-by-point comparison in the matter of *background, details,* and *mood* may be made between this happy morning song and Shelley's "Dirge," beginning "Rough wind that moanest loud." How do you account for the difference between the last lines of the two lyrics? Discuss.

HOME THOUGHTS FROM ABROAD

ROBERT BROWNING

Homesickness strikes suddenly sometimes. A sudden fragrance on the wind, a hint of rain in the air—and our hearts are miles away! Browning found rare happiness in Italy and in another poem, "De Gustibus," expresses a preference for his southern home   But once on an April day, his thoughts flew to England—England in the spring!

OH, TO be in England
Now that April's there,
And whoever wakes in England
Sees, some morning, unaware,
5   That the lowest boughs and the brushwood sheaf
Round the elm tree bole are in tiny leaf,
While the chaffinch sings on the orchard bough
In England—now!

And after April, when May follows,
10   And the whitethroat builds, and all the swallows!
Hark, where my blossomed pear tree in the hedge
Leans to the field and scatters on the clover
Blossoms and dewdrops—at the bent spray's edge—
That's the wise thrush; he sings each song twice over,
15   Lest you should think he never could recapture
The first fine careless rapture!
And though the fields look rough with hoary dew,
All will be gay when noontide wakes anew
The buttercups, the little children's dower
20   —Far brighter than this gaudy melon flower!

FOR INTERPRETATION

1. It is the little details in a picture—whether on canvas or in the memory—that give the touch of reality. Mention the details that make Browning's description of spring in England sound real. What birds does he name? what trees? what flowers? what unexpected bits of detail?

2. What makes the blossoming pear tree lean to the edge of the field with one bent spray? What do you learn in lines 14–16 about the way a thrush sings?

3. How does spring in England compare with spring in your home state? Discuss.

4. With what feelings would an English soldier on duty in Africa or Australia read this poem? Discuss.

From SAUL

ROBERT BROWNING

A verse from 1st *Samuel* was the inspiration for one of Browning's fine dramatic monologues: *And it came to pass, when the evil spirit was upon Saul, that David took an harp, and played with his hand: so Saul was refreshed, and was well, and the evil spirit departed from him.* Browning has the shepherd boy, David, describe how he found the king stretched rigid in his tent and how he played the man back to health. David sang, as he played, of the sheep in the fields, of night under the stars, of the harvest and reapers. In the lines quoted below, he bursts out into a song of young manhood that triumphs even over a desert country and finds joy among rocks, and pleasant sleep in dried river channels.

B1   "OH, OUR manhood's prime vigor! No spirit feels waste,
           Not a muscle is stopped in its playing nor sinew unbraced.
B   Oh, the wild joys of living! the leaping from rock up to rock,
           The strong rending of boughs from the fir-tree, the cool silver shock
5   Of the plunge in a pool's living water, the hunt of the bear,
           And the sultriness showing the lion is couched in his lair.
           And the meal, the rich dates yellowed over with gold dust divine,
           And the locust-flesh steeped in the pitcher, and the full draught of wine,
           And the sleep in the dried river-channel where bulrushes tell
10   That the water was wont to go warbling so softly and well.

U   How good is man's life, the mere living! how fit to
      employ
      All the heart and the soul and the senses forever in
      joy!"

FOR INTERPRETATION

1. Browning was familiar with life in hot countries and has given a realistic picture of rural Palestine about the time of David. Name in order the activities David mentions, matched with the lines that describe them, thus (1) mountain climbing—"the leaping from rock up to rock."

2. What was the food that David ate with so much relish? For what purpose might David be tearing the boughs from the fir tree?

. 3. Do you think any young man might enjoy doing the things David describes? Which ones especially? Upon what other factors would his pleasure depend?

4. What makes it possible for David to sing whole-heartedly, "How good is man's life, the mere living!"? Would Saul agree with him? Why or why not?

MY LAST DUCHESS

(FERRARA)

ROBERT BROWNING

Here again is a dramatic monologue. The setting for this one might be given as follows:

The place: A ducal palace in Ferrara, Italy.

The time: During the Italian Renaissance, probably the fifteenth century.

The speaker: The Duke of Ferrara, no longer young.

The listener: The representative of a neighboring count, come to make arrangements for an approaching marriage between the Duke and the count's daughter—especially the arrangements about the dowry. The business over, the Duke in an affable mood draws aside the curtain before the portrait of his "last" Duchess. (We do not know how many wives had preceded her.) With considerable pride, he shows forth the painting—

THAT's my last Duchess painted on the wall,
Looking as if she were alive. I call

That piece a wonder, now: Frà Pandolf's hands
Worked busily a day, and there she stands.
5 Will 't please you sit and look at her? I said
"Frà Pandolf" by design, for never read
Strangers like you that pictured countenance,
The depth and passion of its earnest glance,
But to myself they turned (since none puts by
10 The curtain I have drawn for you, but I)
And seemed as they would ask me, if they durst,
How such a glance came there; so, not the first
Are you to turn and ask thus. Sir, 'twas not
Her husband's presence only, called that spot
15 Of joy into the Duchess' cheek: perhaps
Frà Pandolf chanced to say, "Her mantle laps
Over my lady's wrist too much," or "Paint
Must never hope to reproduce the faint
Half flush that dies along her throat:" such stuff
20 Was courtesy, she thought, and cause enough
For calling up that spot of joy. She had
A heart—how shall I say?—too soon made glad,
Too easily impressed: she liked whate'er
She looked on, and her looks went everywhere.
25 Sir, 'twas all one! My favor at her breast,
The dropping of the daylight in the west,
The bough of cherries some officious fool
Broke in the orchard for her, the white mule
She rode with round the terrace—all and each
30 Would draw from her alike the approving speech,
Or blush, at least. She thanked men—good! but
thanked
Somehow—I know not how—as if she ranked
My gift of a nine-hundred-years-old name
With anybody's gift. Who'd stoop to blame
35 This sort of trifling? Even had you skill
In speech—(which I have not)—to make your will
Quite clear to such an one, and say, "Just this

3. FRÀ PANDOLF—Brother Pandolf. Like "Claus of Innsbruck" in the last
line of the poem, the name is fictitious. Many of the Renaissance painters
were monks. And it was a matter of pride among the nobility to be patrons
and connoisseurs of art.
25. MY FAVOR—My gift—probably a jeweled brooch.

Or that in you disgusts me; here you miss,
Or there exceed the mark"—and if she let
40 Herself be lessoned so, nor plainly set
Her wits to yours, forsooth, and made excuse
—E'en then would be some stooping; and I choose
Never to stoop. Oh, sir, she smiled, no doubt,
Whene'er I passed her; but who passed without
45 Much the same smile? This grew; I gave commands;
Then all smiles stopped together. There she stands
As if alive. Will 't please you rise? We'll meet
The company below, then. I repeat,
The Count your master's known munificence
50 Is ample warrant that no just pretence
Of mine for dowry will be disallowed;
Though his fair daughter's self, as I avowed
At starting, is my object. Nay, we'll go
Together down, sir. Notice Neptune, though,
55 Taming a sea horse, thought a rarity,
Which Claus of Innsbruck cast in bronze for me!

45. I GAVE COMMANDS—When Browning was asked if he meant that the Duke gave commands to have the Duchess murdered, he replied, "Yes, I meant that the commands were that she should be put to death," and then he added after a pause, "or he might have had her shut up in a convent."

FOR INTERPRETATION

This monologue is best understood when it is read aloud in a conversational tone of voice. The reader must pay careful attention to punctuation marks, for the end of Browning's sentences seldom fall at the ends of the lines. Imagine the portrait on the wall. The Duke is speaking first about it as one of his choice works of art valued because it is by "Frà Pandolf." But he is led from comments on the painting to a discussion of the faults—as he saw them—of the lady painted upon it.

One of the "tricks" of the dramatic monologue is that the speaker betrays his own character as he talks. Have you ever overheard some loud-spoken stranger holding forth with—"And *I* said ———— ————. And *I* told him ———— ————," and so on, and so on—with the result that all your sympathies were won toward the person who was *being told?* Well, that sort of thing sometimes happens in a dramatic monologue. The person speaking is sure that he is right. When he finishes, we may be sure that he is wrong.

See what you think of the Duke when he finishes speaking—and of the Duchess whom he criticizes so callously.

1. If you were preparing this script for a dramatic reading, what stage directions would you insert, and where? For example, what direction would you give for line 5? Where else would you give directions?

2. It is not difficult to read the character of the Duke as he betrays himself. Which lines tell us that he is *proud* and *domineering?* Which lines show that he is *jealous?* that he was *unreasonably* jealous? that he was *cruel?* that he is *remorseless?* Is there anything else that you learn about him? Discuss.

3. Similarly make a list of the adjectives with which the Duchess might be described and point out the words of the Duke that give us each impression. How do we know that she was innocent of any misdemeanor which might have justified the Duke's jealousy? How old do you think she was? On what evidence do you base your opinion?

4. What impression do you think the Duke's words would make on the representative of the count? How should you like to be the young woman who is to become the *next* Duchess?

5. Do you believe the words of the Duke in lines 51–52? Why or why not? Why do you think he has selected this particular bride? Discuss.

6. Turn back to Blake's poem, "The Clod and the Pebble." Which stanza describes the Duke's kind of "love"? Show how that stanza applies to the situation suggested in the monologue.

7. Bearing in mind what you have learned about Italian life in the fifteenth century, do you believe that the character of the Duke is overdrawn? Discuss.

PROSPICE

(LOOK AHEAD!)

ROBERT BROWNING

"Faces front!" The crisp command suggests Browning's attitude toward death. His thoughts about it were expressed in the following poem written in the first year after Mrs. Browning had died. The poet admits the instinctive fear men have of this last experience; but he finds in it a challenge, to be met face forward, strongly, even gladly, in expectation of what lies ahead.

Twenty-five years passed before Browning's call came. He met it just as he had looked forward to it—a momentary paying of "glad life's arrears."

> FEAR death?—to feel the fog in my throat,
> The mist in my face,

When the snows begin, and the blasts denote
I am nearing the place,
5   The power of the night, the press of the storm,
The post of the foe;
Where he stands, the Arch Fear in a visible form,
Yet the strong man must go:
For the journey is done and the summit attained,
10   And the barriers fall,
Though a battle's to fight ere the guerdon be gained,
The reward of it all.
I was ever a fighter, so—one fight more,
The best and the last!
15   I would hate that death bandaged my eyes, and forbore,
And bade me creep past.
No! let me taste the whole of it, fare like my peers
The heroes of old,
Bear the brunt, in a minute pay glad life's arrears
20   Of pain, darkness and cold.
For sudden, the worst turns the best to the brave,
The black minute's at end,
And the elements' rage, the fiend-voices that rave,
Shall dwindle, shall blend,
25   Shall change, shall become first a peace out of pain,
Then a light, then thy breast,
O thou soul of my soul! I shall clasp thee again,
And with God be the rest!

FOR INTERPRETATION

1. The first five lines of the poem suggest what time of year? what weather conditions? Life has been a journey *in what direction?* Which word tells you? What is a *guerdon?* What is the last battle to be fought *ere the guerdon be gained?* What lines later on in the poem tell what will be *the reward of it all?*

2. Men often speak of "fighting" death in the sense of trying to prevent it. Obviously that is not what Browning means when he speaks in lines 13–14 of "one fight more, the best and the last!" What do you think is the poet's meaning? How do later lines in the poem help explain it? Discuss.

3. What kind of death is Browning referring to in lines 15–16? What are "arrears"? Explain the figure, "in a minute pay glad life's arrears."

4. Give a specific illustration of a case where *the worst* suddenly turned into *the best* for someone not afraid to face it. What do you think Browning meant by "the worst" in this particular instance? How can it turn into "the best"—only under what conditions? Discuss. What had robbed death of its greatest threat, or tragedy, for Browning?

5. In what lines does the poet visualize the actual experience of dying? Explain them. After the dying is over, what joys does he expect? Compare the conclusion of this poem with the closing lines of Mrs. Browning's sonnet, "How Do I Love Thee."

6. Review the account of Browning's life. Show how his experiences and his character account for his attitude toward death. Why do you think that almost every poet writes at least one poem about death?

From RABBI BEN EZRA

ROBERT BROWNING

A true test of man's optimism lies in his feeling about growing old. A good many people think that they can face death more easily than the infirmities of old age. Robert Herrick, you remember, wrote——

> "That age is best which is the first,
> When youth and blood are warmer;
> But being spent, the *worse* and *worst*
> Times still succeed the former."

But Robert Browning had a philosophy of life that was equal to even this test. Old age? It should be the best time of life. In "Rabbi Ben Ezra," a poem of many stanzas, he gives the reasons for his belief. The first and last stanzas express the germ of his idea. The lines are supposed to be spoken by Ibn Ezra (more fully, Abraham Ben Meir ibn Ezra), a famous Jewish scholar of the twelfth century, but the thoughts are Browning's.

> GROW old along with me!
> The best is yet to be,
> The last of life, for which the first was made:
> Our times are in His Hand
> 5   Who saith, "A whole I planned;
> Youth shows but half: trust God, see all, nor be afraid!"

So take and use Thy work;
Amend what flaws may lurk,
What strain o' the stuff, what warpings past the aim!
10 My times be in Thy hand!
Perfect the cup as planned!
Let age approve of youth, and death complete the same!

FOR INTERPRETATION

In his development of the poem Browning uses the figure that each life is like a piece of clay in the potter's hand. God is the craftsman who spins the wheel and designs the vessel—vase or cup. Youth could be just the base or the crude beginning. It takes the whole of life to show the Maker's design.

1. Browning was about fifty-two when he wrote "Rabbi Ben Ezra." How old a man do you think is talking in the poem? What relationship, not often recognized, does the poet see between *youth* and *age?* Quote the lines from the first stanza that express it. Is the idea logical? Discuss.

2. If we think, as the poet did, of youth as a preparation for age, what are some of the things that young people should be gathering and preserving for enjoyment in the "best" time of life? Are material things the most important? Discuss. In Browning's opinion, what two words in the first stanza are essential if one is to enjoy old age? Why?

3. To whom are the lines of the last stanza addressed? How can you tell? What expressions in the last stanza refer to the figure of the clay and the potter? In what sense will "Age *approve* of youth"? Why does the poet say that death will—not *destroy* the cup of life—but *complete* it? Discuss.

4. Was the truth of Browning's philosophy proved in the lives of any of these writers—Tennyson, Shelley, Burns, Wordsworth, Byron, Keats, Browning himself? In the cases where your answer is "No," explain why or how the ideal was defeated.

Other poets reflected new influences and foreshadowed modern trends.

HOW DO I LOVE THEE

ELIZABETH BARRETT BROWNING

The face of all the world is changed, I think,
Since first I heard the footsteps of thy soul
Move still, oh still, beside me as they stole
Betwixt me and the dreadful outer brink
Of obvious death, where I, who thought to sink,
Was caught up into love, and taught the whole
Of life in a new rhythm.

There is no over-statement in these lines from the seventh of the "Sonnets from the Portuguese." When Browning first came to see her, Elizabeth Barrett had been given only a few months to live. She had almost stopped writing, and had reconciled all her thoughts to death. Forty-four sonnets tell the story of the transformation that Browning's love brought into her life. The poems were intended for him alone to read. But he believed that they were truly great and should be published. It was a gesture toward disguising their personal meaning that gave them the printed title, "Sonnets from the Portuguese."

One needs to read the whole cycle to learn the story. But one sonnet —the forty-third—is a perfect summing-up of Elizabeth's love. Indeed it is a question whether anything in literature has surpassed these fourteen lines in defining the love that may exist between man and woman.

G	How do I love thee? Let me count the ways.
G1	I love thee to the depth and breadth and height
	My soul can reach, when feeling out of sight
	For the ends of being and ideal Grace.
G2 5	I love thee to the level of every day's
	Most quiet need, by sun and candlelight.
G3	I love thee freely, as men strive for right;
G4	I love thee purely, as they turn from praise,
G5	I love thee with the passion put to use
10	In my old griefs, and with my childhood's faith.
G6	I love thee with a love I seemed to lose
	With my lost saints—I love thee with the breath,
	Smiles, tears, of all my life! and, if God choose,
G	I shall but love thee better after death.

FOR INTERPRETATION

1. In order to see the full meaning of the sonnet, you must be sure to understand some of the expressions in it, considering it first line by line. What is the meaning implied in the expression, "when feeling out of sight for *ends of being* and *ideal grace*"? What word usually covers this human experience? Why is the word *freely* good to use in connection with men's striving for *right*? What is the thought suggested in the line, "I love thee *purely*, as they *turn from praise*"? Do all men and women turn away from praise? What kind of motives do we usually find in people who are not interested in winning honor or praise? Are the emotions of children usually more intense than those of grown-ups? What kind of faith do children give to their beliefs?

2. Considering the sonnet as a whole, which lines express the *idealism* that is a part of true love? Which lines express love's kindness and consideration in everyday living? Which lines express the intensity of love? the unquestioning assurance of love? Which lines sum up the range of Elizabeth's love? Which lines express the deathlessness of love?

SHAKESPEARE

MATTHEW ARNOLD

An unscaled mountain peak, lifting its summit to the stars, seemed to Matthew Arnold the most appropriate symbol of the genius of Shakespeare—a poet *out-topping knowledge.*

OTHERS abide our question. Thou art free.
We ask and ask: Thou smilest and art still,
Out-topping knowledge. For the loftiest hill
That to the stars uncrowns his majesty,
5   Planting his steadfast footsteps in the sea,
Making the Heaven of Heavens his dwelling-place,
Spares but the cloudy border of his base
To the foil'd searching of mortality:
And thou, who didst the stars and sunbeams know,
10   Self-school'd, self-scann'd, self-honor'd, self-secure,
Didst walk on earth unguess'd at. Better so!
All pains the immortal spirit must endure,
All weakness that impairs, all griefs that bow,
Find their sole voice in that victorious brow.

FOR INTERPRETATION

1. Can those who live on the lower slopes of a mountain comprehend its greatness? Explain. With what words does Arnold describe a mountain reaching from seashore to a peak? Explain the meaning of lines 7–8. What does "mortality" mean in this line?

2. Point out the likenesses that Arnold sees between Shakespeare and such a mountain. In what respects is the figure appropriate?

3. Explain and comment on the four adjectives used of Shakespeare in line 10. Do you question the appropriateness of any of them? If so, which? And why?

4. What do you think the last three lines mean? Of what was Arnold thinking when he wrote the last line? Which line or lines in the sonnet do you consider the finest tribute to Shakespeare?

THE BLESSED DAMOZEL

DANTE GABRIEL ROSSETTI

One of the most strangely appealing poems of the nineteenth century was written by an English-Italian poet and painter before he had reached his twenties. And although the author, Dante Gabriel Rossetti, fulfilled his early promise by writing a good deal of excellent poetry, "The Blessed Damozel" remains his best known and perhaps most typical work.

Rossetti has told us that the poem was suggested to him by Poe's "The Raven." Not wishing to compete against the American poet in portray-

ing earthly grief, Rossetti decided to turn things around and present the
sorrow of a maiden in heaven for her lover left on earth. And like "The
Raven," the poem has taken on added pathos from the fact that its author
later lost a wife whom he adored and the verses became a sort of pre-
painting of that separation.

One should read the poem, not looking for hidden meanings—there are
none—but merely to enjoy its music and its exquisite word-paintings
which glow like jeweled-toned murals in some old cathedral.

> THE blessed damozel leaned out
> From the gold bar of Heaven;
> Her eyes were deeper than the depth
> Of waters stilled at even;
> 5 She had three lilies in her hand,
> And the stars in her hair were seven.
>
> Her robe, ungirt from clasp to hem,
> No wrought flowers did adorn,
> But a white rose of Mary's gift,
> 10 For service meetly worn;
> Her hair that lay along her back
> Was yellow like ripe corn.
>
> Herseemed she scarce had been a day
> One of God's choristers;
> 15 The wonder was not yet quite gone
> From that still look of hers;
> Albeit, to them she left, her day
> Had counted as ten years.
>
> (To one, it is ten years of years.
> 20 . . . Yet now, and in this place,
> Surely she leaned o'er me—her hair
> Fell all about my face. . . .
> Nothing: the autumn fall of leaves.
> The whole year sets apace.)
>
> 25 It was the rampart of God's house
> That she was standing on;
> By God built over the sheer depth
> The which is Space begun;

So high, that looking downward thence
30   She scarce could see the sun.

It lies in Heaven, across the flood
      Of ether, as a bridge.
Beneath, the tides of day and night
      With flame and darkness ridge
35 The void, as low as where this earth
      Spins like a fretful midge.

Around her, lovers, newly met
      'Mid deathless love's acclaims,
Spoke evermore among themselves
40   Their heart-remembered names;
And the souls mounting up to God
      Went by her like thin flames.

And still she bowed herself and stooped
      Out of the circling charm;
45 Until her bosom must have made
      The bar she leaned on warm,
And the lilies lay as if asleep
      Along her bended arm.

From the fixed place of Heaven she saw
50   Time like a pulse shake fierce
Through all the worlds. Her gaze still strove
      Within the gulf to pierce
Its path; and now she spoke as when
      The stars sang in their spheres.

55 The sun was gone now; the curled moon
      Was like a little feather
Fluttering far down the gulf; and now
      She spoke through the still weather.
Her voice was like the voice the stars
60   Had when they sang together.

(Ah sweet! Even now, in that bird's song,
      Strove not her accents there,

       Fain to be hearkened? When those bells
         Possessed the mid-day air,
65   Strove not her steps to reach my side
         Down all the echoing stair?)

       "I wish that he were come to me,
         For he will come," she said.
       "Have I not prayed in Heaven?—on earth,
70   Lord, Lord, has he not prayed?
       Are not two prayers a perfect strength?
         And shall I feel afraid?

       "When round his head the aureole clings,
         And he is clothed in white,
75   I'll take his hand and go with him
         To the deep wells of light;
       As unto a stream we will step down,
         And bathe there in God's sight.

       "We two will stand beside that shrine,
80   Occult, withheld, untrod,
       Whose lamps are stirred continually
         With prayer sent up to God;
       And see our old prayers, granted, melt
         Each like a little cloud.

85   "We two will lie i' the shadow of
         That living mystic tree
       Within whose secret growth the Dove
         Is sometimes felt to be,
       While every leaf that His plumes touch
90   Saith His Name audibly.

       "And I myself will teach to him,
         I myself, lying so,
       The songs I sing here; which his voice
         Shall pause in, hushed and slow,
95   And finds some knowledge at each pause,
         Or some new thing to know."

(Alas! We two, we two, thou say'st!
Yea, one wast thou with me
That once of old. But shall God lift
100   To endless unity
The soul whose likeness with thy soul
Was but its love for thee?)

"We two," she said, "will seek the groves
Where the lady Mary is,
105   With her five handmaidens, whose names
Are five sweet symphonies,
Cecily, Gertrude, Magdalen,
Margaret and Rosalys.

"Circlewise sit they, with bound locks
110   And foreheads garlanded;
Into the fine cloth white like flame
Weaving the golden thread,
To fashion the birth-robes for them
Who are just born, being dead.

115   "He shall fear, haply, and be dumb:
Then will I lay my cheek
To his, and tell about our love,
Not once abashed or weak:
And the dear Mother will approve
120   My pride, and let me speak.

"Herself shall bring us, hand in hand,
To Him round whom all souls
Kneel, the clear-ranged unnumbered heads
Bowed with their aureoles:
125   And angels meeting us shall sing
To their citherns and citoles.

"There will I ask of Christ the Lord
Thus much for him and me:—
Only to live as once on earth
130   With Love, only to be,

As then awhile, for ever now
Together, I and he."

She gazed and listened and then said,
Less sad of speech than mild,—
135   "All this is when he comes." She ceased.
The light thrilled towards her, filled
With angels in strong level flight.
Her eyes prayed, and she smiled.

(I saw her smile.) But soon their path
140   Was vague in distant spheres:
And then she cast her arms along
The golden barriers,
And laid her face between her hands,
And wept. (I heard her tears.)

FOR INTERPRETATION

1. Describe the first picture of the Damozel, as she is presented in the first three stanzas. Which details make her seem most real?

2. Who speaks in the stanzas within the parentheses? What is the purpose of these stanzas?

3. What setting is suggested by "the rampart of God's house" (l. 25)? What details in the fifth and sixth stanzas give the effect of a *celestial* scene? What lines in the eighth stanza give the maiden a touch of realness in her heavenly setting? What is she doing in stanza 9—or trying to do? How has the scene changed in stanza 10?

4. What sounds on earth seemed to her lover to be messages from her?

5. What is the subject of the Damozel's song? Tell briefly, in your own words, what she describes. What expressions in stanzas 13–16 indicate Rossetti's familiarity with ecclesiastical subjects? What religious faith is suggested by his details?

6. What question troubles the lover on earth?

7. Describe the series of pictures presented in the Damozel's song. Describe the picture of the maiden as she appears in the next-to-the-last stanza; in the last stanza. What touches give these last pictures the semblance of reality?

8. What story does the poem suggest? How much do we know about the earthly lover? about the girl in heaven? Discuss.

9. Which stanzas of the poem would you choose to illustrate, if you were a painter? Select three or four, and tell what kind of illustrations you would do—in oil, or wash, or crayon; in modernistic or impressionistic or realistic style; and so on.

LOST DAYS

DANTE GABRIEL ROSSETTI

An American poet once wrote——

> "Our slender life goes rippling by, and glides
> Into the silent hollow of the Past.
> What is there that abides?"

It is a similar question that Rossetti asks in his sonnet, "Lost Days." If nothing abides, then are our days lost indeed—each one a "murdered self."

THE lost days of my life until today,
What were they, could I see them on the street
Lie as they fell? Would they be ears of wheat
Sown once for food but trodden into clay?
5   Or golden coins squandered and still to pay?
Or drops of blood dabbling the guilty feet?
Or such spilt water as in dreams must cheat
The undying throats of Hell, athirst alway?
I do not see them here: but after death
10   God knows I know the faces I shall see,
Each one a murdered self, with low last breath.
"I am thyself,—what hast thou done to me?"
"And I—and I—thyself" (lo! each one saith),
"And thou thyself to all eternity!"

FOR INTERPRETATION

1. What different ways of wasting or misusing time are suggested in the first eight lines by:
  a. The trampled ears of wheat?
  b. The squandered coins?
  c. The drops of blood on *guilty* feet?
  d. The spilt water?
From what you know about Rossetti's life, did he *lose* some of his days?

2. In what sense is it true that each wasted day is a "murdered self"? What, on the other hand, may be said of past days that have been wisely used? Can you think of a good figure for a poet to use in representing such days?

3. What, according to Rossetti, will be the saddest reproach for wasted time as each soul reaches eternity? Discuss.

AN APPLE GATHERING

CHRISTINA ROSSETTI

What is the story that Christina Rossetti tells in "An Apple Gathering"?
Was the lover's choice something more than between blossoms and
apples? See if you can fit a meaning to the stanzas.

I PLUCKED pink blossoms from mine apple tree
    And wore them all that evening in my hair:
Then in due season when I went to see
    I found no apples there.

5 With dangling basket all along the grass
    As I had come I went the selfsame track:
My neighbors mocked me while they saw me pass
    So empty-handed back.

Lilian and Lilias smiled in trudging by,
10   Their heaped-up basket teased me like a jeer;
Sweet-voiced they sang beneath the sunset sky,
    Their mother's home was near.

Plump Gertrude passed me with her basket full,
    A stronger hand than hers helped it along;

826

15   A voice talked with her through the shadows cool
       More sweet to me than song.

Ah Willie, Willie, was my love less worth
    Than apples with their green leaves piled above?
I counted rosiest apples on the earth
20   Of far less worth than love.

So once it was with me you stooped to talk
    Laughing and listening in this very lane;
To think that by this way we used to walk
    We shall not walk again!

25   I let my neighbors pass me, ones and twos
    And groups; the latest said the night grew chill,
And hastened: but I loitered; while the dews
    Fell fast I loitered still.

FOR INTERPRETATION

1. What evening do you think is referred to in the second line of the poem? Why does the girl remember it? Which stanza tells us who was with her in the springtime?

2. In the fall, what has she lost besides the apples? Why? Whose was the voice "more sweet than song" that talked with Gertrude when she brought her apples home?

3. Do you think the blossoms and the apples are symbolic? If so, what meaning lies behind them? Discuss.

4. What kind of boy was Willie? What kind of girl was his sweetheart? Is there a moral to the poem? Or does it merely suggest an unhappy romance? Discuss.

From THE BALLAD OF READING GAOL

OSCAR WILDE

"The Ballad of Reading Gaol" covers six weeks of prison life; but for the imaginative reader, "The First Day" seems to have compressed the whole bitter tragedy. It tells its story so well that it needs no explanation except for the reminder that the English word *gaol* has the same pronunciation and meaning as our word *jail*.

THE FIRST DAY

HE DID not wear his scarlet coat,
   For blood and wine are red,
And blood and wine were on his hands
   When they found him with the dead,
5 The poor dead woman whom he loved,
   And murdered in her bed.

He walked amongst the Trial Men
   In a suit of shabby gray;
A cricket cap was on his head,
10 And his step seemed light and gay;
But I never saw a man who looked
   So wistfully at the day.

I never saw a man who looked
   With such a wistful eye
15 Upon that little tent of blue
   Which prisoners call the sky,
And at every drifting cloud that went
   With sails of silver by.

I walked, with other souls in pain,
20 Within another ring,
And was wondering if the man had done
   A great or little thing,
When a voice behind me whispered low,
   "That fellow's got to swing."

25 Dear Christ! the very prison walls
   Suddenly seemed to reel,
And the sky above my head became
   Like a casque of scorching steel;
And, though I was a soul in pain,
30 My pain I could not feel.

28. CASQUE—A kind of helmet.

> I only knew what hunted thought
> Quickened his step, and why
> He looked upon the garish day
> With such a wistful eye;
> 35   The man had killed the thing he loved
> And so he had to die.

FOR INTERPRETATION

Before discussing the poem, read the biographical sketch of Oscar Wilde.

1. The title of the poem, "The First Day," gives us a clue to the meaning of the second stanza. Who would the "Trial Men" be? Why would the man described be wearing a "suit of shabby gray" and a "cricket cap"? What would he be wearing on the *second day?*

2. Where do you think Wilde was when he saw the man in gray? What surroundings are suggested by the lines, "That *little tent of blue* which prisoners call the sky"?

3. What meaning is suggested by the first two lines of the fourth stanza? What is the significance of "other *souls in pain"?* of "within *another* ring"? Why, in the fifth stanza, could Wilde no longer feel the pain in his own soul?

4. What "hunted thought" quickened the other man's step? Why did he look wistfully at the sky? Would all his anguish be because he had to die? Discuss.

5. Why could Wilde write so truly of prison life?

EXTENDED ACTIVITIES

ALFRED, LORD TENNYSON (1809–1892)—"THE LADY OF SHALOTT," "ULYS-
SES," "LOCKSLEY HALL," "BREAK, BREAK, BREAK," "IN MEMORIAM,"
"FLOWER IN THE CRANNIED WALL," "CROSSING THE BAR"

By the middle of the nineteenth century the writing of poetry had
become a recognized and comparatively dignified profession. The rebellious, unhappy lives of the early romantics had wrought some feeling
of sympathy for artists. And there were a few parents who were proud
to recognize signs of poetic genius in their offspring. Such parents had
Alfred Tennyson, the fourth child of twelve of an Episcopalian preacher.

Tennyson's father, a man of intelligence
and understanding, indulged his noisy
brood's poetic and dramatic ventures and
was the first to foresee Alfred's career.
When the boy was in his early teens, the
father wrote, "If Alfred die, one of our
greatest poets will have gone."

At school the sensitive boy found his
regimented life far different from the noisy
family comradeship he had known. His
father, respecting the boy's shyness, permitted him to return home instead of railing at him and stopping his allowance. At
home, Alfred was tutored by his father and
prepared for Cambridge. He disliked college life, but met there Arthur Hallam and
the two became close friends. At eighteen,
Alfred and his brother published with their
father's help, *Poems of Two Brothers*. The fact that scathing criticism of
the immature volume failed to discourage the young poet is tribute to
his genius and courage. Two more volumes of poems were published
before Tennyson was twenty-one.

The death of his father in 1830 left Alfred as the eldest son at the
head of a large and demanding family. The next fourteen years during
which he wrote continually were not particularly happy. Criticism of his
poetry was almost entirely adverse. At twenty-seven he met and fell in
love with Emily Sellwood, but his responsibilities and meager income
made marriage out of the question. Her parents finally asked that they
break the engagement. The sudden death of his beloved college friend,

Hallam, left Tennyson unhappy and confused. He continued to write but published nothing for almost ten years. However, in 1842, a volume called *Poems by Alfred Tennyson* was kindly received, and he was granted a government pension. When he was forty-one, he met again the patient Emily. The two resumed their engagement and were married. In the same year, 1850, he was named Poet Laureate. From that time his fame and happiness increased yearly. Queen Victoria and Prince Albert admired and welcomed him; the *Idylls of the King* and *In Memoriam* were brilliantly successful.

The career of the tall, handsome poet, white-bearded and keen-eyed reflects the Victorian era. Tennyson's early work had been offensive to a slow-thinking public because of its "modern" tendencies—its preoccupation with science, and its liberal social and religious views. In his mature years the public's thinking had caught up with the poet's; the music of his lines charmed the successful Victorians; his patriotism reflected theirs. At his death Tennyson was in the heart of the empire, second only to Victoria herself.

ROBERT BROWNING (1812–1889)—"THE YEAR'S AT THE SPRING," "HOME
   THOUGHTS FROM ABROAD," "SAUL," "MY LAST DUCHESS," "PROSPICE,"
   "RABBI BEN EZRA"

It is impossible to imagine Robert Browning as an old man, warming his rheumatic knees in the sun. He is forever young, forever boisterous, and forever charming. With him and of him we can chant, "How good is man's life, the mere living!"

Robert's father had determined that his son should be reared as happily as possible. The boy's education was as unusual as it was excellent. His father read him the tales of Troy in place of nursery rhymes, sang him to sleep with lyrics from the Greek, taught him Latin grammar by twisting it into grotesque rhymes. From his gentle and devout mother, Browning inherited a love for drawing and music, and a faith that remained steadfast in an age of doubt. At two, Robert made his first drawing; at twelve he arranged a book of his own poems. As he grew older he educated himself from his father's rich store of books. He attended a school in the neighborhood for four years; had a French tutor from the age of fourteen to sixteen, and in his eighteenth year attended some Greek lectures at London University. This was the extent of his schooling yet he was one of the best educated men of his day.

Browning began writing poetry early. By the time he was twelve he had composed a number of poems, somewhat after the style of Byron and tried to find a publisher who would bring them out. When he was twenty-one his first published poem, "Pauline," appeared. He paid the printer with a hundred and fifty pounds given him by his aunt. Not a single copy of the poem was sold. It was fortunate that he did not have to depend upon poetry for a living. His next book met with little more approval, but in literary circles he was winning grudging admiration. About this time he began corresponding with the then famous poet, Elizabeth Barrett. He was a struggling young writer writing fan mail to the invalid poetess. Through a mutual friend, meetings were arranged despite the vigilance of Miss Barrett's father and the animosity of Miss Barrett's dog, Flush. In 1846 the two eloped, sailed for Italy, and remained there for sixteen years, ideally happy. Elizabeth and Italy matured Browning's genius; he wrote rapidly and brilliantly. In Italy and England he was hailed as one of the greatest poets.

After his wife's death he returned to London, continued his writing with rare courage, and even aided in the editing of his wife's works; but he refused ever again to return to Florence where they had spent their life together. The fame and recognition denied him in his earlier years came—with interest—in his later days; but it touched him little. Oxford, Cambridge, and Edinburgh honored him with degrees; London society sought his company; a Browning Society for the study of his works was formed. To the end Browning himself retained his optimism and his boyishness; his interest in painting, in music, in people, and in life.

ELIZABETH BARRETT BROWNING (1806–1861)—"HOW DO I LOVE THEE"

It is one of the vagaries of fickle popularity that a woman, who after the death of Wordsworth was seriously considered for the poet laureateship, should today be remembered for a handful of love sonnets and because she became Mrs. Robert Browning. The sentimental appeal of Elizabeth Barrett's life will never lose its charm for youthful romantics. The eldest of a family of eleven, she was hailed as a prodigy when she read Greek at eight and wrote an epic at twelve. Father and family doted on the frail, tiny child. A fall from her pony at fifteen resulted in a spinal injury; the tyrannical devotion of her father, her grief at the death of her mother and a favorite brother forced upon her an invalid's life. For years she was confined to her room, her writing, her books—and her pet cocker spaniel. Throughout England Miss Barrett's fame was celebrated; she was often called the greatest living poet.

At this time she began corresponding with an impetuous young poet, quite unknown, but whose verses pleased her. At last the poet came to call, Robert Browning—yellow-gloved, bewhiskered and dashing. The rest of the story is familiar history—the father's displeasure, Robert's insistence, her own growing love, and their final elopement. The years in Italy where they went to live saw her health recovered; she walked, rode horseback, and became almost robust. After their son's birth, Mrs. Browning was less well. She still wrote—some of her "Sonnets from the Portuguese," her most beautiful lyrics, belong to this period—but Robert's fame was overshadowing hers. Her death in 1861 ended one of the happiest marriages in all literature. The world has Robert Browning to thank for Elizabeth Barrett's best work just as the world must thank Elizabeth for the best in him.

MATTHEW ARNOLD (1822–1888)—"SHAKESPEARE"

> "Ah, love, let us be true
> To one another! For the world, which seems
> To lie before us like a land of dreams,
> So various, so beautiful, so new
> Hath really neither joy, nor love, nor light,
> Nor certitude, nor peace, nor help for pain;
> And we are here as on a darkling plain·
> Swept with confused alarms of struggle and flight,
> Where ignorant armies clash by night."

The closing lines of Matthew Arnold's famous poem, "Dover Beach," are not somehow the lines one might expect from a busy Inspector of Schools. But Matthew Arnold's life held far more richness than his prosaic educational post would suggest. He was another of the bright galaxy of great intellects of the Victorian period. Son of one of the great headmasters of Rugby, he won scholarships and awards at Rugby and Oxford. No bookworm or literary recluse, Matthew was always popular with students and professors. After taking his degree with honors he traveled widely in France and learned to love it nearly as much as his own England. A few years after his return to England he was named Inspector of Schools. He fulfilled his onerous duties with complete diligence, married well and happily, and for recreation dabbled at poetry as he had at Oxford. The British school system improved vastly under his supervision. His poetry was the least successful of his endeavors, but his literary criticism soon won him an expert's rating. His classical training and tastes made him a severe but just critic. For ten years he was professor of poetry at Oxford, a distinguished, scholarly professor with a dry wit and a taste for fishing during the holidays. In the fields of education and literature he was recognized by the Victorians as their own best critic. Today his principles of criticism are somewhat outmoded, but his essays and the lovely "Dover Beach" are still widely admired.

DANTE GABRIEL ROSSETTI (1828–1882)—"THE BLESSED DAMOZEL"; "LOST DAYS"

Although his own life was full of tragedy, Rossetti's influence on his own and succeeding age was completely wholesome and good. Not since the time of the strange William Blake had art and poetry fused to such brilliance in a single artist. Rossetti found more understanding from his own age than had Blake, but nonetheless much of the world was unsympathetic both to him and to his work.

More Italian than English, Gabriel Rossetti was the son of an exiled Italian, a professor at the University of London, and a half-Italian mother. At school the nervous little boy learned little; at home the household was filled with the music of Italian. Gabriel, his sister, and brother drew and wrote, learned literature from their father and religion from their mother. At fourteen, he left school to prepare to be a painter. Thoroughly disgusted with the teaching methods of the Royal Academy of Art, he soon began experimenting with his own theories. With other young artists, he organized a group called the Pre-Raphaelites, who denounced the still prettiness of the paintings then fashionable and substituted realistic detail and actual form. A few distinguished critics—Ruskin among them—befriended the shabby group. Realizing Rossetti's superior ability, Ruskin would buy enough of the young man's canvases to assure him a livable income. Along with his painting, Rossetti wrote poetry. The same results brightened both: color and form and reality.

It was a slim existence at best and Rossetti's problems were complicated by his love for his pretty and consumptive model, Elizabeth Siddall. Elizabeth posed as the Beatrice of Rossetti's illustrations of Dante Alighieri's epic *The Divine Comedy*. Without complaint she suffered long hours of immersion waist deep in a pool that Gabriel might get the right effect of her long rich hair against the water. The two were at last financially able to marry, but Elizabeth by then was rapidly dying. Frantic at her death, Rossetti buried with her all his poems wrapped in the beautiful auburn hair. Years later the poems were recovered; success came at last to both poetry and painting, but the prosperity had come too late for Rossetti's enjoyment. His health and mind had failed under repeated criticism and his last years were spent wandering and friendless.

CHRISTINA ROSSETTI (1830–1894)—"AN APPLE GATHERING"

Christina Rossetti, sister of Gabriel, found life nearly as uncompromising in its severity as her brother. Educated like him at home, she early showed great poetic promise. She was a beautiful girl, slim and nun-like; her brothers and their friends loved to paint the stillness of her face, a stillness that covered deep and often melancholy emotion. After an unhappy romance ended because of a difference in religion, Christina turned entirely to poetry and religion. She wrote continually, refused to see even the artist friends of her brothers, and with her mother lived a life of complete seclusion. The discipline she enforced on herself showed in the perfectness of her poetry.

OSCAR WILDE (1856–1900)—"THE BALLAD OF READING GAOL"

Oscar Wilde in 1881 was the rage of London. In velvet jacket, knee breeches, and carrying a single flower he lectured before literary circles on "beauty" and dazzled society with his wit. Unfortunately, he could never appear in public without affectation and when he began to write some truly excellent comedy as in *Lady Windermere's Fan* and *The Importance of Being Earnest,* no one really appreciated its worth. The memory of the single flower and long hair was too recent. In reality he was an intelligent young man, a thoroughly competent journalist, and the best writer of farce since Sheridan. London society grew tired of the obnoxious "bohemian." Then Wilde fell into disgrace and spent two years in prison. Upon his release, he hastened to Paris; and there he spent his last years. Little of his work is now read except his two plays and a few poems, the best of which is the vivid "Ballad of Reading Gaol."

OF LITERARY FORM AND STYLE

VICTORIAN POETRY

Even poetry in the Age of Victoria reflected those influences which made the period so predominantly prosaic. Not that the verse was "prosey"—by no means. Those men who did take poetry for their field of expression possessed great gifts, and their work is lyrical and appealing. It does, however, show new interests and new trends in thought. Like the prose, it was mostly romantic in theme and mood; but poetic form was granted important enough to be worked over—to be made polished and fine.

The significant thought of the period finds voice in the works of two great poets—Alfred Tennyson and Robert Browning. The works of the lesser poets reflect several varying phases or aspects of Victorian England.

There was, for example, Elizabeth Barrett Browning who began writing light occasional verse, who then became a crusader in the interests of social reform, and who after her marriage produced her finest work in a cycle of love sonnets. Then there was Matthew Arnold, the scholar, who became almost pure classicist in his devotion to art and to the beauties of the past. There was also the group, during the closing years of the century, that was known as the "Pre-Raphaelites"—men who found in-

spiration in the simple, imaginative, but primitive art of the days before Raphael. Their poetry was melodious, often medieval in subject,
and symbolic rather than realistic. They glorified the ballad form, making of the once-simple folk song a highly artistic, though quite artificial,
form of story-telling. Their work may be studied in the poems of William Morris and the two Rossettis, Dante Gabriel and Christina. Alger-
non Charles Swinburne, once greatly admired for the musical effects of his
lyrics, is now seldom read because of the general lack of substance in his
work. And then there was that strange genius, Oscar Wilde, who composed some impressionistic poetry of unforgettable vividness. And last,
there was the versatile Robert Louis Stevenson, whom some readers remember more affectionately for his delightful *Child's Garden of Verses*
and a few simple songs like "Requiem" than for any of his more pre-
tentious work. Such is the kaleidoscopic picture discovered in a brief
survey of Victorian poetry.

THE POETRY OF TENNYSON

Alfred Tennyson was both the official and actual spokesman for Victorian England. Poet Laureate for forty years, he continued to write
throughout the period and to grow in power. He was England's greatest
laureate because of an unusual combination of qualities. He was a gifted
poet and a sincere, earnest worker. He was possessed of a genius
broad enough to take inspiration from all sources—nature, human affairs,
men and women, philosophy, science—there seems no field that he left
untouched. A versatile craftsman, he could use almost every poetic form
with grace. Moreover, he reflected the idealism of his age in an ennobling
attitude toward life, constant and sincere. The age, as we have seen,
taking its cue from the Queen, was a period of upward-striving. True,
there were gaps between ideal and performance, but the directing influence was good. And Tennyson speaks for it at its best. It might have
been of himself, rather than Sir Galahad that he was writing in the
lines—

> "My strength is as the strength of ten
> Because my heart is pure."

His greatest works, *The Idylls of the King* and *In Memoriam* are truly
representative of the man. The legends of Arthur had fascinated him
from childhood; and he used Arthurian themes off and on for a period of
sixty years. The *Idylls* gave expression to his idealistic and poetic spirit;
but they are far more than pretty tales of a king "swearing men to vows
impossible" and maidens dying all for love. Tennyson knew men and
women. The workings of the human heart and will he understood, and
so the action in each separate idyll is as carefully motivated as in a true
short story. We still read the *Idylls* with profit because they deal with
human truths—the longing of man to build something lasting and noble;
the idealism—sometimes blind—with which he chooses his love; the cor-

roding effects of jealousy and falsehood; the struggle between conscience and desire; the disastrous blight of sin; the reality of penitence and forgiveness—all of these, timeless in their application, Tennyson has woven into the fabric of his dream.

In Memoriam, on the other hand, is a thoughtful group of lyrics bound together by the theme of his grief in the loss of a friend. It is significant because it expresses the doubts, fears, hopes, problems of his time—all reconciled at length by an encircling faith.

The appeal of Tennyson is almost universal. Boys like him for the swing and action of his shorter narratives. Girls like his romances. Men and women appreciate his thoughtful weighing of the problems of life. And the world respects the faith that gave meaning to his own life and to his works.

QUESTIONS IN APPRECIATION:

"The Lady of Shalott"

1. Study the poetic form of "The Lady of Shalott." What devices have been used for musical effect? What device does Tennyson use that Shelley did not? Describe the stanza form of the poem. How has Tennyson avoided monotony in his use of refrain? Select for class comment what you consider the four most effective figures of speech in the whole poem.

2. What lines or words in Part I suggest a fairy-tale mood? What two lines in Part II make the most subtle appeal to our feelings? What is the mood for the first four stanzas of Part III? What words or expressions help build up that mood? How does the mood change in the fifth stanza? In what lines? What successive feelings are aroused by the various stanzas in Part IV? What is the prevailing mood? Select for reading aloud the lines which seem to you to touch the feelings most deeply. What is the general emotional effect of the poem? Discuss.

3. Notice the way in which Tennyson has woven together the four parts of the story. What lines in Part I point forward to the subject of Part II? How do lines 71–72 prepare for the tragedy of the rest of the poem? What lines in Part III lead naturally into the thought and mood of Part IV?

4. List reasons for the almost universal appeal of this poem.

"Ulysses"

1. What are the important differences in form between "Ulysses" and "The Lady of Shalott"? Why are the differences so great? What form is it that Tennyson has used for "Ulysses"? Do you think the effect of the poem would be stronger or weaker if Tennyson had used rhyme? What kind of poetic effects can be obtained in unrhymed verse? Point out, and be prepared to read aloud at least two exceptionally poetic passages from "Ulysses."

2. Do you think that the poem reflects in any way the spirit of nineteenth-century England? The poem was considered by many of Tennyson's contemporaries as one of his finest. What would be some of the reasons for their preference? Discuss.

"Locksley Hall"

1. The lines in "Locksley Hall" are unusually long. What meter has the poet used? What rhythm? Is the form one that is easy or hard to read? to memorize?

2. Would you say that the subject of these lines is "typically Victorian"? Why or why not?

3. Point out a good example of Tennyson's ability to express scientific ideas in poetic language.

4. Point out an example of his ability to see straight in matters of social science. How does he give poetic expression to the idea of *arbitration* among nations? Quote the lines.

"Break, Break, Break"

1. Would you call this poem an elegy? Why or why not?

2. What is the poetic effect of the two lines that open the first and last stanzas of the poem?

3. What details make the poet's experience seem real to us? What other poem or poems have you read that express a somewhat similar sense of loss? Discuss.

4. In what respects is the poem a true lyric? Check point by point against the discussion of lyric poetry in the *Appendix*.

"In Memoriam"

1. What is the unusual feature of the stanza form which Tennyson used for the lyrics of *In Memoriam?* How does it differ in poetic effect from other poems by Tennyson?

2. Why do you think the poet did not include "Break, Break, Break" with this cycle of lyrics? How does it differ from them in form? Is there a different treatment of subject? Discuss.

3. *In Memoriam* was so favorably received that it was largely responsible for Tennyson's being appointed Poet Laureate. What features of the poem would especially recommend it to English readers of the middle nineteenth century?

4. Which of the general characteristics mentioned in the discussion of Tennyson's poetry are apparent in the lyrics of *In Memoriam?* Check them, point by point.

5. Do you find the lyrics hard to understand? worth studying? Do you like this kind of poetry? Why or why not?

"Flower in a Crannied Wall"

1. "Flower in a Crannied Wall" is one of the most simply expressed

of all of Tennyson's poems. Does it have the effect of being a *simple* poem? Why or why not?

2. Why do you think the poet uses only common words and no elaborate figures of speech in this lyric?

"Crossing the Bar"

1. What other images besides that of the ebbing tide has Tennyson used to suggest the closing of a life?

2. Contrast the form of expression and the emotional effect of "Crossing the Bar" with the form and effect of Shelley's "Lament." Is each poem representative of the life and spirit of the man who wrote it? Discuss. Make a similar comparison between Keats's "When I Have Fears That I May Cease to Be" and "Crossing the Bar." If the life situations had been reversed, do you think Tennyson might have written a poem like Keats's sonnet, and Keats a poem with the mood and meaning of "Crossing the Bar"? Discuss.

THE POETRY OF BROWNING AND THE DRAMATIC MONOLOGUE

Just as Tennyson is the idealist among the poets, Browning is the optimist. And the optimism has worth because it was borne out by his experiences. He believed that life at any stage was good and worth living; and he found it so. With Tennyson's "Ulysses" he could say, "All times I have enjoyed greatly."

His zest in living he passes on to others in rugged, vigorous lines. One feels as he reads that Browning wrote by inspiration. His lines must have come bubbling forth like water out of a jug. We can scarcely see him pausing to count feet or mark accents. His own feeling on any occasion set the general pattern of a poem, and a musical ear kept him true to the form. Some of his verse just won't scan systematically. In the first two lines of "Up at a Villa—Down in the City" there is a combination of *dactyls, iambics,* and *anapests;* yet the lines read easily. He is like a musician who plays by ear; and because the ear is good, he comes out all right.

Browning liked to use a conversational style, with broken and incomplete sentences. His verse—like Carlyle's prose—is peppered with dashes and exclamation points. The result is a lively, vigorous spirit and a natural-sounding speech. To speed up the movement, he often "telescopes" his thought, omitting important words. Hard words he avoids, being content with the strong common symbols of daily speech. It is the broken, compressed sentences, not the vocabulary, that makes certain Browning poems seem hard for the beginner. But once initiated, readers like the crisp, individualized style.

The poet liked people, and most of his work concerns them. He understood all kinds—English and Italian, past or present, painters and priests and vagabonds. His best medium for portraying them was the *dramatic monologue,* which he perfected. His technique was to provide a chosen character with a listener and a situation—always implied in the lines of the poem—and then allow him to reveal himself through his own speech. Sometimes the reader is in complete sympathy with the character. In "Saul," for instance, we are carried along with the youthful David and his songs. In "Fra Lippo Lippi" we laugh with—not at—the irrepressible painting monk. But often the monologist betrays his own guilt or weakness; and we see the defects as clearly as if another were counting them off. The monologues are as interesting and varied as the scores of persons they portray.

Young people usually make their first acquaintance with Browning through his excellent narrative poems—poems like "Hervé Riel," "Incident of the French Camp," "The Pied Piper of Hamelin," and "How They Brought the Good News from Ghent to Aix." They will enjoy in his works of wider range some of the same qualities—natural swinging rhythm, force, directness, action, and personality. Browning's poetry—whatever he wrote—has the tonic effect of a fresh, clean wind.

QUESTIONS IN APPRECIATION:

"The Year's at the Spring"

Notice the unusual rhyming scheme of the poem. What is the effect of the rhyme when the poem is read aloud? Have you ever heard this poem sung? What kind of musical setting do you think it should have? How is the lyric typical of Browning himself as well as of the girl who is supposed to have sung it?

"Home Thoughts from Abroad"

1. Read aloud "Home Thoughts from Abroad." What is its general rhythmic effect? Does it read easily? Does it sound musical? Are you conscious of rhyming words? What mood or feeling does the sound suggest?

2. Notice the form of the poem on the printed page. Can you discover any regular pattern or rhythm or rhyme? How do you account for the effectiveness of its sound? Discuss.

3. How has Browning helped us to see England in April and May? Why do you think people who have never been in England enjoy the poem?

4. Why do you think Browning closed the poem with a reference to the melon flower?

"Saul"

1. Read aloud the lines from "Saul." What effect do they have? Mark the rhythm of the passage. How has Browning secured the sound effects you have noticed?

2. What words in the passage are suggestive of action? of strength?

What words or expressions suggest pleasant or sharp *sensations?* How many of our sense images are appealed to? Name illustrations for each.

3. What line is an excellent example of *onomatopoeia* in combination with *alliteration?* What is the most vivid metaphor in the selection? What other figures of speech seem especially effective?

4. In what respects is this poem typical of the man who wrote it?

"My Last Duchess"

1. What do you think gives "My Last Duchess" its conversational tone when read aloud? Is it the choice of words? the kind of sentences? the verse form? or what? Discuss.

2. An interesting comparison in poetic effects may be made by reading aloud the first ten or twelve lines of Pope's "The Rape of the Lock," and then reading the first twelve and a half lines of "My Last Duchess." An examination will show that both poems are written in *iambic pentameter;* and that the lines of both rhyme in pairs. Yet the effect is totally different. Why? What is the difference between Browning's form and the *heroic couplet?* Would you like the effect of this poem better if it were in heroic couplets? Why or why not?

3. What makes the conversation of the Duke sound true to life? Notice the skill with which Browning has the Duke unconsciously disclose the fact that his former Duchess was a charming, lovable person. Quote some of the lines which have this effect. Can you discover the author's special technique? Discuss.

4. What is the effect of having the Duke turn from the portrait to a mention of the dowry of his next bride? of having him call attention to the statue of Neptune as they descend the stairs?

5. What gives this type of monologue its *dramatic* effect? Discuss.

"Prospice"

1. How does Browning secure the effect of vigor, action, and courage in "Prospice"? In giving your answer consider these features—the verse form used (rhythm and rhyme, and so forth), the kind of sentences (long, smooth, flowing, or short, abrupt, choppy, etc.), the kinds of words used (which predominate—adjectives and adverbs, or nouns and verbs?), the number and kinds of figures of speech.

2. Compare "Prospice" in its message and its poetic effect with Tennyson's "Crossing the Bar." What points—if any—do the poems have in common? In what respects are they different? Show how each poem is truly representative of the man who wrote it, and of his age at the time of writing.

"Rabbi Ben Ezra"

1. Describe the stanza form in which the poem is written. What effect does the poem have when read? Why?

2. From your previous readings in English poetry select a poem which

presents interesting contrasts in feeling and form on the subject of youth and age. Point out the most important differences between the poems, and explain—so far as you can—what causes those differences.

OTHER VICTORIAN POEMS

"How Do I Love Thee"

Mrs. Browning used the more difficult Italian pattern for her "Sonnets from the Portuguese" and handled it flawlessly. But the remarkable quality of the sonnets is the sincerity and truthfulness which shine through the poetic lines. From the first sonnet, which tells how she turned from what she thought was the grasp of death to see that it was love that was holding her, to the last one in which she presents the sonnets to her husband, like a sheaf of the flowers he has brought her,—the reader has the feeling that this is a true love story being unfolded. Besides those already referred to, sonnets of special interest are those near the beginning in which Elizabeth sees herself as a sad, helpless invalid in no way worthy of Robert's love, and in which she thinks she must for his sake turn away from it—such a sonnet as the fifth one, or the ninth. And then there are three representing different stages in the development of their courtship—XVII (quite Victorian in its sentiment!), XX, and XXVIII. To them all, Sonnet XLIII provides a fitting climax. Robert Browning is not the only critic who has ranked these sonnets next to Shakespeare's.

1. Notice how the simplicity and quietness of Mrs. Browning's words give the effect of sincerity. Which lines particularly show this simplicity of style?

2. There are few figures of speech, and those few carefully chosen. Point them out and explain them. Are they "elaborate" figures or "natural" ones? Discuss.

3. Show how Mrs. Browning builds up to a climax in answering the question, "How do I love thee?"

4. What other poems do you know that may be compared with this in impressiveness, in emotional sincerity, and in the beauty of thought and expression? Discuss.

"Shakespeare"

1. Part of the challenge of the sonnet form is that within the fourteen lines the poet should develop a large and significant idea. To what extent has Arnold met this challenge?

2. What modification of the sonnet form has he used? What are his most effective lines? How does the sonnet compare in style and thought with other sonnets you have read?

"The Blessed Damozel"

1. What were the principles of the pre-Raphaelite school? In what

respects is "The Blessed Damozel" representative of pre-Raphaelite poetry?

2. What other Victorian poem is most like "The Blessed Damozel" in its combination of melodious form with fantasy and pathos? Which of the two poems do you like better? Why?

3. If you do not remember it clearly, review Poe's poem, "The Raven." What are the principal differences between it and "The Blessed Damozel."—(a) What is the most important difference between the subjects of the two poems? in the principal characters? in the basic symbolism? (b) What are the differences in color, lighting, and special effects? (c) What difference is there in the feeling or mood created by each? What causes the difference? Which poem has the more unreal atmosphere? Which is the more suggestive of real grief? Why? Which one is *dramatic* in effect? Which one is *pictorial?* (d) Both poems are musical, but in different ways. What are the chief differences in sound effects? Is the verse form of each poem suited to its subject matter and mood?

4. Select for reading aloud four or five stanzas from "The Blessed Damozel"—stanzas that you like particularly well. If the whole poem were to be read with a musical setting, what musical selections would you choose as the background for each separate part?

"Lost Days"

1. Is the subject "Lost Days" appropriate for a sonnet? Why or why not?

2. Do the figures of speech in lines 3–8 help make the meaning clear, or are they confusing? Would it be better if the poet had expressed the thought more directly?

3. Which part of the poem contains the more powerful imagery, the first eight lines or the last six lines?

4. What is the total effect of the poem? Would you count it a good sonnet? Why or why not?

"An Apple Gathering"

1. How does the poem, "An Apple Gathering," show that Christina Rossetti shared her brother's artistic sense? What *pictorial* qualities does the poem have?

2. Show how the first stanza suggests the thought of the whole poem. Explain the figure of speech used in the fifth stanza. Is the same figure referred to elsewhere in the poem? Explain.

3. Quote the lines that take the strongest hold on our feelings. Does the poem, as a whole, have an emotional and imaginative appeal? Discuss. In what respects is it representative of the pre-Raphaelite poets?

"The Ballad of Reading Gaol"

1. Notice that the treatment of the first three stanzas is almost purely

objective. What significant things did Wilde *see?* How much of the story can be guessed from these three stanzas?

2. Explain why we say that the treatment of the last three stanzas is *subjective.* Whose thoughts are we sharing?

3. What color marks the first stanza? the second stanza? the third stanza? How do you explain the absence of color in the last three stanzas?

4. Why do you think Wilde wrote the first stanza? Couldn't the story have been told just as well beginning with the second stanza? What is the poetic effect of the poem? What lines contribute most powerfully to that effect? Read aloud the stanza which you consider the best piece of poetic writing.

5. In what important respects does the poem differ from other Victorian poetry?

FOR FURTHER READING

ARNOLD, MATTHEW, *Sohrab and Rustum*

BESIER, RUDOLPH, *The Barretts of Wimpole Street* (drama)

BOAS, LOUIS, *Elizabeth Barrett Browning*

BROWNING, ELIZABETH BARRETT, *Sonnets from the Portuguese*

PALGRAVE, FRANCIS TURNER, *The Golden Treasury, Book V*

PEABODY, JOSEPHINE PRESTON, *The Piper*

TENNYSON, ALFRED, *Idylls of the King; Enoch Arden*

WILDE, OSCAR, *The Importance of Being Earnest* (drama)

WOOLF, VIRGINIA, *Flush*

⌥ APPENDIX ⌥
THE TYPES OF LITERATURE

By the time the student has reached the senior high school level, his experience in reading will have shown him that all literature is divided into groups or *types* depending upon differences in form and in purpose. The two major classifications as to form are *prose* and *poetry;* the two general classifications as to purpose or content are *fiction* and *non-fiction.* There is some overlapping in these main divisions. Libraries use an arbitrary system: under the heading "fiction" they classify all prose stories and novels; under the heading "non-fiction" they catalogue everything else, including poetry and drama. Studies in literature actually follow the library precedent; and for all practical purposes the term "fiction" is understood to include all prose stories written, not to give information, but to entertain.

The usual classifications within the field of fiction are made on the basis of length. Thus book-length fiction is called a *novel;* a story which can be read at a single sitting is called a *short story;* a narrative considerably longer, yet not book length is called a *novelette;* and a short story compressed to about a thousand words is called a *short short story.* There are, however, certain other qualifications which distinguish each type. These will be considered in the following pages.

The remaining mass of literature is separated roughly into *poetry* and *non-fiction prose.* Non-fiction prose comprises chiefly those types of literature that deal with facts. The material is usually informational; and although it may be entertaining, it reflects actual rather than imagined experiences. It includes such widely different forms as *history, biography, travel accounts, essays, letters, diaries, news articles, public addresses,* and the like. Of these many forms, literature is chiefly concerned with the *essay* and with *biography.* In special instances, any of the other types may be so well written as to challenge the attention of the student. An anthology of literature, then, may present an unusual oration or a radio talk or a letter. Even a news-story or an editorial—if well-written—may be lifted from the level of daily journalism to a place in abiding literature. Our type discussions, however, will deal with the more exclusively literary forms—the *essay* and *biography,* with brief definitions of such kinds of miscellaneous prose as have been important in the development of English literature.

One other type has been placed arbitrarily in the non-fiction classification —the prose *drama,* and this, notwithstanding the fact that its materials are dependent upon the imagination just as are those of the story and novel. The field of modern drama embraces the *full-length play,* the *one-act play,* the *radio play,* the *scenario,* the *pageant,* and the *revue.* The student of literature is interested in the first three forms because they may be satisfactorily reproduced in print.

The differences between prose and poetry are primarily differences of form. They will be discussed in some detail in the section on poetry, as will be also the various type-forms of verse.

THE NOVEL AND THE NOVELETTE

We have said that a piece of book-length fiction is commonly called a novel. Yet there are critics who insist that the term "novel" is more properly reserved for realistic fiction, and that the term "romance" should be used for highly imaginative fiction. *Good-bye, Mr. Chips* is a novel because, although the characters and events are imaginary, they are so lifelike as to seem real. Men like "Chippy" have spent their lives in quiet devotion to teaching in any of scores of British schools. They have been shy, sometimes, or "queer." No one guesses—least of all the boys who storm through their classrooms—what bits of romance are hidden in their memories. And no one realizes, except possibly the boys one by one, what impress they have made on hundreds and hundreds of human lives. But they are human and real. So are the school boys, and all the details of English school life. On the other hand, there are books like *Lost Horizon* by the same author, James Hilton, in which the main events are clearly the product of fancy and so improbable that no one is expected to believe they ever happened. Such stories are *romances* not *novels*. It is important to remember this special meaning of the term *romance*. It does not designate a story with a strong love interest, but rather a highly imaginative tale. On the basis of this distinction, *Ivanhoe* with its tournaments, sieges, and hairbreadth escapes is really a romance. *The Mill on the Floss*, by George Eliot, and Dickens's *David Copperfield* are novels; their characters and events, though fictitious, are like the people and events of daily life.

A genuine *novelette* partakes of all the characteristics of the novel, but in abbreviated form. It is not only longer than a short story; it takes a fuller view. Our interest is not confined to a single character. We are concerned with the community which forms its setting and with the interplay of personalities. The novelette, however, has proved much more popular in America than in England.

THE SHORT STORY

In the first place, as we have seen, a short story is fiction that is short. But it has also certain distinctive characteristics. Brander Matthews in 1885 used these words to characterize the short story: "A true short story differs from a novel chiefly in its essential unity of impression. . . . It deals with a single character interest, a single event, a single emotion, or the series of emotions called forth by a single situation. . . . Thus the short story has what the novel cannot have, the effect of 'totality' as Poe called it, the unity of impression." The writer must introduce his characters and set his scene briefly, vividly. Every element must work toward the one pre-determined effect.

Until recently the formula for building a short story was pretty well standardized. It had to be set up carefully, like a house of cards. First there had to be the introduction with a bit of setting and a few stage props. Then came the body of the story in which the reader saw the characters perform, and in which the plot rose step by step to its climax. The climax had to come near the end of the story, with only the *denouement* remaining —the untangling of the problem, the gust of wind that knocked over the house of cards.

Since 1920, the rules governing short-story writing have been much relaxed. New techniques have been tried; and perhaps the only requirement left is that there must be some opposition or struggle involved and that the story must leave one definite impression. Like the novel, the good story presents a picture from life. And like all true literature, it must carry the reader outside and beyond himself. Much popular fiction lacks this artistic touch. It follows closely a pattern that the public likes. Stories may be surcharged with energy so that hero, girl, and reader arrive breathless at the finish. The average reader wants to be pleasantly amused, frightened, or saddened for a little while. And hundreds are the writers who cater to such tastes. But in all the welter of popular fiction, good stories—brilliant stories—are appearing. To find them out, the reader needs to apply his test—does any story leave a single, unforgettable impression, a sense of our having touched a bit of life? Then be sure it is a good story.

The very newest child in the fiction family is the *short short story*. It, too, owes its popularity to the magazine. It is designed to tell its tale on one page, or less. The first short shorts followed one pretty definite pattern, a pattern not unlike the one devised by O. Henry in which the plot led up to a surprise ending with an ironic twist. The chief character was often a criminal, and the "surprise" usually made him the victim of a trap of his own setting. Within the last year or two the pattern has been changing; and some magazines are featuring short shorts that meet, in limited fashion, the requirements of a good short story. They present etchings from life in "postage stamp" size.

THE ESSAY

It is not easy to define an essay. Perhaps the closest one can come to the truth is to say that it is an attempt to put on paper some ideas on a chosen subject which interests the writer and which he hopes will interest the reader. He may be in earnest or he may be joking. He may tell a little story or assume an impersonal aloofness. All that we require of the essayist is that he follow a train of thought to something like a conclusion, and that along the way he point out to us some new ideas. He may lead us by a devious and rambling path, but, if he keeps the mood which attracted us to him, we shall vote him delightful company, and part from him with regret.

It has been the custom to classify essays as *formal* or *familiar*. In the formal essay, the author has taken his subject seriously. He is definitely trying to instruct or to convince the reader. His style is therefore dignified, and perhaps impersonal. Bacon's essay, "Of Studies," is formal. Essays of literary criticism like de Quincey's "On the Knocking at the Gate in *Macbeth*" are formal. So, too, are some of the thoughtful discussions appearing today in the better type literary magazines.

The informal or familiar essay is much lighter in subject and manner. It may range all the way from the absurdities of "Frozen Words" or "A Dissertation on Roast Pig" to the pleasant whimsicalities of our present-day essayists—Rose Macaulay, G. K. Chesterton, J. B. Priestley, and the like. The first familiar essays expressed the authors' fancies in playful or whimsical style, but through an assumed personality like the "Isaac Bickerstaff" of the *Spectator* papers. But Lamb, de Quincey, and Coleridge made the familiar essay completely personal.

The first two decades of the twentieth century have produced some essayists of delightful style; but today the essay—both formal and familiar—is largely being replaced by the less clearly defined "magazine article." Usually the articles are informative in subject—about contemporary affairs, interesting places, personalities—and the "discussion" style is popular, especially on matters of opinion or belief.

BIOGRAPHY

A *biography* is a life story. The *autobiography* is self-told. Actually biography is personalized history. In fact, the first biographies appeared in the earliest histories. The stories of Moses, of David, of Solomon are told in the historical books of the Old Testament. The New Testament contains four separate biographies of Jesus of Nazareth. An interest in the personalities of history led a Greek of the first century to write a series of forty-six accounts of Greek and Roman heroes—the famous *Parallel Lives* by Plutarch.

This pioneer biographer had a surprisingly "modern" point of view. In explaining his method, Plutarch said——

> I record not history, but human destiny. The evidences of vice or virtue are not confined to famous accomplishments; often some trivial event, a word, a joke, will serve better than great campaigns and battles as a revelation of character.

And so he told, among other things, how Cleopatra would dress up like a boy and go rioting about with Antony, or how she ordered her servant to slip beneath the water and fasten a salted herring on Antony's hook when they went fishing.

Biography has swung through many changes in treatment since the days of Plutarch. There was a time when it was stiff and formal, when it concerned itself only with heroes, and chiefly with their virtues. There was a period when the biographer was prejudiced, when he wrote either to denounce his subject or to praise him extravagantly. And then, not many years ago, we passed through the unpleasant "debunking" period, when the author in an attempt to avoid sentimentalism, went to the other extreme and over-emphasized weaknesses and failures. Such writers seemed to delight in dragging good names through the mire. Fortunately the public has tired of sensational muck-raking. Biography has had a rebirth. In any such work, the reader has a right to expect *information as accurate as may be attained, enlivened by sidelights of human interest.* Modern biography is providing just that—authentic records of men and women, as readable as fiction because the author has tried to re-create persons of flesh and blood.

It is not easy to write good biographies. If the author is too close to his subject, it is hard to keep an unprejudiced viewpoint; if the author is too far removed in time, it is hard to get trustworthy information. If a man writes about himself, he must avoid the unpleasant extremes of boastfulness and false modesty. However, the excellent biographical writings of the last few years prove that such difficulties can be overcome. The successful method seems to be an *objective* approach. Whether the author writes of himself or of some one else, he can tell what happened, what the subject of the account *did*, what he said, how he felt. This he may do without comment, without his—that is, the writer's—censure or praise. If he is a good reporter and story-teller, he thus makes it possible for the reader to estimate the character of the subject. Some good autobiographies have won the approval of the reader by centering attention, not upon the author but upon the scenes through which he moved and the personalities he met.

The appeal of biography is two-fold. Since life for each of us is a series of adjustments to our circumstances, we like to read of another's failures and successes. In them we find sign-posts of warning or guidance for our own living. And then we are by nature curious. We like to know about other people—what they are like, what they have done, where they have gone. Through biography we may satisfy these curiosities. There are few quirks of personality, few far-off places that we cannot explore through the pages of a book. And because we realize that such accounts are not fiction, we must have confidence in the author. Reliable, sympathetic biography is a high literary art.

MISCELLANEOUS PROSE

HISTORICAL PROSE:

The *chronicle,* the *diary,* and the *journal* are forms of contemporaneous history. That is, each one records events while they are taking place. In the chronicle, the things recorded are of public importance, whereas the diary is a recording of events of interest to a given individual. A journal, like a diary, is a personal recording of events, but usually with the idea that it will be read by others. A *history* is written long enough after the events described so that the author will have a proper perspective of the field. History is written primarily for the purpose of instruction; but when it is artistically done and when it furnishes real insight into the life of the past, it becomes a significant type of literature. Among the important literary histories by English authors, three are especially outstanding: *The Decline and Fall of the Roman Empire* by Edward Gibbon, *The French Revolution* by Thomas Carlyle, and *History of England* by Thomas Macaulay.

OTHER TYPES OF PROSE NARRATIVES:

The *prose tale* is, of course, almost as old as speech, but in England, it has almost no literary importance until late in the fifteenth century. At that time appeared Sir Thomas Malory's *Le Morte d'Arthur*, a prose collection of the legends of King Arthur and his knights. During the Age of Elizabeth, a number of *prose romances* appeared, imaginative stories told in leisurely style, the best known being Sir Philip Sidney's *Arcadia.*

The *parable*, the *fable*, and the *allegory* are stories designed to illustrate general truths or to present moral lessons. The parable is based on an incident from life. The characters are real men and women in natural situations. The fable uses personified animals as its characters in situations that are lifelike and often humorous. An allegory is a story in which characters and events are symbolic rather than realistic. It may be fairly short, or extended to book length as in Bunyan's *The Pilgrim's Progress.*

PROSE SATIRE:

A *satire* is a piece of literature which holds up to ridicule human follies and vices. The best known prose satires in English literature are the light essays of manners written during the eighteenth century, especially those by Addison and Steele; and the prose tales, like *Gulliver's Travels* by Jonathan Swift.

LETTERS:

It is to be expected that interesting people should write interesting *letters*. From earliest times it has been the custom to save, collect, and sometimes publish the correspondence of famous or unusual personalities. Some English letters of special interest are those written by the fourth Earl of Chesterfield to his son instructing him in the etiquette of the eighteenth century; the letters exchanged between Elizabeth Barrett and Robert Browning before their marriage; the collected letters of Robert Louis Stevenson; and those of Charles L. Dodgson (Lewis Carroll). It is possible, in fact, for one to read the collected letters of almost any favorite author.

ORATORY:

An *oration* is a formal address, elevated in tone and usually delivered on some notable occasion. The most famous British orations have been given in Parliament; and England's greatest orators have been her statesmen. One of the first brilliant speakers of whom there is 'record was Sir Francis Bacon. Ben Jonson wrote concerning his addresses in Parliament, "No man ever spoke more neatly, more pressly, more weightily, or suffered less emptiness, less idleness in what he uttered. . . . His hearers could not cough, or look aside from him without loss. . . . The fear of every man that heard him was lest he should make an end." Another powerful Parliamentary speaker was Edmund Burke, whose speeches were so flawlessly organized and so eloquently expressed that for generations they served as models of persuasive prose. Among the present-day speakers, the most picturesque and effective is Prime Minister Winston Churchill. He is terse and original in his expression besides being courageous about speaking out his convictions.

DRAMA

Plays of all kinds are classified as *drama*. Technically speaking, a drama is a piece of literature designed to be acted, or in the strict Greek sense of the word, to be "done." Since the acting instinct is strong in all peoples, dramas—however crude—have been preserved in tribal rites, in folklore, or in the written word of nearly every racial group. The first English plays were merely "done," but they early found their way into manuscript or printed record. Today successful plays appear on the stage, in the movies, over the radio, and in print almost simultaneously.

Literary drama should present a picture or section of actual life in rapid, vivid action. It is dependent for expression on actors and their voices, gestures, movements, and reactions. Each player must give a faithful interpretation of the character he assumes. Characterization must be developed swiftly, and the play must move rapidly to its conclusion. Drama, like fiction, centers around a *plot*—that is, an outline of events, the general scheme of the story. A thread of events, the *rising action,* leads to the big dramatic moment, the *climax.* This moment is the turning point of the plot. It is followed by the *falling action,* which leads to the solution, or *denouement.* Both characters and plot are developed in harmony with the *setting*—that is, with the place of the story, and the time.

Since the play is to be acted, explicit directions for the setting, for staging, for acting, and for interpretation must be included. In the printed play these directions usually appear in italic type. However, they are very important; and the reader must not skip them, else he would lose much of the significance of the drama.

Given characters, plot, setting, the final test of the play is that it must "act." The playwright must know his medium. He must so handle his materials that dialogue and action tell his story in lifelike fashion. "Act-ability," not easy to define, is readily recognized once the players take to the stage. It is the most important element of every type of drama.

TYPES OF THE DRAMA—COMEDY AND TRAGEDY:

Dramas fall into various classifications according to action and form. If we think of the plot of a play as a conflict between two opposing forces, such as between man and a personal weakness, or between man and his environment, the outcome of the conflict determines the classification. If in the struggle, the man is victorious, the play is a *comedy;* if he is overcome by the opposing force, it is a *tragedy.* The student must understand that a comedy is not necessarily funny and that tragedy does not always end in bloodshed or death.

Tragedy has changed greatly in form in its evolution through the years. Greek drama imposed rigid rules limiting details of setting and action. The theme must concern the destruction of the hero because of his own shortcomings. It was intended to reconcile the spectator to a universe in which guilt is punished and justice upheld. But men discovered that justice is not always done in life. The individual is sometimes victim of a vicious environment. The emphasis accordingly shifted from what the hero *does* to what he *suffers.* Modern tragedy usually ends with a man's failure to make peace with his universe. Thus the range of what was suitable material for tragedy, has been extended.

Comedies may be of the *romantic* type, the *melodramatic,* or the *farci-cal.* A romantic comedy usually is a light play that ends happily. A special type of romantic drama is the *fantasy,* which has its setting in an imaginary land and which uses whimsical or supernatural characters. The *melodrama* is characterized by rapid action, sentimental scenes, and thrilling situations. The sudden arrival of the hero just in time to rescue the heroine is a stock situation. The solution of the difficulty is often unexplained or unexpected. Melodrama provides exciting but not profound entertainment. It is still popular in motion pictures. Comedies which are out-and-out funny, filled with laughable situations, are called *farces.*

A *pageant* is the presentation of a subject—usually historical—by means of a succession of short scenes covering a relatively long period of time. If the production portrays the current scene and is characterized by music, dancing, wit, and humor, it is called a *revue.*

The *one-act* play is a special form of dramatic technique in which the author presents a single dramatic incident. It has somewhat the same relation to the full-length play that a short story has to the novel.

The *radio play* is a recent dramatic development, requiring a specialized technique. Characters, dialogue, and sound effects are its mediums. Instead of the stage directions which supplement action in a written drama, the radio play makes use of an announcer. Occasionally the announcer is woven into the thread of the plot and becomes a sort of incidental character.

erials that dialogue and action tell his story in lifelike fashion. "Act-
ty," not easy to define, is readily recognized once the players take to
stage. It is the most important element of every type of drama.

S OF THE DRAMA—COMEDY AND TRAGEDY:

ramas fall into various classifications according to action and form.
ve think of the plot of a play as a conflict between two opposing
es, such as between man and a personal weakness, or between man
his environment, the outcome of the conflict determines the classifi-
n. If in the struggle, the man is victorious, the play is a *comedy;*
e is overcome by the opposing force, it is a *tragedy.* The student
understand that a comedy is not necessarily funny and that tragedy
not always end in bloodshed or death.

agedy has changed greatly in form in its evolution through the
. Greek drama imposed rigid rules limiting details of setting and
n. The theme must concern the destruction of the hero because of
wn shortcomings. It was intended to reconcile the spectator to a
erse in which guilt is punished and justice upheld. But men discov-
that justice is not always done in life. The individual is sometimes
m of a vicious environment. The emphasis accordingly shifted from
the hero *does* to what he *suffers.* Modern tragedy usually ends with
n's failure to make peace with his universe. Thus the range of what
suitable material for tragedy, has been extended.

medies may be of the *romantic* type, the *melodramatic,* or the *farci-*
A romantic comedy usually is a light play that ends happily. A
al type of romantic drama is the *fantasy,* which has its setting in an
inary land and which uses whimsical or supernatural characters. The
drama is characterized by rapid action, sentimental scenes, and thrill-
ituations. The sudden arrival of the hero just in time to rescue the
ne is a stock situation. The solution of the difficulty is often unex-
ed or unexpected. Melodrama provides exciting but not profound
tainment. It is still popular in motion pictures. Comedies which
ut-and-out funny, filled with laughable situations, are called *farces.*
pageant is the presentation of a subject—usually historical—by
s of a succession of short scenes covering a relatively long period
ne. If the production portrays the current scene and is characterized
usic, dancing, wit, and humor, it is called a *revue.*
e *one-act* play is a special form of dramatic technique in which the
r presents a single dramatic incident. It has somewhat the same
on to the full-length play that a short story has to the novel.
e *radio play* is a recent dramatic development, requiring a special-
technique. Characters, dialogue, and sound effects are its mediums.
ad of the stage directions which supplement action in a written
a, the radio play makes use of an announcer. Occasionally the an-
cer is woven into the thread of the plot and becomes a sort of inci-
l character.

Biography has swung through many changes in treatment since the days
of Plutarch. There was a time when it was stiff and formal, when it concerned itself only with heroes, and chiefly with their virtues. There was
a period when the biographer was prejudiced, when he wrote either to
denounce his subject or to praise him extravagantly. And then, not many
years ago, we passed through the unpleasant "debunking" period, when
the author in an attempt to avoid sentimentalism, went to the other extreme and over-emphasized weaknesses and failures. Such writers seemed
to delight in dragging good names through the mire. Fortunately the
public has tired of sensational muck-raking. Biography has had a rebirth.
In any such work, the reader has a right to expect *information as accurate
as may be attained, enlivened by sidelights of human interest.* Modern
biography is providing just that—authentic records of men and women,
as readable as fiction because the author has tried to re-create persons of
flesh and blood.

It is not easy to write good biographies. If the author is too close
to his subject, it is hard to keep an unprejudiced viewpoint; if the author
is too far removed in time, it is hard to get trustworthy information. If
a man writes about himself, he must avoid the unpleasant extremes of
boastfulness and false modesty. However, the excellent biographical
writings of the last few years prove that such difficulties can be overcome.
The successful method seems to be an *objective* approach. Whether the
author writes of himself or of some one else, he can tell what happened,
what the subject of the account *did,* what he said, how he felt. This he
may do without comment, without his—that is, the writer's—censure or
praise. If he is a good reporter and story-teller, he thus makes it possible for the reader to estimate the character of the subject. Some good
autobiographies have won the approval of the reader by centering attention, not upon the author but upon the scenes through which he moved
and the personalities he met.

The appeal of biography is two-fold. Since life for each of us is a
series of adjustments to our circumstances, we like to read of another's
failures and successes. In them we find sign-posts of warning or guidance
for our own living. And then we are by nature curious. We like to
know about other people—what they are like, what they have done, where
they have gone. Through biography we may satisfy these curiosities.
There are few quirks of personality, few far-off places that we cannot
explore through the pages of a book. And because we realize that such
accounts are not fiction, we must have confidence in the author. Reliable,
sympathetic biography is a high literary art.

MISCELLANEOUS PROSE

HISTORICAL PROSE:

The *chronicle,* the *diary,* and the *journal* are forms of contemporaneous history. That is, each one records events while they are taking

place. In the chronicle, the things recorded are of public importance, whereas the diary is a recording of events of interest to a given individual. A journal, like a diary, is a personal recording of events, but usually with the idea that it will be read by others. A *history* is written long enough after the events described so that the author will have a proper perspective of the field. History is written primarily for the purpose of instruction; but when it is artistically done and when it furnishes real insight into the life of the past, it becomes a significant type of literature. Among the important literary histories by English authors, three are especially outstanding: *The Decline and Fall of the Roman Empire* by Edward Gibbon, *The French Revolution* by Thomas Carlyle, and *History of England* by Thomas Macaulay.

OTHER TYPES OF PROSE NARRATIVES:

The *prose tale* is, of course, almost as old as speech, but in England, it has almost no literary importance until late in the fifteenth century. At that time appeared Sir Thomas Malory's *Le Morte d'Arthur,* a prose collection of the legends of King Arthur and his knights. During the Age of Elizabeth, a number of *prose romances* appeared, imaginative stories told in leisurely style, the best known being Sir Philip Sidney's *Arcadia.*

The *parable,* the *fable,* and the *allegory* are stories designed to illustrate general truths or to present moral lessons. The parable is based on an incident from life. The characters are real men and women in natural situations. The fable uses personified animals as its characters in situations that are lifelike and often humorous. An allegory is a story in which characters and events are symbolic rather than realistic. It may be fairly short, or extended to book length as in Bunyan's *The Pilgrim's Progress.*

PROSE SATIRE:

A *satire* is a piece of literature which holds up to ridicule human follies and vices. The best known prose satires in English literature are the light essays of manners written during the eighteenth century, especially those by Addison and Steele; and the prose tales, like *Gulliver's Travels* by Jonathan Swift.

LETTERS:

It is to be expected that interesting people should write interesting *letters.* From earliest times it has been the custom to save, collect, and sometimes publish the correspondence of famous or unusual personalities. Some English letters of special interest are those written by the fourth Earl of Chesterfield to his son instructing him in the etiquette of the eighteenth century; the letters exchanged between Elizabeth Barrett and Robert Browning before their marriage; the collected letters of Robert Louis Stevenson; and those of Charles L. Dodgson (Lewis Carroll). It is possible, in fact, for one to read the collected letters of almost any favorite author.

ORATORY:

An *oration* is a formal address, elevated in tone on some notable occasion. The most famous Brit given in Parliament; and England's greatest orator men. One of the first brilliant speakers of who Sir Francis Bacon. Ben Jonson wrote concerning ment, "No man ever spoke more neatly, more p or suffered less emptiness, less idleness in what he u ers could not cough, or look aside from him without every man that heard him was lest he should m powerful Parliamentary speaker was Edmund Burk so flawlessly organized and so eloquently express they served as models of persuasive prose. A speakers, the most picturesque and effective is F Churchill. He is terse and original in his expres rageous about speaking out his convictions.

DRAMA

Plays of all kinds are classified as *drama.* drama is a piece of literature designed to be acte sense of the word, to be "done." Since the acting peoples, dramas—however crude—have been pre folklore, or in the written word of nearly every English plays were merely "done," but they ear manuscript or printed record. Today successf stage, in the movies, over the radio, and in prin

Literary drama should present a picture or rapid, vivid action. It is dependent for expres voices, gestures, movements, and reactions. E faithful interpretation of the character he as must be developed swiftly, and the play must clusion. Drama, like fiction, centers around a of events, the general scheme of the story. *rising action,* leads to the big dramatic moment, is the turning point of the plot. It is follow which leads to the solution, or *denouement.* Bo developed in harmony with the *setting*—that story, and the time.

Since the play is to be acted, explicit direc staging, for acting, and for interpretation mu printed play these directions usually appear i they are very important; and the reader mus would lose much of the significance of the dra

Given characters, plot, setting, the final test "act." The playwright must know his medium

POETRY

Although most people can tell at a glance whether a piece of literature is poetry or prose, the term *poetry* is hard to define. Let us consider first some of the differences between the two kinds of literature. Prose is, of course, the most natural form of expression. The poet has taken the materials of prose—words and sentences—and fashioned them into a special form that pleases with its melody and fancy. For poetry is an art, like music and painting, which adds to our enjoyment of the pleasant things of life or to our perception of its deep experiences. Like other artists, the poet is chiefly concerned with preserving in suitable form some worth-while thought or experience or impression. The painter uses a brush or crayon; the poet uses words.

There is one other important distinction of poetry. Prose is acceptable if it has made its meaning plain; poetry must not only express its message but do so in a way to stir one's feelings and set the imagination playing. As with the other arts, its success depends upon its ability to *suggest* meanings beyond those actually expressed. When we look at a great painting, we see more than is on the canvas. Similarly a true poem opens the doors of our imagination and excites us to some new or deeper feeling. In fact it is generally conceded that the imaginative and emotional elements of poetry are essential and that literature expressed in the form of poetry but without imaginative appeal should be designated merely as *verse*.

We have noted that poetry is an art which preserves in words a significant thought or experience; that like all arts, it appeals to the emotions and to the fancy; and that it is expressed in a special form of melody and grace. From this summary we may draw a definition: *Poetry is an artistic expression of a significant idea or experience in words designated to delight the ear and appeal to the imagination and feelings.* Not all so-called poems measure up to every element of this definition. Some emphasize feeling rather than melody; others emphasize melody at the expense of meaning. Our definition describes an ideal which is attained by the highest type of poetry.

The Ornaments of Poetry

Since most of the classifications of poetry are made on the basis of form and since the musical effect of any poem is dependent upon the use of various poetic devices, it is necessary for the student of literature to be familiar with these devices and with the vocabulary of versification.

CONVENTIONS OF FORM:

Poems are read from the printed page, either silently or aloud. Thus they appeal both to the eye and to the ear. To please the eye, poetry is spaced differently from prose. Poems are set off in lines or stanzas rather than in paragraphs. The lines emphasize the devices of rhyme and rhythm. Their lengths are determined by the number of accented and unaccented syllables. Each line of a poem usually begins with a capital letter. A group of lines forming a poetic unit is a *stanza*. Stanzas are set off as units of form regardless of whether or not the thought is complete. Lines within a stanza are often indented to indicate correspondence in length or in rhyme. These mechanics of arrangement help one to read poetry with full appreciation of its melody.

THE TERMS OF VERSIFICATION:

A single line of poetry is called a *verse*. The length of a verse is measured by the number of syllables it contains—especially by the number of accented syllables. Anything written in measured lines is said to be written "in verse." The term *verse* is sometimes used as a synonym for *poetry;* but more often it is used to discriminate between true poetry and something written in poetic form but without imaginative appeal.

The unit of measure of a line of poetry is a *foot*. A poetic foot is a group of syllables containing one accent. The kind of foot depends upon the position of the accented syllable.

The *meter,* or measure, of a line depends upon *the number of feet* it contains. The names given to the various meters are derived from the Greek numerals combined with the word *meter;* thus—

A line of one foot is *mono'meter.*   A line of five feet is *penta'meter.*
A line of two feet is *di'meter.*   A line of six feet is *hexa'meter.*
A line of three feet is *tri'meter.*   A line of seven feet is *hepta'meter.*
A line of four feet is *tetra'meter.*   A line of eight feet is *octa'meter.*

The meters most commonly used in English poetry are *trimeter, tetrameter,* and *pentameter.*

The *rhythm* of a line depends upon the *kind of feet* that it contains. As we have mentioned before, the kind of foot is determined by the position of the accented syllable. In general, then, in English verse the effect of rhythm is secured by the arrangement of words so that the accented syllables come at regular intervals. These different kinds of feet determine the rhythms of English verse:

An *iambic* foot consists of two syllables with the accent falling on the second syllable. The name *Ma-rie'* is an iambic foot. The following line is in *iambic pentameter* because it contains five iambic feet:

The cur/few tolls/ the knell/ of part/ing day/.
—Gray's "Elegy Written in a Country Churchyard"

A *trochaic* foot consists of two syllables with the accent falling on the first syllable. The name *Ma'ry* is a trochaic foot. The following line is in *trochaic trimeter* because it contains three trochees:

Hail to/ thee blithe/ spir-it/.—Shelley's "To a Skylark"

A *dactyllic* foot consists of three syllables with the accent falling on the first syllable. The name *Ma'ri-lyn* is a dactyl. The following line is *dactyllic hexameter* because it has six dactyllic feet:

Had Í but/ plént-ty óf/ món-ey, ∧ /món-ey é/nough and tó/ spare ∧ ∧ /.
      —Browning's "Up at a Villa—down in the City"

Notice that in this line the third and sixth feet are incomplete, with pauses like *rests* in music taking the place of unaccented syllables. But because the accented syllables are there, the feet are counted. The six accents make it a hexameter line. Poems that use the three-syllable rhythms usually contain some irregular feet.

An *anapestic* foot consists of three syllables with the accent falling on the third syllable. The name *An-toin-ette'* is an anapestic foot. The following line is anapestic tetrameter because it consists of four feet and three of them are anapests:

   Not a drúm/ was héard/, not a fu/ner-al nóte/.
      —Wolfe's "The Burial of Sir John Moore"

An *amphabrachic* foot consists of three syllables with the accent falling upon the second syllable. The name *Lu-el'la* is an amphabrachic foot. The following lines are amphabrachic tetrameter:

   I sprang tó/ the stírrup/ and Jóris/ and he ∧ /.
   I gallóped/, Dirk gallóped/, we gallóped/ all thrée ∧ /.
     —Browning's "How They Brought the Good News"

The last foot in each line lacks an unaccented syllable. The amphabrach is sometimes called the "rocking-horse" rhythm.

The *iambic* rhythm is the most commonly used in English verse. Poets like Shelley and Tennyson who like to get varied musical effects will experiment with unusual combinations of rhythm and meter. They are especially fond of the three-syllable rhythms. In his "Indian Serenade" Shelley gets a lyric effect by having a trimeter line begin with an anapest while the last two feet are iambic. Compare these two effects:

I a-ríse/ from dréams/ of thée/, I ríse/ from dréams/ of thée/,
In the fírst/ sweet sléep/ of níght/, The fírst/ sweet sléep/ of níght/,
While the wínds/ are bréath/ing lów/ While wínds/ are bréath/ing lów/
And the stárs/ are shín/ing bríght/. And stárs/ are shín/ing bríght/.

Tennyson uses one of the longest lines in English poetry, trochaic octameter, in his "Locksley Hall"—

Mén my/ bróthers/, men thé/ wórkers/, éver/ réaping/ sómething/ new ∧ .

Skillful poets make many irregular combinations of feet and measures, the essential requirement being that the lines read smoothly aloud. Browning, for example, allowed frequent irregularities in his verse; but his natural sense of rhythm made the effect always musical.

Dividing a line into feet and stressing the accented syllable is called *scanning*. We scan poetry only in order to determine how a poet has achieved a given rhythmic effect. When reading poetry for enjoyment, we read it naturally and expressively, the poet's manipulation of accents providing the necessary rhythm.

The *movement* of a poem and, to a large extent, its *feeling*, depend upon the poet's choice of rhythm and meter. Short iambic lines usually give the effect of rapid action. Iambic and trochaic feet make *strong* lines. The line most commonly used in serious English poetry is *iambic pentameter*. The various three-syllable feet give a light or dancing rhythm, the extra unaccented syllables having the effect of grace notes in music. The poems of Shelley, Byron, and Tennyson afford interesting studies in verse forms. The poems of Browning are the hardest to scan.

RHYME:

One of the most popular of all poetic devices is *rhyme*, or a correspondence in sound of the last syllables in two or more lines of verse. To form a true rhyme, the consonant preceding the last accented vowel must be different from the consonant in the matching line; the remaining sounds should be identical; thus—

> Willows whiten, aspens qui'*ver*,
> Little breezes dusk and shi'*ver*.
> —Tennyson's "The Lady of Shalott"

> Oft, in the stilly ni*ght'*
> Ere Slumber's chin has bou*nd' me*,
> Fond Memory brings the li*ght'*
> Of other days a-rou*nd' me*.
> —Moore's "Oft, in the Stilly Night"

Single-syllable rhymes like *night* and *light* are called "masculine rhymes." Rhymes of two or more syllables like *quiver, shiver*, or *bound me, -round me*, are called "feminine rhymes." Some feminine rhymes have as many as three syllables—*near' to me, dear' to me.*

Rhyming schemes, or patterns, in poetry are indicated by letters of the alphabet, using the same letter to indicate lines that rhyme with each other. Thus the scheme of a poem like "The Rape of the Lock" in which the lines rhyme in pairs is indicated a a b b c c (A A B B C C), and so on. The rhyming scheme of "The Lady of Shalott" is a a a a b c c c b.

STANZA PATTERNS:

To indicate the stanza pattern of any poem, one should name the rhythm and meter and give the rhyming scheme if rhyme is used. For example, the stanza form of Tennyson's "In Memoriam" consists of four *iambic tetrameter* lines, rhyming a b b a.

The student should be familiar with the following stanza forms or verse patterns:

The *ballad* stanza usually consists of four iambic lines, the second and fourth lines rhyming. The first and third lines are tetrameter; the second and fourth are trimeter.

It was/ a moth/er and/ a maid/
That walked/ the woods/ a-mong/, a
And still/ the maid/ went slow/ and sad,/
And still/ the moth/er sung/. a
—"The Milk White Doe"

The *Spenserian* stanza consists of nine lines, the first eight in iambic pentameter, the ninth in iambic hexameter. The rhyming scheme is a b a b b c b c c.

Verses that rhyme in pairs are called *couplets*. The *heroic couplet* is composed of iambic pentameter lines, with the pauses in thought coming at the ends of the lines. Each couplet usually expresses one complete thought. The poetic effect is entirely different when the pauses come within the lines instead of at the end. Browning's "My Last Duchess" is written in iambic pentameter couplets, but they are not *heroic* couplets because the main pauses come within the lines.

Blank verse is unrhymed iambic pentameter. Other forms without rhyme are called merely "unrhymed verse."

The *sonnet* pattern will be described in the discussion of various types of lyrics.

REFRAIN:

A *refrain* is a line or portion of a line which is repeated at regular intervals within a poem. In the old ballads, the refrain was often sung or recited after each line of the poem. See "The Riddling Knight" for illustration. Modern poets like to weave the meaning of the refrain into the thought of the verse and to vary the refrain slightly to keep it from becoming monotonous. Notice Tennyson's skillful use of refrain in "The Lady of Shalott."

ALLITERATION:

Alliteration is the poetic device of having two or more words in one line (or in adjoining lines) begin with the same letter, thus—

Roll on, thou *d*eep and *d*ark blue ocean, roll!
—Byron's "The Ocean"

Care should be taken not to overdo the use of alliteration or it may become awkward as in these lines from Swinburne's "A Child's Laughter"—

*W*elling *w*ater's *w*insome *w*ord,
*W*ind in *w*arm *w*an *w*eather.

857

ASSONANCE:

Assonance is the repetition of the same vowel sound within a line or in adjoining lines of poetry. In the line from Byron's stanzas on "The Ocean," quoted above, you will see that there is a repetition of *o*'s; and Swinburne has made *a*'s predominant in the lines quoted from "A Child's Laughter." Assonance, however, is not particularly noticeable in English poetry.

ONOMATOPOEIA:

Onomatopoeia is the use of words which imitate in sound the ideas or meanings which they denote. Almost all names for sounds and many words for movement are examples of onomatopoeia: *hum, buzz, murmur, thud, crash, wiggle, zigzag*, and the like. Browning combined onomatopoeia and alliteration pleasingly in these lines from "Saul"—

> And the sleep in the dried river-channel where bulrushes tell
> That the water was wont to go warbling so softly and well.

SUMMARY:

It is through the use of these sound effects—rhythm, rhyme, refrain, alliteration, assonance, and onomatopoeia—that writers are able to build up poetic forms pleasing to the ear.

Choral Reading

An English poet, John Masefield, is responsible for the revival of an ancient art in the modern practice of choral reading. The early Greeks had used choruses of men to set the mood for the next act of a great play. At an annual poetry-reading festival in England, Masefield suggested to Miss Marjorie Gullan that many voices reading together might sound more impressive that the accustomed solo readings. She agreed to try it and became the pioneer in the modern revival.

Miss Gullan's ideas found their way into the schools of America, where choruses were naturally available. Students began to hear poetry ringing with the strength of many voices, bringing alive the sounds the poets had striven to create in words.

Human voices differ in tone. Just as singing voices are classified according to the range of which the singer is capable, so speaking voices can be classified as to natural quality or timbre. For the purposes of choral reading, speaking voices can be classified as *light, medium,* or *dark.* In this book, the letters L, M, and D designate these groups. B and G are used for boys and girls, as the contents sometimes call for such division. A small number after the letter or letters may indicate that one voice is appropriate to read a certain passage. U means *unison,* or all voices reading together.

For the best blend of voices, each person should so control his own voice that he can hear the voices on either side of him. After a discussion of the possible ways of reading a passage, the group should agree on matters of emphasis, volume, tempo, and pauses.

While choral reading may furnish attractive features for school assembly programs or for public performances, such a purpose need not be in view when it is practiced in an English class. It is, in itself, such an enjoyable and profitable activity that it may be used freely as a classroom device.

The Types of Poetry

Narrative Poetry

Like prose, poetry is usually divided into two main classifications depending upon whether or not it tells a story. Story-telling verse is called *narrative poetry*. It again is divided into classifications, depending largely on length.

THE EPIC:

An *epic* is an extremely long narrative poem. It has been best defined by the Greek Aristotle, who said that an epic is an "imitation of life which is narrative in form and poetic in meter. . . . It has for its subject a single action, whole and complete. . . . The characters celebrated should be of lofty type and consistently presented. . . . Its subject matter should deal with the probably impossible rather than with the improbably possible." The conditions necessary for developing an epic seem to be an heroic age or period for background; a good story from the past, about a character whose exploits are legendary rather than historical; and an inspired poet. Sometimes the identity of the poet is unknown.

There are two types of epic—the *national* or *folk epic,* and the *literary epic.* The folk epic originated among the people, and passed through a long period of telling and retelling before it reached its written form. The poet who finally made it a unified poem is usually unknown. *Beowulf* is an excellent example of a folk epic. It reflects the life and thought of the people who produced it.

The *literary epic* is the conscious product of one known writer. But the poet chooses his material from traditions respected, and perhaps still believed, by his countrymen. Thus to some extent, the literary epic also reflects the thought and opinions of the age in which it was written. Milton's *Paradise Lost* is one of the famous literary epics of the world. The scenes pictured go back to the beginnings of the world, preserved largely by Hebrew and Christian tradition; but the acceptance and interpretation of them by Milton was representative of the Puritan theology of his day.

The essential elements of any epic may be summarized briefly as follows:
Plot: A unified story whose direct action is short, but whose implied action is on a sweeping scale.
Characterization: One heroic central character, plus some superhuman agents.

859

Setting: The distant past, of legendary rather than historic record.
Mood: Noble and dignified; usually also religious and sublime.
Poetic form: Majestic verse which employs certain arts or devices, such as a *formal introduction* called the "invocation"; a *roll-call of important characters;* and *lofty speeches* descriptive of persons, places, and events.

For a more complete discussion of the epic, see PROSE AND POETRY OF THE WORLD, pages 871–874.

THE BALLAD:

A *ballad* is a short narrative poem, originally designed to be sung. The *folk ballad* is the product of the people, often of the poor and uneducated classes. It uses commonplace words or dialect. Its authorship is unknown. Most English folk ballads sprang up between the twelfth and the sixteenth centuries. They were preserved orally for generations. The *literary ballad* is any fairly short story-telling poem. It may be a conscious artistic imitation of the folk ballad. The subject of the ballad is usually a popular hero or a lovely lady, and more often than not, the story is tragic. Both the folk and literary ballads make use of refrains. In the folk ballad, the refrain was usually sung after each line or stanza of the story, whether or not it fitted in with the meaning. The writer of the literary ballad plans his refrain to fit the sense of the stanzas. A most interesting use of refrain in an artistic ballad may be found in "Sister Helen" by Dante Gabriel Rossetti.

THE POETIC ALLEGORY:

Like the prose allegory, a *poetic allegory* tells a symbolic story in which characters, places, and events represent abstract ideas, general truths, or actual persons and real life situations. The poetic form may be whatever the poet wishes to make it. The most famous allegory in poetry is Spenser's *The Faerie Queene*. In it there is a double significance, for the characters represent not only various virtues and vices such as *holiness, hypocrisy, religion,* but also various people in Elizabethan England such as the Queen and her favorite courtiers. "The Vision of Piers Plowman" is another long poetic allegory.

THE IDYLL:

An *idyll* is a rather long narrative poem written in simple or romantic style on a theme of home or country life. Tennyson was particularly fond of the idyll. His *Idylls of the King* tell the story of King Arthur in musical blank verse; and his *Enoch Arden* tells a familiar story of love and sacrifice in an English seaport town.

OTHER NARRATIVE VERSE:

There are other narrative poems that are hard to classify. Scott's three long narratives—*Marmion, The Lay of the Last Minstrel,* and *The*

Lady of the Lake—have too much action to be called idylls and yet are not long enough nor dignified enough to be considered epics. We call them usually just "narrative poems." Similarly Byron's "Don Juan" defies classification. And there are other stories in English verse which cannot and need not be fitted into any special type grouping. Some may be recognized by their purpose. "The Rape of the Lock" is of course a satire because it was written to ridicule London society. But not all satiric verse is narrative. In reading these longer poems, the important thing is to understand the author's aim and to enjoy the story.

Dramatic Verse

In a sense, of course, all good drama presents a story, but because of its specialized form, drama in verse is not considered under *narrative poetry* but under *drama*. In dramatic construction it follows the same plan as prose drama. The poetic form is usually blank verse and is best exemplified in the plays of William Shakespeare, which combine to a remarkable degree the intensity of action vital to drama and the depth of thought and power of expression inherent in great poetry.

Lyric Poetry

Most short poetry which tells no story is classified as *lyric*. The name lyric, derived from *lyre*, originally denoted a short poem to be sung to the accompaniment of a stringed instrument. It was an expression of feeling, of joy or praise or grief or love. Today its meaning has been expanded to include any poem of distinctly musical form, revealing the feeling or fancy of the writer. There are many specialized types of lyrics, such as the *song*, the *elegy*, the *ode*, and the *sonnet*.

THE SONG:

The *song* is a true lyric. Genuine songs are written to be sung, and hence are short and tuneful. For many of our most delightful songs we are indebted to the fact that English plays included incidental music. Elizabethan England, especially generous, has given us such songs as Shakespeare's "Hark, Hark! the Lark" and "Who Is Sylvia?" or Ben Jonson's "Drink to Me Only with Thine Eyes." The Scotch and Irish poets have given us innumerable bits of song, composed often to some existing folk tune. Tennyson inserted bits of lyric like "Sweet and Low" or "The Splendor Falls on Castle Walls" in many of his longer poems. And some poems like his "Crossing the Bar" have inspired poets to write the music that would make them songs. One other lyric of the sort should be mentioned—a brief, unpretentious bit of verse to which the author attaches no other title than the word "Song." Blake wrote a great number of them, and most poets have some to their credit. A glance through the authors' names in any collection of "Home Songs" discloses a surprising number of famous poets who have contributed words to the world's music.

THE ELEGY:

An *elegy* is a lyric written to honor some one who has died. It may pay tribute to a group of people as in Gray's "Elegy Written in a Country Churchyard" or to a single individual as in Shelley's "Adonais," written for John Keats. A short poem written to be inscribed on a tombstone is called an *epitaph*. Gray's "Elegy" concludes with an epitaph for himself.

THE ODE:

An *ode* is a longer lyric on a serious subject, characterized by dignity of style. The form most often used for the ode consists of stanzas of uneven length, in iambic lines of varying meter, the verses rhyming but in no regular pattern. Wordsworth's "Ode on Intimations of Immortality" is an example of this sort of ode. In American literature, Lowell used a similar form for his Harvard Commemoration Ode. Keats, however, developed a regular stanza pattern for each of his odes; and Shelley invented an intricately beautiful stanza for his "Ode to the West Wind."

THE SONNET:

A *sonnet* is a lyric of fourteen iambic pentameter lines. There are two kinds of sonnets—the Italian, or regular; and the Shakespearean, or Elizabethan. In the *Italian sonnet* the first eight lines, or the *octave*, rhyme a b b a a b b a. The last six lines, or the *sestet*, may rhyme in various ways, preferably using only two rhymes, though three may be permitted—c d c d c d; or c d c d e e; and so on. The octave presents a problem or states a case or introduces a subject; the sestet solves the problem or draws a conclusion. In the Shakespearean sonnet there are three sets of four lines rhyming alternately, and a closing couplet. The rhyming scheme is thus a b a b c d c d e f e f g g. Spenser used a special interlocking rhyming scheme in his sonnets, a b a b b c b c c d c d e e. In the Elizabethan (Shakespearean) sonnet, the closing couplet should contain the most striking thought of the poem; and in any kind of sonnet the last line should present a climax of beauty and significance. You will find many sonnets in the pages of this book, in both the modern and the earlier writings. You will note that they are in each case, on a serious, thoughtful subject or that they express an experience or impression of unusual beauty. Because the form is so exacting, the subject of the sonnet should be a worthy one. In fact, part of the challenge of writing a sonnet is to compress into its fourteen lines a truly significant thought or experience.

There are other lyric forms, many of them; but those which we have defined are the types most often referred to by name. You will need to be familiar with them in order to discuss lyric verse intelligently.

Some Miscellaneous Verse Forms

There are a number of unusual poetic styles that do not fit into any of the ordinary classifications of narrative, dramatic, or lyric verse.

The *dramatic monologue* is not properly drama because it is not intended for stage presentation; it may imply a story, but not necessarily so, and it certainly is not lyric. It is a dramatic character sketch in which the speaker unconsciously reveals his own personality. It is defined in the discussion on Browning, because Browning used the form most successfully.

Then the writers of the age of Queen Anne demonstrated that any kind of writing—letters, essays, political comment, criticism, and so on—can be done in verse if the writer wishes. However, much of this verse was the artificial product of an artificial age. It was usually presented in heroic couplets and falls largely into two groups—*didactic* and *satiric*. Any kind of writing for the purpose of instruction is called *didactic*. Among the examples of didactic verse are Pope's "Essay on Criticism" and his "Essay on Man." *Satiric* verse may be in any form—lyric or narrative, rhymed or unrhymed—the distinguishing feature lying in its purpose to ridicule some one or something. The famous satires in English literature were those by Dryden and Pope and one in imitation of them—"The Dunciad" by Byron. However, modern writers are often satiric, especially in their light verse; and some of the funniest of the Gilbert and Sullivan lyrics were satiric in intent—such as "The Ruler of the King's Navy."

Again we say that the classification of the odds and ends of verse is not important; the thing that matters is intelligent reading of the selection and an appreciation of the author's purpose and effect.

Figures of Speech

Figurative language, which uses words, not literally but imaginatively, is part of all our speech. Everyday talk is full of such non-literal expressions as "My teeth were clicking like castanets" or "The pitcher burned a hot one across the plate." Slang, except for ejaculations is made up almost entirely of figures of speech like, "Don't be an apple-polisher" and "He thumbed a ride home."

But figures of speech are most effective when they add vividness or beauty to poetry and to literary prose. In fact, figurative language is so much a part of poetry that an acquaintance with the most common figures of speech is necessary for a complete appreciation of the art.

SIMILE:

A *simile* is an expressed comparison between two things of unlike nature. The simile is usually indicated by the comparative adverbs *like*, *as*, or *than*.

> Her eyes as stars of twilight fair;
> Like twilight's, too, her dusky hair.
> —Wordsworth's "She Was a Phantom of Delight"

> Her hair that lay along her back
> Was yellow like ripe corn.
> —Rossetti's "The Blessed Damozel"

METAPHOR:

A *metaphor* is an *implied* comparison between two things of unlike nature. *Like, as,* or *than* are omitted.

> If sapphires, lo, her eyes be sapphires plain;
> If rubies, lo, her lips be rubies sound.
> > —Spenser's "Amoretti"

> She was a phantom of delight.
> > —Wordsworth's "She Was a Phantom of Delight"

PERSONIFICATION:

Personification gives to the lower animals, to inanimate objects, or to abstract ideas the characteristics of persons. It is a specialized metaphor.

> Now came still Evening on, and Twilight gray
> Had in her sober livery all things clad.
> > —Milton's "Evening in Paradise"

> I bring fresh flowers for the thirsting flowers.
> > —Shelley's "The Cloud"

APOSTROPHE:

Apostrophe is an address to the dead as if living, to the absent as if present, and to animals, objects, or ideas as if they were persons.

> Roll on, thou deep and dark blue Ocean—roll!
> > —Byron's "The Ocean"

> O wild West Wind, thou breath of Autumn's being.
> > —Shelley's "Ode to the West Wind"

HYPERBOLE:

Hyperbole is obvious exaggeration.

> For lo, my love doth in herself contain
> All this world's riches that may far be found.
> > —Spenser's "Amoretti"

> At every word a reputation dies.
> > —Pope's "The Rape of the Lock"

PARADOX:

A *paradox* is an apparently contradictory statement, which is nevertheless true. Tennyson used many interesting paradoxes in *Idylls of the King.* When Gareth wanted to say that his mother tried to spoil him, he expressed it thus:

> Good mother is bad mother unto me;
> A worse were better.

When the poet commented on Lancelot's loyalty to the queen which made him false to Arthur, he wrote——

> His honor rooted in dishonor stood
> And faith unfaithful kept him falsely true.

CONTENTS BY TYPES

866

HISTORICAL BACKGROUNDS

MODERN ENGLISH LITERATURE

869

ACKNOWLEDGMENTS

For the courteous permission to use the following selections, grateful acknowledgment and thanks are extended to the following authors, agents, periodicals, and publishers.

The Atlantic Monthly: "The Return" by Lord Dunsany.

Brandt & Brandt: "England Is My Village" from *England Is My Village* published by Reynal & Hitchcock. Copyright, 1941, by Helen Rees.

Chatto & Windus: "Apologia Pro Poemate Meo" by Wilfred Owen, by permission of the author's estate.

J. M. Dent & Sons, Ltd.: "The Donkey" by Gilbert Keith Chesterton.

Dodd, Mead & Company: "The Soldier" by Rupert Brooke; "The Monkey's Paw" by W. W. Jacobs.

Doubleday, Doran & Company: "Gunga Din" from *Departmental Ditties and Barrack-Room Ballads* by Rudyard Kipling, copyright, 1892, 1927; "For All We Have and Are" from *The Years Between* by Rudyard Kipling, copyright, 1914, 1919; "Recessional" from *The Five Nations* by Rudyard Kipling, copyright, 1903, 1931; reprinted by permission of A. P. Watt & Son and Doubleday, Doran & Company, Inc., publishers.

Robert Thomas Hardy, Inc.: "To a London Three-Year-Old" by James Hilton.

Harper & Brothers: "All Yankees Are Liars" from *Sam Small Flies Again* by Eric Knight; "The Disillusioned" from *The Balconinny* by J. B. Priestley, by permission of the author.

Leland Hayward, Inc.: "When Green Buds Hang," "Here Dead We Lie," and "I Did Not Lose My Heart" from *More Poems* by A. E. Housman, by permission of the author's estate.

Henry Holt and Company, Inc.: "Silver" from *Peacock Pie* by Walter de la Mare; "Peace" from *Collected Poems*, 1941, by Walter de la Mare; "Loveliest of Trees" from *The Shropshire Lad*, Authorized Edition, by A. E. Housman.

Houghton Mifflin Company: "My America" from *The Pilgrim's Way* by Lord Tweedsmuir, by permission of A. P. Watt & Son, London, and the author's estate.

Alfred A. Knopf, Inc.: "Hate Not, Fear Not" from *Country Sentiment* by Robert Graves; "The End of an Age" from *The New World Order* by H. G. Wells.

Little, Brown & Company: "The Beaches of Dunkirk" from *Action Stations* by "Bartimeus"; a selection from *The Wind Is Rising* by H. M. Tomlinson; by permission of Little, Brown & Company and The Atlantic Monthly Press.

J. B. Lippincott Company: A selection from *If Judgment Comes* by Alfred Noyes. Copyright, 1941, by Alfred Noyes.

David Lloyd: "Sheep" from *The Poems of W. H. Davies* (1934) by permission of Jonathan Cape, Ltd. Copyright, 1916, by William H. Davies.

The Macmillan Company: "An Old Woman of the Roads" from *Poems* by Padraic Colum; "The Ice-Cart" from *Collected Poems* by W. W. Gibson; "The Man He Killed" and "Weathers" from *Collected Poems* by

Thomas Hardy; "A Consecration" and "Rounding the Horn" from *Poems* by John Masefield; "To the Four Courts, Please" from *Collected Poems* by James Stephens; "The Lake Isle of Innisfree" and "An Irish Airman Foresees His Death" from *Collected Poems* by William Butler Yeats.

The Poetry Bookshop, London: "Real Property" by Harold Monro.

Matson and Duggan: "The South Country" by Hilaire Belloc.

Captain Francis Newbolt: "He Fell Among Thieves" by Henry Newbolt.

Princeton University Press: Translations from *Old English Poetry* by J. Duncan Spaeth: selections from *Beowulf;* "The Ploughman's Charm"; "Northumbrian Hymn"; and three "Riddles."

G. P. Putnam's Sons: "The War of the Unknown Warriors" from *Blood, Sweat, and Tears* by Winston Churchill.

Random House, Inc.: "The Landscape Near an Aerodrome" from *Poems,* by Stephen Spender, copyright, 1934, by The Modern Library, Inc.; "Prelude" from *The Complete Works of John M. Synge,* copyright, 1935, by The Modern Library, Inc.

Siegfried Sassoon: "Aftermath" and "Dreamers."

Charles Scribner's Sons: "Reminiscences of Conrad" from *Candelabra* by John Galsworthy; selections from *Victoria Regina* by Laurence Housman.

Time Magazine: "A Sergeant's Prayer" by Hugh Brodie.

The Viking Press, Inc.: "Piano" from *Collected Poems of D. H. Lawrence,* copyright, 1929; "The Open Window" from *The Short Stories of Saki* (H. H. Munro), copyright, 1930; by permission of The Viking Press, Inc., New York.

PRONUNCIATIONS

This list contains pronunciations for the more difficult and unusual proper names used in this book. The diacritical markings used are as follows: āle, senàte, ăm, àsk, câre, ärm, ēve, ĕvent, ĕnd, evēr, īce, ĭll, ōld, ȯbey, ŏdd, ôrb, fōōd, fŏŏt, then, ūse, ùnite, ŭp, ûrn, and menü.

A

Achilles, à-kĭl'ēz
Admiralty, ăd'mĭ-răl-tĭ
Adonais, ăd-ô-nā'ĭs
Adonis, à-dō'nĭs
Æon, ē'ŏn
Æsc, ĕsk
Afghan, ăf'gàn
Aglaura, à-glô'rà
Alighieri, Dante, ä-lê-gyâ'rē dän'tā
Althea, ăl-thē'à
Amalek, ăm'à-lĕk
Amoretti, ăm-ô-rĕt'ĭ
Apollyon, à-pŏl'ĭ-ŏn or à-pŏl'yŭn
Apologia Pro Poemate Meo, à-pō-lō'gĭ-à prō pō'ĕm-āt mē'ō
Areopagitica, ăr-ê-ŏp-à-gĭt'ĭ-kà
Arethusa, ăr-ê-thū'sà
Ariel, ā'rĭ-ĕl
Armada, är-mā'dà
Armour, är'mēr
Artoys (Artois), àr-twä'
Ashur, ăsh'ûr
Atheling, ăth'ĕl-ĭng
Attila, ăt'ĭ-là

B

Babylon, băb'ĭ-lŏn
Bacchus, băk'ŭs
Baiac, bä'yä
Banquo, băng'kō or băng'kwō
Bartimeus, bär-tĭ-mē'ŭs
Bastille, bàs-tēl'
Beaumont, bō'mŏnt
Bede, bēd
Belloc, Hilaire, bĕ-lŏk', ē-lâr'
Bellona, bĕ-lō'nà
Beowulf, bā'ô-wōŏlf
Boleyn, Anne, bōŏl'ĭn, ăn
Bologne, bô-lŏn'
Bordeaux, bôr-dō'

Boswell, bŏz'wĕl
Brobdingnag, brŏb'dĭng-năg
Brontë, brŏn'tā
Brunanburh, brōō'nàn-bûrg
Brut, brōōt
Buchan, bŭk'àn
Bysshe, bĭsh

C

Caedmon, kăd'mŭn
Caius Julius, kā'yŭs jōōl'yŭs
Camelot, kăm'ê-lŏt
Campion, kăm'pĭ-ŭn
Canterbury, kăn'tēr-bĕr-ĭ
Canute, kà-nūt'
Carew, kà-rōō' or kā'rĭ
Carlyle, kär-līl'
Celt, sĕlt or kĕlt
Celtic, sĕl'tĭk or kĕl'tĭk
Champ Elysses, shän-zā-lē-zā'
Chaos, kā'ŏs
Charing Cross, chär'ĭng
Charlemagne, shär'lê-mān
Chaucer, Geoffrey, chô'sēr, jĕf'rĭ
Childe Harold, chīld hăr'ōld
Claus of Innsbruck, klous ĭns'brōōk
Cloonah, klōō'nà
Coleridge, kōl'rĭj
Cologne, kô-lōn'
Colum, Padraic, kŏlm pä'drĭk
Compiègne, kôn-pyĕn'é
Constant, Monsieur, kôn-stän' mē-syû
Covent, kŭv'ĕnt
Coverley, kŭrv'ēr-lĭ
Cowper, kōō'pēr or kou'pēr
Crichton, krī'tŏn

D

Damozel, dăm'ô-zĕl
Dauphine, dô'fēn

874

Davies, dā′vēz
Defoe, dĭ-fō′
De la Mare, dĕ-là-mär′
Dianeme, dī-ăn′ê-mē
Disraeli, dĭz-rā′lĭ
Don Juan, dŏn hwän′
Donne, dŏn or dŭn
Dramatis Personae, drăm′à-tĭs pēr-
  sō′nē
Dumfries, dŭm-frēs′
Dunciad, dŭn′sĭ-ăd
Dunsany, dŭn-sā′nĭ
Dunsinane, dŭn-sĭ-nān′

E

Eglantine, ĕg′lăn-tīn
Elia, ē′lĭ-à
Endymion, ĕn-dĭm′ĭ-ŏn
Euphues, ū′fû-ēz
Evelina, ĕv-ê-lī′nà
Exeter, ĕk′sê-tēr

F

Fascist, făsh′ĭst
Faerie Queene, fā′ēr-ĭ kwēn
Faustus, fôs′tŭs
Ferrara, fĕ-rä′rà
Fleance, flē′åns
Forres, fôr′ĭs
Forsyte Saga, fôr-sīt′ sä′gà
Fra Pandolf, frä pän′dôlf

G

Gaelic, gāl′ĭk
Gallipoli, gà-lĭp′ô-lē
Galsworthy, gôlz′wûr-thĭ
Gaunt, gänt
Gawayne, gô′wån
Geat, yĕ′ät
Gestapo, gê-shtä′pō
Gibbon, gĭb′ŭn
Glamis, glämz
Gloucester, glôs′tēr
Gorboduc, gôr′bō-dŭk
Goth, gŏth
Graymalkin, grĭ-màl′kĭn
Grendel, grĕn′dĕl
Gunga Din, gŭng′gà dēn′

H

Hakluyt, hăk′lōōt
Hautboy, hō′boi

Healfdene, hĕlf′dēn
Hecate, hĕk′åt
Hengist, hĕng′gĭst
Heorot, hā′ô-rōt
Hermes, hûr′mēz
Hesperus, hĕs′pēr-ŭs
Hezekiah, hĕz-ê-kī′à
Hippocrene, hĭp′ô-krēn
Hohenzollern, hō′ĕn-tsŏl′ērn
Holinshed, hŏl′ĭnz-hĕd
Horsa, hôr′sà
Ho-ti, hō′tē
Housman, hous′man
Hrothgar, hrŏth′gär
Hudribas, hŭ′dĭ-brăs
Hygelac, hĭg′ê-lăk
Hyperion, hī-pē′rĭ-ŏn

I

Ian, ē′än
Il Penseroso, ēl pĕn-sĕ-rō′sō
Isaiah, ī-zā′yà

J

Jubal, jōō′băl

K

Korzeniowski, kôr-zĕn-yôf′skĭ
Kubla Khan, kü′blà kän′
Kyowowy, kī-ō-wow′ĭ

L

L'Allegro, lä-lā′grō
Lancaster, lăng′kăs-tēr
Laureate, lô′rê-åt
Layamon, lä′yà-mŏn
Leigh, lē
Llewellyn, lōō-ĕl′ĭn
Le Morte d'Arthur, lê môrt där′thēr
Livy, lĭv′ĭ
Loch Katrine, lŏk kăt′rĭn
Louis, lōō′ĭs or lōō′ĭ
Lucasta, lû-kăs′tà
Lucrece, lû-krēs′
Lyly, lĭl′ĭ

M

Maenad, mē′năd
Maeonides, mē-ŏn′ĭ-dēz
Magna Carta, măg′nà kär′tà
Majuba, mà-jōō′bà

875

Mannyng, măn'ĭng
Marseilles, mär-sālz'
Medieval, mē'dĭ-ē-văl
Mephistophilis, měf-ĭs-tŏf'ĭ-lĭs
Milne, mĭln
Miscellany, mĭs'ĕ-lā-nĭ
Montaigne, Michel de, mŏn-tān' mē-shĕl'
Muse, mūz

N

Naseby, nāz'bĭ
Nazi, nä'tsĭ
Neville, nĕv'ĭl
Nineveh, nĭn'ê-vĕ
Nottinghamshire, nŏt'ĭng-ăm-shĭr
Noyes, nois or noiz

P

Pepys, pēps or pĕps
Phineus, fī'nŭs or fĭn'ē-ŭs
Phoebus, fē'bŭs
Picardy, pĭk'ȧr-dĭ
Pict, pĭkt
Piers, pērs or pērz
Plantaganet, plăn-tăj'ê-nĕt
Prelude, prĕl'ūd
Prospice, prŏs'pĭ-sē
Proteus, prō'tŭs or prō'tē-ŭs
Provençal, prȯ-vän-säl'

R

Rabbi Ben Ezra, răb'ī bĕn ĕz'rȧ
Raphael, răf'ā-ĕl
Reformation, rĕf-ȯr-mā'shŭn
Renaissance, rĕn-ĕ-säns'
Rhys, rēs
Rossetti, Dante Gabriel, rȯ-sĕt'ê dän'tä gā'brē-ĕl
Rouncival, roun'sē-văl

S

Saki, sä'kĭ
Sassoon, Siegfried, să-sün' sēg'frēd
Scotia, skō'shĭ-ȧ
Semele, sĕm'ê-lē
Sennacherib, sĕ-năk'ĕr-ĭb
Siward, sē'wȧrd
Southey, south'ĭ or suth'ĭ

Spaeth, späth
Stoke Poges, stōk pŏgz or pŏg'ĭs
Strachey, Lytton, strā'chē lĭt'ôn
Struther, Jan, strŭth'er jăn
Synge, sĭng

T

Tabard, tăb'ȧrd
Telemachus, tê-lĕm'ȧ-kŭs
Teutonic, tû-tŏn'ĭk
Thames, tĕmz
Thamyris, thăm'ĭ-rĭs
Thomas à Becket, tŏm'ăs ä bĕk'ĕt
Tiresias, tī-rē'shĭ-ăs
Tophet, tō'fĕt
Toulon, tōō-lôn'
Trafalgar, trăf-ăl-gär' or trȧ-făl'gȧr
Triton, trī'tŏn
Tudor, tū'dôr
Tyndale, tĭn'dāl
Tyre, tīr

U

Ulysses, ū-lĭs'ēz
Una, ū'nȧ

V

Vicar, vĭk'er
Victoria Regina, vĭk-tō'rĭ-ȧ rē-jī'nȧ
Vortigern, vôr'tĭ-gērn

W

Wihtgils, wĭt'gĭlz
Wilde, wīld
Witan, wĭt'ăn
Worcestershire, wŏŏs'tēr-shĭr
Wordsworth, wûrdz'wûrth
Wyclif, wĭk'lĭf

X

Xanadu, zăn'ȧ-dōō

Y

Yeats, yāts or yēts
Ypres, ē'pr

Z

Zephirus, zĕf'ĭ-rŭs
Zion, zī'ŏn

INDEX OF AUTHORS

INDEX OF TITLES

879